PROMOTED

To

Grandma

Making the the most of your new role

This edition published in 2019
By SJG Publishing, HP22 6NF, UK

Author: Emma Hill
Editor: Helen Redding
Illustrator: Victor McLindon
Cover design: Milestone Creative

ISBN: 978-1-911517-69-6

Printed in China

Introduction

Your time has come! Being a grandma is one of the most rewarding relationships you can have – imagine the same unconditional love you feel for your children, yet with fewer struggles and a whole lot more fun. So, get ready for sticky fingerprints, precious cuddles, snotty noses, gummy smiles, tears and tantrums … and to fall in love all over again.

Promoted to Grandma provides a mix of tips and pearls of wisdom to impart to your grandchildren (that will make you sound like a pro!) along with light-hearted, amusing and sentimental quotes to help you embrace your new role and celebrate the journey into grandparenthood. Whether you're going to be a hands-on childcare provider or grandparent from further afield, your loving, guiding influence will be needed.
So let the adventures begin!

WORDS OF

Wisdom

"If becoming a grandmother was only a matter of choice, I should advise every one of you straight away to become one. There is no fun for old people like it!"

HANNAH WHITHALL SMITH

"We should all have one person who knows how to bless us despite the evidence, Grandmother was that person to me."

PHYLLIS THEROUX

"A house needs a grandma in it."

LOUISA MAY ALCOTT

"Grandmother – a wonderful mother with lots of practice."

UNKNOWN

"Her grandmother, as she gets older, is not fading but rather becoming more concentrated."

PAULETTE BATES ALDEN

"*Perfect love sometimes does not come until the first grandchild.*"

WELSH PROVERB

THINGS TO DO NOW YOU'RE A

Grandma

Most new parents love the idea of keeping a record of their baby's first year, but have their hands far too full to actually do it. Why not go undercover and quietly compile a keepsake journal for them? Collect photographs and mementos, make a note of your grandchild's milestones and record them in a beautiful journal that you can gift to the parents on baby's first birthday.

Don't expect new, inevitably exhausted, parents to host you. Get up and make the tea! Bring cookies to go with it … and wash up afterwards.

Dig out the toys that belonged to your children. Finally, you will be thanked for never throwing anything away!

Beware of 'granimosity'. Accept graciously that your grandchildren have other grandparents in their lives and don't enter into competition with the in-laws. Just be thankful that your grandchildren have other people who love them as much as you do.

Make sure there are child-friendly areas in your house where you won't be stressing about the mess they're making (because they will make one!).

WORDS OF
Wisdom

"A grandchild is like a fine jewel set in an old ring."

ANNE LAMOTT

"The only people interested in hearing about your grandchildren are other grandparents who want to tell you about theirs."

BRYNA NELSON PASTON

"A grandma's heart is a patchwork of love."

UNKNOWN

"Most grandmas have a touch of the scallywag."

HELEN THOMSON

"When you have a grandchild, you have two children."

JEWISH PROVERB

"When it seems the world can't understand, your grandmother's there to hold your hand."

JOYCE K. ALLEN LOGAN

OUT OF THE MOUTHS OF

Babes

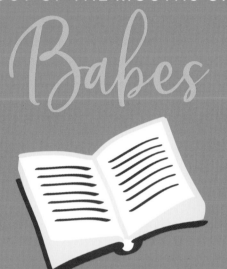

Whilst reading my grandson a bedtime story, he looked over at me thoughtfully and said: "Nana, you look like you're going to break." I told him I was absolutely fine and asked why he thought that. "You're full of cracks," he said.

Playing 'I Spy', my granddaughter chose something beginning with 'g'. When we asked for a clue she said it's something "pink-colored, sort of wrinkled with some white on top". The answer was 'grandma'!

My granddaughter walked into the room and said: "Old lady, will you play with me?" Taken aback by her rudeness, my daughter asked her why she'd called me that. "Because Grandma calls me young lady," she replied, her face the picture of innocence.

When I told my grandson where milk comes from, he asked: "But Gran, how do the cows sit on those bottles?"

WORDS OF
Wisdom

"Grandmothers always have time to talk and make you feel special."

CATHERINE PULSIFER

"If I had known how wonderful it would be to have grandchildren, I'd have had them first."

LOIS WYSE

"A people without history is like wind on the buffalo grass."

SIOUX PROVERB

"Being pretty on the inside means you don't hit your brother and you eat all your peas – that's what my grandma taught me."

LORD CHESTERFIELD

"Grandmother-grandchild relationships are simple. Grandmas are short on criticism and long on love."

UNKNOWN

"*Grandmas never run out of hugs or cookies.*"

UNKNOWN

INSPIRATIONAL

Grandmas

You're never too old to follow your dreams! Life is far too short for regrets and that's a great lesson to teach your grandchildren. Be bold, be adventurous and you'll be surprised by what you can achieve – just like these incredible women ...

THE GYMNAST – JOHANNA QUASS

German Johanna Quass is 92 years old and is the oldest gymnast in the world. She took part in her first competition in 1934 and, unbelievably, is still competing at an amateur level. World War II and having a family interrupted her gymnastics. However, aged 57 she decided to try training and competing professionally again to great success. The grandmother-of-two still trains for an hour every day. She says that, "When there is movement, there is life."

THE TRAVELLER – EVELYN HANNON

Pioneer Canadian travel blogger Evelyn Hannon has been writing about solo female travel in her Journeywoman magazine and online since 1994. For 25 years she's travelled the world compiling tips and advice for women who want to do the same. Now in her late 70s she enjoys taking her grandchildren on her travels: "This is my grandmother-journeywoman way of providing them with 'on-site' training for their own future solo adventures. It's the circle of life!"

THE BODYBUILDER – ERNESTINE SHEPHERD

American grandmother Ernestine Shepherd is best known for once being – at the age of 74 – the world's oldest competitive female bodybuilder. Ernestine didn't even start exercising until she was 56 years old! Now in her early 80s, she's still actively bodybuilding. She gets up at 3am every day and runs 80 miles a week. According to Ernestine: "If ever there were an anti-aging pill, I would call it exercise".

THINGS TO DO NOW YOU'RE A

Grandma

Get tech savvy! If you live some distance away from your grandchild, now is the time to shake off any techno-reluctance. FaceTime, Skype or WhatsApp video calls will all enable you to chat virtually face-to-face, to see them grow, lose teeth and change hairstyles. Just a few clicks and you can be on the receiving end of a chocolate-smeared gummy smile. Whilst it's never going to beat real-life interaction, it really will help to bridge the distance between you.

Bite your tongue! If you disagree with a parenting decision it is not your place to comment.

In terms of childcare, only take on what you can manage and don't be afraid to say no. If you overstretch yourself and become exhausted you will end up helping nobody.

Encourage and support the new parents. Simply telling them they're doing a great job will help to get them through those first few exhausting weeks.

Invest in a wipe-clean tablecloth. You'll soon discover why ....

WORDS OF

Wisdom

"Just about the time a woman thinks her work is done, she becomes a grandmother."

EDWARD H. DRESCHNACK

"A grandma's name is little less in love than is the doting title of a mother."

WILLIAM SHAKESPEARE

"The first step a grandchild takes is to your heart."

UNKNOWN

"Grandma always made you feel she had been waiting to see just you all day and now the day was complete."

MARCY DEMAREE

"It's impossible for a grandmother to understand that few people, and maybe none, will find her grandchild as endearing as she does."

JANET LANESE

"Grandchildren do for me with a smile what an entire bottle of medicine could never do."

UNKNOWN

YOU KNOW YOU'RE A GRANDMA

When...

- Your iPad screen is smeared with little fingerprints and banana.

- You've fallen in love all over again.

- You stop strangers in the street to show them photos of your little darlings, whether they've asked to see them or not.

- You have Peppa Pig on series link.

- You have to open a gate to get up your stairs.

- You're exhausted ... but happy.

- Memories from your children's childhoods, and your own, come flooding back.

—

YOUR LIVING ROOM IS STARTING TO RESEMBLE A TOYSHOP.

—

You get more pleasure from

Buying Toys

than treating yourself
to new shoes.

THINGS TO DO NOW YOU'RE A

Grandma

Plant something together in your garden as a physical reminder of the happy times you spend together.

As they grow up, invite your grandchild to help you with small chores around the house and reward them with plenty of praise when they complete their tasks. Even very young children can help load the washing machine and wipe down surfaces. This is great for their independence and confidence.

Talk about something other than your grandchild to any friends you would like to retain in your life.

Wave goodbye to fresh, unblemished walls and say hello to sticky handprints, scuffs and permanent marker pen.

Tread lightly with your grandchild's parents and express yourself gently. It's all too easy for advice or innocent parenting comments to come across as veiled criticism.

WORDS OF

Wisdom

"A grandmother is a mother who has a second chance."

UNKNOWN

"If grandmas hadn't existed, kids would have inevitably invented them."

ARTHUR KORNHABER, M.D.

"If your baby is 'beautiful and perfect, never cries or fusses, sleeps on schedule and burps on demand, an angel all the time,' you're the grandma."

TERESA BLOOMINGDALE

"A Grandmother is a special person who causes a joyful happening in the heart of a child."

UNKNOWN

"The best babysitters, of course, are the baby's grandparents. You feel completely comfortable entrusting your baby to them for long periods, which is why most grandparents flee to Florida."

DAVE BARRY

"All Grandmothers like letters. Even if they just consist of a squiggle and a dirty finger mark."

UNKNOWN

BEING A GRANDMA

True or False?

Times they are a-changin' and many myths need to be debunked to drag the image of grandmas into the 21st century. Can you use your grandma radar to detect which of these facts are true and which are false?

FACT: Grandmas sit in their comfy armchairs and wait for their grandchildren to come to them.
FALSE! Grandmas run after their grandchildren – through parks and fields, up and down stairs, over chairs, under tables. All in pursuit of that wonderful moment when you envelope them in a hug.

FACT: You must be old to be a grandma.
FALSE! Certainly not! In the US, the average age of a grandparent is 48. Country music star Loretta Lynn was a grandma at just 29. Whoopi Goldberg became a grandma at 34. Even if your 20s and 30s seem an eternity away, never forget that old adage that age is just a number.

FACT: Being a grandma is a lot of responsibility.
TRUE! Research has shown that a grandparent/
grandchild relationship is second in importance
only to the parent/child relationship. As a grandma,
you're in a unique position to have an influence on
the lives of your grandchildren. Set a good example
with your commonsense and wisdom but also show
them the power of having fun!

FACT: Grandmas are frail and need someone to take
care of them.
FALSE! Grandmas are doing it for themselves! As
health levels and life expectancies rise, grandmas
are getting fitter, stronger and more badass. Did you
know that the world's oldest female yoga teacher,
Tao Porchon-Lynch, is 99 years old, loves wine
and never drinks water? The healthier you are, the
longer it will take your grandchildren to exhaust you
– no matter how hard they try!

THINGS TO DO NOW YOU'RE A

Grandma

Practice the art of folding and unfolding the buggy (they're not as simple as they used to be!)

Maintain your grandchild's routine when you're looking after them. It's a way of showing respect to the parents and their decisions, plus you'll avoid having a cranky baby on your hands (there is a reason for that scheduled nap!).

Celebrate the milestones. No doubt you were too busy to really do this as a parent, so indulge now with your grandchildren. Record the early smiles, those first steps, first words ... and enjoy every special moment.

Become a role model.

Prepare to be in demand again!

Shower them with love but don't stuff them with food! Spoiling with too many sweet treats will have a negative impact in the long run. Don't teach them to associate comfort with eating.

WORDS OF

Wisdom

"You know you're a grandparent when you laugh when your grandkids do the same things that made you so angry when your kids did them."

UNKNOWN

"Becoming a grandmother is wonderful. One moment you're just a mother. The next you are all-wise and prehistoric."

PAM BROWN

"A grandmother is both a sword and a shield."

FREDRIK BACKMAN

"There's no place like home ... except Grandma's."

UNKNOWN

"A grandchild is the reward for everything you've done right in your life."

UNKNOWN

"The very old and the very young have something in common that makes it right that they should be left alone together. Dawn and sunset see stars shining in a blue sky; but morning and midday and afternoon do not, poor things."

ELIZABETH GOUDGE

OUT OF THE MOUTHS OF

My three-year-old granddaughter brought a coloring book to me and asked me to read it. I proceeded to make up words to go with each picture. When I finished 'reading', she said, "I don't think I've heard that story before."

One day I babysat my two grandsons while my daughter went to the hair salon. When she arrived home the five-year-old told her how beautiful she looked. Then he looked back at me and, obviously not wanting me to feel left out, said, "and Grandma, you look nearly beautiful."

Grandma said I can be anything I want if I go to university, so I'm going to be a mermaid.

I asked my grandson if he was hungry, he replied: "If it's dinner I'm not hungry, if it's a cookie I am hungry!"

YOU KNOW YOU'RE A GRANDMA

When...

- You know all the words to *The Gruffalo* and the order in which *The Very Hungry Caterpillar* ate all that food.

- All the photos on your phone feature your grandchild. And you show them to everybody and anybody who stands still for long enough.

- Your medicine cabinet is stocked with cough mixture and Band-Aids.

- You own a porcelain item – possibly a plate, maybe a mug – that features a footprint.

- You say "Oh okay, just this once" rather a lot.

- You feel like the proudest woman in the world.

- You're embarking on one of the best journeys of your life.

- You have more grey hairs than ever!

You always have

Ice Cream

in the freezer and sprinkles in the cupboard.

THINGS TO DO NOW YOU'RE A

Facilitate sleep. It's what new parents need above and beyond anything else so, if you can, offer to take the baby out for a walk whilst they get some much-needed shut-eye.

Let the parents make their own mistakes. You can't swoop in and show them how to do things – your way is not the only way.

Remind the world you're a grandma at every given opportunity! (Keep photographic evidence to hand at all times and always be ready with a cute anecdote.)

Learn how to soothe your grandchild to sleep.

Resist going on a shopping spree for the new baby without asking the parents what they actually need.

Re-learn how to dress a wriggling, slippery eel-like creature fresh from the bath.

YOU KNOW YOU'RE A GRANDMA

When...

- You start shopping for Christmas presents in April.

- You have a smile on your face ... and bags under your eyes.

- You can take delight in a baby breathing down a telephone.

- You've found yourself rocking a parcel to sleep in the post office line.

- You inadvertently accessorise with stickers ... on your jumpers, shoes, back, forehead ...

- You refer to yourself in the third person: "come to Grandma for a cuddle."

- You've marvelled over travel systems (and secretly wondered what was wrong with a good old-fashioned pram).

Your cupboards contain treats. Lots of treats.

Your back lawn is for

fun and games,

not for admiring from through
the window.

YOU KNOW YOU'RE A GRANDMA

When...

- You know the names of all the Teletubbies and can sing the theme tune too.

- Your heart is bursting with love (and your cupboards are bursting with toys).

- Your jewellery collection contains several bracelets made of little plastic beads ... and they're more precious than any diamonds.

- You are familiar with all the actions to 'Wheels on the Bus'. And you have to do them around 250 times a day!

- Random items of half-eaten food fall out of your clothing when you get undressed at night.

- Your Band-Aids feature pictures of Mr Bump or Elsa.

- Your fridge door is covered in 'artwork'.

Your fingernails (and some of your fingers and furniture) have been painted a shade of

Glittery Blue.

WORDS OF

Wisdom

"Grandmas don't just say 'that's nice' – they reel back and roll their eyes and throw up their hands and smile. You get your money's worth out of grandmas."

UNKNOWN

"My grandmother is my angel on earth."

CATHERINE PULSIFER

"If you would civilize a man, begin with his grandmother."

VICTOR HUGO

"If a child is to keep alive his inborn sense of wonder, he needs the companionship of at least one adult who can share it, rediscovering with him the joy, excitement and mystery of the world we live in."

RACHEL CARSON

"You are the sun, Grandma, you are the sun in my life."

KITTY TSUI

"*She loved them so much that she felt a kind of hollowness on the inner surface of her arms whenever she looked at them – an ache of longing to pull them close and hold them tight against her.*"

ANNE TYLER

OUT OF THE MOUTHS OF

Babes

My three-year-old grandson told me he was going fishing with his dad. "Are you going to use worms?" I asked him. He gave me a funny look and replied: "no, Nana, a fishing rod!"

I had my grandkids stay for a sleepover. I put them to bed then went to wash my hair. I could hear them getting increasingly boisterous instead of going to sleep, so I hopped out of the shower, flung on a dressing gown and wrapped a towel around my head to go and tell them to calm down. When I'd left the bedroom I heard my grandson whisper to his sister in a trembling voice: "who was that?"

"Where's my kiss?" I once asked my two-year-old granddaughter. "In your lips," she replied.

I was in the swimming pool with my granddaughter and said, "I'm going to get out now, my skin's getting all wrinkly." "But Granny, you were wrinkly before you got in," she exclaimed.

WORDS OF
Wisdom

"Love is the greatest gift one generation can leave to another."

RICHARD GARNETT

"Grandkids bring you into a sweeter, slower present. They show you the future at a time when a lot of your friends are thinking about the past. And they take you back to childhood – theirs, the parent's, your own: a three-time admittance to wonderland."

ADAIR LARA

"When a child is born, so are grandmothers."

JUDITH LEVY

"Grandmothers are just antique little girls."

UNKNOWN

"You better arm yourselves to answer your grandchildren's questions ... no matter what the question is ... without being judgmental."

JOSH MCDOWELL

"Good grandmas have sticky floors, messy kitchens, laundry piles, dirty ovens and happy grandchildren."

UNKNOWN

THINGS TO DO NOW YOU'RE A

Grandma

Watch for signs of parental stress and offer to babysit so the new parents can get some rest and enjoy some vital me-time.

Learn from your grandchild. Notice the joy and fascination with which a baby or young child explores their environment and try to see the world through their eyes. You may have been around the block a few times, but they'll teach you how to view things with a brand new perspective.

Pass on some family history, whether in the form of a recipe, a skill, a tradition or words of advice.

Don't let becoming a grandma make you feel old. Far from it, you'll soon be reliving your own childhood and embracing your inner child as you play alongside your grandchildren.

You've done the hard bit with parenting. Now enjoy all the fun and the cuddles without the longer-term responsibility.

WORDS OF

Wisdom

"Truth be told, being a grandma is as close as we ever get to perfection. The ultimate warm sticky bun with plump raisins and nuts. Clouds nine, ten, and eleven."

BRYNA NELSON PASTON

"Now that I've reached the age where I need my children more than they need me, I really understand how grand it is to be a grandmother."

MARGARET WHITLAM

"A grandmother pretends she doesn't know who you are on Halloween."

ERMA BOMBECK

"Sometimes our grandmas and grandpas are like grand-angels."

LEXIE SAIGE

"The reason grandchildren and grandparents get along so well is that they have a common enemy."

SAM LEVENSON

"The joy of grandchildren is measured in the heart."

UNKNOWN

OUT OF THE MOUTHS OF

Babes

One day, I was doing DIY jobs around the house so just put on some old sweatpants. My granddaughter, who is used to seeing me in floral dresses, said: "I don't like what you're wearing Grandma, it doesn't look pretty." Thinking I was teaching my granddaughter a valuable life lesson I told her, "you don't always have to look pretty, darling", to which she replied: "well, you could at least try!"

I was attempting to get my four-year-old grandson out of the house in a hurry one day. "Come on," I called up the stairs, "I'm losing my patience." A few minutes later he still wasn't down. "What are you doing?" I asked. "We need to go now!" Sweet as anything he calls out: "I'm just looking for your patience, Nana."

I asked my granddaughter if she'd like an apple. "Eww, no thanks, Grandma." So I offered apple slices instead. "Ooh, yummy, yes please!" she replied.

I took my four-year-old granddaughter to a restaurant one day. Whilst we were waiting for our food to arrive, she turned to me and said: "Grandma, why are they called waiters when we're the ones doing all the waiting?"

THINGS TO DO NOW YOU'RE A

Grandma

–

Mellow out over mess. It's fine to have some areas of your house off-limits to grandchildren, but rushing for the wet wipes every time a child touches your precious white sofa is not cool.

–

Babyproof your house! Those precious ornaments all at optimal grabbing level? You might wish to hide them away.

Remember, their mom (or dad) knows best!

Get clued up on modern parenting methods. Read a recent babycare book, or do some research online. Much of the official advice that you were given as a parent will have changed and now be deemed old-fashioned.

Don't become so caught up in grandma duties that you forget to be a supportive parent to your newly overwhelmed adult children.

WORDS OF
Wisdom

"The birth of a grandchild is a wonderful and exciting event! That wonder and excitement continues throughout life."

TOM POTTS

"Like many men and women who make egregious and irretrievable mistakes with their own children, she would redeem herself by becoming the perfect grandmother."

PAT CONROY

"Grandparents are extremely rich folks with silver in their hair and gold in their hearts."

MAMUR MUSTAPHA

"I am convinced there's a gramma gene that disables the word 'no'."

LESLEY STAHL

"A grandparent is old on the outside but young on the inside."

UNKNOWN

"A grandma is a

Hug

waiting to happen."

UNKNOWN

OUT OF THE MOUTHS OF

Babes

My three-year-old grandson had proudly put his shoes on by himself. I gently pointed out to him that he'd put them on the wrong feet. He frowned at me and said in a cross voice: "Nana, I know that these are MY feet!"

A four-year-old was asked where his grandma lived. "At the airport," he replied. "Every time she comes to visit we go and pick her up from the airport, then when she's ready to go home we drop her back there afterwards."

When my two-year-old granddaughter was being potty trained, she toddled off to use the potty at my place. "Don't forget to wipe," I called out to her when she'd finished. "Oh, I did that first," she replied.

After giving my grandson a kiss, he started rubbing his cheek. Feeling a little saddened, I asked him why he was rubbing off my kiss. "I'm not rubbing it off," he replied, "I'm rubbing it in!"

HOW TO BE A FUNKY

Grandma

How can you get down with the kids? Tuning into their wavelength is a great chance to build strong bonds and be a wonderful role model. Try these cool tips for being a funky grandma ...

Retune your radio. Find a station that plays all the latest music. Dazzle your grandchildren with your knowledge of Jay-Z and Ariana Grande tunes. Be sure to be humming along to something by Ed Sheeran while you're cooking tea. (You can always switch stations once they've gone home.)

Be open-minded. Societal norms change whether you like it or not, so be a great role model by going with the flow. Let your grandchildren know they can come to you for support and you'll lend a listening ear, you'll never judge them and that you'll always love them.

Embrace color. Who said that getting older means you have to get more drab? Choose the neon pink silk scarf over the brown woolly one. Ditch your navy go-to handbag for something more colorful – and maybe even fluffy. You'll be teaching your grandchildren an important lesson about individuality – forge your own path and don't be afraid to be bold.

Take your grandchildren clothes shopping and let them choose what they want. Don't try and guide them towards the sensible waterproof jacket – let them choose the pink, fluffy unicorn hoodie, smile and tell them how amazing they'll look. You might have to deal with their less accommodating parents, but it'll be worth it for the brownie points!

Is a funky grandma scared to try new things? No! Show your grandchildren that it's good to challenge yourself. Ride a rollercoaster, book a trip to a little-visited destination, or start a new hobby like photography. You're never too old to try something different and your spirit of adventure will rub off on your grandchildren.

WORDS OF
Wisdom

"The complete family is a family that consists of three generations."

DANIEL SEKER

"It's such a grand thing to be a mother of a mother – that's why the world calls her grandmother."

UNKNOWN

"Grandparents are the best kind of grown-ups."

UNKNOWN

"I loved their home. Everything smelled older, worn but safe; the food aroma had baked itself into the furniture."

SUSAN STRASBERG

"Grandmas hold our tiny hands for just a little while, but our hearts forever."

UNKNOWN

YOU KNOW YOU'RE A GRANDMA

When...

- Your NutriBullet is used more for puréeing root veg than green juicing.

- You never get tired of a grandchild falling asleep on your lap ... though you may feel like closing your eyes to join them in their nap.

- Someone in the world thinks you're the best thing in the universe.

- You've become a soft touch – just one cute smile and a pair of chubby cheeks is all it takes to persuade you!

- You've done the hardest job in the world, and now you're doing the most fun one.

- Your kitchen cabinet is now full of plastic plates and bowls with TV characters on them.

—

Your laundry basket is full again.

—

Amongst your most

Precious Possessions

are scribbles on paper and

scavenged pine cones.

WORDS OF
Wisdom

"A grandma's love will never grow old."

UNKNOWN

"A mother becomes a true grandmother the day she stops noticing the terrible things her children do because she is so enchanted with the wonderful things her grandchildren do."

LOIS WYSE

"Grandchildren are a grandparent's link to the future. Grandparents are the child's link to the past."

UNKNOWN

"The old are the precious gem in the centre of the household."

CHINESE PROVERB

"Uncles and aunts, and cousins, are all very well, and fathers and mothers are not to be despised; but a grandmother, at holiday time, is worth them all."

FANNY FERN

"Everyone needs to have access both to grandparents and grandchildren in order to be a full human being."

MARGARET MEAD

"Grandmas are moms with lots of frosting."

UNKNOWN

OUT OF THE MOUTHS OF

Babes

I was telling my grandson about my childhood, how we used to skate on the frozen lake down the road from our house, and how in summer we fished there and took piles of jam sandwiches to picnic on. He looked at me in wonder and said: "I really wish I'd got to know you sooner, Nan."

One day I was babysitting my three-year-old granddaughter. After I had been reading to her for a while, I let her have some television whilst I settled down to read my own book. She looked over at me and asked: "What are you doing, Gran?" I told her I was reading. Looking confused she said, "but you're not saying anything!"

I was looking after my recently potty-trained granddaughter when I needed to visit the bathroom. In she burst, clapping her hands as I was washing mine. "Well done, Nana," she declared. "You went potty like a big girl!"

I told my three-year-old granddaughter that her birthday would soon be here. A week later, hands on hips looking exasperated, she asked me: "well, is it coming in the front door or the back door?"

WORDS OF

Wisdom

"It's amazing how grandparents seem so young once you become one."

UNKNOWN

"A Grandmother is a safe haven."

SUZETTE HADEN ELGIN

"Holding these babies in my arms makes me realize the miracle my husband and I began."

BETTY FORD

"Grandmothers are voices of the past and role models of the present. Grandmothers open the doors to the future."

HELEN KETCHUM

"Between the earth and sky above, nothing can match a grandmother's love."

UNKNOWN

"A Grandmother thinks of her grandchildren day and night, even when they are not with her. She will always love them more than anyone would understand."

KAREN GIBBS

THINGS TO DO NOW YOU'RE A

Grandma

Read to your grandchild at any available opportunity. It's bonding time when you can sit quietly for a cuddle as well as being good for their future learning.

Choose a name. Not theirs, yours! Are you going to be known as a traditional 'Grandma', 'Nanny' or 'Granny'? Or perhaps you'd like to be addressed in a less conventional way? Maybe you'd like the name to emerge organically, perhaps arising from a grandchild's early mispronunciation.

Instead of a gift, consider taking your grandchild out for a day trip. Making memories with them is far more precious than any material goods.

Share family traditions. Talk of the happy rituals you have always enjoyed as a family and get your grandchildren involved and feeling a part of these as early as possible.

Find the fun! Show them that getting older doesn't necessarily mean slowing down. Make dens in the garden, bake up a storm in the kitchen, go on nature hunts, jump in puddles …

WORDS OF

Wisdom

"My grandchildren multiply the joy my daughters bring me."

ALEXANDRA STODDARD

"If nothing is going well, call your grandmother."

ITALIAN PROVERB

"All grandchildren are brilliant, beautiful and take after their grandma."

UNKNOWN

"Young people need something stable to hang on to – a culture connection, a sense of their own past, a hope for their own future. Most of all, they need what grandparents can give them."

JAY KESLER

"Grandchildren are like snowflakes … each one is beautifully unique."

UNKNOWN

"The most precious jewels you'll ever have around your neck are the arms of your grandchildren."

UNKNOWN

WORDS OF Wisdom

"It is as grandmothers that our mothers come into the fullness of their grace."

CHRISTOPHER MORLEY

"I used to think I was too old to fall in love again. Then I became a grandma."

UNKNOWN

"The idea that no one is perfect is a view most commonly held by people with no grandchildren."

DOUG LARSON

"While one's child takes a part of one's heart to use and misuse as they please, a grandchild is different. Gone are the bonds of guilt and responsibility that burden the maternal relationship. The way to love is free."

KATE MORTON

"Grandchildren don't make a woman feel old; it's being married to a grandfather that bothers her."

UNKNOWN

"A garden of love grows in a grandmother's heart."

UNKNOWN

INSPIRATIONAL

Grandmas

When asked who has been inspirational or influential in their lives, many people will mention their grandma. Take a look at some women who have done amazing things in their lives with children, grandchildren and probably pet dogs, in tow.

THE ATHLETE – FLO MEILER

Great-grandmother Flo Meiler took up track and field sports at the age 60. At 65, she tried the pole vault for the first time, proving you're never too old to try something new! Flo now holds numerous world and US records for her age group. At 83-years-old, Flo is still competing in the pole vault. Clearly, she's super healthy, but Flo does admit to a weakness for French fries and chocolate-covered almonds.

THE SUPERMODEL – DAPHNE SELFE

Daphne is the UK's oldest model and is still landing roles in major fashion and beauty campaigns at the age of 90. She started out as a model but left the fashion world to bring up her three children, only to be rediscovered at the age of 70. Daphne now travels the world and is the iconic face of older models. She once said in an interview: "My grandchildren laugh when they see me in the paper, but they think it's quite cool; I think it gives them a certain kudos at school."

THE JUDGE – RUTH BADER GINSBURG

Grandmother of four, Supreme Court Justice Ruth Bader Ginsburg was only the second female justice in the history of the US. Nominated in 1993 at the age of 60, she continues to serve in the Supreme Court. She has been incredibly influential in furthering the rights of women and has been on the Forbes list of the 100 Most Powerful Women. She's stood up to her more conservative colleagues when she's believed decisions to be regressive, rightfully earning her place in women's history.

WORDS OF

Wisdom

"… they showered us kids with love and left the parenting to Momma and Daddy. That's the beauty of being a grandparent – the hard work belongs to someone else."

PAULA DEEN

"You make all your mistakes with your own children so by the time your grandchildren arrive, you know how to get it right."

LIZ FENTON

"A grandmother is a babysitter who watches the kids instead of the television."

UNKNOWN

"A grandmother is a little bit parent, a little bit teacher, and a little bit best friend."

UNKNOWN

"My grandmother is over eighty and still doesn't need glasses. Drinks right out of the bottle."

HENRY YOUNGMAN

"Grandchildren make our laughter longer."

UNKNOWN

OUT OF THE MOUTHS OF

Babes

I was babysitting my granddaughter one night and declared it was time for bed. "Why?" she asked, and I told her because her father said bedtime is 7 o'clock. "You don't have to listen to him," she replied. "You're his mother!"

My four-year-old grandson was watching me put moisturiser on one day. "What's that for, Gran?" he asked. "It's to stop me getting wrinkles," I told him. "I don't think it's working," he replied.

My three-year-old granddaughter asked me how old I was. When I told her I'd soon be 65, she exclaimed: "65!!? I didn't know numbers went that high!"

I was explaining to my excited grandson that we couldn't predict the exact date when his new baby sister would be born. "You were due on 18th March," I told him, "but you arrived on 15th March." He thought for a moment and then piped up with: "Oh, I'm so lucky to have been born on my birthday!"

THINGS TO DO NOW YOU'RE A

Grandma

Keep treats on hand to comfort, bribe or coerce!

Never address your grandchild's parents with a sentence that begins "In my day...." Understandably, their backs will be up before you've even finished what you're saying.

Avoid playing favorites among your grandchildren. Even the youngest of children will pick up on it.

Play, play, play! And show your grandchild your silly side. Teach them that growing older doesn't mean life has to become all serious.

Get the tissues ready, and not just for snotty noses – you're about to cry. A lot. At that song on the radio, a certain advert on the television, a sad story in a newspaper ... Having a grandchild makes you more emotionally vulnerable.

WORDS OF

Wisdom

"There's no greater music than the sound of my grandchildren laughing."

SYLVIA EARLE

"Just when you think you know all love is ... along come grandchildren."

UNKNOWN

"I thought I had forgotten how to hold a baby – but my arms remember."

UNKNOWN

"A grandparent has been there, done that child-raising stuff, and has the wisdom of experience. And so in some ways, they're free to love without the anxiety of being the actual parents."

JEWELL PARKER RHODES

"Some moments can only be cured with a big squishy grandma hug."

DAN PEARCE

"Being a grandmother is our last chance to act like a kid without being accused of being in our second childhood."

JANET LANESE

OUT OF THE MOUTHS OF

Babes

After getting dressed up for a special evening out, I asked my three-year-old granddaughter if I looked beautiful. She replied, "Grandma, you would be just beautiful if it wasn't for your face."

My granddaughter and I were on the bus one day when a man came and sat on the seat in front of us. She turned to me and asked in a loud voice: "Why does that man have a circle of skin in the middle of his hair?"

My granddaughter was singing in the back of our car when she suddenly started crying. When I asked her what the matter was she said: "I'm crying at how beautiful my voice is."

I asked my five-year-old grandson what he wanted to be when he grows up. "A machine," he answered. When I asked him why, he explained: "you can replace the parts in a machine when they wear out."

HOW TO BE A FUNKY

Grandma

So, you think you've got the moves, the wardrobe and the A.T.T.I.T.U.D.E. but are you really a groovy grandma? Chill out and follow these nifty tips for being hip …

Chances are you already have a mobile phone and have at least had a try of a tablet (one that's not been prescribed by your doctor!) so you're already somewhere up there on the cool grandma stakes. But if you want to know what on earth your grandchildren are talking about, then read articles about technology trends so you know what the Next Big Thing is before they do – guaranteed to impress! Be the one to embrace the latest gadgets, even if you have to get someone else to show you how they work.

One of the most important things you can do for your grandchildren is to stay healthy. Eat well, sleep well, exercise and make time to relax. Don't ignore aches or dismiss niggles. If you're worried something isn't right, then see your doctor. If there's one thing that's going to stop you joining your grandchildren on the dancefloor for an encore of the Cha Cha Slide it's being unwell.

Grandmas are famed for their uncool gifts. You can be the grandma to turn that around – say no to socks, jumpers, talcum powder or soaps-on-ropes! If you really want to earn some brownie points, then a really well-thought-out gift is the way to go. Think about what your grandchild is interested in and don't go for the obvious. The internet is great for finding quirky gifts and things that can be personalised. Thoughtfulness is a wonderful way to demonstrate your love for someone – and your hip grandma rating will rocket.

WORDS OF

"Family faces are magic mirrors. Looking at people who belong to us, we see the past, present and future."

GAIL LUMET BUCKLEY

"Grandma serves kisses, counsel and cookies daily."

UNKNOWN

"A grandmother always has time for you, even if the rest of the world is busy."

G. SAUNDERS

"Grandmothers and roses are much the same. Both are masterpieces of nature, just with different names."

UNKNOWN

"A grandma is warm hugs and sweet memories. She remembers all of your accomplishments and forgets all of your mistakes."

BARBARA CAGE

"I've found something that my grandchildren can wear out faster than their shoes – their grandma!"

UNKNOWN

THINGS TO DO NOW YOU'RE A

Grandma

Lose your inhibitions. Your grandchild wants you to wear her

tiara to the park,

do it! Get down on all fours and roar like a lion – go for it...

Decide the ways in which you can help as a grandparent. How much time you are prepared, and able, to dedicate to childcare should be determined from the offset.

Become a storyteller. No digital device can ever compete with a real-life, loving person telling stories. Share anything from favorite fairy tales to memorable moments from your own life.

Make your home a haven for your grandchild, somewhere they look forward to spending time.

Always be prepared with tissues for snotty noses, Band-Aids for grazed knees, and cuddles to make it all better.

"Being a grandparent is my Happily Ever After."

UNKNOWN

Albert F. Schneider, Jr.
408 Constitution Ave.
Hellertown, Penna.
Moravian College

Building
a Successful Marriage

Building

JUDSON T. LANDIS

Professor of Family Sociology,
University of California at Berkeley

and

MARY G. LANDIS

THIRD EDITION

a Successful

Marriage

Englewood Cliffs, New Jersey

PRENTICE-HALL, Inc.

Prentice-Hall Sociology Series

Herbert Blumer, Editor

Building a Successful Marriage, THIRD EDITION

Landis and Landis

L. C. Cat. Card No. 58-9189

FIFTH PRINTING.........JUNE, 1961

Printed in the United States of America
08698-C

To our children

Judson and Janet

Preface

Most of the readers of this book will be either approaching marriage or already married and learning that marriage is a growth process that constantly requires new understandings and new adjustments. We hope that this third edition of BUILDING A SUCCESSFUL MARRIAGE will continue to prove useful to college classes seeking insight into mate selection, courtship, and the patterns of adjustment in marriage, and to readers who hope to build successful marriages.

We have tried to retain from the earlier editions all the materials that have stood the test of objectivity, scientific validity, and usefulness in meeting the special needs of young people. But we have rewritten some sections in the light of our further thinking and experience with young people and in view of new and enlightening research. We have discovered that many research findings, as well as conclusions reached through study and through counseling with people of all ages, have increased meaning for us as we ourselves advance through the stages of the family life cycle. At this point, as we enter the twenty-ninth year of our own marriage and begin to adjust to the empty-nest stage of life after watching our children grow through childhood and into young adulthood, we find that we can approach some topics in this book with more confidence than when the first edition was written. But always questions arise which suggest the need for new and continuing research, for careful analyses of findings, and for objectivity in presenting data.

A chapter on love is now included for the first time (Ch. 9). This chapter deals with the subject of love not from a philosophical or theoretical viewpoint but in an attempt to provide ideas and insights which may help the young person to assess realistically his own emotional experiences and relationships.

We have endeavored to include in this edition new research findings that are relevant for the college population today. In order not to unduly increase the size of the book we have eliminated use of research data that are based upon dating and courtship behavior of a generation ago, except when the older researches are concerned with matters of permanent relevance as is the Terman study of psychological factors in marital adjustment, or in cases in which the older research findings are valuable for purposes of comparison with new data.

A new chapter has been added on dating, and both chapters on dating (4 and 5) are the outgrowth of studies of dating practices today. Dating is treated as a growth process which can prepare for successful marriage. New materials have been added on maturity for marriage (Ch. 8), and on remaining single (Ch. 6). A study of 200 couples engaged in 1957 has contributed toward bringing the engagement chapter up to date.

Other subjects now given an expanded treatment are: changing sex roles, marriage involving separation, marriage while the man is in military service, premarital sex behavior, fertilty and infertility, adoption, and bringing up children.

For greater convenience, the review questions and suggested readings are listed at the ends of the chapters rather than in the appendix. Outlines for self-study have been included with many of the chapters to help stimulate the reader's thinking.

We are grateful to many people for the valuable contributions they have made either directly or indirectly to our work. We are indebted especially to all those who have cooperated in research; the young parents who gave their histories of adjustment to first pregnancy, the couples who reported upon their adjustments to the problems of early marriage, the older couples who supplied information on the length of time required after marriage to adjust in various relationships. We are also indebted to the many thousands of students who have contributed to our knowledge and our thinking by their discussions in classes and their evaluations of the text and lecture materials, and by their enthusiastic cooperation in a number of research projects relating to court‑ ship, engagement, maturation and dating, effects of divorce on children, experiences with adult sexual deviates, physical and emotional changes accompanying the menstrual cycle, and others.

The study of student dating in eleven colleges was possible only because of the generous cooperation of the following: Eugene P. Link, State University of New York, New Paltz; Kenneth Cannon and Fern Brown, University of Nebraska; Gus Turbeville, University of Minnesota, Duluth Branch; B. F. Timmons, University of Illinois; Freda Wallin, Stanford University; J. Shailer Arnold, Fullerton Junior College; Marion B. Smith, Louisiana State University; Lawrence S. Bee, University of Kansas; Arlie E. McGuire, University of Dubuque; and Charles B. Spaulding, Whittier College. We are grateful to Russell R. Dynes of Ohio State University and Roberta D. Ortenburger of the University of Oklahoma, whose comments and suggestions on the second edition were most helpful.

Our colleagues in different schools and universities have helped us greatly. Their comments and criticisms as they have used the book in classes over the years have served as constructive guides for us in this revision.

Judson T. Landis

Mary G. Landis

Berkeley, California

Contents

Building
a Successful Marriage

What is successful marriage?

Attitude toward permanence of marriage

Divorce a hazard

Marriage as a way of life

Social changes and marriage stability

Successful Marriage

Why marry?

How successful are marriages in the United States?

Building successful marriages around the world

This year more than 3,000,000 Americans will marry. For many of them, the wedding will mark the beginning of a life of expanding happiness and fulfillment. They will be able to build a relationship that will enrich their own lives, and contribute also to the good of society. But a certain proportion of the marriages will not be successful. Some of them will mean unhappiness and personal deterioration for the individuals; some will end in divorce—the public acknowledgment of failure.

The future of any marriage will be affected by such factors as the personality traits of the husband and wife, their family backgrounds, and some of the attitudes they hold. In truth, their attitudes will have far more to do with the success of their marriage than will the intensity of the love they feel for each other on their wedding day. Their marriage will be affected in great measure by their concept of what marriage is, their ideas of what it will require of them, and what they hope to receive from it.

· · · 1

What is successful marriage?

Poets, cynics, and philosophers have all tried epigrammatic summaries of marriage. But marriage cannot be defined in a sentence. In a successful marriage, each partner, because of the marriage, becomes a more integrated person, better able to meet and cope adequately with the vicissitudes of life. Successful marriage is based upon cooperation. It includes the most rewarding comradeship. In a good marriage, each partner is all that he himself is capable of being; moreover, his personality expands and takes on, to some extent, the attributes and capacities of his mate. Both husband and wife are aware that an interdependence exists by which the two stand together, so that pleasures are enhanced through the sharing, and blows that life may offer are cushioned.

This union of personalities is not a gift presented by fate to people who are lucky in love, nor is it a benefit conferred by the words of the wedding ceremony. It must be created by the marriage partners, and can be achieved through cooperative effort over a period of time. It will not be achieved by people who, though united legally in marriage, are striving each to go his independent way and to retain his individual freedom. No absolute freedom exists for anyone, either outside of marriage or within it. But in marriage each partner gives up a measure of personal freedom in exchange for the element of togetherness that is one of the permanent values of married life.

People approaching marriage usually are hoping for happiness as a pair; they are seldom aware that the scope of marriage is broader than the two who marry. Yet people who can build a good marriage are making a positive contribution to the world about them. They will be more effective in all life's relationships. They are not so likely to be among the problem individuals who trouble society.

A successful marriage usually includes children and a home life that provides a healthy emotional climate for the children. Through children, marriage happiness is extended and perpetuated. Sociologists have discovered that in our society successful marriages run in families. Hence, the couple who marry with an intelligent understanding that they have committed themselves to living together in harmony, with tolerance for each other's faults, and with respect for each other's virtues, and who abide by their decision unalterably, are setting a pattern for the successful marriages of their children.

Attitude toward permanence of marriage

One of the important elements in building a good marriage is a consciousness of the fact that marriage commits both partners to a permanent relationship. When people say the words, "I take thee . . . for better, for worse, for richer, for poorer, in sickness and in health . . . until death . . . ," they are contracting for a lifetime of cooperation in all areas of living. Successful cooperation is not possible when any limitations are set upon it. Today, when divorce is relatively easy, it might seem questionable to imply the logic of taking the marriage vows literally—"for better, for worse, until death." But commitment to marriage as a lifetime undertaking is the only logical starting point from which successful marriage can be built.

This point can be illustrated by the experiences of two couples. Two engaged girls were comparing their attitudes toward marriage and divorce. Helen said, "John and I both have divorced parents, and we know that divorce doesn't necessarily solve the problems of an unhappy marriage; so we are going to wait a few months to be married, and we have agreed that no matter what comes up after we marry, we will work our way through it together. Once we marry, we intend it to be for life." Ruth said, "Tom and I don't feel just that way. We are going to be married at once because we think the only way we can find out whether marriage to each other is the thing for us is to try it. We've agreed now that if it doesn't work out, we'll call it off without bitter feelings."

So Tom and Ruth were married, and in the normal course of events disagreements arose. Some were only minor; others would have required both to make serious adjustments. But according to their thinking, why should either of them make the effort to change or to compromise? They both felt that if their marriage was not going to succeed they should find it out while they were still young enough to make a fresh start with someone else. So, when differences arose, Tom and Ruth refused to compromise, and tried to force concessions from each other. Their marriage lasted a year. Both were disillusioned to find that the divorce involved more unhappiness and bitterness than they had thought possible; they could not end their marriage with nonchalance, even though they were not willing to compromise and cooperate.

Helen and John continued dating for ten months following their engagement and then were married. They also found points on which they disagreed. But after ten years of married life, Helen said, "We figured that since we were together for life, the sooner we reached agreement on the points where we differed the happier we would be. We always understood each other better and had more respect for each other's viewpoint after we had talked over our differences. Sometimes one of us changed to the other's way of thinking, but more often we compromised." Their marriage has been increasingly successful.

It is true that in both these marriages personality traits and other factors contributed toward the success or failure. However, there were no insurmountable barriers to happiness in either case. The crucial factor was the willingness or unwillingness to work at creating a successful marriage. With Helen and John, the willingness to work at building a good relationship was based in part on their feeling that their marriage was for life—literally "for better or for worse."

Divorce a hazard

In a sense, easy divorce as it exists in our society is a hazard to successful marriage, since people may sometimes think of it as a ready solution to problems that arise in marriage. The alternative of escape through divorce may prevent some couples from facing in a mature manner the problems of marriage. Yet these problems, through the solving, might well become stepping-stones to deeper and more lasting happiness. The point is sometimes made that in former times, when divorce was not socially acceptable, many people suffered through life in unhappy marriages because they had no escape. That is true. It is also true that many marriages which formerly might have been successful now end in divorce. If they had no easy way out, the partners in these marriages would recognize the necessity for working through problems to success.

One of the things that people contemplating marriage need to know is that divorce is seldom a satisfactory solution to problems. The emotional traumas involved and the personality damage inflicted by the experience of failure that divorce represents are often worse than the difficulties from which people escape through divorce. Certainly, where marriage has failed beyond any possibility of recovery, divorce may be the only course of action. But more realistic preparation for marriage and the recognition that being in love is not the only prerequisite for marriage should lead to more careful and rational mate selection, less haste in entering marriage, and fewer marriages ending in divorce.

Marriage as a way of life

Almost all people who want to achieve success in marriage can do so if they are prepared for their task.

It is necessary to know that all marriages include the pleasant and the unpleasant, the happy and the unhappy, and hard work and commonplace everyday living as well as ecstasy. Too much emphasis is often placed on "happiness," so that some people approach married life expecting it to be one long emotional spree. Disappointment is inevitable for them. None of us could endure for long a life made up of nothing but parties. Party clothes, party conversation, and party food would eventually become intolerable. For life to be interesting and worth while we must have also the commonplace, the difficult, the drab. These elements are present in even the best of marriages. Whether one is married or single, overconcentration on a search for "happiness" as an end may limit one's efforts to build into life those things that give permanent zest to living.

Marriage is a way of life that requires much of the individual. How well a person understands himself and his own personality

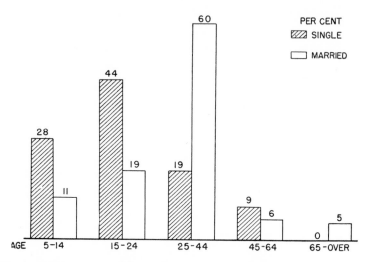

Fig. I PERCENTAGE OF 450 MARRIED AND SINGLE OLD PEOPLE CHOOSING DIFFERENT PERIODS IN LIFE AS THE HAPPIEST. When a large group of old people between the ages of 65 and 100 were asked at what time they had been happiest in life, over half said the best years were those when they were married and had children at home. The comments indicated that their happiness in life was closely related to marriage and family living. The unmarried felt the happiest years had been during childhood and youth. Data from Judson T. Landis, "What Is the Happiest Period in Life?," *School and Society,* 55:1432 (June 6, 1942), 643-645.

needs and how well he habitually gets along with himself and with others will have a great deal to do with the success of his marriage. Marriage does not change basic personality. Sometimes people marry hoping that marriage will work miracles in their lives and bring them happiness, even though they do not have the habit of happiness. That is expecting too much of marriage. Those who marry with an intelligent evaluation of their own marriageability and an appreciation of their obligations, as well as their privileges, are likely to achieve greater success and happiness.

Social changes and marriage stability

It is true today as never before that the outcome is in our own hands when we marry. In former generations, individual choice and responsibility were not so great. The institutional aspects of marriage exerted pressures that are almost nonexistent today. Law, tradition, religion, and social custom—all operated as external controls to give permanence to marriage. The marriage relationship was carefully defined and regulated by society. Since tradition and social pressure favored male domination in marriage, adjustment was not necessarily shared equally by husband and wife.

Moreover, life in the United States was predominantly rural. Consequently, families were generally held together by many bonds that no longer exert a strong influence. A farm family worked together to produce a living. Their isolated mode of life made it possible for all members of the family to be held readily accountable for their goings and comings. Members of the family depended on each other for recreation and social life. In many ways, the family was forced by circumstances to build together all that was worth while in life.

These conditions have changed. Man's position as the dominant head of the family no longer goes unchallenged. The population of the United States is no longer predominantly rural. The conditions under which people live in cities make it more difficult for them to maintain a stable family life. Crowded living conditions, the anonymity of the individual, freedom from social controls, the opportunities for varied recreational activities that separate rather than unite the family, and the lack of any necessity or opportunity for working together to make a living—all affect the stability of marriage.

Formerly, other practical considerations helped maintain the permanence of marriages. A man had to depend on a wife to keep his clothes in order, to prepare his food, to make a home for his aged parents, and to rear his children. A woman had to have a husband to support her and to give her the social standing that was impossible for a spinster to attain. Now a man can depend on the cleaner and tailor to care for his clothes. He can eat in restaurants or he can do his own cooking, thanks to modern preserved and frozen foods. The state provides for his aged parents through old-age assistance, or they may provide for themselves through social security and retirement plans.

Fig. 2   MARRIAGE SUCCESS AND FAILURE. For every four marriages today, one will end in failure, according to present marriage and divorce rates.

As for the woman, the many lines of work now open to her mean that she can earn her own living. Although marriage still has a greater prestige value than spinsterhood, the stigma of spinsterhood has been greatly reduced. Some career women prefer single independence to marriage.

All this means that some of the pressures governing marriage as an institution in our culture have decreased. It does not mean that marriage today is any less necessary or important to people than it formerly was. People are marrying today in greater numbers and at younger ages than ever before.

Why marry?

Although some of the utilitarian reasons for marriage have been minimized by scientific and technological changes, the basic needs that impel people toward monogamous marriage remain unchanged. In fact, the very changes that have decreased the power of external controls on marriage stability have given greater force to the affectional function of marriage. Greater population mobility, the anonymity of the individual in the city, the loosening of bonds with family members—all these factors emphasize for the individual his need for some one person with whom he can build a life of comradeship and understanding.

Marriage satisfies certain personality needs that are difficult to satisfy outside marriage. Strauss asked 173 men and 200 women who were engaged or who had been married less than a year to list the personality needs that they hoped to have satisfied in marriage [1] (see Table 1). The results show that the things that

TABLE 1 PERCENTAGES OF 373 MEN AND WOMEN
STATING VARIOUS PERSONALITY NEEDS
THAT THEY HOPED TO HAVE SATISFIED THROUGH MARRIAGE

Personality need	Men	Women
Someone to love me	36.4%	53.5%
Someone to confide in	30.6	40.0
Someone to show affection	20.8	30.0
Someone to respect my ideals	26.0	26.0
Someone to appreciate what I wish to achieve	28.3	24.0
Someone to understand my moods	23.1	27.5
Someone to help make my decisions	15.0	32.5
Someone to stimulate my ambition	26.6	21.0
Someone to look up to	16.2	29.0
Someone to give me self-confidence	19.6	24.0
Someone to back me in difficulty	16.2	25.5
Someone to appreciate me just as I am	20.2	20.5
Someone to admire my ability	18.5	19.5
Someone to make me feel important	20.8	17.0
Someone to relieve my loneliness	18.5	18.5

[1] Ernest W. Burgess and Harvey J. Locke, *The Family*, p. 369. New York: American Book Company, 1953.

men and women desire from marriage do not differ greatly. A greater percentage of the women expressed felt personality needs. This may indicate that, while both sexes have the same needs, women may be more conscious of their needs than men are.

Happy marriages are those in which both husband and wife find fulfillment of a majority of these needs. In many marriages both partners either consciously or unconsciously seek to give to each other the love, understanding, and moral support that enable the mate to feel that he counts for something. In many marriages enough of these needs are met so that both partners are fairly well satisfied with the bargain, and the marriage may be called successful. In other marriages, one or the other may be entirely unaware of the personality needs of the mate and may make no effort to contribute to their satisfaction. The consciousness of these needs, nevertheless, impels people toward marriage, and in successful marriages, most or many of these needs are met for each other by the two partners.

How successful are marriages in the United States?

Although there is evidence of the instability of some marriages and the unhappiness of others, the over-all picture is that most marriages do meet the needs of the members of the couple. In general, people consider their own marriages to be happy. The marital tangles and family break-ups that make headlines are the exceptions, not the average American marriage.

Several different kinds of studies have been made of marital happiness in the United States. In some studies the couples have rated their own happiness; in others, friends have rated the happiness of the couples. Other studies have used a combination of factors to determine the happiness of marriages. Studies in which the husband and the wife rated their marital happiness independently of each other show a high percentage of agreement between partners. There is also a close relationship between happiness ratings given by the married people themselves and the score rating assigned to them on the basis of other factors by those doing the research or by friends who base their ratings on observation of the marriage.[2]

In five studies of marital happiness, from 63 to 85 per cent of the marriages were rated as happy or very happy (see Table 2).

TABLE 2   COMPARISON OF RESULTS
OF DIFFERENT MARITAL HAPPINESS STUDIES

Happiness rating	Burgess and Cottrell [a] (N-526)	Terman [b] (N-792)	Lang [c] (N-17533)	Landis [d] (N-409)	Landis [e] (N-2640)
Happy or very happy	63.0	85.0	62.0	83.0	74.0
Average	14.0	9.0	19.0	16.0	21.0
Unhappy or very unhappy	22.0	5.0	20.0	1.0	5.0

[a] Burgess and Cottrell, *Predicting Success or Failure in Marriage*, p. 34. Englewood Cliffs, N. J.: Prentice-Hall, Inc., 1939.

[b] Lewis M. Terman, *Psychological Factors in Marital Happiness*, p. 78. New York: McGraw-Hill Book Company, Inc., 1938.

[c] Burgess and Cottrell, *op. cit.*, p. 139.

[d] Judson T. Landis, "Length of Time Required to Achieve Adjustment in Marriage," *American Sociological Review*, 11:6 (December, 1946), 674.

[e] Judson T. Landis. Study of 3,000 students in 11 colleges. Rating of parental marital happiness by children in families without divorce (1952-1955).

The Burgess and Lang studies showed a larger percentage of unhappy marriages because they included some people who were divorced. The Terman study and our studies included only those people who were and who had been living together for some time, an average of 11 years in the Terman study and an average of 20 years or more in our studies. In the latter three studies, it must be recognized that many of the unhappy marriages had been eliminated through divorce.

Terman asked those in his study whether they would marry the same person if they had their lives to live over. Eighty-three

[2] For a summary of the different methods of measuring happiness in marriage, see Ernest W. Burgess and Leonard S. Cottrell, Jr., *Predicting Success or Failure in Marriage*, pp. 38-44.

per cent of the husbands and 86 per cent of the wives said they would.[3]

Thus, the evidence shows that the majority of marriages are happy. This does not mean that marriage does not involve some struggle. Actually, marriage requires more than some people are capable of giving. Such people are unmarriageable; if they do marry they account for a large proportion of the marriage failures. But, in the average marriage, couples find the rewards worth the effort and they struggle willingly and successfully to make the necessary adjustments.

Building successful marriages around the world

Social changes affecting marriage and the family are not a situation peculiar to the United States. All over the world such changes are recognized and are being discussed and studied by thoughtful people. The trend in many other countries of the world, as in the United States, is away from the type of marriage that is rigidly defined and controlled by outside forces and pressures, toward marriages that are formed by choice and that succeed on the basis of cooperation and mutual adjustment. The trend is toward more marriages that depend for survival on the meeting of the personality needs of both spouses.

The rate of change varies greatly in different countries. Social change in any area of living results in confusion or turmoil for individuals and sometimes for whole segments of a society. Therefore people in all countries are concerned with the implications of successful marriage for stable social organization. When professional workers in the field of marriage and the family from different countries discuss together different aspects of family problems, the similarity of problems is striking, whether the representative is speaking for Thailand, Pakistan, Burma, Brazil, a European nation, or the United States. Concern is universal

[3] Terman, *op. cit.*, p. 53.

about increases in divorce, the changing roles of women and men, and parent-child relationships. Always there are those who believe that resistance to change is the answer, that more stringent laws or more restrictive controls will contribute to more successful marriages. But in society and in human relationships, it is not possible to turn the clock back.

For students of marriage and the family today, for professional workers concerned with family stability as it affects social organization, and for individuals who hope to make a success of their own marriages, it is necessary to understand not only social changes taking place, but the nature of marriage itself as a relationship involving all aspects of personality and of living.

People who marry today have opportunities to prepare for marriage that were not available in the past. Continuing research and scientific study of the problems of family living will provide further information to help people everywhere build good marriages.

Review questions

1. What is meant by saying that a young couple's attitudes toward marriage will have more to do with their happiness than the intensity of their love at the time of the wedding?

2. What is a successful marriage?

3. In marriage, each partner gives up some of his personal freedom. What does he gain in exchange?

4. What is meant by the statement that those who can build a good marriage are making a positive contribution to the world about them?

5. Successful marriages run in families. Why?

6. How does a person's attitude toward the permanence of marriage affect his chances for a successful marriage?

7. Have you known couples who entered marriage with the attitude of Ruth and Tom?

8. "Some marriages that formerly might have been successful now end in divorce." Explain.

9. Is divorce necessarily a solution to serious difficulties in marriage?

10. Why is the idea that marriage will mean complete happiness a handicap?

11. Name several social changes that have affected the stability of the American family.

12. In what ways are the sexes less dependent on each other today than they were 100 years ago?

13. Contrast urban and rural living as they affect family relationships and stability.

14. Why is the affectional function of the family more important today than ever before?

15. What are some of the personality needs fulfilled in marriage?

16. Approximately what proportion of marriages are happy in the United States?

17. Why are marriage and family problems similar in countries around the world?

Suggested readings

Baber, Ray E., *Marriage and the Family*. New York: McGraw-Hill Book Company, Inc., 1953. Ch. I, "The Family in Transition."

Becker, Howard, and Reuben Hill, eds., *Family, Marriage, and Parenthood*. Boston: D. C. Heath and Company, 1955. Ch. XXVI, "Plans for Strengthening Family Life."

Burgess, Ernest W., and Harvey J. Locke, *The Family*. New York: American Book Company, 1953. Ch. XVI, "The American Family in Transition."

Burgess, Ernest W., and Paul Wallin, *Engagement and Marriage*. Chicago: J. B. Lippincott Company, 1953. Ch. I, "Marriage in Transition," and Ch. II, "The Study of Modern Marriage."

Cavan, Ruth Shonle, *The American Family*. New York: Thomas Y. Crowell Company, 1953. Ch. I, "Issues in the American Family at the Mid-Century."

Christensen, Harold T., *Marriage Analysis*. New York: The Ronald Press Company, 1958. Ch. II, "An Overview of Family Organization," and Ch. III, "Family Changes Within the United States."

Landis, Judson T., and Mary G. Landis, eds., *Readings in Marriage and the Family*. Englewood Cliffs, N. J.: Prentice-Hall, Inc., 1952. Part I, Reading 1, "The Contemporary American Family as an Anthropologist Sees It," Margaret Mead; Reading 2, "Cultural Configurations in the American Family," John Sirjamaki; Reading 3, "The Changing Functions of the Family," William F. Ogburn; Reading 4, "The Family in a Changing Society," Ernest W. Burgess; Reading 5, "The Changing Family," Paul H. Landis.

Nimkoff, Meyer F., *Marriage and the Family*. Boston: Houghton Mifflin Company, 1948. Ch. IV, "Modern American Family."

Changing status of women

Sex dissimilarities

Mortality and morbidity

Differences in muscular strength and coordination

Rate of growth

Pyschological differences

Role Concepts and Sex Differences

Achievement differences

Reasons for achievement differences

The double standard and biological factors

The preceding chapter discussed the importance of the attitudes that people hold concerning the nature of marriage—the demands it makes and the rewards it offers. Another important element is the attitude each person has about his or her role in life. What rights, privileges, and obligations are mine because I was born a male? Or, what rights, privileges, and obligations are mine because I was born a female? The success of some marriages is jeopardized at the outset because the partners hold set ideas about man's place or woman's place in life, and are unable to adapt themselves to the various roles required of them in marriage. No final answer can be given to many of the questions that will be raised in this and the following chapter; our purpose is to present facts and ideas that may help the reader to evaluate his own attitudes about sex roles in modern life.

Changing status of women

.. 2

A few generations ago higher education was not open to women; they had few opportunities to train for work other than household tasks, and therefore were economically dependent on the men of their families. Until fairly recently, the legal rights of women as individuals, in the United States, were few. American mores still followed the pattern advocated by the bachelor, Paul: "If the woman would learn anything let her ask her husband at home." [1]

The accepted attitude toward women was expressed in a book published in 1881, *Decorum: A Practical Treatise on Etiquette and Dress of*

[1] I Corinthians 14:35.

Fig. 3 EDUCATION TODAY PREPARES BOTH MEN AND WOMEN FOR CAREERS AND FOR MARRIAGE. Courtesy of *California Monthly*.

the Best American Society. The author offers the following advice to gentlemen: "When addressing ladies, pay them the compliment of seeming to consider them capable of an equal understanding with gentlemen . . . they will appreciate the delicate compliment." In the same treatise on decorum the author says, "Young married ladies must never appear in any public place unattended by their husbands or by elder ladies. This rule must never be infringed." And, "Of late years ladies have taken to rowing; this can be managed in a quiet river or private pond but it is scarcely to be attempted in the . . . public parts of rivers unless superintended by a gentleman." For the edification of all concerned, he comments, "Most women are naturally amiable, gentle and complying."

Perhaps the author of *Decorum* was whistling in the dark, for even as he wrote, some able women—despite their amiability and gentleness—were devoting their lives to battling for the "rights" of women. Since then much has been written and said about sex equality, and public opinion regarding the place of women has changed. Most universities are open to women on an equal basis with men. Although university education is still geared to train for what has been traditionally considered as masculine achievement, women can prepare themselves for almost any occupation or profession they choose. It has now become the accepted custom for unmarried American women to hold jobs outside the home. Formerly it was proper for the unmarried woman to make herself useful within the shelter of the home of her parents or brothers. Now, however, even among married women, 50 per cent hold outside jobs during the first year of marriage.

Yet laws that discriminate against women still remain on the statute books of several states. In some states women are barred from holding certain public offices; in others they may not sign contracts without their husbands' consent. In most states, however, women are free to enter almost all occupations, although disparities often exist between the pay received by women and men of equal training.

All inequalities that still exist are targets for those who are battling for complete freedom, or equality, for women. A proposed amendment to the federal Constitution reads: "Men and women shall have equal rights throughout the United States and every place subject to its jurisdiction." The amendment is supported by powerful groups of organized women, such as the National Federation of Business and Professional Women. It is opposed by some equally intelligent and powerful groups, such as the League of Women Voters.

Some of those opposing such an amendment believe that *complete* "equality" would actually discriminate against women because it would place upon them equal responsibility with men, and would deprive them of certain protections inherent in their present inequality. It would fail to recognize that nature has already given women certain inescapable obligations and responsibilities that men will never be able to share equally. Opponents of the amendment feel that these obligations require for women exemptions from some of the responsibilities borne by men.

Sex dissimilarities

The picture is a complicated one. Some of the restrictions placed on women by our moral and economic double standard have no justification; they are simply relics from less enlightened times. Others have a logical and firm basis in the scheme of things as set up by nature, and legislating against them or agitating about them will not alter the facts. The facts concerning the nature, physical make-up, and functioning of men and of women point neither to equality nor to inequality. The more accurate concept is that major dissimilarities do exist, but the words "equal" and "unequal" are inapplicable when we compare the capacities and abilities of the sexes. Men and women are complementary to each other; an acceptance of their biological and cultural differences is important if they are to fulfill their roles constructively and happily.

Traditionally, woman has been thought of as the weaker sex. But careful study of children and adults in all phases of their growth and achievement forces a redefining of terms. Studies show that in rate of development, both physical and mental, the female leads. In muscular strength, the male leads. The female has greater resistance to disease and death, and to emotional pressure, than the male. Also, the differences in body chemistry of the two sexes may account for behavior dissimilarities. We will consider in more detail some of these basic differences.

Mortality and morbidity

Women sometimes say of their husbands, "He doesn't get sick very often, but when he does, things seem to hit him awfully hard!" Wives who make that observation are not just describing an individual husband's reaction to illness; they have discovered a fact well known to doctors. Men are not sick so often as women, but when illness strikes them, it does hit harder. The death rates for males are higher from the time of conception on through every age. Biologists tell us that at least 120 males are conceived to every 100 females, yet at birth the sex ratio has dropped to 105.5 males to 100 females. The great surplus of males conceived do not survive to be born. During the first four months of pregnancy, at least four times as many male as female fetuses die. The proportion of deaths gradually decreases until the eighth month of pregnancy, when the average is 55 males to 45 females. One-fourth more boys than girls die during the first year after birth. And, vital statistics show that this ratio occurs quite consistently year after year. When conditions are improved so that the total infant mortality rate is lowered, as it has been in America during this century, the proportion of male to female deaths becomes even greater. In other words, the greater resistance of the female enables her to profit more from better environment than the male is able to do. Mothers often assume that girls are more delicate than boys, but it is the boys who have less resistance and hence are in more serious danger when disease strikes. As adults, more women than men have occasion to consult doctors, many of the occasions arising from conditions related to the reproductive processes. Although they may require more medical attention, women may still be in relatively good health. Men, on the other hand, less frequently need to consult doctors, but they are susceptible to the more serious diseases, and, once ill, they are much more likely to succumb.

Various explanations have been advanced for the higher mortality rates of males. The fact is cited that their lives naturally expose them to greater dangers. But their higher mortality in the early months following conception as well as during the first twelve months after birth, and the fact that they fall victim to almost all the major diseases in greater numbers than females do, force the conclusion that males

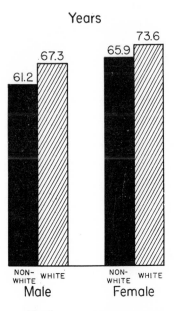

Fig. 4 LIFE EXPECTANCY FOR MALE AND FEMALE, NON-WHITE AND WHITE, UNITED STATES, 1955. Among both white and non-white, the female lives longer than the male. Data from Metropolitan Life Insurance Company, *Statistical Bulletin,* 38 (July 1, 1957), 4.

simply have been equipped by nature with less ability than females to resist or survive illness and infection. The difference in the mortality rates of men and women is reflected in women's greater life expectancy, which is more than six years longer than men's. Today, the average life expectancy for white women is about 74, for white men, slightly over 67. Should we say that men are the "weaker" sex?

Differences in muscular strength and coordination

Although females show from the beginning a natural ability to withstand illness, males from early infancy show development of a different type of strength. Observers who have tested large numbers of infants and young children report that boys consistently show greater muscular strength than girls do in the pre-school years. Girls during this time develop a finer motor coordination. They are able to do things that require use of fingers, such as buttoning clothing, but boys can lift heavier objects and can throw and climb more easily.

It is sometimes believed that the difference in performance between the sexes, particularly the difference in play activities, is due to conditioning. That is, girls are given dolls and encouraged to dress them and play with them, whereas boys are given blocks to build with, or trucks and wagons. The theory is that since boys are shamed if they wish to play with dolls they become conditioned to playing in traditionally masculine ways. Certainly all human beings are to some degree conditioned by the culture in which they live. But it seems logical that inherent biological differences between the sexes account for some of the differences in performance. Since the boy's larger muscles are growing and developing strength at a greater rate, it is natural for him to feel the need for pushing, lifting, climbing, or entering into any type of play activity that makes use of his muscular strength. The girl's muscles are not so strong but they are more finely coordinated, and her finger dexterity is better, hence she enjoys activities like stringing beads or dressing dolls. Nursery-school teachers report that little girls like to tie and untie their shoes and usually learn to lace their shoes considerably earlier than little boys do. While a girl works at lacing her shoes, her brother may be busy lining

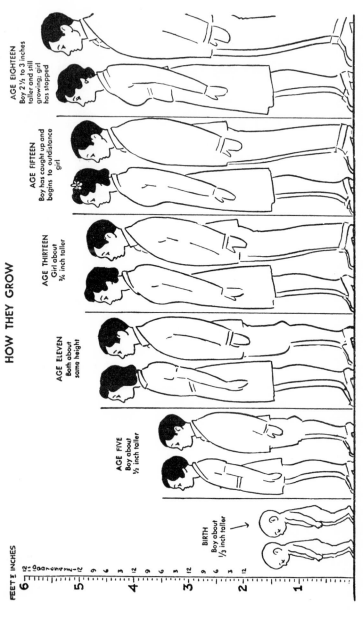

HOW THEY GROW

FEET & INCHES

AGE EIGHTEEN
Boy 2½ to 3 inches taller and still growing; girl has stopped

AGE FIFTEEN
Boy has caught up and begins to outdistance girl

AGE THIRTEEN
Girl about ¾ inch taller

AGE ELEVEN
Both about same height

AGE FIVE
Boy about ½ inch taller

BIRTH
Boy about ⅓ inch taller

Fig. 5   By permission, Amram Scheinfeld, *Women and Men*, p. 54. New York: Harcourt, Brace and Company, 1943.

26

up the chairs and pushing them along in imitation of a train. In institutions for blind and deaf children who have no contact with a normal social environment it has been observed that sex differences in activities are even more pronounced than with normal children.

Rate of growth

While the average little boy is developing muscular strength, his sister is growing at a faster rate. From infancy until middle adolescence, girls usually show faster physical growth, with accompanying differences in emotional and mental development. At birth, the male is slightly taller, on an average, than the female. By age eleven, the girl has caught up with the boy in size, and at thirteen she is almost an inch taller than he is, and slightly heavier. The girl continues to be taller until about the fifteenth year, when the boy passes her in height. She passes the boy in weight at about the twelfth year and continues to outweigh him for some time. The most marked difference in rate of development is evident during the years of early adolescence. Girls of twelve and thirteen are usually well into puberty, and their figures show signs of their growing maturity. They are "boy conscious" at this age, and are chagrined over the fact that many of the boys are not only smaller than they are, but also seem completely disinterested in girls. The average boy enters puberty somewhat later than the girl does. Our study of 3,000 college students showed that, of those who entered puberty between the ages of 10 and 16, the average age for women was 12.5, and for men, 13.3 years.[2] The boy's most rapid growth comes between the ages of 15 and 18 to 20.

[2] In later chapters we will refer again to our study, "Background Factors Related to Maturation and Dating," made from 1952-1955 in these schools: University of Illinois, University of Nebraska, Louisiana State University, State University of New York (New Paltz), University of Minnesota (Duluth Branch), University of Kansas, Stanford University, University of Dubuque, Whittier College, Fullerton Junior College, University of California (Berk-

Society recognizes the earlier physical maturity of girls by setting the legal age for marriage earlier for women than for men.

Psychological differences

Tradition has ascribed mental superiority to the male. A tendency still exists to give each sex a blanket rating of either superior or inferior. But what are to be used as standards for determining superiority or inferiority?

Sex differences in aptitudes begin to show up in early childhood and become more pronounced as individuals mature. Tests that attempt to measure intelligence bring out these differences. Boys on the average make higher scores in the phases of tests that measure mechanical ability, mathematical reasoning, and comprehension of abstract meanings; girls do better in language skills, hand skills, social knowledge, and memory. College entrance examinations show the same differences—boys tend to excel in mathematics and science; girls in language ability. Mentally, as well as physically, girls seem to reach their peak at an earlier age than boys.

Results of intelligence tests emphasize that the sexes think *differently*. It would be difficult, if not impossible, to determine how much of the difference is due to capacity and how much is due to the cultural environment. Some of the most significant differences cannot be tested—for example, various types of social intelligence at which women excel.

Observers who have worked closely with children are able to note differences and similarities that are not measured by the

---

eley). Most of those participating in the study were enrolled in marriage and family classes. Of the sample, 12 per cent were freshmen, 26 per cent sophomores, 24 per cent juniors, 35 per cent seniors, and 3 per cent graduate students. Eight per cent were married, 12 per cent formally engaged, and 16 per cent had an "understanding to be engaged." Most of the remainder were dating. The students in the study were probably a fairly representative sample of college people who elected a marriage and family course in these years. We do not know how or whether students in marriage and family classes differ from averages of the total student body.

regulation mental tests. The Yale Clinic of Child Development has contributed much to our knowledge of the characteristics of children at each age. Gesell and Ilg in their discussion of the child from five to ten, have described some of these characteristics.[3] They state that at the age of six, girls are usually better in reading, writing, and drawing, whereas boys are better in number work and in listening to stories. Girls may advance more rapidly in the early grades. Girls (at eight) are more inquisitive and more demanding of facts about sex than boys—girls may think the subject through far enough to ask more specific questions than boys will ask. Boys are more apt to learn about sex from observing the mating of animals. However, they may be slow to transfer their accidental knowledge about animals to humans. At ten years, according to Gesell and Ilg, sex differences have become more pronounced. The psychology of a ten-year-old girl is significantly distinguishable from that of a ten-year-old boy of equivalent background and experience. The girl has more poise, more folk wisdom, and more interest in things related to marriage and the family. Comparing girls and boys as groups, girls tend to show a more precocious interest in sex. Their questions are more comprehensive, and less dependent on the stimulus of information picked up from other children. The questions seem to come from a more integrated curiosity.[4]

This partial picture of some of the characteristics that emphasize differences between the sexes demonstrates that neither sex can be called superior or inferior. Rather, the evidence suggests the inadvisability of attempting to compare or to measure the differing characteristics of the sexes by identical standards.

[3] See Arnold Gesell and Frances L. Ilg, *The Child from Five to Ten,* pp. 176-177. New York: Harper & Brothers, 1946.
[4] *Ibid.,* p. 317.

Achievement differences

Another phase of the subject that cannot be overlooked is that in many types of achievement, males have the advantage. Although girls advance more rapidly than boys and maintain higher scholastic averages throughout many of their school years, the boys catch up and forge ahead during late adolescence when the girls seem to reach a leveling-off period.

A striking illustration of this process is found in Terman's study of 1,300 superior children. The careers of these gifted children have been followed since 1921-1922, when they were in the elementary grades. It was found that the girls, during adolescence, began to fall behind in relative achievement, and that three times as many boys as girls continued their high level of achievement. The subsequent history of this group shows far greater achievement among the men in proportion to their numbers than among the women.

Similar results have been found by others studying achievement records of children.[5] A list of the outstanding people in almost all fields of endeavor in the past and in our own time would be made up largely of men. The great artists, musicians, and scientists of the past have been men.

Reasons for achievement differences

Many explanations have been offered for men's relative monopoly in the field of achievement. Most acceptable to man's ego is the traditional explanation that he is intellectually superior. But the explanation is not that simple. Terman says, "The woman who is a potential poet, novelist, lawyer, physician, or scientist

---

[5] According to studies made at Harvard under Dr. Psyche Cattell, and a study of musical talent by Amram Scheinfeld, girls show musical talent earlier, but develop it to a lesser degree later on than boys do. For a summary of the studies by Terman, Cattell, and Scheinfeld, see Amram Scheinfeld, *Women and Men*, pp. 301-315. New York: Harcourt, Brace and Company, 1944.

usually gives up any professional ambition she may have had and devotes herself to home, husband, and children. The exclusive devotion of women to domestic pursuits robs the arts and sciences of a large fraction of the genius that might otherwise be dedicated to them. Data strongly suggest that this loss must be debited to motivational causes and to limitations of opportunity rather than to lack of ability." [6] Other researchers have attempted to explain achievement difference in terms of "drive." They believe that man's drive to achieve is related to his sex drive, and hence is not subject to the limitations placed upon woman by her sex. It must be recognized that although "drive" may be continuous in the male, woman's "drive"—because of the recurring changes in hormone balance and physical functioning that accompany menstruation and childbirth—fluctuates periodically or may be entirely absent at times.

Undoubtedly the traditional concept of man as a doer, accomplishing great things in the world, serves as a stimulus toward achievement for men. Conversely, the traditional concept of the place of woman cannot but inhibit achievement in the lives of a great many women. This inhibiting influence may be the reason for the intellectual lag observed in girls during late adolescence. At this time girls become acutely aware of what is expected of them by the opposite sex. Perceptive girls recognize that intellectual superiority is not always an advantage to them; they sense that if they show mental ability beyond that of the male, they may arouse masculine resentment.

Thus, to conform to the roles expected by the group, the boy will do his best to excel, whereas the girl may not be so strongly motivated toward achievement except within certain well-defined feminine areas.

[6] Lewis M. Terman, "Psychological Approach to the Biography of Genius," *Science,* Vol. 92 (Oct. 4, 1940), 293-301.

The double standard and biological factors

Is it possible to eliminate entirely the so-called double standard? Girls sometimes resent the fact that their brothers are so much freer to come and go at will, to be out later at night, and, in general, to have fewer restrictions on their activities. It is true that the male has greater freedom of action. The biological results of sexual freedom will not affect his life to the same extent that they will affect the life of the female. Then too, the unprotected female is simply not as safe as the male because she has less physical strength with which to protect herself.

Another factor is that, although modern social institutions have taken over some of the functions formerly performed by mothers, the child still is more closely associated with the mother than with the father. The child's physical connection with the mother before birth and his dependence upon her in the early months of his life are arrangements made by nature, and they do limit the mother's freedom more than the father's. It seems logical that with the greater freedom of the father should go a greater responsibility for the support and protection of his wife and children.

The problem of the proponents of sex equality is to distinguish between laws that are purely discriminatory and those that have a basis in nature. The changing status of women has already placed on them many added responsibilities which may or may not have been balanced by the removal of certain restrictions. In some states women are now equally responsible with men for the support of the children. In others they are subject to the same alimony requirements that men are subject to, in case of divorce. Clearly, there is confusion in the thinking of those who attempt to legislate concerning equality between the sexes.

A better understanding is needed of the biological facts as well as the social facts about sex differences. It is even more necessary, if individual marriages are to be successful, that men and women discard outmoded ideas about the superiority or inferiority of either sex. It is necessary to accept and try to understand not only the physical differences that exist, but also the cultural changes that are affecting man-woman relationships. The next chapter will explore further some cultural trends in sex roles, and their effect upon marriage success.

Review questions

1. Why do some women's groups oppose legislation designed to give women complete "equality" with men?

2. What do you understand by the statement that the sexes are neither equal nor unequal but have a complementary relationship?

3. Which is the "weaker" sex as measured by morbidity and mortality? Cite statistics to support your answer.

4. Give some reasons for the greater life expectancy of women.

5. What are some of the observable differences in muscular strength and coordination of pre-school boys and girls? Are these differences due to cultural conditioning?

6. How does the rate of growth differ in boys and girls?

7. What mental differences between boys and girls have been revealed by intelligence tests?

8. Give some of the findings of the Yale Clinic of Child Development concerning characteristics of the sexes at different ages. Do the findings show that boys or girls are superior?

9. What have been the results of Terman's study of the achievements of gifted children?

10. Give some reasons that would help explain the greater achievement of the male in our society.

11. Why do girls show a lag in intellectual development during late adolescence?

12. Is there a biological basis for the so-called double standard in morals? Explain.

Suggested readings

Gesell, Arnold, and Frances L. Ilg, *The Child from Five to Ten.* New York: Harper & Brothers, 1946.

Scheinfeld, Amram, *Women and Men.* New York: Harcourt, Brace & Company, Inc., 1943. A scientific discussion of the differences between the sexes.

Some developments affecting role definitions

*Nature of homemaking today impels
more masculine participation*

Diversity in role patterns

Attitudes of young people toward their future roles

Role Concepts as a Factor in Marriage

Why role concepts should be flexible

Reactions of men to their role situations

Some problems in adjusting to role requirements in marriage

For more than two decades much discussion and writing has been concerned with problems relative to the redefining of masculine-feminine roles in life. This redefining is a major social change which has occurred in this century. What has taken place is not a reversal of roles but a readjustment forced by the exigencies of modern life so that roles of men and women now overlap rather than being distinctly different and separate as they were in the past.

Much of the discussion about problems arising from role transitions overlooks the fact that the social developments affecting roles are a factor in the lives of men as much as in the lives of women. It is not simply a matter of women's conflicts and frustrations, nor a question of whether women should be workers or homemakers. Some people see the problem in those terms; they fear that for women to wear slacks and do "man's work" may confuse sons about who is mother and who is father, and may make boys uncertain about their own masculinity. Similarly it is implied that the man who wears an apron and does housework or bathes the baby is depriving his son of a needed masculine model.

All kinds of attempts to turn the clock back toward traditional masculine-feminine patterns have been proposed. In a number of states during the 1930's, laws were proposed, although few were passed, that would have prescribed what clothes women could or could not wear in public. In the same decade, a time of economic depression, some state laws prohibited the employment of women in jobs that were believed to be the prerogative of men. More recently it has been suggested that colleges and universities stop educating women to compete in the same fields with men. At the opposite extreme we have proposals (which still assume that changing role concepts are primarily a problem of women) that governmental agencies provide for child care so that all women may work just as men do.

Patterns of masculine-feminine behavior and functioning must be viewed much more broadly than simply as a problem of women, wives, or mothers. Men also must be able to come to terms with the requirements that modern life makes upon them as men and as husbands and fathers. These requirements are different from those that men knew in other generations.

Many people approaching marriage do not realize the significance that role concepts assume in marriage. Attitudes and views concerning the role or function that each believes will be his or hers in marriage have many implications for mate choice and these attitudes affect the quality of the relationship two people are able to build in marriage.

Some developments affecting role definitions

During the late 1920's and in the 30's a process occurred that was, in effect, a social revolution. Young adults broke with tradition in many areas of living. Within the space of a few years, social customs moved out of the Victorian era and away from long accepted standards to a freer way of living. Social drinking for both sexes came into existence instead of drinking being done by men with men, in saloons to which women did not go. Smoking began to be a feminine as well as a masculine custom, and the word "sex" become mentionable in public. These and many other changes that took place within a few years during the 20's and early 30's in the United States represented more than changes in social customs or readjustments in moral viewpoints. They were visible evidence that, as part of the aftermath of World War I, women relinquished a place in which they had been secluded, protected, and controlled by the tradition of masculine dominance, in exchange for a different level of companionship with men, and more equal participation in all areas of life, including the right to vote and to hold public office.[1]

These social changes had already altered American attitudes when World War II came along, bringing some extreme economic developments that had a profound effect upon the lives and activities of men and women. During World War II the scarcity of workers made it a patriotic duty for women to work even if they were married and had children. After the war, the steady rise of inflation meant that what had in many cases been intended as a temporary situation became permanent. Many couples accepted the idea of two breadwinners as a necessity whether or not they approved in theory of the departure from tradition. In other cases economic pressure may have been a secondary factor, for some women continued working because they found certain satisfactions in work other than homemaking, and some husbands found that they preferred a working wife.

Today many working wives and husbands are too busy to give much thought to theories about "woman's place" or "man's place" in life, or in the family. They are occupied with living and adjusting in the world in which they find themselves. Thus the man who, a few years ago, before he married, might have argued that a woman's place is at home, may freely concede today that it is necessary for both of them to help provide adequate support for the family. The same husband is also likely to agree that under the circumstances a husband must do his share of the housework and child-rearing. Therefore many young people today know and accept a type of family life in which there are no well-defined and exclusive roles for either men or women. They have found that the success and happiness of their own family life is based upon

[1] For an analysis of the social revolution in the United States between 1918 and 1929, see Frederick Lewis Allen, *Only Yesterday*. New York: Harper & Brothers, 1931.

cooperation and adaptability. Many college students have grown up in families in which both father and mother have worked to make a living and keep a home, both working outside the home and both doing whatever is necessary at home.

Nature of homemaking today impels more masculine par-ticipation.   Modern advances in business, manufacturing, and production mean that the nature of the work to be done in the home has changed. Many services once performed by housewives are now done outside the home. Such tasks as canning foods, baking, and dressmaking are not considered a part of the work of the average housewife, but rather are done by professionals. Labor-saving equipment has shortened the time required for many tasks that are still done at home, and has helped also to break down traditionally established ideas of man's work or woman's work. Boys and men, who might never have thought of doing the family laundry when it had to be done by hand, now in many families as readily load and start an automatic washing machine as they run a lawn mower.

Diversity in role patterns

Clearly, the changes that have taken place in conceptions of masculine and feminine roles are not from one precisely defined status to another equally unambiguous one. Rather roles have been broadened for both men and women, so that today married couples and families function in a very wide variety of masculine-feminine patterns.

In 1957, we asked 465 students what tasks their fathers did in the home. Of the total group of fathers reported on, 47 per cent helped buy the groceries; 37 per cent helped dry the dishes; 29 per cent helped with the cooking; 23 per cent helped wash the dishes; 14 per cent cleaned the house; 13 per cent set the table for meals; and 9 per cent did the laundry.

Although in the homes represented by this particular sample of students the fathers have been quite active participants in

Fig. 6 MANY FAMILIES NEED TWO BREADWINNERS. Almost half of all wives work outside the home during the first years of marriage, and more than one-fourth of the total labor force is made up of women. Courtesy of *California Monthly*.

homemaking tasks, it is still true that there are many families in which the division of labor remains traditional—families in which a boy has never seen his father wash or dry dishes, shop for groceries, or cook a meal.

Patterns of authority and dominance-submissiveness differ in families just as much as work patterns do. In some families the father is the autocratic head and the mother is passive and subservient. In other families the mother is the dominant figure and the father is little more than a figurehead. There are also many families in which life is quite thoroughly compartmentalized, the father having absolute authority and responsibility in some matters and the mother having complete authority and re-

Fig. 7 "Sure, I'm in favor of women having equal rights; but you'll never get them back to that!" Reproduced, courtesy of *Ladies' Home Journal*, Curtis Publishing Company.

sponsibility in others. Then there are families in which all members share responsibility, and in which the achievements of each member are a source of pride and satisfaction to the others, regardless of sex. Neither parent in such a family sees the achievements of the other as a threat to his own self-esteem.

Attitudes of young people toward their future roles

Unmarried university students, when queried about the expectations they have concerning their own future roles as husbands and wives, are inclined to express traditional attitudes. In fact, university girls tend to express more traditional attitudes than university boys do. For example, when the same 465 university students who reported on their fathers' participation in home-making were asked what tasks they themselves thought the husband *should* help with in the home, a larger percentage of men than of women thought the husband should help with seven of the eight tasks listed. In general, a slightly larger percentage of the men expressed the opinion that the husband should do more of the household tasks than they reported their own fathers were in the habit of doing (see Table 3).

Similar results were obtained by the Purdue Opinion Panel in 1955 when a national sample of high-school youth were questioned, more boys than girls agreeing with the statement that the good (ideal) wife expects her husband to help with housework and child care.[2]

Does this mean that these girls, a few years hence when they are married and have small children, actually will not want or appreciate help from their husbands? Will the boys, a few years from now, be disappointed at their exclusion from a share in homemaking tasks?

A theory, which might be offered to explain this discrepancy between the expressed expectations of girls and boys, is that

[2] *The Purdue Opinion Panel*, Lafayette, Ind.: Purdue University, 15:1 (February, 1956), 20a.

girls before marriage may be more influenced by romantic ideas about roles of men. A girl may visualize herself as a future wife buying the groceries, doing the laundry, getting meals, and in general playing the traditional role of taking care of a man. Over half can envision the future husband drying dishes—a companionable activity—but only one in ten can see him setting the table.

TABLE 3   PERCENTAGES OF 165 MEN AND 300 WOMEN REPORTING HOUSEHOLD TASKS PERFORMED BY THEIR FATHERS AND THOSE THEY THOUGHT A HUSBAND SHOULD DO

Household tasks	Father did		Husband should do	
	Men	Women	Men	Women
Repairs	81.0%	84.0%	75.0%	85.0%
Cooking	30.0	29.0	28.0	13.0
Setting table	15.0	11.0	38.0	11.0
Drying dishes	47.0	32.0	61.0	53.0
Washing dishes	39.0	20.0	32.0	22.0
Cleaning house	16.0	13.0	23.0	12.0
Laundry	12.0	7.0	13.0	5.0
Buying groceries	53.0	43.0	67.0	44.0

Almost all can see him making repairs around the house but only one in twenty can see him helping with the laundry. When the romantic vision of the future gives place to the reality of actual experience, many girls will change their ideas about what the husband should do in the home. This will be especially true in cases where both marriage partners are working at outside jobs.

Why role concepts should be flexible

Individual students sometimes express the view that as children they resented being left as much as they were, by their working mothers. Some of them say that when they become parents they will be willing to live on a lower economic standard in order to give their children a full-time mother. Some of the people who grew up during the post-war, working-mother years may carry out their resolve to try to live out in their own married lives a role division based on traditional standards. But the wide variety of patterns in today's homes makes such decisions difficult. The girl who felt neglected because of her mother's many other interests and who, as a result, has decided to be a full-time housewife may marry a boy who would prefer a wife who can share all interests with him rather than being the traditional housewife. Or he may believe that two incomes are necessary for a successful family. The boy whose father supported the family and functioned as the head of the household in the traditional manner may marry a girl whose parents worked together at household tasks, made all decisions together, and earned a living cooperatively. Such a couple may have very different ideas about what masculine-feminine pattern is "right."

It becomes necessary for people to review their judgments and ideas concerning the roles that are desirable for men and women, and to try to determine from what sources they have derived their ideas. Perhaps most important of all is that people become aware of the diverse definitions of masculine and feminine roles in life today, and become able to recognize that there is no "right" or "wrong" role for a man or for a woman. Each married couple must work out the husband-wife pattern according to the capacities and the adaptability of the partners and the circumstances of their lives. Set and rigid ideas based upon one's own family pattern may cause trouble.

In the average marriage the husband and wife must harmonize their feelings about roles. A girl who has a strong drive toward achievement and a desire for personal recognition, and a boy whose ego needs are such that he must be the dominant-superior one in the family, are likely to be an unhappy match, whether or not the wife ever holds a job outside the home. But a couple who are cooperative and who can give to one another recognition and respect for ability or achievement in whatever line it may be have a good chance of happiness, regardless of how they work out the division of labor and authority.

During courtship and dating years, couples need to try to understand each other's true attitudes, recognizing that true attitudes toward others are not necessarily the same as the opinions one may express ahead of time when the discussion is more or less theoretical and academic.

A crucial point is how each member of a married pair feels about the part he or she plays in life, and especially whether each feels his contribution is accepted and valued by the other. Some men who believe that they want their wives to play a traditional role actually do not have a high regard for that role. They place a higher value upon work in the competitive world than they do upon homemaking. One woman expressed her feelings this way, "My husband just thought of me as 'the little woman.'

Fig. 8 "Oh, Bert, I think the novelty of housework has worn off." Reproduced, courtesy of *Ladies' Home Journal,* Curtis Publishing Company. By permission, Mary Gibson.

He didn't seem to think anything I did was of any real importance until I went out and got a paying job. No matter how much I accomplished at home, he seemed to think my days were just a breeze. He wanted me to stay at home and be a housewife, but he certainly puts more value on what I'm doing now."

Reactions of men to their role situations

Men, like women, react in many different ways to the role requirements made of them in marriage today. Some men accept as logical and potentially rewarding the concept of equal husband-wife sharing in almost all aspects of family living.

A man said, "Both my wife and I have college degrees in chemistry. At first we worked together in a research lab, but now that we have three children Margaret has given up all outside work and devotes herself to the home and children. I think she works too hard at home, but when I suggested that she come back to the lab part-time and hire more help at home she was shocked. I have tried to help with the housework, but she shoos me out of the kitchen and says, 'Go on and do your reading. I've got things under control.' It is almost as if she didn't want me to help; it is as if she felt, 'Since this is my job I'm going to do it alone. This is one place where I'm in charge.' I would be happier if we could work together. I think we're both missing something."

Some other men will feel insecure in any but the traditionally-accepted masculine role. Not all men could be as comfortable in a cooperative, equalitarian, and many-faceted role as the young engineer who answered his doorbell at dinner-time and stood on the porch talking with a colleague about plans for a business meeting, wearing a kitchen apron and holding his baby son tucked against his shoulder.

One study of fathers' conceptions of their roles showed that the fathers who were interviewed saw themselves as taking an active part in the physical care, teaching, discipline, and play of their children. They were reasonably content with their roles although some of them felt that it was difficult to find enough time for their activities and responsibilities at home in addition to working as a full-time breadwinner.[3]

Some problems in adjusting to role requirements in marriage

Clifford Kirkpatrick has developed some theories on conflicts arising from inconsistencies in the attitudes of both men and women concerning roles. His views are pertinent here. He recognizes that cultural changes have opened a wide range of roles to women, other than the traditionally accepted wife-and-mother role; and that men are confronted with the necessity for adjusting to life in a role far more complicated and different from the traditional role as dominant family-head. Kirkpatrick's hypothesis is that both sexes are inconsistent: women tend to want to have the privileges and rewards of several major roles, such as wife and mother, companion, and partner, while accepting the obligations of only one; and men are inclined to want their wives to accept the responsibilities of several roles, while they are willing to give them the privileges and rewards of only one or two. Kirkpatrick points out that unfairness results in cases where wives claim and get the privileges of more than one role without accepting the corresponding obligations, or where they accept the obligations of several roles without receiving corresponding privileges. Some wives expect to be treated as though they were the mothers of a half dozen well-brought-up children in a well-kept home, although they have no children and actually contribute little to the comfort, well-being, or economic success of their husbands. Other wives may rear children, carry the full load of homemaking and, in addition, earn almost as much as the husband does, without receiving any special recognition from their hus-

---

[3] R. J. Tasch, "The Role of the Father in the Family," *Journal of Experimental Education*, 20 (1952), 319-362.

bands for their contribution.[4] Kirkpatrick says, "Naturally it is easy for husbands and wives to regard the distribution of obligations and privileges from different points of view."

Jacobson found in a study of 100 divorced and 100 married couples that divorced couples show a greater disparity in their attitudes toward the roles of the husband and wife than do married couples.[5]

People naturally see situations in the light of their own personal desires, and in marriage it is easy to be concerned with only one's own needs and expectations without being able to see the other side of the question. The person who can recognize at the outset that he tends to be inconsistent in what he would require of the mate and in what he is willing to concede in return will have a better chance for success in marriage.

Every person, in order to remain mentally and emotionally healthy, must feel that he or she is of worth, and that the way he is expending his emotional and physical energy is of value and importance to the mate and to others.

If one feels undervalued, or dissatisfied with the role that marriage seems to require, that one may retaliate by subtly undermining the mate's self-esteem and satisfaction with his or her own role. Even though such retaliation is without rational intention, it may still be effective in undermining the mate's self-confidence and puncturing his ego. The result may be mounting conflict in various areas of the marriage, with neither partner able to diagnose the trouble.

A husband may unconsciously undermine his wife's ego because he does not value highly her work as a housewife. The

[4] For a report of Kirkpatrick's research, see Clifford Kirkpatrick, "Inconsistencies in Marriage Roles and Marriage Conflict," *The International Journal of Ethics*, 46 (1936), 444-460. (Reprinted in Judson T. Landis and Mary G. Landis, *Readings in Marriage and the Family*, pp. 386-392. Englewood Cliffs, N. J.: Prentice-Hall, Inc., 1952.

[5] Alver Hilding Jacobson, "Conflict of Attitudes Toward the Roles of the Husband and Wife in Marriage," *American Sociological Review*, 17:2 (April, 1952), 146-150.

husband's self-esteem also may be threatened by certain situations. Some men will develop feelings of inadequacy and suffer ego damage if: (a) the wife makes more money, (b) the husband feels his wife is more intelligent, (c) the wife has to get a job to support or help support the family, (d) the wife has greater capacity for sexual enjoyment, (e) the wife has more education, (f) the wife plays the partner role but is superior to her husband, (g) the husband expects the wife to get her ego-satisfaction and status through living in his shadow, but she feels that she must achieve these satisfactions independently of him.

In a period when ways through which the sexes meet each other's ego needs are not firmly fixed and well-defined, it is increasingly important for husbands and wives to be aware of the necessity for understanding this phase of their relationship. Couples contemplating marriage need to give thought to how well they understand each other and to what kinds of situations are tolerable or intolerable to each. A competitive attitude toward each other during courtship may indicate conflicting role expectations. The young woman who has a strong drive to achieve on her own should consider whether her prospective husband is one who could accept her achievements or one whose self-esteem would be threatened by her achievements.

Objectivity is needed by both men and women in interpreting the contribution each can make in any particular marriage. People going into marriage will have a better chance for happiness if they recognize that although the sexes are different and possess different potentialities and needs, neither is born to dominate or to be dominated; neither is inherently superior or inferior; and no set boundaries delineate what is man's place and man's work or what is woman's place and woman's work. They must become able to think of themselves and of each other as individual people rather than as sex prototypes. The two sexes are mutually dependent; satisfying relationships depend on cooperation and shared responsibility.

OUTLINE FOR SELF-STUDY: ROLE EXPECTATIONS

Think through the following outline, deciding upon the answers to the questions. Then write a short analysis of your own attitudes toward the roles of men and women with attention to what role definitions you think you will be able to live with comfortably in marriage.

I. Role situations in your family background

1. How would you classify the interaction between your grandparents: Husband dominant? Wife dominant? Equal sharing in decisions and in dominance? Sharing in tasks? Sharing in interests? Does one of the pair "speak for" the two of them?
2. With the above questions in mind, what type of interaction seems most common among your aunts and uncles?
3. Apply the same questions to your own parents' interaction. Is one dominant? Does one make most of the decisions? Is one more likely than the other to "speak for" the two of them? Would you classify your family as a father-dominated or a mother-dominated family? An equalitarian type of family?
4. If you have married brothers and sisters, apply the same questions to their interaction with their spouses, as well as you can.

II. Your feelings about the roles of men and women in marriage

1. As you think about your different married relatives do you find that you approve in general of one type of husband-wife interaction pattern ("role situation")?
2. Which type of husband-wife interaction is especially distasteful to you among your relatives? Just why do you find this type of interaction distasteful?
3. Among non-relatives what husband-wife role patterns do you find difficult to understand or appreciate?

III. What is your reaction to the following statements?

1. "In the sight of God there is equality between men and women but when it comes to governmental arrangements in the home the husband is the head. God says he cannot answer prayers which come from a woman who doesn't take her God-given place in the home." . . . Billy Graham
2. I would vote for a woman for a public office such as the senate or the vice-presidency. Qualifications are what matter, not the sex of the candidate.

3. Women have as much right as men have to work at full-time jobs outside the home.
4. It is natural that men should dominate and women play a submissive role.
5. If women would stay in the home, families in the United States would be happier.
6. Women who compete in a man's world outside the home are unfeminine and less attractive than women who remain housewives.
7. I think the career-type of woman is more interesting and attractive than the home-type.

IV. In my association with the other sex I have found that:

1. I tend to be competitive toward the other sex.
2. I get along better when the male is definitely dominant and the female is submissive.
3. I am happier when I am dominant in the relationship.
4. I like to date those who let me make most of the decisions.
5. I am unhappy dating those who expect me to make many decisions.
6. I often feel pushed around by my dates.
7. I like to date people who are as intelligent or more intelligent than I am.

Review questions

1. What are some of the viewpoints expressed by people concerned about the changes in the pattern of men-women roles?
2. What are some of the solutions that have been attempted or proposed to deal with the shift away from former concepts about "woman's place"?
3. What changes in social customs during the 1920's indicated the coming rearrangement of role patterns of men and women?
4. What changes have caused many men to accept the idea that the wife must help support the family?
5. List some developments that have encouraged male participation in household tasks.
6. Describe some of the diverse kinds of role situations in families today.
7. Summarize the findings of the study of student attitudes concerning the husband's participation in household tasks. How do you

explain the greater willingness of men to say they will help with household tasks when they marry than of girls to say they think a husband should help?

8. Do you think a girl could be happy playing the subservient role during courtship and not be happy in that role after she is married?

9. What inconsistencies did Kirkpatrick find in the attitudes of men and women in his study of roles?

10. How may the egos of both husbands and wives be threatened in modern marriage?

Projects and activities

1. Repeat the study given on p. 42 with the class and have it summarized for class discussion.

2. *Panel discussion.* The married students in the class discuss changes in their conception of roles from the time they became engaged to the present. If there are not enough married students in the class, single engaged students take part in the discussion, bringing out their attitudes about roles in marriage. What patterns do they anticipate in their future marriages?

3. *Panel discussion.* Invite some older couples from the community to come to class and discuss role situations in marriage.

4. *Socio-Drama.* Write and present a skit that illustrates role patterns today. The scenes might show: the women in the neighborhood gathered for tea and talking about women's roles; a group of husbands discussing their common problems; a family scene that illustrates some possible problems involving several family members.

Film

Who's Boss? Competition in marriage resulting from the confusion in husband-wife roles is the theme of this picture. Illustrates many of the factors discussed in this chapter. McGraw-Hill Book Company, Inc. 20 minutes, sound. Can be had through most rental services.

Suggested readings

Baber, Ray E., *Marriage and the Family.* New York: McGraw-Hill Book Company, Inc., 1953. Ch. XI, "The New Status of Women," and Ch. XIII, "Some Social Implications of Women's New Activities."

Bowman, Henry, *Marriage for Moderns.* New York: McGraw-Hill Book Company, Inc., 1954. Ch. IV, "Marriage Versus Careers."

Burgess, Ernest R., and Harvey J. Locke, *The Family.* New York: American Book Company, 1953. Ch. IX, "Expectations and Roles."

Gruenberg, Sidonie M., and Hilda Sidney Kretch, *The Many Lives of Modern Woman*. Garden City, N. Y.: Doubleday & Company, Inc. 1952.

Komarovsky, Mirra, *Women in the Modern World*. Boston: Little, Brown and Company, 1953.

Landis, Judson T., and Mary G. Landis, eds., *Readings in Marriage and the Family*. Englewood Cliffs, N. J.: Prentice-Hall, Inc., 1952. Part XIII, Reading 1, "Cultural Contradictions in Sex Roles," Mirra Komarovsky; Reading 2, "Cultural Contradictions in Sex Roles: A Repeat Study," Paul Wallin; Reading 3, "Inconsistency in Marriage Roles," Clifford Kirkpatrick; Reading 4, "Problems of the Modern Homemaker-Mother," Della Cyrus.

Metheny, Eleanor, and James A. Peterson, *The Trouble With Women*. New York: Vantage Press, Inc., 1957.

Nimkoff, Meyer F., *Marriage and the Family*. Boston: Houghton Mifflin Company, 1947. Ch. IV, "Modern American Family."

Dating customs today

Dating begins early

Patterns of dating

College and non-college steady dating

Meanings of steady dating

The desire to date

Who is a good date?

Rating and dating

Purposes to be achieved during dating experiences

Dating

Acquiring social competence

Developing self-understanding and an understanding of others

*Dating offers an opportunity to discover
and test conceptions of sex roles*

To assess life values and goals

To examine habitual ways of meeting problems

Dating, as practiced in the United States, is a social custom peculiar to this country. Observers from other countries and also many Americans from the older generation, whose social customs differed from those of today, view the current dating system with bewilderment or with alarm: Will dating, beginning at such early ages lead to too early marriage or to too much sexual freedom? Is the custom of steady dating conducive to immorality?

Whatever the answers to these and other such questions, the current dating system evolved gradually and will not change suddenly. Thoughtful young people need to (1) take a clear and critical look at dating customs as they presently exist, (2) determine what purposes or functions the dating stage of life potentially serves, and (3) assess the contribution of their own dating experiences to their growth into maturity and toward achieving lifetime goals.

Dating customs today

Dating begins early. The dating period starts for many people when they are about 14, and is past by the time they are 19 or 20. Over 34 per cent of all the girls in the United States marry before they are 20, and one-half are married before they are 21. Half of the boys marry by the time they are 23. These figures are for the average of all young people, based on census findings. However, the bulk of the early marriages that lower the average age at marriage are not among the college-educated part of the population. College-educated people tend to marry somewhat later than those with fewer years of

55

education, but there is evidence that college students begin dating as early as do the rest of the population.

The average age at which 3,000 college students reported that they had had their first date was 13.9 for boys and 13.6 for girls.[1] Slightly more boys had first dated at the age of 11 or younger, and slightly more boys had not dated until they were 16 or older. Since boys are somewhat older than girls when they marry, and since they begin dating at approximately the same age as girls do, the dating stage of life lasts longer for boys than for girls.

Patterns of dating

Data from our study of the dating experiences of 3,000 college students show that two-thirds of these students had dated while they were in junior-high school, 95 per cent had dated while they were in senior-high school, and 98 per cent in college. As to the extent of the dating with different people, 21 per cent of the women and 15 per cent of the men had dated at least 15 different people during their high-school years, and 41 per cent of the women and 27 per cent of the men had dated at least 15 different people while in college. In another study of dating patterns among high-school and college people in Ohio, Lowrie found that in general the earlier the individuals began to date the more

[1] See p. 26 for a listing of the 11 colleges participating in this study.

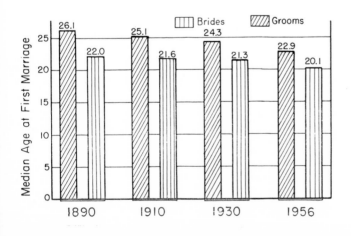

Fig. 9 BRIDES AND GROOMS TODAY ARE YOUNGER THAN THEY USED TO BE.

frequently they dated.[2] He also found that the girls dated more frequently than the boys of the same age, girls tending to date boys somewhat older than themselves.

TABLE 4   YOUNG PEOPLE TODAY START DATING AT A MUCH EARLIER AGE THAN THEIR PARENTS DID

Age at first date	Burgess-Wallin study of 1,000 engaged couples (1936)		Landis study of 3,000 students in 11 colleges (1952-1955) *	
	Men	Women	Men	Women
Under 14	15.0%	16.0%	39.0%	47.0%
14	16.0	20.0	21.0	25.0
15	18.0	21.0	16.0	13.0
16	19.0	23.0	12.0	9.0
17	14.0	10.0	5.0	3.0
18 or over	18.0	10.0	7.0	3.0

* All of those studied in 1952-1955 and 70 per cent of those studied in 1936 had some college education.

College and non-college steady dating.   The evidence suggests that people who go to college may have a steady dating pattern somewhat different from that of the non-college population.

In our study of 3,000 students in 11 colleges, the students were asked whether at present they preferred to go steady or to date with a number of different people. Approximately two out of three of the 2,100 students who were not engaged or married said they preferred to "date the field." In contrast, a study in one large high school showed that 80 per cent of each class in the upper three years of high school favored going steady.[3] In a national study of high-school students in 1948, the Purdue Opinion Panel found that 42 per cent favored steady dating; in a repeat

[2] Samuel H. Lowrie, "Factors Involved in the Frequency of Dating," *Marriage and Family Living*, 18:1 (Feburary, 1956), 50.
[3] El Camino High School, Sacramento, California (1956).

study in 1957, 50 per cent favored steady dating. In the repeat study in 1957, one-fourth of the high-school respondees were undecided, and only 18 per cent were opposed to steady dating.[4]

According to the reports of their steady dating as given by the 3,000 college students, 76.0 per cent had never gone steady in junior high, 42.0 per cent in senior high, and 35.0 per cent in college. The data indicate that the young people who went to

Steady Dating Studies	Number Dated 1927–1929			
Burgess–Cottrell Study of 526 Married Couples	26.0 %	17.0 %	31.0 %	26.0 %
	None	1	2 or 3	4 or More

	1936		
Burgess–Wallin Study 1,000 Engaged Couples	31.0 %	45.0 %	24.0 %
	None	1 or 2	3 or More

	1957		
Landis Study 200 Engaged Couples	27.0 %	46.0 %	27.0 %
	None	1 or 2	3 or More

Fig. 10 NUMBER OF THOSE DATED ON A STEADY BASIS (EXCLU-SIVE OF CURRENT ENGAGEMENT OR MARRIAGE PARTNER). These studies show little change in the pattern of steady dating in the past 30 years. Couples in the 1936 and 1957 studies were not yet married and might have more steady dating partners before marriage. The majority of all the respondents had attended college.

college actually did little steady dating in junior- and senior-high school. Only one in four had had two or more steadies in high school and, at the time of the study, less than one in five had had two or more steadies in college.

In a new study in 1957, of 200 engaged couples one or both of whom were college students, we found that approximately three

---

[4] *The Purdue Opinion Panel,* Lafayette, Ind.: Purdue University, 8:1 (November, 1948), 26; 15:3 (April, 1957), 4.

out of four of the 400 men and women had dated ten or more people during their lives, but three out of four had never gone steady or had gone steady with only one or two people before meeting the fiancé(e).[5]

The pattern of steady dating among young people who have finished high school but who do not go to college may or may not be different from that of college young people.

It is possible that planning to go to college may deter some people from very much steady dating in high school. Moreover, people who do not plan to go to college may be more inclined to go steady with the ones they do date, since their school life ends with high school and they will soon be earning their living and hence be free to marry early. This theory seems to be supported by another Purdue Opinion Panel poll which found that twice as many of the girls whose mothers had a grade-school or high-school education were going steady as the girls whose mothers had a college education. The same report also found that more girls whose mothers had not gone to college married or became engaged in high school than girls whose mothers were college educated.[6]

Meanings of steady dating.   The term *steady dating* has no universally accepted definition. It may mean one thing in one section of the country and another in other sections. The term varies in meaning with the age of the young people. In grammar school, children have "secret" steadies. Actually the two may do

---

[5] Later references will be made to this study of 200 engagements. Students in family sociology classes at the University of California in 1957 were asked to give questionnaires to engaged student couples they knew. The engaged couples were asked to fill in the questionnaires independently of each other and to mail them separately to the researcher. Of the 200 couples 77 per cent were formally engaged and 23 per cent had an "understanding" of engagement. Only if both the man and the woman returned a questionnaire were their responses included in the study. Some questions were included from the study of 1,000 engagements in 1936 by Ernest W. Burgess and Paul Wallin, *Engagement and Marriage.* Philadelphia: J. B. Lippincott Company, 1953.

[6] *The Purdue Opinion Panel,* Lafayette, Ind.: Purdue University, 15:1 (February, 1956), 4a.

no dating at all, but they are "going steady" because they "like" each other. In some high schools going steady represents social success and is accorded social recognition and status. Therefore, many people of high-school age go steady although they do not intend to become engaged or marry. On most college campuses, students may be dating steadily but they are not likely to call their dating with any one person "going steady"; they consider "going steady" to be high-school terminology. When college students say they prefer to date the field, they mean they have not yet found the one person whom they hope to marry, or they feel they are not yet ready to marry; therefore they will continue to date casually until they find someone with whom the dating goes on to the point that both are ready to consider becoming "pinned." Thus on many college campuses people date and become pinned, but they do not "go steady." Some of the differences that exist between the patterns of steady dating in high school and in college are due in part to differences in definition at the different levels.

The desire to date

Most young people, whether or not they feel ready to enter into any permanent relationship, want to have dates. Among the very young, to begin to date represents growing up and becoming a part of the social world. The pressure of social custom and the influence of the peer group motivates toward early dating; developing biological impulses are not necessarily the motivating force. During the first dating experiences of some young people, physical responses or urges toward the other sex may be incidental or even absent. Data on the age at which the 3,000 college students had begun dating show, for example, that those boys and girls who had reached puberty at age 12 or younger were more likely to have begun dating at 12 or younger than were those who reached puberty at later ages. However, the data show also that a considerable group (about 14 per cent) began dating at 12 or younger although they did not reach puberty until age 15 or older, and another group (about 25 per cent) did not begin to date until 16 years or older although they reached puberty at 12 or younger. These data show that the social practices of a community are an important factor in determining when young people begin to date.

Fig. 11   "There's always hope ... my mom didn't hook anyone till she was twenty-three!" By permission, Consolidated News Features, *San Francisco Chronicle*, and Marty Links.

In the later teens the pressure to date increases. A writer in a popular magazine, commenting on American dating customs, says, "Romance, like success, is a relentless necessity in America. A silent telephone is something to be kept secret, like the rejection of your credit application. . . . As the weekend nears, a festive desperation shivers across the land; there is no defeat more catastrophic than a good book (alone) on Saturday night." [7] In addition to social pressure is the fact that as people get older and go into the late teens or the twenties they are aware that the time to marry is approaching. Not only does society expect them to marry, but most people themselves feel the need for companionship with someone of the other sex and for a permanently established physical relationship. So the motivation toward dating becomes ever stronger.

Who is a good date?

In one study among our students 90 per cent said they considered themselves good dates. They thought they themselves measured up on a series of elementary dating skills, yet when they rated the other sex, each sex was quite critical of the other sex's dating ways. Girls made the following criticisms of boys most often:

1. Lack of respect and courtesy; rudeness, inconsiderate behavior.
2. Overindulgence in or overemphasis on drinking.
3. Failure to plan for the date, leaving it up to the girl to decide.
4. Aggressive attempts to neck, especially on first dates; attitudes that suggest a pattern of sexual exploitation.
5. Too much conceit, boastfulness, and self-centeredness.

Boys gave the following as their most common criticisms of girls:

1. Too hard to please; act conceited, self-centered, and artificial.
2. Too expensive; they are "gold diggers."

[7] Frederic Morton, "The Art of Courtship," *Holiday*, 21:3 (March, 1957), 157.

3. Too much emphasis on "rating" in choice of dates.
4. Too much insistence on being asked far in advance for dates.
5. Being habitually late for dates.

Many of the actions or ways on both lists suggest an underlying lack of self-confidence in the dating relationship, or a lack of finesse in social situations. An overemphasis on drinking may be an indication that a boy feels ill at ease. Artificial, aloof, and self-centered behavior on the part of the girl may be a defense for feelings of uncertainty. Are girls "gold diggers," or is it that some-

Fig. 12 By permission, United Feature Syndicate.

times boys do not know how to suggest entertainments within their budgets? Is the boy being thoughtful or thoughtless when he lets his date plan the activities for the evening? Some of the criticisms suggest that communication may be poor between two people who are dating each other. Both may be unsure how to interpret actions or how to evaluate each other's motives and intentions.

Rating and dating

Some years ago, Willard Waller offered a theory concerning the dating behavior of college students.[8] From his observations and research he concluded that students want to date those who rate on campus, and that the rating of an individual is a major factor in the choice of dates. The factors that cause a student to

[8] Willard Waller, "The Rating and Dating Complex," *American Sociological Review*, 2:5 (October, 1937), 727-734.

rate on campus vary somewhat among colleges. On many campuses reputation as an athlete, membership in certain fraternities or sororities, and certain social skills contribute to a higher rating. On some campuses scholastic achievements and leadership in activities are important factors. Among students on the campuses that Waller observed during years of economic depression, men with plenty of money and a car had a distinct advantage in rating over other men, and a girl's rating depended upon popularity as a date, good clothes, attractive appearance, and some other factors, such as conformity to dating customs.

College students are at the age when dating very often results in marriage. The person who is a B.M.O.C. may or may not have the personality traits that make for happiness in marriage. An individual's rating on campus may have little relationship to his or her desirability or undesirability as a permanent mate. If the college years are spent in trying to date those whom others consider good dates, the most favorable part of the dating period may be wasted. This is especially true of college girls, since their chances for marriage are reduced if they do not form a permanent attachment during the college years.

In many cases a high rating among one's associates on campus or anywhere else indicates that one does possess superior qualities of personality and character, or special abilities. But because the influence of the peer group is so strong there is always danger that one may put too much emphasis on what others think or appear to think, to the neglect of his own perceptions of another personality, and without recognizing or understanding his own needs in a relationship.

Many college men say that they ask as long as three weeks ahead of time in order to get even a movie date with certain girls who rate as good dates. When asked, "What do you mean by a 'good date'?" one group of college men summed it up thus: "A girl who is tops in date-rating is good-looking and she dresses well; she's a *nice* girl—not snobbish or conceited, has good manners, and isn't too naive or too young-acting. And she's usually a girl who's accepted in the best social groups."

This description of a girl who rates on a campus today agrees in some ways with Waller's findings of years ago, but it seems also to include specific recognition of personality traits, which may not have been considered so important in some student generations.

Some people who have worked with students on university campuses for a number of years believe that today a larger proportion of students are aware of the implications of their dating. Since they are seriously interested in finding a good marriage partner, they do not allow campus rating to overshadow other qualities that may be more important in mate choice.

In a repeat of the Waller study at the University of Michigan, Blood found that students consistently chose six out of thirty-seven items as being the most important in their choice of dates regardless of whether the dating was casual or serious. The characteristics which received this universal approval from all segments of the student population, were: (1) is pleasant and cheerful, (2) has a sense of humor, (3) is a good sport, (4) is natural, (5) is considerate, and (6) is neat in appearance. Blood concludes that, "Students have grown up enough so that they can afford to be themselves rather than needing to masquerade behind the dating paraphernalia of yore—cars, pins, and raccoon coats. While the rah-rah days survive to some extent in particular segments of the student body, even there they fail to assume primary importance." [9]

Purposes to be achieved during dating experiences

Acquiring social competence.   Possibly the lowering of the average age at marriage and the increased emphasis upon preparation for marriage has caused people today to be more realistic

[9] Robert Blood, Jr., "Uniformities and Diversities in Campus Dating," *Marriage and Family Living*, 18:1 (February, 1956), 37-45.

Fig. 13 WITH THE DECREASING AGE AT MARRIAGE TODAY, A
GREATER PROPORTION OF COLLEGE DATING IS SERIOUS DATING.
Courtesy of *California Monthly*.

about the purposes of dating. In the 1930's when Waller was studying campus dating, economic conditions were such that marriage could not be considered seriously by many students.

Fig. 14 "Why shouldn't he be smooth—he's got a half dozen technical experts and a director standing right there telling HIM how!" By permission, George Lichty and Chicago Sun-Times Syndicate.

Marriage while in college was out of the question. Since World War II, economic conditions have made it possible for people to marry much younger, and marriage before graduation from college has become acceptable. During the early dating experiences, whether people are in the middle teens and quite unaware of implications of dating for their future, or older and conscious of the approaching need to find a permanent mate, dating should help the individual acquire a measure of competence in associating with other people of both sexes. When people first venture into the "couple world," they are occupied for a time with learning social skills. Motivation is strong at this time to study other people in social situations and to observe what is acceptable and what is unacceptable behavior. Such matters as how to ask for a date in a direct way that is likely to bring the desired response, how to refuse a date with friendly tactfulness, how to accept a date gracefully, how to carry one's responsibility in conversation without overdoing it, how to dress appropriately for different occasions, are skills which—if acquired early in the dating experience—will free the individual to begin to make progress in the more important growth processes involved in the dating stage of life.

For many people, making friends with members of the other sex and getting dates is not easy. In the study of the 3,000 college students, we found that 55 per cent reported some difficulty in making friends with the other sex in adolescence, and only one-fourth of the students at the time of the study felt very confident in associating with the other sex. One in ten had little or no confidence. If the students studied are typical of college people, it seems that developing confidence in associating with the other sex is somewhat of a problem for the majority of young people. Of the college people studied, those who were from happy homes, those who felt they were above average in physical appearance, and those who rated their own personalities as above average were more confident in dating and associating with the other sex than those who gave themselves lower ratings on these points.

Parents' Marital Happiness

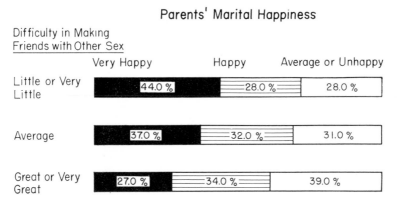

Fig. 15 DIFFICULTY IN MAKING FRIENDS WITH THE OTHER SEX IN EARLY ADOLESCENCE AND PARENTAL MARITAL HAPPINESS AS GIVEN BY 3,000 STUDENTS.

Developing self-understanding and an understanding of others. Until the dating years most people are not much concerned with self-evaluation nor have they much impetus to try to change their habits or personalities. But, whether cause or effect, dating is often accompanied by a growing awareness of many aspects of personality in oneself and in other people. The young adolescent may make little constructive progress here; this function of dating may not be achieved in his early experiences. Even many older young people allow their dating to be more or less random activity, their goal being only to keep in the social swim. But many people, during the dating years, become increasingly interested in their own personality growth and needs. Setbacks or failures in heterosexual associations may jolt a person into looking at himself objectively for the first time. As a result, he may begin to understand himself and begin also

Fig. 16 DATING OFFERS OPPORTUNITIES TO DEVELOP SELF-UNDER-STANDING AND AN UNDERSTANDING OF THE INTERESTS AND PER-SONALITIES OF OTHERS. Courtesy of *California Monthly.*

to achieve a broader conception of personality and how it functions. Successful marriages are based on: companionship, the ability of two to meet each other's personality needs, similar values and goals in life, and mutual respect. Therefore, maturity in understanding personality is important for people if their dating is to lead to mate choice for successful marriage.

Dating offers the opportunity for one to recognize that there are a great many different types of personalities; some are congenial, others much less so; some are fun on dates but would make poor husbands or wives; some that are attractive at first prove after longer acquaintance to be selfish and self-centered, and likely to take the joy out of life for their mates. Perhaps most important of all, however, is that dating experiences may

enable one to evaluate his own interaction with other personalities: What kinds of reactions do I bring out in others? What
specific traits or types of people bring out the best or the worst
in me? Why do I react as I do in my associations with others?
A measure of self-understanding is necessary, and it can be at-
tained by young people who are able to be somewhat objective
during dating.

A case may illustrate some of the kinds of things that can be
learned through dating. This case also shows how too much
emphasis on the rating of a date may blind one to other qualities
important in the relationship of the two. A college senior tells
her experience:

"I dated Stan all through our junior year. I felt that a lot of girls
envied me because Stan was so outstanding on campus. He was
popular and good-looking, and belonged to one of the best fraternities. I was always proud to be seen with him. I felt sure that
I was in love with him, and I hoped to be engaged to him.

"From the first I felt that my parents were not enthusiastic about
Stan for me. I knew they would rather I dated boys who
belonged to my own religion, which Stan did not. And a few times
they were upset when Stan came for me and had been drinking
too much. I felt that they didn't have a chance to see Stan at his
best. But sometimes it bothered me when I thought about being
engaged and married to a man of a different religion from mine
and my family's. And I always wished Stan wouldn't drink as
much as he did. But on our campus no issue was made of drinking
and I thought I just needed to grow up and develop a more sophis-
ticated attitude about some things. Stan often told me that I was
naive and teased me about being old-fashioned. I never quarrelled
with Stan, but sometimes when he was tired or irritated about
something he would say cutting things that almost crushed me.
He was always sweet and apologetic afterwards though, and it
was easy to forgive him. I talked it over with my roommate, and
she said that emotional upsets between people in love are to be
expected, and that I should appreciate his apologizing—that some
men wouldn't—and that I didn't know how lucky I was to be dating
Stan. We made an attractive couple, I know. He is tall and blond
and I am tall too, but not so tall as he. I think he enjoyed the
impression we made as much as I did. In general, I knew that
I was not so happy as I had always been before, but I thought it

was because my parents' negative attitude toward Stan made it hard for me to be as carefree as I usually am in my friendships.

"While Stan and I were apart during the summer vacation, I had some dates with Bill, whom I've known all my life. Bill certainly isn't glamorous, but I was amazed at what a good time I had with him. He is considerate, and he never belittles me, as Stan sometimes does. We found that we think alike on so many things. Suddenly I realized that I felt like myself again, happy almost all the time, and comfortable with myself and my family and in my friendship with Bill. I could act as I felt and not have to worry about being naive or unsophisticated. When school started again this fall I decided not to date Stan any more, even if my friends do think I'm passing up a wonderful chance. But I've learned a few things about myself. I know now that how I feel about my relationship with a man is more important than how popular he is or how he rates with other people on campus. I know now what some of the qualities are that I hope to find in the man I marry—and something about qualities that I hope I never have to live with."

Dating offers an opportunity to discover and test conceptions of sex roles. The average person is likely to take for granted whatever type of masculine-feminine dominance-submissive pattern existed in his own parental family. But after dating different people, he may discover that the pattern accepted for so long is not the most satisfactory for his own relationships. Or he may discover that in no other pattern can he be comfortable. Marriage counselors' files hold many cases of married couples who seek counseling because of conflicts arising from differences in attitudes about roles. Typical of such cases is the strongly dominant girl married to a man who either rebels against any kind of feminine dominance or seems to accept it but reacts by losing his self-confidence and becoming less effective in all areas of living. Another example is the case of a man who grew up in an equalitarian home where both parents were strong personalities who were able to live cooperatively, yet with considerable independence. This man married an extremely dependent girl whose security was threatened if she had to make independent decisions or act in any situation without the decisive reassurance of her husband. In their relationship the wife often felt let-down or rejected, while the husband missed equalitarian companionship and felt her dependence as pressure.

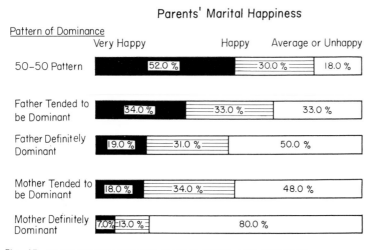

Fig. 17 INTERACTION PATTERN IN THE HOME AND PARENTAL MARITAL HAPPINESS AS REPORTED BY 3,000 STUDENTS.

There are unlimited gradations in the attitudes and feelings that different people have about dominating or being dominated. Dating different people should help the young person to become more aware of what his own feelings are here, and more aware of the different ways in which other people react to situations that he finds satisfactory or unsatisfactory. One girl explained what she had learned in this area in these words:

"I think the first boy who made me see myself differently from the way I had before was Bob. He apparently had much the same type of relationship with his younger sister that my brother had with me. Bob was definitely protective and possessive. He was the big, strong type who wanted to lash out at the world for criticizing its feminine members. He felt like apologizing

Fig. 18 THOSE WHO MARRY HAVING SIMI-LAR GOALS AND VALUES WILL FIND THEIR COMMON INTERESTS A BOND IN MARRIAGE. Courtesy of *California Monthly*.

every time someone told a joke about women drivers. He was so helpful I felt smothered."

A girl with different attitudes and needs might not have felt smothered, but might have delighted in Bob's attitudes. The important thing is for each person to know his or her own true feelings and attitudes about dominance-submissive patterns.

To assess life values and goals.   The dating years are a good time for the young person to give some thought to the values that he lives by, what he hopes to accomplish in life, and what things matter to him most as he considers choosing a vocation. College students in general have certain somewhat broadly similar values or they would not be attending college. However, wide differences exist among college people in specific predominant values. The prime standard for some is making money; with others, position or status is of first importance; others are chiefly oriented to the purpose of having the "good life," or toward some type of service to mankind—with a very great range of possible definitions of "service." Dating should help an individual to determine in some measure just what his own orientation is, how well it fits with that of the people he finds congenial, and to what extent he might be able to change if the circumstances of his life made change necessary. This may be illustrated in one way by the experience of people who date outside their own religion. Many college students discover for the first time, as they date, just how much their religion is their own and how much is a previously unquestioned part of their family background.

To examine habitual ways of meeting problems.   Most people by the late teens have already established quite habitual ways of meeting problems in life. Some people learn while still very young to know and accept their own weaknesses, and they are able to act constructively when confronted with defeat or frustration. One shy nine-year-old boy said, "I used to be afraid of a lot of things, and when I'm afraid I get a stomach-ache. I used to think I was sick when I had a stomach-ache. But I found out that there are two kinds of stomach-aches, the kind when you're really sick and the kind that just means you're afraid; and I can tell the difference. I'm still afraid sometimes, but not as much as I used to be; and when I get that kind of a stomach-ache now I just go on doing whatever I have to do and pretty soon I feel o.k. again."

This boy at nine had made good progress in self-understanding and in coping with a personal weakness. Sometimes people many years older have not gone so far. When they meet frustrating situations or encounter difficult problems, they cannot face their true feelings; they try such escapes as over-eating, illness, blaming others for all their troubles, excessive drinking, or aggressive and antagonistic behavior toward those who are close to them— friends, wives, husbands, or roommates. Such ways of reacting to problems are quite easy to recognize in others, especially when one's judgment is not clouded by the euphoria of being in love. Therefore, during the casual-dating stage of life, it is important to be intelligently alert to kinds of behavior that are likely to lead to poor mental health, not only in associates but in ourselves. It is never too late to learn and to begin to change habit patterns. The person who can discover tendencies toward poor mental health in himself and go on to change and improve his ways, need not handicap his life by going beyond casual dating with another who has unconstructive ways of facing life and who is neither aware nor able to learn better ways.

Review questions

1. Why do some people view with alarm the current dating customs?
2. How should thoughtful young people look upon dating?
3. What is the average age at first marriage for men and women in the United States today?
4. What evidence might support the belief that steady dating finds

greater support among high-school students than among college students?

5. How does steady dating in college differ from steady dating in high school?

6. What determines the age at which young people begin to date? Explain.

7. What are some of the criticisms the sexes have of each other as dates?

8. What are the characteristics of the men and women who rate as dates on your college campus?

9. What did Blood find in his study of student preferences in casual and serious dating?

10. What are some of the elementary skills that should be learned during the early years of dating?

11. What are some of the specific things to be learned about ourselves and others through dating?

Projects and activities

1. Write a few paragraphs describing the rating and dating pattern on your campus. Make a survey of 25 men and 25 women to find what the most desired traits are in a date. Compare or contrast these with qualities that are desirable in a mate.

2. *Panel Discussion.* A panel of four boys and four girls discuss the criticisms each sex has of the other in dating on your campus.

Film

Choosing Your Marriage Partner. A young man is trying to decide which of two girls to marry. He is advised to consider maturity, family background, harmony of personalities, and so forth. Coronet Instructional Films, 15 minutes, sound.

Suggested readings

Baber, Ray E., *Marriage and Family Living.* New York: McGraw-Hill Book Company, Inc., 1953. Ch. V, "Mate Selection and Courtship."

Becker, Howard, and Reuben Hill, eds., *Family, Marriage, and Parenthood.* Boston: D. C. Heath and Company, 1955. Ch. VIII, "How Mates Are Sorted."

Blood, Robert O., *Anticipating Your Marriage.* Glencoe, Ill.: The Free Press, 1955. Ch. I, "Dating."

Burgess, Ernest W., and Paul Wallin, *Engagement and Marriage.* Chicago: J. B. Lippincott Company, 1953. Ch. III, "Dating," and Ch. IV, "Going Together."

Cavan, Ruth Shonle, *The American Family*. New York: Thomas Y. Crowell Company, 1953. Ch. XII, "Social Relationships Preparatory to Marriage."

Duvall, Evelyn Millis, *Family Development*. Chicago: J. B. Lippincott Company, 1957. Ch. XI, "Families with Teenagers."

Landis, Judson T., and Mary G. Landis, eds., *Readings in Marriage and the Family*. Englewood Cliffs, N. J.: Prentice-Hall, Inc., 1952. Part III, Reading 1, "Courtship Practices and Contemporary Social Change in America," Niles Carpenter; Reading 2, "Changing Courtship Customs," John F. Cuber; Reading 3, "Some Changes in Courtship Behavior in Three Generations of Ohio Women," Marvin R. Koller; Reading 4, "The Rating and Dating Complex," Willard Waller; Reading 5, "Dating Theories and Student Responses," Samuel H. Lowrie; Reading 6, "Courtship in a Group of Minnesota Students," Clifford Kirkpatrick and Theodore Caplow. Part IV, Reading 1, "Cultural Factors in Mate Selection," August B. Hollingshead; Reading 2, "Homogamy in Social Characteristics," Ernest W. Burgess and Paul Wallin.

Peterson, James A., *Education for Marriage*. New York: Charles Scribner's Sons, 1956. Ch. IV, "Factors in Adolescence," and Ch. V, "Dating as a Factor."

Waller, Willard, *The Family* (Revised by Reuben Hill). New York: The Dryden Press, 1951. Ch. VIII, "The Social Context of Courtship," Ch. IX, "Bargaining and Exploitative Attitudes," and Ch. X, "Courtship as an Interactive Process."

Dating should mean learning

To consider ego needs and their fulfillment

To recognize and evaluate possessiveness and jealousy

Developmental tasks of the dating years

Coming to terms with sex impulses

Definition of terms in use

Who initiates love-making?

Who draws the line?

A matter of communication

Coping with the sex element

Dating (continued)
—A Growth Process

To recognize exploitative behavior

Age as a basis for exploitation

*The influence of one-sex groups
as a basis for exploitative attitudes*

Getting dates

Student opinions on mate choice

Everyone has certain basic needs. Each individual needs to feel valued and appreciated. He needs to feel that at least part of the time he is receiving the undivided attention of some special person, and that at least one person who matters to him, freely recognizes his worth as a person.

Dating should mean learning

To consider ego needs and their fulfillment. An objective evaluation of one's own ego needs and one's ability to meet the needs of others is important during the dating years.

With the small child, ego needs are all-encompassing; the child does not hesitate to express his feelings with such phrases as: "Watch me!" "Listen to me!" "Let *me* talk!" "Look what *I* can do!" But a part of maturing is becoming able to appreciate that others have the same needs, and to learn to receive pleasure and a sense of fulfillment through meeting the needs of others as well as through having one's own needs met.

Most people have at some time dated someone who has not yet grown up to the point where he or she is aware in any sense of the needs of others. With such a person a relationship tends to be all one way. He is happy and expansive, often a very interesting date, as long as he is the center of attention. His conversation is fascinating as long as the subject remains close to himself or his interests, experiences, exploits, possessions, or feelings. But let the conversation drift to the interests of the other person, and this date becomes bored or tired or remembers other obligations and has no more time to talk.

Like everyone else, this person enjoys being

praised. But it may never occur to him or her to give praise to other people. One young man whose friend complained that he was too critical, said, "Well, I don't go round passing out compliments. I don't praise someone unless I mean it. No one could say I'm a hypocrite. I think a little honest criticism is good for people." This was a rationalized defense of his habitually disparaging attitudes toward others.

In order to build good relationships, it is necessary to look for the good and the worth in others and to give recognition freely. Satisfying relationships with friends, dates, and later in marriage, cannot be one-way relationships. There must be giving as well as receiving, not just occasionally, but most of the time.

The time when self-centered egotism can be observed in oneself and when one can become able to recognize it in others at least cost is during casual dating. Lynn, a college freshman, said of two boys she was dating, "I listen to Bill's problems all the time, and I'm glad to do it if it helps him. But it seems that if I start talking about my problems, some way or other we are off the subject right away. With Jerry, it's just the opposite. I have to watch myself, because he always seems so interested in what I'm interested in that first thing I know we are talking about *me* all the time and I think afterwards that I must have sounded awfully self-centered and childish."

Our study of college students showed that both the men and the women felt the other sex to be self-centered. This may be because everyone is naturally somewhat self-centered; and the dating years are the time when this trait becomes evident to others and if one is alert, to oneself. This is the time when it pays to work at overcoming this tendency, and at cultivating a genuine interest in and appreciation for others.

To recognize and evaluate possessiveness and jealousy. Feelings of possessiveness and jealousy are natural, and most people have some measure of these feelings. But because they are "natural," insofar as they begin to show up quite early in life, many people have the mistaken idea that such feelings are acceptable or even desirable. Sometimes it is mistakenly believed that possessiveness or jealousy is proof of true love. The maturing person will work to overcome his tendency toward possessiveness and his feelings of jealousy. In reality possessiveness is never acceptable except perhaps in small children, when it can be overlooked as normally to be expected for the age. The mother in the following situation did not become unduly upset by her child's actions:

> A mother was sewing, her three-year-old son playing contentedly on the floor, when a neighbor came to call. Almost as soon as the two women began to talk interestedly with each other, the three-year-old left his toys and climbed upon his mother's lap. He became very loving, and put his arms around her neck so closely that she could not see around him. The mother tried to turn him around in order to continue her conversation, but he put his hands on her cheeks and held her face toward his, saying, "Look at *me*, mother. Talk to *me*." The mother said, "Later, son," and gave him a cookie from the coffee table, got a different book for him and settled him again on the floor where he appeared to be contented for a moment. Then he laid down his book and walked over to the caller, kicked her in the shin, and said, "Why don't you go home?"

In dating relationships most people have acquired more finesse than the three-year-old. They are beyond shin-kicking, but in some cases not far beyond. And the motivation for the possessive behavior which they do show is identical with that of the three-year-old. They cannot willingly share any part of the attention of a loved one with others.

Usually, uncontrolled possessiveness accompanied by jealousy in an adult or a person in the late teens or in the twenties indicates insecurity and a lack of self-confidence. This lack in the person himself is the basis for his inability to have confidence and trust in relationships with others. The jealous, possessive person tries to force loyalty and reponse. In his relationships he tends to be demanding rather than trusting. A fairly well-adjusted person is likely, after a time, to find that a relationship with an extremely possessive person is an intolerable burden. After dating such a person for a while one may begin to feel boxed-in and over-controlled. The casual dating stage is the time to find out whether this kind of possessive control is endurable. For most people it is not.

Dating offers excellent opportunities for the young person to study himself and others for overly possessive attitudes and behavior. It is well to remember that no one of any age has achieved perfection in all attitudes and feelings; possessive tendencies, or urges to dominate, and some jealous feelings may occur at times in everyone's life. The important thing is that to achieve maturity and to build permanently happy and mutually satisfying relationships we must work to overcome undesirable tendencies in ourselves, and we must be realistic about the characteristics of other people, especially those we date.

Developmental tasks of the dating years

The term "developmental tasks" is used to refer to the challenges that confront people at each stage of life. Always some of these developmental tasks present themselves as problems. During the dating years some matters that arise as problems can be recognized as necessary and important learning tasks, stages in growth toward permanent and satisfying heterosexual relationships.

Coming to terms with sex impulses. A developmental task that creates problems is the necessity for coming to terms with one's sex nature and impulses within the context of dating activities.

The fact that sexual maturity is reached and sex impulses become strong before people are ready for marriage creates problems that must be faced realistically. These problems may be viewed as falling largely within the following categories: (1) How far should one go with physical intimacies during dating?

(2) How control the limits of physical intimacy? (3) How recognize and cope with exploitative behavior in dating situations? (4) What are desirable and workable standards? (5) How distinguish between physical attraction and love or how relate them?

Ideas about "how far to go" in casual dating have changed during the past several years. There was a time when, for most people, the first kiss meant engagement. That view would be the exception today. In 1957, in a dating study, we asked 465 college students the meaning of a kiss. Forty-nine per cent of the men and 30 per cent of the women said a kiss meant nothing more than an expected way of saying good night on casual dates. In other words, about half of the men and a third of the women considered a kiss as meaning little more than a handshake. However, 55 per cent of the men and 79 per cent of the women (some students, especially girls, agreed with both statements) said a kiss should be reserved as something special for a person really cared for. This may be interpreted to mean that with many people the kiss would not come on the first date but after enough dates to provide some basis for the two people to like or care for each other.

Definition of terms in use.   Certain terms have come into use in reference to degrees of love-making on dates. Terms in current use may vary somewhat from year to year, but some terms have been used rather consistently for the past several student generations. In our study of the 465 students in California (1957), the term "necking" was used by 70 per cent of the men and women to refer to a moderate or light degree of physical intimacy (usually defined as physical contact above the neck), and 70 per cent used the term "petting" for more extreme physical intimacies. Petting is not carefully defined, but may include any contact to the point of sexual intercourse.

Our student responses showed that the women were much more careful in making distinctions and giving terms a definite meaning; the men were not so apt to make distinctions between necking and petting, or between petting and sexual intercourse.[1]

Who initiates love-making?   It is usually assumed that the male initiates love-making, because of his stronger sex drive, or because he thinks he is expected to do so. In the study of the 465 university students, 84 per cent of the men and 97 per cent of the women said that the man had initiated the love-making on the last date reported upon. An unexplained discrepancy is the fact that 16 per cent of the men said the woman had initiated the love-making, but only 3 per cent of the women said that they had started it. Does this indicate a breakdown in communication between people dating each other—the boy interpreting as encouragement or invitation actions or words which the girl means otherwise? Does it represent a tendency for girls to express the traditional viewpoint that "of course" it is the boy who starts love-making? Over half of the women (58 per cent) reported that the man had tried to go further in necking and petting than she wished. In a study of University of Florida students, Ehrmann found that almost one-third of the men tried to do more extreme necking or petting than the women permitted.[2]

In a study of University of Michigan students, Blood found that students' attitudes toward necking and petting may differ by whether the dating is casual or serious. He found that 39.0 per cent of men said they preferred, in casual dating, girls who did not have a reputation for petting while 75.0 per cent held this view concerning girls dated seriously.[3] In other words men seem

[1] A term used by almost a third of both men and women for casual love-making was "making out." Confusion about the meaning of this term was apparent. Approximately 10 per cent considered it to mean extreme physical intimacy, while the rest did not use it in that sense. Possibly the term "making out" will soon disappear from use as have "smooching" and "sparking," which were used for a time but did not survive. The terms "necking" and "petting" have now been in use on college campuses for at least twenty years.

[2] Winston W. Ehrmann, "Student Cooperation in a Study of Dating Behavior," *Marriage and Family Living*, 14:4 (November, 1952), 322-326.

[3] Robert Blood, Jr., "Uniformities and Diversities in Campus Dating Preferences," *Marriage and Family Living*, 18:1 (February, 1956), 44.

to hold two views on petting, depending upon their interest in the girl; in a casual date, petting may be all right, but if the man is serious about the girl he is likely to prefer that she not have a reputation for petting. Blood did not find the same inconsistency in the women students; three-fourths disliked men with "fast" reputations, either for casual or serious dates.

Who draws the line?   In response to our query about who is responsible for drawing the line in necking or petting, 64 per cent of the men and 40 per cent of the women thought both had equal responsibility. However, almost a third of the men and 60 per cent of the women thought it was chiefly the responsibility of the woman. Almost none of the women and only 5 per cent of the men thought it was chiefly the responsibility of the man to draw the line. The feeling that the woman should draw the line represents some survival of the double standard in sexual morality; the assumption of equal responsibility may represent an emerging single standard of sexual morality.

A matter of communication.   Necking and petting seems to be an area of dating behavior in which communication breaks down. Of two student generations queried (in 1952 and again in 1957), approximately a third of the men said that they thought girls expected them to pet, but only 6 per cent of the girls said that this was true.

Kirkpatrick and Kanin, in a study among women at the University of Indiana in 1955, found that 56 per cent had had dating experiences during the school year in which they had experienced "offensive male sexual aggression." [4] Without doubt some of the offensive behavior was due to poor communication on what each thought the other desired or expected.

Coping with the sex element.   It becomes necessary to understand physical expressions of sex for what they are, and not

---

[4] Clifford Kirkpatrick and Eugene Kanin, "Male Sex Aggression on a University Campus," *American Sociological Review*, 22:1 (February, 1957), 52-58.

to identify all necking and petting behavior with love. With the approach of physical maturity, strong impulses arise to express sexual drives through close contact with a member or members of the other sex. During the dating years the young person decides how far he will go toward satisfying his impulses.

Those who date several different people during the dating years will find people with widely varying standards. If the young person is to be comfortable in his associations, he must know what he considers desirable and undesirable, right and wrong. This is not only true in deciding how far one will go in necking and petting but also on moral issues such as honesty and loyalty, and on social habits such as drinking and smoking.

Counseling sessions with college students and research studies have shown that most young people plan to save complete sexual union until they are married. However, engaged couples often find it a problem to keep love-making within the limits that they have mutually agreed upon.

In more casual dating, both girls and boys need to know how to draw the line tactfully and effectively. This is not always easy, especially for a girl who is inexperienced with boys, or lacking in confidence. The key to the problem is learning to say no graciously, without appearing to be judging others and

Fig. 19 By permission, The Hall Syndicate, Inc., © 1957.

Dennis the Menace
By HANK KETCHAM

"SURE they're fightin'! He's a soldier, isn't he?"

their standards. Listed below are some techniques offered by 200 college girls for controlling necking and petting on dates:

1. Be honest—say no sincerely and politely.
2. Keep talking. Keep up an interesting conversation.
3. Avoid situations that are an easy set-up for necking and petting.
4. Plan dates thoroughly.
5. Double date or date in groups.
6. Let the boy know your attitude from the start.
7. Keep an early curfew.
8. Plan after-date activities.
9. Use reason, discuss your viewpoints.
10. Don't prompt necking or petting by your actions.
11. Set point beyond which you don't go.
12. Divert date's attention.
13. Ask to be taken home.
14. Don't date fellows overly interested in necking and petting.
15. Refrain from long "good nights."

Most of the above techniques might seem to refer to dates before engagement, although some of the suggestions would be applicable after engagement also. With engaged couples who have a real meeting of minds and who do agree about wanting to draw the line, such techniques would not be necessary since the girl would not have to take most of the responsibility for control.

Statements by the men and women in our 1957 study of engagements show a fairly high degree of agreement on setting the limits of intimacy. A summary of their statements is given in Table 5.

Another 25 per cent of the engaged men and women said that in their engagement "the girl draws the line." That statement may represent a form of agreement or it may mean disagreement, but it is nevertheless significant.

Kirkpatrick and Kanin in their study of sex aggression at Indiana University, found that while less serious types of male aggression were concentrated in occasional dating experiences, in a minority of cases the more serious types of aggression were likely to occur when couples were pinned or engaged.[5] Those findings suggest that where there is serious disagreement between an engaged couple about limiting intimacies, the engagement may represent an exploitative attempt rather than a serious intention to marry.

TABLE 5   FEELINGS OF ENGAGED COUPLES
TOWARD LIMITING INTIMACIES

Statement	Men	Women
We are in agreement that we want to save intercourse for marriage.	65%	77%
After discussing it, we mutually agreed on a set limit.	75%	80%
We never discussed it, but there was mutual agreement.	17%	9%
There is much conflict on how far we should go.	3%	6%

To recognize exploitative behavior.   During the courtship period exploitative behavior is not uncommon. Certain circumstances or conditions, such as differences in social class, differences in age, and traumas of certain courtship experiences, are conducive to an unfair or unjust utilization of an individual by one of the other sex. Exploitation usually indicates a one-sided emotional involvement. The exploited one is emotionally involved, but the other is after selfish gratification, or is motivated by other considerations.

Men from a higher *social class* are in a position to exploit women from the lower social classes. White men can sometimes exploit Negro women. College men sometimes use their position to exploit non-college girls.

In the study of University of Florida students, Ehrmann found

[5] *Ibid.*, p. 55.

that when college men dated girls of a lower social class they were more apt to go as far as they could with the girls. On the other hand, if they were dating girls of their own social class, they did not try to go farther than the girls thought was right.[6] If the girls were from a higher social class, the men did not try to go so far as they did with girls of their own social class. Ehrmann points out that a girl from a lower social class dating a boy from a higher class may permit or even encourage the boy in exploitative behavior because the stakes are high: There is a chance that she will win the gamble and he will marry her.[7] In cases of this type it would seem that a form of exploitation is reciprocal. Both are exploitative, but from dissimilar motives and with different considerations at stake.

Age as a basis for exploitation.   Older, experienced men may exploit the affections of young girls to gain sexual gratification. Because society recognizes that older men may take advantage of young girls, it protects girls until a certain age through laws on statutory rape. After the girl reaches the specified age, she is supposed to be worldly-wise enough to be able to protect herself from exploitation.

Exploitative behavior is carried on by women as well as by men. Boys are not protected by law from exploitation by older women, but this certainly occurs. Young women also exploit older men, as well as men their own age, by using physical charm to keep a man or men emotionally involved. The feminine exploiter may take advantage of the emotional involvement of men not only to have the convenience of their devotion, but to exploit them economically in typical "gold digger" fashion. Men exploit usually to gain sexual gratification. Women more often exploit to gain prestige, status, or economic advantages.

[6] Winston W. Ehrmann, "Student Cooperation in a Study of Dating Behavior," *Marriage and Family Living*, 14:4 (November, 1952), 322-326.

[7] Winston W. Ehrmann, "Influence of Comparative Social Class of Companion upon Premarital Heterosexual Behavior," *Marriage and Family Living*, 17:1 (February, 1955), 48-53.

The influence of one-sex groups as a basis for exploitative attitudes.   Before boys mature enough to become interested in girls, they may form gangs and companionship groups of their own sex, and have hostile attitudes toward girls. Some boys carry over into adulthood this immature behavior pattern of hostility to girls and loyalty to boys. These immature males have the attitude that it is smart to exploit women and to have sex relations if possible, but to remain free of permanent involvements. Such a man may boast to his friends about the number of conquests he has made and may report current progress in each affair. Often such reports are exaggerated, since this kind of exploitative behavior grows out of a need to establish status through sexual prowess. However, exploitation motivated by sex hostility is often a part of the pattern with immature persons.

Not all exploitative behavior, of course. is consciously exploitative. Nevertheless, one of the tasks of the dating years is to learn to recognize such behavior, and to avoid being a victim of it.

Getting dates

When the sexes are fairly equally distributed, as on a college campus, young people can usually get acquainted with members of the opposite sex if they make an effort. As women pass the age of 25, however, it becomes increasingly difficult for them to meet eligible men, because of the dearth of marriageable men in the age groups over 25. The first thing the person who wishes to date must do is to mingle in groups that present eligible prospects. The college boy or girl who sits in his or her room night after night should not feel resentful because of a lack of dates. The office girl who spends her evenings at home or at a boarding club with other girls will meet few eligible males. When an insurance company hires a new salesman, it requires him to interview a given number of prospects each day. The company knows that if a man sees enough prospects, sales are sure to result. How-

Fig. 20 THE CUSTOM OF COFFEE DATES BEFORE A FIRST DATE PROVIDES AN OPPORTUNITY TO GET ACQUAINTED IN AN INFORMAL SITUATION. Courtesy of *California Monthly*.

ever, if he sits behind his desk and worries about making his contacts, he will make few sales.

The same rule applies to people who are interested in dating. They will have to circulate where they will meet people. College students should go to dances, informal parties, the student union, the coke or coffee bar, athletic events, and the many other places where students congregate. Conditions in many of the larger colleges make it difficult for the sexes to meet under circumstances where they can get dates. Large numbers of students commuting from home to school, lack of housing facilities on campus, and heavy enrollments may make it difficult to have many activities or events that take in all students. Even in small schools the students who commute often find it difficult to get acquainted, since they are seldom on campus except for classes.

We asked students at the University of California, where one-third are commuters, the best ways for meeting members of the other sex on campus. They gave their answers in this order:

1. In regular classes and in the library
2. In activities related to school
3. At parties and dances (going stag)
4. Introduced by friends or relatives
5. By having blind dates
6. At fraternity-sorority functions
7. Through campus organizations
8. At religious group functions
9. At living group (dormitory) functions
10. At student "hangouts" or sport events

In some schools the library is called the "date bureau" because so many people meet for the first time there.

Students who commute and who wish to date should participate in activities that will help them meet others who are interested in dating. Over four-fifths of the California students queried felt that members of fraternities or sororities had an advantage in getting dates. Students in any sort of organized living group

Fig. 21 PEOPLE FIND CONGENIAL FRIENDS THROUGH PARTICIPAT-
ING IN STUDENT ACTIVITIES. Courtesy of *California Monthly*.

felt that they had a distinct advantage over those living alone or
at home. People who do not live in any organized group with
others will find at almost all universities that most of the religious
denominations maintain student centers or student foundations
near the campus. At these centers students meet for lunch, for
discussions, and for social activities. The student with any religious interest or religious affiliation should use the opportunities
offered by the church of his choice. There he will be likely to
become acquainted with others with similar interests.

Young people not in college should become active members
of community groups for which they are eligible. If a woman is
working in a place where there are no unattached men, or in an
occupation in which it is impossible to meet men, she may well
change jobs or move to a new community. Certainly, single people
should be as realistic about meeting good dates and a possible

future mate as the insurance salesman is in trying to meet prospective buyers.

In summary

The purposes and tasks of the dating stage of life discussed in
this and the preceding chapter have ranged from the necessity
for achieving a measure of self-understanding and understanding
of others, to the question of getting dates, a point that might
seem to be a relatively elementary subject. However, all of the
challenges and problems of dating are interrelated in their importance. No one of them can be regarded as elementary or
insignificant, because even small developmental tasks, which may
seem to depend simply on learning techniques or rules for action,
contribute to growth in personality. Progress through the dating
years should be an intelligent advance toward mature conceptions
of the potentialities of human relationships, and should serve as
valuable preparation for later successful marriage.

Student opinions on mate choice

During the past 25 years, three studies have been made of
university student opinion on mate choice. Do you agree or disagree with the majority opinion on the items summarized in
Table 6?

TABLE 6 OPINIONS ON MATE CHOICE GIVEN BY 3,000 STUDENTS FROM 11 COLLEGES (1952-1955), 2,000 STUDENTS AT MICHIGAN STATE UNIVERSITY (1947), AND 642 STUDENTS AT NEW YORK UNIVERSITY (Early 1930's) *

Questions	Men, percentage answering yes			Women, percentage answering yes		
	1952 -1955	1947	1930	1952 -1955	1947	1930
All other factors being satisfactory would you marry:						
1. A person of lower economic rank?	95	94	93	77	69	82
2. A person from a family you consider inferior to your own?	82	79	78	63	58	75
3. A person decidedly not good looking?	37	39	32	75	74	79
4. A person of unattractive disposition and personality?	—	2	2	—	2	4
5. A person of lower moral standards than your own?	16	11	29	9	4	20
6. A person of a different religious faith (Catholic, Jewish, Protestant) than your own?	55	47	58	56	59	42
If so, would you be willing to adopt his faith?	23	25	9	38	40	5
7. A person of less intelligence and (or) education than your own?	83	83	76	37	37	18
8. A person who had had premarital sex relations?	73	67		74	48	
9. A person who had been divorced?	56	54		49	48	
10. A person who would not have children?	23	21		12	23	
11. Would you want your mate to have less education than you have, the same education you have, or more education than you have?	Less 9		17	Less 1		0
	Same 82		78	Same 18		36
	More 9		5	More 81		64
12. Do you want your mate to be older than yourself, the same age, or younger?	Older 1		1	Older 86		94
	Same 25		24	Same 11		6
	Younger 74		75	Younger 3		0

* Adapted by permission from *Marriage and the Family* by R. E. Baber, copyrighted, 1939, by McGraw-Hill Book Co., Inc., p. 149. 1930 information from Baber; 1947, 1952-1955 information from studies by J. Landis. All students answered "yes" or "no" to the first ten questions. The "no" answers are omitted in order to make the table less complicated.

OUTLINE FOR SELF-STUDY: DATING

I. Being a good date

1. What specific traits are you working on to improve yourself as a date? Can you see progress?
2. What criticisms do you think others might have of you as a date? Consider whether the criticisms are justified.
3. How important do you think "rating" is with you in dating? Has "rating" become more, or less, important with you since you first started dating?

II. Learning through dating

1. What specific social skills did you acquire through dating in junior high school? In senior high school? In college? Which of your social techniques could still be improved?
2. What values and goals do you have that seem to differ from the values and goals of some people you have dated? Can you determine just how important these values are to you?
3. What role seems to be most natural for you? Dominant and decisive? Equalitarian and cooperative? Easily dominated? A combination of some of the above?
4. What roles have you had to play at times in dating that did not seem to fit you? Has the role that you feel most natural playing become more set as you have dated more people?
5. Can you think of one or more specific traits or ways of reacting to situations and people that you have discovered in yourself through dating experiences?
6. When you have had a bad day, how do you work off your negative feelings? Do you take it out on others? Do you relieve your feelings through activities such as reading, working, playing, or in other ways? Are you inclined to give vent to your feelings by: slamming doors, brooding, drinking, overeating, speeding in a car, making those about you suffer?
7. How well do you know your own ego needs? Are your feelings often hurt? Do you often need to be complimented? Are you "burnt up" often? Have you established the habit of complimenting people for the good things they do or say, or for traits you see in them?
8. What type of people whom you date seem to give you a special sense of well-being? Does any type leave you feeling deflated or insecure? In this same way try to evaluate your effect on those you date.

9. Have you ever been possessive or jealous of those you have dated? Have you ever dated a person who was jealous or possessive? If you have a tendency toward jealousy or possessiveness, what steps are you taking to curb this tendency?

III. Evaluation of your dating progress to date

1. Compare yourself with your five best friends in general progress in dating, i.e., frequency in dating, confidence in dating, being a good date, learning about yourself and others through your dating.
2. In your dating pattern can you see progress toward becoming better prepared to make a wise choice of a mate?
3. Has your dating helped you toward a realistic understanding of what love is or may be?

Review questions

1. "I think a little honest criticism is good for people." What is one explanation for this attitude?
2. What does extreme jealousy or possessiveness often indicate?
3. What is the meaning of the term "developmental task"? How does it apply to dating?
4. What are some of the developmental tasks associated with the sex impulse and dating?
5. What meaning do most students today place on a good-night kiss on casual dates? Do you agree with this meaning?
6. What did Blood find in dating preferences for casual and serious dating? Did he find the same attitudes held by both men and women?
7. What are student beliefs about who should draw the line in love-making?
8. What evidence is there that there may be poor communication between boys and girls in love-making?
9. What techniques did college girls list as helpful in controlling the extent of intimacy during dating? If couples are engaged, is it necessary for either to have to draw the line?
10. What is meant by exploitation? What are some common patterns of exploitation?
11. What policy should one follow if he wishes to meet date prospects?
12. What are some of the most common places where couples first met at one university? Where do people meet at your school? Do commuting students find it difficult to meet possible dates at your school?

Projects and activities

1. *Panel Discussion.* Four boys and four girls discuss the common problems of getting dates on your campus.
2. *Panel Discussion.* A group of students discuss the problem of poor communication betwen boys and girls on dates.

Film

It Takes All Kinds. Demonstrates different types of personalities through reactions to frustration. Gives insight into personalities which might or might not meet one's personality needs in marriage. McGraw-Hill Book Company, Inc. 20 minutes, sound.

Suggested readings

Blood, Robert, "Uniformities and Diversities in Campus Dating Preferences," *Marriage and Family Living,* 18:1 (February, 1956), 37-45.
———, "A Retest of Waller's Rating Complex," *Marriage and Family Living,* 17:1 (February, 1955), 41-47.
Ehrmann, Winston W., "Influences of Comparative Social Class of Companions Upon Pre-Marital Heterosexual Behavior," *Marriage and Family Living,* 17:1 (February, 1955), 48-53.
Kanin, Eugene J., "Male Aggression in Dating-Courtship Relations," *American Journal of Sociology,* 43:2 (September, 1957), 197-204.
Kirkpatrick, Clifford, and Eugene Kanin, "Male Sex Aggression on a University Campus," *American Sociological Review,* 22:1 (February, 1957), 52-58.
Smith, William M., "Rating and Dating: A Re-Study," *Marriage and Family Living,* 14:4 (November, 1952), 335-340.
Waller, Willard, "The Rating and Dating Complex," *American Sociological Review,* 2:5 (October, 1937), 727-734.

Meeting others, a problem for the unattached

Relationships with parents and failure to marry

Sibling relationships and failure to marry

Fear of marriage

Some Will Never Marry

Physical and psychological reasons

Living a single life

For some people dating is a social custom followed with pleasure, but with little serious purpose; for others it is a course of action directed, whether consciously or unconsciously, toward the goal of finding a permanent lifetime mate. Dating, for most people, eventually leads to marriage. In the United States today, 93 per cent of the women and 92 per cent of the men aged 45 and over are married or have been married; these percentages have increased steadily during the past seventy years.

Nevertheless, a certain percentage of the population does not marry. Some young people pass through the years when most people are dating, but for any of a number of reasons they fail to date, or they have few dates, and they fail to go on to serious dating and eventual marriage. It is much more difficult for people to find eligible prospects for marriage after they are out of school. The difficulty in finding mates is not so much because of differences in the sex ratio as in the conditions of urban living in the United States today.

The sex ratios are sufficiently equal for young people of marriageable age so that, from a numerical point of view, most people should be able to find mates. However, numbers do not tell the whole story. A larger percentage of males than females of marrying age are unmarriageable for physical, mental, or emotional reasons, and men tend to date and marry women who are younger. The average man of 35 marries a woman 6½ years younger, and there are more women in the age group from 25 to 29 than there are men in the age group from 30 to 34. Furthermore, there are more single women than single men working in cities, except in certain highly industrialized cities that attract males. Professor Ogburn estimates that cities lower the percentage married by at least 10 per cent, or in other words, at least 10 per cent more people of comparable age would be married if they lived in rural areas.[1]

Conditions in cities, with their heterogeneous religions, occupations, and nationalities, make it difficult for those interested in finding dates or marriage partners to become acquainted with other interested people of their socio-economic background.

It is true also that in rural as well as in urban places women in certain occupations, such as teaching, library work, and social work, have fewer opportunities to meet eligible men than women in some other occupations have.

Meeting others, a problem for the unattached

In some cities social clubs are organized specifically for unmarried adults between certain ages with few, if any, other restrictions than age and marital status placed upon membership. Naturally such clubs provide opportunities for members to find mates, although the specific purpose of the group is usually social rather than matrimonial. Typical of such a group is the Berkeley Club, a social club for unmarried adults from twenty-five to forty-five years of age, in Berkeley, California. The group organizes social events such as dances, hikes, and barbecues, and members participate in special interest sections concerned with art, music, dramatics, and other creative activities, or they join others interested in tennis, swimming, or other active sports.

Organizations like the Berkeley Club serve a desirable purpose in an urban environment where it is difficult for unattached adults to meet others of their age group in an acceptable social situation.

Most large city newspapers carry advertisements of matrimonial

[1] W. F. Ogburn, with the assistance of Clark Tibbits, *Recent Social Trends in The United States,* p. 681. New York: McGraw-Hill Book Company, Inc., 1933.

and introduction services that are commercial enterprises operating for profit. These organizations print descriptions of their
clients and make them sound interesting. "Gentleman, late twenties, college degree, holds good position, wants plain home-type
girl of Protestant faith"; "Nurse, attractive, wholesome, early
30's, very congenial, responsible, good cook, likes to stay home,

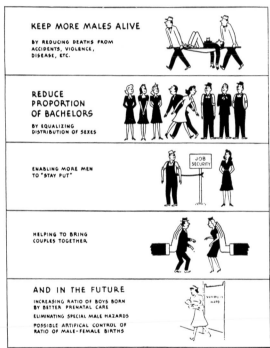

Fig. 22 POSSIBLE
WAYS TO PROVIDE
MORE ELIGIBLE
MEN IN THE MAR-
RIAGE MARKET. By
permission, Tony
Barlow and *Col-
lier's*.

interested in bachelor or widower." To sign up with a commer-
cially operated organization may seem a peculiar way to begin
a romance and to find a mate, but thousands seek such services
because they have not been able to meet eligible persons any
other way. Some unscrupulous people make use of "Lonely Hearts
Clubs" to exploit lonely and unattached persons. The fact that

any organization set up to help lonely people get acquainted with congenial companions or possible marriage partners is a profitable field for swindling, emphasizes the problem unattached adults face, especially in large cities.

Relationships with parents and failure to marry

Not all those who remain single do so because of the difficulty of meeting possible mates. A factor which must be considered in explaining failure to marry is that many people are slow to achieve emotional independence in their relationship with their parents. This slowness or failure may be due to a combination of traits in parents and children. Some parents consistently dominate the child and demand undivided devotion. From earliest childhood their children are so impressed with their obligations to the parent that it is hard for them ever to break away and marry. In studying large families Bossard and Boll found that children of large families, especially girls, tend to stay single.[2] In some cases this is because older children must take over many of the duties of the parents in caring for younger children. Some of these people are highly marriageable, but they pass the time for marrying before they are able to be free from the burdens they carry in their parental family.

Some parents, because of their own disillusionment with marriage, condition their children against marriage. One young man patiently courted a girl whose mother had done everything in her power to condition the girl against marriage. The marriage was held up for 10 years by the mother. Every time the wedding was planned, the mother became ill, and the wedding had to be postponed. Finally, after several attempts, the couple married in spite of the "heart attack" the mother was having. After the wedding, the mother quickly recovered from her attack. The fact that she was able to prevent the marriage for so long showed that this

---

[2] James H. S. Bossard and Eleanor Stoker Boll, *The Large Family System,* p. 284. Philadelphia: University of Pennsylvania Press, 1956.

was not a one-sided attachment; the daughter was immature in her extreme devotion and submission to the will of the mother. After the marriage, the husband wanted children, but the wife postponed having them year after year so that she could be free to care for her mother during her frequent illnesses. A convenient time never came for her to have a child. Such cases as this are not at all infrequent.

Sibling relationships and failure to marry. Some young people do not become interested in marriage because they are content with an already-satisfying emotional relationship with someone, such as a brother or a sister as well as a parent. The security that they feel in the established relationship prevents their feeling a need for cultivating heterosexual relationships outside the family. Sometimes the strong reliance placed upon the secure relationship within the family may be based in part on fears of sex or of marriage, or on a lack of confidence in associating with the other sex. They cling to a relationship that they feel adequate for, and accept it as a satisfactory substitute for other relationships.

Fear of marriage. Some people court and become engaged, but avoid marriage itself. The spinster may hesitate to give up her job with its economic security to face the uncertainties of marriage; or the bachelor who has been fairly content in his single state may shrink from the added responsibility for another person that marriage means. Some women who have been conditioned to fear sex experience and child bearing will postpone or avoid marriage even if they do become engaged. People may be unaware of their real reasons for stopping short of marriage. The spinster or the bachelor may rationalize concerning economic or personal independence, without recognizing their underlying fear concerning ability to cope with a close relationship such as marriage. And no doubt many women find rational reasons for postponing marriage without recognizing that conditioned fearful attitudes toward sexual experience and childbirth are influencing their thinking. Some of these women, when they reach their late twenties or the thirties will say of their experience, "Why is it that all the 'good men' are either married or for some other reason not possibilities for marriage? I've had romances, and still have them.

Fig. 23 "Do you believe the silly superstition that daughters instinctively look for boys who resemble their fathers?" By permission, Consolidated News Features, *San Francisco Chronicle,* and Marty Links.

But the men I get to know well are never anyone I could possibly consider marrying."

Some unmarried men say almost the same thing about the women they know. Such a feeling is usually sincere. The one expressing the viewpoint believes that it happens to be his or her misfortune not to be able to find the right person to marry. But, many times, underlying that kind of experience is a more or less unrecognized inner resistance to marriage in the person himself.

If the years pass, and one is never able to find anyone among all those in the world who seems an available possibility as a marriage partner, some thoughtful evaluation of one's own attitudes is desirable, and in some cases help from a qualified counselor may prove valuable.

Physical and psychological reasons. The failure of some people to marry may have a physical or psychological basis. Married people have a lower death rate at every period of life than do single people, or those whose marriages have been broken by death or divorce.[3] The greatest difference is found among people under the age of 45. Until recently, because of the higher death rate of married women in childbirth, single women in the age group from 20 to 24 had a lower death rate than married women. But this is no longer true. Among males aged 20-44, the death rate for the married is only about half that for the single. Deaths from almost all causes are lower among married men. The differences in the death rates are not so great among females, although married females have the lowest rates. By far the highest death rates, even higher than among the single, are among the divorced and widowed.

Marriage may contribute to longevity and mental balance because two people care for each other, but the larger factor is probably a selective process which may operate. Those who do not marry tend to include an undue proportion of the handi-

[3] Metropolitan Life Insurance Company, *Statistical Bulletin,* 38 (February, 1957), 4.

capped. And among those who fail in marriage and return to a single state are found a higher proportion of people with emotional handicaps as evidenced by the much higher suicide and death rate of the divorced and widowed. The crisis of becoming widowed or divorced is doubtless an added factor in the higher death rate of this group, especially among the men.

The fact that the difference between the death rates of married and single women is not great might be explained in terms of what one sociologist calls the "mating gradient."

The term "mating gradient" refers to the fact that, on the average, men tend to marry beneath them in social and economic status. Evidence seems to indicate that men also tend to select mates who are physically and emotionally less fit than themselves. Folsom suggests that the operation of the mating gradient would seem to leave an unmarried residue on the upper rungs of the female ladder and on the lower rungs of the male ladder.[4] This selective factor would certainly be a partial explanation for the difference in the longevity and mental balance of the single female and the single male. The less able males tend to be among the permanently single, but that is not so true of females.

Living a single life

Our discussion thus far may seem to imply that since most people do marry, finding a mate and marrying is the desirable course of action for everyone. Such is not necessarily the case. Without doubt many people who might live happily and successfully, permanently single, are forced toward marriage by social pressure. They can hardly ignore social attitudes that assume the married state to be the inevitable eventuality for all "normal" people. They know that to remain single is to choose deliberately to belong to a special minority group. Here it would be well if social attitudes could be changed toward a more realistic assess-

[4] Joseph Kirk Folsom, *The Family and Democratic Society*, pp. 490-491. New York: John Wiley & Sons, Inc., 1943.

ment of situations. For not only will there always be some people qualified for marriage but unable to find suitable mates, but also there are many people who are better suited for single than for married living. The latter should be able to remain single without any social stigma.

Research has concentrated on the satisfactions and problems of married living, while folklore and hearsay predominate in thinking about single living. A number of single women have given us their case histories. They have discussed their reasons for remaining single, and summarized what they consider to be the advantages and disadvantages of single living. Some professional women state candidly that they have put success in a career ahead of marriage for reasons that seem to them valid. One said, "I don't think I could have managed the double or triple life that married career-women must lead. Either the marriage or the career would have suffered. I love children but that need in my life is met by my nieces and nephews who live near me and are very dear to me."

An advantage of singleness that was suggested in many different ways by the single women is perhaps a negative one, but nevertheless real. This is the fact that single living does not require so much of the individual in the day-to-day affairs of living. To share and cooperate in all phases of life does not come easily to all people. Probably the greatest problem of married people is in learning to be successful in cooperative, joint living. The single person is free to live according to his own preferences; he escapes the necessity for changing and adjusting to the preferences of another person, or for coping with conflicts in a relationship if he is unable to change. The single women mentioned also some material advantages; two definitely cannot live as cheaply as one. The single person responsible for himself or herself only, is able to plan for activities and expenditures which might be out of the question after marriage. Of course, some of the available activities must be done alone rather than in the

Fig. 24 SOME WOMEN DO NOT FEEL THEY CAN FULFILL THE RE-
QUIREMENTS OF TWO CAREERS AND, THEREFORE, DECIDE TO RE-
MAIN SINGLE. Courtesy of *California Monthly.*

company of a companion. And some pleasant pursuits such as
travel are less pleasant without companionship. But loneliness—
a disadvantage mentioned often by the single—is also a specter
in the lives of many married people. The absence of loneliness is
not absolutely guaranteed by marriage.

Disadvantages other than loneliness weigh against the advantages of being single, and certain of the disadvantages loom larger for some single people than for others. There is the necessity for creating a satisfactory social life in a society organized on a couple basis. There is the embarrassment resulting from the never-ending matchmaking efforts of friends and family. There is the lack of an organized and regular sex life, which lack is felt as deprivation by many unmarried women as well as men. Single women also mention their regret that they have never had children. And, if single people live and work away from their families or kinship groups, they feel the lack of relationships that provide emotional security. As one said, "No one around here would know or care what happened to me, as long as I don't fail to show up for work. I don't really matter to anyone."

It is possible that the person making that last statement would feel the same at times, even if married. For the feeling that "nobody loves me" is not necessarily associated with circumstances and conditions of life; it may arise from personality traits within the individual. Whether those with such traits are more or less likely to marry we do not know.

In summary

Most people do marry. Dating as practiced by people during their early adult years, especially during the school and college years, tends to lead to marriage.

But for a certain proportion of people experience does not follow that pattern. They do not date or their dating does not lead to mate choice. If they wish to marry, these people will need to be objective about the facts of their lives: where they live, the type of job they hold, and the resulting opportunities or lack of opportunity for finding a mate. They will need also to consider their personality make-up, and attempt to determine whether they do really want to marry, all things considered.

Marriage is not inevitable for everyone, without any conscious effort to find a suitable mate; nor is marriage necessarily the most desirable life for everyone. Nevertheless, the average person considers marrying and is interested to know as much as possible about marriage, since it is the way of life for the majority of people. Even for those who for various reasons remain permanently single, to be "marriageable" is necessary insofar as to be marriageable implies the ability to live effectively with others.

Review questions

1. What percentage of people marry in the United States? How does the percentage of women who marry in the United States compare with that of other western countries?
2. It takes greater effort to find an eligible mate in the city than in the country. Why?
3. Is the sex ratio on your compus favorable to the men or to the women?
4. What are some of the common reasons why some people do not marry?
5. Which live longer, the married or the single? What are some of the probable explanations for this difference?
6. What do you understand by the "mating gradient"?
7. Should all people marry? Discuss.
8. What are some of the advantages of living a single life?
9. What are some of the disadvantages of living a single life?

Film

Feelings of Hostility. Shows how disappointment creates crises in a girl's life, how her mother mishandles the situation, and how this results in the girl's inability to establish a love relationship with the other sex in maturity. Gives insight into why some do not marry. National Film Board of Canada. 30 minutes, sound. Distributed by McGraw-Hill Book Company, Inc.

Suggested readings

Bossard, James H. S., and Eleanor Stoker Boll, *The Large Family System.* Philadelphia: University of Pennsylvania Press, 1956.
Bowman, Henry A., *Marriage for Moderns.* New York: McGraw-Hill Book Company, Inc., 1954. Ch. III, "The Permanently Unmarried."

Klemer, Richard H., "Factors of Personality and Experience Which Differentiate Single from Married Women," *Marriage and Family Living*, 16:1 (February, 1954), 41-44.

Landis, Judson T., and Mary G. Landis, eds., *Readings in Marriage and the Family*. Englewood Cliffs, N. J.: Prentice-Hall, Inc., 1952. Part II, Reading 1, "The Family Cycle," Paul C. Glick; Reading 2, "Statistical Perspective on Marriage," Kingsley Davis; Reading 3, "Mate Selection," Paul Popenoe. Part IV, Reading 4, "Cupid Is My Business," Clara Lane.

Moore, H. K., "The Wife and the Spinster," *Family Life*, 11:5 (May, 1951), 1-4.

Popenoe, Paul, "The Old Bachelor," *Family Life*, 13:5 (May, 1953), 1-2.

Marriageability

Most people hope to make good marriages. But concepts that verge on the superstitious are still widely held. Some people go on the assumption that marriage can only be a leap in the dark—that one responds to an irresistible attraction or an indefinable emotion called love, and makes the plunge, hoping to be lucky-in-love and end up happily married.

Successful marriages do not have such haphazard, unpredictable bases. The quality of a marriage depends on the marriageability of the two people involved, and many traits and habit patterns combine to determine the marriageability of each individual.

Personality traits and successful marriage

The wedding does not change basic personality structure. If change occurs quickly after the wedding it is more likely to be that people revert to their real selves, and traits or tendencies that may have been suppressed or controlled during courtship become evident again. To marry with the idea that one is going to make changes in the spouse or in his ways after marriage is to invite trouble. It is true that a good marriage promotes growth in both partners so that over a period of time people do change in many ways, but probably not in the kinds of ways that a hopeful fiancée may have in mind when she says, "That habit of his irritates me, but after we're married I'll get him to change." The growth changes that occur under the impact of a good marriage will be gradual and will require time, sometimes a lifetime. The changes will also tend to go in directions and remain within limits set long be-

117

fore marriage by the early developmental experiences of each person. For this reason, it is wise for people choosing mates to be alert to traits of marriageability or unmarriageability already developed in themselves and others, for such traits are significant indications concerning the potential quality of a future marriage.

Some people are definitely more marriageable than others. They would have a better than average probability of making a success of any marriage they might enter. Others would have difficulty no matter whom they married.

Traits of happy and unhappy husbands and wives

Lewis M. Terman made an analysis of the traits of 792 couples.[1] He found differences between traits common among people who were happily married and those unhappily married. The happily married women were more likely to show these characteristics:

1. Have kindly attitudes toward others.
2. Expect kindly attitudes from others.
3. Do not easily take offense.
4. Not unduly concerned about the impressions they make upon others.
5. Do not look upon social relationships as rivalry situations.
6. Are cooperative.
7. Do not object to subordinate roles.
8. Are not annoyed by advice from others.
9. Frequently have missionary and ministering attitudes.
10. Enjoy activities that bring educational and pleasurable opportunities to others.
11. Like to do things for the dependent or underprivileged.

[1] Lewis M. Terman, *Psychological Factors in Marital Happiness*, pp. 142-166. New York: McGraw-Hill Book Company, Inc., 1938. Terman and his associates made a study of 792 couples, who were in the middle and upper-middle classes, living in urban and semi-urban California. The couples had been married varying lengths of time, from less than one year to more than 30 years, the average being 11 years. Approximately one-third (38 per cent) were college graduates. Each spouse was asked to fill out a detailed questionnaire independently of the other. The study was anonymous; the chief purpose was to determine what psychological factors are associated with marital happiness. Data were collected in the early and middle 1930's. We shall refer to the Terman study occasionally throughout this book.

12. Are methodical and painstaking in their work.
13. Are careful in regard to money.
14. In religion, morals, and politics tend to be conservative and conventional.
15. Have expressed attitudes that imply a quiet self-assurance and a decidedly optimistic outlook upon life.

The unhappily married women showed a different set of personality characteristics. In general, they were as follows:

1. Are characterized by emotional tenseness.
2. Inclined toward ups and downs of moods.
3. Give evidence of deep-seated inferiority feelings to which they react by aggressive attitudes rather than by timidity.
4. Are inclined to be irritable and dictatorial.
5. Have compensatory mechanisms resulting in restive striving, as evidenced by becoming active joiners, aggressive in business, and over-anxious in social life.
6. Strive for wide circle of acquaintances; are more concerned with being important than being liked.
7. Are egocentric.
8. Have little interest in benevolent and welfare activities unless these activities offer personal recognition.
9. Like activities fraught with opportunities for romance.
10. Are more inclined to be conciliatory in attitudes toward men than toward women.
11. Are impatient and fitful workers.
12. Dislike cautious or methodical people.
13. Dislike types of work that require methodical and painstaking effort.
14. In politics, religion, and social ethics are more often radical.

Terman found that happy husbands were inclined to have the following characteristics:

1. Have even and stable emotional tone.
2. Are cooperative.
3. Show attitude toward women that reflects equalitarian ideals.
4. Have benevolent attitude toward inferiors and the underprivileged.
5. Tend to be unselfconscious and somewhat extroverted.
6. Show superior initiative.
7. Have a greater tendency to take responsibility.
8. Show greater willingness to give close attention to detail.

9. Like methodical procedures and methodical people.
10. Are saving and cautious in money matters.
11. Hold conservative attitudes.
12. Have a favorable attitude toward religion.
13. Strongly uphold the sex mores and other social conventions.

Unhappy husbands showed personality traits that were somewhat comparable to those of the unhappy wives, although not the same in all cases:

1. Are inclined to be moody and somewhat neurotic.
2. Are prone to feelings of social inferiority.
3. Dislike being conspicuous in public.
4. Are highly reactive to social opinion.
5. Often compensate for a sense of social insecurity by domineering attitudes.
6. Take pleasure in commanding roles over business dependents or women.
7. Withdraw from playing inferior role or competing with superiors.
8. Often compensate by daydreams and power fantasies.
9. Are sporadic and irregular in their habits of work.
10. Dislike detail and methodical attitude.
11. Dislike saving money.
12. Like to wager.
13. More often express irreligious attitudes.
14. More inclined to radicalism in sex morals and politics.

A study of the personality characteristics in the four classifications above suggests that the people who were unhappy in marriage had characteristics that would tend to make them unhappy in their associations, whether they were married or single. The marriage relationship is not so different from other personal relationships. We do not rationally choose friends who are uncooperative, selfish, moody, aggressive. People who show more positive attitudes, those who willingly share, and those who are dependable in the day-to-day affairs of life are more satisfactory friends. They are also more marriageable.

Most people will marry regardless of the level of their marriageability, since about ninety-three out of a hundred Americans eventually do marry. However, with many couples during the courtship period the elements of sex attraction and love fantasy may be so dominant in their relationship that they cannot evaluate each other's real personality. After marriage, they may become aware of traits in each other that make living together difficult.

Husband-wife grievances

In order to find what common grievances married people hold against their spouses, Terman asked the 792 couples to rank 57 common grievances according to their seriousness. The 28 most serious are given in Table 7.

It will be noticed that these grievances have little to do with the conditions of the marriage; rather, they are almost entirely personality faults. Terman points out that this holds true for the first 20 items on the husbands' list, and for all but one of the first 20 on the wives' list. "A majority of the faults are of the kind commonly thought to be indicative of emotional instability, neurotic tendency, or marked introversion, as these terms are used in the current literature of personality psychology." [2]

The most serious grievances from the husbands' point of view are that the wives nag, are not affectionate, are selfish and inconsiderate, complain too much, interfere with hobbies, are slovenly in appearance, and are quick-tempered. The wives counter that their husbands are selfish and inconsiderate, are unsuccessful in business, are untruthful, complain too much, do not show affection, do not talk things over, and are too harsh with the children.

It is interesting to note that among the first eight grievances three are the same on both lists. The husbands put in third place and the wives in first place that the other is selfish and inconsiderate. One-third of the least happy husbands and wives, but only 3 per cent of the more happy spouses listed this complaint.

[2] Terman, *op. cit.,* p. 101.

TABLE 7   RANK ORDER OF MARITAL GRIEVANCES
ACCORDING TO SERIOUSNESS
AS GIVEN BY 792 HUSBANDS AND 792 WIVES *

Order for husbands	Order for wives
1. W. nags me	1. H. selfish and inconsiderate
2. W. not affectionate	2. H. unsuccessful in business
3. W. selfish and inconsiderate	3. H. is untruthful
4. W. complains too much	4. H. complains too much
5. W. interferes with hobbies	5. H. does not show his affection
6. W. slovenly in appearance	6. H. does not talk things over
7. W. is quick-tempered	7. H. harsh with children
8. W. interferes with my discipline	8. H. touchy
9. W. conceited	9. H. has no interest in children
10. W. is insincere	10. H. not interested in home
11. W.'s feelings too easily hurt	11. H. not affectionate
12. W. criticizes me	12. H. rude
13. W. narrow-minded	13. H. lacks ambition
14. W. neglects the children	14. H. nervous or impatient
15. W. a poor housekeeper	15. H. criticizes me
16. W. argumentative	16. H.'s poor management of income
17. W. has annoying habits	17. H. narrow-minded
18. W. untruthful	18. H. not faithful to me
19. W. interferes in my business	19. H. lazy
20. W. spoils the children	20. H. bored with my small talk
21. W.'s poor management of income	21. In-laws
22. In-laws	22. H. easily influenced by others
23. Insufficient income	23. H. tight with money
24. W. nervous or emotional	24. H. argumentative
25. W. easily influenced by others	25. H.'s insufficient income
26. W. jealous	26. H. has no backbone
27. W. lazy	27. H. dislikes to go out with me
28. W. gossips indiscreetly	28. H. pays attention to other women

* By permission from *Psychological Factors in Marital Happiness* by L. M. Terman, Copyrighted, 1938, by McGraw-Hill Book Co., Inc., p. 99.

Selfishness is not a trait that suddenly afflicts people after they marry. It was undoubtedly very evident before marriage to anyone who was not involved emotionally.

Complaining is in fourth place on both lists. Again, the person who has a complaining attitude toward life developed that attitude long before marriage. Chronic complainers usually do not recognize that they are complaining; the habit reflects an attitude toward life that may be traceable to some other personality difficulty.

One-third of the less happy husbands and wives said that the spouse was not affectionate enough. In some cases, failure to show affection may be due to selfishness or thoughtlessness. In other cases, it may mean only that one comes from an undemonstrative family. In some families the pattern does not include much show of affection; caresses between parents and children are rare even though the family may be a "close" and happy one. The pattern of the parental family is often carried over into their own marriages by the children. A person brought up in a family where there were frequent demonstrations of affection may expect this outward demonstration of affection in marriage. The lack of such expression may cause the person to feel insecure and uncertain of the love of the spouse.

Many of the other grievances listed are simply the outward indications of unhappy temperaments. *One of the most important characteristics of a marriageable person is the habit of happiness.* It would be impossible to overestimate the value of cultivating this trait in oneself and of seeking it in a marriage partner. As

Fig. 25 WHAT COMES OUT OF MARRIAGE DEPENDS ON WHAT GOES INTO IT, AND AMONG THE MOST IMPORTANT THINGS . . . ARE THE ATTITUDES, PREFERENCES, AVERSIONS, HABIT PATTERNS, AND EMOTIONAL RESPONSE PATTERNS. . . .Courtesy of *California Monthly.*

Terman sums it up, "What comes out of marriage depends on what goes into it, and among the most important things going into it are the attitudes, preferences, aversions, habit patterns, and emotional response patterns, which give or deny to one the aptitude of compatibility. In a large proportion of unsuccessful marriages, it is possible to discover in the husband or the wife, or perhaps both, numerous elements of the unhappy temperament and evidence that these elements have played a casual role." [3]

Important characteristics in marriageability

Adaptability.   The marriageable person has developed, or is in process of developing, adaptability.

Young people who have been brought up in such a way that they find it easy to adjust to new situations and to many different kinds of people will fit more easily into marriage. Some people have rigid personalities; they find it difficult to change their ways, to accept new ways, to make new friends, or to fit into any situation that is different from what they have always been used to. Since marriage requires many adjustments, the person who does not look upon change as a threat to his security will make a better marriage partner.

In comparing groups of divorced and happily married couples, Locke found that the happily married men and women rated higher on adaptability. He considered as more adaptable those who could "give in" in arguments, who were not dominating, who were slow to anger, and who were quick to get over anger.[4]

Burgess and Wallin concluded that some of the 1,000 couples they studied during engagement who had low marital-prediction scores still made happy marriages, possibly because of a high rating on general adaptability.[5] Burgess and Wallin have made a

[3] Terman, *op. cit.*, pp. 110-111.
[4] Harvey J. Locke, *Predicting Adjustment in Marriage*, p. 192. New York: Henry Holt and Company, 1951.
[5] Ernest W. Burgess and Paul Wallin, *Engagement and Marriage*, pp. 620-655. Chicago: J. B. Lippincott Company, 1953.

perceptive analysis of the components of adaptability. They point out that adaptability involves three elements: understanding; knowledge of the different kinds of responses appropriate to specific situations; and the ability to incorporate these responses into one's behavior.[6] In other words, the adaptable person can perceive not only "How would I feel in his place?" but "How does *he* feel, and what is it in the situation that underlies his feeling?" Then, in addition to this understanding of another's feelings, the adaptable person has learned by experience and observation what kinds of responses or actions would be most helpful to the other person and to the quality of the relationship between the two of them. But knowledge is not enough; some people who know what actions or responses would be most helpful to the other person and to the relationship involved still cannot act according to their knowledge. Habit patterns are too strong for them. The adaptable person becomes able to *do* the things he knows. Some people may know how not to "rub other people the wrong way," but they may still be too rigid and inflexible to act according to the knowledge. Such a person will say, "I know I'm stubborn, but that's the way I am. I can't help it." Or, "I criticize. I think people ought to be able to take honest criticism. Oh, of course I know she doesn't like it, and it causes trouble between us, but I can't help it. I've always been this way."

A young husband who was seriously working at his marriage described his experience:

> "I realize that it is much easier for me to criticize than to praise. It seems to come naturally to say, 'The roast is a little overdone, isn't it?' when what is really going through my mind is that this is a darn good dinner. Sometimes when I've definitely made up my mind to compliment my wife on some special thing, because she deserves the compliment and I know how good it makes her feel for me to tell her so, I find myself coming out with something that sounds a lot more like a criticism than a compliment. She stayed up half the night lately to type a paper for me, and I

[6] *Ibid.*, p. 635.

wanted to say something about it the next day. I heard myself saying, 'I guess late at night is not your best time for typing. I found some of the funniest mistakes when I proofread that paper this morning.' Now, why couldn't I have said, 'Thank you, Honey, for staying up and missing your sleep to type my paper last night. I appreciate it.'? That was what I *meant*, but as usual what I *said* just hurt her feelings."

This man had developed insight enough to understand some of his wife's feelings, and to know what was wrong with his own habitual responses to situations. But he was struggling to become able to incorporate his knowledge into his behavior. The ability to act and respond to situations flexibly is a most important part of the adaptable personality.

Empathy.   To be able to perceive accurately the feelings and attitudes of others is called empathy; the ability to empathize is extremely important in the adaptable, marriageable personality. The person who rates high in empathy can use his perceptive understanding of the feelings of his mate as a regulator of his own responses and behavior in ways that add greatly to the success and happiness of the marriage. It must be said here that the empathic ability of the two partners in a marriage also arms them with weapons that they may use against each other, if they lack the will or the motivation to build a good marriage. A wife or a husband thus is able to inflict hurts to the mate far more serious than any outsider could ever inflict, simply because he or she knows so well the inner strengths and weaknesses of the mate. Spouses who are empathic know what will hurt as well as they know how to give emotional support and to build up the mate.

Empathy differs from sympathy in that to sympathize with another is to "feel for him" whether or not one can understand how he really feels; but to empathize is to be able to be sensitively aware of another's true feelings, even if they are not the kind of feelings one might have oneself in the same situation. The small child who says unexpectedly to a guest, "You don't

Fig. 26 EMPATHY IS THE ABILITY TO PERCEIVE ACCURATELY THE
FEELINGS AND ATTITUDES OF ANOTHER. Courtesy of Coronet
Films.

like me, do you?" or to his mother who is patiently helping him get ready for school, "Why are you mad at me this morning, mother?" is probably putting into words the true feelings or attitudes that he has sensed in the other person at the moment. Some degree of empathy is part of everyone's natural endowment. But as people grow older, their empathy may decrease because their own anxieties and motivations or the pressure of their neurotic needs prevents the effective functioning of empathy. So there are people who reach an age for marrying but who have trouble understanding others; their assessment of situations, actions, and feelings is more often erroneous than accurate. Their failure in empathy leads to misunderstandings and to strains growing out of misjudging of actions and misinterpreting of words.

The most marriageable people are those whose own motivations and emotional tensions are not so dominant in their lives that their ability to empathize is weak or non-functioning. Moreover, the most marriageable people use their empathic ability positively, as a basis for becoming more adaptable in their behavior in relationships with others. They are able to control their words and actions so that they do not say the thing that hurts, or do the thing that is sure to rub the other person the wrong way or complicate a difficult situation. The person who is habitually tactless either lacks empathy, or has not yet become able to regulate his responses and behavior toward the goal of building good interpersonal relationships.

How can one evaluate the functioning of empathy in oneself and in others?   It is possible to recognize failure in empathic processes in an individual in several ways. There is the "tactless" person. Also, for example, the person has failed in empathy who in a group will drive through with his own ideas or plans, successfully overruling all objections from others, and then feel happy and satisfied with his successful dominance, without sensing that even though others have outwardly agreed with him it was not their choice. The person who gets her own way and then is all smiles and happiness, unaware that the one who has given in to her is not quite so happy as she is; the one who frequently expresses pronounced or forceful opinions before drawing out any views from anyone else, and then concludes that all are in agreement with him since no one offers any dissenting argument—these are not empathic. Many situations that occur in every-day associations with people bring out the presence or absence of a perceptive understanding of other people's feelings.

The young person who is working to improve his own level of marriageability will need to try to be objective in observing his own interaction with other people. "Do I ride roughshod over other people's wishes or preferences?" "Do I tend to talk when I ought to listen?" "Do I usually get my own way?" "Do I make quick judgments of other people, and rate them without bothering to get to know them well?" Such questions as these may possibly be helpful. One does not create empathy in himself; he must rather allow it to begin to function, by taking himself out of the way of his understanding of other people.

Ability to work through problems. The ability to work through problems is another important point in marriageability.

Almost all problems that confront people in the normal course of events in life have the possibility of some kind of solution. The solution may not always be a satisfactory or happy one, nevertheless it is possible for the average person to formulate for himself some fairly satisfactory way of coming to terms with problems in his life. The test of one's approach is whether the policy he follows in relation to problems results in bettering or worsening his effectiveness as an individual functioning in a situation, in a group, or in interpersonal relationships.

An illustration may clarify this point:

> Don, a college sophomore, whose parents were unable to help him financially, was invited to live with his aunt and uncle in a university city and to attend school there. The aunt and uncle were anxious to help Don in every possible way; they provided

him with his board and a comfortable room, and also gave him an allowance to cover school expenses. However, they had no children of their own and their ideas about what the life of a college student should be like seemed to Don to be very unrealistic. They thought he should be in his room studying every weekday evening except Saturday and on that night they thought he should be in by midnight. They checked up on his progress constantly, inquired into his assignments, and in general showed so much interest that Don felt overwhelmed by supervision.

The situation soon became a serious problem to him. He was irritable and unhappy, and frequently frustrated because he controlled his impulses to blow up and tell his aunt and uncle to leave him alone and let him handle his own affairs. He became aware of an inclination to let his studies slide and to spend more and more time fooling around with other students, enjoying himself all he could, partly from a feeling that he wasn't going to be in college long anyway since the situation at his uncle's was getting him down. When his midterm grades showed that his average was dangerously low, he realized that something must be done. He tried to face the problem objectively. He came up with this summary of possible alternatives: He might quit school and go home. He ruled that out as accepting unnecessary failure. If he stayed, he might try to adjust completely to his relatives' rigid ideas in order to avoid conflicts. He felt that he could not do that. He might try to support himself in school and move out of their home. He knew that would hurt them and they would not understand his doing it. Moreover, he found that to support himself in school was not immediately possible anyway, although he concluded that by careful planning he could do so another year by carrying a lighter study load and working more. The only possible and reasonable alternative that he could see at the moment was to try to find some compromise with his relatives and continue the present arrangement. This he set out to do.

He was able to have some frank and friendly discussions with his aunt and uncle, trying to show them that he appreciated their help and seriously intended to make a success of his education; but at the same time he gave them exact information about what rules governed the activities and hours of other students on the campus, and he tried to get them to see why it was so difficult for him to live by a rigid set of rules that applied to none of his associates.

There was no quick and final solution, but Don was able to pin point the problem for himself and for his aunt and uncle. The trouble arose from a natural difference in viewpoints because of differences in age and experience; there was not a difference in basic motives or intentions. After he had analyzed the problem so objectively, much of Don's frustration disappeared, and he could use patient persistence to build a better understanding with his relatives and to work out irritating details of policy.

Many people have never set up a positive system for facing problem situations in their lives. They do not assess a problem realistically and choose ways of acting that will bring constructive results. Instead, they give up easily and consider a situation hopeless, or they regress to some form of immature emotional behavior that may create new problems or cause the old ones to snowball into unmanageable proportions.

People who can face problems realistically and seek intelligent solutions are more likely to be successful in married living. The need for an established way of meeting problems constructively arises at times in every marriage. For example, for some couples early in their marriage, there may be excessive control or dominance coming from one or both sets of parents-in-law. The person who does not let problems overwhelm him nor force him into irrational or destructive action, can meet such in-law situations with some objectivity. He has learned through practice that there are positive ways of working out even the most difficult problem situations.

In such a problem as strained relationships with in-laws, the solution might be found in temporary acquiescence; in escape— putting distance between the in-laws and the couple; in frank and open discussion of the situation; in making greater efforts to understand and accept the motives back of the problem behavior; even in limiting contacts with the in-laws, or in making changes in living arrangements, or in financial plans. But whatever the eventual solution may be, the one who has an habitual policy of facing problems constructively will find his own good solution; he will not just go through random or destructive motions based on emotion, and so complicate his problem.

Family background as part of marriageability

The statement is sometimes made that a child is headed for a happy marriage or for the divorce court by the time he is ten years old because of the training and conditioning he has received up to that time. Researchers who have tested this hypothesis by investigating the background factors in the lives of people and attempting to relate these factors to success in marriage have concluded that young people are usually conditioned early in life in ways that will make them good or bad risks in marriage. Although the studies were made in different parts of the country, they produced many of the same conclusions concerning the background factors that make for happiness in marriage. Terman [7] found the following ten circumstances most predictive of marital happiness:

1. Superior happiness of parents
2. Childhood happiness
3. Lack of conflict with mother
4. Home discipline that was firm, not harsh
5. Strong attachment to mother
6. Strong attachment to father
7. Lack of conflict with father
8. Parental frankness about matters of sex
9. Infrequency and mildness of childhood punishment
10. Premarital attitude free from disgust or aversion toward sex

Terman believes that anyone who passes on all ten of these points is a distinctly better-than-average marital risk. Burgess and Cottrell [8] found the following background factors most important in predicting success in marriage:

[7] Terman, *op. cit.*, pp. 110-111.

[8] Ernest W. Burgess and Leonard S. Cottrell, *Predicting Success or Failure in Marriage.* Englewood Cliffs, N. J.: Prentice-Hall, Inc., 1939. Burgess and Cottrell conducted a study of 526 middle-class couples living in and about Chicago. The couples had been married from one to six years, an average of three years. Approximately 60 per cent had some education beyond high school. Married, separated, and divorced couples were included in the study. In most cases, the wife completed the questionnaire. The chief purpose of the study was to determine the factors and personality traits predictive of success

1. Happiness of parents' marriage
2. Superior family background of husbands and wives
3. Similarity of family backgrounds
4. Husband and wife not "only" children
5. Husband closely attached to father and having little or no conflict with mother
6. Wife's close attachment to mother
7. Husband and wife reared in country
8. Husband and wife attended Sunday School beyond 18 years of age (as adults)
9. Husband and wife had several friends of the same and the opposite sex
10. Parental approval of marriage

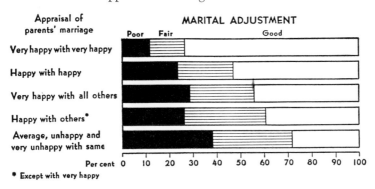

Fig. 27 APPRAISAL OF THE HAPPINESS OF PARENTS' MARRIAGE (COMBINED RATINGS) AND ADJUSTMENT OF THEIR CHILDREN IN MARRIAGE. If both sets of parents had very happy marriages, the children have a much better chance for happiness in marriage. From Ernest W. Burgess and Leonard S. Cottrell, *Predicting Success or Failure in Marriage*, p. 101. Englewood Cliffs, N. J.: Prentice-Hall, Inc., 1939.

These two lists agree in general. Both are concerned with the happiness of the parents' marriage, and the relationship of the

or failure in marriage. The data for the Burgess-Cottrell studies were collected during the early 1930's. Charles E. King repeated the Burgess-Cottrell study with a group of 466 Negro couples and found the same relationships between premarital factors and marital adjustments. See Charles E. King, "The Burgess-Cottrell Method of Measuring Marital Adjustment Applied to a Non-White Southern Urban Population," *Marriage and Family Living*, 14:4 (November, 1952), 280-285.

child with his parents. People from homes where the parents had happy marriages, and from homes in which a satisfactory relationship existed between the parents and their children, have an advantage in developing traits of marriageability. People reared in homes in which the parents were unhappy, and in which there was constant parent-child friction have some handicaps for successful marriage. It is also true that divorce tends to run in families. Reports from approximately two thousand students at the University of California concerning the marital records of their parents, grandparents, aunts and uncles, showed a significantly greater proportion of divorces in families whose grandparents had divorced, than in families whose grandparents had remained married.[9] (See Fig. 28.)

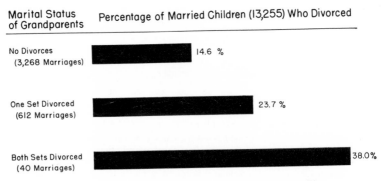

Marital Status of Grandparents   **Percentage of Married Children (13,255) Who Divorced**

No Divorces
(3,268 Marriages)   14.6 %

One Set Divorced
(612 Marriages)   23.7 %

Both Sets Divorced
(40 Marriages)   38.0%

Fig. 28 PERCENTAGE OF PARENTS, AUNTS, AND UNCLES OF 1,977 COLLEGE STUDENTS WHO HAD DIVORCED, AND THE MARITAL STATUS OF THE GRANDPARENTS.

[9] Judson T. Landis, "The Pattern of Divorce in Three Generations," *Social Forces,* 34:3 (March, 1956), 213-216. In studying the dating and engagement histories of these 1,977 students, it was found that a slightly higher percentage of the students who came from homes in which there had been divorce among both their parents and their grandparents went steady with and became engaged to people from homes broken by divorce. However, any tendency of children from divorced families to marry children from divorced families would not be sufficient to explain the high divorce rate among children of divorced parents.

The evidence shows then that people seem to be conditioned by their family background in ways that affect their marriageability. Those reared in happy homes have an advantage in that their parents were able to give them an example of successful family living. Nevertheless, those reared in unhappy homes are not doomed to failure. Research in the past has been based almost entirely on success or failure among people who had had no formal preparation for marriage. Today the young person can evaluate his own marriageability and overcome many of the effects of whatever handicaps he may have. With a rational approach to marriage, people can and do break cycles of unhappiness that may have run in their families. Those who have not had the background of happily married parents need to be alert to recognize danger signals that might warn of special problems ahead because of traits in themselves or in the person they consider marrying, and to avoid rushing into marriage if doubts exist about a relationship. By such alertness, they can avoid repeating the mistakes their parents may have made.

On the other hand, young people who have grown up in happy families, with parents who had good marriages, are not automatically assured of successful marriages themselves. It is necessary for every couple, no matter what their backgrounds, to approach marriage intelligently, and to work at building happy and successful relationships within marriage. Important as background is, it can never guarantee happiness in marriage any more than it can doom one to unhappiness.

In this chapter we have discussed a number of different considerations that have to do with marriageability. The most important aspects of marriageability are related to personality and to one's habitual ways of meeting life situations. Habits and personality patterns are closely related to the family background and life experiences of the individual, but can, nevertheless, be modified.

OUTLINE FOR SELF-STUDY: YOUR MARRIAGEABILITY

Think through the following outline, and decide upon your answers to the questions. Then write an assessment of your own marriageability as revealed by your study and thinking.

I. *Your personality traits*

1. Which of the personality traits found in the Terman study of happy husbands and wives do you have?
2. In general, do you have an outgoing and accepting attitude toward others. Are you often critical of other people?
3. Do you find it easy to work happily with others? When you work with others do you tend to feel either that you are pushed around, or that you have a hard time getting the others to cooperate with you or accept your leadership?
4. Do you find it easy to live with yourself? Do you tend to feel depressed when alone, or do you have a fairly sustained sense of well being?
5. Are you cautious in making most decisions? Or do you act first and think later?
6. In general, do you find it easy to live within the accepted conventions of society?
7. Can you accept things as they come in life, or do you often complain about circumstances or wish life were different?
8. Do you lose your temper?
9. What kind of personality or self do other people reflect back to you? You can judge this by whether you usually feel liked, responded to, and accepted by others.

II. *Handling problems in your life*

1. How do you react to failure or disappointment? Would an outside observer say your habitual way of reacting is mentally healthy? Will it lead to living harmoniously with others?
2. If some circumstances in life are difficult for you, or put you under pressure, can you make an objective evaluation of the problem situation and take positive rather than negative action? Think of a specific problem you have had. How did you meet it? Did your course of action result in an improvement in your situation, or growth in yourself? What was constructive or what was destructive in the way you met that problem? Did you learn from it so that you could handle a similar problem that might arise more constructively?

III. Assess your adaptability and empathy

1. How do you fit into new situations? If your family has moved, what difficulty, if any, did you have fitting into a new community? When you first went to college, did you adjust readily to living away from home?

2. Do you make friends easily? How many friends have you kept for two or more years?

3. How do you rate in empathy? Can you size up situations and people as they really are, or does it sometimes seem that everyone is out of step except you? Do you have a reputation for being considerate of other people's feelings? Do other people seem to get annoyed with you for reasons that are unclear to you?

IV. Assess your family background

1. How many happy marriages can you count among your grandparents, aunts and uncles, cousins, and brothers and sisters? How many divorces or unhappy marriages are there in your immediate background?

2. If there has been divorce or unhappiness in your family, have you tried to figure out the causes of the failures? How have the failures affected your thinking about marriage? What are you doing in a positive way to prepare for success in your future marriage?

3. What are your relationships with your parents and brothers and sisters? Friendly and close? Indifferent? Antagonistic? Can you recognize what traits in yourself may contribute to the kinds of relationships you have with your family members? How will these traits affect your future relationship in marriage?

4. Do you know which of your family's values are a part of you that you will take into marriage? (Making money? Service to others? Religious values? Participating in civic and community affairs? Having the respect of friends and associates? Material possessions—keeping up with others in standard of living? Success in a vocation?)

Review questions

1. How much change in the personality traits of your spouse can you expect after marriage? Will annoying personality traits disappear after marriage if two people love each other?

2. What were some of the personality traits which Terman found to be characteristic of happily married men and women? Of unhappily married men and women?

3. Why is it difficult to recognize undesirable personality traits during courtship?

4. What does Terman's study of husband-wife grievances reveal about personality traits?

5. Why is the habit of happiness important in marriageability?

6. Why is adaptability important in marriageability? What elements are involved in adaptability?

7. Define empathy. How might empathic ability be used destructively in a marriage?

8. What factors might prevent empathy from functioning effectively?

9. How can one recognize the failure to empathize in others? In oneself?

10. What is a good test of whether one is facing problems in life constructively?

11. What are some constructive steps in meeting a problem?

12. What family background factors seem to be important in predicting success or failure in marriage? Do research studies agree on this subject?

13. Divorce seems to run in families. How might this be explained?

14. Does a happy family background guarantee success in marriage for the children? Explain your answer.

Projects and activities

1. Make a list of ten personality traits that you find hard to tolerate in others. Now make a self-analysis and try to determine why you cannot tolerate these traits in others.

2. *Panel discussion.* A group from the class discuss ways they have observed by which others meet their problems or handle their aggressive feelings.

3. Write a paper on your marriageability, taking into consideration personality traits and family background.

4. *Socio-drama.* Try writing and acting a skit which brings out some personality traits that would make for happiness or unhappiness in marriage.

Film

Choosing for Happiness. Two college girls consider different men they have dated as possible husbands. All fail to meet the needs of Eve because she herself is probably unmarriageable at her present stage of maturity. McGraw-Hill Book Company, Inc. 20 minutes, sound.

Suggested readings

Baber, Ray E., *Marriage and the Family.* New York: McGraw-Hill Book Company, Inc., 1953. Ch. V, "Mate Selection and Courtship."

Becker, Howard, and Reuben Hill, eds., *Family, Marriage, and Parenthood.* Boston: D. C. Heath and Company, 1955. Ch. VI, "Producing Marriageable Personalities."

Burgess, Ernest W., and Harvey J. Locke, *The Family.* New York: American Book Company, 1953. Ch. XIII, "Mate Selection."

Burgess, Ernest W., and Paul Wallin, *Engagement and Marriage.* Chicago: J. B. Lippincott Company, 1953. Ch. XIX, "Adaptability."

Landis, Judson T., and Mary G. Landis, eds., *Readings in Marriage and the Family.* Englewood Cliffs, N. J.: Prentice-Hall, Inc., 1952. Part IV, "The Influence of Parent-Images upon Marital Choice," Anselm Strauss.

Peterson, James A., *Education for Marriage.* New York: Charles Scribner's Sons, 1956. Ch. IV, "Factors in Adolescence," and Ch. V, "Dating as a Factor."

Emotional maturity

Objectivity

A realistic conception of marriage

*Maturity for marriage includes
a conception of love based on truth*

A philosophy to live by

A reasonable evaluation of self

An evaluation of family background

The mature person meets problems constructively

Has an understanding of human motivations

Can think independently

Maturity for Marriage

Takes responsibility for mistakes

*Has a sense of proportion about present desires
and future goals*

Is ready to sacrifice for others

Has outgrown immature sex attitudes

Can assess his own level of maturity

Age as a factor in readiness for marriage

In most of the states in the United States, girls may legally marry at 18 and boys at 21 without parental consent, and in many states the legal ages are much lower. Chronologically, therefore, there is no question about when people are mature enough to marry.

People of the courtship age are interested in knowing whether there is a "best" age for marriage. Because of the many variables that must be taken into consideration, it is difficult to isolate the age factor. To illustrate, college people seem to have happier marriages than non-college people, if divorce rates of college and non-college people are taken as a measure; and college graduates marry at a later age than non-college graduates. Is it the age at marriage or the college experience that results in happier marriages among college graduates? Or are there selective factors that may differentiate college and non-college people and that affect marital success? The question of what age is best emerges as less to the point than the question of what level of maturity is necessary before one is old enough to marry.

Emotional maturity

A factor of greatest importance in the success or failure of any marriage is the emotional maturity of the partners. Emotional maturity can be defined as the level of one's development in ability to see oneself and others objectively, to be able to discriminate between facts and feelings, and to act on facts rather than on feelings. The child of ten is not expected to be emotionally mature; he is developing satisfactorily if he is as

141

mature as other children of his age. So at each stage of life a certain level of maturity is necessary if one is to function adequately at that level. Problems arise when the emotional growth of people is arrested at immature stages; especially are problems likely to be acute if one or both partners in a marriage have not achieved a satisfactory level of maturity.

Certain traits discussed in the preceding chapter, such as the ability to use empathy in constructive ways, are characteristic of mature adults. The level of maturity an individual has achieved may also be measured by the degree of flexibility or adaptability with which he reacts in his relationships with other people. The rigid, inflexible person, like a small child, clings to certainty, sameness, and habit. Growth toward understanding and cooperation in a close relationship, such as marriage, is handicapped by this type of immaturity.

Objectivity

One of the most important characteristics of maturity is objectivity, the ability to get outside ourselves and see ourselves and our interests realistically, to look at external facts as separate from our feelings about them. Small children view most of the circumstances of their lives subjectively. They are self-centered. But with increased maturity should come the ability to see things in their true relationships, the ability to stand aside as it were, and judge events more impartially—to recognize that the world does not necessarily revolve about one's own life and experiences. Without objectivity, an individual will have distorted ideas about himself, his needs, and "rights." He will fail to evaluate his own motives. Few people can be completely objective, but the person who is growing toward a maturity adequate for marriage is able through his experiences and observations in living, to be objective in his attitudes and judgments. He perceives the relative importance of events as they relate to himself and other people, and can act according to intelligent perceptions.

Fig. 29 THERE IS SOME RELATIONSHIP BETWEEN CHRONOLOGICAL
AGE AND MATURITY FOR MARRIAGE. Courtesy of *California
Monthly.*

A realistic conception of marriage

The mature person comes to see marriage for what it is. He knows that marriage is not an easy escape from reality and from personal problems, but rather a way of life that may bring new problems and that certainly will bring greater responsibility, but which also has the potentiality for greater fulfillment of personal needs and deeper personal happiness. He sees marriage as most rewarding if the total relationship between the two partners is a mutual meeting of personality needs. He can accept also the fact that marriage is not merely a personal matter between two people. It is an institution designed by a civilized society to protect and give security to children born into that society and to guarantee the stability and continuity of the whole social group. The many legal and social regulations and prohibitions that affect marriage are evidence of society's stake in each marriage. The person who is mature enough for marriage is aware of these larger implications of his marriage as well as its meaning for his own personal life.

Maturity for marriage includes:

A conception of love based on truth. A mature understanding of the nature of love may develop slowly as one goes through adolescence and early adulthood. The individual may have gone through a process of experiencing different levels and types of love. He knew a type of love in junior high school, possibly had several "loves" in high school. Each of these experiences taught him something about the nature of love. If he gets safely through this part of life, he has probably come to realize that he could love people whom he could not possibly live with in marriage. He has learned that love must be supported by a broad foundation of common interests, common goals in life, sincere acceptance of each other, and basic respect; and that love, to grow and become more satisfying in marriage, must be based upon a total relationship between two people. The mature person sees "romantic love," as pictured in movies, plays, and in fiction, for what it is, a form of fantasy experience that has little relationship to the type of love that can provide happiness in marriage.

A philosophy to live by. The mature person is developing a philosophy that will guide him through the future. He is coming to terms with the universe about him in his moral philosophy, his religious concepts, and in his responses to and functioning among other people. He has at least a measure of security concerning his philosophy of life because he is finding that it is

Fig. 30 "I shut my eyes during the kissing scene and make believe he's choking her." By permission, Ray Helle and *The Saturday Evening Post.*

workable in that it enables him to cope with difficult circumstances or situations in his life. He still tests and evaluates his basic attitudes, and will continue to do so throughout life if his maturing continues; but he has already lived long enough and matured enough to have made the major shifts and reshufflings in his philosophy that are characteristic of adolescence or of the person who is still in the early stages of growing up. At this point his directions are set, even if the exact course is not charted. He is thus ready to choose a marriage partner wisely, and the one who chooses him does not have to make a blind choice.

A reasonable evaluation of self. The mature person has made a fairly accurate and objective evaluation of himself. He sees his strengths and weaknesses, and he is working to overcome the weaknesses if possible. If he has weak points within his personality that he cannot change, he accepts them without great sorrow or feelings of guilt. He builds on his strengths and makes the most of himself in terms of what he has to work with. He recognizes that there are some things he cannot do well if at all, but he also knows the things he can do well. He accepts without great regret his inabilities and limitations, and appreciates and uses his assets.

An evaluation of family background. Before a person is mature enough for marriage he needs to be able to view and understand his own family background and the contribution it has made to his personality, and the implications it may have for his marriage. Since most research shows that a child's chances for success in marriage are determined to some extent by the success or failure of his parents' marriage, and by the emotional climate of his home, the mature person is not afraid to look at his family background and attempt to evaluate it objectively. If he sees marriage failure and unhappiness in one or more generations in his immediate past, he can think constructively about the situation and try to avoid a repetition in his own life, just as he would face the fact of a family history of tuberculosis, or migraines, and try to live in such a way as to avoid becoming a victim so far as it might be within his control. If there has been unhappiness in his family he does not accept it as inevitable for his own marriage. Rather, he attempts to determine how this unhappiness has affected him, and he takes positive action to overcome his handicaps. The mature person does not harshly blame his parents for their weaknesses and failures; he gives them credit for the strengths and achievements that he can see in their lives. Similarly he does not take for granted that he is all set for happiness if his parents have been happy; he tries to understand the techniques of living that have meant happiness in his family. Especially he attempts to assess his own contribution to the emotional climate in which he has grown up, in order to be able to contribute positively to the happiness of his future marriage and family life.

The mature person:

Meets problems constructively. Another trait that distinguishes the mature person from the immature, no matter what the chronological age may be, is that the mature person has learned how to meet his problems in constructive ways. He is not easily thrown into confusion, discouragement, or disorganization by disappointments or frustrations in life. He has been able to use his past experiences as means of growth so that he has established more or less habitual policies that enable him to cope with emergencies and crises in life. This phase of maturity will significantly affect his ability to build a successful marriage.

Has an understanding of human motivations. The mature person has not only given thought to his own personality and family background but he has gained some understanding of human personality and how it functions. He has come to recognize types of behavior in himself and others in relation to inner motivations. He can see aggressive and domineering behavior as indicative of feelings of insecurity; he sees heavy drinking, the use of drugs, certain physical illnesses, moodiness, or clinging dependence as means sometimes used to escape from problems in life; he sees rebellion against society as an immature way of gaining attention; he recognizes jealousy as an inability to cope with feelings of inadequacy; he knows that gossip is motivated by a desire to build oneself up by pushing others down. These perceptions and understandings of the motivations that influence behavior should enable the mature person to be charitable in his judgment of others, and also to be wiser in choosing a marriage partner. Sometimes behavior patterns that might for a time seem charming or desirable in a girl friend or boy friend—such as an adoring possessiveness—when understood, may constitute a warning about a personality or a relationship.

Can think independently.   The mature person has achieved some degree of independence in his thinking. He has profited by what he has been taught at home, but he has reached the point where he can think for himself. If at one time in his growing up he threw overboard much of what he had been taught, he is now past the stage of immature rebellion against authority and has integrated his ideas based on life experiences with attitudes derived from his background so that he can be relatively unemotional and independent in his decisions.

Takes responsibility for mistakes.   The mature individual has become able to accept responsibility for his own mistakes. He has grown beyond blaming others for his weaknesses and refusing to recognize his own faults. When he makes a mistake, he accepts it and tries to learn from the experience. Many people in their teens have developed to the extent that they rationally try to learn and do learn from their mistakes. A 17-year-old girl expressed an attitude that is predictive of the eventual achievement of a level of maturity adequate for successful marriage:

> "I think it's safer to try to learn from my mistakes than to try to dodge what happens. I've found out that if I try to duck responsibility for something and tell myself, 'Oh, well, it wasn't my fault

anyway,' it seems that the same kind of thing happens again later, and it hits me harder the next time. I think it's easier to learn all you can from each experience so that you won't have to learn it later the hard way."

Has a sense of proportion about present desires and future goals. The small child wants what he wants when he wants it. The mature individual recognizes his wants, but he can also look ahead and make choices. He wants a secure job, but he is willing to take years of training to be ready for that job. He wants a high income and money to spend, but he is willing to work and learn and enjoy the present, while moving toward the future goal. He has strong sex urges toward the girl he dates, but he knows what he wants in the future in a marriage relationship and he keeps a sense of proportion about the place of sex in the present framework of his life. He would like to have a good car now but, if necessary, he will settle for whatever transportation he can afford at present so that he can afford to marry his girl next summer. The mature person does not deny his desires and wants, but he is willing to plan and to wait, and, if necessary, to make sacrifices today in order to carry out plans that he has decided will mean greater over-all satisfaction in the long run.

Is ready to sacrifice for others. Marriage is a cooperative venture involving two people who are willing to sacrifice for the partnership and for each other. The maturing person begins to appreciate that much of life consists of exchanges. At one level the child gives obedience in exchange for protection or for approval. At another level the worker gives his time, energy, and ability in exchange for a material reward in the form of a paycheck. On the far deeper level of relationships within marriage and the family, each person gives of himself; he gives emotional support, acceptance, and cooperation as a part of a mutual exchange that adds up to a satisfying relationship. In material and practical matters, too, he recognizes the necessity for giving. Mature parents, no matter how young, are willing to lose sleep to sit up with a sick child, to get up for the baby's two o'clock feeding when they are dead tired, and to give up buying things they want for themselves or for the house in order to provide for their children.

Fig. 31 By permission, United Feature Syndicate.

Some "adults" marry, never having reached this level of maturity. They cannot think first of the needs of a spouse or a baby and forget themselves; so the grocery money goes for a new hair style, or for a few rounds at a bar; the babies are slapped for crying, or children are left to their own resources while the parents attempt to escape back into the freedom they had before marriage. This type of immaturity, the inability to sacrifice for others or for the partnership, can be seen daily in our world. It accounts for much marital break-up and is responsible for many personality maladjustments in children. In contrast to such immaturity is this statement by a 19-year-old husband and father who, in discussing his job and financial budget, said,

> "I think our biggest problem is to make my paycheck cover all the things we need. We've had so many unexpected expenses. We didn't plan to have a baby the first year, but he came, and of course we're glad we've got him. . . . He wasn't very husky at first and we've had a lot of extra medical bills. Sometimes I get under pressure just trying to figure out which one of all the places to put each dollar, but it hasn't been too bad because so far we've managed to get along. I think sometimes about all the money we used to spend just fooling around going to shows and such things before we were married; it was a lot of fun, and it would be nice if we could go out together once in a while for an evening now, but there's no money for baby-sitters or for shows. I don't waste

much time thinking about it; I'm too busy supporting the three of us to waste time wishing we could do things we can't do. I'll tell you, you have a different feeling about your job when you've got two other people to take care of than you have when you're just working to earn money for a good time for yourself."

Has outgrown immature sex attitudes. For many reasons, people may have immature attitudes toward the place of sex in life. This is partly because of the way sex education of children is handled. Because of the negative attitudes expressed by some people, children often learn to think of sex as dirty and vulgar, or secret and sinful. Some people need many years after they have reached biological sexual maturity to grow to the place where they can view sexual feelings as a positive force in personality and sexual impulses and responses as a wholesome expression of love between two people. As they grow older, they may go to one extreme or the other in their sex attitudes—either denying their real feelings or overemphasizing sex in life while at the same time failing to recognize the true value of sex in all its aspects as a factor in successful marriage.

The person who is mature enough for marriage will have reached the point where he can consider whether or not his attitudes about sex are positive and wholesome, and where he can work to change his attitudes if change is needed. To change attitudes is not easy, but it can be done. Some people will need the help of a counselor, but the person who is achieving maturity in other areas of his life will take whatever steps are desirable in order to increase his growth toward maturity in sex attitudes.

Can assess his own level of maturity. Perhaps one of the more significant measures of progress toward maturity is the ability to be fairly objective in assessing one's own level of maturity. The immature person is usually not aware of much need to grow or change. The less mature he is, the more readily he may plunge into marriage with little or no understanding of the obligations and responsibilities he is assuming, and no thought about whether he is ready or willing to accept the obligations. The mature person will not be unduly fearful of assuming responsibility, but he will face the fact that with marriage he is assuming responsibility. He will consider, before he takes the step, whether he is ready for it. We quote from a self-evaluation written by a college student:

> "I'm in love with Ted, but I'm not going to get engaged because I know I'm a long way from being ready to marry. I want to marry and have children some day, but right now I just couldn't face all that responsibility. It's a problem in some ways, because I think it would be nice to have the children while I'm young—perhaps in the early twenties—so I'd have all the energy it takes to be a good mother—but when I see other girls almost my age with babies, I feel sorry for them. I still want to have fun before I get tied down to that. And another thing, I've been in love two or three times, but so far, it has not lasted. Each time after the affair has ended I have found someone else who turns out to be more nearly the type I'd like to marry some day. I'm still not sure enough about some things in my own personality or sure enough of my judgment of another's personality to make a choice that would have to be permanent. In the last year I've learned several things about myself. . . . Perhaps in another year or so I'll be more nearly ready to marry."

The person who made this self-evaluation had made more progress toward the maturity necessary for marriage than many others her age who are only vaguely aware that marriage means babies, and babies mean responsibility as well as sweetness. She was achieving a realistic attitude toward love and marriage, and some objectivity about her own level of maturity.

Age as a factor in readiness for marriage

All the characteristics discussed in this chapter require time and experience for development. Some people mature more easily and quickly under the impact of life experiences, but most people need years—chronological maturity—in order to develop a sound readiness for marriage. For this reason, although it is difficult to isolate the age factor, evidence indicates that the more successful marriages are not the very youthful marriages.

In our country, dating that starts at an early age may result in emotional involvements that lead to early marriages. Many of those who marry young would, a few years later, choose an entirely different type of spouse from the one chosen at 18. Between the ages of 16 and 22, the individual's conception of a desirable spouse will change as much as, or more than, his ideas about a vocation. If the 16-year-old takes a job, he is more apt to drift into it, but the 22-year-old has given his vocation more serious thought and can approach a special field with greater certainty and confidence. That may have some relationship to the fact that college graduates tend to have relatively fewer marriage failures than non-college people; many of them do not marry until after college—they have had the four college years in an environment that exposes them to opportunities for growing toward at least certain kinds of maturity before they undertake marriage.

Studies made of the relationship between age at marriage and happiness in marriage are summarized in Table 8.

TABLE 8   STUDIES OF THE BEST AGE FOR MARRIAGE
AS JUDGED BY MARITAL SUCCESS AND FAILURE

	Poor	Good	Excellent
Burgess-Cottrell (526 marriages)			
Men	Under 22	22-27; 31 and over	28-30
Women	Under 19	19-27	28 and over
Hart-Shields (500 marriages)			
Men	Under 24	24-28	29
Women	Under 21	21-23	24
Terman (792 marriages)			
Men	Under 22	22 and over	22 and over
Women	Under 20	20 and over	20 and over
Landis (409 marriages)			
Men	Under 20	20-29	30 and over
Women	Under 20	25 and over	20-24
Landis (544 marriages)			
Men	Under 20	20 and over	20 and over
Women	Under 18	18-21	22-27

All the above studies show that the chances for happiness in marriage are less when men marry before the age of 20 and when women marry before the age of 18. Three of the studies show that men who married as they approached their thirties were more likely to find happiness in marriage than those who married at younger ages.

In our study of 409 older-generation couples,[1] we found that it took longer for the men and women married under the age of 20 to reach good working arrangements in sex relations, spending income, associating with mutual friends, in-law relationships, and in social activities and recreation. The couples who were 20 years old or over when they married made the adjustments in less time than those under 20, and, in general, those who were married at 30 and over made the adjustments in less time than any other age group. The men who married at an early age had much more difficulty than the women who married at an early age, and the men who married at 30 years and over had less difficulty than the women who married at 30 years and over. Only 47 per cent of the men who married under 20 said the sex adjustment was satisfactory from the beginning of the marriage; 83 per cent of the men who were 30 and over when they married said the sex adjustment was satisfactory from the beginning. In general, this is the pattern existing between age at marriage and adjustments that take place after marriage.

In his study of divorced and happily married couples in In-

---

[1] This study was an analysis of the experience of 409 couples to determine how long it takes to work out adjustments after marriage, and to discover what factors are associated with happiness in marriage. The couples had been married from three to 40 years, an average of 20 years, and all were still married. Each spouse was asked to fill out an anonymous questionnaire independently of the other. The couples were largely residents of the middle west, Michigan, and Illinois; and they were of the middle or upper class economically. One-third of the participants were college graduates, and many of them were the parents of college students. Data were collected in 1945. For a summary of the study see: Judson T. Landis, "Length of Time Required to Achieve Adjustment in Marriage," *American Sociological Review*, 11:6 (December, 1946), 666-677.

diana, Locke found that a much larger percentage of the divorced women had married before the age of 18 and of the divorced men before the age of 21. The divorced women had married two years younger and the divorced men one year younger, on an average, than the happily married women and men.[2] A far-reaching study by the Bureau of the Census shows approximately the same results.

In the Bureau of the Census survey, women were asked how many times they had been married and their age at first marriage. For the women who had been married once, the median age at first marriage was 21.1 years; for those who had been married more than once, the median age at first marriage was 19.0 years. The report shows that the pattern has held constant for the past 35 years; that is, those remarrying were married for the first time when they were approximately 2 years younger than those married only once.[3]

Figure 32 summarizes our study of the divorce rate in 3,000 marriages. All the couples in this study were the parents of college students, and therefore would not represent a cross section of the population. The divorce rate decreased in these families as the age at marriage increased. If one spouse was under 20 and the other over 20 at marriage, the divorce rate was higher than if both were over 20 years old at marriage.

All of these findings emphasize the fact that chronological maturity age is related to the other kinds of maturity necessary to make a success of marriage. Certainly age cannot be isolated as the sole factor responsible for the higher proportion of failures among youthful marriages. One hypothesis is that more of those who marry early do so to escape unhappy home surroundings or to

[2] Harvey J. Locke, *Predicting Adjustment in Marriage: A Comparison of a Divorced and a Happily Married Group*, pp. 101-102. New York: Henry Holt and Company, 1951.

[3] Bureau of the Census, *Current Population Reports, Population Characteristics*, Series P-20, No. 67 (May 2, 1956), 3.

defy parental dominance than is true of those who marry later. To choose marriage as a hoped for means of escape from pressures may represent immature judgment and lack of the experience in problem-solving needed to make a success of marriage. Some who marry as an escape might not have the judgment to make a wiser choice even if they were much older, but many of them, if given time, would achieve a level of maturity not present when they marry at a very early age.

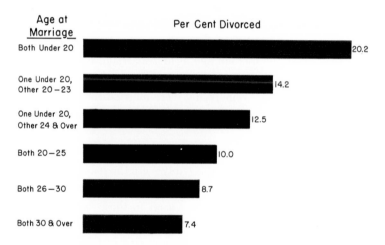

Age at Marriage	Per Cent Divorced
Both Under 20	20.2
One Under 20, Other 20 – 23	14.2
One Under 20, Other 24 & Over	12.5
Both 20 – 25	10.0
Both 26 – 30	8.7
Both 30 & Over	7.4

Fig. 32 AGE AT MARRIAGE AND THE DIVORCE RATE.

Undoubtedly, some early marriages are handicapped at the outset because they are entered into hastily, after short acquaintance, often without due consideration of the realities that will have to be faced after marriage.

Many youthful marriages are forced by pregnancy; if it were not for pregnancy, the couples would never have married each other. All studies that have been made of forced marriages show a high failure rate. Our study of 1,425 marriages of high-school students in 75 California high schools in 1957 revealed that if both members of the couple were in high school at the time of the marriage, between 44 and 56 per cent of the marriages were forced by pregnancy. Of the marriages that had taken place three years before the time of the study, one in five had already ended in annulment, divorce, or separation.

It is often believed that people who are older when they marry will have greater difficulty adjusting in marriage because they have become "set" in their ways. However, the studies on age for marriage do not show that this is true. The older person will have learned many things that may give him certain advantages. He has had an opportunity to observe the successful and unsuccessful marriages of his acquaintances. He has had the opportunity to become more realistic in his ideas of what marriage is. Moreover, since the man's sex drive decreases somewhat by the late twenties and thirties, while the woman's sex drive tends to reach its maturity in the late twenties and thirties, a couple may arrive at mutually satisfying sex adjustments more easily if they marry late. Older people may also base their mate selection upon a broader companionship basis, with sex interest exerting a less decisive influence.

The woman who marries at a later age knows what it is to be a single adult, and she has had time to decide whether she is willing to work at achieving a happy marriage. The girl of 18 may have more confidence that she could remarry if her marriage failed, and so lack so strong an incentive as the older woman would have for making difficult adjustments.

Any one or more of these factors may operate to increase the probability of success in marriages not made at very young ages. Nevertheless, the crucial factor in marriage success or failure is the level of maturity in all areas of life that has been reached by the two partners in a marriage. The studies showing the relationship between marriage success and age at marriage underline the truth that most people require years of living before they develop the maturity adequate for marriage success.

OUTLINE FOR SELF-STUDY: MATURITY FOR MARRIAGE

Much of the success of any marriage depends upon the maturity of the two people involved. Study yourself on the following criteria. If you find it difficult to rate yourself, ask a friend or a member of your family to help you. Few people are mature on all points, so do not be discouraged if you find some immaturities in yourself.

I. Have you developed a measure of objectivity?
1. Can you see yourself as you look to other people?
2. Can you see others as most other people see them?
3. Can you discriminate between facts and feelings about yourself, other people, and things?
4. Do you act on the facts in a situation, in spite of your feelings?

II. Have you developed a measure of maturity in handling frustration?
1. What was your pattern of behavior when your wishes were blocked at age 5? Age 10? Age 15? Your present age? Can you see growth toward maturity in your changing pattern of behavior?
2. As you think of mistakes you have made in the past, can you think of specific things you have learned from your mistakes?
3. How many times during the past month have you blamed others for something that was really partly your fault?

III. Are you developing characteristics of a mature adult?
1. Do you have a philosophy of life that enables you to meet unalterable situations with poise?
2. Do you practice a reasonable measure of self-discipline in getting your work done or meeting responsibilities and obligations?
3. Do you live in the present and plan for the future, leaving the past behind, except insofar as you can profit by having learned from experience?
4. Can you support yourself financially?
5. Have you had the experience of earning your own money and living within a fixed budget?
6. Have you developed a degree of other-centeredness? Do you find it easy to fit in with and to meet the ego needs of others?
7. How many strong prejudices do you have? (Prejudice relates to matters like being a good or a poor student, or living in a certain region, or to social and financial standing, as well as to race.

politics, religion, and many other matters.) Do you have fewer than, more than, or about the same number of strong prejudices as you had five years ago?

IV. *Are you approaching a maturity adequate for marriage?*

1. Can you look at your family background and assess its contribution to your attitudes, views, and feelings about marriage?
2. Have your experiences with love and affection enabled you to grow in your understanding of love?
3. Do you see sex in marriage as a desirable and wholesome relationship designed to bring satisfaction and security to both partners?
4. Have you become emotionally weaned from your parents so that your spouse will have little reason to feel that you are too dependent on them?
5. Have you grown to the place where you can think first of your responsibilities to others and sacrifice your personal needs when necessary?

Review questions

1. Why is it difficult to isolate the age factor in determining success in marriage?
2. Define emotional maturity.
3. Why is objectivity important in developing maturity?
4. What is a mature conception of marriage?
5. How should the mature person view love? What may contribute to a person's ability to see love in this light?
6. Why is developing a philosophy of life a part of maturity?
7. How does the mature person evaluate himself and his family background?
8. What are some of the understandings the mature person has of human motivations?
9. Why do some people have difficulty in developing mature attitudes and feelings about sex?
10. The maturing person can assess his own maturity. Discuss.
11. Cite evidence from research studies which indicates that, generally speaking, youthful marriage is not desirable.
12. Cite factors other than age which may explain the greater failure of youthful marriages.
13. Is there evidence to support the belief that as people grow older they get "set" in their ways and cannot adjust in marriage?

Projects and activities

1. Make an analysis of your own emotional maturity. Then prepare two lists, one giving the ways in which you are quite mature and the other giving ways in which you still need to grow.

2. *Role playing.* Two couples discuss their future marriage, one couple taking the part of two 18-year-olds and the other couple the part of two 23-year-olds. Each couple brings out attitudes to represent the maturity of the age group they represent.

Film

It Takes All Kinds. Presents a series of people, each one reacting to an identical tense situation, and each one disclosing the essential pattern of his or her personality. Study each person as he reacts to frustration, and judge whether you think his behavior is mature or immature. McGraw-Hill Book Company, Inc., 20 minutes, sound.

Suggested readings

Blood, Robert O., *Anticipating Your Marriage.* Glencoe, Ill.: The Free Press, 1955. Ch. VI, "Deciding When to Get Married."

Bowman, Henry A., *Marriage for Moderns.* New York: McGraw-Hill Book Company, Inc., 1954. Ch. V, "Age for Marriage."

Christensen, Harold, *Marriage Analysis.* New York: The Ronald Press Company, 1958. Ch. VI, "Social and Emotional Maturity."

Monahan, Thomas B., "Does Age at Marriage Matter in Divorce?," *Social Forces,* 32:1 (October, 1953), 81-87.

Love

At every age people are interested in the concept of love. But during the college years when the time for marriage is near, the question of love, what it means and how one can recognize it or understand it, becomes crucial. One may have taken for granted that when true love comes it will be a transforming experience, recognizable as unique from any other emotional experience or feeling in the past. Such a one may find himself responding to another person or to several others with feelings that are hard to identify—feelings that are in some ways familiar from all the way back into childhood, and that in other ways are new, unfamiliar, and thrilling. So questions arise: "Could this be love?" "Is it possible that love can come this way with so little fanfare?" "I seem to find in my feelings for this person some of what I feel for my brother and for my sister, even some of what I feel for my parents, and a great deal of the same kind of unromantic attachment that I have for some of my life-long friends. I thought *love* would be unique in all ways, unlike anything I'd ever felt before, overwhelming, and when it came, absolutely recognizable. Does my uncertainty mean that my feeling for this person can't be love?"

A young man, after four years of marriage, said, "I wonder sometimes how Carol and I ever happened to get married at all, because the way we feel about each other now is so far beyond what we felt for each other when we were married. It seems as I look back, that we just dated, decided we were in love, and—since everyone approved and encouraged us—went ahead and got married. But now we have grown close

163

to each other. We think together; where we differ, we can talk over our differences freely, and we never seem to have any need to win out over each other in differences. What we are to each other has grown so much that now when I think of love it seems that what we married on was only the smallest beginning of a love."

Love does not come labeled

Love grows; it does not strike as a lightning-sudden emotional experience. It is not easily and quickly recognizable as unique, because love—adult, lasting love between a man and a woman—includes many familiar elements of experience. It grows out of the character and personality each has developed through all the experiences of life from childhood. Love does include one special element not consciously present in many other relationships—the element of sexuality. But that element alone cannot identify an emotional experience as love, because with physical maturity the element of sexual attraction and response may enter into many associations. To be physically attracted to people of the opposite sex is a part of adult interaction and may continue to occur throughout life, dissociated from any love-relationship.

So, what is love? How can it be recognized? How know the pseudo from the real? Above all, how can we know whether the feelings and responses that we interpret as love are the kind of love that will grow and last for a lifetime in marriage?

The answers would not be hard if we were not all so handicapped by exposure to the romantic superstitions widespread in our culture. A multitude of almost totally irrelevant emotions and relationships are mistakenly included among our ideas and concepts of love.

Mistaken conceptions of love

Almost anything passes for love. "I'm madly in love with a singer who's appearing in a night club in my city. So far, I haven't been able to meet her. I'm desperately afraid that when I do manage to meet her I'll find out that she's married or engaged to some other man."

"I love this boy. I'm either in the heights or in the depths all the time, so that I can't study or do anything else. I know true love isn't supposed to run smoothly, but I never dreamed it would be so disorganizing as this. We have some violent quarrels. When he's angry or has been drinking, he is rough and cruel; but he's terribly sweet afterwards; and I can't stay away from him or get him off my mind."

Is it love that these statements are describing?

Fig. 33 By permission, United Feature Syndicate.

"I think I'll make up with Alvin—I always have that empty feeling when I'm not in love with anyone!"

To students of human emotional development, it seems most unfortunate that such aberrant emotional episodes are ever associated in anyone's mind with love. For love is not violent, uncontrollable, and unpredictable emotion. It is not a long-distance attraction to an unknown person. It is not a paralyzing or disorganizing—or even an ecstatic—compulsion that holds two people together.

What love is

To put it most simply, love is the concern of two people for each other. *You love a person if his well-being, his growth toward his greatest potential in all facets of his personality, matters to you as much as your own,* probably not more, but as much. This means that if you love someone, it is because of what you are, yourself. Your concern for your own growth toward your best potential is a reality in relation to which you will develop the deep, permanent concern for the welfare of another person, which is love. So it must be said that if emotional growth has been healthy in the individual his love for another person is an ability, or a capacity, which is a part of his basic character.

Love is a two-way thing. A one-sided attachment that reaches out with desire or frustration toward another person who does not share or respond, is not love. A "love" that clutches and clings, and attempts to control the object of the emotion, is not real love, but rather is the expression of neurotic needs or pressures. People who can accept themselves as they are and who have a firm self-respect can give acceptance and respect—love—to another person. They have no need to cling in the desperate fear of losing the love of the other, nor do they need to control and dominate a loved one. If one dominates, or demands and requires, while the other does most of the giving, adjusting, and acquiescing, love either will not grow in the first place, or it will wither and deteriorate into mere bondage.

Love: motivation toward cooperation

Two people who love each other can work together, at least in some areas of life. Certainly they will have some problems; cooperation does not come entirely naturally to people. But when two love each other, they have a motivation which enables them to cope with the problems and potential frustrations of living in partnership rather than as completely independent individuals. They are motivated to work at the cooperation which is an essential part of love.

The motivation to cooperate is strong in lovers for several reasons: The relationship with the loved one is a chosen relationship; in this way it is different from love relationships with members of one's own family, which are in a sense thrust upon one unasked and without choice. When the adult or even the adolescent has chosen another and committed himself to loving the chosen one, there is a strong urge to prove the rightness of the choice, to "make it work," even if doing so requires adjustment and cooperation that might be withheld or unwillingly given in other relationships. The rightness of one's own perceptions and judgments is at stake.

A second and perhaps stronger motivation toward cooperation and adjustability is based in the fact that the love relationship brings security and reassurance to the individual. One feels deeply, whether on the conscious level or not, that the emotional support which comes as a result of loving and being loved is worth working for and, if necessary, sacrificing to maintain. This second motivation becomes effective in a love that can develop into a permanently sustained relationship. It may not be operative in affairs that have some earmarks of love, but which are based primarily in neurotic needs. In the neurotically based relationship compliance is likely to be required rather than cooperation offered: "If you love me, you will do what I want," and its counterpart, "If you loved me, you wouldn't ask anything of me."

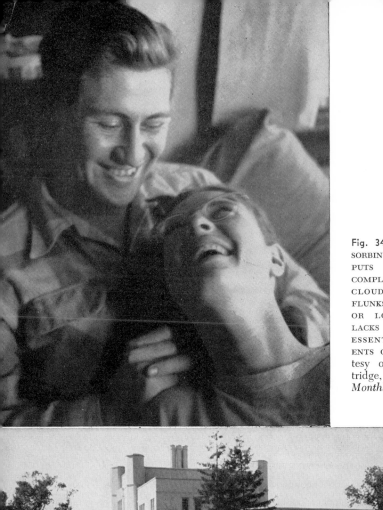

Fig. 34 THE ALL-AB-
SORBING "LOVE" THAT
PUTS A PERSON SO
COMPLETELY IN THE
CLOUDS THAT HE
FLUNKS OUT OF SCHOOL
OR LOSES HIS JOB
LACKS SOME OF THE
ESSENTIAL INGREDI-
ENTS OF LOVE. Cour-
tesy of Rondal Par-
tridge, and *California
Monthly.*

These attitudes mean in reality, "I want what I want when I want it, and I'll use love to bargain with or as a form of coercion." Love as a motivating force toward building a rewarding cooperative relationship is not a factor in such affairs.

The subject of why the positive motivations are effective in a true love relationship needs to be explored further.

Through every stage of life the need to love and be loved is among the most urgent of human necessities. The importance of meeting this need in small children, if they are to have a healthy emotional growth toward maturity, is quite generally recognized. But the fact that the need is perhaps equally strong in people of every age is not so generally faced. Emotional growth goes on throughout life; either progress continues toward greater maturity, or a measure of emotional deterioration and retrogression occurs. Nothing in personality is fixed or static. Therefore, just as being freely loved and loving in return gives the small child security and self-confidence, so loving and being loved gives security and confidence to the adult. The man or woman who is loved and accepted by one person can live and function in other relationships more effectively. He is more free to be himself without defensiveness; he can worry less about protecting his ego from hurt. He can therefore be more outgoing and confident in all his relationships.

These emotional effects of love mean that people who love and are loved are not completely absorbed with love; they are more fully functioning personalities in all aspects of life. The all-absorbing "love" that puts a person so completely in the clouds that he flunks out of school or loses his job, lacks some of the essential ingredients of love. For love never makes the individual less effective, less fully functioning; rather it promotes growth and increases awareness of meanings, needs, and opportunities in the world about one.

To say that love means adjustability and cooperation is not to imply that if two people are truly in love, all will be sweetness and light under every circumstance. Two people remain two people, with all their individual faults and foibles, no matter how much in love they are. But the motivations that function in the love relationship mean that, even under the pressure of difficult or irritating circumstances, the basic attitude of two who love each other is supportive toward each other rather than destructive. They can be generous in judging each other, can think the best instead of the worst. In short, they have a basis for getting together in differences. Their relationship can survive their individual faults and peculiarities, even though these may cause some friction. That is to say, love is not necessarily blind. Rather, love that can survive the shocks and shifting requirements of a lifetime of two people together is not blind at all. It sees clearly, but can judge kindly and give acceptance and understanding, instead of the unrelieved condemnation that might come, even justifiably, from others.

Companionship as a part of love

In a love that is adequate for a lifetime of marriage, for the two to be congenial friends is more important than any other phase of their relationship. This does not mean that they both necessarily have to like to fish or climb mountains or dance, or even read the same books, although if they happen to like doing the same things, their friendship-love will be more rewarding. But it is essential that they share feelings about some values that matter most to them both. Burgess and Locke have made the point that a sharing in intellectual, religious, artistic, or altruistic interests means more to a relationship than a sharing in matters like athletic interests or other general activity interests that might involve a smaller part of the whole personality.

Two who love each other must be friends in the same sense that any two people of the same sex are friends. This means they enjoy each other's company because of genuine congeniality, aside from sex interest; they want to confide in each other, to talk things over, and to share amusement, ideas, disappointment, or grief. They tend to see life through each other's eyes. They are at ease and comfortable with each other, as good friends always are.

Outside of sex and "love," two people who are not at ease and comfortable with each other and able to be themselves happily when together do not make any pretense of remaining close friends. They seek other, more congenial company. But, because of mistaken ideas about what love is like, and also because sex impulses can skew a relationship, two people who have no basis for companionable friendship may believe themselves to be in love, and marry. Many of such couples do make lasting marriages. They work out some kind of adjustment that enables them to make a home and rear children. But missing from their relationship are some of the elements that would add joy and confidence to a relationship heavily weighted with duty and obligation. Certainly, duty and obligation have a place in any sustained relationship, but when love is based firmly in companionable friendship such words take a different meaning.

Love at first sight

If love needs time to grow, if it grows upon cooperation and companionship, then what about love at first sight?

Of his life-long love a man said, "I fell in love at sight when I was 17. My heart did a flip-flop the minute I looked at her. I dated other girls, even had other romances, but five years after I met her, and after we'd gone through college together, I married my first-sight love. Now, after thirty years of being married to her, the magic is still there. I think I kept my eyes open during our school years together. If I had found that my heart had fooled me about her, I would have fought off the spell, because above all I wanted a good marriage. But I was lucky. She turned out to be all that I dreamed she was the day I met her."

Another first-sight love: "I fell in love at sight with a man I met last month on a bus. We're planning to be married at once, but my parents are terribly opposed. They object to his age and they say I don't know anything about him or his past or future. I say that the instant he spoke to me I knew I loved him, and that's enough."

An objective outsider would recognize at once that the love affair in the second case has little chance to eventuate in the kind of successful marriage that grew out of the at-sight response in the first case. What was different about the two affairs, and what was similar? Were they both "love at first sight"?

Both included the one element that characterizes love at first sight: an immediate, strong attraction to another person. In some cases, this attraction may be almost entirely physical. Perhaps in the case of the girl and the man on the bus, the tone of his voice or the look in his eyes when he spoke to her provoked a response that was new or more violent than she had ever before experienced so suddenly toward a stranger. In some such affairs, the attraction is mutual; both are aware almost from the moment of their meeting of a response to each other that exerts a compulsive pull toward physical intimacy.

In other cases, the immediate attraction may arise more predominately from the fact that the two see in each other's appearance or manner, or in the circumstances under which they meet, the "ideal" they have been looking for in a mate. Chance may bring about their meeting at a moment in their lives when both are in an attitude of openness and readiness to embrace figuratively and literally the embodied "ideal." This second factor, perhaps, operates in at-sight affairs more often than pure sex attraction does. What brings people to the point of emotional readiness to fall in love at sight is an interesting question. Sometimes there is a special need at the moment to escape from certain problems in the circumstances of life, or in one's own emotional life. Emotional or material complications may exert a strong pressure toward sudden falling in love. Dr. David Rioch, a psychiatrist, says that among his clients have been a number of people who fall suddenly in love when confronted with a crisis in life or with the necessity for making a major choice or decision. To quote him, "When the time comes that one must 'go on to the next thing' such as at the end of the college years or after the death of a parent or loved one, love offers an out that is not publicly disapproved, rather it is an out that society even approves and looks upon with sentimental fondness." [1]

At such a time two people meet. It makes little difference whether the immediate mutual attraction is chiefly physical or whether it is a response to a conception of an ideal. In either event the resulting flare-up is what is known as love at first sight. The urge is strong to make fast the bonds for all time without delay. If such a couple marries at once their marriage has about the same chance to be successful as any other unpremeditated, wild plunge has for producing a happy outcome. But some couples so attracted to each other go ahead with caution to become well acquainted. They take time to discover each other's true attitudes, beliefs, habits, and tastes. Some such couples scarcely know at what point in their association they pass the phase of rather superficial attraction and progress into a relationship enriched by the other elements necessary to real love. All their lives they may be staunch believers in love at first sight, because that is the way it seemed to happen to them. If on becoming better acquainted with each other they had discovered no sound basis of congeniality, the early attraction would have had little chance to survive.

The cases of love at first sight that do not end in happy marriage are probably far more numerous than those that do. They receive less attention, however, for when the affair turns out to be a passing thing those involved forget that it was "love" and

[1] Dr. David Rioch, Director, Division of Neuro-Psychiatry, Walter Reed Medical Center. Gimbel Lectures, Stanford Medical School, April, 1957.

relegate it to its place with other short-lived infatuations. In other words, the emotional response was not love; not all of the elements necessary for the growth of love were present.

In summary, when all aspects of the subject of love are considered, it becomes clear that love is not an isolated emotion or condition that exists in one's experience. It is a sharing that involves the personalities and lives of two people. The feeling of despair or frustration that one may have because he desires another or wishes for the companionship of another is of course a reality in experience, but it is not love. *Love, then, is a relationship as distinguishable from a feeling.*

Love includes the physical. Two who love each other desire and enjoy the closest physical intimacy; sex enhances their association in all other phases of living. But sex is far from the main ingredient. It may hold a relatively small place in some loves—in others, a large place. Love depends for permanent survival upon the knowledge two have of each other's true selves, their acceptance of each other as worth loving, their shared values and purposes, their respect for each other, and the trust and confidence that grows out of the total relationship which has been built between them.

SOME QUESTIONS TO THINK ABOUT
IN ORDER TO EVALUATE A LOVE

1. Are you comfortable and at ease with him or her? Able to be yourself without strain?
2. Since you have been in love, are you more inclined to live up to your best conception of yourself and your abilities?
3. Are you conscious of a continuing stable bond between the two of you, even when you have no feeling of love?
4. Does this person matter greatly to you regardless of emotion or lack of emotion at the moment?
5. Would you love him or her just as much even if he were sick instead of well, or even if his handsomeness or her beauty should be marred or disfigured?

6. Is he or she physically attractive to you so that you have no inclination to be apologetic or defensive about his or her physical characteristics?
7. Are you proud to be seen together?
8. How well do you agree on the things worth sacrificing for in life?
9. Do you find it easy to talk over points of disagreement and reach an understanding? (Have you known each other long enough and well enough so that you have discovered your inevitable points of disagreement?)
10. Do your disagreements result in a better understanding of each other? (For disagreements to result in tabling and blocking off the issue, or in the same one always giving in, is a danger signal.)
11. Do you have confidence in his or her judgment? Do you respect his or her general mental ability?
12. Do you confide in this person freely, with complete confidence that what you say will be understood, judged kindly, and never divulged no matter what the temptation?
13. Are you happy and satisfied with the way he or she shows affection for you?
14. As you look toward the future as realistically as you can, do you feel that the two of you have in your relationship the elements that will enable you to cooperate and if necessary sacrifice for your continuing pair-unity?

Review questions

1. What are some mistaken conceptions of love?
2. Define love.
3. How does love serve as a motivating force toward cooperation?
4. What basic needs fulfilled by love make it possible for those who love and are loved to be more fully functioning in their other associations?
5. If two people love each other, will there ever be times when they disagree? Quarrel? Have emotional explosions? Ridicule each other?
6. How important is companionship in love? Is it possible to have a happy marriage without companionship?
7. What are some of the situations that may predispose an individual toward falling in love at sight?
8. Do first-sight attractions usually end in successful marriage? Explain.
9. What is meant by the statement that love is an ability or a capacity in the person who loves?

Projects and activities

    1. From different sources, find as many definitions of love as you can and bring them to class. For a beginning see Burgess and Locke, *The Family,* Ch. XII.
    2. Make a study of love stories in current magazines, or in movies. In how many of the cases was it "love at first sight"? Evaluate the fictional loves on the basis of the concepts in this chapter.

Suggested readings

Becker, Howard, and Reuben Hill, eds., *Family, Marriage, and Parenthood.* Boston: D. C. Heath and Company, 1955. Ch. VII, "Steps in Love and Courtship."
Blood, Robert O., *Anticipating Your Marriage.* Glencoe, Ill.: The Free Press, 1955. Ch. IV, "Growing in Love."
Bowman, Henry A., *Marriage for Moderns.* New York: McGraw-Hill Book Company, Inc., 1954. Ch. II, "The Reasons for Marriage."
Burgess, Ernest W., and Harvey J. Locke, *The Family.* New York: American Book Company, 1953. Ch. XII, "Love and Courtship."
Christensen, Harold T., *Marriage Analysis.* New York: The Ronald Press Company, 1958. Ch. X, "Love Development Through Dating and Courtship."
Duvall, Evelyn Millis, and Reuben Hill, *When You Marry.* Boston: D. C. Heath & Company, Revised 1953. Ch. I, "What You Bring to Marriage," and Ch. II, "Love Enough To Marry On."
Folsom, Joseph K., *The Family and Democratic Society.* New York: John Wiley & Sons, Inc., 1943. Ch. XI, "Love as Experience and Relationship."
Landis, Judson T., and Mary G. Landis, eds., *Readings in Marriage and the Family.* Englewood Cliffs, N. J.: Prentice-Hall, Inc., 1952. Reading 5, "The Family and Romantic Love," Andrew G. Truxal and Francis E. Merrill.
Waller, Willard, *The Family* (Revised by Reuben Hill). New York: The Dryden Press, 1951. Ch. VI, "The Sentiment of Love."

Marriage Under Special Circumstances

According to the American stereotype, two young people grow up, finish their education, the man gets a job so he can begin to support a family, they marry and spend the rest of their lives together. But today more and more marriages do not conform to the stereotype. Cultural changes in our society, and military requirements that affect the marriage plans of a great many couples, mean that large numbers of marriages are made under special circumstances. These marriages may require special adjustability if they are to be successful. People need to recognize what some of the problems are and to consider their ability to cope with them.

Marriage while in college

Many students now in college are deciding whether to marry immediately or to postpone marriage until their education is completed. Before World War II, marriage while in college was rare. Student marriages were generally disapproved by parents and college administrators. Some colleges automatically dropped students who married before graduation. But the second world war and the Korean war changed that situation. When the boys returned from these wars, they married and had children and yet continued their education.

College administrators came to see advantages in having married students on campus, and several studies made in midwestern colleges revealed that the married students in the studies were making better grades than the single students. Riemer found that the married students with children made better grades than any other

179

students.[1] Our study of 3,000 students in 11 colleges showed that the men who were married as college students had, when they were in high school, made lower grade averages than had the men who were single as college students. But the married men were making better grades in college than the single men were. Married women students had, in high school, made about the same grade averages as the women who were single in college, but the married women were making much better grades in college than the single women were. Various explanations might be offered for the better achievement of the married students. It is possible that certain selective factors determine which students will marry in college and that these factors are related to achievement. The more settled life, and the decrease in social activities requiring time and energy may also affect achievement.

Immediately after the wars, some people believed that the tendency to marry while in college was a wartime phenomenon and that when the older G.I.'s were graduated the college campuses would return to "normal." College administrators took temporary measures to house the married students. On some campuses today, married students live in the old "temporary" structures, which are now sub-standard housing. The trend toward marrying while in college has continued. There are more married students today on some campuses than there were in the years just following World War II. Of the 3 million college students in 1956, about 16 per cent were married. Table 9 gives the percentage of married students at one university by 5-year periods for the past 15 years.

Attitudes toward college marriages have clearly changed, although for various reasons the majority of students still prefer to remain single while in college. In 1952, we asked 450 of the students in our marriage classes, "If you found the one you hoped to marry eventually, would you marry while an under-

---

[1] Svend Riemer, "Married Students are Good Students," *Marriage and Family Living*, 9:1 (February, 1947), 11-12.

Fig. 35 ONE STUDENT OUT OF SIX WHO REGISTERS IN AN AMERI-
CAN COLLEGE TODAY IS MARRIED. Courtesy of *California Monthly*.

TABLE 9 PERCENTAGE OF MARRIED UNDERGRADUATE STUDENTS
AT THE UNIVERSITY OF OREGON *

Year	Men	Women
1941	5.5%	2.2%
1946	23.5	7.9
1951	23.9	7.7
1956	27.1	10.9

* Lester A. Kirkendall, "Married Undergraduates on the Campus: An Appraisal"
The Coordinator, 5:2 (December, 1956), 54-63.

graduate?" One-fifth of the boys and half of the girls said that
they would marry while they were undergraduates. Four out
of five men and women said that they would marry if they were
in graduate school. The students expressed the belief that their
parents are in approximate agreement with them about marriage
while in college; that is, about the same percentages felt that
their parents would approve if they chose to marry while in

Fig. 36 "...All I had when I went to college was a jalopy
...it never occurred to me that I had to have a wife, too!"
By permission, George Lichty and Chicago Sun-Times Syndicate.

college. In 1957, we asked 465 of our students the same questions about marrying while undergraduates and graduates, and found that sentiment had increased in favor of marrying as an undergraduate in college. Thirty per cent of the men and 57 per cent of the women in 1957 said they would favor marrying as undergraduates.

Some advantages of college marriages

In 1947, we attempted to learn some of the advantages and disadvantages of college marriages by means of a detailed study of 544 college married couples.[2] Most of the men in these marriages were G.I.'s, so it was a group of men and women older than the average college population of today. However, some of the findings are applicable to any college marriage. Many of the advantages the married students listed had to do with the emotional security that marriage provided. Many of the men felt that marriage gave more stability to their lives, made life more purposeful, and made it easier for them to settle down to work. This feeling of stability might have had something to do with the higher grade averages made by married students. Almost all the husbands felt that a wife was a help in college rather than a hindrance. A few complained that the wives had too much company, interrupted study, or wanted to go out evenings. However, most were not critical. Almost half the wives in this study were working to help support the family, so they were contributing economically to the husband's education.

Success of college marriages

Two studies, ours in 1947 and one by Christensen and Philbrick[3] at Purdue University in 1950 (346 couples), asked mar-

[2] Judson T. Landis, "On the Campus," *Survey Midmonthly*, 84:1 (January, 1948), 17-19.

[3] Harold T. Christensen and Robert E. Philbrick, "Family Size as a Factor in the Marital Adjustments of College Students," *American Sociological Review*, 17:3 (June, 1952), 306-312.

ried students this question, "Knowing what you know now, would you marry before finishing college if you were unmarried?" In both studies, three-fourths of the couples said that they would marry while in college if they had it to do over again. The one-fourth who would not, or who were uncertain, felt there had been too many difficulties in earning a living, in finding housing, and in doing satisfactory college work. Although these were the reasons given by those who would hesitate to try a college marriage if they had it to do over again, other factors revealed by the research studies suggest that the real reasons may have been deeper. Many of the couples who doubted the wisdom of their college marriage felt that perhaps they had made a marriage that might end in failure. If they had waited to marry and had become better acquainted, they might not have married each other at all. The Christensen-Philbrick study showed a much lower happiness rating among those who would hesitate to marry while in college if they had it to do over again.[4]

It is difficult to get accurate information on the success of college marriages. In our study, 95 per cent of the couples gave a self-rating of happy or very happy. Since none had been married for very long, a high happiness rating was to be expected; ratings by the same couples might have been different after more years of marriage. However, Riemer found in one study of students in a student housing project that the divorce rate was lower than the usual rate during the first four years of marriage among other college-educated groups.[5] Although some of the evidence seems to indicate that students who marry while in college make a better-than-average success of their marriages, it may also be true that they are making more than an average effort at building good marriages.

---

[4] *Ibid.*, p. 310.
[5] Svend Riemer, "Youthful Marriages." Paper delivered at the Annual Meeting of the National Council on Family Relations, Lake Geneva, Wisconsin, September, 1951.

Some considerations in college marriages

Many of the factors that are important in contributing to success in marriage are about the same whether people marry in college or after college. But additional problems arise in college marriages that are not necessarily present in other marriages.

Willingness to give up life of a single student. Most young people enjoy the social side of college life. In the process of dating and enjoying college social life they may find one person whom they want to marry, but they still may not be ready to sacrifice their other activities for marriage. These students are not ready to settle down to marriage even if they are in love. A complaint that single college girls sometimes make about the married men on campus is that the men "don't act like they're married." The man who is not ready to give up his single habits is not ready for marriage, whether he is in or out of college. Since college marriages are so generally accepted, couples may be swept along into marriage after a short engagement without realistically facing what it will mean to be married on campus.

Readiness for parenthood. Although most couples who marry in college may plan to postpone having children until after graduation, they must accept the eventuality of parenthood. The girl who said, "We are not going to have a baby for three years since it will be that long before my husband finishes his graduate work," expressed the confident attitude of many couples approaching marriage. In studying 212 college couples at Michigan State University who had had their first baby, we found that only slightly over one-third had planned the first pregnancy.[6] Christensen and Philbrick found the same percentage of planned pregnancies among the 346 couples studied at Purdue University.[7] Since the wife often works to supplement the income or is

---

[6] Shirley Poffenberger, Thomas Poffenberger, and Judson T. Landis, "Intent Toward Conception and the Pregnancy Experience," *American Sociological Review*, 17:5 (October, 1952), 616-620.

[7] Christensen and Philbrick, *op. cit.*, p. 309.

also a student, an unplanned pregnancy may upset carefully devised plans. A survey by the Health Information Foundation found that in 1956 the average cost for medical and hospital expenses connected with having a baby were $225. However, costs vary greatly in different communities. In many places couples must have a minimum of $400 to cover the obstetrician's fee and the hospital charges. This initial cost of a baby, in addition to all the continuing expenses would be too much for many college couples unless the wife continues working.

College couples in the Purdue study who felt children were a disturbance to college performance listed the following as the most common disturbances: "They increase the economic demands; they complicate the housing situation; the added noise and distraction make studying difficult; the added responsibility requires extra time, such as for night duty during infancy or illness, and for play 'when daddy comes home.' " [8] In studying college couples with children, at an Oregon college, Johannis found that two-thirds of the husbands and wives felt that children created special problems such as, "crowded space with too little room for the children's play, excessive costs for housing in relation to current income, and difficulty in arranging for child care while the mother worked or father and mother went out at night." [9]

Students who have doubts about their willingness or ability to take on the responsibilities that come with parenthood, in addition to being students, might better postpone marriage until they feel ready to cope with the eventuality of parenthood.

Willingness of the husband to help the wife. When both members of a married couple are attending classes and perhaps working part-time or when one is in school and the other working, their lives become very full; they find it necessary to organize

---

[8] *Ibid.*, p. 312.

[9] Theodore B. Johannis, "The Marital Adjustment of a Sample of Married College Students," *The Coordinator*, 4:4 (June, 1956), 29.

their activities with great efficiency. If, in addition, there are children to care for, couples need to be supermen and superwomen in order to meet all their responsibilities adequately. The success of college marriages means that many young couples are adequate for all these requirements. But a man or boy who expects to be waited on, who considers it beneath his masculine dignity to do dishes, scrub floors, or diaper babies, is likely to be a problem husband in a college marriage. And a girl who wants to be free

Fig. 37 "I feel sort of funny, getting a bachelor's degree!"
By permission, Bo Brown and *The Saturday Evening Post.*

from hard work and struggle, and who cannot be happy if she has to miss any of the whirl of college social life, should not marry while she is still in college. For even if there is plenty of money, working together at marriage while both are students requires unselfish cooperation and some sacrifice of personal preferences.

Present income and parental support. Economic conditions and opportunities for part-time employment will have much to do with how frequent college marriages continue to be. During the 1950's it has been possible for most students to earn their living by holding part-time jobs. Most couples have been able to support themselves without having to depend on their parents.

In 1947, it cost an average of $148 per month for the college couples in our study to live. Most of those couples were living in college housing projects. In 1952, we found that the average had advanced to $222 per month. In 1958, the cost was from $280 to $300, depending on whether couples had a child and whether they lived in college housing.

Students thinking of marriage often reason that since their parents support them while they are single, why shouldn't the support continue after marriage? The traditionally accepted viewpoint is that marriage means the end of parental support, especially for the girl. Once married, she is to be supported by the husband. However, approximately one-fourth of our students questioned in 1957 expressed the belief that parents should continue support for the daughter who marries in college. Many parents are uncertain about what is the wisest policy here. If they can afford it, they would like to continue the financial backing so that their children may finish their education. But they recognize that certain problems may arise if they continue to support their married children even though the children are still students. Few parents can look upon their children as independent married adults as long as the parents are contributing a major part of their children's support. The situation may be more complicated because of the fact that the money contributed is for the use of the child-in-law as well as the "own" child. In-law friction may easily arise in such cases.

Many cases have come to our attention in which the young people are willing to accept the parental support, but they are not willing to accept any control or "interference" that may come with parental support. If there is to be parental subsidy, parents and children need to be objective about the situation. Otherwise, misunderstandings may bring disillusionment and disappointment to parents, and unhappiness to children. Many of the married students who try to face problems realistically feel that they must earn their own way after they marry. In 1957 we asked 376 of our students who were single and being supported by their parents whether they thought the parents should continue the support if the student should marry. Half of the men and 39 per cent of the women thought parents should continue support.

The majority of student couples agree that if they are to marry while in college both will have to do all they can to help with their own support. If the husband only is a student, the wife usually works; if both are students, both hold part-time jobs if they can. Many students solve the problem by waiting to marry until at least one of them is within a year of graduation, since financial arrangements are much easier to make for one year than for three or four years.

The precedent has been set, and young people will continue to marry while in college, especially if economic conditions are favorable. The more general acceptance of the fact that married women may continue indefinitely to work outside the home, the tendency for people to marry at younger ages than formerly, widespread knowledge of contraception, and a gradual change in the attitudes of parents toward continuing to help support sons or daughters after marriage—these and other factors will operate to establish the custom of college marriages more firmly within our mores.

Nevertheless, those who are considering such marriages need

to be realistic in recognizing that they face certain alternatives that do not usually confront couples who marry after their education is complete. If they want to live as responsible adults, independent of outside financial help, they will have to work harder than couples who marry later. If, on the other hand, they marry expecting help from parents or others, they will, during their college years, be in something of an interim state—no longer mere dependent children, but not independent married adults either. They also need to face the fact that *both* will have to be willing to work at all household tasks and to care for any children that may come.

For married students the future is now.   Sometimes married students sacrifice too much of the present for what they think of as the future. They may put too much of their thinking on the life they hope to have after the education is finished and the husband can begin the work that is to make their living. They think of the present arrangement in which the wife works to support them both, or in which both work in order to remain in school, as an interim. Some such couples are working so hard that they have little time or energy to enjoy life together or to appreciate fully the positive values in their present life as a married couple. But the first years of marriage are very important in establishing patterns of response and habits of mutual enjoyment in a relationship. Too great a sacrifice can be made in order to keep on schedule toward a planned graduation. Some couples who decide to marry now and undertake the additional responsibilities that come with marriage while in college ought perhaps to be willing to take more time to finish their education. If both must work, they might choose to think in terms of five years rather than four for getting the college degree, and in terms of spreading the graduate work over more years. Such a plan may involve less strain and allow more time for pleasant living and for building satisfying relationships without any sacrifice of permanent goals.

College communities offer special opportunities for young married couples to live an enriched life. There are large numbers of other couples of the same age, with the same interests, and with many of the same goals. There are many people with children of the same age. Practical courses in marriage and the family and in child development are available, as well as opportunities to enjoy cultural advantages at little expense. All of these things are an important part of education, and students who marry while in college should benefit from these advantages.

Many college administrations are now improving housing provisions for married students. Permanent, modern apartment houses are being built on college campuses so that couples no

Fig. 38 APARTMENT HOUSES FOR MARRIED STUDENTS AT PURDUE UNVERSITY. Many university administrations have now concluded that marriage while in college is here to stay, and they are building permanent apartment houses for the married students. Courtesy of Purdue University.

longer face all the inconveniences of a few years ago when colleges made no provisions for students with families. Purdue, Michigan State University, Brigham Young University, and others, have housing areas with excellent facilities for recreation and for the education of the children of married students.

People contemplating a college marriage, like those contemplating any other marriage, must have perspective on life as a whole and a realistic conception of successful marriage. If they are willing to begin at once to work at building together the kind of cooperation and mutual support that is necessary for a good marriage, they can cope with whatever special problems are involved in marriage while in college.

Marrying a divorced person

With the present high divorce rates, a considerable proportion of marriages involve one member who has been married before. An analysis of remarriage in the United States reveals that the divorced have a tendency to marry those who have also been divorced.[10] However, many people marrying for the first time marry divorced people. Are there special problems in marriages of this type? How may a previous divorce affect a second marriage?

A young woman went to a marriage counselor for what she considered to be a routine premarital consultation. She told the counselor happily about her wedding plans and asked for any advice he might offer to help her make a good beginning in marriage. Incidentally, she mentioned that her mother had not yet been told of her engagement, because it was something of a problem to know how to break the news that her fiancé had only recently been divorced. There had never been a divorce

[10] *Socioeconomic Characteristics of Persons Who Married Between January 1947 and June 1954: United States.* Washington, D. C.: U. S. Department of Health, Education, and Welfare, Vital Statistics-Special Reports, 45:12 (September 9, 1957), 286.

in the girl's family and she felt that her mother might be prejudiced and doubtful about her daughter's marriage to a divorced
person. The girl said to the counselor, "I feel that my future
husband's having been divorced is of absolutely no importance
as far as our happiness is concerned. All that is in the past. It was
not his fault in any way and now that divorces are so common,
it would be silly for anyone to attach any importance to whether
or not a person has been married before."

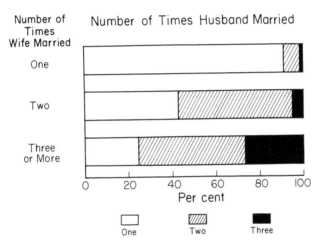

Fig. 39 PEOPLE MARRYING FOR THE FIRST TIME TEND TO MARRY
OTHERS MARRYING FOR THE FIRST TIME. Divorced people tend to
marry divorced people. *Socioeconomic Characteristics of Persons
Who Married Between January 1947 and June 1954: United
States.* Washington, D. C.: U. S. Department of Health, Education, and Welfare. Vital Statistics—Special Reports, 45:12 (September 9, 1957), 286.

That view is often expressed by young people contemplating
marriage to a divorced person. Nevertheless, the truth is that
marriage to a divorced person does include special factors that
differentiate such marriages from first marriages for both partners.
These marriages differ in the following ways.

Society's attitude toward second marriages. Public custom is to smile with approval upon "first" marriages. The wedding is acknowledged, approved, supported, and celebrated with an enthusiasm that is not always readily given when one partner has previously been married and divorced. The difference may be only slight, but it is represented by the attitudes of some ministers who will not officiate at a wedding if one partner has been divorced. Even if there is no disapproval from any source, many of the couple's friends may assume an attitude of watchful waiting to see how it turns out, in contrast to the attitude of optimistic acceptance that usually accompanies the wedding that is a first for both.

Hollingshead [11] made an interesting study of a large group of marriages in New Haven, Connecticut, which brought out rather clearly how society feels about first weddings in contrast to weddings in which one or both have been married before. The biggest difference was found where both had been married before. For example, if neither had been married before, 81 per cent were given showers by friends; if both had been married before, only 32 per cent were given showers. If the wife had been married before, the pattern of activities connected with the wedding was similar to that if both had been married before. However, if only the husband had been married before, the wedding activities approached those in cases in which neither had been married before. Clearly, friends, family, and society in general will come to the aid of the woman and help her get off to a good start in a first marriage, as they will not do if it is her second marriage.

Families have doubts. Family doubts or outright opposition, which are factors to be reckoned with in the success or failure of any marriage, are more likely to be present when one

---

[11] August B. Hollingshead, "Marital Status and Wedding Behavior," *Marriage and Family Living*, 14:4 (November, 1952), 308-311.

partner has been divorced. The family of the one with no previous marital record is likely to view the marriage with mingled hope and fear for the future, whether or not the fears are justified by the circumstances of the previous marriage.

TABLE 10 VARYING PATTERN OF WEDDING ACTIVITIES ACCORDING TO PREVIOUS MARITAL STATUS OF SPOUSES *

	Both first marriage	Wife first, husband before	Husband first, wife before	Both married before
Engaged	89.0%	74.0%	69.0%	54.0%
Engagement ring	84.0	64.0	60.0	43.0
Shower	81.0	57.0	27.0	32.0
Formal wedding	70.0	29.0	25.0	6.0
Church wedding	81.0	45.0	23.0	25.0
Cases where bride's family paid for wedding	46.0	23.0	15.0	3.0
Reception	88.0	79.0	52.0	45.0
Wedding trip	95.0	79.0	76.0	62.0

* Adapted from August B. Hollingshead, "Marital Status and Wedding Behavior," *Marriage and Family Living,* 14:4 (November, 1952), 308-311.

The family of the divorced partner cannot help but make comparisons between the new spouse and the former one. Is the new choice better or worse? Views will vary, depending on family attitudes toward the circumstances of the first marriage and divorce. Consequently, the first marriage and divorce are one of the facts of life that will enter into in-law relationships and associations with friends, even when it is possible for the married pair to feel honestly that "all that is past."

If there are children. In addition to factors related to family and social attitudes many second marriages involve children from the previous marriage. Marriage to a divorced person with children makes it necessary for the second mate to adjust to emotionally weighted circumstances. Some people find it very difficult to accept situations that arise if husband or wife has visitation rights with children in custody of the former mate. To know that the spouse sees the former mate when visiting the children may arouse feelings that make trouble in a second marriage.

If the previously married mate has financial responsibilities for the children another kind of adjustment is necessary. Financial pressure may be severe if the husband must pay alimony or child support. Few men can earn enough money to support adequately two families. Not infrequently it becomes necessary for a second wife to work to help support her family because of financial pressures arising from obligations her husband has to a first family.

The person who has not been married before needs to be thoughtfully aware of these situations and many more that inevitably exist in marriages involving children by a previous marriage.

Success and failure in second marriages

Some of the earlier research studies were inconclusive on the success of second marriages. However, recent evidence seems to leave little doubt here. Two states, Iowa and Missouri, now keep records on number of times married for all couples who make application for a marriage license. Monahan has made a detailed analysis of the data in these two states and has found that second marriages are not so enduring nor so successful as first marriages. He also found that the divorce rate increases with successive marriages.[12] This finding is supported by information collected by the Bureau of the Census on previous marital status. The census data reveal a much higher failure rate in second marriages, 20.5 per cent of divorced men and 23.0 per cent of divorced women having had two or more marriages. Only 13.5 per cent of

[12] Thomas P. Monahan, "How Stable Are Remarriages?," *The American Journal of Sociology,* 58:3 (November, 1952), 280-288.

married people living with spouses had had a previous marriage ended either by death or divorce.[13]

Some reasons explaining the higher failure rate in marriages after divorce may be these: (a) Divorced persons tend to marry other divorced persons. Therefore both people in the marriage may have traits that make it difficult for them to adjust in marriage. (b) Any moral compunctions against divorce would have been faced and overcome at the time of the first divorce, so there might be less hesitation to resort to divorce a second time. (c) Divorce may represent an attitude of trying to escape problem situations in marriage, rather than the habit of working through problems to solutions other than divorce. (d) Divorce is often a traumatic experience. Marriages made after divorce may be the result of "rebound" or of other conditions unfavorable to a wise choice. The shorter acquaintances, shorter engagements, and larger percentage who do not get engaged among those who have been married before, as revealed in the Hollingshead study, would tend to support the theory that those marrying for a second time often "jump" into a second marriage as an attempt to compensate for failure in a first marriage.[14]

How much did the divorced person learn from marriage failure? A question of great importance for the young person who considers marrying a divorced person is the attitude of the previously married one. If he (or she) feels sure that he was wholly blameless in the marriage failure that occurred, there is good reason to question whether he is good material for a second marriage. For marriage failure, like marriage success, can be achieved only by two working at it together. We have often wondered at the naïveté of young people who say, "I know he'll make a wonderful husband (or she'll make a wonderful wife). He had a rough time in his first marriage, but none of it was his

---

[13] Bureau of the Census, *Current Population Reports, Population Characteristics,* Series P-20, No. 21 (December, 1948).

[14] Hollingshead, *op. cit.,* p. 310.

fault." The divorced person who has learned from his experience and is able to see where he himself failed and so contributed to the first marriage failure is far more likely to make a success of a second marriage. Many people do learn by bitter experience, not how to control the second mate better, but how to understand their own weaknesses and strengths, how to choose more wisely a second time, and how to work more effectively at building a successful marriage.

Among the people who make a success of a second marriage are those who have achieved greater maturity by the time they marry again, or who have been able to learn from their mistakes, whether the mistakes were in the choice of a mate or in meeting problems. They are able to do better in a second marriage. In the very unhappy group of those who fail a second time may be found those who could not accept any of the responsibility for the first failure, but blamed the mate for all their problems. When they make a later marriage they will expect the next mate to make up for all their early troubles; they will set impossible standards for the mate and none for themselves. A young person considering marriage with a person previously married and divorced should ask above all, "What has he learned that might have helped in his first marriage, and that would help make a better thing of our future marriage?"

To brush aside the thought of the former marriage and to tell oneself, "All that is of no importance to our happiness," is to invite unhappiness. A previous marriage is a fact of life in a second marriage.

Marriages involving separation for military service or other reasons

For many young men, active military duty begins following graduation from college. The military service may not involve an extended separation from fiancée or wife. At best, however, couples marrying just before military service cannot start their married life under circumstances that are ideal for beginning to build the relationships basic to a successful marriage. Such questions must be faced as: Should they marry at once or postpone marriage until the intensive early part of his military service is past? And, if they marry now shall she follow him so that they may share as much time as possible, even though it may mean loneliness and some discontent for her when he has little free time? These and other questions can be answered more satisfactorily by couples who have given some thought to the implications for their relationship of any kind of separation, whether brief or extended, and avoidable or unavoidable.

Whether separation occurs during engagement or after marriage, it is a circumstance that needs to be thoughtfully considered by people who are hoping to build a permanently happy relationship. Many people who face separation because of military service or some other unavoidable circumstance naturally feel impelled to win some measure of security by marrying quickly in order to ensure their future together, even though for the present they must be apart.

Some potentially good relationships cannot survive a separation of more than brief duration. In other cases, a separation may help one or both to become more objective about a relationship that would have little chance of being permanently satisfactory if it survived; thus, the separation serves to break up a potentially disastrous relationship. Clearly, it is better in such cases if the separation occurs before, rather than after, marriage.

Postponing adjustments. In cases where separation must occur soon after marriage, the adjustments which inevitably must be made in learning to live with each other are postponed. Time passes; a couple may be married a year or more without having had the opportunity or the necessity to make adjustments that are usually made very soon after marriage. Usually when a married couple are together during the first year of marriage, they go almost everywhere together; they try their best to please each other in every way possible. And in the process they tend to grow closer together in their habits and their ways of reacting to situations. They may never again have quite so strong an urge to work at giving their marriage a good start. With couples who undergo early separation, the situation is different. After their separation has ended, and they come together to begin life as a married couple, they learn that the interim has not been a blank; both have necessarily continued to live and grow, but not together. Even if they have been completely faithful to each other and have kept in touch through frequent letters, they now face the task of starting to build a marriage as a bride and groom when they no longer are bride and groom. The love affair that was climaxed by their wedding is now history, and society does not give them the help toward a good marital start that it so willingly extends to brides and grooms.

Loneliness and the married feeling. Many couples who have had to be separated soon after marriage say that they have never got to "feeling married." Therefore, while they are apart they are tempted to date others just as if they were in fact single. The temptation may be increased by the loneliness arising from the separation. Many people cannot endure the strain of long-continued loneliness; their emotional balance may depend on their ability to push their love for the absent one back into the periphery of their lives and thoughts. Yet if they do this, the two will inevitably be farther apart when they are reunited.

A reasonably long acquaintance is important to the success of all marriages, but long and thorough acquaintance is much more important before marriages that are to be followed by separation. Since absence does not always make the heart grow fonder, couples need to have time to get to know each other well and to be sure of their love for each other before they marry, so that when the natural doubts arise later during separation they will have the confidence that comes with a long and deep under-standing of each other. Even when a marriage is a potentially good one, if the acquaintance before marriage is short, there is no basis of understanding and confidence to tide the couple over the periods of loneliness, doubt, and uncertainty that inevitably follow separation.

Age, a factor. The age of the young people is very important in these situations. All the handicaps that ordinarily exert pressure on marriages of the very young will be intensified by separation. Couples contemplating such a marriage should be very sure that they are looking at marriage as a lifetime proposition and that they are not being impelled into it by the emotions accompanying the approaching separation.

Alternatives, if marriage would involve separation. Some couples feel they should marry before separation because they are afraid they will lose each other if they do not. This may be true. But would their love survive if they were married? The fact of a wedding ceremony will not necessarily insure the survival of an emotional attachment. If their love for each other is not well established, it might be safer for them to part as an engaged, rather than as a married couple. Sometimes questionable behavior during a separation can be accepted and forgiven by an engaged couple, while it would be grounds for divorce if they were married. If they can survive an engagement apart, they have a better chance to make a success of marriage once they are together. If they cannot survive such an engagement, less damage will have been done than if they had married and their separation had resulted in a broken marriage. How facing the alternatives may work out is illustrated by the experiences of two couples related below:

> "Bob and I became engaged at Christmas time and in February he went to Pensacola to enter officers' training school. We couldn't bear the thought of losing each other and we almost decided to marry then. It would have meant being apart for six months as a married couple instead of as an engaged couple, because he wouldn't be free to marry until August if we waited. I felt absolutely sure of our love for each other, and yet I kept wondering

why I was afraid I would lose him if we waited to marry until after my graduation and his first few months were over with. I wondered if perhaps I really trusted him less than I thought. We had a hard time deciding, but at last he left and I stayed to finish the year and graduate in June. I have been so happy that we made this decision. We write to each other every day, and once in a while he phones me. I miss him terribly, so much so that sometimes when he phones me I just can't think what I want to say and the conversation is not very satisfactory. But just the same I think that through our letters we have come to understand each other even better, and above all we now feel secure about our future relationship. The separation has not raised doubts in our minds but has made us able to decide that our wedding is worth waiting for. In the years after we are married I'll never wonder whether I would have lost him if we'd waited. I *know* we can be faithful to each other."

However, another girl said:

"I made the same decision that you did. I wanted to graduate before we married so I let Tom go without me. We planned to be married a few months later. But we hadn't been apart two months before he was dating other girls where he was stationed. I was terribly upset at first, then I began to realize that another boy whom I sometimes studied with was more my type. I began going out with him, and now Tom and I have decided it would have been a mistake if we had married. It just didn't last when we were apart."

It was fortunate that the second couple parted as an engaged, rather than as a married couple. The first girl and her fiancé, however, probably would have survived the separation happily whether married or not. The point is that an impending separation should not be allowed to rush a couple into marriage, unless marriage would be the right thing for them if there were no danger of any separation.

Parenthood and separation. Marriage results in children even with the contraceptive information available today. Many couples who know that a child needs both parents decide to wait to marry until they can rear their children together. If a child is born when the parents are separated for much of the time, an adjustment for all three—father, mother, and child—will be necessary later. At best, much greater effort must be made if all are not cheated of the privilege of growing to understand one another during the child's infancy.

Thus far our discussion seems to have presented only the negative aspects of marriages that involve separation. These negative aspects are facts that have to be faced. However, there is another side to the question. If a couple are mature, well acquainted, sure that they meet each other's personality needs, and believe that if no separation loomed they would have no serious doubts about their marriage, then they should be able to marry and survive the separation.

Building ties when separated. If separation cannot be avoided, the problem becomes one of continuing to build a good relationship through letters. Many people find this hard; others find it quite natural and easy to put some of themselves into letters. For almost all who have had a long courtship or have been married for some months before the separation, letter writing should be easier. The two have become well enough acquainted so that they have a life in common made up of friends, family, economic plans, and many other things. It is important that all communication between a couple separated by circumstances beyond their control be directed toward maintaining as much as possible the feeling of togetherness. A man who was drafted and sent to a distant state far from his wife and month-old child said concerning their letters:

> "I write to her every day even if it is only two lines. I think it helps her to know that she can depend on me. She knows I think of her even if I'm too tired to say anything worth the postage stamp. When I write about any of my friends here I try to choose my words carefully and to be clear about what I'm saying, not leaving anything hanging in the air that might raise unanswered questions or make her wonder if I might be holding something back."

Certainly the time of separation is no time to use techniques to test the love or loyalty of the other. For the man to say that he is going into town with the boys, or for the wife to say she was at a party and saw an old boy friend, might start a misunderstanding that would be hard to overcome. When people are separated there will inevitably be some uncertainties, and to create unnecessary ones can only be destructive.

Reunion after separation.   Although there has been constant letter writing, most couples are not prepared for some of the readjustments that may come with reunion. During the absence each may tend to build up an idealized picture of the other and of their relationship. During the separation they do grow apart in some ways; instead of thinking together as one, they have been thinking as two independent individuals. Each may have some new ways or new ideas which may seem out of character to the other. They may have forgotten each other's annoying habits and mannerisms. When they are united, they must again face the realities of being just ordinary human beings with the usual faults and idiosyncrasies. For some it will take time to get back to their old basis of living as husband and wife. For those who had a hasty marriage following a short acquaintance, it may mean starting almost from the beginning of courtship and —for the first time—really getting to know each other.

Many people have had the experience of meeting a friend after a long absence. The two are happy to meet, greet each other with enthusiasm, and then stand with nothing to say; an unexpected distance has developed with time and change. Married people may have an experience similar to this when they get together after long separation.

For those with a firmly based relationship, the strangeness can be temporary and quite easily overcome. Most of the factors involved in relationships for married couples who are necessarily separated need not be crucial or damaging, if the problems are understood and approached constructively. Knowing what some of the problems are likely to be and facing these situations together can be more than half the battle.

Marriage while in the service

Factors affecting mate choice: marriage readiness. Many young men will continue to go into military service unmarried and without any serious attachment to a girl back home. Some college men today keep their relationships with women on a light level because they do not feel that they want to marry until after their military service is over and they are ready to become established in a job. However, many men reach the point of readiness to marry during the time that they are in the service and away from their accustomed associations. In such cases they are likely to find a girl among whatever group they are associating with at that time. Before they left for the service, many of these men probably knew a number of girls who would have made excellent wives, if the men had been at the point of readiness to choose a wife.

This matter of marriage readiness accounts for some of the marriages between American servicemen and girls from Germany, Japan, England, and other countries where American men are stationed.

Loneliness in a new environment. Being in military service usually means being away from friends and family and accustomed activities. A man may especially miss companionship with a girl or girls whom he knew and dated in civilian life. In the relatively impersonal and routinized world in which he now lives, he feels more than previously the need for close personal ties with someone. If he finds a girl whom he enjoys dating, his dating may develop quite rapidly into serious courtship. Possibly the necessity for him to adjust to the new kinds of experience he finds in the service or in any other situation that keeps him far from home may push him toward marriage readiness. If he meets the girl's parents and is accepted and welcomed by them, he may feel that he has found a home to replace his own. Under these conditions some young men marry quickly without stopping to consider as many background factors as they would do if they approached marriage in their home environment.

Points to consider before a service marriage. Certainly some successful and happy marriages have been made between couples who met in the girl's home state or city while the man was in military service or working far from home. The boy who has given some thought to what he hopes for in his future marriage and who is aware of the relevance of background factors to marriage success can, if he becomes ready to marry, find a wife while he is far from home. But in order to avoid a hasty or unwise marriage, the unattached young man should recognize and consider the following points before he becomes involved in serious courtship while far from his usual associations.

1. You are likely to feel more lonely at times than you have ever been before.
2. You may feel more strongly than before your need for companionship with girls or a girl.
3. Because of your own special needs, you may find it hard to be objective about traits in the girls you date.
4. A military uniform tends to obscure social differences; there is a chance that you might marry into a social class that would be out of character for you or which would require very difficult adjustments for your bride after your service is ended.
5. Since, during your service, you adjust to many differences in people and circumstances, temporarily you may forget how people back home feel about marriages across interracial lines, across some internationality lines, and marriages involving extreme contrasts in social background. Because you can look about you and see other servicemen contracting "mixed" marriages, it may seem that such a marriage is no different from any marriage you might make at home; therefore it may be difficult for you to use the same level of judgment that you would use under other circumstances.
6. If you do find someone who meets your needs and with whom there seems a possibility of building a good marriage in the environment in which you meet, you should still try to look ahead to the future after service is past. Does the girl have

the temperament and adjustability that would enable her to leave her home or her country and family and adjust happily in whatever situation her marriage to you would place her? Will she be accepted by your family and friends? If there is a difference in race, certain problems will arise even if your family is not opposed to a mixed marriage. You may have difficulty finding housing, finding friends to associate with, and facing discrimination from other sources.

7. In all your relationships, it will be especially important to maintain a perspective view of your life as a whole—your background and your future after the period of temporary service is past. Try to make decisions in the light of your lifetime values and the goals you have for your future.

In summary

The choice of whether or not to marry under the special circumstances discussed in this chapter confronts many college students today. Each person so confronted must consider the factors involved and the alternatives open to him. Many people are able to make a success of marriage even under the most difficult of circumstances. Whether or not circumstances are difficult is not so important as whether the individual is able to view the situation realistically and to evaluate accurately his ability to cope with eventualities, before making a lifetime decision.

Review questions

1. What changes have encouraged an increase in marriages among college students? Is marriage while in college increasing or decreasing?

2. What opinions do students express about their attitudes and their parents' attitudes concerning marrying while in college?

3. Give some of the advantages and disadvantages of college marriages.

4. Why would some couples hesitate to marry in college if they had it to do over again? What seems to underlie their doubts?

5. What special problems should couples consider if they plan to marry while in college?

6. How much does it cost a college couple to live today?

7. Should parents continue to support their son who marries while still a student? Should the parents of a girl continue her support after marriage? What opinion did students express on these questions?

8. If students are to marry while both are in college, what philosophy, which might benefit their marriage, might they adopt? Do you think it reasonable to expect students to look at life in this way? Discuss.

9. What are college administrators now doing to recognize the needs of married students?

10. Comment on the following statement: "Yes, he has been married before, but that is no concern of mine. He was not to blame, and I am marrying him as he is today."

11. In what respects do second marriages differ from first marriages?

12. What did Hollingshead find in his study of ritual and ceremony accompanying first and second marriages?

13. Why is there a higher divorce rate in second marriages?

14. What attitudes characterize those divorced persons most likely to make a success of second marriages? What attitudes characterize those likely to repeat failure if they marry again?

15. What are some factors involved in separation during the early years of marriage?

16. Should a couple marry if there is danger that the separation ahead might result in their not marrying each other? Discuss.

17. What techniques can separated couples use in letter writing to build ties?

18. Why is reunion after separation sometimes difficult?

19. What is meant by the term "marriage readiness"? Why may this apply to men in the service?

20. What are some specific points for a man to consider before marrying while away from his usual environment?

Projects and activities

1. Make an anonymous class survey to find what class members think about marriage while in college, parental support for college marriages, and whether the wife should work to put her husband through school.

2. Collect figures on the cost of living from several married students and report to the class.

3. *Panel Discussion.* The married students in the class discuss the financial aspects of being married while in college.

4. *Role-Playing.* Alice and Bill are juniors at the university. They have been supported by both sets of parents since marrying a year ago. Bill has planned to go on to graduate school. Alice has found that

she is pregnant. *Scene.* Alice is reading a letter from her parents in which they say that since their agreement was to support Alice through college, they feel that if she must drop out of school on account of the baby, Bill should take over the responsibility for support.

5. *Panel Discussion.* The married students who married before the man's military service and those students who are engaged and facing military service discuss the pros and cons of marriage and military service. Or: The single men who have been in the service and the single men who face a term of service discuss the pros and cons of marriage and military service.

Suggested readings

Becker, Howard, and Reuben Hill, eds., *Family, Marriage, and Parenthood.* Boston: D. C. Heath and Company, 1955. Ch. XXIV, "War and the Family."

Bernard, Jessie, *Remarriage.* New York: The Dryden Press, 1956.

Bowerman, Charles E., "Assortative Mating by Previous Marital Status," *American Sociological Review,* 18:2 (April, 1953), 170-177.

Duvall, Evelyn M., and Reuben Hill, *When You Marry.* Boston: D. C. Heath and Company, Revised 1953. Ch. XXI, "Families in an Uneasy World."

Goode, William J., *After Divorce.* Glencoe, Ill.: The Free Press, 1956.

Hill, Reuben, *Families Under Stress.* New York: Harper & Brothers, 1949.

Koos, Earl Lomon, *Marriage.* New York: Henry Holt and Company, 1957. Ch. 18, "Marriage in a War Minded World."

Landis, Judson T., "On the Campus," *Survey Midmonthly,* 84:1 (January, 1948), 17-19.

Landis, Judson T., and Mary G. Landis, eds., *Readings in Marriage and the Family.* Englewood Cliffs, N. J.: Prentice-Hall, Inc., 1952. Part VII, Reading 2, "Separation and Marital Adjustment," Margaret Mead; Reading 3, "Separation and Adjustment—A Case," John F. Cuber; Reading 9, "Adjustment of the Divorced in Later Marriages," Harvey J. Locke and William Klausner.

Riemer, Svend, "Married Students Are Good Students," *Marriage and Family Living,* 9:1 (February, 1947), 11-12.

Waller, Willard, *The Veteran Comes Back.* New York: The Dryden Press, 1944.

Society's attitude toward premarital sex union

Conformity or nonconformity to moral codes

Attitudes of young people on premarital conduct

Premarital experience related to marital adjustment

Experimentation as preparation for marriage

*Kinsey's findings on premarital experience
and marital responsiveness*

*Effect of premarital experiences
upon a couple's over-all relationship*

Premarital pregnancy

Premarital
Sexual Relations

Premarital experience as an obstacle to marriage

Overemphasis on sex

A man's sex experience as preparation for marriage

Learning together in marriage

Deferred marriage

A problem that arises among all groups of young people is the necessity for making decisions on the question of sex conduct before marriage. A great many young people who are hoping to make good marriages, and who want to avoid mistakes that they might regret at a later time, have questions concerning premarital coitus. The questions place emphasis upon moral, ethical, and empirical considerations in varying degrees. Is premarital sexual intercourse wrong? Is it good preparation for marriage? Is there danger to future happiness from emotional pressures resulting from over-repression of sexual drives? What is society's true attitude today toward sex experimentation before marriage?

Society's attitude
toward premarital sex union

The present adult generation has seen many changes in the mores concerning marriage and the family. Among these changes has been the widespread acceptance of divorce as an alternative to coping with the common problems of marriage. Another change has been the greater freedom in the association of the sexes, with the virtual disappearance of chaperonage. Some observers of American life have superficially concluded that all standards have changed equally and that premarital sex union is no longer contrary to the mores. However, the majority of children in American families are still brought up believing that sexual intercourse is to be reserved for marriage and that sexual promiscuity is a deviation from acceptable moral standards.

Our society is inconsistent in its attitude toward

sex conduct. It no longer rigidly controls or enforces moral standards, and in fact makes it easy for people to break the rules, yet it has not changed the penalties for those who fail to live up to socially approved standards. The disappearance of active chaperonage and the acceptance of early dating means that most young people are on their own morally for a number of years before marriage. But public opinion still condemns premarital coitus as a serious form of antisocial behavior for women; pregnancy before marriage is still looked upon as a tragedy and disgrace in the middle- and upper-middle-class family. And there has been little change in social attitudes toward the unwed mother and her child; in almost all states, the child born outside of marriage does not have the same legal rights that other children have.

Conformity or nonconformity to moral codes

Various attempts have been made to determine how prevalent among young people is the disregarding of standards concerning sex conduct. Studies made by Ehrmann at the University of Florida,[1] and our study of 3,000 students in 11 colleges and universities in 1952-1955 show that a high percentage of university girls (from 88 to 91 per cent) say that they have refrained from having premarital sex relations. In the Kinsey research, 81 to 83 per cent of the college girls aged 16-20 reported having had no premarital sex relations.[2] These are findings for college and university girls, not for women in the general population among whom the picture might be different.

[1] Winston W. Ehrmann, "Two Methods of Measuring the Individual's Control of Pre-marital Dating Behavior." Paper delivered at Annual Meeting of the National Council on Family Relations, Lake Geneva, Wisconsin, August 29, 1951. Winston W. Ehrmann, "Student Cooperation in a Study of Dating Behavior," *Marriage and Family Living,* 14:4 (November, 1952), 322-326.

[2] Alfred Kinsey, Wardell B. Pomeroy, and Clyde E. Martin, *Sexual Behavior in the Human Female,* p. 288. Philadelphia: W. B. Saunders Company, 1953.

The research findings show that if a college girl has premarital coitus it is most likely to take place during engagement and with her future spouse. The percentage of virgin girls late in the engagement period or at marriage would not be so high as the statistics given here on the virginity of college girls in general. Burgess and Wallin found in their study of 1,000 couples engaged in 1936 that a considerably higher percentage of girls had had premarital sex relations by the date of the wedding.[3]

Some misimpressions are current about sexual promiscuity among American girls and women because of interpretations given to some of the publicized Kinsey findings. It must be noted that the over-all findings of the Kinsey research on the American female are not generally applicable to a representative group of young women. The segment of the Kinsey findings that was gathered specifically from college girls aged 16-20 agrees in general with the findings of other researchers for this group, and other evidence supports the reliability of the findings for this part of the population in the Kinsey research. But conclusions based upon the Kinsey findings for the entire sample of American females are not widely applicable for the following reasons: The sample of women [4] was heavily weighted with women who had married late (average age at marriage 27),[5] who had failed in marriage (almost one-third) [6] and who had had many premarital pregnancies (15 per cent having had two or more).[7] The 2,094 women in Kinsey's group who had experienced premarital coitus, had indulged in coitus approximately 460,000 times or an average of 220 times each.[8] Many of these women had their experiences

[3] Ernest W. Burgess and Paul Wallin, *Engagement and Marriage,* p. 331. Chicago: J. B. Lippincott Company, 1953.
[4] See Judson T. Landis, "The Women Kinsey Studied," *Social Problems,* 1:4 (April, 1954), 139-142.
[5] Kinsey, Pomeroy, and Martin, *Sexual Behavior in the Human Female,* p. 426. Philadelphia: W. B. Saunders Company, 1953.
[6] *Ibid.,* p. 32.
[7] *Ibid.,* p. 327.
[8] *Ibid.,* p. 327.

over a number of years and with a great variety of partners (almost half had from two to over twenty partners).[9] Thus the sample was in no way representative of the average girl, college or noncollege, who marries in her late teens or early twenties.[10]

Whatever the statistics may be about the incidence of premarital sexual experience among young people today, it must be recognized that shifts that occur in the mores concerning various types of behavior are not always in the direction of removal of taboos. In moral standards there is a tendency for reaction to occur after some behavior patterns have been tried. Attitudes tend to change in swings or cycles so that on some points the younger generation may tend to be more "moral" than their parents. Therefore the mass of figures that have been gathered about the incidence of premarital sexual experience do not provide an answer for the individual who must formulate his own behavior code.

Attitudes of young people on premarital conduct

Between 1940 and 1952-1955, three studies were made of the opinions of college students on sex standards for men and women outside of marriage. The students were asked to check one of four statements that most nearly represented their opinion. The first study was made of 173 students at Cornell in 1940-1941 by Rockwood and Ford.[11] We made a similar study among 2,000 students at Michigan State University in 1947, and repeated it in 1952-1955 with 3,000 students in 11 colleges. Table 11 summarizes the results.

It is interesting to note that in all three student generations approximately two out of three students stated that they believed in no sexual relations for either sex outside marriage, three-

---

[9] *Ibid.*, p. 336.

[10] See Lewis Terman, *Psychological Factors in Marital Happiness*, p. 321. Ernest W. Burgess and Paul Wallin, *Engagement and Marriage*, pp. 330-331.

[11] Lemo D. Rockwood and Mary E. Ford, *Youth, Marriage and Parenthood*, p. 40. New York: John Wiley & Sons, Inc., 1945.

fourths of the girls and over half of the boys holding to this belief. If attitudes about sex standards have been greatly modified by the social changes of recent years, the change is not revealed in these studies.

TABLE 11 PERCENTAGES OF STUDENTS
CHECKING EACH OF FOUR STATEMENTS
REPRESENTING ATTITUDES ON PREMARITAL SEX STANDARDS
(3,000 Students in 11 Colleges in 1952-1955,
2,000 Michigan State University Students in 1947,
364 Cornell University Students, 1940-1941)

	Men			Women		
Approved standard	11 Colleges 1952-55	M.S.U. 1947	Cornell 1940	11 Colleges 1952-55	M.S.U. 1947	Cornell 1940
Sexual relations:						
For both	20%	16%	15%	5%	2%	6%
None for either	52	59	49	65	76	76
For men only	12	10	23	23	15	11
Between engaged persons only	16	15	11	7	7	6

These studies show that approximately two out of three of the girls of each college generation gave as their reason for refraining from premarital sex experimentation "family training" or "sorrow of parents" (see Table 12). In the 1952-1955 study, men who had refrained from premarital coitus also gave this as the second most common reason for their virginity.

Regardless of how emancipated young people may be, many of them can indulge in premarital coitus only with some degree of emotional conflict. Since girls are quite universally conscious of the attitudes of their parents and families toward their sex conduct, many are not happy in relationships that they fear will bring sorrow or disgrace to their families.

It is possible that so few students in the later studies checked fear of pregnancy as an inhibiting factor, not because they had no fear, but because they felt there were better reasons than fear.

They had a more positive reason for maintaining virginity before marriage. In collecting dating and courtship histories, we have noticed that engaged couples are frank to say that they do heavy petting and that they are having difficulty refraining from sexual relations, but a great many of them say "that is one thing we wish to save for marriage." Because this statement had been made to

TABLE 12   PERCENTAGES OF 614 COLLEGE MEN AND 1,735 COLLEGE WOMEN FROM 11 COLLEGES IN 1952-1955 AND 174 CORNELL WOMEN IN 1940, GIVING VARIOUS REASONS FOR HAVING REFRAINED FROM PREMARITAL SEX RELATIONS

Reason for chastity	Men 11 Colleges 1952-55	Women 11 Colleges 1952-55	Women Cornell 1940-41
I want to wait until married	50%	81%	—
Family training	41	66	71%
Religious beliefs	33	32	21
Fear of pregnancy (causing)	27	27	68
Fear that sexual relations will stand in the way of marriage	19	21	42
Fear of social ostracism	12	17	22
Other	9	3	—

us over and over again in conferences with young couples, we put the statement "I want to wait until married" in the 1952-1955 study. Among both men and women, this was the most common reason chosen; 50 per cent of the men and 81 per cent of the women checked it.

The positive motivation for this idealism concerning sex and marriage has its source in family attitudes and teachings, in religion, in a conscious desire to have a good marriage, and in an awareness of society's standards and expectations. The negative motivations, such as fear of venereal disease, fear of pregnancy, and fear of social ostracism, still exert some pressure, but they have lost a measure of the force they exerted in former generations. The positive motivations and the basic idealism of young people are now the major factors.

Premarital experience related to marital adjustment

Many people are especially interested to learn whether premarital experience has any effect upon later marital happiness. First it is necessary to distinguish between different kinds of premarital experience. Experiences with prostitutes or with casual dates, which would be classified as promiscuity, may be different in their effects from premarital experiences that occur during engagement or between two people who are involved in serious courtship. Effects of casual premarital experiences will be considered later in the chapter. At this point our discussion is concerned with experiences between people seriously dating or engaged.

Research studies have attempted to discover effects of premarital sexual relations upon later marital happiness. Some findings seem to indicate that those who have had premarital experience are less well adjusted in marriage, but a causal relationship between the premarital experience and the poor marital adjustment cannot be assumed, because of the fact that so many complicating factors are related to premarital experience as well as to marital adjustment.

To illustrate:

> A couple steady-dating during their senior year in high school indulged in sexual intercourse. Just after graduation, when they were both seventeen, the girl learned that she was pregnant. When they told their parents that they intended to be married, both families objected. The boy's family felt that the girl was from an undesirable family, a family of less wealth, social standing, and education. The girl's family had had high hopes for the future of their daughter, since she had made a brilliant scholastic record in high school. She had talked of becoming a doctor and her family was anxious to help her toward her goal. Both families agreed to the wedding only when they were told of the pregnancy.
>
> After five years of marriage this couple was extremely unhappy. The wife held a deep resentment because she had not been able to go to college or prepare for the career she had hoped for. She also rejected her baby from the time of its birth, and it developed into an unhappy, problem child. She was unable to respond sexu-

ally to her husband throughout almost all the marriage, although she had enjoyed coitus before marriage. An offhand diagnosis would seem to be that the premarital coitus and resulting forced marriage were the whole cause of the trouble, since the wife rejected everything associated with the premarital experience. But analysis of the factors involved in the case brought to light other circumstances that made diagnosis much less simple. Although the wife's mother seemed conscientious and anxious to help her daughters, this daughter, at 22, stated that for as long as she could remember she had felt a bitter antagonism toward her mother. She was intensely attached to her father and said she had always resented being a girl and wished she were a man. Moreover, all through the young couple's marriage a violent antagonism persisted between the two parent-in-law families, both of whom blamed the child-in-law for all the marital difficulties, as well as for the original sexual activity that had caused the marriage.

The young couple was also plagued with financial difficulties, for the husband had trouble holding a job. His family sympathized with him in his job difficulties, always making excuses for his failures and blaming circumstances or other people. They were willing to help him with gifts of money, and they resented the fact that his wife felt that he ought to be able to support her and the baby without financial help from his parents.

Would it be possible to isolate any one factor and say that it was solely responsible for this marriage failure? This case illustrates the difficulty of determining what causal relationship exists between premarital experience and later success or failure in marriage. Certain types of personality weaknesses or maladjustments may contribute to excessive sexual emphasis before marriage, and these same factors may contribute to failure in marriage. Research studies have shown a combination of background factors to be related to marriage failure. Among people whose marriages end in divorce are more who: are from unhappy or divorced homes; had no close relationship with parents; were from families with no religious affiliation or with antagonistic attitudes toward religion; have, themselves, no religious affiliation or are antagonistic toward religion. In our research with the 3,000 college students and also in the study of 200 engaged couples, these same factors were found to be significantly associated with nonvirginity in college students, both men and women. These findings emphasize the unsoundness of attempting to isolate any one factor in experience and assess exactly the importance of that factor as causal in marriage failure or success.

Experimentation as preparation for marriage

Because studies have shown that the sex adjustment in marriage is often difficult, some young people believe it would be wise to experiment before marriage in order to learn whether or not they are well mated. But such experimentation may create doubts that have no sound basis. The experimentation can only tell people that they are physically fit for mating. This they may safely assume without experimentation, since only an extremely small percentage of human beings are not biologically equipped to mate. There is the possibility that experimenting before marriage will be disappointing because of the conditions under which such experimentation must take place. The couple may conclude that they are not well matched, whereas, if they had waited until they could start their sex life under the more ideal conditions of marriage, they would have found the experience mutually successful. The problems that are basic in difficult sex adjustments in marriage are not biological but psychological; and the psychic elements in sex adjustment require time and patience if a happy and permanently good sex adjustment is to be achieved.

Burgess and Wallin, in their study of 1,000 engaged couples and of 505 of the couples who later married, found no difference between the sex adjustments of those couples who had had premarital sex relations and those who entered marriage as virgins; but they also found that more of those engaged couples who were having premarital coitus eventually broke their engagements.[12]

[12] Ernest W. Burgess and Paul Wallin, *Engagement and Marriage,* pp. 367-371. Chicago: J. B. Lippincott Company, 1953.

A major objection to premarital coitus as preparation for marriage is that it is difficult for a couple to achieve, outside marriage, sexual union that is complete in all its psychic and emotional aspects. Such factors as the fear of discovery and the fear of pregnancy, or in some cases surroundings that are much less than ideal, may affect the premarital sexual experience. Couples whose marriage to each other might have the possibility of great happiness may become doubtful after they have experimented sexually. In some of these cases the disillusionment results in the breaking off of a love affair that might have led to a successful marriage. This is suggested by the Burgess and Wallin findings that fewer of the engaged couples who had premarital coitus eventually married each other than of the couples who did not have premarital coitus.

Although it is true that any two people may not be equal in sex drive, there is no sure way before marriage for a couple to determine whether or not they match in sex drive.

Kinsey's findings on premarital experience and marital responsiveness

At this point it is necessary to consider the relevance of certain of the Kinsey findings. In spite of the fact that the women in the Kinsey study were not representative of the American college population, one specific item from the Kinsey research is often cited as if it were relevant for college students who are interested in reliable data concerning the effects of premarital experience upon later marriage success. Kinsey's conclusion is emphasized that women who had had premarital coitus and had enjoyed the experience were more likely to enjoy coitus early in marriage. Therefore students ask, "Does this not mean that premarital experience is conducive to a good sexual relationship in marriage?" Many people overlook Kinsey's further findings in the same connection: that there was little difference in the development of enjoyable sex responses between women who were virgins at marriage and the group who had had and enjoyed coitus before marriage.[13] Moreover, a significantly higher percentage of the premaritally experienced group than of the virgin group had extramarital experiences and also continued sex relations with other men after their marriages had failed.[14] Thus, their premarital experiences certainly could not be construed as having contributed to marital success. Further, almost half the women Kinsey studied who had had premarital coitus had not enjoyed the experience, and among this group were the greatest percentage of women who never enjoyed coitus in marriage, even after 15 years of marriage.[15]

A careful study of Kinsey's findings and of the analysis of their data by the Kinsey group of researchers clearly shows no possible basis for concluding that premarital sex experience is a causal factor in good sex adjustment in marriage; their own analysis and analyses of their findings by other researchers lead rather to the opposite conclusion. The Kinsey data show that sexually responsive women who choose to experience sex relationships within marriage rather than premaritally or extramaritally, achieve more stable and successful marriages, and in addition they experience just as much specific sex enjoyment.

The moral training and the psychological conditioning of young people in our society are such that most people are able to discover the true nature of their sex responses and experience the most mutually satisfactory sex relationship when they can live together under the suitable conditions of marriage. Even when differences exist in sex drive and responsiveness couples in marriage can, as time passes, adjust to and cope with such differences.

---

[13] Alfred Kinsey, Wardell B. Pomeroy, and Clyde E. Martin, *Sexual Behavior in the Human Female,* p. 406. Philadelphia: W. B. Saunders Company, 1953.
[14] *Ibid.,* p. 427.
[15] *Ibid.,* p. 406.

Effect of premarital experiences
upon a couple's over-all relationship

It is significant that in the Burgess-Wallin study many engaged couples who reported premarital coitus said they felt their sex relations had increased their feeling of closeness, and in a study by Kirkendall a number of engaged couples who had decided against having premarital sex relations reported that they felt their decision not to have intercourse had drawn them closer together. These findings seem to imply that to be able to discuss important matters of policy and conduct with frankness and mutual trust and to reach an agreement that both can accept with confidence and respect for each other, means closeness in a relationship, whether the decision is to go ahead into premarital sexual union or to refrain from it.

Nevertheless, for many couples the decision to go ahead brings inevitable results regardless of their feeling of closeness at the time. For several years Kirkendall has been having systematic interviews with college-level men in an attempt to discover what effects premarital experiences may have upon attitudes and relationships. Kirkendall says that although his sample is admittedly a select, one-sex group, the interviews show that premarital intercourse inevitably affects interrelationships, since sex is too intimate a part of one's emotional nature, and intercourse has too much cultural meaning for it to be neutral in its consequences. He reports that in many cases men expressed "no regrets" about their relationships, at the same time indicating that by no regrets they meant that no premarital pregnancy had occurred, nor was there any discovery or public embarrassment over the affair; yet they related in detail experiences which had obviously resulted in hurt feelings, recriminations, bitterness, distrust, and suspicion. Kirkendall states that the interviews have forced the conclusion that "practically all premarital coitus in the pre-engagement period, and an undetermined portion of intercourse in the engagement period, occurs under conditions which, both then and eventually, result in more suspicion and distrust, and less ability to set up a good relationship." [16]

His hypothesis is that underlying the feelings of distrust and disrespect that often arise in connection with premarital experience is the fact of conflicting motivations that may exist in the two partners, women being more likely to regard intercourse as a move toward insuring a continuing, stable relationship, and men's interest more likely to be chiefly in securing emotional and physical satisfaction. He notes the comments of some engaged couples: "Once we began to have intercourse, I (the man) seemed to lose interest in getting married," and, "We began to make sex more and more the focus of our relationship." And another comment, which brings up a different aspect of the problem, "Even though we loved each other, the nagging fear of pregnancy spoiled the relationship for us."

Premarital pregnancy

The ratio of illegitimate births to legitimate births continues about the same in our population from year to year, regardless of advances in contraceptive knowledge. Whatever attitudes may be held about premarital pregnancies, they are eventualities that can hardly be faced realistically ahead of time. When the situation is purely hypothetical, a couple may believe that they could handle the situation fairly well. But when the case is no longer hypothetical and a girl finds or suspects that she is pregnant, serious decisions must be made and no happy solution is possible. The least unhappy solution is to be found in marriage, if the man and woman are suitable marriage partners. In many cases, however, marriage for couples caught in these circumstances may not be the answer. The girl may consider abortion, which not only means extreme risk to her life and health but involves moral and

---

[16] Lester Kirkendall, "Premarital Sex Relations: The Problem and Its Implications," *Pastoral Psychology*, (April, 1956).

legal considerations. Moreover, legal definition may distinguish between abortion and infanticide, but the girl who is involved lives with her own concepts of the difference. The other alternative is to try to make plans that will enable the girl to go safely through the pregnancy and give birth to the baby. This solution means that the parents must be trusted to help.

Many girls will not hesitate to give the baby for adoption, believing that that would be best for the baby and for themselves. Adoption is probably best for the baby, for he can be given the advantages of a happy home and loving parents. Under the best possible circumstances, parents or friends may be able to make the whole experience fairly smooth, with a minimum of publicity for the mother. After the baby is adopted, the mother may feel that the entire experience is in the past. But if she later marries happily and has other children, her love for them may bring her a new awareness of the one that had to be given away, and as time passes and she watches her children grow up, the more painful will be the thought of the first-born whom she was not able to know. Young people may be totally unconscious of this side of unmarried parenthood during the time when a premarital pregnancy is only a problem to be solved, but it is a consideration that arises later and inevitably means sorrow. Later sorrow and mental conflict operate also in the case of the illegitimate father, and for many of the same reasons.

Numerous other considerations enter into the situation once a premarital pregnancy occurs, so that even among the most emancipated groups in present-day America premarital pregnancies are tragic for all concerned. This is a practical reason why many young people choose to save sexual relations for marriage.

Premarital experience as an obstacle to marriage

One reason that young women cite for refraining from premarital unions is the possible "injury to chances for marriage afterwards." What about this reason? Some girls who consent to coitus do so in the belief that their chance for marriage with the man in the case will be increased thereby. If the affair is between two people who are dating casually or who are not engaged and close to marriage, the more realistic attitude is probably that expressed by the girls in the studies who believed that sex relations before marriage hindered chances for marriage. We cite a case:

> R. B. had been reared in an upper-class home, was intelligent, and above average in personality and appearance. He considered his standards of conduct average or above. He came for counsel in sorrow over his broken engagement. He stated that it was important to him to marry a girl whose standards of conduct were high and in whom he could have complete confidence. Therefore, in his dating, if he liked a girl and found her attractive it had been his policy to go as far as possible in his petting. He said, "If she permits coitus with me, I can usually be pretty sure I am not the only one, so I look for another girl." His problem was that he had at last found a girl with whom he was seriously in love. He hoped to marry her, but in pursuance of his usual policy he had finally, after having become engaged to her, succeeded in having coitus. At that point he found himself overwhelmed with doubts and unhappy about the planned marriage, even though she assured him that he was the only man with whom she had ever been intimate and that she had consented to it only because they were engaged. Finally he had broken the engagement but was extremely unhappy about it, as was the girl.

Most girls will be indignant at the unfair attitude of the young man in this case, but his attitude is not uncommon. Boys may express what they believe to be modern attitudes, especially late at night when the moon is bright and there has been extensive necking or petting. However, they often react emotionally in another way when they are faced with the situation in their own marriage, that is, after they are married to a girl whom they know to have been a non-virgin. There are many other situations in which people can express a rational attitude toward or acceptance of a fact, yet be unable to accept it on an emotional level.

In the study of 3,000 students in 11 colleges, three men out of four could say rationally that, other factors being satisfactory, they would marry a girl who had had premarital coitus. But further evidence suggests that it is doubtful whether that large a percentage would emotionally accept previous non-virginity in their wives.

To our query of students on this point, 65 per cent of *non-engaged* men said they would not marry a girl who had had premarital coitus with several different people, but 89 per cent of the *engaged* men said they would not marry such a girl. Evidently the ability to rationalize sexual promiscuity decreases as the individual approaches marriage with a specific person. The same trend was noticed in the opinions of the women in the study.

Overemphasis on sex

Most of the considerations relative to premarital sex experience are as important for the man who wishes to make a successful marriage as for the woman. From the viewpoint of the young man, one of the chief hazards of premarital coitus, aside from the danger of being forced into a marriage with a girl whom he might not have chosen for his wife, is the danger of exaggerating the sex element in courtship to the neglect of other important considerations.

Certain objectives need to be accomplished in courtship as a preliminary to a permanently successful marriage. Marriage counselors are constantly called upon for help by troubled couples who have been carried into marriage by an overwhelming sex interest only to find later that they have nothing else in common. The danger here is greater for the young man than for the girl because, in our society, since boys are brought up to be less inhibited than girls, a boy may be more easily blinded to other qualities, if a girl provides sexual response. The boy who hopes to make a good marriage needs to avoid obsessive sex interest and to be realistic in looking for other qualities. To illustrate how this may work in an individual relationship:

A couple came to the counselor with their problems. They had become engaged after a short acquaintance and had now been engaged for almost a year. The boy said, "She is competitive toward me. Any success or recognition that I get seems to upset her unless she can top it by some achievement of her own. And she has to dominate everything; when we are out with other people she does all the talking, even answers for me before I can get a word in. Sometimes I get so fed up with it that I feel like violence."

The girl's version was, "He is terribly hot-tempered and has no self-control. He tends to blow his top over almost anything and two or three times he has gotten into such a rage that he struck me. I come from a family who never would get violent no matter what happened. I'm so unhappy I don't know what to do."

The most natural reaction of the listener would be to wonder why in the world the couple didn't break their engagement and get it over with. Clearly there were danger signals flying all around them, warning that they could not get along with each other if they married. But in conferences with each one separately it came out that they began having sex relations not long after they became engaged. Neither one of them had ever had such experience before. They both said it was their feeling that they would rather have saved their sex life until after marriage, but once they had had sex experience together both had found it the most satisfactory part of their whole association, and they continued, since they were engaged and felt that they were "practically married."

The girl's attitudes were complicated and confused because of the fact of their sex experiences. She feared that she would suffer from feelings of guilt if she did not marry him. She wondered also if she would ever be able to enjoy sex with a different man. She worried about whether she would feel that she must tell any other man whom she might later marry about her experience. And she said, "I just feel *married* to him on account of all this, even though at times I think I really hate him." The boy was just as troubled. He wondered if some other girl whom he might later marry would be as good a sex partner as this girl was. He felt responsible for having caused his fiancée to drop her standard of premarital virginity. He frankly said that, although in many ways his fiancée irritated him beyond control, still he enjoyed the fairly regular sex experience he had with her so much that he did not want to break up with her and go back to casual dating again. If this couple had refrained from intimacies long enough to explore and understand all facets of their responses to each other in other areas of life, they would have broken their engagement with little or no hesitation.

The truth is that sex relationships are one of the basic elements in a happy and successful marriage—but only one. There are many others. A couple will have a better chance of finding in their marriage all the necessary elements for happiness and success if they do not allow sex to take over as a dominating factor in their association before marriage.

The happiest marriages are between those who can avoid becoming involved in premarital sexual intimacies while they look for personality traits in each other and determine how companionable they are in all parts of life.

A man's sex experience as preparation for marriage

College students, especially men, sometimes raise the question: Isn't it in some ways an advantage to sex adjustment in marriage if the man has had some previous experience? This viewpoint overemphasizes techniques in coitus and overlooks the fact that mutuality and psychic identification are extremely important elements in a successful sex relationship in marriage. It can be fairly safely assumed that adults will have little difficulty in the matter of learning techniques for physical performance; the problems more likely to be encountered in sex life in marriage are in the realm of the emotional and psychic. Therefore, experience with a prostitute or with girls who are casual dates and whose habits might verge upon promiscuity can teach a man nothing that he could not learn better in marriage. The advantages are in favor of the husband and wife who can learn together, and in so doing build an increasingly satisfying relationship. Casual experiences do not create awareness of the importance of sympathy and identification with a loved personality as satisfying essentials of sexual union. The more casual premarital experience a man has had, the more fixed may become a pattern of sex expression based almost exclusively upon individual physical gratification. After marriage it may be difficult for him to realize the need for a wider and more inclusive emphasis. If his conception of marital consummation is exclusively physical, and the physical response of his wife is not just according to his premarital pattern, he may be disillusioned and inclined to seek response elsewhere, thus destroying the possibility of the physical and psychic identification that might have been developed.

Learning together in marriage

Our consideration of premarital sex relations is oriented to the goal of building successful marriages, which meet the needs of both partners in all of the various areas of living. No matter how absorbing or overwhelming the sex phase of life may seem during dating, courtship, and engagement, sex remains but one segment of life, even married life. Therefore, the most valid test of a premarital policy is: how does the policy contribute to the building of a permanently rewarding relationship for both partners? Viewed in that light, temporary, immediate gratification of sexual desires becomes less important. Experimentation for the sake of experimentation or for variety in experience can be seen as undesirable.

Learning together in marriage can be far more satisfying for both husband and wife; together, two people can grow into new stages of sexual experience and eventually achieve a far richer sexual relationship than would be possible outside of marriage, or than is likely to develop if there has been experimentation on a casual basis before marriage.

Two people who meet each other's needs in other areas of life—and this they need to find out before they become involved in sexual relations with each other—can with confidence expect to be able to create together in marriage a sex relationship not possible outside of marriage.

Deferred marriage

Currently there is much discussion of the problems of those who, because of early dating, have become ready to marry, but who are unable to marry because they have several years of professional training ahead of them, or because they may not have reached the point of financial independence that will allow them to marry. Various solutions have been suggested. A certain school of thought assumes that young people are faced with exactly three alternatives. They must either: (1) marry at very early ages, (2) have sex expression through promiscuity or premarital relationships, or (3) inhibit their natural urges to the point of dangerous self-repression, which may result in inability to adjust to normal marriage later.

Several fallacies exist in such reasoning. The first one is the assumption that marriage is only legal sexual indulgence; in other words, if sex urges are strong, young people should marry early with no consideration given to the fact that in general very young marriages are not as successful as those made after maturity has been achieved.

The second fallacy is the assumption that the alternative is either premarital indulgence or dangerous repression. That assumption ignores the possibility of deliberately avoiding overemphasis on sex in courtship, of developing absorbing interests, and engaging in activities that preclude concentration on sex urges. It does not recognize the existence of self-control and cooperation to avoid overemphasis on sex, as distinguished from over-repression or dangerous inhibition. The majority of young people are aware of normal sex urges, certainly, but they have also a reasonable measure of perspective on life needs as a whole, and the ability to plan and build for permanent happiness.

The third fallacy of those who hold that youth must either marry early, be promiscuous, or be over-repressed, argues that control of sex impulses before marriage leads to over-repression that may handicap later marital adjustment. It is true that marital adjustment is sometimes handicapped by the strong inhibitions of one partner or the other, but these inhibitions do not arise from repression in young adulthood. They are developed early in childhood and are usually due to the faults in our system of sex education of young children. If overly strong inhibitions are present, they have been built up long before late adolescence. They can usually be broken down gradually by intelligent effort in marriage, but to attempt to throw control aside and indulge in sexual experimentation before marriage would only result in greater mental conflict for overly inhibited individuals.

Normally well-adjusted young people will suffer no ill effects from following a plan which includes self-control and emphasizes avoidance of excessive sex interest until they can marry. The advantages are all on the side of this course of action. Here, as in many other phases of marital and premarital experience, the long-time viewpoint is of fundamental importance. What is most desirable for life as a whole? The permanent happiness of a good marriage must be weighed against other considerations.

Review questions

1. In what ways is society inconsistent relative to premarital sexual behavior?

2. What do various studies show about the virginity rate of college girls?

3. In what ways was the sample of women studied by Kinsey and his associates not representative of the average college student or college graduate?

4. What do college students give as the approved sex standard before marriage? Do student generations change in their attitudes on sex standards?

5. What are the most common reasons students give for refraining from premarital intercourse?

6. Why is it difficult to determine the effects of premarital coitus upon marital adjustment? What does the case cited in the text show?

7. Explain why premarital coitus cannot determine for a couple whether they are well mated sexually.

8. What is meant by saying that the psychic is as important as the physical in sex expression? What bearing does this have upon premarital coitus?

9. Were the virgins or the non-virgins in the Kinsey study more successful in having stable marriages?

10. What are some of Kirkendall's findings on the attitudes of college men toward their premarital sex experiences?

11. Discuss some of the problems involved in premarital pregnancies from the point of view of society; the woman; the man; and the child.

12. Why might engaged men express less willingness than non-engaged men to marry a girl who had had premarital coitus with several different men?

13. Summarize the evidence concerning premarital coitus as preparation for marriage for men; for women.

14. Is control of sex impulses during the later teens a handicap to adjustment in marriage? Explain.

Suggested readings

Bowman, Henry A., *Marriage for Moderns*. New York: McGraw-Hill Book Company, Inc., 1954. Ch. VIII, "Courtship and Engagement."

Burgess, Ernest W., and Paul Wallin, *Engagement and Marriage*. Chicago: J. B. Lippincott Company, 1953. Ch. XI, "Sex and Engagement," and Ch. XII, "Assessing Premarital Intercourse."

Christensen, Harold T., *Marriage Analysis*. New York: The Ronald Press Company, 1958. Ch. IX, "Maintaining Sex Standards."

Duvall, Evelyn Millis, and Reuben Hill, *When You Marry*. Boston: D. C. Heath and Company, 1953. Ch. VII, "Does Morality Make Sense?"

Landis, Judson T., and Mary G. Landis, eds., *Readings in Marriage and the Family*. Englewood Cliffs, N. J.: Prentice-Hall, Inc., 1952. Part XIV, Reading 1, "Sexual Behavior, What Is Acceptable?," George P. Murdock, Luther E. Woodward, and Frederick DeWolfe Bolman; Reading 2, "Sound Attitudes Toward Sex," Lester A. Kirkendall; Reading 3, "Penicillin Is Not Enough."

Mixed Marriages

The novelty of extreme differences in background or personality make-up of two individuals is sometimes believed to be conducive to romance. Among groups of young people discussing marriage or courtship these questions often arise, "How much does it matter whether we are of the same nationality or religion? Why are parents often opposed to their children marrying across religious lines? Is it all just prejudice? How great do differences have to be to constitute a 'mixed marriage'?"

The time to consider these questions is before the final choice of a mate has been made. Many marriages take place between people of widely different backgrounds; the success of such marriages varies with the individuals who make them. The chance for success is greater if those who marry across lines of difference are aware at the outset that they will have to work harder for success than they would have to do if they married someone with a background similar to their own. All couples have some problems after they marry; in a mixed marriage the number of problems is increased and some problems that would normally exist are intensified. Any marriage that involves extreme difference may be called a mixed marriage, although the term is usually applied to those in which there is a difference in race, nationality, or religion, since these differences show the problems of mixture most clearly.

There are enough differences among the teachings of the Protestant, Catholic, and Jewish faiths to make interfaith marriages one of the more difficult types of mixed marriages. Interfaith marriages are opposed by all three faiths.

Protestant-Catholic marriages

Many devout members of both faiths look upon those who leave the church as lost souls. This conviction is probably the chief reason for church opposition to interfaith marriages. Protestants fear that if a Protestant marries a Catholic, the children born will be brought up to be Catholic and so will be lost to Protestantism. Catholics fear that the Catholic who marries a Protestant will become a lukewarm church member and that the children may be lost to the faith.

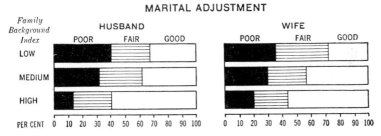

Fig. 40 INDEX OF SIMILARITY IN FAMILY BACKGROUND AND ADJUSTMENT IN MARRIAGE. Young people who come from similar backgrounds have fewer handicaps to happiness in marriage. From Ernest W. Burgess and Leonard S. Cottrell, *Predicting Success or Failure in Marriage*, p. 79. Englewood Cliffs, N. J.: Prentice-Hall, Inc., 1939.

Catholic program to prevent mixed marriages. The Catholic church has been more aggressive in its program to prevent interfaith marriages and to guarantee that if such marriages are made the children will be brought up in the Catholic church. Catholic literature devotes considerable space to shaping the attitudes of young people against interfaith marriages. In stating

Fig. 41 SIMILARITY IN INTERESTS, IN FAMILY BACKGROUNDS, IN GOALS IN LIFE, IN RELIGION, ALL ADD TO SATISFYING COMPANIONSHIP IN MARRIAGE. Courtesy of *California Monthly*.

the Catholic point of view, Edgar Schmiedeler, formerly Director of the Family Life Bureau of the National Catholic Welfare Conference, says, "Mixed marriages lead in many ways to a watered-down type of religion; and a watered-down type of religion does not make a cement which firmly and effectively binds the family group together. Since courtship is the beginning which leads ultimately to a marriage contract, the sound starting point toward this goal will be to avoid courtship with any and all non-Catholics." [1]

If a Catholic decides to marry a Protestant in spite of church pressure, the church asks that the Protestant take instruction in the Catholic faith. Classes are arranged for this purpose. The marriage must be performed by the Catholic church to be valid in the eyes of the church. Before marriage, the Protestant member must sign an agreement that the children will be brought up in the Catholic faith, that the marriage will not be broken except by death, and that no other marriage ceremony will be held. The agreement is reprinted here:

Ante-Nuptial Agreement

To Be Signed by Applicants for Dispensation from Impediment of Mixed Religion or Disparity of Cult.

Non-Catholic Party

I, the undersigned _____ of _____, not a member of the Catholic Church, desiring to contract marriage with _____ of _____, who is a member of the Catholic Church, propose to do so with the understanding that the marriage bond thus contracted can be broken only by death.

And thereupon in consideration of such marriage, I, the said _____ do hereby covenant, promise, and agree to and with the said _____ that he (she), the said _____ _____ shall be permitted the free exercise of religion according to

[1] Edgar Schmiedeler, *Marriage and the Family*, pp. 111-112. New York: McGraw-Hill Book Company, Inc., 1946.

the Catholic faith without hindrance or adverse comment and that all the children of either sex born of such marriage, shall be baptized and educated only in the faith and according to the teachings of the Roman Catholic Church, even if the said _____ shall die first.

I hereby promise that no other marriage ceremony than that by the Catholic priest shall take place.

I furthermore realize the holiness of the use of marriage according to the teaching of the Catholic Church which condemns birth control and similar abuses of marriage. I shall have due respect for the religious principles and convictions of my Catholic partner.

Witness my hand this _____ day of _____19_____ at _____ in the County of _____, and State of _____.

Signed in the presence of
Rev._____   _____
                                                    Signature of Non-Catholic

Catholic Party

I, the undersigned _____ a member of the Catholic Church, of _____ Parish, _____, wishing to contract marriage with _____, a non-Catholic, hereby solemnly promise to have all the children of either sex, born of this marriage, baptized and reared only in the Catholic faith.

Furthermore, I promise that no other marriage ceremony than that by the Catholic priest shall take place.

I also realize my obligation in conscience to practice my religion faithfully and prudently to endeavor by prayer, good example and the reception of the Sacraments, to induce my life partner to investigate seriously the teachings of the Catholic Church in the hope that such investigation may lead to conversion.

Witness my hand this _____ day of _____19_____ at _____ in the County of _____, and State of _____.

Signed in the presence of
Rev._____   _____
                                                    Signature of Catholic

A priest has specific instructions stating the conditions under which he may grant a dispensation for a mixed marriage. First the priest must be morally certain that the promises in the ante-nuptial agreement will be kept by the couple. With the granting of the dispensation, he becomes a third party to the marriage and is thus morally obligated to see that the agreement is carried out. This obligation of the priest often is not understood or recognized by Protestants who marry Catholics and later feel that their marriage suffers from interference by the priest as a third party and outsider.

Legality of ante-nuptial agreement. The question often arises whether the ante-nuptial agreement is a legal agreement that is enforceable. Usually this agreement has not been considered legally binding; its force has existed in the moral responsibility people feel when they have given their word by signing the ante-nuptial agreement. Recently, however, the legality of the agreement was tested in the courts when a Catholic man sued his former wife because she was not bringing their son up in the Catholic faith as she had promised at their marriage. The Court of Appeals of the state of New York decided the case by a split vote of five to two, which in effect upheld the right of the mother to rear the child in her faith after her divorce from the child's father.

Whatever force the ante-nuptial agreement may or may not have, it represents an effort of the Catholic church to develop a program to deal with a type of marriage considered by the church to be a major problem.

Protestant opposition to mixed marriages. What is the attitude of the Protestant church? The majority of the some 250 different Protestant denominations frown upon interfaith marriages, but go little further. They do not, as denominations, devote much time to discouraging their young people from marrying Catholics. They do not require the Catholic to agree that the children will be brought up in the Protestant faith, and they do recognize the validity of marriages performed by the Catholic church. The Protestant denominations are probably as much opposed to interfaith marriages as the Catholics are. From the viewpoint of holding their members, they have reason to be more opposed because of the definite program of the Catholics for seeing that the children of interfaith marriages are brought up Catholic. The Protestants' lack of a planned program to prevent or control interfaith marriages is due in part to the lack of organization among the many Protestant denominations.

Contrasts in beliefs affect marital adjustment. Although the churches emphasize that interfaith marriages lead to lukewarm religious attitudes and oppose them on that basis, other factors are involved that are of concern to those interested in the stability of marriage and family life. The difference between Catholics and Protestants in belief concerning birth control, for example, is a potential hazard to the success of an interfaith marriage. A couple might be able to differ on points of religious belief without the differences having any major effect upon marital happiness, but some Catholic-Protestant differences are vitally associated with marital relationships. Contrasting views about birth control, or about the training and education of the children will intrude into the daily life of the mixed couple. Moreover, attitudes of the two in-law families are likely to be a larger factor affecting the adjustments of a mixed couple, than is true of couples who are of the same backgrounds.

Attitudes of Catholic and Protestant young people on mixed marriages. In spite of church attitudes and contrasts in beliefs, are Catholic and Protestant young people willing to cross church boundaries and marry? Our study of 3,000 students in 11 colleges included questions about willingness to marry outside their own faith. Results showed that 55 per cent of the 3,000 students said that, other things being equal, they would marry into a different faith. Willingness to marry outside the faith was closely related to the family religiousness; that is, students who said their families were devout were much less likely to say they would marry outside the faith than those who reported that their families were slightly religious or indifferent to religion. Of these students, the Catholics were much more willing to marry outside the faith than were the Protestants, but less willing to change to the faith of the spouse than the Protestants. Of the Catholics, 72 per cent said they would marry outside the faith, but only 11 per cent said they would change to the Protestant faith; while of the Protestant students, 51 per cent said they would marry outside the faith, but of these 37 per cent said they would change to the faith of the spouse. Prince found, in studying 1,293 students at the State University of Idaho, the same pattern among Catholic and Protestant students.[2] In our study, Protestant girls expressed greater willingness to change faiths than did Protestant boys.

In practice, a great many young people do marry outside their faith. A study of ecclesiastically valid marriages (those sanctioned and performed by the Catholic church) in all sections of the country showed that in some dioceses three-fourths of all Roman Catholics marry outside the church, and that for the country as a whole more than one Catholic in four marries outside the church. The greater proportion of mixed marriages are contracted by Catholics of higher socio-economic status, and Catholics who are not in closely-knit ethnic groups.[3] In addition to the one-fourth who marry with the approval of the Catholic church, the Bishop's Committee estimates that each year from 15 to 25 per cent more Catholics make ecclesiastically invalid marriages.[4] Several studies show that it is the Catholic girl who is more likely than the Catholic boy to marry outside the faith.

Divorce rates in mixed and non-mixed marriages.   People who do not accept official statements from the church as controlling factors when it comes to choosing a marriage partner are nevertheless deeply interested in the results of research concerning the chances for success in Catholic-Protestant mar-

[2] Alfred J. Prince, "Attitudes of College Students Toward Inter-faith Marriages," *The Coordinator* (September, 1956), 11-23.
[3] John L. Thomas, "The Factor of Religion in the Selection of Marriage Mates," *American Sociological Review*, 16:4 (August, 1951), 467-491.
[4] For a summary of studies, see John L. Thomas, *The American Catholic Family*, p. 154. Englewood Cliffs, N. J.: Prentice-Hall, Inc., 1956.

riages. In states with large Catholic populations, college students are constantly asking for the facts about how these marriages work out.

Three large studies have been made to determine the divorce rate in mixed Catholic-Protestant marriages. These studies did not distinguish between ecclesiastically valid marriages and marriages in which the parties were of different faiths but married without the sanction of the Catholic church. One of these studies was our analysis of data from 4,108 mixed and non-mixed marriages among the parents of college students in Michigan. Special attention was given to: conflict situations resulting from religious differences; types of solutions attempted for the conflicts; the adjustments reached by the parents on the religious training of the children; and the eventual denominational choice of the children. Using separation and divorce as an index of failure, the study showed that mixed marriages in which both husband and wife hold to their separate religious faiths have a much higher rate of failure than other marriages. Where both parents were Catholic, the divorce rate was lowest, only 4.4 per cent of the marriages ending in divorce; if both were Protestant, 6.0 per cent ended in divorce. Of the marriages in which neither parent claimed any religious faith, 17.9 per cent ended in divorce. The highest divorce rate of all existed in marriages in which the husband was Catholic and the wife Protestant. Of this group 20.6 per cent were divorced.[5]

The two other studies of mixed marriages were made in widely separated parts of the country and show approximately the same results. These studies did not analyze the divorce rate by the

[5] New studies support the evidence that it is the Catholic husband-Protestant wife combination that results in the highest divorce rate. See Loren E. Chancellor and Thomas P. Monahan, "Religious Preference and Inter-religious Mixtures in Marriages and Divorces in Iowa," *The American Journal of Sociology*, 61:3 (November, 1955), 233-239. Also: Thomas P. Monahan and William M. Kephart, "Divorces and Desertion by Religious and Mixed-Religious Groups," *The American Journal of Sociology*, 59:5 (March, 1954), 454-465.

different possible combinations, that is, by whether the father was Catholic or Protestant and by the divorce rate when one spouse drops his religion and takes up the religion of the other. Ashley Weeks analyzed the marital status of 6,548 families of public and parochial school children in Spokane, Washington. He found a

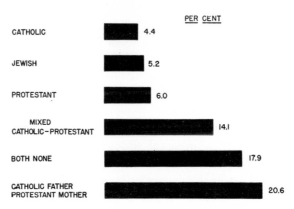

Fig. 42 RELIGIOUS AFFILIATION AND PERCENTAGE OF MARRIAGES BROKEN BY DIVORCE OR SEPARATION (4,108 MARRIAGES).

divorce rate of 3.8 among Catholics, 10.0 among Protestants, 17.4 in mixed marriages, and 23.9 if there was no religion.[6] Howard Bell analyzed the marital status of 13,528 families of mixed and non-mixed marriages in Maryland, and found a divorce rate of 6.4 among Catholics, 4.6 among Jews, 6.8 among Protestants, 15.2 in mixed marriages, and 16.7 if there was no religion in the home.[7] All these studies seem to show that both Catholic and Protestant authorities are justified from the viewpoint of family stability in discouraging young people from entering mixed marriages. However, the research studies on mixed religious marriages have dealt with couples who have children. It is possible that the divorce

[6] H. Ashley Weeks, "Differential Divorce Rates by Occupation," *Social Forces*, 21:3 (March, 1943), 336.

[7] Howard M. Bell, *Youth Tell Their Story*, p. 21. Washington, D. C.: American Council on Education, 1938.

rate is no higher than average in mixed marriages where there are no children. On this point existing data are as yet insufficient.

Tentative explanation of higher divorce rate. What are the explanations for the higher divorce rate in mixed marriages? One factor is that during the period of courtship it is hard to be realistic about marriage and easy to minimize the difficulties ahead. A man may sign away his birthright and that of his future children under the influence of love, but regret it later. Their religion may not seem so important to young unmarried people as it will seem later when they have children. Professor Baber, who made a number of case studies of mixed marriages, found that one-half of the conflicts that occurred in the Protestant-Catholic marriages he studied were over religion, and that often these conflicts centered around the training of the children. He found that the mixed marriages in which the parents were "indifferent" to religion were almost as likely to have conflict over religion as those in which the parents were "devout." [8] Although a person may not be much interested in religion, if he has been exposed to the religious teachings of a certain faith for a period of years it is difficult for him to forget this training. It is also difficult for him to be entirely indifferent about the training of his children. He may never bother to give his children religious training in his own faith, but he will often resent their being brought up in a contrasting faith. The attitudes and feelings of the two families will add to the conflict here. Both sets of grandparents will not only be watching and hoping to see the children brought up in the "right" church, but the grandmothers may feel that they must take an active hand in the children's religious upbringing just as the priest feels morally obligated to bring pressure on the Catholic spouse if the children are not baptized in the Catholic faith.

Another factor in Catholic-Protestant marriages may be that those who are already weak in their respective faiths may more

[8] Ray E. Baber, *Marriage and the Family*, p. 104. New York: McGraw-Hill Book Company, Inc., 1953.

readily marry outside the faith. It will be remembered that our study of 3,000 students revealed that those from homes where the family had been indifferent to religion were much more willing to say they would make mixed marriages. If the members of a mixed marriage are only nominal participants in their faiths they approach the group who claims no religious faith at all and so their failure rate might tend toward that of the non-religious group with the very high divorce rate revealed by the studies.

Religious faith of children in Protestant-Catholic marriages. Since the non-Catholic is required to sign a statement that he will bring up the children in the Catholic faith, the question of the religious training of the children would seem to be settled at marriage. Most young people are honest in their intentions when they sign the agreements about the instruction of the children, but it is difficult for young unmarried people to project themselves ahead and to know how they will feel when they have their children. After they are married and the children arrive, many people find that some things begin to matter to them more than they had anticipated. At this time, or later when the children are old enough for the beginning of instruction, the entire question will come up for rethinking, and some agreement will have to be reached. The study of mixed marriages among the parents of college students gives some indication of what the eventual decision was about the religious upbringing of the children in these marriages. There were 305 marriages of mixed Catholic-Protestant backgrounds; however, in 113 marriages one spouse had dropped his faith to accept the faith of the spouse. There were, then, 192 marriages that were mixed in that each spouse maintained his original faith. In these 192 marriages, half of the 392 children had been reared in the Protestant faith. The remainder had been reared in the Catholic faith (45.0) or had no faith (5.0). The most common tendency seems to be that the children, especially the daughters, follow the faith of the mother. Approximately 65 per cent of the boys followed the faith of the mother, while 75 per cent of the girls followed the faith of the mother. It is not surprising that the children tend to follow the faith of the mother since it is usually true that the mother is closer to the children and, in many homes, takes greater responsibility for their religious training.

Parental policy on religious training in Protestant-Catholic marriages. The students who were the products of Protestant-Catholic marriages were asked to describe the policy of their parents on religious instruction. A ranking from most common practice to least common practice revealed the following:

1. Mother took all the responsibility for the religious training. (36 per cent)
2. Our parents told us about both faiths but let us decide for ourselves when we were old enough. (27 per cent)
3. The responsibility for religious instruction was equally divided between our parents. (20 per cent)
4. We took turns going to both the church of my father and the church of my mother. (7 per cent)
5. Father took all responsibility for the religious training. (4 per cent)
6. Some of us went with my father to his church and some went with my mother to her church. (3 per cent)

In these findings, the dominance of the mother in the religious training of the children is observable since in 36 per cent of the families the mother took all responsibility for the religious instruction of the children, while in only 4 per cent of the families the father took all the responsibility.

There is some evidence that the Catholic father makes a stronger effort to defend his faith than the Protestant father does, in that the Catholic father has more to do with the religious training of the children. The Catholic father's insistence upon having a place in the religious instruction of the children may be one factor explaining the high divorce rate when Catholic men marry Protestant women. In marriages of this combination the divorce rate was 20.6, while it was only 6.7 per cent when

Protestant men marry Catholic women. Half of the nominally Protestant men who had married Catholic women were non-church members, and they were willing to let the wife rear the children in the Catholic faith without much conflict.

The Catholic father is more likely to be a participating church member and to feel that the children should be brought up in his faith. It may be quite a blow to him if his wife later finds that she is not willing to live up to the agreement that she signed before the marriage. Serious conflict seems to result in these mixed marriages unless the father gives up and lets the mother have complete charge of the religious instruction, or unless the mother gives up and lets the father have complete charge. The latter solution would be difficult, since the mother is usually closer to the training of the children than the father is, and it would be more difficult for her to give up or to ignore the religious training of the children.

Another factor explaining the lower divorce rate in Catholic mother-Protestant father unions is the hesitation of the Catholic mother to seek a divorce. Three out of every four divorces in the United States are granted to women. This does not mean that men furnish all the grounds for divorce, but simply that the wife is more likely to be the one who petitions for the divorce. There may be as much difficulty in the Catholic mother-Protestant father unions as in any other combination, but they are less likely to end in divorce because the wife does not believe in divorce. She is more likely to stay in the marriage even if it is unhappy. On the other hand, if a Catholic father-Protestant mother union is unsatisfactory, the Protestant wife will not be so hesitant to ask for a divorce. Consequently, the divorce rates in the two different combinations of Catholic-Protestant mixed marriages are different.

Parental conflict in Protestant-Catholic marriages. Each student was asked to state the degree of difficulty the difference in religious belief had created in the parents' marriage. The ranking was on a five-point scale, from no handicap at all to a very great handicap. Approximately a third of the students felt that the Protestant mother-Catholic father combination had been a serious handicap, whereas one-fifth of the students from the opposite combination felt that the difference in religion had been serious. Only 3 per cent of the students from families where both parents were Protestants, and only 4 per cent where both parents were Catholic, stated that religion had been a point of conflict in their parents' marriage. Two studies, one by Burgess and Cottrell,[9] and one by Dyer and Luckey, found no significant difference between the happiness of couples in mixed and non-mixed religious marriages. However, the couples in these studies were in the early years of marriage and had not yet faced the problems arising when consideration must be given to the religious education of the children.

Change to faith of spouse. In approximately one Protestant-Catholic marriage in three, the couple attempted to resolve their differences over religion by one of the spouses accepting the faith of the other, usually before marriage. Of the 305 mixed marriages in this study, 113 had tried this solution. In 56 of the marriages the Protestant member had changed to the Catholic faith, and in 57 marriages the Catholic member had changed to the Protestant faith. What evidence we have indicates that the marriage has a better chance for success when this solution is attempted. Among the cases in which one spouse changed to the faith of the other the divorce rate was not as high as in cases in which each held to his own faith.

The lower divorce rate among the couples who become of the same faith is due in part to the removal of conflict over the religious training of the children. In these marriages from 90 to 95 per cent of the children followed the faith agreed upon by the

[9] E. W. Burgess and L. S. Cottrell, *Predicting Success or Failure in Marriage,* pp. 87-88. Englewood Cliffs, N. J.: Prentice-Hall, Inc., 1938. See also Dorothy T. Dyer and Eleanore Luckey, "Religious Affiliation and Selected Personality Scores as They Relate to Marital Happiness of a Minnesota College Sample." To be published.

couple. In only 5 per cent of the cases did the children follow the faith renounced by the one spouse. These findings suggest that when one member gives up his faith and accepts the faith of the other at the time of marriage he seems to hold to his bargain, at least to the extent that he does not interfere with the religious instruction of the children.

Summary of problems in Catholic-Protestant marriages. Our investigation of marriages in which couples have tried mixed Catholic-Protestant unions indicates that this type of mixed marriage presents serious difficulties. Many hurdles must be overcome before a successful and happy marriage can be achieved. Although the church tries to help young people avoid trouble and although young people think they have removed causes for friction before they enter marriage, most of the causes making for friction must be faced repeatedly after marriage. Agreements made in good faith before marriage may have to be altered later, and they cannot be altered without conflict. These conflicts arise from the differences in belief concerning the religious instruction of the children, birth control, divorce, and other points.

A Catholic young person may be sincere in agreeing with the Protestant partner before marriage that birth control will be practiced in marriage; but he may find later that his conscience will not permit him to stand by his agreement. A Protestant may agree before marriage that birth control will not be practiced, but after the arrival of a few children he may feel that it is unreasonable for the spouse to expect the agreement to be kept. Before marriage acceptance of the theory of the "safe period" may seem to be a solution to the difference in beliefs over birth control, but when a couple finds the "safe period" to be unreliable, the question of using contraceptives will have to be faced and settled all over again.

In places where there are parochial schools, the question arises whether the children will be sent to the public or to the church school. Often the Protestant member objects to sending the children to the parochial school when it seems to him the children could as well go to a public school.

Even if the married couple themselves can bridge the gap in religious differences, their families present a further problem. Often parents cannot understand how their children can marry outside the faith. They may use every possible means to prevent the marriage. If the marriage takes place, the parental opposition can be an important source of in-law friction. An illustrative case follows:

> Jane, a Protestant, and John, the only son of devout Catholics, were engaged. John insisted that they be married by a priest because of the feelings of his parents. Jane at first refused to sign the agreement requiring the children to be brought up in the Catholic faith. Two priests refused to marry them, but a third, realizing that they would be married by a Protestant minister otherwise, persuaded Jane to sign the agreement and married them, even though Jane stated that she considered the signing of the agreement a mere formality. Jane knew that John's mother had used every possible means to try to persuade John not to go ahead with the marriage.
>
> When the first baby was born, the mother-in-law repeatedly suggested making plans for the Catholic baptism of the child, without response from Jane. One day Jane phoned her mother-in-law and invited her to attend the christening of the baby by a Protestant minister. The mother-in-law, shocked and hurt, refused to attend. John took no active part in the controversy, but left all decisions in the matter to Jane.
>
> The marriage has lasted for 12 years and is fairly happy. Jane takes all responsibility for the religious training of the three children, who are being brought up in the Protestant faith. John attends the Catholic church several times a year on special days with his mother. Jane privately tells her friends, "He would never go to the Catholic church at all if I didn't insist on it, but I think he should do at least that much to please his mother." Jane and John's mother have as little as possible to do with each other and there is mutual antagonism.
>
> All Jane's resentment seems to be directed toward John's mother and not toward John. But it would not have been so directed if John had made any effort to control the upbringing of the children. If John himself had had any stronger religious convictions, he could not have adjusted to the complete domination of the family

life in this area by his wife. One reason why this marriage was able to survive seems to be the fact that John had been dominated by his mother until his marriage, and the pattern continued after marriage with the wife substituted for the mother. There was little conflict, since the husband could accept the situation and the wife could enjoy her position of dominance.

Jewish-Gentile marriages

The Jewish-Gentile marriage is mixed not only in religion but also in additional aspects of culture. Differences in food habits, holidays, and days of rest are involved. Because of these cultural differences and also because the Jews have strongly urged their people to marry within their group, relatively few Jewish-Gentile marriages take place.

Jews recognize two types of Jewish-Gentile marriages, intermarriage and mixed marriage. Intermarriage is marriage between a converted Gentile and a Jew.[10] Orthodox, conservative, and reform rabbis will perform marriages of converted Gentiles and Jews; however, this type of marriage is discouraged, since Jews do not feel that Gentiles converted to Judaism are faithful Jews. When the Gentile does not accept Judaism, the marriage is termed a mixed marriage. No orthodox rabbi and few reform or conservative rabbis would officiate at a mixed marriage.

By a margin of only two votes, the Central Conference of American Rabbis meeting in Montreal in 1947 defeated a resolution which would have completely forbidden marriage between Jews and unconverted Gentiles.[11] One study of Jewish-Gentile intermarriages in New Haven between 1870 and 1950 shows that approximately 5 per cent of the Jewish marriages were interfaith.[12] Other studies of interfaith marriages in New York, Cin-

---

[10] Solomon B. Freehof, "Report on Mixed Marriages and Intermarriage," *Yearbook*, Vol. 57. Philadelphia: Central Conference of American Rabbis, 1947.

[11] *Family Life*, 7:9 (September, 1947), 8.

[12] Ruby Jo Reeves Kennedy, "Single or Triple Melting Pot? Intermarriage Trends in New Haven, 1870-1950," *American Journal of Sociology*, 57:1 (July, 1952), 56.

cinnati, and Stamford all show a low interfaith marriage rate among the Jews.[13] In interfaith marriages, the Jewish man is much more likely to marry outside the faith than is the Jewish woman. Baber found in a study of 130 Jewish-Gentile marriages in New York City that Jewish men marry Gentiles about twice as frequently as do Jewish women.[14] Another study of 59 inter-marriages revealed that the Jewish partner was male in 40 of the 59 cases.[15] The greater tendency for the Jewish man to marry outside the faith is because the young men have greater freedom to mingle with Gentiles and are not so carefully super-vised as are Jewish girls. One student of interfaith marriages points out that the male friends of Jewish girls are very carefully checked, more carefully than in the case of Gentile girls. Al-though Jewish boys are also closely guarded, they take advantage of the wider mobility that is a prerogative of their sex. However, the interfaith marriage rate of the Jewish men is still low because of parental supervision of dating. "One or two dates with a Gen-tile girl are sufficient for the relationship to become a topic of gossip in the community. In such cases word usually reaches Jewish parents quite rapidly, and they plead with their sons to confine their interest to Jewish girls."[16]

In our study of the attitudes of 3,000 students, we found that the Jewish students from homes that were indifferent to religion were much more likely to favor marrying outside their faith. The men were more willing to marry outside their faith than the women, but if the women said they would marry outside their faith more than a third said they would change their faith to that of the spouse; only 12 per cent of the men said they would change their faith.

[13] Milton L. Barron, "The Incidence of Jewish Intermarriage in Europe and America," *American Sociological Review*, 11:1 (February, 1946), 11-12.
[14] Baber, *Marriage and the Family*, p. 102.
[15] Barron, *op. cit.*, p. 12.
[16] Barron, *op. cit.*, p. 12.

Conflict in Jewish-Gentile marriages.   Most of the differences we have discussed in relation to Protestant-Catholic marriages exist in Jewish-Gentile marriages as well. In addition, cultural differences make adjustment more difficult in Jewish-Gentile marriages than in the Protestant-Catholic marriages. Discrimination has forced Jews to emphasize family and group solidarity. The Jewish family is a closely knit in-group into which it is often difficult for an outsider to fit. Family resistance to accepting the member from the out-group is often shown by both the Gentile and the Jewish families. Slotkin [17] found in his study of 183 Jewish-Gentile intermarriages that 57 per cent of the intermarried people were either partially or entirely accepted by both families, 20 per cent of the Jews were not accepted by their own families, and 23 per cent were not accepted by the family of the spouse, 16 per cent of the Gentiles were not accepted by their own families, and 27 per cent were not accepted by the family of the spouse. The higher percentage of non-acceptance by the Jewish families indicates stronger pressure toward endogamy on the part of the Jewish group.

Baber found that the children of Jewish-Catholic marriages and Jewish-Protestant marriages were brought up in the Jewish faith more frequently than in either the Catholic or the Protestant faith. This would seem to indicate that the Jewish parent dominates in the religious training. It means also that in Jewish-Gentile marriages the father more often dominates, since in such marriages the Jewish partner is more often the man. Baber found that half the conflicts occurring in these marriages were over religion, and the children were usually involved. Conflict was as frequent in marriages in which the spouses were indifferent as in those where the spouses were devout.[18] This finding is contrary to the

---

[17] J. S. Slotkin, "Adjustment in Jewish-Gentile Intermarriages," *Social Forces*, Vol. 21 (December, 1942), 226-230.
[18] Baber, *Marriage and the Family*, p. 103.

beliefs of many people who contend that if neither spouse is religious little trouble over religion will develop.

Another factor that stands in the way of successful Jewish-Gentile marriages is the prejudice that some Gentiles hold against Jews. In some sections of the United States, anti-Jewish campaigns and discriminatory attitudes still exist. Because of these

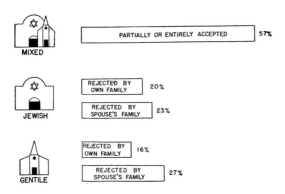

Fig. 43 FAMILY ACCEPTANCE AND REJECTION IN JEWISH-GENTILE MARRIAGES. Young people in love may bridge the gap in a mixed marriage, but it is more difficult for their families to merge their mixed backgrounds. Data from J. S. Slotkin, "Adjustment in Jewish-Gentile Intermarriages," *Social Forces,* Vol. 21 (December, 1942), 226-230.

attitudes on the part of some Gentiles, and because the Jewish people have tried to preserve their culture, they suffer as a minority group. The Gentile who marries a Jew is conscious of Gentile attitudes and sometimes attempts to avoid being identified with Jews as a group, even though he loves the individual one whom he has married. If the family lives in an area where discrimination exists, the Gentile is pained to see his children suffer as Jews.

Ann, a college girl in a midwestern school, fell in love with a Jewish boy from New York who was taking part of his aviation training in Illinois. They decided to marry, but Ann's parents objected. Ann could not understand why her parents opposed the marriage. She was not acquainted with prejudice against Jews. In her town there was only one Jewish family, and they were highly respected. In her college no distinctions were made between Jewish and Gentile students. Ann and Art, her fiancé, planned that after marriage they would live in the East near his family. An older friend, from whom Ann sought advice, suggested that the marriage be postponed and that Ann go to New York City for a semester and take work toward her degree, meanwhile using the opportunity to become acquainted with Art's family. The plan was agreed upon, and Ann spent a semester in the eastern school, after which she decided that her parents were right in opposing the marriage. Art's family treated her with kindness and tried to make her feel that they would accept her as a member of the family, but at times she felt uncomfortably aware that they were not happy about Art's decision to marry outside his own faith. She felt that she could accept Art's religion and she liked his family, but she found it difficult to adjust to family customs that were quite different from those of her own family. She also concluded that she did not love him enough to endure with him the discrimination that she found to exist in many places where she went with him. She realized, too, that she would be half-hearted in her acceptance of his life and that she might not be willing to have her children brought up in his faith and subjected to the discrimination which she had observed. She decided not to go ahead with the interfaith marriage.

This girl did well to analyze carefully before marriage her true attitudes and feelings concerning the different backgrounds of herself and her fiancé. This analysis enabled her to recognize that she was not capable of overcoming the difficulties that would be involved in the intended marriage. Some young people in a similar situation may find that, to them, the difficulties would not be insurmountable. Such persons may well decide, after careful self-analysis, to proceed with an interfaith marriage. However, they should be fully aware that it is easy to underestimate the importance of cultural and religious differences when one is emotionally involved during the courtship period, and that it is hard to be realistic about the future. One tends to put future problems out of mind and avoid facing them before marriage.

Mixed marriages between Protestants

Before leaving the subject of mixed religious marriages, we should point out that marriages between members of Protestant groups may include almost as many problems as the interfaith marriages here discussed.[19]

Marriage between a member of one of the conservative Protestant denominations that condemn dancing, motion pictures, smoking, and reading newspapers on Sunday as sinful, and a Protestant who knows nothing of such beliefs or considers them remnants of fanatical attitudes of a past generation, could involve as many wide differences as any interfaith marriage. The difference in religious beliefs would enter into many phases of living, just as in other interfaith marriages.

Further, the individual who has a religious orientation to life may find that his is a mixed marriage if he marries someone who is not religiously oriented. The spouse who is religiously oriented represents the sacred point of view in contrast to the secular or naturalistic viewpoint.[20] The contrasts in beliefs between the religiously oriented and nonreligiously oriented may be as great as the contrasts between Jews and Gentiles or Catholics and Protestants. Our study of mixed and nonmixed religious marriages, with a total of 125 couples in which the wife was a church member and the husband was of no religious faith, revealed that 16.0 per cent had ended in divorce. If the wife had been Prot-

[19] For a study of mixed marriages of Lutherans, see James H. S. Bossard and Harold C. Letts, "Mixed Marriages Involving Lutherans—A Research Report," *Marriage and Family Living*, 18:4 (November, 1956), 308-310. See also James H. S. Bossard and Eleanor Stoker Boll, *One Marriage, Two Faiths*. New York: The Ronald Press Company, 1957.

[20] For a discussion of sacred and secular points of view see Howard Becker and Reuben Hill, eds., *Family, Marriage, and Parenthood*, pp. 19-21. Boston: D. C. Heath and Company, 1955.

estant, the divorce rate was almost as high (19.0 per cent) as when the Protestant wife had married a Catholic. The high divorce rate in this combination of spouses may result in part from a clash of sacred and secular values. Available information seems to indicate that young people should compare and contrast their religious values and philosophies as well as the differences in their specific religious faiths.

Internationality marriages

Many mixed marriages involve more than one type of mixture. With increased differences between the backgrounds of a couple, more adjustability and more intelligent effort is required of each member of the pair if they are to build a good marriage.

The complicated set of differences that may be involved in a marriage can be recognized in this case:

> At the time the case came to our attention the couple had been married for fourteen years. They lived on the plains of western Oklahoma in the dustbowl area of the 1930's. Their house was a fairly comfortable four-room farm house set in the midst of acres of wheat land. There was no tree on their land; nor were there any trees in sight in any direction from their house. The husband was a hard-working man of crude appearance. He owned his land, but he was not well off. By careful management he was able to make the income from his wheat farming carry them from year to year.
>
> The wife was of French parentage. She had met and married her husband while he was serving in France with the American forces during the first world war. She had never been happy in the marriage, and through all the years she was never able to adjust to the circumstances of their lives. Her reasons for her unhappiness were, "He told me he had a big American ranch, and I pictured beautiful trees and hills like my own France. So I left my family and came with him. This is what he brought me to. At home we had lots of fun and music, and I gave music lessons to the children of the village. But here it is always quiet—he never talks and he never laughs. When I've wanted a piano he says we can't afford it. In my family we could get along without a tractor but not without a piano. My family were so happy for me when I had a chance to marry him, so when I was disappointed, I couldn't write and tell them. It seemed better to stay and try to

make the best of it, but I don't know if I did right. He doesn't think I am a good farmer's wife."

From a French village to an Oklahoma wheat farm proved too great a step for this wife. The husband also was unhappy in the marriage. It was impossible for him to understand how his wife could look upon the vast wheat fields of his native state as less desirable than the small crowded village from which she had come. All of her feelings about their home baffled and irritated him. He saw her as simply unwilling to accept the good life that he provided for her. But the two were in agreement in trying to stay together. The husband felt responsible for his wife's support, and she was unwilling publicly to admit defeat.

It will be seen that this marriage involved several kinds of differences. The most obvious was the nationality difference. They had to learn to understand each other's language. But more crucial in the marriage may have been the differences in their conceptions of what made life worth living. The fact that they spoke a different language in so many important areas of living was the real problem.

Many internationality marriages involve a difference in religion as well as in customs and manner of living. For two people to be from different countries—nationality differences alone—may be of little importance to their happiness if they happen to be of the same religion, of approximately the same economic level, and if the things they value in life are not far different.

In 1956 it was estimated that 11,000 servicemen married foreign brides in Europe. In numbers, English brides ranked first, German second, and French third. The Air Force recognizes problems in mixed marriages and attempts to prevent hasty marriages by insisting on eight months in the foreign country before a serviceman may marry. It is provided also that the chaplain must do all he can to appraise the probable success of a proposed marriage and give his approval before a couple may marry.

Internationality marriages may require special adaptability. As means of travel and transportation become ever more advanced so that the world becomes smaller and smaller, more and more young people will consider marrying others from far distant parts of the world. This is especially true on university campuses where outstanding young people come from all over the world to study. Any girl who contemplates marriage with a man from a different part of the world should study carefully in an effort to get a realistic picture of family life in the country he comes from. She should also study herself and take time to try to know whether or not she is willing to work at adjusting to the life into which her marriage will take her. For although ways are changing in countries all over the world and women are achieving an improved status in many countries, still, changes are uneven or slow, and the American girl who marries today or tomorrow into a contrasting culture from her own must be ready to do the adjusting herself. She cannot count on bringing about changes in the ways of the world into which she will move.

All marriages require the willingness and the ability to adjust to differences. An American girl married a man from Pakistan and fled his country later with the complaints, "His mother sat on the floor to sew! They expected me to stay behind a wall with the other women! They always had tea instead of coffee; and I couldn't bear their food!" This girl probably would have had trouble even if she had married a man from her own home state. She would have found habits in her mother-in-law that were different from her own mother's habits; she would have encountered in her husband's family life ways that she was not used to. Her attitudes were probably too rigid to enable her to accept and adjust to the differences that are to be expected in any marriage; so naturally she had no chance at all for success when she married into a culture extremely different from her own.

Interracial marriages

Some internationality marriages include also a difference in race. Such marriages were relatively rare in the United States a generation ago. But the world wars, the Korean war, and the continued stationing of American men in all parts of the world have meant an increase in interracial marriages. More than

21,000 G.I.'s married Japanese girls after World War II. Many more married Chinese and Korean women. Moreover, the various governmental educational programs that bring young men from all over the world to American universities in increasing numbers have meant that more American college girls now marry men with contrasting racial and religious as well as nationality backgrounds. Interracial marriages are viewed with alarm and strongly opposed in many parts of the United States, especially by the parent generation. In many of the states, laws specifically prohibit marriages between people of different races. Whether or not such attitudes are justified, the views of society affect the lives of people who make these marriages.

Some problems of interracial marriages. Some specific problems must be faced in interracial marriages. The children of mixed racial marriages are sometimes subjected to discrimination by both the races represented in the marriage. People who can endure criticism or prejudice when it is directed against themselves sometimes suffer intensely when such attitudes strike at their children. For this reason some of the most difficult problems arising in mixed racial marriages, as in marriages of mixed religion, are in relation to the children. Parents may possibly change their religion when they see that their differences are the cause of insecurity or confusion for their children, but they cannot change their race. The fact that there is no sound biological basis for the opposition to interracial marriages becomes merely an academic point; the social problems create hazards for such marriages.

Couples of mixed race may have trouble finding satisfactory housing in the United States because of social attitudes. They may also be deprived of congenial companionship among other married couples in their community unless they can find and associate with other "mixed" couples. Young people who make mixed marriages while in a university community, where attitudes may be more inclined toward acceptance of such marriages, often encounter new problems after they leave the university community and settle elsewhere. Whether or not such problems are distressing or traumatic to a couple will depend on their own sets of values, and on the quality of the relationship they have been able to achieve in their marriage. In some cases if the mixed marriage was made hastily and without realizing that special problems will inevitably arise, one or both may tend to react by blaming the other mate for troubles, so that when the pressure of opposing backgrounds becomes severe the marriage will not survive.

It is important to recognize that interracial marriages, and inter-nationality marriages involving religious and cultural differences, inevitably require far more of the individual than is required in the usual type of marriage between people of relatively similar backgrounds.

This part of our discussion of mixed marriages may seem to be pessimistic, but it is, rather, realistic. Certainly, some marriages involving several different kinds of mixtures and with the potential for the whole range of

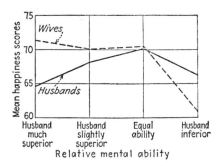

Fig. 44 CURVES OF MEAN HAPPINESS ACCORDING TO RATED MENTAL ABILITY OF SPOUSES. By permission, from *Psychological Factors in Marital Happiness* by Lewis M. Terman, Copyrighted, 1938, by McGraw-Hill Book Co., Inc., p. 193.

mixed-marriage problems, turn out to be successful and happy. When such is the case, the success is due to special qualities of flexibility within the two individuals themselves. They have the ability to face their problems, to do what they can about them, and to accept with a fair amount of equanimity circumstances or situations which many other people might consider unendurable.

Differences in intelligence or education

Differences in intelligence are less serious than some others, but may still constitute a mixed marriage and involve hazards to happiness for one or both spouses. Terman found that in cases where the husband was far superior to the wife in intelligence, the husbands rated low in happiness, although the wives rated high.

TABLE 13 PERCENTAGES OF 6,166 MARRIAGES ENDING IN DIVORCE BY EDUCATION OF SPOUSES

Education of spouses	Study 1 [a] Number of marriages	Per cent divorced	Study 2 [b] Number of marriages	Per cent divorced
Total cases	3,796	6.3	2,370	10.1
Both grade-school graduates	793	6.4	190	8.4
Both high-school graduates	1,054	6.7	318	12.9
Both college graduates	422	5.7	153	6.5
Husband 1-4 years more education	646	6.8	824	9.6
Husband 5-8 years more education	58	5.2	176	10.9
Wife 1-4 years more education	721	6.1	454	6.8
Wife 5-8 years more education	102	1.9	255	6.3

[a] Parents of students at Michigan State University.
[b] Parents of 3,000 students in 11 colleges.
It is interesting to note that in these studies there were a large number of cases of women who had married men with several years less education than theirs, and that in these marriages the divorce rate was low. Analysis of the data showed, however, that in this type of marriage the husband and wife were older at marriage than the average of other couples. The age factor would make for a lower divorce rate in these marriages regardless of education.

If the intelligence ratings were reversed, the husband being inferior to the wife, the wife's happiness score was low. Couples with the highest rating for both husband and wife were those in which the husband and the wife were equal in intelligence.

Several studies have been made in an attempt to discover whether educational differences of the spouses affect adjustment in marriage. The majority of these studies show that the same amount of education is slightly favorable to good adjustment in marriage.[21] Possibly if someone from a family of highly educated people who place great value upon education married into a family with little or no formal education, the marriage would involve elements of a mixed marriage, since educational differences may represent significant differences in family background in other matters such as viewpoints, values, and goals in life.

Physical differences

Physical differences such as a difference in height do not constitute a mixed marriage. Such differences are noted here only because they tend to loom large in the minds of people, sometimes larger than other differences that are not so readily visible but which have serious implications for marital success.

It is not a physical difference, but rather the attitude held toward a difference, that may cause problems in a marriage. A tall woman who feels embarrassed and conspicuous when dating a man shorter than herself might adjust more happily in a marriage with a man her own height or taller. A man who feels inferior and conscious of his shortness when with taller girls might better marry a girl no taller than he. The reason for this is that if he is uncomfortable about their difference in height his attitude may have the effect of causing his wife to feel disparaged and uncomfortable about her own tallness. People who feel there is something wrong with their physical appearance as a couple may have the effect upon each other of destroying self-confidence rather than of building up each other's self-esteem. In such cases although the height difference in itself is of no significance, feelings about it may have an adverse effect upon the relationship.

Age differences

Various studies have attempted to determine whether age differences between spouses affect the happiness of marriages. The

---

[21] Kirkpatrick, Hamilton, Landis, Terman.

findings of Burgess are representative. Burgess found no consistent relationship between age of the spouses and their marital happiness, although the age combinations with the largest percentage of good adjustments were those in which the wife was older than the husband. After analyzing these data, Burgess states, "When we summarize the findings regarding age differences, the popular romantic notion that, for marital happiness, the husband should be somewhat older than the wife, is not substantiated for the group studied." [22]

If a woman marries a man ten years older than herself, it may mean that she has been conditioned to respect older men or has idolized her own father; she finds greater happiness in marriage to an older man because of such conditioning. Similarly, the man who marries an older woman may marry her because he needs to be mothered and because she wants to mother someone. The marriage may be above average in happiness because it meets the needs of both.

Only in cases where age differences are extreme, such as a variation of twenty years or more, might age differences constitute a mixed marriage, and not necessarily in all of such cases. But if, because of great disparity in age, the two belong to two different generations with contrasting values, recreational and cultural interests, and viewpoints, their differences may be as great as if they married into a different culture from their own. Such a marriage could involve many of the problems occurring in mixed marriages of other types.

Summary

A mixed marriage may result from a combination of factors, all of which make for extreme difference. The greater the number of contrasts, the more hurdles will have to be surmounted to achieve happiness in the marriage.

[22] Burgess and Cottrell, *op. cit.*, pp. 161-164.

Consideration of all types of mixed marriages forces the conclusion that whether the difference is in race, religion, nationality, or in certain other characteristics and circumstances in the individuals' make-up or background, a marriage that involves differences serious enough to make it a "mixed" marriage will put special requirements on the partners. Further, it seems that the differences in mixed marriages do not usually decrease with the passing of time after marriage. They tend to become magnified in the minds of the couple and their families. To achieve happiness in such marriages, individuals must be mentally and emotionally mature and must possess more than average understanding and tolerance.

When considering any marriage one needs to evaluate honestly his or her own marriageability and the strength of his determination to work at making a good marriage no matter what circumstances may arise. This is more true of those making a mixed marriage than of the usual couple.

Review questions

1. Define mixed marriage. How do the adjustment problems of mixed marriages differ from adjustment problems in other marriages?

2. What are the four items one agrees to in signing the ante-nuptual agreement? Is the agreement legally enforceable?

3. In what way does the priest become a third party in a marriage in which he has granted a dispensation for a mixed marriage?

4. What differences in belief make Protestant-Catholic marriages mixed marriages?

5. What are the attitudes of Catholic and Protestant young people toward marrying outside their faith, as revealed by the study of 3,000 students? Toward changing to the faith of the spouse?

6. What percentage of Catholics marry outside their faith?

7. What are some of the factors explaining the higher divorce rates in mixed marriages?

8. What has research revealed about the faiths of children reared in Catholic-Protestant marriages? How is this explained if agreement has been made before marriage that the children will be reared in the Catholic faith?

9. What seems to be the most common parental policy on religious instruction?

10. Give some of the reasons for the higher divorce rate in Catholic father-Protestant mother marriages.

11. What agreements made before marriage are often renegotiated after marriage?

12. What is the position of the three large Jewish groups toward mixed marriage? Toward intermarriage?

13. Cite factors that make for conflict in Jewish-Gentile marriages.

14. Do differences in intelligence or education between spouses make for unhappiness in marriage? High divorce rate?

15. What do research studies show in regard to differences in age of spouses and happiness in marriage?

Projects and activities

1. Have a rabbi, a priest, and a minister present their views on mixed marriages to the class.

2. In order to break down religious, nationality, and racial prejudice there should be a biological fusing of different groups; or we might say that for the good of society one should make a mixed marriage. Is it possible to harmonize this point of view with what has been said about mixed marriages in this chapter?

Film

This Charming Couple. Focus is on the unreality of romantic love as well as on a type of couple combination that approaches a mixed marriage. McGraw-Hill Book Company, Inc. 20 minutes, sound.

Suggested readings

Bossard, James H. S., and Eleanor Stoker Boll, *One Marriage, Two Faiths.* New York: The Ronald Press Company, 1957.

———, and Harold C. Letts, "Mixed Marriages Involving Lutherans," *Marriage and Family Living*, 18:4 (November, 1956), 308-310.

Bowman, Henry A., *Marriage for Moderns.* New York: McGraw-Hill Book Company, Inc., 1954. Ch. VIII, "Choosing a Marriage Partner—Mixed Marriages."

Cavan, Ruth Shonle, *The American Family.* New York: Thomas Y. Crowell Company, 1953. Ch. X, "Cross-Cultural Marriages."

Chancellor, Loren E., and Thomas P. Monahan, "Religious Preference and Interreligious Mixtures in Marriages and Divorce in Iowa," *The American Journal of Sociology*, 61:3 (November, 1955), 233-239.

Golden, Joseph, "Characteristics of the Negro-White Intermarried in Philadelphia," *American Sociological Review*, 18:2 (April, 1953), 177-183.

———, "Patterns of Negro-White Intermarriage," *American Sociological Review*, 19:2 (April, 1954), 144-147.

Landis, Judson T., and Mary G. Landis, eds., *Readings in Marriage and the Family*. Englewood Cliffs, N. J.: Prentice-Hall, Inc., 1952. Part VIII, Reading 1, "Marriages of Mixed and Non-Mixed Religious Faith," Judson T. Landis; Reading 2, A Study of 48 Interracial Marriages," Ray E. Baber.

Monahan, Thomas P., and William M. Kephart, "Divorce and Desertion by Religious and Mixed-Marriage Groups," *American Journal of Sociology*, 59:5 (March, 1954), 454-465.

Slotkin, J. S., "Jewish-Gentile Intermarriage in Chicago," *American Sociological Review*, 7:1 (February, 1942), 34-39.

Strauss, Anselm L., "Strain and Harmony in American-Japanese War-Bride Marriages," *Marriage and Family Living*, 16:2 (May, 1954), 99-106.

Thomas, John L., *The American Catholic Family*. Englewood Cliffs, N. J.: Prentice-Hall, Inc., 1956.

Average time—first date to engagement

Importance of becoming well-acquainted

Becoming engaged and engagement rituals

Meaning of rings and pins

Significance of engagement

Permanence of engagement

Why engagements are broken

Recovering from emotional involvement when engagement is broken

When an engagement must be broken

Length of engagement

Recognizing danger signals

Engagement

Engagement as a bridge to successful marriage

Coitus during engagement

Confessing the past

The premarital examination

Parental approval and planning the wedding

The honeymoon

In the past, a promise to marry constituted a legal contract. If a man broke his engagement against the will of the girl, she could sue him for damages. Society took a firm position to force a man to go ahead with marriage after he had once declared his intention to marry, because a woman's future was endangered if she had been jilted. Today a broken engagement is not so serious a handicap for a woman, since women are freer to be active in hunting husbands. A jilted girl has resources other than sitting by the fireside, suffering from a broken heart. In fact, the trend toward equality in responsibility as well as in privileges has gone so far that, in states where breach of promise suits are still legal, suits are occasionally filed by men as well as by women.

Formerly it was not unusual for the parents of a girl to approach the man she was dating, if he had not proposed within a reasonable time, and ask whether he had "serious intentions." Parents were realistic in recognizing that it was not fair for a girl to have her time taken up with the attentions of a suitor who did not intend to marry her. Further, they felt a man should not be too slow in making up his mind. Parental action of this type is relatively unusual in our day. Parents may worry over the fact that a daughter is wasting her best years on a man who is not a marriage prospect, but they will hardly feel that they can ask him to declare his intentions.

Average time—first date to engagement

How long does it take young people to become well enough acquainted so that they feel ready to become engaged? According to the love stories

271

presented in novels and plays, it would seem that two people meet, fall in love, and become engaged—the time required for the procedure being negligible. But in real life people take somewhat longer. The majority do not rush into engagements. Some years ago we asked over 500 single and married students who had been engaged to state how much time had elapsed between the first date and the engagement. A summary is presented in the table below. It is interesting to note that nearly half dated for a year or more before becoming engaged, that 53 per cent were engaged within the first year of dating, and that 27 per cent were engaged within less than five months.

TABLE 14   AVERAGE LENGTH OF TIME ELAPSED IN 546 COURTSHIPS
FROM THE FIRST DATE TO ENGAGEMENT

Length of time	Number	Percentage
1-2 weeks	11	2.0
3-4 weeks	15	3.0
1-2 months	50	9.0
3-4 months	70	13.0
5-8 months	105	19.0
9-11 months	39	7.0
1-2 years	142	26.0
3 years up	114	21.0
Total	546	100.0

In the study of 200 engagements in 1957, those who were formally engaged told how much time had elapsed during each stage of their courtship. The total time was about the same as for the students who had reported ten years earlier. The couples in 1957 reported an average of 4½ months of casual dating with each other, 8 months of dating steadily, 10 months during which they had an "understanding"; they had been formally engaged an average of 6 months at the time of the study, and they planned to wait another 6 months before marrying. The average time from first date to marriage would be approximately 3 years. Thus the research on engagements among today's college students, as well as among students ten years ago, contradicts the idea that boy and girl meet, fall promptly in love, and soon marry. Rather, the pattern suggests that college couples are inclined to approach engagement and marriage cautiously.

The 200 engaged couples described the progress of the development of their love from the first dates to engagement. With most of these couples love developed gradually as they became well acquainted with each other.

TABLE 15   DESCRIPTION OF THE PROGRESS OF LOVE UP TO ENGAGEMENT AS GIVEN BY 200 ENGAGED COUPLES

Progress of love	Men	Women
We both fell in love at first sight	3.0%	3.0%
I fell in love at first sight	2.5	2.0
Fiancé(e) in love at first sight	2.5	1.0
One fell in love first, the other later	27.0	26.0
It was a gradual falling in love for both	65.0	68.0

Importance of becoming well-acquainted

It is more important than ever before that people become thoroughly acquainted before engagement or marriage, since marriages are no longer held intact by institutional forces and the stability of a marriage depends upon qualities within the marriage itself. Marriages last if comradeship, cooperation, emotional security, and affectional satisfaction are present. If some of these elements are not present, there is a good chance that the marriage will be unhappy, whether or not it ends in divorce. Couples who are friends for a reasonable length of time, during which they become well acquainted before they become engaged, have a better chance for happiness. Terman found that husbands were happiest who had been acquainted with their wives for three years or more before marriage. He found that wives were happiest who had been acquainted with their husbands for at least a year before marriage. These findings suggest that a woman may be able to learn as much about a man in one year as he can learn about her in three. Burgess and Cottrell found that the chances for happiness were best if couples had dated each other for three or more years before marriage. All available evidence indicates that the period of time during which a couple associates together in various activities before undertaking marriage is important in building a good relationship.

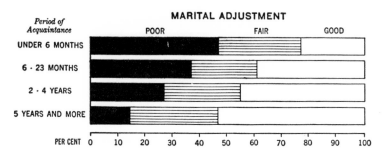

Fig. 45 DURATION OF ACQUAINTANCE BEFORE MARRIAGE AND MARITAL ADJUSTMENT. From Ernest W. Burgess and Leonard S. Cottrell, *Predicting Success or Failure in Marriage*, p. 165. Englewood Cliffs, N. J.: Prentice-Hall, Inc., 1939.

Becoming engaged and engagement rituals

Our study of engagements in 1957 showed that there had been a definite proposal of marriage by the man in about 70 per cent of the cases. In these cases most of the girls (89 per cent) said that the proposal was not a surprise, and 86 per cent accepted at once. If there has been good communication and a satisfying relationship between a couple for about a year, as was true of these couples, the marriage proposal and acceptance are not likely to be a sudden development. Almost a third of the couples said that there was never any formal proposal and acceptance, but that "we just understood that we were engaged."

As for the places in which couples get engaged, more than half of this group became engaged while in automobiles, and about one-fourth while at the home of one of them.

Half of the men in this group of engaged couples went through the formality of asking the girl's parents for permission to marry her. However, the custom is not the same as in former generations when the man was expected to go alone to the girl's father and ask him for his daughter's "hand in marriage." In two-thirds of the cases in which parental permission was asked, both members of the engaged pair went, together, to ask for parental approval, and they consulted both parents together, not just the father.

"Okay! You just made yourself a deal."

Fig. 46 By permission, Walter Goldstein and *The Saturday Evening Post*.

The table below summarizes other rituals observed by the engaged couples. Notice that a larger percentage of the girls than of the boys reported having certain rituals.

TABLE 16   PERCENTAGES OF 200 ENGAGED MEN AND 200 ENGAGED WOMEN REPORTING SPECIFIC RITUALS DURING ENGAGEMENT

Rituals	Men	Women
Using pet names	55.0%	65.0%
Using a special language	34.0	63.0
Considering a certain song "our" song	49.0	51.0
Sharing special jokes	56.0	63.0
Going to certain places	70.0	76.0
Observing significant dates	78.0	84.0

Meaning of rings and pins

The ancient Egyptians used the ring as the symbol of a pledge. This custom has come down to us and is widely followed in present-day engagements. The man gives the girl a ring as a seal upon the agreement. The wearing of a fraternity pin on college campuses is a custom similar to the wearing of an engagement ring, but it has a slightly different meaning.

Over 700 students at Michigan State University were asked to check this statement: "If a girl wears a boy's fraternity pin at MSU it means they are engaged." A much larger percentage of girls than boys interpreted wearing the boy's pin as a sign of engagement. (See Fig. 47.) When we asked 465 students at the University of California in 1957 what wearing a fraternity pin meant, 59 per cent of the boys and 77 per cent of the girls answered, "engaged to be engaged." Again, we notice that the girls seem to take pinning more seriously than the boys do. Twenty-five per cent of the boys said it meant "going steady," while only 10 per cent of the girls thought it had this meaning. Although confusion exists, it seems that a new step in the court-ship process has evolved. Instead of casual dating, going steady, engagement, and marriage, the pattern on college campuses seems to be: casual dating, dating steadily, becoming pinned or engaged to be engaged or having an understanding, formal engagement, marriage. Undoubtedly, on almost all campuses, a girl accepts a boy's fraternity pin only when some sort of an "understanding" has been reached. But evidence suggests that these understandings are not generally considered to be quite so binding as an engagement announced and sealed with a ring.

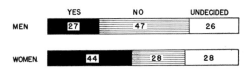

Fig. 47 ANSWERS GIVEN BY MEN AND WOMEN STUDENTS TO THE STATEMENT, "IF A WOMAN WEARS A MAN'S FRATERNITY PIN IT MEANS THAT THEY ARE ENGAGED."

The fact that in the polls of student opinion there was such a difference between the meanings the boys and the girls attached to pin-wearing suggests a reason why the understandings indicated by acceptance of the pin are not considered strictly binding. A girl will learn to take "pinning" lightly if she accepts a pin in the belief that it means a tentative promise to marry and later realizes that it did not have that meaning for the boy who gave it to her. So, although pinning is a common custom, its meaning varies. The giving of a ring is more universally accepted as indicating a serious intention to marry.

Significance of engagement

When a couple becomes engaged, they usually believe that the matter is settled for all time. However, as they come to know each other better through engagement, they sometimes find that they are not suited for each other and decide to break the engagement. Thus engagements today differ from those in earlier days, when the promise to marry was considered a legal contract that must eventuate in marriage. In those days the engagement was a period specifically for planning the wedding and making the trousseau. In practice, it has now become, in addition, a period of more intimate acquaintance during which both partners may more accurately evaluate marriage desirability. Today we recognize that many promises to marry never should have been made and that it is better to break an engagement than to go into an unhappy marriage that may end in divorce. It is more desirable, however, to delay an engagement until after the two have come to know each other well and have associated together long enough to build up a strong basis of friendship and affection. There is then less likelihood of a broken engagement and the emotional upheaval that may result for one or both.

Permanence of engagement

Quite a large percentage of engagements are broken. Of the 1,000 engaged couples studied by Burgess and Wallin in the late 1930's, 39 per cent of the men and 51 per cent of the women had broken one or more previous engagements or they later broke the engagement in force at the time they responded in the study.[1] In our studies of students after World War II we found that of 143 married students one-third had been engaged at least one time before the engagement that finally resulted in marriage. In studying 307 single students who had been or who were engaged, we found that approximately half had already broken at least one engagement. The students in this study were largely men who had been in military service. Women as well as men would probably show a higher incidence of broken engagements during and after a war. The 3000 students studied in the 11 colleges in 1952-1955 had a much lower broken-engagement record. Twenty-six per cent of the women and only 16 per cent of the men had broken one or more engagements. Only 12 per

[1] Ernest W. Burgess and Paul Wallin, *Engagement and Marriage*, p. 273. Chicago: J. B. Lippincott Company, 1953.

cent of the 200 engaged student couples in our 1957 study had broken one or more engagements. However, some of the current engagements will be broken; almost 20 per cent of the engaged couples said they had at times regretted becoming engaged and had thought of breaking the engagement. The broken engagement rate today is probably less than it was among the students studied after World War II, but it seems safe to assume that one-fourth or more of engagements among college students today do not end in marriage. It is well to keep this in mind as we discuss the engagement period. In discussing engagements here, we have not made a distinction between "formal engagements" and "private-understanding engagements." Among those who have formally announced their engagements there will probably be fewer who break their engagements than among those who have "private understanding engagements."

Why engagements are broken

The fact that a large percentage of engagements are broken may indicate that people become engaged sooner than they should; that engagement is not taken so seriously as it was at one time; or that young people today have a chance to get better acquainted during the engagement period than was true in the days when courtship was more strictly supervised, and are realistic enough to recognize when there is little possibility of the planned marriage being successful.

Table 17 summarizes the reasons given by 678 students who

OUT OF 100 ENGAGED COUPLES

Fig. 48 MANY EN-
GAGEMENTS DO NOT
END IN MARRIAGE.

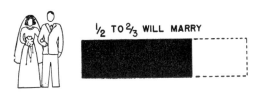

½ TO ⅔ WILL MARRY

had broken one or more engagements in the 1952-1955 study. The causes of broken engagements as given by the students can be grouped as follows: (1) one or both lost interest, (2) separation, (3) incompatibility, (4) contrasts in family background, (5) influence of family and friends, (6) other factors, such as fear of marriage. In their study of engagement, Burgess and Wallin found about the same factors most frequently associated with broken engagements: slight attachment, separation, parental opposition, cultural divergencies, and personality difficulties.[2]

TABLE 17   PERCENTAGES OF 678 STUDENTS IN 11 COLLEGES GIVING SPECIFIC REASONS FOR BROKEN ENGAGEMENTS

Cause of break-up	Men (N-169)	Women (N-509)
Parents	13.0%	18.0%
Friends	2.0	3.0
Mutual loss of interest	17.0	14.0
Partner lost interest	18.0	9.0
I lost interest	20.0	34.0
Separation	23.0	26.0
Contrasts in background	13.0	27.0
Incompatibility	16.0	17.0
Other	13.0	12.0

Loss of interest. More than half the boys and girls said that the reason the engagement was broken was that one or both lost interest. A higher percentage of girls said that they had lost interest, and a smaller percentage admit that it was the boy who lost interest. Kirkpatrick,[3] in his study of broken love affairs among Minnesota students, observed this same tendency. Are girls quicker to perceive that a planned marriage would be unworkable and so "lose interest"? Or are the girls unwilling to admit

[2] *Ibid.*, p. 273.
[3] Clifford Kirkpatrick and Theodore Caplow, "Courtship in a Group of Minnesota Students," *American Journal of Sociology*, 51:1 (September, 1945), 114-125.

that the man in the case lost interest and broke the engagement? Or are today's men students more chivalrous than they get credit for being, allowing a girl to feel that she was the one who lost interest when an engagement goes flat?

Engagements after a short acquaintance are often based upon some superficial attraction which may wear off as the couple becomes better acquainted. Love-at-first-sight engagements are frequently of this type, since they are based on attraction rather than on common bonds. Therefore, they may not survive the more careful scrutiny of the engagement period. The element of adventure or new experience, which may have represented romance when the couple became engaged, may wear off during the engagement period and leave little to hold some couples together.

Separation. When engaged couples separate to attend different colleges, the engagement has little chance of withstanding the four years of separation. Both are constantly in the company of other attractive young people: they enter into activities common to students and usually become interested in dating someone among the new acquaintances. Thus they gradually drift apart. If an engaged young man goes to college, leaving his high-school fiancée at home, there is a good chance that he will find someone else and will wish to break the engagement. At first, he may feel the separation keenly and tend to withdraw from the life about him; but if he is normally gregarious he will be drawn into association with others. Gradually, new interests will take precedence over the old. We have mentioned the high percentage of broken engagements among young people of the war generation. However the students in 1952-1955 gave separation as the second most common cause of broken engagements.

An important factor causing broken engagements is the rapid emotional maturing of people of the courtship age. The young person who becomes engaged while in high school but who does not plan to be married before finishing college will change and mature greatly during the four years. His conception of a perfect mate will be modified so that the high-school sweetheart may later fail to measure up. Many people find that the mate they choose at 22 bears little resemblance to the one they would have chosen at 18. Many of the broken engagements are those which were made at an early age when the couple were immature; these engagements could not stand the test of more mature judgment. Young people in college not only mature, but their interests and values may be changed by college experience.

Incompatibility. During the engagement period the couple usually spends more time together than during the period when their dating was casual. They now have a chance to see each other in more varied real-life situations. With extra time to spend together, they may learn whether they have many interests in common. Sometimes they discover that they have few activities which they can enjoy together and they come to the conclusion that there would be little to make for permanent companionship in their marriage. In such cases they are wise to break the engagement.

As they become more intimately acquainted, each will get a better understanding of the real personality of the other. On occasional dates it is quite easy to be on "good behavior," but when a couple is together constantly after becoming pinned or engaged, each has an opportunity to observe the other's accustomed behavior around his family and friends. If a young man sees his fiancée behave rudely and selfishly in her own home, he may realize for the first time that the girl has these personality traits; and the girl whose fiancé has always treated her with devoted attention may be shocked to see that he shows little thoughtfulness or consideration for his mother and sisters. Habitual behavior has a way of showing itself if given time, and true attitudes on many matters, such as likes and dislikes concerning people and activities, and each one's true interests, are likely to come to light if people are together enough. An advantage of longer engagements is that they offer opportunities for a couple to be more realistic about their compatibility or incompatibility.

The pinned stage of a romance may accomplish many of the purposes of engagement. A pinned couple may associate together in almost all ways as if they were engaged, but if it seems best not to go on to marriage they can break off their relationship early enough so that both may be spared many of the unhappy emotional effects that would accompany a broken engagement.

Cultural contrasts. Many "mixed" engagements do not survive the contrasts in backgrounds. A Catholic boy may become engaged to a Protestant or Jewish girl, but on becoming more thoroughly acquainted with the girl's beliefs and the problems involved in a mixed marriage, he may decide that he should not go on with the wedding plans. Engagements are often entered into before the young people have had any opportunity to know each other's family. If it is a mixed engagement of nationality or race, the couple may have thought the difference was of little importance while they were dating; but as they approach the reality of marriage and become better acquainted with the future in-laws, each may find it more and more impossible to accept the cultural background of the other. So resistance to the engagement on the part of the family or families may also contribute toward breaking a "mixed" engagement.

Friends and family. Although a modern youth is free to marry whomever he chooses, he is influenced by what others think of his choice. During engagement, the friends and families have an opportunity to come to know the prospective husband or wife. Most young people find it hard to go ahead with a marriage if the fiancé(e) is looked upon unfavorably by friends and family. Most girls are sensitive to how the fiancé is "going over" with family and friends. If a girl recognizes that her fiancé does not seem to her people to be very desirable, it not only wounds her pride but may also cause her to look at him more candidly herself. She may begin to see him as others see him and decide to break the engagement.

Two separate studies of divorced people, one by Goode and one by Locke, support the conclusion that the degree of approval of friends and family is rather closely related to how marriages succeed.[4] Goode points out that one factor in the greater success of approved marriages might be that friends and family who approved of the match will pitch in to help marriages succeed when crises arise. If there has been disapproval, active support for maintaining the marriage might be lacking since the family felt pessimistic about the outcome from the beginning. Goode and Locke also found that it was the wife who was more conscious of the disapproval of her family.

Other factors.   After longer acquaintance, a girl may decide that the man she loves could not support her in the manner that she would like, or a man may decide that the girl has expensive tastes and that he could not support her. During the financial planning that usually must be done by an engaged pair the economic values are more likely to be revealed so that each comes to know how the other thinks. A clash in economic values may cause the couple to decide that the marriage would be unwise.

Sometimes an extreme parental attachment on the part of one partner does not show up until the couple have become thoroughly acquainted during engagement. A girl may admire the man's devotion to his mother and she may interpret his behavior as evidence that he will treat his wife the same way. In some cases that would be the correct assumption. However, if the son's devotion is so strong that he can see no reason why, as newlyweds, they should live alone when Mother's home is open to them, the fiancée may recognize the danger signal and postpone marriage until the partner is willing to start married life in a separate

---

[4] William J. Goode, *After Divorce*, pp. 81-85. Glencoe, Ill.: The Free Press, 1956. Harvey J. Locke, *Predicting Adjustment in Marriage*, p. 119. New York: Henry Holt and Company, 1951.

place. If the man never reaches that point, the girl will be well out of a situation that might have meant an unhappy marriage. Devotion to parents is right in its place, but successful marriage requires a mature independence from parents.

Some girls go into marriage recognizing that the man is overly attached to his mother and that their lives will always be dominated by the mother. A few can adjust to that situation and make the marriage a success in spite of it. Most girls, however, cannot happily accept such a situation. If the boy recognizes his too great dependence on his mother, there is some hope that he may eventually become emotionally mature. However, the girl who marries such a man is apt to be disappointed if she allows her happiness to depend on ending the maternal domination. If she doubts whether she could accept this domination, she would do well to break the engagement.

So there are many reasons why couples break their engagements, and most of the reasons are sound. Engagement provides the couple with an opportunity to hesitate on the verge of marriage and to make sure the marriage has a chance for success. However, too many broken engagements in the experience of one person may be evidence of resistance to marriage or may mean that the individual is reckless or superficial in his approach to relationships with others—becoming engaged for exploitative and selfish motives without having a serious intention to marry.

Recovering from emotional involvement when engagement is broken

Much has been written and spoken about "broken" hearts resulting from broken engagements. Spinsterhood and bachelorhood in other generations was often explained by the story of how Auntie had her heart broken when she was young and never got over it, or how Uncle Joe's sweetheart died before their wedding and there never was another girl to replace her in his affections. To get some idea of how long it takes people to get over the emotional shock of a broken engagement, we questioned 320 formerly engaged people. Their responses are summarized in Table 18.

TABLE 18   LENGTH OF TIME TO GET OVER
THE EMOTIONAL INVOLVEMENT OF THE ENGAGEMENT
REPORTED BY 320 FORMERLY ENGAGED STUDENTS

Length of time	Men (N-249)	Women (N-71)	Total (N-320)
1-2 weeks	21.0%	24.0%	22.0%
3-4 weeks	12.0	7.0	11.0
1-2 months	17.0	18.0	18.0
3-5 months	19.0	17.0	18.0
6-12 months	4.0	4.0	4.0
13-23 months	13.0	21.0	15.0
2 years and over	14.0	9.0	12.0
Total	100.0	100.0	100.0

Some of the students in this study were war veterans who had been away from home and in the service when the engagement was broken. Some of the men stated that these circumstances prevented their forgetting the broken engagement as easily as they would have ordinarily. If the engagement was broken by the girl at home while the man was in some isolated region where there were no girls of his own kind, it was natural for him to brood over the affair more than if he had been able to shift his attention to a desirable substitute or to mingle socially with suitable girls.

The fact that almost 70 per cent of the people felt that they had recovered from the emotional upset caused by the broken engagement within five months, almost a fourth of them within two weeks, suggests that this kind of emotional crisis is most often temporary, and without permanent ill effects.

When one is in the midst of the emotional turmoil that may occur at the time of a broken engagement, the experience seems unique. The tendency is to feel that no one else has ever endured

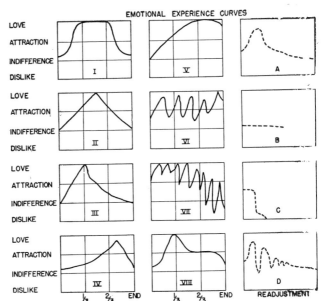

Fig. 49 EMOTIONAL TRENDS IN THE COURTSHIP EXPERIENCE OF COLLEGE STUDENTS AS EXPRESSED BY GRAPHS. Of 400 university students who had had 900 love affairs, the largest percentage thought Graph I most nearly represented their emotional trends toward the loved one during the love experience.

quite the same ordeal. It is helpful in such circumstances if one can realize that not only have others suffered similarly but that the experience tends to follow a rather specific pattern.

Kirkpatrick and Caplow [5] made some interesting studies of the patterns of emotional trends in the courtship experience of college students. The students cooperating in one phase of their studies checked graphs representing their feelings during the readjustment period after broken love affairs had ended.

Over half said Graph B among the four graphs in Fig. 49 represented their feelings. That is, their feelings approached indifference to the former loved person and no serious trauma remained. Fifteen per cent indicated that there was a temporary flare-up of affection for the loved one, which soon decreased and became indifference (Graph A). Another 15 per cent went through a period of recurring up-surges in affection for the former loved person before tapering off to a state of indifference (Graph

[5] Clifford Kirkpatrick and Theodore Caplow, "Emotional Trends in the Courtship Experience of College Students as Expressed by Graphs with Some Observations on Methodological Implications," *American Sociological Review*, 10:5 (October, 1945), 619-626.

D). In 11 per cent of the cases, what had been love turned into dislike (Graph C). In approximately 90 per cent of the terminated love affairs reported in this study, a normal state of adjustment, indifference to the former love object was achieved.

In our study among students in 1952-1955, we included a section adapted from Kirkpatrick's study of adjustment reactions to broken love affairs among University of Minnesota students.[6] Table 19 summarizes the responses of over 1,700 of the 1952-1955 students who had broken off serious love affairs. It is interesting that the adjustment reactions are quite universal and that men and women resort to the same ones with about the same frequency, except that women "preserve keepsakes" and remember unpleasant associations more than men do. You will notice that most of the adjustments are normal and acceptable reactions, although some tend to be neurotic, or if they became extreme, would have to be classed as neurotic. The girl who constantly daydreams about the former lover, refuses to date others, and imagines how unhappy the former lover is with his new girl friend or wife, is developing an unhealthy mental state and may need counseling to reorient her life.

The findings on how long it takes to get over broken engagements point up a common relationship in love affairs: the one-sided involvement. One member of the couple may feel that he is very much in love and wish to continue a relationship while the other has already decided that she is not in love and may be plotting her escape from the affair. When the affair is ended, one is relieved, the other hurt.

The emotional upset for the one hurt by the breaking off of a love affair or engagement may be compared with a case of

[6] Clifford Kirkpatrick and Theodore Caplow, "Courtship in a Group of Minnesota Students," *The American Journal of Sociology*, 51 (September, 1945), 114-125. Reprinted in Judson T. Landis and Mary G. Landis, eds., *Readings in Marriage and the Family*, pp. 79-90. Englewood Cliffs, N. J.: Prentice-Hall, Inc., 1952.

TABLE 19   PERCENTAGES OF 1,745 STUDENTS FROM 11 COLLEGES
GIVING ADJUSTMENT REACTIONS
WHEN MOST SERIOUS LOVE AFFAIR ENDED

Reaction	Men (N-577)	Women (N-1,168)
Remembered pleasant association	75.0%	74.0%
Got dates with others	72.0	75.0
Daydreamed about partner	34.0	29.0
Preserved keepsakes	13.0	34.0
Avoided meeting him (her)	25.0	24.0
Read over old letters	17.0	26.0
Attempted to meet him (her)	24.0	19.0
Remembered unpleasant association	14.0	24.0
Frequented places of common association	17.0	18.0
Liked or disliked people because of resemblance	12.0	14.0
Daydreamed	10.0	14.0
Avoided places of common association	10.0	13.0
Resolved to get even	2.0	3.0
Imitated mannerisms	0.5	4.0
Thought of suicide	1.0	2.0

measles, in that it follows a definite course. Mothers of children ill with measles sometimes become frantic with worry during the time when the disease is at its worst stage, just before recovery begins. At this point the family doctor will attempt to comfort the mother and the patient by telling them that it is a "typical" case, that there are no complications, and that if the patient is kept comfortable and given reasonable care, nature will bring about recovery. When several children in succession in a family have to be nursed through the measles, the mother learns to ease each child through by giving good care and by encouraging the patient to recognize that the disease is taking its course and will soon be over. Friends and family of the person suffering from a broken love affair have much the same role. They can do little except to try to live peaceably with the emotionally upset individual, meanwhile hoping there will be no "complications," such as a sudden marriage on the rebound or an unhealthy clinging to grief.

It is hard, however, to convince the victim of a broken love affair that his is a "typical" case. A part of the process of attaining maturity is learning by experience that recovery, in the sense of regaining emotional balance, is possible from even the most devastating loss or bereavement. The person who can apply himself to absorbing tasks as soon as possible after emotional loss can hasten such recovery. The students who reported broken love affairs said that "getting dates with others" was one of their most common adjustments to a broken affair. That is a good adjustment if the dates are an attempt to fill time and enjoy life by mingling with others, and not an attempt to get even with the former love. But sometimes people who date others in order to forget a former love allow themselves to fall quickly in love on the rebound. Rebound loves and marriages may result in far more permanent pain than that which they are designed to cure.

When an engagement must be broken

To end an engagement when one of the pair has concluded that the marriage cannot work out is sometimes very difficult. Some engagements are broken in immature ways, with a careless disregard for the feelings of the partner, or even with a deliberate attempt to hurt. It is humiliating to both men and women to have their affections suddenly repulsed and to have to face friends and family with the announcement that the fiancé(e) has broken the engagement. But in some cases, even if the one who breaks the engagement shows all possible consideration for the feelings of the other, the one most hurt by the break may regress to an immature level of behavior in an attempt to hold the unwilling partner. Threats of violence to himself are common. Sometimes threats are made to "tell" things that might be damaging to the partner, and pathological individuals may even resort to threats against the life or person of the partner. These are ways of reacting to situations in which the individual feels extremely frustrated. A small child may react to a blocking of his wishes by running away or by telling his mother that he will run away. It is not that he wants to leave home, but in his childish way he is attempting to bring sorrow to his mother by harming himself. The immature adult who threatens suicide when a love affair is ended against his will does so because he wishes to force the loved one to worry over him, to fear that he will harm himself, and to feel responsible for his behavior. He hopes it will cause the loved one to decide she loves him too much to risk allowing him to harm himself. Sometimes in fiction or movies the jilted lover drinks to drown his sorrow until his former sweetheart comes back to him, then they marry happily.

Fig. 50 "When we break up, Melvin, I'm certainly going to miss your candy." By permission, Walter Goldstein and *The Saturday Evening Post.*

If one partner threatens violence when the engagement is broken, the one wishing to break the engagement should look upon the threats objectively. In the first place, there is little chance that they will be carried out. The small boy who starts to run away from home to hurt his mother seldom runs more than a block. Making threats is an indication of immaturity and instability and should be recognized as convincing proof of the desirability of breaking the engagement. If fiction pictured life situations rather than romantic fantasy, it would tell what happened later in the married life of the girl who weakened and married the man after he proved his love for her by turning to liquor. Instead of living happily ever after, she would be spending the rest of her life trying to pacify a husband who resorted to sulking, temper tantrums, or drunkenness whenever things failed to go according to his wishes. Immature patterns of behavior do not change with marriage, any more than selfishness is cured by marriage.

The quick marriage to someone else, which is another form of immature reaction, is an attempt to save face and at the same time to hurt the former partner by demonstrating that she (he) has been quickly forgotten. Marriages for spite, or on the rebound, have little chance for happiness. The innocent mate in the rebound marriage is to be pitied. Courtships in which one or both partners have not had time to get over previous love affairs should not end in engagement or marriage until ample time has elapsed so that both may evaluate their chances for happiness as carefully as if it were the first love affair. They need to be sure that they have had time to let their wounded affections heal and that no spite or "rebound" is involved. Quick marriage after a broken affair usually indicates that the person is seeking an escape and that his emotions may still be involved with the former loved one.

When an engagement must be broken, it is better if both can recognize that a one-sided affectional attachment would result in unhappiness in marriage. Impossible as it may seem at the time, the rejected one will find that there are others whom he can marry, who have all and sometimes more of the desirable traits of the ex-partner. Unfortunate is the person who thinks that he has only one possible mate in the world, and that this one has rejected him. It is better to be philosophical about the whole matter.

Length of engagement

How long should engagements be to result in the best adjustment in marriage? Some people can get thoroughly acquainted during a relatively short period of engagement, whereas others may be engaged for years without having settled many of the questions that should be faced during the engagement period.

In the past, when engagements were for the purpose of planning and preparing for the wedding, short engagements were considered desirable. Since couples are permitted greater freedom in expressing affection during engagement, long engagements mean more possibility that the problem of premarital sexual intercourse will arise. Formerly the logical solution to the problem was to recommend short engagements so that couples could be ushered quickly and safely into marriage.

Research studies show that longer engagements are among the factors predictive of happiness in marriage. A summary of studies dealing with the length of engagement and happiness in marriage is presented in Table 20. All studies indicate that short engagements are more likely to be followed by poor adjustment in marriage. Our study of 544 couples found the lowest percentage of very happy marriages among those who had not been engaged at all. It also revealed that those couples who met under favorable circumstances (home, school, church, in contrast to blind dates, pick-ups, or places of commercial recreation) were also the ones who were acquainted longer and who had longer engagements. This suggests that other factors which are also predictive of success in marriage go along with longer engagements.

In comparing the length of engagements of a matched sample of divorced and happily married couples in Indiana, Locke found short engagements, under one month for men and under six months for women, much more prevalent among the divorced, and relatively long engagements, 12 or more months, much more prevalent among the happily married.[7]

TABLE 20 LENGTH OF ENGAGEMENT
AND CHANCES FOR HAPPINESS IN MARRIAGE
AS REVEALED BY STUDIES OF MARRIED COUPLES

Adjustment in marriage	Terman [a] 792 couples	Burgess-Cottrell [b] 526 couples	Landis [c] 544 couples
Poor	Under 6 months	No engagement, or under 9 months	No engagement, or under 6 months
Good	6 months-4 years	9-23 months	6-23 months
Excellent	5 years and up	2 years and up	2 years and up

[a] Terman, *Psychological Factors in Marital Happiness*, p. 199.
[b] Burgess and Cottrell, *Predicting Success or Failure in Marriage*, p. 168.
[c] 544 student couples studied at Michigan State University in 1947.

It might be expected that short acquaintances would be followed by long engagements, but the opposite seems to be true. Those who are acquainted the longest before engagement tend to have the longest engagements.[8] The type of person who will take time for courtship may also take time to approach marriage after the engagement. This willingness to proceed carefully is part of the explanation for the greater success of marriages following longer engagements.

Another factor in the success of marriages following longer engagements is, of course, the weeding out of the poorer marital risks. Many of the people who were not engaged or who were

[7] Locke, *Predicting Adjustment in Marriage*, pp. 93-94.
[8] Goode, *After Divorce*, p. 80.

engaged for a short time would not have married had they attempted a longer engagement. One study showed that 5 per cent of the applicants for marriage licenses in California failed to return to get their licenses at the end of the three-day waiting period.[9] The additional three days were all the time some of those couples needed in order to realize that they did not wish to marry each other.

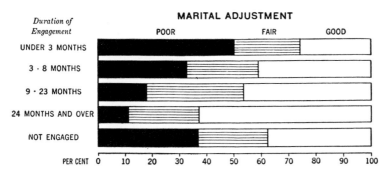

Fig. 5I DURATION OF ENGAGEMENT AND MARITAL ADJUSTMENT. Long engagements often weed out couples who would not make a go of marriage. Better a broken engagement than a broken marriage. From Ernest W. Burgess and Leonard S. Cottrell, *Predicting Success or Failure in Marriage,* p. 168. Englewood Cliffs, N. J.: Prentice-Hall, Inc., 1939.

Certainly, time alone is not the crucial factor. But the time factor may be an indicator of other elements in the engagement. Research findings probably mean that most people do need more than a few weeks or months to achieve certain growth tasks which are important functions of the engagement period. Time is needed for two people to become able to understand accurately each other's attitudes and viewpoints, since communication is not accomplished by words alone. For example, on such matters as feelings about having children a couple may have wide differ-

[9] Paul Popenoe, *Modern Marriage,* p. 176. New York: The Macmillan Company, 1940.

ences in attitudes. In a short engagement, the subject of having children may be touched on, if at all, in a romantic, idealized way—"when we are married and have children." The one who hopes to have several children and who especially values family life with children may just assume that the other feels the same. But sometimes as time passes he or she may discover that the real attitudes of the fiancé are not in agreement here at all. In a longer engagement such attitudes are more likely to come out. The couple may then be able to talk over their feelings in a way that amounts to true communication. They may reach a compromise in their attitudes and so be able to go into marriage with an understanding that will help them to avoid shock or disillusionment after marriage, even though they do not feel exactly the same on such an important matter. Or, as time passes, their discernment of their real differences in this or in any other area of life may cause them to conclude that they are too far apart to marry happily. In a short engagement the wedding day will come before there has been time enough to think constructively or objectively about values that are mutual or that may be antagonistic.

Of course a couple might be engaged for two or more years during which they merely marked time, so that when they marry their tasks of adjustment will be much the same as those who have had very short engagements. For example: Mrs. B. went to a counselor after six months of marriage. She was disappointed and disillusioned. She explained that their engagement had lasted for almost two years, and remarked, "I always thought that after that long an engagement a marriage couldn't fail. But we hadn't been married more than a few weeks before I saw all kinds of things in him that I never had even thought of. He seems to be a completely different person from the man I was engaged to."

An examination of the facts in this case showed that although the engagement had lasted for almost two years, the couple had actually been together for not more than a total of a month, if all the days they had spent in each other's company were added together. Moreover, most of the times that they had been together had been on special occasions when it was easy for each to show a public face that was attractive to the other. Their true selves had little chance to show, and their association remained on the level of dating, with no real exploration of the attitudes, values, or traits that would be important in their marriage. The wife commented during her talk with the counselor, "I never once saw John before our marriage except when he was dressed in his best and ready to give me his whole attention, and every time he saw me I knew in advance that he was coming and had time to be at my best for him." Clearly this couple went through a relatively long engagement without coming out of a dream world long enough to make any progress at building the basis for a sound relationship.

So, while all the evidence shows that engagements are more likely to lead to successful marriage if they are fairly long, an important consideration is what use a couple makes of the time during which they are engaged. Our discussion of the purposes and some of the problems of the engagement period includes the pinned stage for those on campuses with that custom. Some of the purposes of engagement may be achieved while a couple are pinned, before the engagement is official; in these cases, the engagement need not be so long as where there is no pinning interim.

Recognizing danger signals

Interviews with many engaged couples have revealed that for some couples danger signals begin to fly after they become engaged; many things in their relationship and in their interaction with each other and with each other's family are clear warnings that there is danger of unhappiness and maladjustment if they marry. Quite often people do not recognize these danger signals for what they are.

John and Barbara met as students at a west coast school, began dating in April and were engaged in October. Just before Christmas John discussed his engagement with a counselor. He said, "I have often had a feeling during our engagement that we might be talking at cross-purposes when we discuss plans for the future. Usually she expresses verbal agreement with my ideas about the kind of life I'd like for us to have, then after I leave her, I feel uncertain. It seems that whenever we talk about something that means a lot to me, I end up with the feeling that none of my ideas or thoughts look very good when brought out into the open. Since we've been engaged I seem to have been discarding as impractical or rather silly, a great many of the hopes I've always had for the future. I realize it's important to be practical but I've always felt that there are some things that can't be judged or decided on the basis of strictly a dollars-and-cents value. Maybe I'm just worrying over nothing or only having a small case of pre-wedding jitters."

John visited Barbara's home in the east for the Christmas holidays and met her family for the first time. Barbara had told him that they were a happy family. During his visit in her home he noticed that her mother was extremely dominating; the 28-year-old brother, who was unmarried and living at home, and the father took orders constantly from the mother, but not without showing antagonism. Barbara's two older sisters, aged 26 and 30, came for Christmas and he learned for the first time that they were both divorced. The whole family had the habit of making jokes at each other's expense, or of openly disparaging each other with no pretense of humor. John came from a family who were mutually supportive toward each other, and he found himself very uncomfortable in the atmosphere of his fiancée's home.

He had known that Barbara had moody spells, but he was now bothered by a similarity between some of her moods and the behavior he observed in her unhappy brother and sisters.

He noticed also that the family valued everything in terms of money. They frankly appraised the cost of Christmas gifts they received, and he realized that the gift he had spent so much careful thought choosing for Barbara, embarrassed her before her family because it was clearly less expensive than some of those exchanged by other members of the family. He began to remember his vague feelings of disappointment on past occasions when he had given her small gifts that were inexpensive or contrived, but that he thought had special significance.

If John had not visited Barbara's family he probably would not have recognized the danger signals indicating that, between him and Barbara, a very great difference existed in conceptions of happiness, in life goals, and in values that make life worth while.

If elements exist in the personalities of two people or in their relationship that would make the success of their marriage extremely difficult or impossible, almost always danger signals are showing. The problem is to recognize such danger signals for what they are.

The discussion below of engagement as a bridge to marriage points out matters that can serve as guides to recognizing danger signals. Vague feelings of uneasiness or disappointment in relation to efforts to grow together in some of the areas of life during engagement may call attention to the presence of danger signals.

Engagement as a bridge to successful marriage

Establishing the habit of talking things over. The habit of talking things over so that the two can understand each other's views and feelings is essential in a successful marriage. This habit may become well established, if people are aware of its importance, during the engagement. Some people communicate more easily than others; they are able to express themselves in ways that are understood and they can draw out expression of feelings and attitudes from others. Other people have difficulty revealing themselves even to those close to them. Some couples may avoid even talking about subjects or areas of life on which they suspect that they do not understand each other or know each other's true feelings. It is worth while for the engaged couple to talk over all the different parts of life that will be important to them in marriage.

Money matters. For example, the handling of money is often a focal point of friction with married couples. An engaged couple needs to discuss frankly their attitudes about money,

What does each one consider worth sacrificing and saving for? Do they agree? How important does each feel it is to have *enough* money, and what is "enough"? In their two parent families how was money handled? Does each think his family had the "right" views about money? Was there friction over money in the parent families? If so, can the engaged couple figure out how the friction might have been avoided or resolved? What ideas do they have about how they will handle such problems that might arise in their marriage?

There is tremendous value for engaged couples in looking at such potential problem areas of life before they are married. At this time in some ways the questions are merely interesting topics for discussion, yet by discussing them frankly viewpoints can be understood and progress made toward mutually satisfactory viewpoints. If such things are not discussed, or if they are only briefly touched upon and then dropped and avoided because the two cannot talk about them freely without creating tension or uncertainty, real difficulties may arise after marriage. After marriage, for most people, money and its use is no longer merely an interesting subject for discussion. It is a matter to be reckoned with. The better they know and understand ahead of time each other's attitudes and habits relative to the use of money the easier this area of their married life will be. It can come as a serious shock to a newly married person to discover that the mate is "extravagant" or "wasteful" or "miserly" or "doesn't have the slightest idea of the value of a dollar"—if financial matters have not been considered during engagement.

Having children. Engaged couples also need to discuss their feelings about children and their conceptions of themselves as future parents. In our study of student attitudes, a fifth of the

---

Fig. 52 ENGAGEMENT IS A TIME FOR GROWING TOGETHER IN UNDERSTANDING AS WELL AS A TIME TO DETERMINE WHETHER THE RELATIONSHIP HAS ALL THE ELEMENTS NECESSARY FOR SUCCESS IN MARRIAGE. Courtesy of *California Monthly*.

students said they would refuse to marry anyone who did not want to have children. A happy marriage, to them, includes children as an essential to completeness. However, a person who feels this way may take it for granted that all other young people feel the same, especially the one he or she loves. Sometimes one partner will avoid discussing the subject because of resistance to the whole idea and an unwillingness to reveal attitudes that might come between the two as an engaged pair. Nevertheless, the subject is one that should be frankly discussed.

Sex and contraception. Attitudes toward the place of sex in marriage, and beliefs or expectations about birth-control need to be compared. This is especially true in marriages of mixed religious faiths, but applies also to nonmixed marriages. If the couple differs on the use of contraceptives in marriage, or if their views about the place of sex in marriage differ greatly, their facing these differences during engagement gives them a chance to try, rationally, to find a common ground of agreement. They may be able to understand and accept each other's views, or to face it if they cannot harmonize their attitudes. Such differences are never any easier to settle after marriage than before; in fact they may be harder to resolve afterwards because of emotional pressures and frustrations that may develop when one feels boxed-in, caught in a marriage situation that seems unresolvable.

It is important for a couple to make serious efforts to communicate with each other about such matters before confronting the actual circumstances. If one partner looks on sex as a wholesome, happy part of marriage, while the other is embarrassed or repelled by the idea of the sex phase of marriage, the couple should recognize the danger of conflict in their future relationship. Such a difference means that greater effort must be made to reach a satisfactory relationship in marriage. An engaged couple, by talking over such areas of difference, can either make progress toward altering and harmonizing their differences, or they can face the question of whether they are well enough in harmony to go ahead into marriage.

Life goals and values. Couples need to compare their standards of what things are worth striving for in life. The woman whose greatest wish is to live in her home town among people she has always known may not find happiness married to a man who would gladly move from place to place if that seemed desirable in order to succeed in a chosen occupation. And he, in turn, might feel hindered and held back if it became necessary for them to live permanently in one place in order to keep his wife happy. However, such a difference need not be so great a problem if it is faced ahead of time rather than coming as a shock after marriage.

Feelings and beliefs about religion need to be shared and understood. The person who values an active religious life may be disappointed and unhappy if married to one disinterested in religion.

Differing attitudes on the value of an education may create problems unless both have completed their education before marriage. It is hard for a young couple to weather student life as a married couple if either one feels that the required sacrifices are unwarranted.

The parent families and roles. Engaged couples also need to take a candid look at their two parent families in the matter of the roles played by the parents. Is the father the traditionally dominant head of the house in one family, while in the other the mother dominates? Are both parent families similar in that they are father-dominated, mother-dominated, or relatively equalitarian in roles? The kinds of masculine-feminine roles played in the parent families will be a factor in the new marriage. It need not be a disrupting factor, but it will definitely be a factor. During engagement it is quite easy to look at the parent families objectively and try to figure out what kinds of roles each one of the engaged pair would be most likely to expect to play if no special thought were given to the matter. Just discussing such a subject and exploring different kinds of attitudes and different kinds of roles that each might be capable of playing in marriage will increase the likelihood that the two can be comfortable in whatever role pattern they eventually create in their own marriage.

Coitus during engagement

One of the problems of a longer engagement may be coping with sex impulses. Premarital intercourse is not good preparation for satisfactory sex relationships in marriage. This subject has been explored in an earlier chapter. Among the strongest reasons for avoiding indulgence in sex relations during engagement is the fact that such indulgence can so easily skew the total association of a couple. Their enjoyment of sex is likely to block them from exploring and evaluating the many other facets of their interaction, all of which are of as much importance to their future life in marriage.

How the question of coitus during engagement is handled by a couple is often predictive of the level of their success in marriage. If one partner is persistent in wanting to indulge in coitus during engagement in spite of the reluctance of the other, especially if the reluctance is based on conscientious beliefs or on a desire to reserve complete sexual indulgence until after marriage, a difference in values and in basic attitudes is apparent. Such persistence, usually on the part of the man, may indicate that an exploitative pattern exists in the relationship. The persistent one is concerned chiefly with his or her own personal gratification and wishes, and has little understanding of or regard for the feelings, beliefs, or needs of the other. Such attitudes are not conducive to happiness in marriage. Arguments or conflicting views about coitus during engagement may need to be recognized as danger signals.

Confessing the past

At some time during engagement one may feel that he must confess the past—if there is anything to confess. What rule should be followed when the urge comes to tell all? One should consider four questions before doing any confessing: (1) *Why* do I feel that I must tell? (2) Will our marriage be happier if I do tell? (3) Will my fiancé(e) be happier if I tell? (4) If I must tell, is the fiancé(e) the best person to tell it to?

If a person will analyze his motives carefully, he may find that he has one of two motives for wishing to confess. He may simply want the pleasure of reliving or exhibiting the past, without realizing that an element of self-aggrandizement is involved in the confessing. On the other hand the urge to confess past incidents or experiences may arise from inner pressures or guilt feelings, which might be less burdensome if they were shared with another. Neither of those motives is sufficient reason for telling regrettable past experiences to the fiancé(e). Confessions made for no other reason than those may only cause unhappiness for the loved one, and may raise doubts and questions that will have an adverse effect on the happiness of the marriage. The very confessing of relatively insignificant past events, may exaggerate the importance of the events out of all proportion. If the urge to relieve guilt feelings by confessing is strong, the confession might better be made to someone other than the fiancé(e). A minister, priest, or marriage counselor who can listen and remain wisely silent and undisturbed, or who is capable of giving wise counsel, would be a better choice.

However, there are certain things which it is necessary to tell to the fiancé(e). In general things ought to be told that would, if known, lead to a better relationship in the marriage, or those that, if found out later, would make trouble in marriage. If either member of the couple has had venereal disease, has had an illegitimate child, has been married before, or has a prison record, the mate should know about it before marriage. These matters could seriously affect the marriage, and their effect might be far more damaging if they were unknown to the spouse until after marriage. Venereal disease can be cured, but the person who marries someone who has had a venereal disease has a right to evidence that a permanent cure has been effected. Previous parenthood, or a former marriage, or a prison record are things that can never be completely buried in the past. Therefore the future wife or husband must be told of these things if they exist.

TABLE 21 PERCENTAGE OF 200 ENGAGED MEN AND 200 ENGAGED WOMEN REPORTING PAST EXPERIENCES OR FACTS IN FAMILY BACKGROUND AND THE PERCENTAGE WHO TOLD FIANCÉ(E) ABOUT THESE FACTS *

	Men		Women	
Experiences or facts	In background	Told fiancée	In background	Told fiancé
Dating history with others	96.0%	96.0%	93.0%	100.0%
Necking experience with others	84.0	73.0	73.0	71.0
Petting experience with others	62.0	63.0	42.0	58.0
Premarital sex relations	33.0	74.0	12.0	67.0
Personality faults	51.0	100.0	59.0	100.0
Serious problems in family	30.0	95.0	43.0	100.0
Insanity in the family	5.0	90.0	5.0	78.0
Personal crimes	7.0	86.0	3.0	83.0
Crime in the family	3.0	83.0	3.0	67.0
A nervous breakdown	2.5	100.0	2.0	100.0
Suspected bad heredity	2.0	100.0	2.0	100.0
Having been married before	2.5	100.0	.5	100.0
Having had venereal disease	1.5	68.0	.5	50.0
Child out of wedlock	.5	100.0	1.0	100.0

* Findings from study of 200 engagements at the University of California in 1957.

The premarital examination

It is advisable to have a premarital examination from a competent physician during the engagement. Many states now require an examination for venereal disease before a marriage license can be obtained. This law is important in helping to prevent the spread of venereal disease. A premarital examination should provide the following: (1) a complete physical examination for both, (2) a pelvic examination of the female, (3) attention to diseases or defects that might be hereditary, (4) an opportunity to secure reliable contraceptive information if it is desired, (5) a blood test, and (6) a chance to ask questions about sex.

People living in parts of the country where special counseling services have been established should take advantage of them. Some counseling services provide a series of tests to determine the chances for success in marriage and to help couples approach marriage intelligently.

A physical check-up will determine the couple's state of health and will reveal any diseases or defects needing medical attention or any conditions that might hinder coitus. If there has been mental disease in either family, the couple will wish to be reassured concerning types of mental difficulty that cannot be passed on through heredity. For couples who do not plan to have children during the first year of marriage, it is important to secure reliable birth-control information. The most generally satisfactory contraceptives necessitate examination by a physician and instruction from him.

Young people usually have questions they would like to ask about sex in marriage. Here the doctor may not be able to give much help. The doctor has been trained in the physical phases of sex functioning; but sex functioning is also psychological and many doctors are not in a position to advise on this important aspect of the subject. However, doctors who have made a study of the psychology of sex and who are interested in this phase of preparation for marriage may be good sources of information.

If there is a Planned Parenthood Clinic in the community, that is usually one of the best places to go for the premarital examination. The doctors working with Planned Parenthood have a special interest in the questions confronting couples approaching marriage. Planned Parenthood centers prefer that couples come to the center at least a month before the wedding date, since the premarital examination and consultations should be completed before the last hurried days preceding the wedding.

Parental approval and planning the wedding

Marriages that are planned and made public have a better chance than those that are secret. Sometimes, when parents are opposed to the marriage, the young people see elopement as their only choice. In a study of 738 elopements, Popenoe found that 46 per cent were caused by parental opposition.[10] A smaller percentage of these marriages turned out happily than of marriages that had parental approval. When "economy" was the motive for the elopement, 63 per cent turned out happily; 60 per cent when "avoidance of publicity," 45 per cent when "parental objection," and 33 per cent when "pregnancy" was the motive. If strong parental opposition exists, the couple should seriously consider whether the reasons for the opposition are valid. If they decide to marry in spite of opposition, they should make every effort to secure the co-operation of the families before the marriage. Often the parents will consent when they see that the young people are determined to marry. If the opposition continues, however, the marriage is handicapped. Family ties of affection are not easily broken, and there is likely to be an emotional reaction either of antagonism toward the parents or unhappiness on the part of the couple who marry despite opposition.

In studying divorced and happily married couples, Locke found parental approval of the prospective mate closely associated with marital happiness and parental disapproval closely associated with marital maladjustment.[11]

Traditionally, the bride plans and pays for the wedding and the groom plans and pays for the honeymoon. In practice, many

---

[10] Popenoe, *op. cit.*, pp. 222-227.
[11] Locke, *Predicting Adjustment in Marriage*, p. 118.

Fig. 53 "... Steady now ... Easy ... Almost there ... Courage ..." By permission, Ted Key and *The Saturday Evening Post.*

such customs are not rigidly followed. Frequently the bride and groom together plan both the wedding and the honeymoon. It would be unwise for any couple to go heavily into debt for the wedding and the honeymoon. Their total bill for the marriage should be in keeping with the income they will have after they are married.

Some ministers like to cooperate in planning church weddings, and because of their experience they can often give helpful suggestions. Whether the wedding is to be large and pretentious or small and simple will depend on the wishes of the pair and their economic level. From the viewpoint of marital success, the important thing is that the wedding marks a change in status which should be looked upon as permanent.

309

The honeymoon

The function of the honeymoon is to give the couple a chance to settle into their new status as a married couple, unhindered by the presence of interested friends and relatives. The absence of any observing friend or relative allows them to express their affection for each other freely, without self-consciousness. On the honeymoon, the husband and wife can begin to form the habits of affectionate companionship that will be basic to their whole married life.

Young people are sometimes disappointed and disillusioned because they approach the honeymoon unaware of its broad, general function, and believing that it will be chiefly a time of perfect sex fulfillment. But sex fulfillment may not be full and complete during the honeymoon. If conditions are ideal, the couple's first attempts at sexual union may be all that they had anticipated. But most couples require time and experience in order to achieve complete and mutually satisfactory sexual response. The honeymoon is the beginning of their sex life, as well as of their companionship as a married couple. But it is only the beginning. They may need weeks or months of living together before their sex experience becomes mutually satisfying—something they may have thought would come automatically as a part of the honeymoon.

The establishment of a pattern of understanding cooperation and unselfish consideration for each other in all their relationships is more important than complete sexual satisfaction for either one on the honeymoon.

In setting the wedding date, girls usually try to plan so that they will not be menstruating during the honeymoon. It is well to plan that way so that conditions may be as ideal as possible for the beginning of sex life in marriage. But many girls find that the added strain of the last few days or weeks preceding the wedding may cause menstruation to be delayed until the relaxation that comes with the honeymoon.

If the honeymoon is to serve its function, a few points must be considered when it is planned:

1. Whether the time is to be only a day or two or much longer, the plans should provide for privacy and anonymity. Most newly married couples want only to be Mr. and Mrs._____, inconspicuous in a world of married people. Anonymity may be found in a hotel in the city or a cottage in the country, on a lake or ocean cruise, or hiking in the mountains. The important consideration is that the couple go where no one knows them.

2. The honeymoon should provide freedom from fatigue and nervous tension. Strenuous travel schedules should be avoided. If a couple tries to cover a predetermined amount of territory and to make sure that they miss nothing of educational or cultural value, they may find themselves working so hard at having a wedding trip that the purpose of the honeymoon is defeated.

3. The kind of plans made should depend upon what activities both can enjoy. If they like to see and do the things that are offered by a large city, they may choose to spend their honeymoon in that way. If they are both enthusiastic campers or if they enjoy hiking or fishing, they may plan a honeymoon of that type. The point is that the honeymoon is a time for them to enjoy each other in an environment that allows them to be themselves and to relax in each other's company.

4. The cost of the honeymoon should be kept well within what they can afford, so that they will be free from financial pressure or worry.

If a couple has made good use of the period of their engagement, the engagement will have served its basic purposes, and a sturdy bridge to marriage will have been built. In such cases, the honeymoon is not likely to offer shocks or unanticipated discoveries. Before the wedding, the two will have come to know each other so well and will have built so much understanding between them that the honeymoon can be a relaxed and happy beginning to their married living.

OUTLINE FOR SELF-STUDY:
TO ASSESS A RELATIONSHIP

If you are engaged or about to be engaged think your way through the following questions and attempt to evaluate your relationship and its potential for success if you marry. (If you are not seriously dating now, apply these points to a dating relationship or love affair you have had in the past. Can you see why the relationship did not survive?)

I. Quarreling in your relationship

Do you quarrel? How often? How intense are the quarrels? Is your quarreling becoming less frequent or more frequent? Have quarrels resulted in blocking off certain touchy issues that are no longer discussed? Have you taken positions in a quarrel, which you find yourself defending in later quarrels? Have some of the quarrels made for a better understanding and more accepting attitudes between you?

II. Your attitudes toward your engagement

Have you ever broken or considered breaking this engagement? How many times? Are you ever bothered by doubts about whether you should go on with your plans? Are you proud and happy about your engagement, confident and secure in your feelings about the future? What attitudes toward your engagement are you aware of among your friends and family? Are you proud of your fiancé(e) around your friends and family? Do you feel uncomfortably apologetic or feel that you must make excuses for things he says or does?

III. Your respect for each other

Do you respect this person and all that he or she represents? In judgment? Ideals? Goals in life? Moral standards? Habits? Vocational choice? Religion? Does your basic respect for all that he or she is enable you to act in ways that make your fiancé(e) feel supported and built up? In turn, does your fiancé(e) respect you and make you feel valued and appreciated for all that you are? Do you respect his or her friends and family? Do you feel that they accept you and think well of you? If you do not, can you weigh honestly the basis of the nonacceptance and determine whether serious differences exist betwen you?

IV. Decision making in your relationship

Think about the pattern of decision making between you. How do you arrive at decisions? Does one tend to have the major voice in decisions, or do you talk things over and decide together? Do you usually feel satisfied about the wisdom of decisions you have made together, afterwards, when you are not with your fiancé(e)? If the present pattern of decision making continues in your marriage, will you both be happy and satisfied with it?

V. *Your confidence in each other's ability to cope with life*

Do you ever feel that you are the victim when your fiancé(e) has a bad day? Do either of you take out unpleasant feelings or aggressions on your friends or family, or do you resort to escapes such as moodiness, brooding, temper spells, reckless driving, or excessive drinking? If your fiancé(e) acts in any of these ways, how do you react now? Can you live comfortably with this pattern? Will you feel the same about it later if the two of you marry and have children to bring up?

VI. *Consider your total relationship*

A love affair may be based on one or two satisfying elements, such as a strong mutual interest in music, sports, or religion, or on a compelling physical attraction. A broader basis is necessary for success in marriage. How many satisfying areas of mutuality do you have? Are there things you cannot talk to each other about because of lack of mutual interest, antagonistic viewpoints, or because certain doubts cause you to block off discussing the topic?

Does the relationship bring out the best in you? How do you feel after you have been together? Elated? Confident? Ambitious? Uncertain? Moody? Depressed?

Have you tried to get each other to change many ways?

Are you more comfortable with each other than with anyone else? Can you be yourself happily in this relationship without strain?

As you look at all aspects of your association with each other—your feelings about each other and about your engagement, your habitual ways of treating each other, your agreement or disagreement on important matters, your ability to talk over and share together all that matters to each of you—can you conclude that your engagement or relationship is a dependable bridge to successful marriage?

Review questions

1. What relationship is there between length of acquaintance and happiness in marriage?
2. What does the wearing of a fraternity pin at your school mean? Are you certain?
3. What is the purpose of the engagement period today? How does this differ from the past?

4. How permanent are engagements today?

5. What are common reasons for breaking engagements?

6. What are some of the most common trends in courtship as represented by graphs?

7. Does the research on broken engagements give encouragement to those suffering with broken hearts? Discuss. Apply this same principle to other emotional crises.

8. What are some common reactions to the frustration which comes with the breaking of an engagement?

9. What should the attitude of the wounded partner be when an engagement is broken?

10. Why are long engagements predictive of success in marriage?

11. Cite some subjects that should be discussed during the engagement period.

12. Give reasons for or against confessing the past.

13. What questions should a person ask himself before confessing his past?

14. Give the chief reasons for a premarital examination.

15. Are elopements as happy as conventional marriages? Why?

16. What points should be considered in planning the wedding and the honeymoon?

Projects and activities

1. As a class, make a survey of student opinion on "being pinned" on your campus to determine what students think it means. Summarize and report to the class.

2. Let each student consult two other students who have broken an engagement to find out just why the engagements were broken. Summarize the class findings.

3. Study several movies to see what pattern of behavior is depicted when the hero or heroine is frustrated in love.

Films

Are You Ready for Marriage? A young couple who want very much to get married discover what it takes to be ready for marriage through discussions with a counselor. Coronet Instructional Films. 15 minutes, sound.

The Meaning of Engagement. Shows engagement as a period of developing psychological unity, learning to know each other, and developing plans for the future. Coronet Instructional Films, 15 minutes, sound.

Suggested readings

Becker, Howard, and Reuben Hill, eds., *Family, Marriage, and Parenthood*. Boston: D. C. Heath and Company, 1955. Ch. IX, "The Engagement."

Bowman, Henry A., *Marriage for Moderns*. New York: McGraw-Hill Book Company, Inc., 1954. Ch. IX, "Wedding and Honeymoon."

Burgess, Ernest W., and Paul Wallin, *Engagement and Marriage*. Chicago: J. B. Lippincott Company, 1953. Entire book, but especially Chs. V through VIII.

Butterfield, Oliver M., *Planning for Marriage*. Princeton: D. Van Nostrand Company, Inc., 1956. Ch. V, "Engagement."

Cavan, Ruth Shonle, *The American Family*. New York: Thomas Y. Crowell Company, 1953. Ch. X, "Courtship and Engagement."

Duvall, Evelyn M., and Reuben Hill, *When You Marry*. Boston: D. C. Heath and Company, Revised 1953. Ch. IX, "Wedding Plans."

Landis, Judson T., and Mary G. Landis, eds., *Readings in Marriage and the Family*. Englewood Cliffs, N. J.: Prentice-Hall, Inc., 1952. Part V, Reading 1, "Marriage Adjustment and Engagement Adjustment," Ernest W. Burgess and Paul Wallin; Reading 2, "Personality and Marriage Adjustment," Robert F. Winch; Reading 3, "A Study of 738 Elopements," Paul Popenoe. Part VI, Reading 1, "Of Weddings," Frank H. Ferris; Readings 2 and 3, "A Hindu Marriage in Bengal," and "A Hindu Wife," D. N. Mitra.

Peterson, James A., *Education for Marriage*. New York: Charles Scribner's Sons, 1956. Ch. X, "The Engagement Period."

Waller, Willard, *The Family* (Revised by Reuben Hill). New York: The Dryden Press, 1951. Ch. XII, "The Engagement."

Problem of regulation

Marriage is a civil contract

Eugenic regulations

Age for marriage

Marriage between relatives

Miscegenetic regulations

Marriage license

Waiting period

Who is qualified to perform marriages

Legal Control of Marriage

Validity of marriage

Common-law marriage

Void and voidable marriages

Legitimacy of children of annulled marriages

Legal status of illegitimates

The state has a stake in every marriage, and exercises control over the making and keeping of marriage contracts through legal requirements and restrictions. The state's basic interest is in the children who may result from marriage, but it is also concerned with the rights and responsibilities of the individuals who marry. Both men and women are guaranteed privileges and assume obligations when they enter into a marriage contract. The children of legal marriages are legitimate and have clearly defined inheritance rights. The laws also attempt to guarantee the children a stable environment for growth. Thus it is necessary to regulate who may marry and to exercise control over the dissolution of marriages.

Marriage laws, like other laws, are designed to protect the interests of both the individual and society. The individual yields a measure of personal freedom for the good of society and is compensated by guarantees of personal security and social stability.

. . 14 Problem of regulation

Almost everyone agrees that laws governing marriage are necessary. There is much disagreement, however, as to the kind and extent of regulation which will achieve the desired ends. Although it is generally agreed that it is not desirable for the biologically unfit to marry and to reproduce, opinions differ concerning who are the biologically unfit and how to control their relationships. Some believe they should be prevented from marrying; others maintain that preventing their marrying will not prevent their reproducing and that it is better to legalize their

317

union to give their children legitimacy. Still others advocate permitting the biologically unfit to marry if they first submit to a sterilization operation.

It is agreed that young people should not marry before reaching a mature stage of development, yet there is no agreement on when people are mature enough to marry. Some state laws permit marriages of boys 14 years old if they have parental consent; other states set the age at 18. Girls may be legally married in some states at 12; in others they are not legally old enough until they reach 16 or 18. Where the age for legal marriage is low, the belief is that a high age requirement would promote sexual promiscuity. In the states where the age requirement is high, the prevailing attitude of the legislators is that, even though more promiscuity may result among those below the legal age for marriage, a higher age requirement makes for more stable marriages and so is best for the individual and for society.

It is common for states to accept marriages as valid even though they do not conform to legal requirements, provided that no one takes action to have such marriages annulled. Those who have the responsibility for administering the marriage laws differ about how far to go in permitting the individual's romantic impulses to take precedence over the established regulations. The problem is to exercise enough regulation to achieve desired ends, but not so much that people will flout the laws, follow their own desires, and form illegal unions.

Marriage laws are in the hands of the separate states, and in attempts to solve the problem of effective control for the good of society, a great variety of laws have been enacted. The result has been confusion. There are 48 different sets of marriage and divorce regulations, since the states have acted quite independently of each other.

Baber points out that a man, by traveling 15 miles to get into three different states, would be considered a married man in one state, a single man in another, and a bigamist in the third.[1] The courts have given contradictory decisions on the legality of divorces granted in one state to citizens of another state. In a test case in 1948, the Supreme Court ruled that the Massachusetts courts erred when they declared divorces invalid that were obtained in Florida and Nevada, and that each state must give full faith and credit to the official acts of other states. Lawmakers are showing an increasing awareness of the complications arising because of the diverse laws, and the present tendency is toward greater uniformity.

We will look at some of the more common regulations concerning marriage. In some cases, the laws of Michigan will be quoted, not because they are "model laws" but because they include most of the regulations found in other states, and because the reader will gain a better understanding of the nature of some of the marriage regulations if specific laws are quoted. The student who is interested in the marriage laws in his own state should read Vernier's *American Family Laws*. This five-volume work, with its supplement, details the marriage regulations in the 48 states, Alaska, Hawaii, and Washington, D.C.

Marriage is a civil contract

Marriage laws specify that marriage is a civil contract between two individuals. The marriage contract differs from ordinary contracts in that (1) it cannot be rescinded or its fundamental terms changed by agreement between the two parties; (2) it results in a *status;* (3) it merges the legal identity of the parties; (4) the tests of capacity differ from those applied to ordinary contracts (in other words, those who may not bind themselves by ordinary contracts may make a valid marriage).[2] Although a

[1] Ray E. Baber, *Marriage and the Family*, p. 75. New York: McGraw-Hill Book Company, Inc., 1953.
[2] Chester G. Vernier, *American Family Laws*, Vol. I, p. 51. Stanford University Press, 1931.

marriage can be entered into easily, it cannot be dissolved by mutual agreement as other civil contracts can be terminated. Society is profoundly interested in the family as an institution, and once the marriage contract is made, society tries to see that the contract is not readily dissolved. To get out of the contract, the individuals involved must go through court procedure.

The important point which makes a marriage contract valid is the consent of the two parties to the agreement. What really marries the couple is their mutual and willing expression of *I do* when they accept each other as husband and wife. The law prescribes a wedding license and someone to officiate, but although both these requirements are met, if one partner has been forced into the marriage by the other, no marriage has taken place, since willing consent was not given by one party to the contract. Coercion or unwillingness on the part of one partner makes the contract void. On the other hand, marriage can take place without either the officiant or the license, if the couple willingly agree to live as husband and wife and do so. This is termed common law marriage and is recognized in many states. The following is an example of a specific law covering the marriage contract:

Michigan 12691. Marriage, as far as its validity in law is concerned, is a civil contract to which the consent of parties capable in law of contracting, is essential.

Contract: Chastity is not a requisite to validity of a marriage and while marriage is, in a very important sense, a contract, it is also a relation governed by rules of public policy, which apply to no mere private agreements. *Intention is the essential ingredient,* as in every other contract, and, when one of the parties, instead of assenting to the contract, positively dissents from it, there can be no legal or valid marriage, although a ceremony is gone through by the officiating minister or magistrate. A contract of marriage cannot be presumed when such presumption would do violence to facts in the case. This section does not make a ceremony essential to validity, and a common law marriage, when shown, binds the parties.

Eugenic regulations

All states have regulations governing the marriage of those who are mentally ill or those whose minds have not developed to an adult stage. People who are not of sound mind cannot make a legal contract of any type, and therefore are incapable of contracting a marriage. Emphasis on this matter is changing, however, so that now the more generally accepted reason for preventing these marriages is the danger that the mentally defective may have defective children. A survey of inmates of the Alabama State School for the Feeble-minded in 1945 revealed the following: 318 inmates had one feeble-minded parent, 325 had two feeble-minded parents, 87 had an insane, hospitalized parent, 15 had a parent in prison, 136 had alcoholic parents, and 46 had syphilitic parents.[3] Three states, Nebraska, South Dakota, and New Hampshire have now amended their laws so that feeble-minded persons may marry if they first undergo a sterilization operation. This is a sound step. For the states to have laws preventing the marriage of mental defectives has accomplished little. In the rare cases where laws preventing mental defectives from marrying are enforced, the mental defectives often have illegitimate children instead of marrying and having legitimate children.

Although all states have some mental requirements for marriage, little is done to enforce these laws. The couple may be required to swear that they are not of unsound mind, but how many mental defectives will state that they are of unsound mind when applying for a marriage license? It is safe to assume that their judgment might be biased.

In 1935, Connecticut passed a new type of venereal disease law, often referred to as the eugenic marriage law. Since 1935 a total of 43 states have passed venereal disease laws. These laws require both men and women to have a physical examination for

[3] Marian S. Olden, "Present Status of Sterilization Legislation in the United States," *Eugenic News* (March, 1946), 10.

TABLE 22   MARRIAGE LAWS (As of January 1, 1958)

State	Minimum marriage age specified in law [a]		Common law marriages are valid	Prohibit marriage of those with transmissible disease in infectious stage	Physical examination and blood test for male and female			Waiting period	
	Male	Female			Date of enactment	[b]	Scope of laboratory test	Before issuance of license	After issuance of license
Alabama	17	14	★	⋯	1947	30 da.	[h]	⋯	⋯
Arizona	18	16	⋯	⋯	1956	⋯	[d]	2 da.	⋯
Arkansas	18	16	⋯	⋯	1953	30 da.	[d]	3 da.	⋯
California	18	16	⋯	⋯	1939	30 da.	[d]	⋯	⋯
Colorado	16	16	★	⋯	1939	30 da.	[f]	⋯	⋯
Connecticut	16	16	⋯	⋯	1935	40 da.	[d]	5 da.	⋯
Delaware	18	16	⋯	★	1947	30 da.	[d]	⋯	★
Florida	18	16	★	⋯	1945	30 da.	[d]	3 da.	⋯
Georgia	17	14	★★	⋯	1949	30 da.	[d]	5 da.[c]	⋯
Idaho	14[e]	12[e]	★★	⋯	1943	30 da.	[d]	⋯	⋯
Illinois	18	16	⋯	⋯	1939	15 da.	[h]	⋯	⋯
Indiana	18	16	★	⋯	1939	30 da.	[d]	⋯	⋯
Iowa	16	14	★★	⋯	1941	20 da.	[d]	⋯	⋯
Kansas	18	16	★★	⋯	1947	30 da.	[d]	3 da.	⋯
Kentucky	16	14	⋯	⋯	1940	15 da.	[h]	⋯	⋯
Louisiana	18	16	⋯	⋯	1954	7 da.	[h]	⋯	⋯
Maine	16	16	★	★	1941	⋯	[d]	5 da.	⋯
Maryland	18	16	⋯	⋯	⋯	⋯	⋯	2 da.	⋯
Massachusetts	18	16	⋯	⋯	1943	30 da.	[d]	5 da.	⋯
Michigan	18	16	★	⋯	1939	30 da.	[h]	5 da.	⋯
Minnesota	16	15	⋯	⋯	1953	⋯	⋯	5 da.	⋯
Mississippi	17	15	★	⋯	1943	15 da.	[d]	3 da.	⋯
Missouri	15	15	★	⋯	1943	⋯	[d]	⋯	⋯
Montana	18	16	★	⋯	1947	20 da.	[d]	⋯	⋯

State	Minimum age, male[a]	Minimum age, female				Year	Waiting period	Disease	Time[b]	[c]
Nebraska	18	16	★			1943	30 da.	(d)		
Nevada	18	16							5 da.	
New Hampshire	14	13				1937	30 da.	(d)	3 da.	
New Jersey	14[e]	12[e]				1938	30 da.	(d)		★
New Mexico	18	16				1957				
New York	16	14				1938[g]	30 da.	(d)	3 da.	★
North Carolina	16	16				1941	30 da.	(d)		
North Dakota	18	15				1939	30 da.	(d)		
Ohio	18	16	★	★		1941	30 da.	(d)	5 da.	
Oklahoma	18	15	★	★		1945	30 da.	(d)		
Oregon	18	15				1937	10 da.	(i)	3 da.	
Pennsylvania	16	16	★			1939	30 da.	(d)	3 da.	
Rhode Island	18	16	★	★	★	1938	40 da.	(d)	1 da.	★
South Carolina	18	14	★	★	★					
South Dakota	18	15	★	★	★	1939	20 da.	(d)	3 da.	
Tennessee	16	16	★			1939	30 da.	(h)		
Texas	16	14	★			1949	15 da.	(d)		
Utah	16	14				1941	30 da.	(f)		
Vermont	18	16				1941	30 da.			★
Virginia	18	16				1940	30 da.	(d)		
Washington	15	15							3 da.	
West Virginia	18	16				1939	30 da.	(d)	3 da.	
Wisconsin	18	15				1939	15 da.	(d)	5 da.	
Wyoming	18	16	★			1943	30 da.	(h)		

a With parental consent.
b Time allowed between date of examination and issuance of license.
c For those under 21 who do not have parental consent.
d Syphilis.
e Common law marriage age.
f Syphilis and other venereal diseases.
g Amended in 1939.
h Venereal diseases.
i Syphilis and gonorrhea.

venereal disease sometime before marriage. The examination is valid for a period of from 7 to 40 days, the time limit varying in different states. If the marriage does not take place within that period, the examination must be repeated. In 32 states the test is for syphilis only, but in the other states the test includes all venereal diseases. The costs of making physical examinations and laboratory tests are borne either by the individual or by the public health authorities. If the tests are not free, some states set the maximum fee a doctor may charge.[4] Today almost all states accept out-of-state laboratory tests for people who are going to another state to be married. (Table 22 gives a summary of the marriage laws in the various states.)

There are few other physical prohibitions to marriage, although it might be desirable to have more. Two states, North Carolina and North Dakota, require a certificate from a licensed physician stating that the man and woman desiring to marry are free from tuberculosis in the infectious or advanced stages. Seventeen states also prohibit the marriage of epileptics.

Age for marriage

States usually set minimum age requirements for marriage—one age which is legal if the parents give their consent, and one age at which young people may marry without the consent of their parents. The most common legal age for marriage with the consent of the parents is 18 for boys and 16 for girls. Twenty states have adopted this standard.

The most common minimum age for marriage without the consent of the parents or guardian is 21 for boys and 18 for girls. Approximately three-fifths of the states have adopted these ages. The next most common age is 21 for both men and women.

[4] For a summary of eugenic marriage laws, see *Premarital Health Examination Legislation, Analysis and Compilation of State Laws.* Washington, D. C.: U. S. Department of Health, Education, and Welfare. Publication No. 383, 1954.

Two states, Idaho and New Jersey, have not passed any laws concerning age for marriage, therefore the common law prevails in these states. The English common law followed the Roman law, which permitted girls of 12 and boys of 14 to marry. States with no laws prohibiting child marriages are not necessarily the states that have the most child marriages. It is not so much the law as the attitude of the people toward child marriages that determines whether children will marry. All the states that have fairly large percentages of child marriages are in the southern section of the United States. There were approximately 8,000 boys and girls of 14 married in the United States in 1950.[5] In the same year there were almost 400,000 boys and girls between the ages of 14 and 17 in the United States who were or had been married; 350,000 of these were girls.[6]

An important reason for discouraging early marriage is that very young people are not likely to be emotionally mature enough to use judgment in selecting mates or to cope with the responsibility of parenthood. Boys who marry early may not be in a position to support families.

It must be remembered that many child marriages are forced because of pregnancy. In most states judges have the right to waive the minimum ages for marriage if the girl is pregnant.

[5] *Sixteenth Census of the United States, 1950,* Vol. II, Parts 1-50. Washington, D. C.: Bureau of the Census.
[6] *Ibid.,* Vol. II, Part 1.

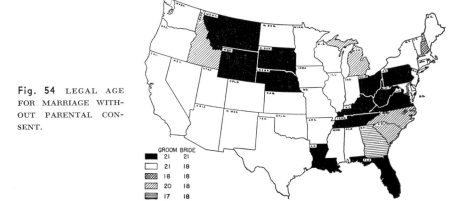

Fig. 54 LEGAL AGE FOR MARRIAGE WITHOUT PARENTAL CONSENT.

Many such marriages do not have a chance for success because of a series of reasons in addition to the immaturity of the couple. In some marriages there is great disparity in age, usually the man is a number of years older than the girl. Recently a man of 70 married a girl of 13. The girl believed herself to be in love with the man and her parents willingly gave their consent to the marriage. That the law does not attempt to judge the results of marriage contracts is shown by the Michigan law which states: "Marriage is a contract which the legislature may not dissolve, though contracted for convenience with unhappy results."

The question arises whether some of the laws make sense. Boys and girls may not vote until the age of 21, yet they may marry several years before this in many states.

Although states prohibit marriages below certain ages, a marriage of people below that age usually stands as valid if it has been consummated. If an interested person takes the case before a court, offers proof of non-age of one or both parties, and asks annulment, the court will probably annul the marriage. Otherwise it stands.

Marriage between relatives

All states prohibit marriages between close blood relatives. Brothers and sisters, fathers and daughters, mothers and sons, grandfathers and granddaughters, grandmothers and grandsons, aunts and nephews, and uncles and nieces, may not marry in any state, with one exception. Rhode Island permits marriage of an uncle and a niece if both are Jewish and if the wedding ceremony is performed by a rabbi. In this matter, Rhode Island suspends its own marriage law in order to accommodate itself to the Jewish law which permits the marriage of an uncle and a niece but not of an aunt and a nephew. The next most common prohibitions against marriages of consanguinity are that first cousins and brothers and sisters of half blood may not marry. Both prohibitions are found in 29 states. Only six states prohibit the marriage of second cousins.[7] Although many states do not permit first cousins to marry within their borders, a number of them do recognize the marriages of first cousins who go to another state to marry and then return to their home state to live. This policy seems inconsistent, but it is commonly followed by states in order to prevent confusion and to guarantee the legitimacy of children born of such marriages.

The strongest objection to marriage of close blood relatives is the incest taboo. However, there is a biological reason for opposing consanguineous marriage, since relatives are more likely to carry the same hereditary defects in their germ plasm. If marriage takes place between closely related people, defects are more likely to show up in the children, who can inherit the traits from both sides of the family. In animal breeding it is common to "line breed" to build up a particular stock. In line breeding, mothers and sons and fathers and daughters are mated. The principle is that superior stock produces superior stock. In stock breeding, the defective strains have been eliminated so that mating of blood relatives does not present the risk that it does in human mating. In humans it is impossible to eliminate the undesirable strain. If first cousins were of the best hereditary stock, from a biological point of view first-cousin marriage would be desirable.

The incest taboo is carried to an unreasonable and illogical extreme in the laws prohibiting marriage because of affinity. There is no biological reason why in-laws or step-relatives should not marry. In Michigan, the law goes so far as to say a man may not marry his stepmother or his wife's grandmother, and goes on to include every possible relative-in-law or step-relative among those an individual may not legally marry. Surely there is no more valid basis for objection to a man's marrying his former wife's grandmother, if he wishes to do so, than to his marrying any other grandmother. Only seven other states have all the

[7] Indiana, Minnesota, Nevada, Ohio, Washington, and Wisconsin.

prohibitions found in the Michigan law.[8] Twenty-six states have no regulations at all on marriages of affinity. The most common regulations are those prohibiting the marriages of step-parents to stepchildren (23 states), parents-in-law to sons- and daughters-in-law (20 states), a man or a woman to granddaughter-in-law or grandson-in-law (18 states).[9] All these prohibitions, when considered objectively, seem to have no reasonable basis. They are simply based on misunderstanding of blood relationship and on the general aversion to incest.

Miscegenetic regulations

Interracial marriages are forbidden in 30 states. The intermarriage of Negroes and whites is more likely to be prohibited in the southern states and the intermarriage of whites and Mongolians in the western states. The following states have no regulation concerning miscegenetic marriages: California, Connecticut, Illinois, Iowa, Kansas, Massachusetts, Michigan, Minnesota, New Hampshire, New Jersey, New Mexico, New York, Pennsylvania, Rhode Island, Vermont, Washington, and Wisconsin.[10]

The following states prohibit marriages of whites with Negroes of one-eighth Negro blood: Florida, Indiana, Mississippi, Missouri, Nebraska, North Dakota, and Texas. Alabama imposes a penalty of from two to seven years in prison for the marriage of a white person to a person of Negro descent.[11]

California's law against interracial marriages was declared unconstitutional in 1948 when a Mexican woman and a Negro man who were refused a marriage license appealed to the courts for a ruling. The court declared the law unconstitutional for several reasons, among them the following: (1) A marriage contract is a fundamental right of free men. (2) Marriage is the right

---

[8] Kentucky, Maine, Maryland, Massachusetts, Rhode Island, South Carolina, and Vermont.
[9] Vernier, *op. cit.*, pp. 183-184.
[10] Vernier, *op. cit.*, pp. 204-208.
[11] *Ibid.*

of individuals and not of special groups. (3) Legislative control of marriage must be based on proved peril to the parties involved or to the state. (4) The law discriminates because of race or color. (5) The law is not meeting a definite need. Since both parties applying for the license were Catholic, they declared that their religious freedom was hampered by the law because they could receive all the sacraments except that of marriage.

J. H. Burma [12] reports that in the two and one-half years following the repeal of the California law, Los Angeles County had 445 marriages between whites and members of other races. In three out of four cases the wife was white and the husband Oriental or Negro. He estimates that only one-half of one per cent of all marriages in Los Angeles County are interracial.

Although interracial marriages are permitted in many states, few interracial marriages actually take place, because of social pressure. It is recognized that often the parties to a miscegenetic union are ostracized by both racial groups.

Biologically there is no reason why the races should not intermarry but the pressure of social attitudes makes it difficult for these marriages to be happy, and the arrival of children presents additional problems. If no stigma were attached to interracial marriage, then no race problem would exist, since the acceptance of biological fusion represents complete acceptance of a minority group. In the United States so much stigma is still attached to such marriages that those interested in successful and happy marriages cannot but discourage them.

Marriage license

All states have adopted the system of requiring a license in order to keep records of marriages. Although their laws require licenses, many states recognize marriages without a license. As we

[12] John H. Burma, "Research Note on the Measurement of Interracial Marriages," *American Journal of Sociology,* 57:6 (May, 1952), 587-589.

have pointed out earlier, it is not the license that marries the couple, and almost half of the states still recognize common law marriage, which takes place without a marriage license. Quakers and some other religious groups are exempted from getting marriage licenses because of their religious beliefs. Georgia, Maryland, and Ohio permit the substitution of the published banns for a license.[13]

A license grants a couple legal permission to be married. However, those qualified to officiate at a marriage may refuse to marry a couple even though a license to wed has been secured. Some ministers are in the habit of questioning couples about their previous marital status and the circumstances of any previous divorce. If a minister concludes that a contemplated marriage has no chance for success, or that for moral reasons the church should not sanction the marriage, he may refuse to perform the ceremony, since the license is permissive and not mandatory.

Here is a typical law regarding the marriage license:

Michigan 12705. It is necessary for all parties intending to be married to obtain a marriage license from the county clerk of the county in which either the man or the woman resides. If both parties are non-residents of the state, it shall be necessary to obtain such a license from the county clerk of the county in which the marriage is to be performed.

Waiting period

Two policies are usually followed if a waiting period is required between the time of the application for a license to wed and the marriage. Most states follow the policy of not delivering the license for some time after the application is made, five days being the most common period of waiting. According to the other method, the license is issued at once but is not valid for a certain number of days. All states except Nevada either require a waiting period or have a venereal disease law, which serves much the

---

[13] Vernier, *op. cit.*, p. 60.

same purpose in that it prevents hasty marriages. In many states, a judge may waive the waiting-period requirement under certain conditions. If the girl is pregnant, if both members of the couple are definitely old enough to know what they are doing, or if other circumstances seem to make the waiting period unnecessary, they may apply to a judge who is permitted to use his power to waive.

Fig. 55 KNOWN FOR ITS EASY DIVORCE LAWS, NEVADA ALSO EX-TENDS A HELPING HAND TO COUPLES WHO WISH TO BE QUICKLY WED. The Gretna Green Chapel, where for fifteen dollars a minister, witnesses, lighted candles, and a license can be purchased as a "package wedding." The justice of the peace in Las Vegas made more money than the President of the United States in 1941. By permission, Press Association.

The waiting-period requirement, like the physical examination for venereal disease, is relatively recent. Most states have passed this requirement within the last 30 years. Maine is the only state which has always required a waiting period or the publishing of banns. The custom of publishing advance notice through the posting of or the reading of the banns started early in the Middle Ages and has continued among Catholics to the present. Publishing of the banns was made mandatory by the Fourth Lateran Council in 1215. It is now recognized that this old church custom was important in preventing hasty marriages. In the 1920's a series of widely publicized "Gin Marriages" awakened many state legislatures to the need for a waiting period before the issuance of marriage licenses. The law reduces the number of ill-advised marriages. In Los Angeles alone, 1,000 marriage license applicants per year do not bother to return to get the license at the end of the waiting period.

When many states did not have a waiting-period law, the effectiveness of such a law in any one state was hampered. Couples wishing to marry could easily cross a state border and be married at once. However, with 47 states now requiring either the waiting period or a venereal disease test, the problem has been largely solved. It is reasonable to expect that before long some form of waiting period will be required in all states. Then the last of the "marrying parsons" who have capitalized on interstate marriages will be forced out of business.

Who is qualified to perform marriages

In all states except two, marriages may be performed by either the civil or the religious authorities. In these two states the ceremony must be performed by the religious authorities.[14] People usually prefer to be married by the clergy; three-fourths of all marriages are performed by a minister, priest, or rabbi. Of all the civil authorities qualified to officiate at weddings, the justice of the peace performs most marriages.

In some states the legality of the marriage is doubtful if the officiant is not properly qualified to perform the marriage. However, in other states the legality of the marriage is not affected

[14] Vernier, *op. cit.*, pp. 81-90.

by the status of the officiant. The important thing is that the couple is acting in good faith. The Michigan law states:

12701. No marriage solemnized before any person professing to be a Justice of the Peace or a minister of the gospel shall be deemed void. *Provided* the marriage be consummated with a full belief on the part of the persons so married that they have been lawfully joined in marriage.

In 41 states, Friends or Quakers and members of other denominations having special methods of solemnizing marriages are exempted from the law that requires an officiant. Members of these sects are permitted to solemnize their marriages according to the method prescribed by their religion. In the Quaker marriage ceremony the man and woman marry each other without the aid of an officiant. The marriage is a civil ceremony in which the groom states, "I, John Jones, take thee, Mary Smith, to be my wedded wife, etc." The bride repeats, "I, Mary Smith, take thee, John Jones, to be my wedded husband, promise to obey, etc." After the pledges have been made, all those present sign the wedding certificate, and the couple are as thoroughly married as they would be if they had been married by a minister with the use of a marriage license.

Validity of marriage

On this point the Michigan law says:

12696. The general rule of law is that a marriage valid where it is celebrated is valid everywhere; and the converse to this is equally general, that a marriage void where it is celebrated is void everywhere. Whatever the form of the ceremony, if the parties agreed personally to take each other for husband and wife and from that time lived together professedly in that relation, presentation of these facts would be sufficient to show marriage as binding upon the parties, which would subject them and others to legal penalties for disregard of those obligations.

In general, the spirit of the above law exists in other states. That is, if a marriage is void where it is celebrated, it is usually void everywhere. Exceptions occur in a few states that make marriages void if the parties married in order to evade a state law. These states are Illinois, Louisiana, Massachusetts, Vermont, and Wisconsin. Twelve other states have passed laws prohibiting out-of-state marriages to evade the state law, but in most of these states such marriages are not considered void.

As the various state laws now stand, it is easier for each state to recognize the marriage laws existing in other states.

Common-law marriage

Common-law marriages are still valid in 21 states. These are marriages in which a man and a woman mutually agree that they will live together as husband and wife. No license or marriage officiant is employed, nor is there any specific ceremony such as the Quakers hold. If the validity of the marriage is questioned, the couple must show that they are living as husband and wife. If either is already married, or if other legal reasons make a regular marriage impossible, the couple cannot marry by common law. In the states where common-law marriages are valid, they are as binding as other marriages. In these states, a common-law marriage must be dissolved through divorce, according to the divorce laws governing all other marriages, before either party may remarry.

Common-law marriages were frequent in Europe during the Middle Ages but were abolished by the Catholic church in the Council of Trent in 1563. England abolished common-law mar-

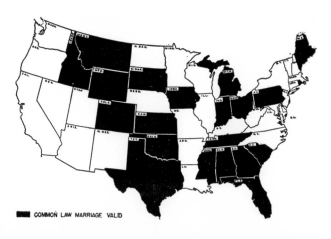

Fig. 56   TWENTY-ONE STATES RECOGNIZE COMMON-LAW MARRIAGE AS VALID.

COMMON LAW MARRIAGE VALID

riages in 1753. Common-law marriages were suited to the frontier life of early America, since it was often impossible to get a minister when people were ready to marry. Love and death could not always wait on the parson. In many frontier communities people who died were buried with little ceremony and the funeral was held weeks or months later when the circuit rider came around. In the same way, couples pledged themselves as man and wife and began housekeeping, sometimes having a wedding later when the circuit rider appeared. Others dispensed with the wedding, and their pledges and their living together as man and wife were accepted as a marriage.

There is now no good reason for the retention of common-law marriages. The American Bar Association, the Commission on Uniform State Laws, and almost all authorities in the field of social reform favor the abolition of common-law marriage.[15] Such marriages have been defended by some on the grounds that they protect the legitimacy of children, since some people will always live together as husband and wife without a wedding ceremony.

However, in such marriages, legal difficulties may arise concerning inheritance or in case of divorce. Relatives may challenge the validity of the marriage, claiming that there was not a marriage but rather merely a temporary relationship and that the surviving member of the pair has no right to inherit as a spouse. Also one member of the pair may repudiate the relationship and claim that the relationship was never agreed upon as marriage, thereby escaping the necessity for securing a divorce or assuming financial responsibility toward the other member. Thus, in practice, common-law marriages have not as much protection for the individual as other marriages, even though they may be legally allowed.

[15] Vernier, *op. cit.*, p. 108.

Void and voidable marriages

Certain marriages are considered void from the beginning and certain others are voidable. In a void marriage it is not necessary to have the marriage annulled or to take any legal recourse. Although there were mutual consent, a license to wed, and a qualified officiant, no marriage took place, since a legal reason such as consanguinity, feeblemindedness, or an already existing marriage prevented marriage.

Some prohibited marriages stand as valid unless reason is shown why the marriage should be declared void. These are voidable marriages and are dissolved through annulment rather than through divorce. Annulment differs from divorce in the following ways: (1) It proceeds on the basis that no valid marriage ever existed between the parties. (2) Property is to be returned to each. (3) Usually neither is entitled to further rights of support; and (4) Children are considered illegitimate unless they are protected by some other law. In some states the difference between annulments and divorce is not clear. There are states that make no distinction between the two, so the only ending for an illegal marriage is divorce. The most common grounds recognized for annulling marriages are non-age, insanity or lack of understanding, force or fraud, bigamy, and impotence.

In most states, those who marry under age are legally married unless action is taken to have the marriages annulled. One-fourth of all annulments are for non-age. A few years ago a Tennessee girl of nine married a man 22 years old. At that time Tennessee had no statute on age for marriage and the old common law prevailed. At common law, marriages of children under seven years of age were void. Since both members of the Tennessee couple and their parents were satisfied with the marriage, nothing could be done to dissolve it. The marriage stood as legal, since the common law provided that marriages of children over seven were voidable but not void. In some states this marriage would not have stood, and the man would probably have been jailed and charges brought against him.

A common reason for having marriages annulled is for force or fraud. The French war bride of a G.I. who had claimed to be the owner of a big plantation in Georgia had the marriage annulled on the grounds of fraud when she found that actually he lived with his parents in a three-room shack on a 20-acre farm. Over one-third of all annulments are for misrepresentations of this type or for fraud due to false promises. Fraud or force may not be the real reason for some of these annulments. Couples must give reasons that are acceptable to the court if they are to get out of a bad marriage, and since fraud is an acceptable reason, that may be the one offered.

One-fourth of annulments are because of bigamy. Although such marriages are usually void from the beginning, it is common to have them annulled through court action. No doubt then remains about the marital status of the party once court action has been taken, whereas confusion might arise if no legal action had been taken, especially in states where the law is confusing.

In addition, annulment can be secured because of mental incapacity, and physical incapacity or impotence. Impotence is not to be confused with sterility, which is inability to reproduce. Impotence is the inability of the male to have sexual intercourse. It is recognized in many states as cause for annulment of marriage. The majority of states recognize mental incapacity, also, as grounds for annulment.

Some causes for annulment, such as insanity or impotence, cannot be used if the marriage has been allowed to stand unchallenged for a certain period of time. Approximately one-third of annulments come within the first year of marriage. Annulments account for only a small percentage of marriage dissolutions, probably not more than 2 per cent. Most people resort to divorce.

Legitimacy of children of annulled marriages

If a couple were never legally married and they had children during the period when they thought they were married, are their children legitimate or illegitimate? Again there is confusion. Several of the states have passed no regulation on this point and still go according to the common law which held that the children were illegitimate.[16] The most common policy of states that have legislated upon this point is similar to the following law, which declares that children of void or annulled marriages are legitimate. This is the law in 21 states:

> **Michigan 12750.** Upon the dissolution of a marriage on account of non-age, insanity, or idiocy of either party, the issue of the marriage shall be deemed to be in all respects the legitimate issue of the parent who, at the time of the marriage, was capable of contracting.

In some states the children of certain types of illegal marriages are considered illegitimate. Children of incestuous and bigamous unions are more likely to be considered illegitimate than the children of other prohibited unions.

Legal status of illegitimates

Although many states have made efforts to legitimatize children born of void and annulled marriages, progress has been slow toward an enlightened viewpoint concerning children born out of wedlock. Sexual immorality has been frowned on, and if the sexually delinquent has become diseased or if pregnancy has resulted, society has had little sympathy. This attitude applied not only to the parent but to the child as well, for the child was stigmatized as illegitimate and made to suffer too. The status of the illegitimate child was such that it was hard for him to live a normal life. It was public knowledge that the child was illegiti-

---

[16] Maryland, Mississippi, North Carolina, Pennsylvania, Tennessee, and Washington.

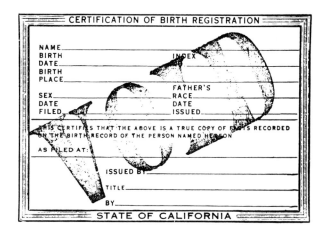

CERTIFICATION OF BIRTH REGISTRATION

NAME
BIRTH
DATE
BIRTH
PLACE

INDEX

SEX
DATE
FILED

FATHER'S
RACE
DATE
ISSUED

THIS CERTIFIES THAT THE ABOVE IS A TRUE COPY OF ... RECORDED ON THE BIRTH RECORD OF THE PERSON NAMED HEREON

AS FILED AT:

ISSUED BY

TITLE

BY

STATE OF CALIFORNIA

Fig. 57 COPY OF A SHORT-FORM BIRTH CERTIFICATE. If requested, the short-form may be secured in some states.

mate; his birth certificate carried the information and under the law he could not inherit property from his father or from his mother.

Some progress can be seen in present-day thinking on the problem of illegitimate children. We now question whether a child in a democracy should suffer because of his origin. We recognize that there are immoral parents, and the emphasis is correctly being shifted from illegitimate children to illegitimate parents.

Four babies out of every 100 born each year in the United States, or from 150,000 to 170,000 at today's birth rates, are from illegitimate unions. The number of illegitimate births has increased with the increasing birth rate, but the ratio of illegitimate to legitimate births has not changed in several years.[17] To register babies born out of wedlock as illegitimate is still the practice in most of the states. Throughout life, whenever the birth certificate has to be shown, the illegitimate birth becomes known to others. Birth records are public records kept at the county seat and, as such, are open to public inspection. Some states have revised their laws so that birth certificates showing illegitimacy are recorded only at the state capitol. In this way greater secrecy is maintained. Even this method, however, is small protection, for the illegiti-

[17] *Vital Statistics of the United States 1949, Part I*, p. 33. Washington, D. C.: Bureau of Census, 1952.

339

macy still shows up on the birth certificate, which must occasionally be shown.[18]

Only a few states have changed their laws so that all citizens receive a short form of their birth certificate which lists only essential facts: name, sex, place and date of birth.

Only two states, Arizona and North Dakota, legitimize *all* children and give them equal rights. The Arizona law states:

Every child is the legitimate child of its natural parents and is entitled to support and education as if born in lawful wedlock, except the right to dwelling or a residence with the family of its father, if such father be married. It shall inherit from its natural parents and from their kindred heirs, lineal and collateral, in the same manner as children born in lawful wedlock. This section shall apply to cases where the natural father of any such child is married to one other than the mother of said child, as well as where he is single.

Arizona and North Dakota are realistic in recognizing the rights of all children regardless of their origin. In 44 states, the "natural" child does not have the right to inherit from his father.[19] In all but one state, Louisiana, the illegitimate child may inherit from its mother. The most common limitation on inheritance is that although the illegitimate child may inherit from its mother it cannot inherit from her lineal or collateral kindred. The Michigan law represents this point of view. It states, "Every child is heir of his mother, but it [illegitimate child] is not allowed to claim, as representing his mother, any part of the estate of any of her kindred, either lineal or collateral."

Although 46 states have laws which may require a father to support his illegitimate child, it is often difficult to prove pater-

---

[18] Arizona, Arkansas, California, Colorado, Connecticut, Idaho, Maryland, Massachusetts, New Mexico, Nebraska, New Hampshire, New York, Oklahoma, and Vermont had eliminated the question of legitimacy from the birth certificate by 1955. *Vital Statistics of the United States 1955*, Volume I, p. 23. Washington, D. C.: Bureau of Census, 1955.

[19] In Arizona, North Dakota, Iowa, and Wisconsin the illegitimate child may inherit from his father.

nity.[20] Unless the mother of the child initiates action to prove the paternity of the child, the father need take no responsibility for its support.

Norway has probably the most advanced legislation on illegitimacy. There the state takes the responsibility for establishing paternity and setting the obligation of support. Full inheritance rights from the father and support to the age of 16 from the parent best able to supply that support are guaranteed by the state.[21] If force is necessary in order to collect the payments for the support of the child, the state takes this responsibility, just as it takes the responsibility for protecting the lives or property of other citizens. This guarantee is of fundamental importance. In the United States, when the mother takes the initiative and establishes the paternity and the court orders the father to support the child, little real guarantee of permanent support for the child is made. If the father falls behind in payments or ceases altogether to contribute to the child's support, it is up to the mother to take legal action. In many cases, however, the mother will be unable or unwilling to take such action and the child is the victim.

A Children's Bureau study of illegitimate children born in 1935 showed that 80 per cent of the white fathers and 86 per cent of the Negro fathers had fallen behind in support payments within two years. Almost half of them had failed to pay as much as half of what was due for the child's support.[22]

In Minnesota and North Dakota, administrative boards have been created to assist unmarried mothers and their children and to aid in the enforcement of illegitimacy laws.

If children born out of wedlock are to have an equal chance

[20] Texas and Virginia have no legislation applying to the father of an illegitimate child.

[21] Helen I. Clarke, *Social Legislation.* New York: D. Appleton-Century Company, Inc., 1940.

[22] M. C. Elmer, *The Sociology of the Family,* p. 389. New York: Ginn & Company, 1945.

with others to become desirable citizens, it would seem that the following policies should be universal:

1. Legitimatize all children and give them equal rights regardless of the circumstances of their birth.
2. Provide birth certificates that do not call for paternity information.
3. Give the state responsibility for establishing paternity.
4. Give the state responsibility for enforcing parental support of all children.
5. Provide adequate financial support for all children in need.
6. Provide more adequate maternity care for unwed mothers.
7. Create general acceptance of the fact that there are no illegitimate children, only illegitimate parents, and that for the good of society all children must be freed from any stigma attached to their birth.

One registrar of births, in a state that still records "legitimate" or "illegitimate" on each birth certificate, when asked why the state did not change its policy on registering births, responded: "It just is not legal to do what some states are doing in not registering the paternity of children. Their action would not stand up in court at all, and there is danger that the practice will result in many legal tangles." This man was sincere, but his attention was focused entirely on an outmoded legal viewpoint rather than on society's obligation to approximately 160,000 children born out of wedlock each year. Considerable evidence indicates that this legalistic way of thinking is giving way to a more socially desirable point of view. Laws need to be adjusted in consideration of their effect on the welfare of young citizens.

An analysis of existing marriage laws points to the conclusion that a great many state laws need intelligent revision. Marriage education in colleges and high schools throughout the country should lead to a better understanding of the broad social purposes underlying legal regulation of marriage and, in turn, to revision of marriage and divorce laws so that they may contribute more effectively to the stability of family life.

Review questions

1. What special problems does the state face when it attempts to regulate marriage?
2. How does a marriage contract differ from other civil contracts?
3. What one thing is essential to make a marriage binding?
4. Give some of the most common eugenic regulations of marriage.
5. Why is it difficult to enforce some of the eugenic regulations?
6. What is the most common legal age for marriage without the parents' consent? With consent?
7. Folkways and mores rather than the law determine the age at marriage. Explain.
8. Give some of the common regulations of marriages of consanguinity. Of affinity.
9. Why is there a great variation among states on marriages of affinity?
10. Summarize the miscegenetic regulations. What is the regulation in your state?
11. Is it possible to marry without a marriage license?
12. Cite evidence to show that requiring a waiting period between the time of application for a license to marry and the marriage is a good regulation.
13. What do authorities think about the policy of recognizing common-law marriages?
14. Distinguish between void and voidable marriages. Give an example of each.
15. How does annulment differ from divorce?
16. Give the most common grounds for annulment.
17. What is the legal status of children of void marriages?
18. What changes are taking place to protect children born out of wedlock?
19. Give some additional recommendations for action to protect the children of unwed mothers.

Projects and activities

1. Special report. Have one member of the class consult Vernier's *American Family Laws*, or a statute book from your state, and give a report on the marriage laws in your state.
2. Special report. Gather all the available information on your state's policy on children born out of wedlock.
3. Have one member of the class get copies of all the legal forms required for marriage and the registration of births in your state. Post these on your bulletin board.

Suggested readings

Becker, Howard, and Reuben Hill, eds., *Family, Marriage, and Parenthood*. Boston: D. C. Heath and Company, 1955. Ch. XIX, "What Family Members Should Know About Law."

Vernier, Chester G., *American Family Laws*. Stanford: Stanford University Press, 1931-1938, 5 vols. and supplement. A complete analysis of American family laws in all 51 jurisdictions.

Adjustability required in all relationships

Patterns of marriage adjustment

Importance of adjustments made early in marriage

The time factor in adjustment

Levels of adjustment in marriage

Time required to adjust and happiness in marriage

Quarreling

Wholesome tension-relievers

Tremendous trifles

Achieving Adjustment in Marriage

Remodeling the spouse after marriage

Courtship patterns carried into marriage

Maturity of married love

Role concepts and marriage adjustment

Before marriage, people in love have a tendency to emphasize the similarities in their ways of thinking rather than the differences. It is easy for the couple to idealize each other and to impute attitudes that may not exist. Each one may oversell himself, and, since both are in a somewhat hypnotic state of euphoria, they may fail to learn much about their points of difference during the courtship period. After they have returned from the honeymoon and are launched upon life as a married couple, true personality traits and value systems may become more apparent. Gradually the two may recognize that they are not in such close agreement on everything as they had thought they were during the engagement period. This realization is a normal part of marriage and occurs quite universally to a greater or lesser degree. If the two people are from about the same type of family background, their values may be very similar. If it is a "mixed" marriage, there may be practically no agreement. Married couples become conscious of differences in several well-defined areas in which they have to build a good, cooperative relationship. As one studies large numbers of marriages that have lasted happily for years, the evidence becomes more and more convincing that successful marriages do not just happen. A conscious recognition of the need to work at building a successful marriage has proved to be the important factor in the success of many marriages, and the failure to recognize the necessity for working at it has resulted in unhappiness in many other marriages.

.. 15

Adjustability required in all relationships

In most situations involving human relationships, elements of conflict are present. Marriage is no different from other human relationships in this respect.

Whenever two or more people attempt to live peaceably and pleasantly together, adjustments must be made. People who live in college dormitories, in sorority or fraternity houses, or in any type of housing where several roommates live together learn that living with others under any circumstances requires cooperation, self-discipline, and a willingness to share and to compromise. One person who is selfish and demanding or thoughtless and inconsiderate of the rights of others can create constant friction and unpleasantness. Learning to get along with room-

TOM HENDERSON

THE SATURDAY
EVENING POST

"Of course, *before* we were married he was the life of every party."

Fig. 58 By permission, Tom Henderson and *The Saturday Evening Post.*

mates or housemates is in some ways a good preparation for later married life. One learns to be tolerant of the wishes and peculiarities of others and develops the ability to use tact and to avoid controversial issues. Married life requires the same finesse. However, in marriage, people are inclined to take their differences more seriously and to go head-on into controversial issues because they feel they belong to each other; they cannot go their separate ways and avoid sore points so easily as with a roommate. In addition, the marriage relationship includes the sex element, which plays an important part. It may serve as a strong bond which holds husband and wife together and which aids them in working out points of difference, or it may serve as a focal point of friction so that they react more emotionally in all other areas requiring adjustability.

Patterns of marriage adjustment

Most people who are in the early years of marriage today probably believe that the joys and satisfactions, and the frustrations and disappointments that they are experiencing in their married living are unique to themselves. It is not likely to occur to them that their experiences tend to fit a pattern which is being repeated in the lives of thousands of their contemporaries. Many married people would probably become less disturbed by the frustrations and disillusionments that may occur at any stage of marriage if they knew how common in human experience are exactly the situations that may distress them. The need is to recognize that certain developmental tasks confront all married couples. And these tasks are somewhat different at each of the four or five stages of the life cycle: (1) in early marriage; (2) when children come; (3) in middle life when the children leave home; (4) when retirement time comes; (5) when crises occur, such as death, serious illness, or financial disaster. Some of the tasks that confront newly married couples are accomplished easily and smoothly, each such achievement contributing to the couple's sense of unity and to their awareness that they are establishing a firm foundation for their permanent happiness and success as a married couple. Some others of the developmental tasks may be more difficult for some couples. Nevertheless *all* couples must build their marriage on the basis of good working arrangements in certain basic areas of living. The specific areas in which adjustability and cooperation are necessary are: sex relations; money matters; religion; social activities and recreation; in-law relationships; associating with friends individually or as a couple; and, after children come, their training and discipline.

It is safe to assume that in all marriages differences of opinion and potential conflict situations will arise in one or more of the areas requiring agreement or cooperation. That is normal. The quality of a couple's over-all relationship will be determined by their ways of meeting these situations. How potential conflict situations are resolved and how soon they are resolved are fundamental to the happiness of the marriage partners.

Ways of solving conflicts in marriage tend to fall within three different patterns. (1) Some couples are able to develop a relationship in which both compromise to a certain extent and find a middle ground of agreement satisfactory to both. Few, if any, couples are in perfect agreement from the beginning in all areas of living. Through compromise, they may reach an adjustment after a few years that gives them a feeling of confidence and security in their marriage. In the most satisfactory adjustments, neither one feels that he has had to make too great a sacrifice in the compromising.

(2) Another type of adjustment is that in which two people may find that they hold quite seriously opposing view-points or they have antagonistic characteristics, but they accept the fact of their differences and *accommodate* themselves to the situation in any one of several ways. They may not be able to reach a compromise that is entirely satisfactory to them both, but their

accommodation involves little or no outwardly expressed aggression or antagonism. They resolve their differences on certain matters by striking an equilibrium in which each tolerates the behavior of the other with little or no protest. Both may recognize that they have not reached a satisfactory agreement, but their state of accommodation will be such that their differences place very little strain upon the marriage. During the process of accommodation, the couple may discuss issues and attempt to reach mutuality of views. Sociologists speak of cooperation, or collective effort for common ends, as a form of accommodation. And certainly such cooperation is a part of the picture in this type of adjustment in marriage. Differences in viewpoint and reactions to undesirable characteristics may be "tabled," as it were, in the interests of other common goals. The undesirable conditions will continue to exist but will not be allowed to hinder cooperation toward mutually desired ends. Examples of this form of accommodation are seen among couples who differ seriously on such points as religion or social activities, but who present a united front for the benefit of their children. Examples are also found among couples whose financial security depends on an absence of conflict and on cooperation between them. Such couples often table their serious differences or at least control their actions so that no outward conflict shows, and concentrate on the cooperative effort that is necessary for their economic advancement and security.

(3) A third form of adjustment in marriage is a state of hostility. Constant quarreling and bickering go on about the points on which the two differ, or tension is produced by antagonisms that are sometimes expressed in words and often made evident by behavior. The members of the couple are not able to cope in any satisfactory way with their differences; they reach an impasse or a relationship that is static and inflexible, and characterized by hostility.

This state of hostility may be illustrated by a couple who differ on recreational interests. The husband does not like to dance but is an enthusiastic golfer. The wife continues to try to force her husband to take her to dances. When he refuses, she may retaliate by hiding his golf clubs, going home to mother, or going to dances without him. Or she may appear to have given up her interest in dancing but continue to hold resentful feelings. This resentment may find expression in a refusal to participate in other activities that the husband enjoys, or refusal to cooperate in sexual intercourse. The husband may retaliate by spending more and more time on recreational interests with others. Thus, a couple may settle into a permanent state of antagonism and conflict. It is a most unhappy type of adjustment to differences.

Another couple with different habit patterns in their ways of facing problems might have the same differences concerning recreational interests, but they might adjust to the situation in a more desirable way through the process of accommodation discussed as the second type of adjustment. They might compromise and each become able to participate in at least some of the recreational interests of the other, whether or not with pleasure. Or they might accommodate themselves to the situation by accepting their difference, each going his or her own way as far as possible, but with little or no hostility over their inability to enjoy the same things.

Importance of adjustments made early in marriage

The process of achieving some level of pair adjustment is in the forefront during the early months or years of every marriage. In successful marriages, adjustments that are relatively satisfactory are made during this early period. Nevertheless, adjustability will be called for throughout the married life of each couple. As they go into new stages of life, they will encounter new conditions which require them to be flexible and to have an open mind toward differences in viewpoint. No matter how satisfying a

Fig. 59 OF MARRIED STUDENTS STUDIED ON TWO CAMPUSES, A
LARGE PERCENTAGE REPORTED HAVING HAD A NEED FOR COUNSEL-
ING ON MARRIAGE PROBLEMS.

closeness two people achieve, they remain two people, and each
will have his or her own way of reacting to new experiences.
When children are born, when children mature and leave home,
when grandparents must move in to live with the family, when
their financial situation changes for the better or the worse, and
when illness or death comes into their lives, new levels of adjustment will have to be achieved by the husband and wife. Relationships do not remain static in the face of changing circumstances
and conditions in life.

However, couples who are able to make satisfactory adjustment in most areas of married living in the early years of their
marriage will usually be able to cope with later requirements that
life makes upon them as a pair. If a good understanding and

mature affection exist between them, they will adjust readily later, scarcely recognizing some of the new developments as potential sources of conflict. But if in some segments of their lives chronic conflict exists before new problems arise, a couple may find that new developments will put an intolerable strain upon their relationship.

The time factor in adjustment

For most people the process of reaching some kind of working arrangement in the areas where they are not together, is not accomplished suddenly. It takes time, and some people become discouraged early. Johannis, in studying 54 college couples in Oregon who had been married approximately three years, found that one-third of the husbands and wives had considered separation since marriage.[1] In our study of 544 college couples at Michigan State University, who had been married approximately two years, we found that one-fifth of the husbands and wives had considered separation.[2]

Research has revealed that certain of the areas of living seem to require more time for adjusting than others, with most couples. Just as there seems to be a pattern in the kinds of adjustments people reach in their marriages, so also the time factor in their progress toward working arrangements falls into a pattern.

We have findings here from the previously quoted study of marital adjustment among 409 married couples who reported anonymously on many phases of their marriages.[3] These couples represent successful marriages, for they had been married from 5 to 40 years; none was divorced. The husbands and wives responded independently of each other concerning the adjustment

---

[1] Theodore B. Johannis, Jr., "The Marital Adjustment of a Sample of Married College Students," *The Coordinator*, 4:4 (June, 1956), 25.

[2] Judson T. Landis, "On the Campus," *Survey Midmonthly*, 84:1 (January, 1948), 19.

[3] Judson T. Landis, "Length of Time Required to Achieve Adjustment in Marriage," *American Sociological Review*, 11:6 (December, 1946), 666-677.

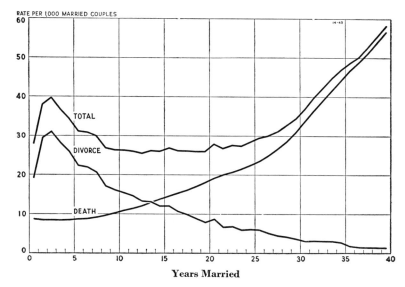

RATE PER 1,000 MARRIED COUPLES

Years Married

Fig. 60 MARITAL DISSOLUTIONS BY DIVORCE AND DEATH IN THE
FIRST 40 YEARS OF MARRIAGE, UNITED STATES, 1947. Marriage
failure as measured by divorce reaches a peak in the second and
third years of marriage. From *Statistical Bulletin,* Metropolitan
Life Insurance Company, 30:11 (November, 1949), 3.

processes in their marriage.[4] Since each one responded independently, it was possible to see how well couples agreed on the
level of their success in achieving working arrangements in the
different areas, and whether they agreed on the length of time
that had been required to arrive at whatever adjustment they
had made. Most couples were in agreement, but about one
couple in ten disagreed. In some cases one spouse would report
that the couple had been in agreement from the beginning of the
marriage, while the other spouse might say that satisfactory adjustments in certain areas had taken years or had never been
made.

Each spouse in the study stated whether he felt they had

[4] In this study of long-married couples, the term adjustment is used to
indicate an established pattern of feeling and acting with which the two
rather habitually confront situations in their marriage.

355

agreed satisfactorily from the beginning of the marriage, whether months or years had passed before satisfactory adjustment was achieved, or whether the couple had never worked out their differences in an area. All checked specifically their success or failure, and the time required to adjust in each of the areas: spending the family income, relationships with in-laws, sex relations, religious life, choosing and associating with friends, and social activities and recreation. Figure 61 summarizes the results of this study.

Notice that more time was required for reaching a plateau of adjustment in sex relations and in spending the family income

Fig. 61 PERCENTAGE OF 818 SPOUSES REPORTING VARIOUS PERIODS OF TIME REQUIRED AFTER MARRIAGE TO ACHIEVE ADJUSTMENT IN SIX AREAS. People who had been successfully married for an average of 20 years had experienced greater difficulty in adjusting in certain areas. From Judson T. Landis, "Length of Time Required to Achieve Adjustment in Marriage," *American Sociological Review*, 11:6 (December, 1946), 668.

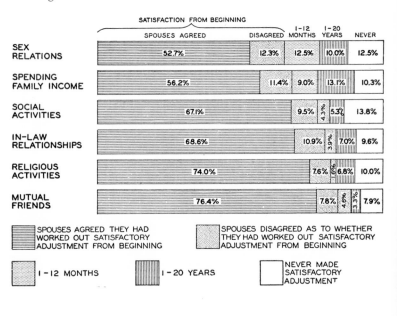

than in any other areas. Approximately half of the couples agreed that their sex adjustment had been satisfactory from the beginning. The remainder (47 per cent) either disagreed on how long it had taken, agreed that months or years had passed before they achieved a good adjustment in sex, or agreed that they had never arrived at a satisfactory relationship. On spending the family income, the picture is about the same. Social activities and recreational interests, and in-law relationships, were equal in time required for adjustment after marriage. Approximately two out of three of the couples had agreed satisfactorily from the beginning; the remaining third had either required time to adjust or had never arrived at a good adjustment. Three out of four of the couples in these marriages had been together from the beginning in religious life and in associating with friends. These two areas presented the least difficulty. The husbands, considered as a group, gave the six areas the same rating on length of time required for adjustment as did the wives as a group. And those who had been married under ten years agreed with those who had been married 30 years or more.

More of those married from 30 to 40 years had achieved a satisfactory level of adjustment in all areas except one—sex. It may be that in these older marriages a better sex adjustment had once existed, but at the time of responding to the questionnaire the couples had reached a period in life requiring a new adjustment. However, the findings give us no reliable clue to why those married the longest reported a less satisfactory adjustment in sex than in the other areas of their marriage.

Levels of adjustment in marriage

After the couples in the study recorded how long it had taken them to reach established levels of adjustment in the various areas of living, they stated whether the working relationship in each area was satisfactory to both, satisfactory to one, or unsatisfactory. The unsatisfactory adjustments might more accurately be called conditions of stalemate or failure to adjust.

The area in which the fewest had arrived at a mutually satisfactory adjustment was in sex relations; the area in which the most had arrived at a mutually satisfactory adjustment was in associating with friends. The adjustments in the various areas were either states of accommodation or of conflict in from one-third to one-fifth of the marriages. In sex relations, over one-third of the couples had either made an adjustment which was a compromise or had continued in conflict. The couples had arrived at mutually satisfactory adjustments in from about two-thirds to four-fifths of their relationships in the seven areas (see Fig. 62).

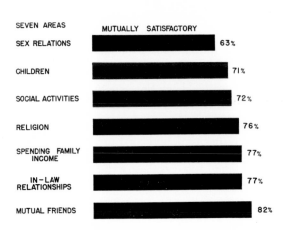

Fig. 62 PERCENTAGE OF 409 COUPLES AGREEING THAT THEY HAD ARRIVED AT MUTUALLY SATISFACTORY ADJUSTMENTS IN SEVEN AREAS.

Fig. 63 TIME NEEDED TO ADJUST IN SIX AREAS IN MARRIAGE, AND HAPPINESS IN MARRIAGE, AS REPORTED BY 409 COUPLES. The sooner couples merge their interests and find satisfactory working arrangements, the more likely they are to find happiness in marriage.

Time required to adjust and happiness in marriage

The study of the 409 couples showed that a close relationship existed between agreement or early adjustment to differences and happiness in the marriages. Over one-half of the couples rated their marriages as very happy if agreement had existed from the beginning or if they had been able to get

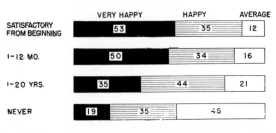

together on differences immediately, whereas only one-fifth rated
their marriages as very happy if they had been unable to adjust
at the beginning.

Some couples rated their marriages as very happy, even if there
was one area in which they had never been able to agree. But
if there was failure to adjust well in two areas, 77 per cent were
average or unhappy, and all those who reported unsatisfactory
adjustments in three or more areas rated their marriages average
or unhappy. Of the 409 couples, only eleven reported failure to
adjust in as many as three areas. It would seem safe to theorize

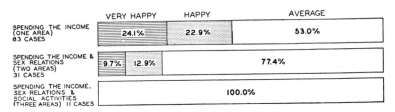

Fig. 64   HAPPINESS OF MARRIAGES IN WHICH COUPLES HAD NEVER
ADJUSTED IN ONE, TWO, OR THREE AREAS. Failure to arrive at
satisfactory working arrangements in three or more areas means
almost certain failure in marriage; if the marriage survives, it
will be average or unhappy.

that the reason there were so few in the study who had failed to
adjust satisfactorily in as many as three areas is because people
who could not resolve their differences in more of the areas of
living probably would not remain married, and divorced or
separated couples were not included in this study. In successful
marriage, if a measure of success is permanence of the marriage,
husbands and wives do manage to work out their differences in at
least four of these major areas of living. In marriages that can be
called happy as well as successful, the man and woman are likely
to have achieved good working arrangements in all of the seven
areas.

Quarreling

Almost all married couples will have some quarrels while they are in the process of developing the many facets of their relationship as a pair. They will discover that some of the quarrels are damaging to their relationship in that the quarrel drives them apart and leaves hurts that are slow to heal. Some others of the quarrels, even though painful, may serve to bring into the open differences that can be resolved, once they are faced. Whether a quarrel is the best way to face differences is the question. Research studies of engaged couples have shown that couples who try to avoid arguments are less likely to break their engagements.[5] The quarreling pattern during engagement is predictive of unhappiness in marriage. Similarly it may be said that a quarreling pattern in marriage is destructive in its over-all effect upon marital happiness. This is true even though some of the quarrels, especially in the early months of marriage, may serve to bring differences into the open.

Many quarrels serve no purpose other than as an outlet for accumulated tensions in one or both partners. It is true that the pace of modern life is such that for almost everyone there are pressures that produce emotional tension, and individuals must find ways to relieve tensions if mental health is to be preserved. The need for tension relievers is sometimes used as a basis for arguing that marital or family quarrels are not only necessary but useful.

Many adults recognize that it is not practicable to express their emotional reactions freely in most of their relationships outside the family. They exercise self-restraint in their dealings with friends, acquaintances, or business associates, because they accept the fact that if they did not, they would soon have few friends and no job. For many people the family serves as a shock absorber, or the place where they relax self-restraint and give vent

[5] Ernest W. Burgess and Paul Wallin, *Engagement and Marriage,* p. 294. Chicago: J. B. Lippincott Company, 1953.

to the frustrations and tensions that accumulate in other areas of life. If we could confine ourselves only to a consideration of the need of the individual for tension release, we might say that to provide a place for such release is a function of the family, or more specifically of marriage. We could then agree that a devoted spouse should accept explosive outbursts of the mate as attempts to make a constructive adjustment to life. Husbands and wives then could feel that in serving as sparring partners, who knew when to retreat and when to meet violence with violence, they would be enabling each other to maintain emotional balance. Unfortunately that is not the effect that quarreling usually has. We cite the case of Sally and Bill, a young married couple:

Bill's work requires him to be in constant contact with other men, many of whom are working under pressure in highly specialized jobs. Bill's immediate superior is a man who is a perfectionist about his work and who has little understanding of human nature. While on the job, Bill works at maintaining harmonious relationships with his co-workers and his superior; this requires serious effort, and sometimes strains his self-control severely. After an especially hard day, Bill comes home to find that Sally has invited the Browns in for waffles and a game of bridge. Bill doesn't like waffles. In his family, waffles were not considered a suitable substitute for a good dinner after a day's work. Moreover, the Browns are a couple he finds hard to tolerate. They have been friends of Sally's since childhood and she can see nothing wrong with them. But to Bill they are just a shallow pair who are not even good bridge players. Their conversation frequently is concerned with occurrences far back in the past before Bill met Sally, and these reminiscences irk Bill.

So the stage is set; conditions are perfect for a good quarrel. Bill explodes. He gives vent to all the resentments that have been accumulating all day long. He goes further and expresses himself freely concerning the Browns and some of Sally's other friends, past and present. While he is getting things off his chest, he tells what he thinks of any family who would let a daughter grow up thinking that *waffles* were a suitable offering for a hungry man who worked hard to support his wife and family. And since he is on the subject of cooking, he throws in for good measure a few references to the good cooking he was used to before he left Mother's house and married Sally.

According to some theories, Sally, after responding with some uncomplimentary references to Bill's family background, his friends, and his general behavior, would dissolve in tears; they would kiss and make up; and their love would be on a better basis than before because of the progress toward understanding growing out of the quarrel. But is that the way it really works? Has enough constructive good been accomplished to compensate for the damage that has been done? One thing has been accomplished that may be considered a step in their adjustment. Sally has decided she will not ask the Browns in any more, because it just is not worth it, if it upsets Bill so. She also secretly resolves that if she is going to have to give up her friendship with the Browns, she is justified in insisting that Bill drop certain friends of his for whom she has no affection. She will take that up later.

The quarrel has served as a tension-reliever for Bill. But he does not feel any better for it. He is ashamed of the things he said about Sally's family, and he realizes that the comparisons he made between his mother's cooking and Sally's will only widen the rift that is already developing between Sally and her mother-in-law. And worst of all, their four-year-old son, Johnny, was wakened by the quarrel and came downstairs crying just after Sally began to cry. When Johnny saw Sally crying he could hardly be comforted. After they got him back to bed, Sally remarked with bitterness that Johnny was getting to be a naughty and unhappy child. She said, "Every time he hears us quarrel he is worse for days."

As might be suspected, Sally and Bill were developing a quarreling pattern. Their quarrels were becoming more frequent rather than less so. Each quarrel added a few more barbs that rankled. Each left a few smoldering resentments that might break out on another occasion. Although some of their quarrels settled issues, inasmuch as one decided to change his attitude, or both decided to compromise, most of the verbal battles settled nothing at all. They simply added scars. Both Sally and Bill grew more adept at responding with remarks that touched sore points. In the quarrel described above, Sally might easily respond to Bill's disparagement of her family by suggesting that a possible reason for the recent failure of Bill's father in a business venture was his inability to get along with co-workers. This reference would be especially puncturing to Bill's self-confidence and would serve to produce still more tension for him on other occasions when he found the going hard in his relationships at the office. Thus a vicious circle: more tension, more quarrels, more emotional scars, and Bill and Sally being driven apart in understanding and affection.

In the average marriage, the quarrels that can be considered constructive are few. The possible benefits—release of pent-up emotional tension for one or both and bringing differences into the open in order to resolve them—may in many cases be gained by more constructive means. An important consideration is that many marital quarrels do not stem from any real differences that need to be resolved, or from any underlying dissatisfaction with the mate. They do not have as their basis a rational attempt to eliminate differences; therefore they can accomplish little con-

Fig. 65 "What do you mean, WE'RE incompatible? You're the one who's incompatible." By permission, Dave Huffine and *The Saturday Evening Post.*

structive good. Disputes between a married couple are no different from those between friends outside marriage. Few friendships can survive constant or frequent quarrels. Friends learn to curb the impulse to say bitter words in the interest of preserving the friendship. Happily married couples practice the same rule. They learn to withhold the bitter criticism or the cutting retort in order to avoid unpleasantness and to enjoy greater happiness. If they find that points of strain develop between them over some matters, they learn to talk these matters over without having to get violent or to be destructively critical in their discussions.

Many couples recognize early in marriage that it is better not to discuss problems or to try to talk about things that might cause conflict late in the day when they are physically tired, certainly never when they are hungry.

One couple, both of whom were working at jobs outside the home, reported that in the early months of their marriage they found themselves involved in frequent arguments or bickerings. Upon analyzing the situation, they realized that their differences invariably occurred late in the afternoon when both were just home from work and were preparing dinner together. They therefore made it a rule to have dinner earlier and to refrain from any but the most casual conversation until after they had eaten and had relaxed. That ended the quarreling. They realized that both had been reacting in a childish manner to fatigue and hunger. It is safe to say that most marital quarrels would never occur if the individuals could analyze the real reasons that provoke the quarrels and recognize immature behavior in themselves for what it is.

It must be said also that rather than relieving pent-up emotional tensions, marital quarrels often contribute to building up greater tension, as illustrated by the case of Sally and Bill. A feeling of mild antagonism or opposition may become much more intense when emotionally expressed. We are inclined, when faced with opposition, to express things more strongly than we feel them, with the result that our feelings become more intense to back up our words. Happily married people know that giving frequent expression to their affection for each other seems to build up and to increase their love. Love thrives on expression and response. So it is with anger, irritation, and criticism. The free and frequent expression of these feelings increases their strength and magnifies the importance of things that might more happily be passed over, overlooked, and forgotten. Angry quarreling, if repeated often enough in a marriage, will inevitably destroy love.

Moreover, many married couples are unaware of the serious effect that quarreling has on children. Research studies have revealed that the quarreling of parents is a source of extreme unhappiness and worry to children who are subjected to it. Even if the parents themselves consider the quarreling to be constructive or attach little importance to it, the effect on the children is not lessened. Couples who know the damaging effect of quarreling on children may feel that they will get their quarreling over with and their adjustments made before they have any children. But there is a strong possibility that if they do much quarreling early in their marriage, rather than getting the quarreling over with, they will establish a habit of meeting problems in that manner, and habits do not change easily.

Some couples, recognizing that points of disagreement are bound to arise in marriage, decide early that they will make it their habit to talk over differences. It is well to agree early that no such discussions will be held when either spouse is under par physically or emotionally. When both are feeling well adjusted with themselves and their marriage, they can discuss differences and be relatively objective because of the more accurate perspective they will have under these conditions.

Couples find it exceedingly rewarding to work at developing the technique of talking things over frankly, with the acknowledged purpose of understanding each other's viewpoint. In taking this rational approach to marital adjustment, they are recognizing that successful marriages do not just happen, but must be built. They are often pleasantly surprised to find that it is possible to reach satisfactory understandings on all important matters without becoming emotionally combative over their differences.

If the conference method of resolving differences has been established early in marriage, it can be working well by the time the children are old enough to take part in family discussions. Children also find conflict-creating situations in the home and need to have an opportunity for expressing their grievances. Effective, democratic family councils can be developed in homes in which the husband and wife establish this pattern early, before children are involved. In order to present a united front on discipline and child-training, the parents will need to discuss some questions privately. But having a voice in determining family policy is an important contributing factor to children's happiness and good adjustment in life. Children coming from homes that have used the family-conference method of settling differences are more likely to fit into the community as desirable members than are children brought up in homes with a quarreling pattern.

Wholesome tension-relievers

If at times too much tension has been built up in outside-the-home relationships, it is possible to find tension-relievers other than warring with the spouse. Some mature people have discovered that taking a long walk or ride will do wonders toward helping them to regain perspective. One businessman, who found his security threatened by a change in ownership of the corporation for which he worked, preserved his emotional balance by using his spare time to grub out trees that he did not want in his garden. He learned that an hour or two of working with the spade and mattock helped his emotional balance and enabled him to live peaceably with his wife and family. Some husbands and wives go to a movie or a concert, read a fascinating book, or take a drive in the country when they feel under emotional pressure. Any activity that enables a person to get away from his problem far enough to look at it objectively is an aid to perspective. And perspective is vital to marital happiness.

Resorting to activities rather than to quarreling is not just an "escape." It is constructive, because often when the individual has refrained from quarreling and has turned to other interests in order to relieve tension he realizes that there was no point worth quarreling over from the beginning; he realizes that the difficulty was within himself and could be corrected only by a change in his own attitude.

Tremendous trifles

When two people live together as intimately as do husbands and wives, it is natural for them to find that many little things come up to cause irritation. Mannerisms or habits that might pass unnoticed in friends or casual acquaintances often assume importance and provoke extreme annoyance when practiced by one's wife or husband. Carelessness with cigarette ashes, turning down the page corner to mark the place in a book, leaving a ring in the bathtub, being slow to come to the table when meals are ready, may become so irritating to the spouse that emotional explosions occur. Baber has called these trivial things, which often cause friction in marriage, "tremendous trifles." [6]

Why these trifles become so tremendous is not easy for the outsider to understand, but that they do harass many marriages is certain. The happy couples are those who can preserve a sense of proportion about the relative importance of events. That requires effort, and the effort will be aided by a sense of humor. A great many things cannot be explained, interpreted, or corrected, but will dissolve into the air if a couple can laugh over them together. A small boy, when taken to task by his mother

[6] Ray E. Baber, *Marriage and the Family,* pp. 221-223. New York: McGraw-Hill Book Company, Inc., 1953.

for some of his annoying ways, said, "I don't know why I do it. Let's just laugh it off." That is often the best solution to annoyances in marriage. Certainly it is a much surer road to peace and happiness than for either spouse to try to change the ways of the other. And as a tension-reliever a hearty laugh is at least as effective as an angry explosion, and it is far more pleasant to live with.

Remodeling the spouse after marriage

Sometimes during the courtship period a man and woman may observe habits and mannerisms in each other which they realize could be annoying in a husband or a wife, but each may pass over such traits with the thought, "He will surely change after we are married." The fact that the future spouse loves so devotedly and is so evidently desirous of making the loved one happy in all possible ways seems conclusive proof that after marriage he (or she) will gladly make every effort to change in any small ways the spouse might wish. So, when they are married and secure in their love, the wife or the husband may begin tactfully to suggest desirable changes. The result is usually disappointing. One reason why "tremendous trifles" become such a problem is that married people find greater difficulty than they had anticipated when they begin remodeling the mate. Not only is it hard for an adult to change ways which have become part of his personality make-up, but the mate who is "worked on" for his faults suffers ego deflation. He wants to be loved for himself, faults and all, and that is probably one reason he married the person he did. He felt that she knew him well and loved him anyway. If the remodeling program had started before marriage, perhaps no marriage would have taken place.

Some people are self-disciplined and mature enough to welcome constructive criticism from the spouse. Such individuals will evaluate criticism objectively and make successful efforts to correct undesirable personality traits in themselves. But for most people contemplating marriage, it is much safer and less likely to lead to disappointment if both members proceed on the assumption that the partner will do little changing after marriage. It is better to face the questions, "Do I love her enough to tolerate these things as trivial?" "Can I refrain from making him uncomfortable by agitating for change?" If the faults loom large and seem very annoying before marriage, there is no reason to believe they will be less irritating after the wedding. No one is without faults. Happy marriages are those between people whose faults are tolerable to each other. Wives have frequently been known to say of someone else's husband, "How can his wife endure that way of his! I couldn't stand it if my husband behaved that way." Yet the wife speaking may have a husband with faults that seem far worse to the other woman. So it is well to look, not for a faultless mate, but for one who can be loved for his personality traits viewed as a whole, and whose faults are those which the one most concerned does not find especially irritating.

Sometimes when spouses have traits or habits which are moderately irritating to each other, they adjust to the annoyances by a form of negative adaptation. This adaptation can be illustrated by a couple in which the wife is an inveterate talker, and overzealous in looking after her husband. Friends wonder how the husband endures her constant directions and suggestions covering every detail of his activities; they marvel at his self-control. The truth may be that through negative adaptation he has reached the place where he is quite unconscious of her talking; he gives the appearance of listening but in reality is occupied with his own thoughts and hears little of what she says. Her habit causes him little if any annoyance and the marriage may be a happy one.

Courtship patterns carried into marriage

During the courtship period, it is natural for a measure of uncertainty to exist. Both partners may need frequent assurances and demonstrations of love. One or the other may occasionally indulge in attempts to keep the other guessing by pretending indifference, or by showing attentions to other members of the opposite sex with the intention of arousing jealousy in the loved one. If the loved one reacts as desired, the little game will be called off until the partner again feels the need for reassurance. Frequent lovers' quarrels followed by affectionate reconciliations often characterize affairs of this type, and each incident leads to new commitments and to a deeper emotional involvement. Although such courtship behavior is not unusual, it is frequently a sign of immaturity. An excessive desire to test and to prove the love of the partner is sometimes an indication of inner insecurity and lack of confidence, which may cause the immature demands for reassurance to be carried over unhappily into marriage.

Granted that a certain minimum of affectional testing may occur during courtship, it is not desirable for this pattern to be carried over into marriage. One of the joys of a good marriage is the calm of emotional security that comes with the knowledge of being wholeheartedly loved. In a happy marriage, both partners express and demonstrate their love so that neither one has occasion for doubt. Attempts to test love by pretending indifference or by trying to arouse jealousy after marriage are almost invariably threats to the success of the marriage.

Maturity of married love

It is unfortunate that in so much popular fiction as well as in motion-picture stories the thrills and delights of being in love are presented as associated quite exclusively with the courtship period. All the uncertainties of courtship are offered as exciting and desirable. The depth of happiness achieved in successful marriage is seldom, if ever, pictured. No doubt one reason is that emotional experiences that have depth and permanence are far more difficult to portray. Only great actors or superior writers can hope to do justice to them. The result is that popular misconceptions exist. "He's just an old married man now," or "She's married and settled down," imply that with marriage, romance ends. Some married people go along with such a viewpoint, making frantic efforts to cling to courtship patterns rather than allowing themselves to grow into the normal patterns of marriage. They fear that they may "settle down like other married people" and "take each other for granted." They fail to appreciate the fact that to maintain the level of obsessive emotionalism of the courtship period for an indefinite time could become extremely wearing. They have not yet learned that the security of married love is one of the most satisfying experiences in life. To fight off mature affection and to try to preserve the courtship type of love experience are in the same category as trying to maintain the appearance and behavior of sweet sixteen when one is 35. That is clinging to immaturity because of a failure to appreciate the pleasures of living on a mature level. Being able to "take each other for granted" and to trust each other without limit is one of the emoluments of a happy marriage. Few other relationships in life offer this benefit.

Role concepts and marriage adjustment

The conceptions that individuals hold concerning their own roles in life and their role expectations from their mates significantly affect their marital adjustment. Like many of our other values in life, our feelings about what is "woman's place" or "man's place," and what are the special prerogatives of each sex, are likely to be more emotional than rational, and it is difficult for us to examine our attitudes objectively. Therefore, much frustration and antagonism may arise in a marriage in which the two hold differing views. Often neither will be able to define his attitudes clearly or to pin down the true basis of certain antagonisms.

An example of such a case may illustrate the point.

> John grew up in a family in which the father had been an invalid for many years and the mother had supported the family by running a small business. As the four sons grew up, they worked and helped support themselves, but they always consulted closely with their mother about their affairs and respected her judgment. John married Margaret, who came from a family in which the father was a very successful professional man, with a dynamic personality. Her family was definitely father-dominated. Margaret's mother happily devoted her full energies to being a good wife and a good mother. She never made decisions without consulting her husband, and she relied on his judgment. After some years of marriage, John and Margaret were still struggling with an inability to understand each other or to feel secure in their relationship. No doubt a number of factors entered in, for it is never possible in a failing marriage to isolate one factor and say that it alone is the cause of all the trouble. But in this case it was apparent to the marriage counselor whom they consulted that a major point in their lack of adjustment was that each looked for a type of dominance in the other that was lacking. John constantly brought home to Margaret his problems from his job and wanted to talk them over with her and get her ideas and suggestions. This seemed to her a burden, and she tended to get worried and upset over his problems; she felt they were not in her sphere and that she was not capable of helping him. Moreover, his dependence on her for help contributed to a feeling of insecurity and inadequacy in her. She herself wanted to lean on him for far more help than she was able to get. She felt that he should make all decisions concerning money matters and problems related to the children. When he left these things to her, she felt that he was "letting her down" and failing to take the responsibility that she had a right to expect of him as head of the house. Both developed rather serious feelings of inadequacy, insecurity, and discontent with the marriage. Neither fulfilled the role that the other felt was "right."

The opposite situation also arises. The husband may be willing and anxious to be recognized as head of the house but may feel that his wife is not willing to accord him his "rightful" prerogatives. Such couples become competitive toward each other and tend to undermine each other's self-confidence by withholding respect and emotional support. Each feels that his or her contribution to the family well-being is undervalued by the other.

A great many marriages involve some differences on this point. And it is always extremely difficult for one mate to force the other to fulfil an unwanted role. Flexibility in attitudes is essential for both, and successful marital adjustment will depend on the perceptive understanding two people have of each other's feelings and needs, and on their ability to adjust in order to meet each other's needs.

Finally—

Since the success of a marriage depends greatly on the material going into the marriage, it is important to choose a mate wisely; but people can learn to become good husbands and wives through thoughtful, cooperative effort. There is hope even for those who have not made a wise choice, if they have an intelligent understanding of the different facets of life in which they must work together, and if they work to establish satisfactory and happy levels of adjustment in their relationships.

"People who share a cell in the Bastille or are thrown together on an uninhabited island will find some possible ground of compromise if they do not immediately fall to fisticuffs. They will learn each other's ways and humours so as to know where they must go warily and where they may lean their whole weight. The discretion of the first years becomes the settled habit of the last; and so, with wisdom and patience, two lives may grow indissolubly into one." [7]

Review questions

1. Contrast the interaction of courtship adjustment with the interaction of marriage adjustment.
2. How does marriage adjustment in a "mixed marriage" differ from marriage adjustment in a conventional marriage?
3. In what ways is adjusting to a marriage partner comparable to living with a roommate?

[7] Robert Louis Stevenson, "Essay on Marriage," *Virginibus Puerisque*.

4. What are the three chief forms of resolving conflict in marriage adjustment? Illustrate each with cases of marriages you have observed.

5. What are seven potential conflict areas in marriage interaction that may call for adjustment?

6. Which areas seem to require the longest time for adjustment? In which areas are the fewest mutually satisfactory adjustments after some years of marriage?

7. Are marriages happier if mutually satisfactory adjustments are reached early in marriage?

8. Is it possible for a couple to have a happy marriage if they have never adjusted in one area?

9. How does modern living cause tensions to be built up in the individual?

10. Differentiate between productive quarrels and destructive quarrels. Is a quarrel in marriage ever strictly constructive and not destructive?

11. What might be the effects on a marriage if one spouse came from a quarreling family and the other from a non-quarreling family?

12. List five advantages of the family conference method of handling family differences.

13. Name several wholesome "tension-relievers" that you have found effective, or which you have observed in your friends.

14. What are "tremendous trifles" in marriage?

15. What is the psychological effect of being "remodeled"?

16. What are the most important factors in determining whether a particular marriage will be a success or a failure?

Projects and activities

1. Write up a case of a family you have observed that uses either quarreling or the conference method of settling family problems.

2. Give a case of a family difference which started as a "productive quarrel" but ended in a family fight.

3. Make a list of "tremendous trifles" which have caused trouble in your family, or some family you know well.

4. *Role-playing.*

(a) John came from a home run by a neat and orderly mother, who always had John's clothes pressed and ready for him. He has been married to Joan for six months and has become annoyed at her housekeeping and her failure to be responsible for having his clothes ready for him.

Scene: John is hurrying to get to work and finds that he has no clean socks. Joan comes into the room at this moment.

(b) John and Joan have been married 6 years and have children 1, 3 and 5 years old. The baby has been sick and Joan has had a hard day. When John comes home from work, dinner is not ready, although Joan knows that this is the evening when John has an early bowling date.

Films

Who's Boss? Use this film here if it was not used at the end of Chapter III.

Marriage Today. Gives a mature concept of marriage and marriage adjustment by showing several couples who have been married for some years. McGraw-Hill Book Company, Inc. 20 minutes, sound.

Suggested readings

Baber, Ray E., *Marriage and the Family.* New York: McGraw-Hill Book Company, Inc., 1953. Ch. VI, "The Husband-Wife Relationship."

Bowman, Henry A., *Marriage for Moderns.* New York: McGraw-Hill Book Company, Inc., 1954. Chs. X and XI, "Personality Adjustment."

Burgess, Ernest W., and Harvey J. Locke, *The Family.* New York: American Book Company, 1953. Ch. XIV, "Marital Success," and Ch. XV, "Predicting Marital Success."

Burgess, Ernest W., and Paul Wallin, *Engagement and Marriage.* Chicago: J. B. Lippincott Company, 1953. "Marital Adjustment."

Cavan, Ruth Shonle, *The American Family.* New York: Thomas Y. Crowell Company, 1953. Ch. XVI, "Marital Adjustment."

Duvall, Evelyn Millis, *Family Development.* Chicago: J. B. Lippincott Company, 1957. Ch. VI, "Beginning Families: Establishment Phase."

Kenkel, William F., "Influence Differentiation in Family Decision Making," *Sociology and Social Research,* 42:1 (September-October, 1957), 18-25.

Kephart, William M., "The Duration of Marriage," *American Sociological Review,* 19:3 (June, 1954), 287-295.

Landis, Judson T., and Mary G. Landis, eds., *Readings in Marriage and the Family.* Englewood Cliffs, N. J.: Prentice-Hall, Inc., 1952. Part X, Reading 1, "Psychological Factors in Marital Happiness," Lewis M. Terman; Reading 4, "Time Required To Achieve Marriage Adjustment," Judson T. Landis; Reading 5, "Predicting Adjustment in Marriage," Ernest W. Burgess and Leonard S. Cottrell; Reading 6, "Learning To Live Together—A Case," Anonymous; Reading 7, "Occupational Factors and Marriage," Meyer F. Nimkoff; Reading 8, "Social Class and Marital Adjustment," Julius Roth and Robert F. Peck.

Peterson, James A., *Education for Marriage.* Chicago: Charles Scribner's Sons, 1956. Ch. XII, "Achieving Individuation and Togetherness," and Ch. XIII, "Early Adjustments in Marriage."

Sex Adjustment in Marriage

A mutually satisfactory sex relationship is one of the important factors that contribute to happiness in marriage. However, people contemplating marriage may assume that sex gratification is the basic and all-important factor upon which the success or failure of marriage depends. Such is not the case. Sexual union is but one of a complicated set of relationships and activities that make up the whole interactional pattern of a marriage.

The sex relationship and adjustment in other areas of life

Conflict in other areas sometimes causes the failure of marriages in which the sex phase of life seems to be satisfactory to both partners. Inability to agree on the use of money, for example, with constantly recurring quarrels over finances, may cause a couple to part in spite of sexual compatibility. Friction over in-laws may create such animosity between husband and wife that they will part regardless of the bond provided by their sex life.

Moreover, if conflict exists in other areas of a marriage, it is likely to be reflected in the sex life of the couple. Since sexual union is the most intimately cooperative activity of marriage, the partners have a tendency to come together less frequently if antagonism exists between them. If they are at odds over other matters, one or the other may even show a definite resistance to sexual union, with the result that other conflicts will become intensified.

Conversely, marriages in which the sex adjustment is poor may endure because of the strength

. . 16

of other bonds. Sharing of interests in children, in friends or relatives, in religion, in recreation or in work, and in many phases of daily living, all make their contribution to a good marriage. Since all facets of a marriage are closely interrelated, it is often impossible to determine whether a poor sex adjustment is a cause or a result of dissatisfactions in other parts of the life of a couple.

Sex relationships, more often than some other phases of marital interaction, seem to be the focal point of tensions, because constantly recurring biological urges force couples to reckon with this part of life. Two people who differ on religion may possibly agree to disagree and live together happily; a couple may have widely divergent ideas concerning the use of money, yet if they have enough money so that their differences do not cause financial hardship, they can tolerate their differences and live in peace.

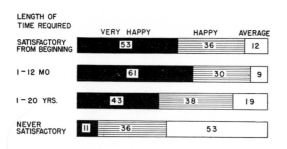

Fig. 66 LENGTH OF TIME REQUIRED TO ADJUST IN SEX RELATIONS AND HAPPINESS IN MARRIAGE (409 COUPLES).

But in the area of sex the issue must be faced; for the sex urge is comparable to hunger in that it seeks periodic satisfaction. It also requires cooperation. Differences here cannot be ignored as can some other differences. Therefore, although sex is not an all-important factor in itself, a mutually gratifying sex relationship will serve to facilitate all adjustments, just as conflicts seemingly unrelated to sex will have repercussions in the sex life of the couple.

Although the place of sex in marriage is too often exaggerated, the contribution it makes to successful marriage is nevertheless important. Certainly few marriages would take place were it not for sexual attraction between the two partners; so throughout life the sex attraction can serve to enhance and to color all the couple's association together. Studies among happily married couples all agree that couples who have achieved the highest degree of mutuality in their sex relations are among the most happily married.

The personality traits that each partner takes into marriage will have much to do with the degree of sexual mutuality achieved. People who are cooperative, perceptive of the reactions of others, and considerate of the needs of others are the ones who seek to share gratification rather than having as their goal self-gratification only. Those who are selfish, impatient, unaware of the needs of others, and unwilling to learn from others will have far less to contribute toward the achievement of a rewarding sex relationship in marriage. These personality factors are of far greater importance in sex adjustment than simple biological adequacy is.

Mutuality in sex life

In earlier days the belief was generally accepted that sex in marriage was to be enjoyed by men and tolerated by women. It was not recognized that husbands had any obligation toward attempting to achieve mutuality in the sex act. And many women accepted a passive role, with the attitude that coitus was one of their marital duties not intended to involve much pleasure. Evidence of too much pleasure in sex experience was to be avoided by self-respecting wives, since it might be taken as an indication of unladylike tendencies. Many exceedingly happy marriages operated on that basis.

Wives who wholeheartedly accepted their role as passive and who entered marriage with no other expectation may have escaped some of the conflicts that many women experience today. Young people now generally believe that sex expression in marriage should be a mutually gratifying experience. In the conception of woman's role in sex relationships, some have gone so far that they attach too great importance to woman's ability to react vigorously in the early days of marriage. Disillusionment may result at this point with newly married couples. For here a cultural lag exists. Our generation has discarded the belief that woman is the passive, man the active, partner in sex experience, and in theory we subscribe to a belief in mutual sharing of sexual pleasure. But the adverse conditioning of girls in the realm of sex goes on, and the general preparation for marriage, which would make mutual sharing a more easily accomplishable fact, has not kept pace with the new attitudes and expectations that young people have concerning marriage.

The crucial period is the first few months or years of a marriage. If too much disillusionment and frustration develops, undesirable patterns may become so set that it will take much intelligent effort by one or both partners to remedy the defects in the adjustment pattern. However, some couples whose early sex life has been a disappointment or a problem, do achieve mutually satisfactory sex adjustments after as long as 10 to 20 years of married life. Therefore, if sex relationships are not what the marriage partners feel they should be, it is worth while to persevere in working to bring about a mutually rewarding relationship. But much conflict in the early years of marriage could be avoided if young people were well prepared, before they marry, with knowledge of the differences in the sexes emotionally and physically.

Causes of poor sex adjustment

Research studies show three broad classifications which include most of the causes of poor sex adjustment in marriage. These are: (1) problems due to biological or organic factors, (2) problems due primarily to a lack of biological and psychological knowledge, and (3) problems due to social conditioning. Relatively few cases fall within the first classification. In one study of 100 couples, 5 per cent had had difficulty because of organic disturbances,[1] and in our study of the 544 couples only 2 per cent had any difficulty that would fall within the first classification.

Most difficulties in sex adjustment are due to causes which fall within the second and third classifications. Both husbands and wives enter marriage with a vast amount of misinformation concerning the role and functioning of sex. Much relearning is necessary. In addition to mistaken ideas about biological and psychological functioning, the wife or husband, sometimes both, may bring to marriage certain attitudes which are the result of unfortunate conditioning during childhood, and which may handicap the establishing of a good sex relationship. Some children, perhaps girls more often than boys, are conditioned to look upon sex with shame, aversion, or fear. When a man and woman have difficulties in the sex phase of their marriage it is sometimes hard to distinguish between causes of failure due to lack of knowledge and those due to social conditioning because, in spite of adverse conditioning, many wives would be able to respond and cooperate in building a good sex relationship if the husbands were well enough informed to understand their wives' reactions.

Time and psychic unity as factors in sex adjustment

Strangely enough, sex adjustment is sometimes difficult just because those going into marriage believe that the one part of marriage that will pose no problems at all is the sex relationship. Many people reason that since sex is based on biological drives, all that is necessary for a successful marriage is that one follow one's biological inclinations. People who approach marriage with this attitude are often among the group who experience early disillusionment. If man lived on the animal level, the simple

[1] E. W. Burgess and L. S. Cottrell, *Predicting Success or Failure in Marriage,* p. 221. Englewood Cliffs, N. J.: Prentice-Hall, Inc., 1938.

following of biological urges would probably accomplish "mating" as it does with other animals. However, human sexual intercourse in a civilized society differs as much from animal mating as man's eating according to socially approved rules differs from the animal's unceremonious devouring of his food. Equally important with biological impulses are many psychic and emotional factors. Results of research among married people indicate that many couples do not immediately achieve a sex relationship that is in all ways satisfactory; they need time and understanding, and some patience, in order to build a good sex relationship.

Our study of the length of time required after marriage for 409 couples to achieve satisfactory levels of adjustment revealed that one-eighth of the couples needed weeks or months but reached a sex adjustment they considered satisfactory within a year. One-tenth of the couples required an average of six years to work out this part of their marriage, some of them requiring as long as 20 years.

In the average marriage there is likely at first to be a measure of uncertainty, awkwardness, and tension in the sex life. Since the newly married couple plans to live together for the next 40 or 50 years, it is surely worth while to proceed slowly at first in order to build a permanently satisfying sex relationship. For, once a good sex adjustment is established, the sex life of the couple will contribute greatly to their feelings of mutual contentment and well-being. Happily married couples, after a few years, report that their sex adjustment becomes an increasingly satisfactory bond in their marriage.

In one study [2] of honeymoon experiences the wives listed as their most common problems on the honeymoon "adjusting sexually" and "lack of adequate sex education." Approximately half of the women in the study said that they had failed to achieve

---

[2] Stanley R. Brav, "Notes on Honeymoon," *Marriage and Family Living,* 10:3 (August, 1947), 60.

complete sexual harmony during the honeymoon. However, three out of four thought that the honeymoon was a complete success. Those findings suggest that in many of the cases happy relationships were being created in all the different areas of life during the honeymoon, so that even though completely satisfactory sex relationships were not established so early, the honeymoon was considered a success.

In his study of married students in Oregon, Johannis found that, of the one-third who reported they had needed marriage counseling during their first three years of marriage, 60 per cent had needed counseling on sex relations.[3] Of the 544 college couples we studied at Michigan State University, the largest percentage of those who needed marriage counseling early in marriage had felt a need for counseling on sex.

All available evidence indicates that a good sex adjustment is usually established gradually, over a period of time, and does not occur suddenly on the honeymoon. It is not unusual for brides to report that sex on the honeymoon was a disappointment or that it did not measure up to their anticipations. In research on this subject, Adams found that one-third of the most responsive wives in the study reported that their first experience of full sexual climax did not occur until after they had been married from three to six months.[4]

Handicap of misinformation

In some ways we are still living in a man's world. The woman who is successful in her contacts with men caters to masculine ego either consciously or unconsciously. She does not deflate a man's ego by showing superior knowledge in the areas that he

[3] Theodore B. Johannis, Jr., "The Marital Adjustment of a Sample of Married College Students," *The Coordinator*, 4:4 (June, 1956), 25.

[4] Clifford Adams, "An Informal Preliminary Report on Some Factors Relating to Sexual Responsiveness of Certain College Wives." State College, Pennsylvania: The Pennsylvania State College, 1953.

feels are his specific province. She is especially careful in the sex realm. Many a husband would be offended or chagrined if his bride questioned his knowledge of sex or tried to educate him on the subject. Many men go into marriage with a smattering of information gathered from "bull sessions," from questionable literature, or from premarital experimentation. The man who has had promiscuous premarital experience is inclined to think he knows women and sex and is therefore prepared for marriage. Actually, he has learned little that will help in working out a good sex relationship with his wife; and his confidence that he knows everything can be a serious handicap. His experience before marriage may cause him to be overly critical of his wife's responses, and may prevent his trying to develop techniques that are important in a permanent marriage relationship. Regardless of how much more accurate and realistic the wife's information may be, she can do little to help this type of husband without deflating his ego. Both men and women need to enter marriage with open minds, ready to learn and to work at reaching a good understanding.

Cultural conditioning of sex response

A complication in sex adjustment in marriage is to be found in the way the subject of sex is handled in our culture. Some children are conditioned so that it may be difficult for them to adjust to normal sex experience when they grow up. When they first begin to ask questions about sex, parents may try to keep them in ignorance, thus forcing them to seek information from undesirable sources. When children engage in any type of sexual expression or experimentation, parents are likely to be worried or shocked, and to show their shock, or to punish the child severely. Consequently the child may conclude that all sex interests are vulgar, shameful, and bad. Girls are likely to be impressed more than boys with taboos in the area of sex, since much greater social stigma is attached to the girl who deviates from socially acceptable behavior. Many parents solve the practical problem of protecting their daughter by over-impressing her with the dangerous aspects of sex activity. Many young married people have stated that their adjustment would have been easier if they could have been told before marriage about "the beauty of sex relations," that "sex is not sordid" and "not to be feared."

Conditioned responses that have been built up over a period of 20 years preceding marriage will not change suddenly with the marriage ceremony. Timidity and reluctance to discuss the whole subject of sex make it difficult for some couples to cooperate where cooperation is essential for success. Much could be said about the need for dropping inhibitions that have been built up during childhood. For most people that is a difficult process. However, an intelligent understanding of themselves and the reasons back of their attitudes will help overcome many of the effects of early conditioning. In time, people can be reconditioned so that their responses are positive and satisfying. As constructive sex education becomes more widespread, more people should become able to establish good marriage adjustments readily.

Another factor, which makes it difficult for some women to respond in the early years of marriage, is that in general girls have associated some unpleasantness with sex for as long as they can remember. Not only have they been punished for any childish infraction of sex taboos, but they are also conscious of the inconvenient or unpleasant aspects of menstruation, and they have heard tales about the pain of childbirth. It is little wonder that some young wives cannot instantly throw off all feelings of resistance toward sexual activity at marriage.

Further, ignorance concerning the facts of physical structure and functioning handicaps many girls. This ignorance is responsible for much of the emotional resistance that some wives have toward the first experiences in sexual intercourse. Dr. Kavinoky, gynecologist of many years' experience, says: [5]

> "It is amazing how often the girl is unaware of the fact that there is an opening in the hymen, that 'breaking the maiden veil' is unnecessary and that there is a deep vaginal canal. This latter is appreciated with such spontaneous surprise (when the girl is informed of it in the premarital examination) that it is hard for us to realize that vagueness about pelvic anatomy and physiology can be the basis for so many groundless fears.
>
> "This discovery of the nature of a vaginal canal, and later a realization of the elasticity of the hymen and of the vaginal canal has a striking effect in the change it causes in the emotional attitude of the young woman. A fearful girl becomes a relaxed, cooperative, and intelligent patient soon after discovering this fact."

The premarital conditioning of the husband usually has been different from the conditioning of the wife. Men grow up thinking of sex expression as something to be enjoyed; they have little reason to be aware of any unpleasant or painful concomitants of sex functioning. If boys are punished for their early experimentations, it is seldom with the zeal that is applied when girls are the offenders. Some parents tend to view boys' infractions of rules on sex behavior as evidence of potential virility, and to be lenient.

If both partners in marriage understand and make allowances for this difference in experience and conditioning, they can more intelligently cooperate toward a satisfactory sex adjustment. Patience may be especially necessary on the part of the husband.

Differences in sex response

One thing that has proved baffling to many husbands is that they find it impossible to understand the reactions of their wives. A young husband who stated that his wife's "sex drive varies with the success of daily affairs" had made a keen observation. The average man finds that he can enjoy sexual gratification regard-

[5] Nadina Kavinoky, M.D., "Premarital Examination," *The Western Journal of Surgery, Obstetrics and Gynecology,* 51 (October, 1943), 412-415.

less of how other phases of the marriage are going. He may be at odds with his wife and critical of nearly everything she does, yet desire coitus. The wife cannot understand this attitude and is often resentful about it. Many wives complain bitterly that husbands show affection only when they are interested in coitus. The woman's viewpoint is likely to be that coitus is the ultimate expression of a love that includes the whole personality. If personality clashes or antagonisms develop over things in the daily association, she is likely to be much less interested in coitus. The fact that her husband can desire it in spite of other personal factors is to her an indication that his interest in her is only physical and for his own gratification.

The husband can be equally resentful of his wife's attitude. To him it may appear that she withholds response from him as a method of revenge or retribution. He naturally interprets her reactions in the light of his own. If he were to withhold response from her, it could be only by a rational and specific effort. What he cannot realize is that her *ability* to respond sexually often depends on her whole general response to his personality. There is probably greater need for an understanding of each other on this point than on any other one thing affecting the happiness of husbands and wives. If a couple can accept the fact that this difference exists, that it is not a peculiarity of their own marriage, but rather a universal difference between men and women in our culture, they can look upon it in a different light. It is often a help to young married couples facing problems to realize that they are not alone; the problems that loom so large in their marriage have been encountered in greater or lesser degree in almost all the marriages they see about them; and the happy marriages with which they are acquainted have been achieved not because these conditions did not exist, but because the couples have accepted them realistically and have worked their way through them successfully.

Strength of sex drive

Different views are held concerning inherent biological differences between the sex drives of men and women. A difference in sex desire appears to exist, but it is impossible to say with certainty how much of the difference is due to cultural conditioning and how much is of biological origin.

Many wives at marriage are sexually "unawakened" and time is required for them to learn to achieve full response and satisfaction in coitus. Women experience some measure of sex desire before marriage, but full response through orgasm is experienced before marriage by only a small percentage of women compared to the proportion of young men who at marriage have been experiencing some form of full sex response for some years. It takes time, therefore, for the average couple to understand each other and to adjust so that they meet each other's sexual needs. In our study of college students in the 11 colleges in 1952-1955 the married women were asked when they first experienced orgasm. Of significance in our discussion here is the fact that 11 per cent of these wives said they had never experienced it, although they had been married an average of three years. Table 23 summarizes this study and compares our findings with those of similar studies by Terman [6] and Thomason.[7] In approximately half the cases in all three studies, the wives experienced orgasm within the first month of marriage, and one-fourth more within the first year of marriage. The remaining fourth took one or more years, or had never experienced it. These studies emphasize the fact that a wide range exists in the ability of wives to respond sexually in early marriage, and that time is required for growth in this area.

The fact that the sex drive in men usually matures earlier than

[6] Lewis M. Terman, *Psychological Factors in Marital Happiness,* p. 306. New York: McGraw-Hill Book Company, Inc., 1938.

[7] Bruce Thomason, "The Influence of Marital Sexual Behavior on Total Marital Adjustment." Paper read at National Council on Family Relations, Rutgers University, September, 1952.

in women means that even when the sex drive of the husband is far beyond that of the wife early in marriage, they can hope to reach a better balance of approximate equality of drive after a time. With many couples the sex adjustment is much more satisfying after as much as ten or more years of marriage. In marriages in which the partners are very unequally matched in sex drive in the early years, both will have to compromise, but they need not conclude that they are permanently handicapped, for time may show that the difference is not so great. It should be noted here that a difference in sex response early in marriage is by no means a universal problem. In the two studies of college

TABLE 23 PERCENTAGES OF WIVES IN THREE STUDIES
STATING VARIOUS LENGTHS OF TIME
BEFORE ORGASM WAS EXPERIENCED IN MARRIAGE

Length of time		Terman (N-792) 11 years	Thomason (N-641) 4 years	Landis (N-114) 3 years
	Married:			
Honeymoon to 4 weeks		51.1%	50.0%	53.0%
One month to 1 year		25.7	27.0	30.0
One year or more		16.0	7.0	6.0
Never		7.1	7.0	11.0
No reply		—	9.0	—

couples in Oregon and in Michigan, approximately one-fifth of the husbands complained that the wife was not responsive enough and one-fifth of the wives complained that the husband was too responsive, but about four-fifths of the husbands and wives reported that they felt that the mate was responsive enough. Thus, with four-fifths of the individuals, differences in responsiveness were not a problem at the time of the study.

In considering differences in response, there is sometimes a concentration on techniques by which husbands may arouse increased response in their wives. The emphasis tends to be upon the physical, ignoring the fact that the wife's response depends on psychological and emotional elements also. Expression of affection and assurances of love and appreciation are elements of great importance. Some husbands are unaware that the mood of the wife changes with the time of the menstrual cycle. Her ability to be aroused and her reaction to coitus may differ with each part of the month. Although variations occur in individuals, studies show that with most women the periods of time just before or just after menstruation are periods of greatest sexual response. Terman found that one-half of the women in his study recognized greater desire just before or just after menstruation, about twice as many after as before.[8] In another study, 181 single college girls kept a record of the day to day changes in their

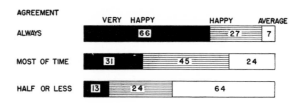

AGREEMENT

Fig. 67   AGREEMENT IN SEX EXPRESSION AND MARITAL HAPPINESS (544 COUPLES).

physical and emotional feelings throughout one or more monthly cycles.[9] One item they recorded was any change in awareness of sex desire. This study showed that if any noticeable upswing in desire occurred it was just before or just after menstruation, with slightly more reporting upswings before than after. These findings and other available evidence suggest that some wives who do not have a strong sex drive may experience full climactic sex response only at one time of the month.

[8] Terman, *op. cit.*, p. 351.
[9] Judson T. Landis, "Physical and Mental-Emotional Changes Accompanying the Menstrual Cycle in Women," *Proceedings of the Pacific Sociological Society.* Pullman: Washington State College, 25:2 (June, 1957), 159-162.

Differences in timing and orgasm response

Although there is reason to believe that no biological difference exists in sex drive, still in our culture a significant difference between the manner and duration of reaction in men and women does exist. Men are more easily aroused and can be more quickly satisfied; women are slower to arouse and are capable of response of longer duration.

It is desirable for the wife to receive emotional release through orgasm in sexual intercourse. However, research shows that in a great many very happy marriages the wife seldom or never experiences what is known as full climactic response and yet receives pleasure and satisfaction from the sex relationship. There are all levels of sexual enjoyment; orgasm is only one. The love play leading to coitus may be satisfying without orgasm. The important test is whether complete and satisfying union is achieved for both. It is not necessary, nor is it possible, for all wives' responses to conform to a typical physical climax. Terman's study of marriage adjustment among the gifted group [10] and their wives found that almost half of the wives who seldom or never experienced orgasm still claimed to derive either complete or fairly complete satisfaction from the sex act. Nevertheless, if the wife expects and desires orgasm and is frequently disappointed, the sex adjustment of the marriage is likely to be adversely affected.

It is important for couples to realize that, in general, men's sex desire and response are more specific and localized than are women's. Women, in average cases, reach a climax more slowly, their reaction is more diffuse, the emotional reaction is of longer duration and slower to subside. Men's response ends more abruptly with the climax of the sex act. If the partners are aware that these differences exist, the differences need not be a barrier to mutuality. If each focuses his attention on the needs and

[10] Lewis M. Terman, "Correlates of Orgasm Adequacy in a Group of 556 Wives," *The Journal of Psychology*, 32 (October, 1951), p. 128.

responses of the other, complete mutuality can usually be achieved in time. Here the husband has more responsibility than the wife, because his responses are likely to be faster than hers. By exercising a measure of control and by studying his wife's reactions, he can make progress toward the goal of a satisfactory sex experience for both. Thus the highest level of emotional and affectional as well as physical union may be achieved.

The successful sex act should result not only in physical release or satisfaction for the husband and for the wife, but in a general sense of well-being for both, in a feeling of security due to psychic as well as physical union.

Other factors

Quite commonly the achievement of a successful sex relationship depends in part on other factors, such as fatigue of one or both partners. The circumstances under which sex union is attempted must also be suitable. There must be privacy, a confidence that there will be no interruption, and pleasant surroundings. If either feels that haste is necessary because of other obligations or impending interruptions, a mutually gratifying experience will be less likely.

One young couple were having conflict in connection with sex in their marriage. They had prepared for marriage by reading and discussing the best information available on all phases of marital adjustment. Yet after three months, they both felt disillusioned. The wife was finding coitus repugnant, and the husband remarked bitterly that he felt he had married a frigid woman. An analysis of the facts revealed that their problem was due almost entirely to the circumstances under which they were attempting to live. They were keeping their marriage a secret from their friends and families. Any time they spent together was of necessity clandestine, and in surroundings very different from those desirable for consummation of marriage by bride and groom. Whenever they were together as man and wife, they felt the pressure to be careful that their relationship not be discovered. These things weighed more heavily upon the wife than on the husband, although she had not recognized the connection between them and her inability to respond sexually. After consulting a counselor, the couple announced their marriage and began living together openly with the inhibiting psychic factors removed. The wife's ability to respond sexually became satisfactory and they reached a much better adjustment in sex relations.

Frequency of coitus

Some people go into marriage hampered by preconceived ideas about just how frequently coitus should occur. But there can be no set rule. Great variations exist, ranging from nightly or oftener at one extreme to only two or three times a year at the other. The matter is entirely up to the couple concerned and should be determined by their mutual desires, the success of their relationship, the type of lives they lead, and other factors. Most couples in time find the level of frequency most conducive to their happiness and well-being.

Terman found that couples of 20-29 reported a frequency of approximately seven times per month. There was a gradual decrease in the frequency of intercourse until the age of 50-59, when approximately three copulations per month were reported.[11] The same study revealed that for each age group the husbands desired coitus more frequently than the wives did. The fact that husbands usually desire coitus more frequently than wives again reveals the importance of cooperation and willingness to compromise on the part of both partners in marriage.

It is not unusual for husbands to behave unreasonably when their sexual desires are blocked. To wives this behavior may

[11] Kinsey found a somewhat higher frequency, from approximately 12 times per month for the 20-29 age group to four times per month for the older group. Kinsey, *op. cit.*, p. 252.

appear to be an immature and undisciplined response to the blocking of desires. In some cases neither husband nor wife will recognize the cause of the husband's behavior; he will simply act generally irritable until the wife loses patience with him and a quarrel results. It is helpful if husbands can analyze their own behavior. Wives can be more sympathetic to husbands' needs if they also understand the causes. Almost all wives are tolerant of the fact that many husbands revert to childish behavior when they are hungry. That is why so many successful homemakers see to it that a comfortable chair, the evening paper, and his slippers are invitingly evident when the man of the house comes home if dinner is not quite ready. And how many times the same wives excuse the explosive behavior of a young son with the explanation, "He is hungry. What he needs is a good dinner."

It is impossible to estimate the proportion of marital difficulties arising because of explosive behavior on the part of husbands who experience blocking of sexual desires. But marriage counselors recognize that in a great many cases that come to them for help this is one of the contributing factors. Unfortunately, no simple and effective remedy can be recommended to solve this problem. If both husband and wife recognize that their needs may differ, and if both are willing to compromise, they can eliminate much unpleasantness and build a sex life that is quite satisfactory for both, even though they must cope with a considerable difference in the strength of their sex drives. However, even in marriages where the spouses are equally matched, there will be times when one spouse is physically or mentally exhausted and not interested in sexual activity, while the other may be very much interested. Sex adjustments that are perfect at all times are probably relatively rare. The tempo of modern living—success and failure in work, sickness of the spouse or the children, worry and anxiety—all affect the desire and the capacity for sexual enjoyment. For these reasons it must be recognized that a successful sex adjustment is one that provides a satisfying experience for both partners most of the time, but probably not all the time. The emotional and psychological factors associated with intercourse, and the integration of the sex act within the framework of a total relationship that is satisfying to both, are the tests of a good sex relationship.

Anxieties over sex experiences early in marriage

Some couples become too anxious to work out a sex adjustment early in marriage and attach too much significance to any early disappointments or failures. Many young wives will not experience full climactic response in the early weeks of marriage even though they are well informed and their husbands are successful lovers, since marriage breaks down the physical barrier to coitus but does not necessarily break down the psychic barrier. Time is required for new conditioned responses to be substituted for old ones. Anxieties generated by early failures sometimes produce a mental state which makes complete sexual response more difficult. Young people who love each other, who are companionable, and who have many things in common still have to learn to live together. In their sex adjustment, as well as in many other adjustments, time will take care of many problems, if they are willing to work at building good relationships.

Lack of standardization in sex teachings and attitudes

When any two young people marry, they are almost certain to bring two different, and often contrasting, sets of attitudes toward sex to their marriage. No institutional provision has existed for teaching young people about sex behavior and sex practices. In all other phases of living most people receive some form of constructive teaching from earliest childhood. Families attempt to inculcate in their children proper concepts of social attitudes and behavior. Newspapers and magazines carry discussions of what is desirable in dress, in manners, and in social customs. Public schools accept the obligation for teaching children many of the standards that will help them get along in the world about them. Only in the field of sex behavior and practices has education been seriously neglected. Here the teaching is almost entirely negative; it consists chiefly in impressing the child with taboos. And even the taboos are not standardized.

Research on sex behavior in marriage indicates that no single pattern of sex practice in marriage is generally accepted as "normal" and proper. Rather, a wide range of practices may be looked upon as normal and right, or as improper and wrong, according to the individual's background. This variation in what is considered right, proper, and normal in sex relations can make for great misunderstanding, even repulsion and disgust, between two young people who come from families or economic groups with contrasting attitudes toward sex behavior and practice in marriage. What one spouse accepts as normal the other may feel is abnormal or perverted.

So, two young people who find differences in their attitudes toward sex expression in marriage will sometimes have difficulty in harmonizing their attitudes. One may be sure his or her standards are best because they are based on religion or morality or "right." The other may be equally sure that desirable practices can be based only on what is "normal" biologically. An added difficulty arises because few couples will be able to recognize rationally even that their fundamental attitudes do differ, or to what extent the differences exist. They will simply go into marriage expecting much from sex relations, and if all is not perfect at once or soon, the husband may decide he has a frigid wife, or the wife may decide she has married a selfish and insensitive husband. Or either one may decide that the other is over-sexed or over-aggressive sexually. The couple may not have analyzed the real problem—a fundamental difference over attitudes toward proper and normal sex expression in marriage. The problem need not affect the marriage adversely, however, if both can be tolerant and understanding on differences in levels and types of "normal" sex expression.

Outside help for problems

Couples who have difficulties in their personal adjustments in marriage are often hesitant to seek outside help. They will readily seek medical help in case of illness, and many will discuss their physical ailments freely with friends and neighbors. But, when it comes to working out husband-wife relationships, many couples feel that they must maintain a pretense of perfect harmony and never openly admit that any serious problems of adjustment have arisen. The attitude of society has supported this viewpoint. Couples have been expected to conceal their hostilities and to work out their problems alone. They could perhaps go to their priest or minister with a confession of failure, or go to a lawyer for advice concerning a divorce, but little or no help was available in working out their problems in a constructive way. Little progress was made toward the understanding and cure of mental illness as long as families hid their mentally ill members and tried to keep secret the illness they felt to be a disgrace. An open recognition of any problem is necessary before progress can be made toward a solution.

So, much frustration, unhappiness, and ultimate divorce can be avoided if couples will acknowledge the common marital difficulties and realize that it is not an admission of defeat to seek help from an outside authority. A shortage exists, however, of people qualified by training, experience, and personality to help married couples who are facing difficulties. Some ministers and doctors have studied to become qualified to handle the special problems of marital adjustment, since they realize there are not enough other qualified counselors. But many more specially trained marriage counselors are needed. It seldom is wise to seek help from neighbors, friends, or relatives, for these people would be inclined to be prejudiced in favor of one spouse or the other, and unable to view the situation objectively.

A trained counselor [12] is in a position to look impartially at the total marriage situation. He may let the couple talk it out, suggest certain readings, or make suggestions according to what he observes as an outsider. In many marriage situations, all one spouse needs is a chance to talk about his problems with an unprejudiced outsider. Others need several sessions devoted to self-analysis in order to find the solution to their problems. As two people live together, they will find solutions to many marital problems without the aid of a counselor. Some excellent help is available in reading material.

A number of books treat of the physiology and psychology of sex. Public libraries are becoming increasingly aware of their obligation to provide such books to meet the needs of the public. However, since in many communities these books are still unobtainable from libraries, those interested will have to buy them in order to read them. It is desirable for couples to own helpful books which may be reread when questions arise after marriage. Much of the material dealing with the subject of sex will have greater meaning some time after marriage. Readers are inclined to skip over important points that may be beyond their present experience.

Sex in marriage a positive value

A satisfying sex relationship is one of the positive elements contributing to the well-being of each partner and of the married pair. The couple who find satisfaction together in the sexual relationship are more likely to have well-integrated personalities and to have a home in which children will find happiness. They will also be able to condition their children to look on sex as one of the normal and desirable satisfactions of living. Just as we

[12] The American Association of Marriage Counselors, Inc., 104 East 40th Street, New York 16, N. Y., will furnish information on qualified marriage counselors in various parts of the United States.

appreciate good food and comfortable shelter, a workable philosophy of life, and the security of religion, so we recognize sex fulfillment in marriage as a positive good. Its value consists not only in its function of reproducing the race but also in its constructive force in promoting the happiness of individuals. It can be the most complete form of love expression, contributing to the mental, emotional, and physical balance which is necessary if two people are to have a happy and successful marriage.

HELPS TOWARD A GOOD SEX ADJUSTMENT IN MARRIAGE

1. Try to become informed accurately before the wedding about the facts of sexual relations in marriage. Read together a good sex manual during engagement, and go to a qualified person for premarital counseling.
2. Learn to talk over sex reactions in marriage in order to be perceptive of the feelings of the spouse. Sex is an area of living in which each one receives greater satisfaction through doing the most he can to bring satisfaction to the other.
3. When differences are discovered and frustrations arise (as is true in all marriages at times), try to accept such differences without resorting to accusations or blame. The task is to recognize that there are differences between the sexes in response and to work to understand and cope with these differences.
4. Keep a perspective on the whole relationship. A sex adjustment is good if the two find satisfaction in most, but not all, of their attempts. In marriages with excellent sex adjustments, times of frustration and failure for one or both will occasionally occur.
5. If possible, develop a sense of humor, which helps to ease failures or embarrassments in sexual matters.
6. Remember that good sex adjustments usually take time. First experiences are only the beginning, not the fatal test of what a sex relationship in marriage is to be.

Review questions

1. How important is a good sex adjustment in marriage?
2. In what ways may failure to adjust in spending the family income affect the sex adjustment?

3. What special factors, which do not operate in the making of other marital adjustments, serve to focus attention on the working out of sex adjustments?

4. Contrast the attitudes of two generations ago toward sex expression in marriage with the attitudes of today.

5. Name the three broad classifications that include most of the causes of poor sex adjustment in marriage.

6. What are some of the specific circumstances that cause poor sex adjustment?

7. Why is "bull session" information often a handicap to a good sex adjustment in marriage?

8. How does cultural conditioning of the sex response before marriage affect marital adjustment?

9. Why must the husband show patience and understanding in the early months of marriage if there is to be a good sex adjustment?

10. What is one common difference in the sex response of men and women which makes for misunderstanding between husbands and wives?

11. Why does there appear to be a marked difference in the strength of the sex drive of the husband and wife in the early months of marriage?

12. Is there a biological difference in the strength of the sex drive in men and women?

13. If a couple finds they are having difficulty in arriving at a mutually satisfactory sex adjustment, where may they get reliable help?

Project

As a special project, two or three students query all agencies in your community that might be doing marriage counseling to learn what facilities are available to the public. Report to the class.

Suggested readings

Baber, Ray E., *Marriage and the Family*. New York: McGraw-Hill Book Company, Inc., 1953. Ch. VII, "Husband-Wife Relationships."

Becker, Howard, and Reuben Hill, eds., *Family, Marriage, and Parenthood*. Boston: D. C. Heath and Company, 1955. Ch. X, "Taking Physical Factors into Account."

Burgess, Ernest W., and Paul Wallin, *Engagement and Marriage*. Chicago: J. B. Lippincott Company, 1953. Ch. XX, "The Sex Factor in Marriage."

Butterfield, Oliver, *Sexual Harmony in Marriage*. New York: Emerson Books, Inc., 1953. This book and the one by Stone and Stone are excellent.

Exner, M. J., *The Sexual Side of Marriage*. New York: W. W. Norton & Company, Inc., 1932.

Groves, Ernest, Gladys Groves, and Catherine Groves, *Sex Fulfillment in Marriage*. New York: Emerson Books, Inc., 1943.

Stone, Hannah, and Abraham Stone, *A Marriage Manual*. New York: Simon & Schuster, Inc., 1952. Those about to be married or in the early years of marriage should read this book.

In-laws and Marriage Adjustment

Some people go into marriage vaguely aware that they are getting, along with a wife or husband, a new family: a mother-in-law, a father-in-law, brothers- and sisters-in-law, even aunts-, uncles-, and grandparents-in-law. Others marry feeling secure in the belief that marriage is for two alone and blissfully unconscious of all the in-laws that are an inevitable result of the "I do." Those who do realize that one marries a family as well as a mate have a wide variety of attitudes. Some who have been conditioned by years of exposure to mother-in-law jokes marry with a fatalistic attitude that in-law trouble is a part of marriage. Some others look forward with pleasure to associating with a larger family group. A person who has had no sister or brother may hope to have the lack filled by a brother-in-law or sister-in-law. Whatever the attitudes of those marrying, in-laws will be a factor in marital adjustment.

In-law adjustment:
a problem of early marriage

. . 17

Just how important are in-law relationships as a factor in marriage? Several research studies have provided some interesting information on this point. When couples who had been married for an average of 20 years were asked what had been their most serious problem in achieving happiness in marriage, the women mentioned in-law relationships second, and the men mentioned in-laws third among six chief areas of daily living.[1] These people had been married long

[1] Judson T. Landis, "Length of Time Required to Achieve Adjustment in Marriage," *American Sociological Review*, 11:6 (December, 1946), 666-677.

enough to have faced most of the issues that arise in married life. Since none of this group was divorced and 83 per cent classified their marriages as happy or very happy, they would tend to understate rather than to overstate the seriousness of in-law friction as it would exist in a representative cross section of marriages.

The second study asked for the same information from 544 couples who were in the early years of marriage.[2] These couples gave in-law relationships first place in their list of difficult areas.[3] Thomas found, in studying 7,000 Catholic marriage failures that had gone through the Catholic separation courts, that although only 7 per cent of all the failures were attributed to in-law problems, in the marriages that had failed during the first year, in-law problems were named as the most common cause.[4] This research, like the other studies, emphasizes the fact that in-law disagreements are a factor affecting the early years of marriage more than the middle and later years, although some couples settle into a permanent state of friction with the in-laws. Some of the younger couples experiencing difficulty early in marriage will in the course of time resolve their differences and reach a good understanding with the in-laws, so that if queried on their relationships years hence, they would probably report their relationships with in-laws to be excellent. The long-married group includes fewer with in-law difficulties, because those who were not able to solve their problems have in some cases ended the marriage by divorce; in other cases the situation has resolved itself through the death of the parents-in-law.

There is a logical explanation for the greater importance given

[2] Judson T. Landis, "On the Campus," *Survey Midmonthly*, 84:1 (January, 1948), 19.

[3] The findings of this research were supported by findings of a study among college married students in Oregon. See Theodore B. Johannis, Jr., "The Marital Adjustment of a Sample of Married College Students," *The Coordinator*, 4:4 (June, 1956), 24-31.

[4] John L. Thomas, "Marital Failure and Duration," *Social Order*, 3:1 (January, 1953), 26.

to in-law relationships by the younger married group. First of all, to make the transition from being an unmarried member of the family into which one was born, to being a member of an enlarged family circle that comes ready-made with the wedding, is one of the major developmental tasks of early marriage. To integrate oneself happily into the family of the spouse, a family whose ways and attitudes may not exactly correspond to the long-accepted ways of one's own family, may require special tact and perceptive understanding. The task is made more complicated by the fact that one joins a new family at the very time when it is necessary also to achieve a new level of independence from the parental family. The married pair must establish a new unit of their own, independent of either parental family, even as—paradoxically— they are joining each other's family as in-laws. People who can view the task of creating good relationships with the new rela- tives-in-law as a challenge which, if adequately met, can add greatly to the happiness of their marriage, will seldom have much "in-law trouble." They can more easily keep a perspective upon situations that arise, not necessarily seeing occurrences as in-law problems.

Specific pattern of in-law friction

The couples in our research who reported that they felt in-laws were a source of friction in their marriages were asked to specify which in-law relationship was the center of the trouble. Table 24 summarizes their responses. They reported the friction to be about equally divided between the mother-in-law and all the other family members combined. In fact, the mother-in-law fig- ures in 60 per cent of the in-law imbroglios, if those cases are counted in which two or more members of the family are in- volved. Studies by Thomas [5] and Duvall [6] confirm the conclusion

[5] John L. Thomas, *The American Catholic Family*, p. 235. Englewood Cliffs, N. J.: Prentice-Hall, Inc., 1956.
[6] Evelyn Millis Duvall, *In Laws: Pro and Con*. New York: Association Press, 1954.

that the mother-in-law is the in-law most often blamed for being difficult.

TABLE 24   PERCENTAGES OF 116 HUSBANDS AND 160 WIVES
REPORTING VARIOUS IN-LAW RELATIONSHIPS
THAT WERE CAUSING FRICTION IN MARRIAGES

	Husband	Wife	Both
Mother-in-law	42.0%	50.0%	46.7%
Father-in-law	15.0	11.0	12.3
Brother-in-law	3.0	6.0	5.0
Sister-in-law	16.0	13.0	13.8
Two or more of the above	24.0	20.0	22.2

The findings suggest that in-law friction has a feminine pattern, since mothers-in-law, sisters-in-law, and wives are involved more frequently than are fathers-in-law, brothers-in-law, or husbands. The brother-in-law seldom receives any blame as a contributor to tense in-law relationships. The pattern as revealed by all the research seems to be that it is the wife who more often thinks that in-laws are a problem, and her feelings are most often directed toward the husband's mother.[7]

In-law adjustments and happiness in marriage

The study of the 544 couples in the early years of marriage revealed a close relationship between happiness in marriage and getting along with the in-laws. Of those couples who had an excellent in-law adjustment, 67 per cent said their marriages were very happy, but if the in-law relationships were fair or poor, only 18 per cent classified their marriages as very happy. The same

[7] On this point in addition to Duvall, Landis, and Thomas, see Sheldon Stryker, "The Adjustment of Married Offspring to Their Parents," *American Sociological Review*, 20:2 (April, 1955), 149-154. Paul Wallin, "Sex Differences in Attitudes to In-Laws, A Test of a Theory," *The American Journal of Sociology*, 59:5 (March, 1954), 466-469. Mirra Komarovsky, "Continuities in Family Research," *The American Journal of Sociology*, 62:1 (July, 1956) 42-47.

association was found in our study of the 409 marriages of couples in the parent generation. Further, the longer it had taken the parent couples to work out a satisfactory relationship with in-laws, the more likely the marriage was to be rated as unhappy.

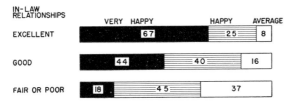

Fig. 68 IN-LAW RELATIONSHIPS AND HAPPINESS IN MARRIAGE (544 COUPLES). Excellent adjustment with the in-laws and happiness in marriage go together.

Ability to create and maintain pleasant and peaceful relationships with in-laws seems to be part of the total personality make-up which is more likely to achieve happiness in marriage. However, the research findings indicate that the whole problem of in-law relationships has not received enough attention in the preparation of young people for marriage.

An analysis of the conflict situation

If we would understand the in-law conflict situation, we must reflect on the family life pattern. For the first 20 years of the child's life his family is a strong "we" group. The mother is wrapped up in the children from the time they are born until they leave home. As small children, they look to her for their every need; to them she represents security. She influences their decisions as they grow older, and many parents sponsor the idea that "mother always knows best." The father is usually more occupied with making the family's living and is not so closely associated with the children. He has many interests outside the home, whereas the mother of necessity must center more of her interests in the home and the children. This pattern may develop in the children a measure of dependence on the mother. Even under the best family guidance, most people have not been completely weaned psychologically when they marry. The marriage takes place today, but a pattern that has been built up over a period of 20 years will not disappear with the wedding ceremony.

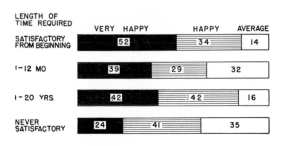

Fig. 69 PERCENT-AGES OF 409 HUS-BANDS AND 409 WIVES REPORTING VARIOUS PERIODS OF TIME REQUIRED FOR ADJUSTMENT IN IN-LAW RELA-TIONS AND HAPPI-NESS IN MARRIAGE.

After the wedding, most mothers will continue to give helpful suggestions to the son and in turn the son will continue to consult with the mother. This same pattern will be found in the wife's family. Here the problem begins in many marriages. Each spouse, while continuing his own accustomed relationships with his family, may feel resentful of the close relationship between the other spouse and his or her family. The offering of parental counsel may seem to the child-in-law to be parental interference, and the fact that the spouse seeks parental advice may be interpreted as an indication that he has more respect for, and confidence in the parents than in the mate.

A natural situation exists with good intentions on the part of all concerned, yet unless the patterns of a lifetime are altered, in-law friction may develop.

Lack of objectivity in in-law relationships

When misunderstandings have developed, both the children and the parents are inclined to lose their objectivity. To the parents, the son-in-law or daughter-in-law may seem to be ungracious and unappreciative, and the son-in-law or daughter-in-law may view all parental interest as interference. Some comments made by young people about their parents-in-law are illuminating here.

> "They try to run our home."
> "They treat us as children."
> "They give us too much advice."
> "—try to help too much."
> "—try to influence our lives."
> "—hover over us."

These are comments more likely to be made by the child-in-law about the spouse's parents, than about his own. This same young person may be continuing to seek counsel from his own parents with no thought that the spouse might interpret the situation as parental "interference." Personal conferences with some of the young people who made such comments about their parents-in-law revealed that frequently they were shocked when they realized that the spouse had exactly the same criticism, but directed at *his* parents-in-law.

It seems that many couples find it hard if not impossible during the early years of marriage to discuss with each other their feelings concerning the in-laws. Each fears he will seem to be motivated by jealousy. The fact that an element of jealousy is actually present does not make objective discussion any easier. We list some further comments made by daughters-in-law, which indicate that an element of jealousy, or at least a competitive attitude toward the parents-in-law, often exists.

> "His mother insists on first place with my husband."
> "They still think he belongs to them."
> "They don't accept my status as daughter-in-law."
> "They try to steal my place as his wife and the mother of his child."

It will be readily seen that the young wife would find it difficult to discuss these complaints lucidly and convincingly with her husband. She will find this inability to talk it over with her husband extremely disconcerting, and may seek to relieve her emotional turmoil by talking it over with her own parents or friends, who may lend a more sympathetic ear.

The comments quoted above are from daughters-in-law, but sons-in-law also may find it hard to accept and tolerate close affectional bonds between the wife and her family. Husbands also become emotional over the spouse's continued dependence on her parents for advice or help.

Parents as a factor in in-law relationships

Some of the parents as well as the children show signs of immaturity in their in-law relationships. Some mothers cling to their children, refuse to let them grow up, and continue to make decisions for them long after the children should be thinking for themselves. This type of mother has herself not matured to the place where she accepts life as it is. She resists the natural course of events, which is that children must grow away from their parents. This means that they are going to think for themselves, and that they will marry and have families of their own who will be more dear to them than their own parents. The mother who fails to accept this viewpoint and who tries to hold the first allegiance of her children will probably have trouble with her children-in-law. On the other hand, some children are late to mature and they continue to cling to their parents. The husband or wife married to an immature spouse may have difficulty in adjusting to the in-law situation.

Regression in parents and children. One aspect of mother-in-law trouble centers in regressive tendencies that may show up in people when they are faced with problems. As one looks back, a past level of life may seem easier and simpler than the present situation. In early marriage the inevitable problems to be solved surprise and baffle some people who believed that marriage would end all problems; their urge is to go back home emotionally and sometimes physically. This tendency toward regression appears in sons and daughters after marriage and also in parents who encourage their married children to come to them with their troubles.

Many mothers experience a crisis in their lives when children marry and leave home. Their lives have been full while the children were home, and when the last one has gone mothers may feel the emptiness deeply. So the married daughter who runs home to mother may find mother waiting with welcoming arms. Both mother and daughter have regressed, and the young husband understandably feels anger toward his mother-in-law, whom he blames for complicating his life.

Fathers are not so likely to follow the lives of the children, since fathers are not usually so close to the children emotionally. The father has his job and is as absorbed in that after the children marry as he has always been. He may even heave a sigh of relief privately when the last daughter is married, since she has been expensive to support during the teen years. It is different with the mother. The loss of the children through marriage and her subsequent loneliness must be taken into consideration when we attempt to understand in-law problems.

Distance is an asset.   The American ideal has been that when young people marry they live alone. In practice, some young people do live with the parents when they marry. If they live with or very near to parents during the first years of marriage, their process of growing up and becoming psychologically weaned from the parents may be delayed. Continuation of the parental-dominance and the child-dependence pattern of the spouse with whose parents they are living is often intolerable for the outsider who has married into the family. The women are more likely to conflict, since the wife is striving to establish herself in her new status and will be quick to resent the mother who continues to hold a dominant place. This type of in-law friction has a much better chance to show itself when the families are living together or near each other.

Contrasting backgrounds as a factor.   Because of the common custom of making jokes at the expense of mothers-in-law, some people go into marriage with a chip on the shoulder, just waiting for the mother-in-law or father-in-law to make a threatening move. They look for any indication of parental interference, and because of the dominance-submission pattern which is carried by both young people into the marriage, it is usually easy to find something that can be interpreted as parental interference. Then the battle is on.

In marriages in which the two young people come from contrasting backgrounds, such as different nationalities, religions, economic classes, or social classes, all the usual factors which make for family misunderstandings are present in addition to the contrast in home backgrounds. These contrasts contribute to friction in in-law relationships. In rural parts of America it is hard to convince many farm parents that a city girl can ever make a good wife for their son. It is difficult for farm parents who feel this way to keep from showing their attitude in some way, and the city daughter-in-law is sensitive to this critical attitude on the part of her husband's parents. As one such wife said after 23 years of marriage, "His folks have never really felt I belonged, just because I came from the city. Nothing I did was right."

Sometimes friction develops because the parents are critical of the changes that come over the young people after marriage. It may be that the parents have taught their son to go to church on Sunday or that card playing is wrong. If after marriage this son stops going to church on Sunday, or takes up cards, the parents can come to but one conclusion: it must be that wife of his. The wife may or may not be partly to blame. Young people will do more as they wish after leaving home and when they have established homes of their own. Some may not have been in sympathy with their parents' beliefs but conformed as long as they lived at home. It is to be expected that the thinking of both partners will be modified by marriage. But when parents cannot accept changes, it is hard for them not to offer reproof or counsel, which the child-in-law will resent.

Age at marriage and in-law difficulties

Our study of the 409 parent marriages revealed that the men who married under the age of 20 took longer to achieve a good understanding with the in-laws than those who married later.

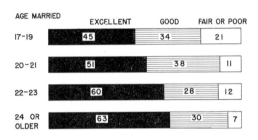

Fig. 70 AGE OF 544 WIVES AT MARRIAGE AND IN-LAW ADJUST- MENT.

Among the 544 couples in the early years of marriage, the wives who married at ages under 20 were having more difficulty with in-laws than were the young husbands. The husbands and wives who married at 24 or over had the best working arrangement with the in-laws. In-law difficulties are much more important as causes of trouble in youthful marriages. Parents may be inclined to interfere more when they feel that the children are not old enough to marry, and married couples who are young and immature may be especially sensitive to parental interference.

Behavior arising from in-law disharmony

So far we have given attention to conflicts between parents-in-law and children-in-law in an attempt to clarify somewhat the background factors of such difficulties. The whole interactional pattern is complicated, for just as the young people fail to understand their parents-in-law, so they are puzzled and frustrated by the reactions of their spouses to the in-law situation. Young husbands complain:

"She takes her mother's advice no matter how bad it is."
"She tells her mother too much about our personal affairs."
"She is too much at their beck and call."

And both husbands and wives complain that the spouse:

"Is tied to their apron strings."
"—wants to live near own folks."
"—is too worried about them."
"—gets homesick."
"—agrees with them (though they're ignorant) just to pacify them."

When the partners find it hard to understand these attitudes in each other, they tend to resort to certain types of behavior that are extremely irritating. The husband or wife may (1) behave in an unpleasant manner to the in-laws; (2) behave unpleasantly to the spouse in the presence of the in-laws; or (3) attempt to thwart the mate in in-law relationships by refusing to have anything to do with the in-laws. Such comments as, "He makes the in-laws feel unwanted," "won't talk to them," "argues with them," give an idea of some overt expressions of feeling toward the in-laws.

Few sons- or daughters-in-law engage in this behavior as a conscious effort to offend the in-laws. In most cases the offenses are no more deliberate than the interference by the parents is a deliberate attempt to make trouble. Frequently the offending actions simply mean that the spouse is ill at ease and unsure of himself in the presence of the in-laws. This is also true in many cases when the wife or husband feels critical of the spouse's behavior toward the mate in the presence of the in-laws. Both husbands and wives are often extremely sensitive to the impression that the mate is making on the in-laws. Since they hope to give the impression that unity and solidarity exist in the marriage, any direct or implied criticism from the partner in the presence of the in-laws is remarkably disturbing.

Again the comments of troubled couples are enlightening.

"He embarrasses me in front of them."
"—ignores me when we are with them."
"—doesn't show any affection when the in-laws are around."
"—criticizes me in front of the in-laws."
"doesn't take my side if I differ with the in-laws."

All these comments indicate that the child-in-law feels the need of "backing" from his mate around the in-laws. He wants the fact demonstrated that he is loved and respected by the spouse. Many of the things a husband does may provoke no irritation at all when he is alone with his wife, but the same words or actions in the presence of the in-laws will cause the wife to feel that she has lost face and has been repudiated before those whom she especially desires to impress. Husbands react similarly to the face-losing situations.

In-law relationships: a "natural" for conflict

It is of the greatest importance for young people entering marriage to have a realistic understanding of the in-law interactional pattern. Happy in-law relationships can contribute much to the joy of a good marriage, yet because of the nature of normal parent-child relationships before marriage, the in-law relationship is a natural set-up for conflict. It helps for young people to realize that most parents are just as interested in the success of the marriage as are the children, and that the children-in-law have just as many attitudes provocative of conflict as the parents have. If the children-in-law can analyze with some objectivity the motives back of their own behavior, they will find it easier to maintain perspective on the entire in-law relationship.

There is truth in the old statement that "it takes two good women to make a good husband." If the young wife finds that she resents the implication of the statement, and that it is painful to her to admit that her husband is the man she chose to marry at least partly because his mother did such a good job of bringing him up, then she needs to re-examine her own attitudes. She will probably find that she is carrying a chip on her shoulder and looking for mother-in-law trouble. Some mothers-in-law, in the interests of peace, fairly scurry to keep out of the way of belligerent daughters-in-law.

Meeting an in-law problem: a case

Nevertheless, some mothers-in-law do interfere and make life difficult for their married children.

> H. R. lived with his mother until he was forty, at which time he married Helen, who was several years younger. They moved into his home, which the mother continued to dominate. It was the mother who always met him at the door when he returned home in the evening and who sat down to discuss with him the happenings of the day. This had been the pattern of their lives for years and the marriage made no change. He asked his mother's advice in all matters and she was included in all plans. Early in the marriage the couple sometimes went out for an evening of dancing or visiting with friends; but as time passed the mother objected to being left alone, so they gave up these evenings out. At first, friends of the couple came in occasionally, but the mother acted as hostess and entertained the guests with stories of H. R.'s activities and interests, so that soon friends ceased to come. Since the mother planned all meals and directed the housework, the wife found herself in the position of a privileged servant in the home rather than of a wife. Any attempts she made to take over responsibilities or make decisions were taken as affronts by the mother-in-law, who would weep and be forced to go to bed with a headache. If the wife attempted to make any plans with her husband, the mother-in-law's feelings would be hurt. She would assume a martyred attitude and explain to the son that his poor old mother was only in the way, that she was unloved and unwanted by the daughter-in-law, and so on. H. R. would then chide his wife for being inconsiderate of his mother and causing her unhappiness in her own home. Helen's friends and relatives marveled at her endurance and privately predicted that some day soon she would pack up and leave. Her own mother, who lived near by and could observe the situation, once said to a friend, "I don't see how Helen can stand that mother-in-law of hers, but she has never said a word about it to me. She keeps her own counsel."

After a few months, Helen accepted a part-time job in a flower and gift shop. She suggested to the mother-in-law that since she had only a little time to help with the work at home she would be glad to take the responsibility for any specific tasks the mother would like her to do, and that she would do these regularly. That suited the mother-in-law well, and she turned certain tasks over to Helen. These Helen did conscientiously, and the mother-in-law was kept busy with the rest of the house. Helen centered her interests in her work and made friends with other young women who worked. She resumed the study of music, which she had dropped at her marriage. Since her husband loved music, they began to have musical evenings at home, which the mother-in-law enjoyed since they centered around her son's chief interest. Gradually friends were attracted back to the home. The mother-in-law was delighted to shine in the role of hostess who provided excellent food and served the guests. Helen acted as accompanist for her husband's singing and mingled with the guests almost as another guest.

H. R.'s mother had always prided herself on her success with houseplants, so Helen's work in the flower shop enabled her to take an active interest in this hobby. She brought her mother-in-law unusual plants and then praised and admired the way they flourished under the mother-in-law's care.

In other words, Helen met her mother-in-law problem in a constructive manner. She loved her husband and hoped to build a good marriage, so she refused to battle with her mother-in-law, but rather sought to understand her and make friends with her. She cultivated other outside interests for herself rather than brooding over the fact that she was not mistress in her own home.

Her success was impressive. It took time. But by the time there were two small children, the home could be called a happy one. The mother-in-law still carried much of the responsibility for running the house, but Helen had her children to care for; she also had many friends, none of whom had ever heard any complaints from her about her mother-in-law. And she had the unquestioned devotion of her husband. A visitor in the home, after the marriage had lasted for 15 years, noticed that the mother-in-law treated Helen with great respect and affection. She frequently quoted her as an authority on almost any subject, "*Helen* does it this way," or "*Helen* says——." Such would never have been the case if Helen had braced herself and battled for her rights rather than being content to work out a solution through compromise, sacrificing some of her preferences for the greater good of a permanently happy marriage.

Few young women would be able to meet the problem as Helen met it. The natural course of action would be for the wife to try to force the husband and the mother-in-law to accord her her rightful place as mistress in the home. Or she might have demanded a home away from the mother-in-law or tried to force the mother-in-law out of the home. In this case that probably would not have worked, and the marriage would not have survived, for the son was certainly too tied to his mother to be able to take positive action against her wishes. In some other situations, to force the issue might be the best procedure, but in any marriage that is complicated by such an in-law problem the important thing is to maintain perspective and to consider the best way to build a good marriage for all of life.

Certainly time is always on the side of the younger generation, the son-in-law or daughter-in-law, for parents grow old and become less able to dominate. Moreover, as time passes many sons and daughters who have been too dependent upon their parents do achieve a more mature independence and come to recognize that the present and future in their lives is more happily tied up in their marriage and not in a parental relationship.

Living with parents

Young people will find most of their adjustments much easier if they can live alone during the early years of marriage. During times of housing shortages or for financial reasons some married couples live with relatives. Many such families realistically face the fact that difficulties may arise, and they work out arrangements which keep emotional tensions and frayed nerves at a minimum. Such arrangements require much compromise. The two generations may not agree on the use of money, what is right or wrong conduct, how to cook a good meal, or how to train children. Research studies by Burgess and Wallin, and by Locke, found that more in-law trouble is likely to occur in situations when the daughter-in-law must live with the mother-in-law, than in cases in which the son-in-law is living in his wife's parents' home.

When couples live with parents, a complicating factor is the tendency for young people to fail to take full responsibility for their own actions. If things go wrong in the household, if the children are spoiled and tempers are short, there is always a scapegoat handy to blame. It is easy to think that things would be otherwise if only in-laws were not present to complicate life. So the presence of the third person in the home does serve to retard adjustments that need to be made in marriage. There is often a tendency for one of the pair to discuss problems with the third person rather than going ahead to work them out with the mate. A wise mother of several children told them all when they married, "If you ever have any trouble in your marriage, don't come to me with it. Send your husband (or wife). I will listen to my child-in-law's side of it, but I don't want to hear any complaints from my own children."

Successful in-law relationships

As we stated early in the chapter, the ability to get along well with the in-laws is one of a number of characteristics that are found in those who have the capacity for meeting adjustment problems constructively. The couples who supplied information on difficulties in this area listed their solutions to the in-law problem. The most successful in their relationships were those who willingly compromised in the interests of harmony, or who made friends with the in-laws and actively liked them. Their comments were of this type:

> "I fit in with their ways of doing things."
> "Made up my mind to get along."
> "I treat them as my own family."
> "I respect their views."
> "We visit them often but not for very long."
> "I am helpful whenever possible."
> "I try to be agreeable and friendly to them."

"I ignore things that irritate."

"I realize they have developed their ways over a long period of time so I don't try to change them."

"I try to be sensible about it and not condemn them for faults because I have faults too."

All these comments indicate a positive frame of mind that will avoid or resolve in-law friction.

A few couples reported that they had met problems by simply not trying to get along with the in-laws. Most of those who had chosen that solution had managed to live as far away from the in-laws as possible and to see as little of them as possible. Comments made by the couples in the study of older-generation marriages revealed that many of the couples in the older genera- tion had met their problems by this substitute solution. That is, they avoided any open conflict with in-laws by having nothing to do with them.

In some cases, to live far away from the in-laws may be the only way to avoid friction. The young person whose emo- tional development has stopped at an immature level may have a better chance to grow up if he is away from his family during the first adjustment period of marriage. Many more tensions would develop for the spouse if they were living near the in-laws during the time that the immature one is "growing up." The too-interested mother may also find interests other than the lives of her children, if the children are not living near her after they marry. So, although putting a wide distance between the married couple and the in-laws is not the most constructive or desirable solution, it sometimes serves to facilitate other adjustments during the early years of some marriages. By thus postponing conflict, some young people may attain a more satisfactory marital adjust- ment and may also achieve greater maturity, so that after a few years they may be able to live near the in-laws and enjoy a pleasant relationship with them. The better solution, of course, is for the young couple to strive to be mature and generous in their attitudes, because pleasant in-law relationships contribute to happiness in marriage.

Do in-laws break up marriages?

Of themselves, poor in-law relationships probably do not break up many marriages, although divorced people often blame the in-laws for the marriage failure. Usually the failure of the marriage is due rather to a combination of factors. It may appear that the mother-in-law is interfering too much in the marriage, but an objective observer might see also that the son is immature

Fig. 71 "We just now finished dinner, Mother. Oh, meat and biscuits and gravy. Dessert and coffee. No, I didn't have a vegetable. Yes, I know I should. Now don't worry. What? Oh, she baked a cake. Ha-ha-ha! You're a scream, Mother! . . ." By permission, Hank Ketcham and *The Saturday Evening Post.*

and dependent and very willing to accept the domination of the mother. He is not mature enough to stand on his own feet. If the wife is also immature and insecure in her affectional relationship with her husband, she will be more determined to battle with the mother-in-law.

Outside interference from in-laws is not likely to break up the marriage of a young couple who are working out their adjustments together, who can freely and objectively discuss their families, and who are secure in each other's affection. Couples or individuals who are inadequate in their relationships with others may resort to many different types of behavior in compensating for their own inadequacies. Many of the comments from young people who complain that they have in-law trouble reveal that the trouble lies within the complaining individuals themselves. Such people would have in-law misunderstanding regardless of whom they had married.

In-law relationships during the later years of marriage

Most of our discussion thus far has been of in-law friction in the early years of marriage, for it is then that it is most likely to occur. In-law problems of later marriage are of a different type. After a few years have passed, the many adjustments facing newly married couples have been worked out and the new family has become a solid unit. Each partner is more sure of his place in the affections of the spouse and does not need so much reassurance around the in-laws. Most people will have achieved by this time at least a measure of maturity. Some comments by the long-married group suggest the nature of the more common problems of the later years.

> "My husband's father lives with us. He has many irritating habits and attitudes which trouble my husband more than they do me."
> "My husband's mother tried to be in full charge of all of us until her health failed and she became a helpless invalid."

And from a husband, "My father was compelled to live with us after my mother died and he was irritable and childish, making it hard for my wife."

The problems of the later years grow more from the necessity for caring for old folks who find it hard to fit into the homes of their children. Sometimes the son-in-law or daughter-in-law on whom the care of the older parent falls feels put upon and believes that some of the other children should carry the load. In such cases friction may develop between the brothers-in-law and sisters-in-law.

OUTLINE FOR SELF-STUDY: IN-LAW RELATIONSHIPS

The key to successful in-law relationships is in developing a mature understanding of the complicated relationships that result when two families are connected by a marriage. You are probably an in-law now, whether or not you are married. If you are not you will be, some day. Consider the answers to the following questions:

1. Have you ever been critical of any in-law (brother-in-law, sister-in-law, mother- or father-in-law) in your immediate family? Try to decide whether your evaluation of the in-law is objective or subjective.

2. Consider the following situation: The son works for his father and some day will inherit the business. After college he wanted to go into a profession but the father insisted that he come home and go into the family business. After two years of marriage, his wife feels smothered by the attention of the in-laws. Her mother-in-law drops in frequently and makes suggestions on such matters as how to decorate the home, how to care for the baby, what to feed her husband. Her husband's younger brothers and sisters stop in every day on the way home from school. The couple is doing well financially but the daughter-in-law feels overwhelmed by her husband's large family.

    Can you put yourself in the place of the wife in this case and understand her feelings? Can you imagine yourself the husband and think of his reactions to his wife's attitude? What advice would you give to each? Why would you so advise them? Can you determine how much of your reaction to the case arises from your own experiences or your attitudes toward your own in-laws?

3. If you are married (or planning to be), what kind of an in-law are you?

   a. Try to assess your level of maturity in your relationships with your in-laws. Can you recognize and accept in yourself immature attitudes toward the in-laws, but at the same time keep from letting your feelings control your actions or words?

   b. Do you habitually look for the best in your in-laws? Do you tend to tell your family and friends about the good things you see in your in-laws? Did you consider the preferences and wishes of both families in planning your wedding? Do you consider your in-laws among your real friends? Do you feel that your in-laws understand and appreciate you?

   c. Have you and your spouse grown together enough so that you can speak of *our* families rather than *my* family and *your* family? Do the two of you make your decisions before you consult your families? Have you arrived at the place where you can communicate freely with your families but at the same time stand as an independent unit living your own lives and making your own decisions?

   d. As you look ahead would you say that you are developing a pattern which will make for a happy family in the larger sense? That is, good relationships between the grandchildren and the grandparents, cousins and cousins, and so forth?

   e. If you feel that you have "in-law problems," would an outsider agree that you have a real grievance or would he conclude that the things bothering you are insignificant or imagined?

Review questions

1. Why are young people often unconscious of the fact that, in reality, marriage unites two entire families?
2. How important are in-laws in marriage adjustment?
3. In what relationships are in-law frictions most common?
4. What is the relationship between the length of time required to

adjust to the in-laws, ultimate adjustment with the in-laws, and happiness in marriage?

5. "In-law friction in the early years of marriage is a normal outgrowth of parent-child relationships." Explain.

6. "They give us too much advice." Analyze this tendency in parents-in-law.

7. Why do couples find it difficult to discuss their in-law differences?

8. Give several reasons why the age from 45 to 60 is a crisis period for the average mother.

9. Why is in-law friction more likely if the children live with the parents-in-law?

10. Discuss in-law problems in "mixed" marriages.

11. Why should in-law friction be more pronounced among those who marry young?

12. What three common forms of interaction between the husband and wife develop from frustrations in in-law relationships? Illustrate each.

13. It has been said that most in-law friction is due to two women trying to be first in the affections of one man. What is the basis for this belief?

14. How do in-law problems among middle-aged couples differ from in-law problems of early marriage?

Projects and activities

1. Make an objective analysis of the in-law relationships in your immediate family. If the in-law relationships are harmonious, why are they this way? If there is difficulty, who is at fault? Write a paragraph describing an in-law relationship pattern.

2. *Role-playing.* a) Jack and Marilyn have been married two years and have been getting along very well. They live away from both families. Jack's mother came to visit them six weeks ago and at present shows no indication of wanting to go home. Marilyn had understood that the visit would be for two weeks. Marilyn has felt "left out" in many of the discussions between Jack and his mother, and she finds herself resenting her mother-in-law.

Scene: Jack's mother is out to a movie for the evening and Marilyn has decided to have a frank talk with Jack. Before she has a chance to say anything, Jack mentions that his mother has been so much help with the washing and housework that he thinks it would be a good idea if she stayed indefinitely.

b) Two young couples are seated playing bridge for the evening. Scene: Couple #1 mentions that they have in-law problems. In the conversation that follows, couple #2 brings out positive feelings about in-laws while couple #1 continues finding fault with their in-laws.

Film

Marriage Is a Partnership. Analyzes the first year of marriage and gives particular emphasis to misunderstandings over and adjustments to in-law relationships. Coronet Instructional Films. 14 minutes, sound.

Suggested readings

Baber, Ray E., *Marriage and the Family.* New York: McGraw-Hill Book Company, Inc., 1953. Ch. VII, "The Husband-Wife Relationship."

Duvall, Evelyn Millis, *In Laws: Pro and Con.* New York: Association Press, 1954.

Komarovsky, Mirra, "Functional Analysis of Sex Roles," *American Sociological Review*, 15:4 (August, 1950), 508-517.

_____, "Continuities in Family Research: A Case Study," *The American Journal of Sociology*, 62:1 (July, 1956), 42-47.

Stryker, Sheldon, "The Adjustment of Married Offspring to Their Parents," *American Sociological Review*, 20:2 (April, 1955), 149-154.

Sussman, Marvin B., "Activity Patterns of Post-Parental Couples and their Relationship to Family Continuity," *Marriage and Family Living*, 17:4 (November, 1955), 338-341.

_____, "The Help Pattern in the Middle Class Family," *American Sociological Review*, 18:1 (February, 1953), 22-28.

Wallin, Paul, "Sex Differences in Attitudes to In-Laws—A Test of a Theory," *The American Journal of Sociology*, 59:5 (March, 1954), 466-469.

Religious affiliation and marital success

A family bond

Nature of religion

Religion and adult needs

Religious philosophy and family living

Religious Attitudes and Marriage

Self-discipline

Religion and happiness

Religion and parenthood

Most people, by the time they reach a marriageable age, have a pattern either of religious orientation or of nonreligious orientation. This orientation will have become a rather fundamental part of their personality structure. It is not easily changed. Couples approaching marriage need to consider whether they are together in their religious attitudes. Their agreement or disagreement and the extent of their religious or nonreligious orientation will affect the happiness and success of their marriage.

Religious affiliation and marital success

Research studies show that in general, in our culture, the presence of a religious faith is associated with more favorable chances for marital success. Burgess and Cottrell found more favorable adjustment in marriage among those who were regular in their religious observances.[1] Our study of 409 couples showed regular church attendance to be among the factors associated with happiness in marriage. In reporting on the happy and the unhappy married men among the group in his study, Terman says, "Unfavorable attitudes toward religion characterize more of the unhappy men. Happily married men are a distinct majority among those . . . who believe it essential that children have religious instruction."[2]

Terman also found that those whose religious training had been extremely strict or rigid tended

. 18

[1] E. W. Burgess and L. S. Cottrell, *Predicting Success or Failure in Marriage,* p. 123. Englewood Cliffs, N. J.: Prentice-Hall, Inc., 1939.
[2] Lewis Terman, *Psychological Factors in Marital Happiness,* p. 164. New York: McGraw-Hill Book Company, Inc., 1939.

to approach the group with no religious training at all, insofar as marital happiness was concerned, although they still had a somewhat higher happiness rating than the no-religion group. In another study relating religious upbringing to marital adjustment, Peterson classified religious backgrounds according to five types ranging from those that rigidly control the individual along puritanical lines and are emotionally oriented, to the agnostic or no-church group.[3] He found the most low-adjustment scores among those individuals who had the rigid type of religious background and the most high adjustment scores among those who were in the religious group classified as liberal.

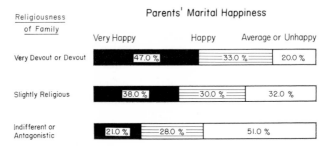

Fig. 72 RELIGIOUSNESS OF THE PARENTS AND PARENTAL MARITAL HAPPINESS AS REPORTED BY 3,000 STUDENTS.

When the measure is marital permanence or marital break-up, studies covering approximately 25,000 marriages have shown that there were three times as many marital failures among people with no religious affiliation as among those within given religions. In marriages between persons of different religions, religion may be a disruptive factor, yet the failure rate of marriages of mixed

[3] James A. Peterson, "The Impact of Objective and Subjective Religious Factors on Adjustment and Maladjustment in Marriage," unpublished Ph.D. Thesis, University of Southern California Libraries, 1951. As quoted in James A. Peterson, *Education for Marriage*, p. 328. New York: Charles Scribner's Sons, 1956.

religions is generally lower than that of marriages where there is no religion (see Fig. 42 on p. 244).

In comparing divorced and happily married couples, Locke found a larger percentage of the happily married couples had had a church wedding, were church members, and were active in Sunday school and church attendance, both before and during marriage. He suggests that being a church member is not only a mark of a conventional person but also of a sociable person, and both characteristics are associated with good marital adjustment.[4]

A family bond

Most churches emphasize the value of religious participation by family groups. In modern life the forces that separate the members of the family and direct their interests into widely divergent channels are more numerous than are the opportunities

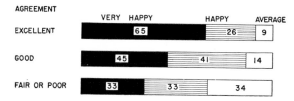

Fig. 73 AGREEMENT ON RELIGIOUS EXPRESSION AND HAPPINESS IN MARRIAGE. Agreement on religion was closely associated with happiness in marriage among 544 couples who were in the early years of marriage.

for participation in any activity as a family unit. Hence for children to participate with their parents in religious worship and in the activities of a church often aids in building family solidarity. Going to church together on Sunday morning, if it is the habitual practice of a family, often acquires special significance for the

---

[4] Harvey J. Locke, *Predicting Adjustment in Marriage*, pp. 239-241. New York: Henry Holt and Company, 1951.

children and for the parents. It is an occasion when they are together as a family, wearing what one child happily called "our Sunday morning faces." The occasion is different from most of their other associations, which for many families tend to fall into a pattern of merely crossing paths as each hurries about the business of his own separate life and activities. A family religion adds to children's feeling of identification with their parents and so contributes to their sense of security. Family religion also serves as a constructive link between the family and the community. But group religious participation by the family is not the major value of religion in family living.

Nature of religion

In order to understand the contribution of religion to marriage and family life, let us consider some aspects of the nature of religion. Philosophers and theologians offer many definitions of religion from which we may choose. William James says, "Religion means the feelings, acts, and experiences of individual men so far as they apprehend themselves to stand in relation to whatever they may consider the Divine." [5] John Dewey: "Whatever introduces a genuine perspective is religious." [6] William Ernest Hocking: "Religion is the habitual reference of life to divine powers." [7] And John Herman Randall: "Religions differ widely but, like art, religions all do the same things for men. They are all man's quest for the divine and his attempt to order life in its light." [8] Randall says further that, "All religions embrace a code for the guidance of living and a set of ideals toward which human life should be directed."

[5] William James, *The Varieties of Religious Experience,* p. 31. New York: Longmans, Green and Company, 1902.

[6] John Dewey, *A Common Faith,* p. 24. New Haven: Yale University Press, 1934.

[7] William Ernest Hocking, *Types of Philosophy,* p. 26. New York: Charles Scribner's Sons, 1929.

[8] John Herman Randall, *Preface to Philosophy,* Part IV, "The Meaning of Religion." New York: The Macmillan Company, 1946.

Summarizing the meaning of these statements, we see that all of them emphasize the orientation of the individual to realities outside his physical existence. Such orientation aids people in developing and maintaining a perspective on life and its problems. Life becomes more than the present moment or the immediate problem. Whatever helps the individual maintain a sense of proportion about factors in his life and the world about him increases his adequacy in a relationship such as marriage.

Religion and adult needs

Few adults are self-sufficient or entirely secure emotionally. It is inevitable that crises arise in life that shake our confidence in material things, even in the permanence of the social environment about us. Change is constant. Political changes, changes in customs and behavior patterns, changes in our manner of life as a result of technological developments, the changes in our closest associations brought about by the death or absence of friends and loved ones—all these things upset our security and we look for something of permanent and unchanging validity to hold to. For many people a religious faith provides the security that enables them to maintain emotional balance in the face of life's vicissitudes. The security that is sought in religion is not dependent on material things; it is a security of the spirit, based on values that, for the individual, have an unchanging validity.

Some people consider religion simply an "escape." If it is such in some lives, it tends to serve as a sane and constructive escape from the confusion and pressures of modern life.

It is true that many unhappy, poorly adjusted, and intolerant people are religious. But extremes in religion may be attempts to escape from realistic acceptance of the responsibility for living and adjusting among others, and are not comparable to a workable religious faith.

There is a difference between a religious faith that is a commitment of the individual to a way of life, and the verbal acceptance of certain dogma. The person with a positive religious faith that impels him to behave toward others according to standards based on respect for others and acceptance of them as individuals of as much worth as himself is more likely to be a well-integrated personality and hence a better risk as a marriage partner.

Religious philosophy and family living

Certain essentials of a religious philosophy are especially relevant to marriage and family living. Central in Judeo-Christian teachings is the individual; the emphasis is on respect for the essential rights of each personality. Ideally a religious faith impels one toward unselfishness and sympathy for the needs of others rather than thought only for one's own personal needs and satisfactions.

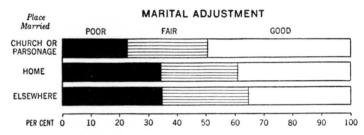

Fig. 74 RELATIONSHIP OF PLACE IN WHICH MARRIED TO MARITAL ADJUSTMENT. People who were married in a church had happier marriages than those who were not. It does not necessarily follow that if all people were married in churches marriages in general would be happier. People who choose to have church weddings may also have other factors in their backgrounds that make them better "bets" in marriage. Ernest W. Burgess and Leonard S. Cottrell, *Predicting Success or Failure in Marriage,* p. 126. Englewood Cliffs, N. J.: Prentice-Hall, Inc., 1939.

The person with effective religious beliefs will not be a blind adherent to a certain creed, but will be capable of growth under the impact of experiences. This capacity, which we might call the absence of a closed mind, may be seen in the answer given by a father to a questioning son. The son, home from school for vacation, stated that his education was providing him with many enlightening facts that were making him more and more skeptical concerning the values he had been taught as a child. His father answered, "You are right to re-examine your set of values. Our philosophy of life is adequate for living only if it is based on truth. We need never be afraid to seek truth; we need only be careful not to stop short of finding it."

The person who has a faith that "works" in his own life makes a good marriage partner. He will not be ready to do battle over nonessentials, but will rather strive to understand the viewpoint of the other person. He will show a willingness to compromise for harmony. He will respect the personality of the partner, refraining from ridicule or the belittling attitudes that are so devastating to the happiness of a wife or husband. He will build up the self-respect and self-confidence of his partner rather than destroy it. His own inner security will be a source of strength to those about him in the times of crisis that come to every family. He will be able to maintain a perspective on life and its values so that when trouble comes he will not go to pieces but will be able to withstand pressure.

Self-discipline

Another characteristic of religion that gives it relevance to family life is that it demands self-discipline. Religious people do many things because they believe they ought to: they refrain from other things because they believe they ought not to do them. They also act or refrain from acting in certain ways solely out of consideration for the feelings and attitudes of others. The attitude that says, "If the taking of meat offendeth my brother, I will take no meat," [9] is one that will make for peace and harmony in the daily contacts in life.

[9] I Corinthians 8:13.

Self-discipline is a valuable asset for those who would work out happy relationships in marriage. No matter how interesting an unpredictable and undependable person may be as a temporary companion, that type of person is usually difficult to live with as a permanent partner in all the affairs of life. Innumerable occasions arise in family living when the course of life and love is smoother and happier for all if each member can be depended on to behave as a disciplined individual—to follow the course of action that is for the best interests of all even when it requires a sacrifice of personal preference.

Religion and happiness

Elsewhere we have stated that some people who are unhappy in their marriages would not be happy in any event, married or single. In order to be able to give happiness to others, it is necessary to have the elements of a happy existence within oneself. Religion should contribute to personal happiness. The religious person has confidence in his own destiny, and he believes in the permanence of certain universal principles. He is not blindly optimistic, for he knows that life and society include evil and ugliness as well as goodness and beauty. But, especially in his attitudes toward others, his lack of pessimism is evident. He will give others the benefit of the doubt, assuming that their motives and intentions are as generous as his own. This attitude contributes to his own happiness because he is not tormented by suspicions and distrustful doubts concerning his associates; it also contributes to the happiness of others by helping them to feel valued as individuals.

Religion and parenthood

The person who has the inner security that results from a religious faith does not find it necessary to strike out at others in the world about him, or to be overly critical, aggressive, or bitter. Consequently, he is far easier to live with. As a parent, he will consider the individuality of each child, not just selfishly as it relates to himself, but in terms of the ultimate possibilities that are within the child. He will seek to understand the child, and to help him develop in his own way toward his highest potentialities. Such a parent will not take the position of demanding instant obedience on the basis of arbitrary parental authority, but will adopt policies designed to help children develop self-control and a positive philosophy of life for themselves. Ideally, the religious parent will not try to force his beliefs on his children, but rather will live so that his children will be inclined to give consideration to the values by which he lives.

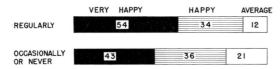

Fig. 75 CHURCH ATTENDANCE AND HAPPINESS IN MARRIAGE. Of 409 couples married successfully for a number of years, those who were regular in their church attendance had higher happiness ratings than those who attended church only occasionally or never.

In summary

The young person contemplating marriage will do well to take stock of his religious attitudes and those of his future mate, remembering that no person is without a religion of some kind. The most irreligious person is nevertheless committed to a set of values. Does this commitment enable him to overcome inner fears and anxieties? Does it direct him toward an understanding of others and a tolerance for the things that matter to them? Does it enable him to face life with equanimity? Or is he seeking security in possessions, in popularity, in dominance over others? Do life's requirements reveal his set of values to be adequate for effective living?

Those who desire a good marriage will want to start with every possible advantage in favor of the success of the marriage; the presence of constructive religious attitudes will contribute favorably to chances for success. Religious attitudes are often a key to the general personality pattern of an individual. This explains in part the greater success of marriages between those who have a positive religious belief.

Review questions

1. What do research studies reveal concerning religion and marital adjustment?
2. How can religious participation serve as a family bond making for family unity? Disunity?
3. What is one of the fundamental contributions of religion to the individual?
4. In what ways does a religious faith fulfill fundamental needs of adults in the modern world?
5. How do you explain the fact that some of the best-selling books in recent years have dealt with religious themes?
6. If it is admitted that religion is an escape, how can religion be defended?
7. List five ways in which religion should contribute to marital adjustment if one follows Judeo-Christian teachings?
8. How should religion bring about self-discipline?
9. In what ways should religious faith contribute to the general happiness of the individual?
10. The person with a religious philosophy probably has what other characteristics that make for successful marriage adjustment?

Projects and activities

1. Have representatives from the Protestant, Catholic, and Jewish faiths talk to your class on the subject of religion and marriage.
2. *Panel Discussion.* What religion means to me.
3. Give a book report on one of the current best-selling books with a religious theme. Analyze the book, and tell why the religious theme has a strong appeal.

Suggested readings

Becker, Howard, and Reuben Hill, eds., *Family, Marriage, and Parenthood.* Boston: D. C. Heath and Company, 1955. Ch. XX, "Religion and Family Life."

Bro, Margueritte Harmon, *When Children Ask*. Chicago: Willett, Clark & Company, 1940. Tells how to answer children's questions about religion.

Duvall, Evelyn Millis, and Reuben Hill, *When You Marry*. Boston: D. C. Heath and Company, Revised 1953. Ch. XIX, "Family Life and Religious Living."

Eakin, Mildred, and Frank Eakin, *Your Child's Religion*. New York: The Macmillan Company, 1942.

Fosdick, Harry Emerson, *On Being a Real Person*. New York: Harper & Brothers, 1943.

Peterson, James A., *Education for Marriage*. New York: Charles Scribner's Sons, 1956. Ch. 17, "Achieving Religious Togetherness."

Finances and Adjustment in Marriage

Almost all married couples find it necessary to compromise and adjust in order to arrive at a good understanding on financial matters. Family discord is frequently attributable to a failure to agree on how to spend the money. It will be remembered that the study of the length of time required to adjust in marriage revealed that it had taken the 409 older couples longer to work out problems centering around the spending of the family income than problems in any other area, except sex relations. Approximately one couple in five had never satisfactorily agreed on finances, although the couples had been married an average of 20 years.

Contrasting economic values

Why should spending money be a problem in marriage? Here it is necessary to look at the values that each partner has brought into the marriage. Our society places emphasis on money and material possessions, but there is no unanimity concerning what things are worth buying. Since most families do not have enough money for all the things that are desired, they must choose carefully in spending. This necessity for choice is the key to the difficulties that the husband and wife experience in the early years of marriage. They have come from families in which standards of value differ.

We observed a young couple shopping together in a super market. The wife was putting items in the shopping cart and the husband was following her, taking certain items out of the basket and placing them back on the shelf. He seemed to be acting more or less automatically, without being aware of the implications of what he was doing. His choice of the items removed from the basket reflected his family values. Expensive items, out-of-season foods, and some things that he apparently considered "unnecessary" to their living were being placed back on the shelves. With just as little thought, the wife went about the store picking up articles that appealed to her without looking at the price tags or examining the labels.

The incident illustrates in a small way how different may be the approach to spending that people from different families have. If we had been able to follow the young couple around long enough to observe developments when the young wife realized that her shopping was being censored, the situation would no doubt have provided a good example also of how such differences in economic values and attitudes can become an emotionally explosive issue.

But contrasts in values may go far deeper than is evidenced by choices made in a super market. For example, in a marriage the husband may be from a family where the available money was spent for good clothes, a good car, and frequent entertaining. With this background, his values may center around making a good impression on neighbors and friends. The wife may come from a family where the chief values were getting an education, or saving for the future, or owning a home. During the courtship period the wife may have been charmed and impressed by the husband's free spending to entertain her. They ate at the best places, and she never had to wonder whether there would be a corsage when they were going to a dance. The fact that her family was more conservative in spending money for such things might mean that she enjoyed them all the more when provided by her fiancé. However, after marriage this same free spending by the husband may prove to be a source of friction. The wife may be conscious of the limitations of their income and may feel that they should be saving money for a home and for other things that are important according to her set of values. To her, the expensive pleasures they enjoyed during the courtship period can now be foregone in order to have money for things she considers of more permanent value. The husband, who has been accustomed to thinking of money as a means of providing pleasure and enjoyment, may not be in sympathy with what he looks on as a sacrifice of the present for the future. He may find it hard to understand the wife's seeming change of attitude after the marriage, since she appeared to appreciate his free spending during courtship. It would take some time for such a couple to get together on use of the income. Patterns of spending and value systems developed over a period of 20 years will be slow to change. In some marriages the partners will never reach complete agreement on the use of money.

During the courtship period a man may be proud of his fiancée because she is always beautifully dressed. He is pleased when his friends admire her appearance. After the wedding he may still wish to be proud of a well-dressed wife, but may find that his income is not sufficient to permit his wife to have the kind of clothes she has been accustomed to buying. The wife may feel that clothes are so important that she would gladly cut down on the food bill in order to enlarge the portion of the budget allocated for clothes. However, if the husband happens to be from a family that believed in "setting a good table," he will not take kindly to the idea of saving on food to spend on clothes. The wife will find it hard to understand how he can have "changed" so, for during courtship he seemed so proud of her appearance.

Some of such differences in viewpoint begin to show up long before a couple marries, if they are alert to observe signs of differences. The boy who is first attracted to a girl and begins to date her because she always looks so charming (an effect helped by her expensive and beautiful clothes), may later become disturbed when he thinks seriously of marrying her. One such girl was hurt and puzzled during her engagement. She said, "Sometimes he sulks and makes critical remarks when I'm wearing a new sweater or a new coat. He never used to be that way. He used to tell me how lovely I looked when I wore something new. What's the matter with him?" In this case the boy was disturbed because, as they came nearer to their marriage, he sensed a difference in their values concerning use of money. He did not believe in spending so lavishly for clothes, no matter how much money one had. In his view, there were more important places to put money. Yet he was in love and resisted believing that they seriously differed on any matter of importance. Therefore, he reacted emotionally by becoming sulky and critical when her new clothes made him conscious of the difference in their views about money. Many couples fail to face their attitudes openly and to try to reach an understanding on such points during their courtship, especially if they are greatly attracted to each other and are being carried along by the sweep of their courtship.

Contrasts in ways of controlling money.   In some families the father takes all responsibility for spending the money, in others the mother; in other families the responsibility is about equally divided between the mother and father. Thus, contrasting family economic systems can be observed. The young man who comes from a family in which the father has taken all responsibility may be inclined after marriage to feel that he should control the money. The fact that his mother always asked his father for money when she wanted it seemed perfectly natural to him. If this young man should marry a girl from a family where the money had been controlled by the mother or controlled democratically by both parents, there is a good chance that misunderstandings may arise. This wife would feel humiliated if she were forced to ask her husband for money and to account to him for every expenditure. The husband might be unaware of her viewpoint and at a loss to understand why his wife should react emotionally to a financial arrangement that seemed reasonable to him. Such a couple faces the problem of harmonizing their ideas concerning the handling of money.

When couples differ greatly on how the money should be used, the feeling of frustrated irritation each may have sometimes affects their behavior in a variety of ways. The husband may become overly critical of the wife's actions in other matters. He may find it easier to be generally critical than to debate with her on the subject of economic values. He may engage in behavior she does not approve of, such as going out with the "boys" in the evening, or drinking too much. Or he may just become surly, moody, and hard to live with, behaving in general like a worried or irritable person. In many cases he will not have analyzed his own attitudes enough to realize why he behaves as he does.

Growing together on economic values

Young married people often feel that it is conceding defeat to admit that they differ widely on economic values or anything else. Many couples in the early years of marriage try to keep up the pretense that they are in agreement on everything. In so doing, they make no progress toward harmonizing their ideas.

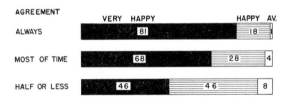

Fig. 76 AGREEMENT ON THE USE OF MONEY IN EARLY MARRIAGE AND HAPPINESS IN MARRIAGE (544 COUPLES).

It is much better for the couple going into marriage to recognize that almost surely they will differ on some matters but to agree that they will discuss differences as they arise in order to arrive at working arrangements as early as possible in marriage. If differences in financial attitudes are extreme, it will take more time and greater effort on the part of both to reach a compromise.

The importance of talking things over in marriage, if couples

are to avoid emotional explosions, cannot be too strongly emphasized. The time to talk things over is when any difference in
viewpoint becomes evident, *before* the situation reaches the point
where either one is ready to do battle. Some men go into marriage
with the feeling that women know nothing about finances or that
it is a sign of weakness for a man to need his wife's advice on
money matters. Most modern women have been brought up to
think that their opinions on money are worth considering. They
feel that they should be consulted when important decisions are
to be made in affairs that will affect their lives. Today relatively
few women will gladly allow the man of the family to handle all
money and make all decisions. It is more satisfactory for couples
to talk matters over and share responsibility for decisions.

Budgeting or financial planning

Since most couples start their marriages on a limited income,
they have to do some careful planning if the money is to meet all
needs. A budget is not primarily a plan to save money; it is a
plan to distribute the income so that the family may have the
things they consider most essential. The term budget has unfortunate connotations for some people. Many have tried to follow
some ideal plan that did not fit their situation. Bigelow [1] states
that a budget "is not a classified system of household accounts.
It is not a hard-and-fast list of predetermined expenditures, an
ironclad arrangement allowing for no variation or flexibility in
the use of income. The family budget is a spending plan. It is a
tentative estimate of the family's income and the family's expenditures for a realistic list of items. It is a guide to intelligent
spending."

Whatever the married couple may call it, they will need to
plan their spending so that they get the most for their money.

Keeping a budget has value in the early years of marriage, for

[1] Howard F. Bigelow, *Family Finance*, Chs. 14, 15. Philadelphia· J. B.
Lippincott Company, 1953.

it causes a couple to plan and study their spending and encourages them to talk money matters over together. It is a good idea for an engaged couple to work out a financial plan before they marry. This means that they will discuss their attitudes on spending money and discover some of their points of agreement and difference at a time when they can discuss their differences more objectively than might be possible later, after they are married and are faced with baffling financial problems. It should also help them to be more realistic about how they will be able to afford to live after marriage, so that there should be less tendency for them to blame each other if they later feel a financial pinch.

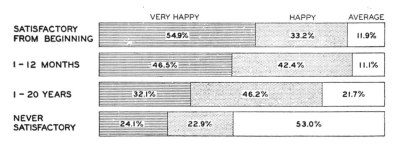

Fig. 77 DEGREE OF HAPPINESS OF 409 COUPLES REPORTING VARIOUS LENGTHS OF TIME REQUIRED TO MAKE ADJUSTMENT IN SPENDING THE FAMILY INCOME. The sooner couples can merge their value systems into one, the greater their chances for happiness in marriage.

However, many couples will not be realistic about money before marriage. If they attempt to discuss the matter and it appears that they differ widely, they will abandon the subject because of a conscious or unconscious wish to believe that they agree on everything. With some couples, one partner may suspect that they are far apart in their views on the use and handling of money but may deliberately avoid discussion of the subject before marriage because of a determination to marry anyway, and a belief that "everything will be all right once we are married."

Fig. 78 WORKING OUT THE BUDGET TOGETHER MAY AVOID MANY UNNECESSARY MISUNDERSTANDINGS ABOUT THE USE OF THE FAMILY INCOME. Courtesy of Coronet Films.

Budgeting as a source of friction

Marital tension is sometimes increased through attempts to follow a budget. A couple may try to follow a theoretically perfect budget plan that may not fit their special situation. If they cannot make the budget work, it is easy to begin to blame each other for the failure. Conflict may also develop over failure of one spouse or the other to record expenses. Perhaps the husband happens to be the one who believes in keeping a budget, and his method includes keeping a record of every cent spent. If his wife is not good at remembering where and for what she spent the money, constant hostility may center around the budget. Such a wife may have no peace because the husband checks up on whether she has recorded her expenditures. A common complaint among young couples is that the spouse will not cooperate in keeping a budget. If following a budget becomes a source of friction, some other financial system should be adopted. Getting more for the family's money through budgeting is good, but if making the budget work can be accomplished only at the cost of peace, the budget should be abandoned or revised.

Some people who object to keeping records use the system of putting money that is to be used for different purposes in different envelopes. The theory is that when a fund is exhausted the expenditures stop. It is not necessary to point out the complications that may arise with that system also.

The budget should never be thought of as a means for one partner to force the other into line in the spending of money. If this attitude exists, something more fundamental is wrong in the relationships of the couple, and budget-keeping will not correct the difficulty. It will simply serve as a focus for their friction.

If a couple does agree on the method of budgeting that they will follow, neither one should become too concerned if the budget does not balance during a given month. Some couples enjoy managing their money to keep a balanced budget. They record expenses strictly and take pleasure in their success in living within the budget over a period of time.

Who should hold the purse strings

No set rule can be stated on who should have control of the spending in a family. One husband said, "My wife was a bank bookkeeper before our marriage—she is a grand family treasurer." He had been married for 25 years and was thankful that he had never had to worry about taking care of the family money. In many families it is more practicable for the wife to manage the money because she has more time to give to the money management or because she has better judgment about its use than the husband. It has been estimated that women do 80 per cent of the spending for the American family. The wife buys the food, clothing, and usually the household furnishings. These constitute the major expenditures for the average family. Since women do most of the spending, there is some logic in the belief that more wives should take over the handling of family finances. One study among young married couples showed that in one-fifth of the couples, the wife handled almost all family finances. That system is probably more general among couples who have been married longer.

Many men appreciate having their wives take the responsibility for money management. Couples who have tried this system are usually enthusiastic about it. The wife plans her expenditures carefully when she knows just how much money there is and is responsible for making ends meet. A wife said, "We had constant arguments over money in the early years of our marriage. I was often irritated because my husband would say there

"We've been married ten years and this is the first week it shows a profit."

Fig. 79 By permission, Joseph Serrano and *Parade Publications*.

wasn't enough money for things I felt we needed. I believed that he just was not in sympathy with what I felt to be 'needs,' and that if he had wanted the things there would be enough money for them. Finally, we decided to try a different system. He turned over his entire salary to me with the understanding that I would handle it. My problem was to make it stretch to cover our fixed obligations and the other things I wanted. I no longer felt critical of him, for often I found there really wasn't enough money for things I felt were 'needs' and I revised my ideas about where the money should go. I enjoy planning and trying to see how I can make the money stretch. And my husband would never go back to the old system. He says it is wonderful not to have to spend time and thought on managing the money."

Of course, such an arrangement is based on mutual confidence. If the husband spent money carelessly, he could upset his wife's financial plans, just as she could upset the family finances by failing to cooperate if the husband were handling the money.

In many families the responsibility is equally divided. The couple has a joint checking account and both use their judgment in the spending of the money. This system is sometimes hard to carry out smoothly in the early years of marriage. Only after people have lived together for some time and have reached agreement on financial planning and spending will they have enough confidence in each other's judgment so that they can handle the money together easily.

Some men feel they must handle the money in order to preserve their sense of importance and dominance in the family. A young man from a patriarchal type of family may feel that to turn over the money management to his wife would be to abdicate his place as head of the house. Perhaps the least desirable way of handling family finances is for the husband to have complete control. However, in many American families this is still the policy. In some cases it works satisfactorily, for some women prefer that their husbands take this responsibility. Some

"Darling, which would you rather do next week, eat or pay the rent?"

Fig. 80 By permission, Stan Hunt and *The Saturday Evening Post.*

husbands attempt to use the allowance system as a means of control; this attempt may indicate that other adjustment failures are present in the marriage. In such marriages the husband may feel that although his wife dominates in many areas of family living, he can occasionally have the last word as long as he holds the purse strings. One woman, after 23 years of marriage, said, "I receive a weekly allowance that is sufficient for food only. I receive money for other things only after an argument." This woman's bitter resentment toward her husband extended into other areas of living, but the focal point of their adjustment failures was in their conflicts over family finance.

452

There are modifications of the three chief plans for managing the family income, which have been discussed in this chapter. In some homes the children are given a part in deciding how the income shall be used. This plan is especially desirable in the purchase of items such as a new luxury. However, small children should not be burdened with all the financial decisions faced by the average family. Financial worries are hard enough for adults, and little is to be accomplished by having children feel too much of the burden of financial responsibilities. As children grow older and have more understanding, they should be encouraged to take more part in money management in the family.

The fundamental thing is agreement. If a couple finds that one system does not work satisfactorily for them both, it is well to try another. Success is more probable if people can throw aside preconceived ideas and be adjustable. Money should smooth the path, not serve as a provoker of family battles.

OUTLINE FOR SELF-STUDY: ECONOMIC VALUES

To examine your own attitudes about money and its handling, think through the following outline. If you are pinned, engaged, or married, it is suggested that the two of you go through the outline together and assess your agreement and your ability to cooperate together in matters involving money.

I. Your family's contribution to your attitudes about money

1. If an outsider were to judge by the way your parents spend their money, what would he conclude your family values most? Would he see this same pattern of values among your grandparents? Aunts and uncles?
2. Did your family use a budget? If so, how did it work out?
3. From your viewpoint, who seemed to have dominance in decisions on spending the money? Who acted as family bookkeeper?
4. As a child did you have any part in making decisions about the spending of the family income?
5. In your family what was the pattern of giving to each of the following: To charity? To a church? To those in need? To friends and relatives?

II. *Your values and spending habits*

1. In general, does your family's way with money seem right and satisfactory to you or do you disagree with some of their values or their financial habits?

2. If you had an allowance as a child try to evaluate the effect upon your present spending habits of the allowance system as you experienced it.

3. As you think of how you spent your allowance or money you have earned through the years, what things do you seem to value most? When you are short of money, what things do you sacrifice in order to get what you want more?

4. What kinds of gifts do you most appreciate? Do you enjoy giving presents to others?

5. Do you usually think it over before making a major purchase, or do you "buy at sight"?

6. Do you find it easier to spend money your parents give you than to spend money you earn yourself?

7. Compare your spending habits with the spending habits of your three best friends, or your fiancée or spouse. Does the comparison show a difference in basic values? If so, how much could you change?

8. Are there any ways in which you think your best friend might reasonably be critical of the way you manage your money?

III. *Your attitudes about money*

What is your reaction to each of the following statements? Do your reactions help to clarify your attitudes?

1. I think the wife and the husband should have equal voice in how the family income is spent.

2. I believe that the one who earns the income should be the one to decide how it is spent.

3. I believe in giving at least ten per cent of my income to charity or to the church.

4. I think giving is not in order until after necessities and debts are provided for.

5. I would rather live in a good neighborhood and economize on food and clothing than to have a poorer house and address but spend more on daily necessities.

6. I would gladly sacrifice a steak dinner once a week in order to talk to my mother long distance.

7. I would gladly give up going to a show occasionally in order to buy a new book.

IV. Some points of parental friction over the use of money, as given by college students

Study each point of difference. With which side of the question do you find yourself agreeing?

1. Father wanted to invest in stocks; Mother wanted to invest in real estate or keep the money in the bank.
2. Father wanted to spend on hunting equipment, a TV set; Mother wanted to spend on things for the house.
3. Father thought Mother spoiled the children by giving money too freely.
4. Father never wanted to talk over money matters with Mother.
5. Mother wanted to pay bills; Father wanted to keep money and then would spend for unnecessary things.
6. Each considered the other extravagant.
7. Mother had to ask Dad for money, and she didn't like it.
8. Dad worried about the future because Mother would not save.
9. Mother thought Dad wasted money on cigarettes and insurance.
10. Mother did not like Dad to pick up the dinner check when with friends.
11. Dad wanted to buy cheap things; Mother wanted only the best.
12. Dad would buy only if he had the cash; Mother wanted to buy on the installment plan.
13. Dad liked to have company; Mother thought it was too expensive.

Review questions

1. What are the basic factors making for misunderstanding between husband and wife over the use of money? Give three illustrations.
2. Why do attitudes toward the spending habits of the spouse sometimes seem to change after marriage?
3. What is the real purpose of a budget?
4. What are some common causes of friction growing out of use of a budget?
5. What are three common family patterns of controlling the family purse?

6. Give some arguments in favor of the wife's having the major responsibility for handling family finances.

Projects and activities

1. Write a few paragraphs describing the "pattern of family spending" in your parents' family. Include such things as budgeting, who took the chief responsibility for spending, chief values of your family as a unit, and chief values of individuals in the family.

2. *Role-playing.* a) Bob and Ruth have been married for eight months. Bob's father had been the one who made all the major decisions about money in the family. Ruth's mother had controlled the money in her home. Bob and Ruth never discussed money before marriage, nor did they talk about who would control the money. Bob followed the example of his father and told Ruth that she would have an allowance for groceries and certain other household items. Ruth is becoming more and more resentful.

Scene: Ruth tells Bob that she is going to get a job, so that she can have her own money.

b) John is free with his money. That was one reason why Mary liked him from the beginning.

Scenes: I. During engagement—John has just presented Mary with a ring, for which he has had to go heavily into debt. II. After five years of marriage, three children, and many debts—John brings Mary an expensive dress as a gift.

Suggested readings

Becker, Howard, and Reuben Hill, eds., *Family, Marriage, and Parenthood.* Boston: D. C. Heath and Company, 1955. Ch. XIII, "Financing the Marriage."

Bowman, Henry A., *Marriage for Moderns.* New York: McGraw-Hill Book Company, Inc., 1954. Ch. XIII, "The Use of Money and Leisure Time."

Bradley, Joseph F., and Ralph H. Wherry, *Personal and Family Finance.* New York: Rinehart & Company, Inc., 1957.

Butterfield, Oliver M., *Planning For Marriage.* Princeton: D. Van Nostrand Company, Inc., 1956. Ch. VIII, "Money Enough for Marriage."

Feldman, Frances Lomas, *The Family in a Money World.* New York: Family Service Association of America, 1957.

Masteller, Kenneth C., *How To Avoid Financial Tangles.* Great Barrington, Mass.: American Institute for Economic Research, 1957.

Buying on a cash basis

Charge accounts

Cash or charge

Where to buy?

Judging goods

Care of purchased goods

When to shop

Organizations to aid consumers

Some methods for making the money stretch

What about borrowing?

Getting
Your Money's Worth

Installment buying

Small-loan companies

Credit unions

Commercial banks

Buying a home

Few people have means that they consider entirely adequate. The family with an income of $5,500 thinks $6,500 would mean luxurious existence, and the family living on $7,000 or $8,000 a year feels the need for $10,000. So it goes. Whatever the actual dollar income, careful management is necessary. A couple can learn much about buying, borrowing, and investing, which will help in family financial management.

Buying on a cash basis

The chief advantage of buying all the family needs on a cash basis is that the policy of paying cash prevents overbuying. Some young married couples who start out on the basis of doing much of their buying on credit learn that it is easy to get in so deep that they have a long, hard struggle to get out of debt. Buying for cash also makes it possible to shop around and buy where quality and prices are most satisfactory.

One disadvantage of operating entirely on a cash basis is that no credit ratings are kept on cash customers. If it does become desirable or necessary to use credit, to establish the credit takes a little longer. Cash buyers also complain that in some stores they are not treated with the consideration that is accorded to the charge customers.

Charge accounts

The chief advantage of charge accounts is their convenience. It is easy to say "charge and send." If articles have been charged and the buyer finds after getting them home that they are not suitable, it is simple and easy to return them and be

· · 20

given credit. With a charge account, the busy housewife can also make use of the shopping service that most large stores provide. She may phone or write a description of the articles she wants and the approximate price she wishes to pay and they will be selected by the shopper and delivered. A third advantage of charge accounts is that a complete record of expenditures comes with the bill at the end of the month. Payment is made in a lump sum and record-keeping is facilitated.

A disadvantage of charge accounts is that sometimes they are too convenient. It becomes too easy to overbuy. One housewife said, "We don't keep any charge accounts because if I have one I buy everything I see that I want as I walk through the store, then we have an awful time paying the bills." That is true of husbands as well as of wives in many cases. If the family finds it impossible to develop sales resistance, it is better not to have charge accounts.

Of course, all the conveniences offered by the charge account are reflected in the prices paid for goods. The store that charges and delivers and then accepts returned goods courteously after the customer changes her mind has to be paid for these services. Enough general mark-up has to be made to allow for the goods that are sometimes returned after being carelessly handled. The salaries of the "shoppers" who fill mail or phone orders must also come out of prices paid by the customer. Many other costs of service are included in prices paid by both charge and cash customers at the better stores.

One housewife said, "I *use* the services offered by the stores where we have charge accounts. I never take the time to go to the stores where my shopping can just as well be done by phone or mail. I realize that I pay for the service in the price of the goods, but I am willing to pay that much in order to save the time, energy, and carfare it would take for me to go and do the shopping. And, too, my sales resistance is not as good as it should be, so when I order by phone or mail, I buy only what are definite needs."

Cash or charge

In making the decision on whether to pay cash or use some charge accounts, a couple or a family must consider their own situation. Can they afford to pay for the services offered by a charge account? Do they need these services? If they have no children, or if they have help in the home so that the housewife has plenty of time and energy for shopping, perhaps she will never need to use a shopping service. If they have no help and if they have small children so that she is closely tied to the home, it may be well worth while to use the shopping service. What about the sales resistance of the family? Have they learned to consider before buying, or is it impossible for them to pass up items that make a momentary appeal? The little boy who said, "I saw a honey of a squirt gun. If I still want it next week I am going to buy it," was beginning to develop the sales resistance that is valuable. He had already learned that a good way to make the money stretch is not to buy until we are sure that we really want or need the thing that looks so desirable at the moment. All these things enter into whether the family should buy only for cash or use credit.

Where to buy?

If the buying is to be on a cash basis, the family will find it worth while to consider the stores that do not offer so many services. There is no point in paying for services that one does not intend to use. Various types of chain stores and affiliations of independent stores can offer lower prices because they have the advantages of mass buying, they offer no special services, and all their sales are on a cash basis.

Judging goods

When it comes to the actual buying of goods, the family buyer can learn much to her advantage. In buying foods, she will do well to read labels carefully and decide for herself which brands and sizes are best to buy. Not all nationally advertised brands are necessarily the best buys. It is sometimes confusing to find in the same store several different brands of the same canned vegetable with quite wide variations in price. Many housewives who have been taught that "it pays to buy the best" will automatically choose one of the higher-priced cans. But other factors than quality often have a part in determining price, so that paying higher prices does not insure getting the best. If the shopper is in doubt, it is a good plan for her to buy one of each price level, take them home and compare them to see for herself what the difference is. Housewives who do this often make interesting discoveries. Sometimes the lowest-priced can of food, or the medium-priced one, will prove to be of the best all-round quality. No hard and fast standard of judging can be given in one simple rule. Unfortunately, the grades and standards stamped on foods are not very enlightening to the buyer. The best thing a house-wife can do is to make it a habit to read labels, note weights, observe whether foods are wet-pack or dry-pack, whether sweetened or unsweetened, and then choose as intelligently as possible, always making tests for herself if she is in doubt. She will eventually learn to recognize good buys or poor buys without so much effort.

Many of the same factors apply to buying clothing and household materials. A high price does not insure quality. Nor is the cheap item necessarily a bargain. Sometimes it is a total waste of money to buy the cheapest; it would be better to pay more and have a more durable item, or to go without. But that is not always the case. It is necessary to learn to distinguish the good from the shoddy, rather than to judge the value of an article by its price. The wise buyer will judge for herself and will learn by experience.

Care of purchased goods

Proper care of clothing and furniture is important as a means of making the money go further. Careful laundering of clothing, dry cleaning when needed, and mending done "in time" will pay well in lengthening the life and adding to the good appearance of clothing. Intelligent care should also be taken of various types of woods and materials. Furniture can become increasingly beautiful with the right care, or it can deteriorate until the family is ashamed of it and will want to replace it. Excellent pamphlets on the care of furniture and clothing are available at little or no cost.

When to shop

Grocery stores usually offer the best prices as well as the best selection of articles in their week-end sales. Most of the grocery buying may well be done once a week when advantage can be taken of these better buying opportunities.

Off-season buying pays dividends. Winter clothes can be bought more reasonably during the January sales when merchants are anxious to clear their stocks so they will not have to hold them over. There are some goods that one would not wish to buy in off seasons because of style changes, but a great many things, particularly children's clothing, can be purchased at these times if foresight is used.

Some goods can be bought *in season* to advantage. This is true of most of the farm products. Family meals may be planned to take advantage of the times when oranges, grapefruit, lettuce, oysters, and other food items are abundant on the market and when the prices are lowest. Canned fruits are often featured in sales during the canning season. If no home canning is done, this season is the time to buy a supply of canned fruits and vegetables.

Organizations to aid consumers

Some progress has been made in setting up private testing agencies to help consumers. The best known of these are Consumers' Research, Incorporated, in Washington, New Jersey, and Consumers' Union, 17 Union Square W., New York, New York.

The two organizations work similarly. They are independent of all business organizations, secure their income from sale of books, reports, and reprints, do not accept money or articles to be tested from manufacturers, and buy on the open market the samples to be tested. We quote from CR: "No manufacturer or dealer, as such, makes any contribution, directly or indirectly, to CR's technical or editorial work, or to any of CR's officers or employees, directly or indirectly, nor will any such contribution be accepted if offered. No one pays in money, goods, or services to have any product recommended or any unfavorable comment made, modified, or omitted from the Bulletin of Consumers' Research." CU follows a similar policy.

CU and CR test articles in their laboratories before rating them. They also make use of the findings of noncommercial technical experts in arriving at their conclusions concerning some articles.

Both CU and CR publish monthly and yearly buying guides. These guides give a rating of all types of articles and explain the basis for the rating given each article. Those who are having their first experience in planning family expenditures will learn much from a study of these guides. It is not desirable to follow blindly the recommendations made by these organizations, but their discussions of the various considerations which determine quality are a most helpful contribution to consumer education. One of the chief values of this type of service is that it will stimulate the buyer to study values and to buy intelligently; it will help consumers to develop resistance to advertising that may be highly attractive but not wholly reliable.

Some methods for making the money stretch

1. Take proper care of clothing, household tools, and equipment.
2. Wear suitable clothes for the type of work being done; that is, washable clothes for gardening or household tasks.
3. Learn to use a screwdriver, hammer, saw, pipe wrench, and paint brush. Although cartoonists enjoy showing the household goods submerged because the man of the house has attempted to fix the plumbing, people of average intelligence can learn to make a great many of the minor repairs that are required about a home. The saving of money will be worth while, and there is a satisfaction in personal achievement.
4. Work at developing the family's own resources in the matter of recreation. A good time need not be gauged by how much it costs.
5. Families who enjoy such activities as vegetable gardening, and preserving by canning or freezing, foods that their garden produces or that are low priced in the markets at certain seasons, may save money by these activities.

What about borrowing?

Whatever the attitude of the family toward borrowing money, borrowing is sometimes necessary. Unexpected expenses may arise, such as illness or accident, before there has been an opportunity to accumulate savings. Some who are accumulating savings toward a home or some other major expenditure prefer to borrow to meet unexpected expenses rather than to dip into accumulated savings. Others will decide to have the new refrigerator, car, or furniture now, and will mortgage their future income to do so.

Several sources of credit are open to people who want to borrow. The interest rates that are charged vary greatly from one agency to another. The rates are charged according to the risks involved in the lending. Some agencies specialize in lending money to high-risk classes of people and therefore charge high rates of interest. The problem for the individual consumer is to find the agency that will lend him money at the lowest rate. It is important to shop carefully before buying credit. Because of a lack of information, many people with a good credit rating pay unnecessarily high interest rates if they borrow money from agencies that specialize in lending to people who have a poor credit rating.

Usually it is cheaper to borrow on property than on a promise to pay. Tangible evidence of ability to repay is worth more to the lender than the borrower's promise to pay. For this reason, agencies that ask the borrower to give collateral can lend money cheaper than those that simply require the borrower's signature. Many people will resist mortgaging the home, car, or furniture to secure a loan, and so will pay unreasonably high rates of interest. Loans that are justifiable and that are not beyond the borrower's ability to repay should be secured as cheaply as possible, even if it does require mortgaging property. If there is danger that the loan cannot be repaid and that the property might be lost, the borrowing should not be done in the first place. Life insurance policies can also be used as collateral. The insured may borrow from the insurance company, or he may deposit his policy with a bank as security for a loan.

Some people are confused about interest rates because they think of all interest rates as being stated on a yearly basis. If the rate of interest is 3 per cent, they assume that means 3 per cent a year. However, it may mean 3 per cent per month. Credit unions may charge 1 per cent per month on the unpaid balance, which is actually 12 per cent per year. The finance company may charge 3 per cent per month on the unpaid balance, which is actually 36 per cent per year. The banks usually charge about 6 per cent per year. A young woman who had worked for a finance company for two summers stated in all seriousness that it was cheaper to borrow from the finance company where she worked than at a bank, because the finance company only charged 3½ per cent. When it was explained to her that that was actually 42 per cent per year she was amazed.

Installment buying

A common method used to get goods without having the cash is to buy on the installment plan. The carrying charges one pays for this privilege must be recognized by the buyer as interest. Since the buyer usually is not posting security, except that he does not own the goods until the last payment is made, the carrying charges in terms of interest may be anywhere from 0 to 500 per cent. A great variety of installment plans are offered to the consumer and it is safe to say that few consumers know what interest rates they are paying when they use installment buying. Even people who work in the time payment departments of large stores may have no conception of the rates the customers are paying.

A buyer went to the time payment office of a large mail-order house and stated that he wished to buy a $100.00 radio on time payments. The girl in charge looked on the time payment chart, observed that the carrying charge would be $9.00 with 10 per cent paid down and the remainder paid in 12 equal payments. The total charge would be $100.00 plus $9.00 carrying charge, or a total of $109.00. When the girl was asked what the interest would amount to she said approximately 9 per cent. The buyer expressed doubt and suggested that they figure it together in detail. Their figures showed that if the buyer purchased and paid according to the plan, he would be paying not 9 per cent but almost twice that. If the interest had been actually 9 per cent on the *unpaid balance throughout the transaction,* the charge would be not $9.00 but $4.82. The girl protested that something must be wrong with the figures, for she had always been instructed to say that the interest was 9 per cent, and certainly it appeared to be so. However, if a person borrowed $100.00 at a charge of $9.00 and retained the entire amount for one year, he would then be paying interest at 9 per cent. But in a transaction in which more than half of the purchase price would be paid within six months but for which the charge was still $9.00, it will be seen that the interest rate would be almost twice 9 per cent. Table 25 shows the method for figuring interest on such a transaction.

TABLE 25   METHOD FOR FIGURING INTEREST AT 9 PER CENT ON THE UNPAID BALANCE OF A $100 LOAN

Balance due	Interest at 1 month at 9%
$99.00	$0.74
90.75	.68
82.50	.62
74.25	.56
66.00	.50
57.75	.43
49.50	.37
41.25	.31
33.00	.25
24.75	.18
16.50	.12
8.25	.06
Total Interest	$4.82

Before buying on time, the wise buyer will not only figure the exact rate of interest he will be paying and consider whether he might better "borrow" elsewhere, but he will also read carefully the terms of his contract. What if he cannot make his payments? What does it say about repossession? What about fines for failure to pay? Does the dealer turn the time payment contract over to some other agency? Can a claim be made on goods other than those purchased? Does the purchaser get a rebate on the carrying charge if the total cost is paid before it is due? The buyer should know the answers to these and other questions before he signs a time payment contract.

Families are offered many tempting things through attractive advertising. They may have a fine new kitchen or a beautiful bathroom with 24 months to pay. All they have to do is to decide whether they want the $4.50 per month bathroom, the $10.00

per month kitchen, or the $12.00 to $15.00 per month kitchen or bathroom. What interest rates will they be paying on the total purchase price? Would they be better off to go to a bank and borrow the total price at around 6 or 7 per cent? Many families who would not mortgage their home to borrow the money at a bank will readily buy on terms that are far more expensive.

A survey of a large number of families in Urbana, Illinois, found that two-thirds of the family heads were unaware of either the dollar carrying charges or the interest rates on their most recent installment purchases. This situation makes it possible for lending agencies to charge almost any amount for credit, and in a way does away with competition among the lending agencies. Recognizing the evils in the installment system, the state of New York in the years 1956 and 1957 passed laws to protect the consumer against unfair lending practices. The legislation proceeds on the theory that an installment buyer should not have to go through the complicated process of attempting to figure interest charges on an installment contract. In most cases the seller must list the installment charges in terms of the cost per $100 per year. Under this law no seller may charge more than $10 per $100 per year for installment sales up to $500, or more than $8 per $100 a year for purchases above that amount. New York consumers can now know exactly what they are paying. If people bother to inquire about what they are paying in terms of interest, the law should not only protect the consumer but it should also force competition among the lending agencies.

Small-loan companies

One of the most highly advertised forms of credit is that offered by small-loan companies. These companies operate under laws enacted to eliminate illegal lenders, but not all states have such laws. The Uniform Small Loan Law was drafted in 1916 by the Russell Sage Foundation after a number of years of research on lending practices. The Foundation has constantly revised its original recommendations in order to keep small-loan laws up to date.

The Uniform Small Loan Law states that those lenders who choose to be licensed under the law may make charges higher than those that are otherwise considered legal, on condition that the lender will submit to rigid regulation and supervision. The Law permits the charging of 3½ per cent per month on the unpaid balance. Some state laws do not permit an interest rate as high as the Uniform Law permits.

Small-loan companies specialize in lending money to borrowers who have little or no security. They may require a chattel mortgage and may take wage assignments as security. But usually all they have as security is the borrower's promise to pay. The rates of interest are extremely high because of the risk involved. Too many consumers who could borrow from banks, from insurance companies, or credit unions, borrow from small-loan companies at a rate of interest that they cannot afford to pay.

However, the small-loan companies still serve a useful purpose. People without security could not borrow money except through illegal lenders or loan sharks if it were not for the small-loan companies.

A report from Kansas, a state without a small-loan law, shows that one illegal lender had charged rates varying from 192 per cent to 418 per cent per year on his more than 2,000 loans in Topeka.[1] Even in states with small-loan laws, consumers must "shop" among the legal lenders, for a legal rate may still be an exorbitant rate.

Credit unions

Credit unions are permitted by the Federal Credit Union Act to charge interest at the rate of 1 per cent per month on the

[1] *Small Loan Laws of the United States*, p. 12. Cleveland: Bureau of Business Research, Western Reserve University, 1952.

unpaid balance. Although this rate is higher than the borrower would pay if he could furnish security and borrow at his bank, it is still a much lower rate of interest than he might pay through installment buying or to a small-loan company. Credit unions are formed by groups of people who have money to lend, or who wish to borrow relatively small amounts without security.

TABLE 26   RATES PER YEAR ON CONSUMERS' CREDIT

Financing agency or type of loan	Common charge	Range of charges
A. Cash lenders		
Savings bank accounts	. . .	3-6
Building and loan ass'n shares	6	6-12
Insurance policies	5	3-6
Credit unions	12	6-12
Industrial banks	15	12-24
Remedial loan societies—other loans	18	15-30
pledge loans	24	9-36
Commercial banks—personal loans	12	8-36
Consumer finance companies—under small-loan laws	30	16-42
Pawnshops	36	24-120
Illegal lenders	260	42-1200
B. Retail installment financing in five states having rate legislation—12 month contract		
New cars	12	8-24
Used cars under two years old	24	9-31
Used cars over two years old	30	9-43
Other commodities	24	9-34
C. Retail installment financing in states without rate legislation—12 month contract		
New cars	12	9-120
Used cars	40	9-275

Commercial banks

Some commercial banks have set up personal loan departments and, although their interest rates are higher than those charged when the borrower has assets, the rates are usually much lower than would be paid to a small-loan company. Table 26 will tell you at a glance the different rates of interest that are usually charged by different types of lending agencies.

Buying a home

Some young couples who have finished their education and who have jobs that will keep them in one community may wish to start saving for their future by buying a home. Below are listed some points to consider when buying a home.

1. Will this house suit the present size and living habits of the family?

2. Is it a house that will sell readily if the family should have to move later?

3. Is it better to buy a new house or an older one? Old houses are usually cheaper, have more space inside and outside, are landscaped, and are likely to be in settled neighborhoods with established schools and shopping services. New houses have the latest conveniences in kitchen, heating, and plumbing, and may need fewer repairs, but usually are less spacious.

4. Does the house fit in with the other houses in the neighborhood? A house should not be noticeably more or less pretentious than the other houses near by. There may be difficulty in selling the house later if it is not in keeping with the neighborhood.

5. Is the house structurally sound? Check the roof, the plastering, the floors, the plumbing, the understructure to see that the house is well built and in good repair. Old houses in many cases were better constructed than some of those being built today. If in doubt about construction have the house inspected by an expert.

6. Does the electric wiring meet present-day standards? Many older houses will need rewiring in order to adequately carry the load of the many electric appliances used today by the average family.

7. What about the heating system? Some old houses will need repairs; in some new houses the system may be inadequate for heating the entire house.

8. In many parts of the country it is important to check for termites and other wood-destroying organisms. An expert will usually do the inspecting for from $5 to $10 and the offer to buy can be contingent upon correction of any such damage.

9. Is there room for an expanding family? Could another room be added easily as the family grows? Are there adequate closets? Is the room arrangement convenient?

10. Is the price right and are the conditions of sale reasonable? How much would a bank lend to help finance the house? The amount the bank will lend is a clue to whether the price is right. Are the payments low enough so that unforeseen expenses could still be met? Is the interest rate on the mortgage in line with current interest rates?

11. Is it necessary to pay the price asked? Almost all old houses and some new houses have two prices, the asking price and the price at which the house will be sold. If the asking price is $15,000, the house will probably be sold for from $10,000 to $14,000, depending upon how many houses are on the market at the time, and whether the buyer has had experience in buying a house. Those buying a home for the first time are often uninformed about the two-price system in real estate selling.

12. Is the title to the property clear? Any offer to buy should be contingent upon guarantee of a clear title. A qualified real estate firm will usually protect the interests of the buyer, but the buyer should make sure this is done.

Fig. 81 "She's checking for termites." By permission, O'Brien and *The Saturday Evening Post.*

OUTLINE FOR SELF-STUDY: USE OF MONEY

I. In order to evaluate your spending habits and your use of goods, consider the following questions.

1. Do you usually keep items of clothing until worn out? What do you do with clothes that you are through with: Give them to someone? Destroy them? Leave them hanging in the closet?

2. Do you feel uneasy until you have paid for something you have charged?

3. Do you prefer to buy a thing you want on time and enjoy it while you pay for it, or do you enjoy more, things that you wait to have until you can pay cash for them?
4. As a child, did you usually have money saved up with which to buy presents?
5. Do you usually look in several different stores before you make an important purchase? Do you go shopping for amusement or recreation, or do you consider shopping "work"?
6. Do you have a tendency to go without things that you need or want, even if you might be able to afford them?
7. How many times have you bought things that you did not need, or that you did not use after you had bought them? How did you feel about the purchase?
8. When you have paid a high price for a possession, do you feel better about the item than you would if you got it as a bargain? Or do you get more pleasure out of your "bargains"?
9. If you had to borrow $300, would you prefer to borrow it from a bank, a loan company, or a relative? Would you resent paying the same interest to each of the three sources?
10. Some people are "compulsive spenders." That is, they cannot resist spending whatever money they have available at any given time, since the act of spending gives them pleasure. They are never sure where their money has gone. At the opposite extreme are people who hate to part with money even for necessities. It is keeping and accumulating money that gives them pleasure. In between are those who see money simply as a useful commodity; they spend or save according to a rational plan based on needs. Try to classify yourself in relation to these three types.

II. Assume that you are married and your take home pay is $300 per month. Make out a budget for two. Include specific amounts for all of the following that you consider necessary in a family budget.

1. Rent and utilities (heat, electricity and gas, telephone, water) $_____
2. Groceries   _____
3. Clothing   _____
4. Furnishings for the home   _____
5. Insurance: life, car, sickness, home   _____
6. Recreation   _____
7. Gifts to charity and friends   _____

8. Taxes _____
9. Transportation _____
10. Auto expenses, gasoline, payments, repairs _____
11. Savings and investments _____
12. Miscellaneous expenses, cleaning and laundry, hair-cuts, dues, subscriptions _____
13. Medical and dental care (not covered by insurance) _____
14. Smoking, drink _____
15. Others, specify_____ _____

Total _____

Review questions

1. What are the chief advantages and disadvantages of buying on a cash basis? Of using charge accounts?

2. How can a housewife learn to judge the value of goods?

3. What agencies have been organized for the specific purpose of protecting the consumer against buying shoddy goods?

4. What are the chief questions a couple should consider before they borrow money?

5. How do you explain the fact that people will shop around for groceries but not for credit?

6. What questions should a buyer ask before he buys goods on an installment contract?

7. Where does one usually pay a higher interest rate, at a bank or on an installment contract? Why is it difficult to figure the interest rate on installment contracts?

8. What are small-loan companies? How are they controlled?

9. Under what conditions should one consider borrowing from a small-loan company?

10. Why are small-loan companies permitted by state laws to charge such high interest rates?

11. What are the small-loan regulations in your state?

12. Where can one usually borrow money at the lowest rate of interest?

Projects and activities

1. *Special reports.* (a) Give a general over-all report on the method and work of Consumers' Union and Consumers' Research. (b) From a recent issue of Consumers' Union or Consumers' Research give the findings and ratings on some consumer goods.

2. Have one student "shop" with all the lending agencies in town to see where he can borrow money and at what interest rate. Report findings to the class.

3. Mr. A. wants to buy a new radio but does not have the cash. He decides to borrow the money. He consults all lending agencies in his community in shopping for the credit. Play the role of Mr. A. and ask all the questions that he should ask each lender.

Posters

1. Make a bar chart showing the varying rates of interest charged by lending agencies in your community.

2. Make a chart with labels from canned goods showing the variation in the price for the same grade of article sold under different brand names.

Suggested readings

Becker, Howard, and Reuben Hill, eds., *Family, Marriage, and Parenthood.* Boston: D. C. Heath and Company, 1955. Ch. XVII, "Designing the Family Home."

Bradley, Joseph F., and Ralph H. Wherry, *Personal and Family Finance.* New York: Rinehart & Company, Inc., 1957.

Duvall, Evelyn, and Reuben Hill, *When You Marry.* Boston: D. C. Heath and Company, Revised 1953. Ch. XI, "Money Matters in Marriage."

Gordon, Leland J., *Economics for Consumers.* New York: American Book Company, 1953. Chs. X and XI, "Producer Made Wants: Advertising"; Ch. XII, "The Profitable Practice of Fraud"; Ch. XIII, "Price Appeal"; Ch. XXIV, "Producer Aids to Consumers"; Ch. XXVI, "Watch Your Weights and Measures"; and Chs. XXVII and XXVIII, "Government Aids to Consumers."

Your Shelter Dollar. Chicago: Household Finance Corporation, 1957.

Buying Life Insurance

Unwise buying of insurance often complicates the financial problems of families. The average couple believes that some insurance is necessary, but they find it difficult to know which of the many types would be most suitable to their circumstances. Consequently, many families simply buy insurance from the first salesman who approaches them, and they usually buy whatever type the agent happens to be promoting. It is the purpose of this chapter to present some facts and considerations that may be useful to those who wish to make sure that their insurance dollars serve them well.

Protection rather than investment

Confusion about life insurance results because people do not have clearly in mind the fact that the chief purpose of life insurance is *protection* and not *investment*.

Some life insurance companies promote the sale of policies that are to be considered by the purchaser as investments along with protection. It will be to the financial advantage of the family of moderate means to disassociate completely their protection needs from their savings or investment program. Protection is simply the provision of an income for the dependents who would be left without support if the breadwinner should die. Insurance that does not include an idea of investment or savings but that does provide the needed protection can be bought cheaply and should be carried by all young husbands and fathers. If it is possible to provide for regular investments at the same time, that may be done also, but it should be done as a separate plan. In

479

our discussions of term insurance and endowment insurance we shall attempt to make clear the reasons why it is to the advantage of the head of the family to have this distinction clearly in mind.

For some reason it is hard for people to look at life insurance as they look at home or car insurance. The average family insures the house for a period of three to five years. If no fire or other disaster occurs, they are thankful, and they do not waste any time on regrets that they had no cash return to show for the insurance. They bought protection, which meant that they could leave the house with the confidence that if catastrophe struck they would have the means to secure another home. It is with the same attitude that they insure the car against fire, theft, or collision. They consider the

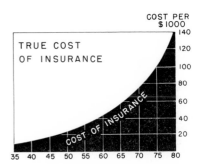

Fig. 82 IF INSURANCE PREMIUMS WERE FIGURED ON A YEAR-TO-YEAR BASIS, ONE WOULD PAY A HIGHER PREMIUM WITH EACH YEAR'S INCREASE IN AGE. From Maxwell S. Stewart, *How to Buy Life Insurance*, p. 3. New York: Public Affairs Committee, Inc., 1941.

money well spent for *protection* and do not regret that they have had no occasion to collect on the insurance. It is this principle on which life insurance should be judged.

Classifications of life insurance

Industrial insurance. Life insurance companies issue policies under three classifications: (1) industrial, (2) group, and (3) ordinary.

Industrial policies are sold in small denominations. The average industrial policy was $350 in 1955. Weekly premiums of five, ten, or twenty-five cents are paid to the agent who goes from door to door collecting. This insurance is sometimes referred to as "burial insurance," since the policies are small and are often taken out by low-income families to cover the cost of burial. The policies may be written as straight life, limited payment life, or endowment policies. (Industrial policies should not be confused with insurance plans which cover employees of certain industries. These are forms of group insurance and are distinctly different.) The purchaser of industrial insurance gets little protection for his money because of the company's expense in writing small policies and collecting the premiums each week. It costs companies 50 per cent more to collect by this method than through the ordinary method of receiving premium payments.

Weekly premium policyholders are usually given an opportunity to save 10 per cent by mailing the premium directly to the company, but most buyers of this type of policy still prefer to pay the agent each week.

The advantages of industrial insurance are that the policies are small and the premiums can be paid conveniently by people who could not get together the total annual premium at one time. The disadvantages are that the premium rates are high because of the weekly collections, the extra expense of handling many small policies, the high lapse ratio which makes it impossible for the company to write off expenses over a long period, and—since no medical examination is required—the high mortality rates among those insured. It has been estimated that 83 out of every 100 who take an industrial insurance policy will drop the policy in a period of less than 20 years. In 1951, 12 per cent of all industrial policies in force lapsed or were surrendered; in the depression year of 1932, almost a third of all such policies in force lapsed.[1]

It is unfortunate that low-income families who need to get the

[1] *Life Insurance Fact Book,* p. 40. New York: Institute of Life Insurance, 1952.

most for their insurance money must buy a type of policy that gives them little protection for the money spent.

Although industrial insurance is a poor buy, 112,000,000 of the 251,000,000 policies outstanding in 1955 were of this type. This figure represents almost one-half of all insurance policies, but only 11 per cent of the face value of insurance policies. As people have become better educated on insurance fewer and fewer are buying industrial insurance. There has been a steady decrease in the total insurance dollar spent for industrial insurance and a steady increase in the amount spent for policies that offer greater protection for the money.

More than a third of all industrial insurance policies are on children under 15 years of age, most of these children under four.[2] The very people who can least afford the security they need have bought insurance that contradicts the soundest principles of life insurance. It should be kept in mind that the chief purpose of insurance is to protect the dependent members of the family in case of misfortune. The Institute of Life Insurance, a national organization of insurance companies, states, "Juvenile insurance should not be considered until the father's life is adequately covered, since obviously his economic value is his family's basic safeguard, and should be the primary consideration in setting up his family's life insurance program."[3]

In summary, we can say that a person gets the least insurance protection for his money in buying an industrial insurance policy. It should never be bought unless it is the only insurance possible for the family, and in those cases it should be placed on the father, not the children.

Group insurance. Group insurance is the term applied to policies that are written to cover a large number of people. It is a relatively new type of insurance but is growing more rapidly

[2] *Ibid.*, p. 27.
[3] Marion Stevens Eberly, *Feminine Focus on Life Insurance*, p. 9. New York: Institute of Life Insurance, 1951.

than all other types of insurance. Half of the country's work force is covered by group insurance policies, which averaged $3,200 per insured worker in 1955. By an act of Congress, all Federal employees are now eligible for group insurance. Usually an institution or industry employing 10 to 25 or more people is eligible to have its employees insured under a group plan. Premiums are paid by contributions from the employer, or from both employer and employee. Group insurance is term insurance and is usually considered a good supplement to other insurance. The amount that can be carried is usually limited.

Group insurance is a good buy for many people. The premiums are low, since the insurance is written on a term basis. Cost of collection is low because: (1) the company pays the premiums in a lump sum, (2) one policy is written to cover the group rather than many, (3) physical examinations are eliminated, and (4) commissions paid for selling the insurance are low.

Group insurance is the cheapest of all forms of private insurance, since it combines the best features of the cheapest ordinary insurance, term insurance, with the advantages of writing insurance by the group method.

Ordinary insurance. Ordinary insurance is sold by all insurance companies and, in terms of face value of policies, accounted for three-fifths of all insurance in force in 1955. It is usually sold in amounts of $1,000 or more. Premiums are paid monthly, quarterly, semi-annually, or annually, by mail. The term really covers four basic kinds of policies: (1) term, (2) whole or straight life, (3) limited payment life, and (4) endowment. The term "ordinary insurance" is used to distinguish these policies from industrial or group insurance.

Term insurance. Term insurance is written for a certain specified length of time, one year, five years, or ten years, and the premiums are figured on the probability of the individual's dying during that period. At the end of the period the insurance expires unless renewed. If the insurance is renewed, the premium is slightly higher, since the insured is older and his chances of dying are greater than during the previous period. Term insurance does not combine any saving principle; it is bought for just the reason that car insurance is bought—protection.

Term insurance has several advantages. Next to group insurance the insured gets the most protection for his money, since he is paying solely for protection and he pays only at the rate of his present death risk. This type of insurance makes it possible for the young person with a limited income to provide well for his dependents in case of his death. Those who have debts can carry enough insurance to cover the debts, with a minimum outlay in premiums. The individual who is not certain about his permanent life insurance program may take out a term policy for protection and in the meantime study all policies to determine his permanent program.

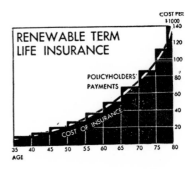

Fig. 83   PREMIUMS ON TERM IN-SURANCE ARE FIGURED TO COVER THE CHANCE OF DEATH FOR THE PRESENT AGE OF THE INSURED. Each renewal calls for higher premiums. Stewart, *op. cit.*, p. 10.

Term policies have the disadvantage of having to be renewed from time to time. As one grows older, the rate becomes higher. This is a disadvantage for those engaged in occupations in which earning power decreases after 50 years of age. Many term policies are non-renewable without a new medical examination; others are non-convertible.

One should give consideration to buying term insurance for immediate protection. During the first 20 years of marriage, when a man may have debts and when his dependency load is greatest, he can buy a maximum amount of protection in the form of term insurance at minimum expense. During that period many married men cannot afford to buy the more expensive insurance policies that combine saving with protection. As the number of dependents decreases and as the man becomes financially able, he can convert his term insurance into some other type of policy if he wishes. If term insurance is purchased, care must be taken to buy a policy that is renewable without a medical examination and one that is convertible to some other type of insurance. Later in life the family head may wish to convert to an annuity policy to provide funds for old age. When the time comes to convert to another policy, he can either take the new policy at his age when converting or start it at the age at which he took out the term policy. He will pay the premium difference between the cost of a term policy and the new policy. Another good plan is to carry the renewable term policy as long as he has dependents and gradually to drop it as the children leave home. Other investments may be made to finance the old age of the head of the household, or he may purchase annuities. Although term insurance does not have a large sale among *ordinary life* policies, the face value of term insurance is now larger than any other type of policy since *group insurance* is term insurance.

Whole or straight life policies. Whole life policies are the most common type of ordinary life policies sold. The policyholder pays a fixed sum each year as long as he lives and the insurance company agrees to pay the face value of the policy on the death of the insured. The policy has been set up to distribute the cost of the protection through the lifetime of the insured, eliminating the necessity for higher and higher premiums as the insured grows older. For a young man, the premiums are higher than would be necessary to cover the cost of protection at his age; for an older man they are lower. Although the face value of the policy is not payable until death, unless the insured lives to be 100, when all whole life policies endow, the insured may at any time withdraw the cash or loan value of the policy. Whole life policies have a cash or loan value chiefly because the younger people in the insured group pay higher premiums than are required by the mortality risk at their age. However, most of the premium is used to pay for protection only.

The chief advantages of this policy are that it distributes the cost over the lifetime of the individual and that it is a permanent plan of insurance for the dependents of the insured. The disadvantage of whole life insurance is that for young people with several dependents it provides less protection for the money. The same amount of money spent on term insurance would provide approximately twice as much protection.

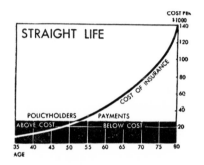

Limited payment policies. All limited payment policies are modifications of the whole life plan. The total cost of the insurance is paid in 10, 20, or 30 years instead of throughout the lifetime of the insured. The advantage

Fig. 84 IN STRAIGHT LIFE POLICIES, PREMIUM COSTS ARE DISTRIBUTED SO THAT A YOUNG MAN PAYS MORE THAN IS NECESSARY FOR PROTECTION. As he grows older, however, he will pay less than is necessary for protection. Stewart, *op. cit.*, p. 8.

is that the insured pays the policy up in a short time and then can forget about it. The great disadvantage of this type of policy is that during the years when the dependency load is greatest the insured is paying large premiums and yet is providing little protection for his dependents during that time. Term or whole life policies would give his family more protection when they need it most.

Endowment insurance. Many people buy endowment insurance because they feel that it is one policy in which the insured does not have to die in order to get something out of his insurance. The endowment policy places emphasis on savings rather than on protection. Endowment policies are usually sold to run for periods of from 10 to 30 years, with the provision that if the insured dies during the period his beneficiaries will receive the face value of the policy. If the insured outlives the contract, he will be paid the face value. What the company actually does is to take out a decreasing term policy to cover the life of the insured in case of death. The rest of the money is invested. If the insured does not die, the term policy is canceled, and the insured is paid the face value of the policy.[4]

The person who is thinking of buying endowment insurance and who has confidence in his ability to invest money may wish to consider another plan for his investments. He may wish to

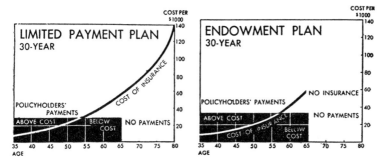

Fig. 85 (*left*) WITH LIMITED PAYMENT POLICIES, PREMIUMS ARE FIGURED SO THAT ONE PAYS THE TOTAL COSTS OF HIS INSURANCE DURING HIS MOST PRODUCTIVE YEARS. Stewart, *op. cit.,* p. 9.

Fig. 86 (*right*) ENDOWMENT INSURANCE CALLS FOR HIGH PREMIUMS FOR A LIMITED PERIOD. Stewart, *op. cit.,* p. 9.

take out the term part of the endowment policy but, instead of having the company invest his money, he may wish to do his own investing. If he knows how to invest wisely, his long-time return

[4] Some companies write participating endowment policies in which the insured gets the $1,000 face value of the policy plus additional earnings.

may be greater than if he had put all his money into the endowment policy. This is especially true in times of inflation such as we have been experiencing during the past 20 years. The man who took out a 20-year endowment policy in 1938 was paid off in cheap money in 1958. If he had invested in property or stocks his investment would have multiplied and kept up with inflation.

Those selling insurance feel that the insurance company is better qualified to invest money than is the individual. They recognize that insurance is not a profitable investment, especially in times of inflation. Companies are now debating and considering what they can do to take care of problems of inflation and deflation. Some consideration has been given to paying annuities in terms of the value of the dollar at the time the annuity becomes due. This is the only way the buyer of insurance could get real protection for his future. If the inflationary trend of the 1950's continues there is inadequate protection in insurance.

Insurance agents argue that if people are not forced to save they will not save, and that therefore the compulsive nature of the insurance contract is a benefit. They support their position by pointing out that in the great majority of cases life insurance is the only savings middle- and low-income families have been able to accumulate. There is some validity to their arguments.

However, when reverses come, the masses of low-income people are forced to drop their insurance. We have already noted the lapse rate among industrial policyholders. The lapse rate on ordinary policies in commercial companies was approximately one-third of the new policies written in 1936. In 1955, with economic conditions much different, the lapse rate was very low, only 3.8 per cent. In some years the number of lapsed policies of ordinary insurance exceeds the number matured in the same year.[5] When policies are allowed to lapse, not all money paid in is lost if the policy has been in force for two years or more.

[5] *Life Insurance Fact Book,* p. 44. New York: Institute of Life Insurance, 1956.

We would emphasize that endowment insurance is largely for the person who wishes to look at insurance as an investment. All other types of insurance will provide more protection for the money. With a $40.00 annual premium, the individual 25 years old can buy approximately $5,000 in protection in 20-year term insurance; $2,000 in whole life insurance; $1,400 in 20-pay life; and $900 in 20-year endowment. It should not be difficult for the man who is interested in protection for his family to decide on the type of insurance suited to his needs.

Buying insurance on children

Parents who wish to provide for their children's college education often consider taking out an endowment policy on each child to mature when the child is ready for college. Some insurance companies make a specialty of selling this type of insurance to parents of young children. Authorities on family insurance are agreed that any insurance to provide for the education of a child should be placed on the one who will be responsible for paying

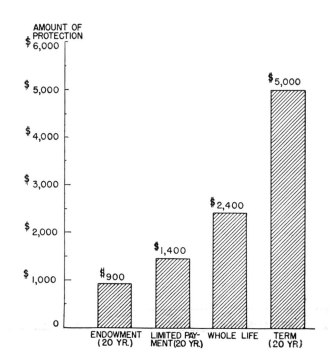

Fig. 87 AMOUNT OF PROTECTION THAT CAN BE PURCHASED FOR AN ANNUAL PREMIUM OF 40 DOLLARS IN DIFFERENT TYPES OF ORDINARY INSURANCE. If a person's needs are for a maximum of protection, he should consider the types of policies that emphasize protection.

for the education of the child and not on the child to be educated. If the father should die before the child reaches college age, the mother might find it impossible to keep up the insurance payments on the child, and there would be little guarantee of a college education. The best endowment for the child's education would be some form of good insurance on the father's life together with a program of systematic saving, so that whether the father lives or dies funds will be provided for the education of the child. Although this is a sound principle in buying insurance, the Survey Research Center of the University of Michigan found in 1955 in a nation-wide survey of life insurance ownership that 53 per cent of the children under 18 years of age were covered by insurance.[6]

Costs of insurance

It is almost impossible for the consumer to compare costs of insurance. The claim is made that competition between companies keeps the cost of insurance about the same in all companies. However, the Temporary National Economic Committee's study of insurance companies showed that the net cost for the same protection varied in different companies from $36.20 to $133.94. Matteson and Harwood [7] found that in two companies the administrative expense was respectively $4.92 and $21.33 per $1,000 of insurance. The cost of insurance varies according to the size and age of the company and its ability to invest funds, to administer the company efficiently, and to keep mortality expenses down through wise selection of insurees.

The insurance consumer is often dazed when he tries to compare costs. He learns that in a mutual company he will pay a high premium but receive a dividend each year, whereas in a

---

[6] *Ibid.*, p. 6.

[7] William J. Matteson and E. C. Harwood, *Life Insurance from the Buyer's Point of View*, p. 45. Great Barrington, Mass.: American Institute for Economic Research, 1956.

joint-stock company he will pay a low premium and receive no dividend. In the mutual company the insured pays more than necessary and the company simply returns his overpayment in the form of a dividend. The insured should not be misled by dividends; what he really wants to know is the net cost of insurance in different companies. Matteson and Harwood,[8] two economists of the American Institute for Economic Research, have made a careful analysis of the net costs of insurance in many different companies operating in the United States to determine how much costs vary from company to company for the same policy. They have taken all factors into consideration in computing the net costs of insurance in the different companies. They state that for the ordinary life policy, the 20-year net cost at age 25 for $1,000 protection varies from $78 in the least expensive company to $126 in the most expensive company. For the 20-payment life policy the 20-year net cost varies from $118 in one company to $221 in another.

It is important for the buyer to determine the best buy in the particular policy that he wants.

Buying life insurance

Determining needs. Because of differing needs, it is impossible to lay down universal rules on what insurance each person should buy. In determining his specific needs the individual should take into consideration (1) age, (2) debts, (3) dependents, (4) present earnings, (5) possible future earnings, and, if married, (6) earning ability of his wife.

People in the teens or early twenties without debts or dependents need not be too concerned about taking out insurance. In the spring of the senior year of college, it is the custom of many insurance companies to advise seniors in college to take out permanent insurance policies. Most college seniors are not

---

[8] *Ibid.,* pp. 66-69.

yet ready to set up a permanent insurance plan. If some temporary protection is needed for the benefit of people to whom one owes debts, a five year term policy can be bought for around $6 per thousand per year. The future of most young people of this age is still too uncertain to make it advisable for them to take out permanent insurance, especially contracts that feature the saving principle. College girls should be especially cautious in buying

Fig. 88 "But what do I get if he lives?" By permission, Chon Day and *The Saturday Evening Post*.

permanent insurance since, if they are single, they do not know what their insurance needs will be when they marry. Then it becomes a joint concern, and the money for insurance should be placed on the husband.

As obligations become greater and as dependents increase, serious thought should be given to protecting the dependents and those to whom debts are owed. During the period of early marriage it would seem that the need is for as much protection as can be purchased for a small cost. Term insurance gives the most protection for the smallest yearly premium. If the wife has special training so that it would not be difficult for her to support herself and the children in case of the death of the husband, it may not be necessary to carry so much protection as in cases where it would be a hardship for the wife to provide for herself and the dependents.

As the man becomes established in his profession, he will wish to consider permanent investments. If he has taken out a ten-year renewable and convertible term insurance policy at age 25, he may, at age 35, wish to convert it to permanent insurance such as a whole life policy. If he can save systematically, he may wish to keep his renewable term insurance until he no longer has a high dependency load, then it can be dropped completely since it will have served its purpose. His need then will be for savings or for an annuity for his own support in old age, rather than for protection for his dependents.

Figure 89 shows the consumption unit responsibility of the male family head in the average American family from age 20 to age 62. An "adult consumption unit" is the amount spent a year for food, clothing, shelter, medical care, recreation, and other items, by an average adult male. At age 20 the average American family head is supporting slightly more than one unit. This responsibility gradually increases until age 39, when a maximum of 3.75 units are being supported. After age 39, the family responsibility gradually decreases as the children take over their own support. In determining insurance needs it is well to plan an insurance program that will take care of the peak family responsibility load in case something should happen to the breadwinner. Some companies are now writing family policies that combine a straight life policy with a term policy. The term part of the policy is gradually decreased and finally dropped when the family is

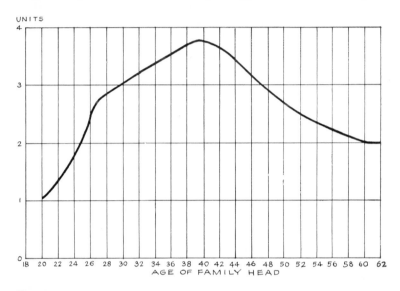

Fig. 89   CONSUMPTION UNITS IN THE AVERAGE AMERICAN FAMILY ACCORDING TO AGE OF MALE FAMILY HEAD. Insurance purchased should provide maximum protection when the breadwinner has the greatest consumption unit responsibility. From Metropolitan Life Insurance Company, *Statistical Bulletin,* 26:5 (May, 1946), 6.

grown; the straight life part continues for life. The combination of straight life policy and decreasing term policy is sound. But many companies are promoting a "family style" policy that covers all family members. The policies usually protect the husband with a straight life or endowment policy and the wife and children with term policies that are decreased and dropped or convertible as the children get older. Such a "family style" policy violates sound insurance principles by placing almost half the protection on the wife and children rather than on the bread-winner. It is well to remember when considering any insurance plan that *the average family needs no insurance on children and little, if any, on the wife; all available insurance money should be spent on the father who is the permanent support of the family.*

Where to buy insurance. After the individual has carefully considered his present needs and future prospects, he is ready to consider where he will buy his insurance. It must be remembered that our discussion is for the masses of people who have limited incomes or who wish to have the most for their money. People with ample funds may spend conspicuously and wastefully for insurance as for other items, without serious results.

The next step is to consider where the most protection can be bought at lowest cost. If the individual is eligible to take out insurance with some special group, he will probably find it to his advantage to do so. Various group plans are available for people in different lines of work. The Teachers Insurance and Annuity Association of America was endowed by the Carnegie Corporation so that insurance could be sold to teachers without profit and with the overhead being paid by the endowment. The Presbyterian Ministers' Fund offers insurance to all Protestant ministers, their wives, and students of the ministry. This is the oldest life insurance company in the United States. The cost of life insurance written for special groups is usually low.

Savings bank life insurance. To eliminate some of the undesirable features of insurance, especially the high costs of protection, savings bank life insurance has been set up in three states: Massachusetts, New York, and Connecticut. People in those states may purchase life insurance over the counter in savings banks. The immediate situation which brought about the development of savings bank life insurance was a series of scandals involving life insurance companies. Louis D. Brandeis, later

Justice of the United States Supreme Court, and other interested citizens, organized and were successful in getting the Massachusetts legislature to pass a bill in 1907 providing for savings bank life insurance. New York passed a similar law in 1938 and Connecticut in 1941. Savings bank insurance is set up especially for low-income people. The growth has been rapid in Massachusetts and New York during recent years.

Savings bank life insurance has many advantages over insurance sold by other insurance companies. Considering the average length of time a policy stays in force, Massachusetts savings bank insurance costs, on the average, about one-fourth less than ordi-

WHY SAVINGS BANK LIFE INSURANCE COSTS LESS

1. BECAUSE YOU DON'T PAY COMMISSION TO AGENTS

2. BECAUSE S.B.L.I. HAS LOWER COST OF OPERATION

3. BECAUSE POLICIES BOUGHT UNDER PRESSURE ARE MORE LIKELY TO LAPSE

4. BECAUSE THRIFTY AND CAREFUL PEOPLE WHO BUY THEIR OWN INSURANCE ARE BETTER RISKS

Fig. 90 From Stewart, *op. cit.*, p. 5.

nary insurance written by the regular companies, and only about one-half as much as industrial insurance. In New York, straight life insurance issued by the savings banks costs approximately 15 per cent less than similar insurance purchased from other companies.[9]

The Temporary National Economic Committee found that in 1936 the number of industrial policies allowed to lapse amounted to 35 per cent of the new policies written, while the lapse in ordinary insurance amounted to 30 per cent of the new policies. The lapse rate of savings bank life insurance was only 1¼ per cent.[10] The difference in the lapse rate is explained in part by the fact that no high-pressure tactics are used to sell savings bank life insurance. It is purchased by people who have given careful thought to their insurance program and who have purchased the insurance without having to be "sold."

Bills for the establishment of state savings bank insurance plans have been introduced in many states, but only those in Massachusetts, Connecticut, and New York have been passed. Old-line companies and their agents have been strong in their opposition to the extension of savings bank insurance. They feel that savings bank insurance is unfair competition.

The life insurance agent.   If a person is not eligible to buy insurance through any group plan, then it is time to seek the agent of a life insurance company. When talking with life insurance agents, it is well to remember several things. In the first place, the agency method of selling insurance has placed emphasis chiefly on one thing: selling. In the companies with the best standards, agents are carefully selected on the basis of personality and then are trained to become masters in the art of salesmanship. The agent's business is to sell insurance and not to be an expert adviser on general family finances. Naturally, a suc-

[9] Maxwell S. Stewart, *Buying Your Own Life Insurance,* pp. 13-14. New York: Public Affairs Committee, Inc., 1947.
[10] *Ibid.,* p. 17.

cessful agent can be expected to push the types of policies that "sell" best.

The American College of Life Underwriters was organized to do something to see that qualified people enter the insurance field. Those who successfully pass the examinations given by this organization are recognized by being designated C.L.U. (Chartered Life Underwriter). In 1956, only 5,000, or 2 per cent of life insurance agents, were C.L.U. men.

Some insurance companies have a good training program for agents before they are permitted to sell insurance. Other companies encourage their agents to take in-service courses to qualify them for their work.

An agent may be sincere in recommending a certain policy, but it is up to the buyer to determine for himself what policy will meet his own needs. He should not feel that he must buy from the first agent with whom he discusses the matter, any more than he must buy the first house a real estate agent shows or the first car an auto salesman demonstrates. The intelligent buyer will shop for insurance just as he shops for anything else and will recognize that each salesman is going to do his best to sell, for that is how he makes his living. The careful buyer will not buy a policy until he has asked the agent to submit his plan in writing so that it can be studied. Then the buyer will be able to compare the policies of the several companies under consideration and he will also avoid haste in buying. Certainly he should never buy any policy he does not clearly understand. Before buying a policy the buyer should also check on the standing of the company.

Paying premiums. The buyer will have a choice of paying premiums quarterly, semi-annually, or annually. The privilege of paying quarterly or semi-annually will add to the cost of the policy. On a $10,000 whole life policy the extra charge per year will be from $10 to $20 more if the buyer pays quarterly.

If one cannot make payments annually, it is much more economical to take out policies for smaller amounts and have them dated so that they come due at different times of the year. There is no extra charge for having more than one identical policy written. Such an arrangement has a further advantage in that if some insurance should have to be dropped, one small unit could be dropped. A few policies written in amounts of $5,000 are cheaper than five $1,000 policies; however, with most policies there is no advantage in buying one large policy rather than several smaller ones.

Beneficiaries. Some people contemplating marriage have insurance policies in force that were purchased for them when they were children. These policies are likely to be industrial endowment policies taken out to provide for the college education of the child. The parents are usually the beneficiaries named on the policy. If the child marries and the policy is still in force, the question arises: Should the beneficiary be changed to the spouse, and when should this be done? Since the parents have paid for the policy, the child may feel that it would not be right to change the beneficiary to the spouse.

If the child is still in debt to the parents for his college education or for other reasons, it might be well to continue the parents as beneficiaries until the debt is paid, that is, if it is a debt that the parents expect to be paid. If there is no recognized debt then old policies or any new policies taken out by either spouse should be changed so that the spouse becomes the beneficiary. Since marriage is a joint venture, a partnership in material things as well as in love, the beneficiaries should be changed at the time of marriage. There is no object in waiting months or years to take care of this important detail. Sometimes couples hesitate to change the beneficiary because they still feel obligated to their parents. A part of growing up is recognizing that one's first obligation now is to the spouse and not to parents. For spouses to change beneficiaries shows confidence and trust in the new relationship.

In summary

If there is a limited income, it is important that all insurance be placed on the one who supports the family. Usually this is the husband. He could support himself and the children if the wife died, but if he died the wife might find it difficult to manage without his support. It must be kept in mind that we are speaking of the average American family with limited money for insurance; the money must buy the greatest possible amount of protection for dependent members of the family. Families with unlimited means may wish to insure all or none of the family members, since their provisions for security are different.

Review questions

1. Why is a discussion of life insurance pertinent in a book on successful marriage?

2. What is the chief purpose of life insurance? Why are some people confused as to its primary purpose?

3. Name the three chief classifications of life insurance policies.

4. Are industrial insurance and group insurance one and the same thing? How does industrial insurance get its name?

5. What are the chief advantages of industrial insurance? The chief disadvantages?

6. Under what conditions should one buy industrial insurance?

7. Why is group insurance a good buy? What are some of the shortcomings of group insurance?

8. What are the four chief types of policies sold under the heading of ordinary insurance? Which of these is the most commonly sold in face values of policies?

9. What is the chief function of term insurance? Are all term policies convertible? Renewable?

10. What advantages does a straight life policy have over a term policy?

11. Do all straight life policies have a cash or a loan value? Explain.

12. What is the principle of the limited payment policy? Under what circumstances would it be unwise to take out a limited payment policy?

13. Why do many people decide that what they need is an endowment policy? What financial plan might offer more benefits than an endowment policy?

14. Is it wise for families of limited incomes to take out endowment policies on their children for the education of the children? Explain.

15. Do insurance policies that offer the same protection cost the same in different companies? Explain why or why not.

16. How can the consumer of insurance determine the true net cost of an insurance policy?

17. What factors should be taken into consideration in determining one's insurance needs?

18. What is meant by "consumption unit responsibility"?

19. Who are the C.L.U. agents?

20. What are the chief advantages of having five $1,000 policies rather than one $5,000 policy?

21. Under what conditions should all the insurance of the family be placed on the life of the breadwinner?

Problems to solve

1. John and Mary Smith are 25-years-old. John is through law school and is starting his law practice. He is in debt several thousand dollars for his college education and, in addition, must meet the expenses of getting started in his practice. John and Mary have one son, James, who is one year old, and they expect another baby in six months. John has no insurance but is interested in buying some. What would you recommend that he buy?

2. John and Mary Smith are now 40-years-old. John is well established in his law practice and all debts have been paid. They have four children now, ages 16, 15, 13, and 10. John followed your advice before and bought the policies recommended. Would you recommend any changes in his policies at this time? If so, what changes would you suggest?

3. An insurance agent has approached you about a policy and has made it sound so good that you feel that you must buy. You have never heard of his company, but he assures you that it is a good one. What should your procedure be before buying?

4. For some 20 years the dollar has been getting cheaper and cheaper, as we have been in a period of inflation. Under these conditions what type of investments offer the most protection for a family? Endowment insurance? Stocks? Bonds? Annuities? Straight life insurance? Buying a home? Real estate? Defend your answer. Which would provide the greatest protection if money were to get expensive, or if we were to have deflation?

5. *Role-playing.* Two scenes between a life insurance agent and a client. (a) Show how life insurance *should not* be bought or sold. (b) Show how life insurance *should* be bought or sold.

Suggested readings

Gordon, Leland J., *Economics for Consumers.* New York: American Book Company, 1953. Ch. XX, "Buying Protection: Principles of Insurance," and Ch. XXI, "Insurance Practices."

Jordan, David F., and Edward F. Willett, *Managing Personal Finances.* Englewood Cliffs, N. J.: Prentice-Hall, Inc., 1945. Ch. XIII, "Buying Life Insurance"; Ch. XIV, "Buying an Annuity"; Ch. XV, "Pension Plans and Social Security"; and Ch. XX, "Making a Will."

Matteson, William J., and E. C. Harwood, *Life Insurance from the Buyer's Point of View.* Great Barrington, Mass.: American Institute of Economic Research (latest edition, usually revised each year). One of the best books on the subject from the consumer's point of view.

Reproduction

Long before the individual reaches the time for marriage he should have a clear understanding of the basic facts of the structure of both male and female reproductive systems; of conception and how it comes about; of menstruation and its relationship to conception; and of the fundamental facts about pregnancy and childbirth. All phases of sex and reproduction have long been beclouded for many people by superstition and hearsay. In this chapter it is our purpose to present briefly but as clearly as possible the essential facts of the reproductive process.

Female reproductive system

The female reproductive system consists of external and internal organs. The external are (1) two labia majora, (2) two labia minora, and (3) a clitoris. All these are called collectively the vulva. The labia majora are folds of tissue that form the outer rim or boundary of the vulva. The labia minora are inside, or between, the labia majora and are thinner, elongated folds of mucous membrane. The clitoris is a small organ situated at the point where the upper edges of the labia minora join. It is exclusively an organ of sensation.

The internal organs are (1) the vagina, (2) the uterus, (3) two fallopian tubes, and (4) two ovaries. The vagina is an elastic passageway between the uterus and the vulva, opening into a small space called the vestibule, between the labia minora. The vagina serves as the female organ of copulation, as well as the birth canal. It also is the passageway for the menstrual flow. The vaginal opening is partially closed by a membrane called the hymen. Superstitions exist concerning the hymen, not only among primitive people but among Americans. Chief among the erroneous beliefs held concerning the hymen is that it is an infallible index to a woman's virginity. Actually its presence, absence, or structure is unreliable as a means for the layman to determine either chastity or unchastity. Natural variations in size, structure, and thickness of the hymen are great— from membranes that are of such slight development that they are hardly discernible, or that are so loose and dilatable that they survive intercourse and even the birth of a child, to others that are very thick and strong with only a tiny opening into the vagina.

The uterus is a pear-shaped, muscular organ normally about three inches long and two inches wide. It serves as the home of the baby during the period of gestation. Its muscular walls increase in thickness and size during pregnancy and serve as the chief force to expel the child during the birth process. The uterus opens into the vagina through the cervix, a muscular ring at the lower end of the uterus. The ovaries are the gonads or sex glands of the female. They have two chief functions. They produce the reproductive cells called ova or eggs, and they manufacture the hormones, which are responsible for the development of female characteristics and for the processes that result in menstruation. The fallopian tubes serve the purpose of conducting the egg cells from the ovaries to the uterus. The meeting of an egg cell with the sperm, and its subsequent fertilization, also usually take place in the larger part of the fallopian tube. Each tube is about four inches long; its smaller end opens into the uterus, and its larger end lies closely about the surface of the ovary but not directly connected to it. The end which is in contact with the ovary is made up of numerous fingerlike projections, which are for the purpose of intercepting the egg when released from the ovary, and starting it on its way through the fallopian tubes to the uterus.

Male reproductive system

The male reproductive system consists of the following organs or structures: (1) two testicles or testes, (2) epididymides, (3) vasa deferentia (the testicles, epididymides, and part of the vasa deferentia are contained in the scrotum), (4) two seminal vesicles, (5) prostate gland, and (6) the penis.

The testes are the gonads, or sex glands, of the male. Each testicle is about the size of a walnut and they are suspended in the scrotum, a pouch or sac hanging between the thighs just behind the penis. The temperature of the testicles is usually somewhat lower than that of the rest of the body. The lower temperature that is necessary for their functioning is probably the reason they are placed outside the body rather than inside, as are the female gonads (ovaries). The testicles have two chief functions. They secrete the male sex hormone (testosterone), which has much to do with the development of male characteristics such as body build, deep voice, and distribution of body hair. Their second function is to produce the reproductive cells, called spermatozoa or sperm cells. The manufacture of sperm cells begins at puberty and continues for many years. The number of spermatozoa produced decreases with age; in some men their production ceases after middle age. However, cases are on record of men as old as ninety who have fathered offspring.

Convoluted along one side of each testicle within the scrotum is the epididymis, a loosely coiled tube into which the sperm cells are emptied for storage. The epididymis is connected to a tube called the vas deferens which serves to suspend the testicle from the body and also to carry the sperm cells up out of the scrotum toward the seminal vesicle and the prostate gland. After the vas deferens leaves the scrotum, it goes up over the outside of the pubic bone and enters the abdominal wall through a very small opening in the muscles. It is this small opening or muscular ring that sometimes becomes enlarged or ruptured, allowing a portion of the abdominal lining or of the intestine to protrude through the opening, in the condition called inguinal hernia.

After entering the abdominal cavity, the vas deferens goes on to join the seminal vesicle, and then passes through the tissue of the prostate gland to enter the urethra. There has been uncertainty about where the sperm are stored for immediate ejaculation. It now appears that they are stored in the ampulla, which is between the vas deferens and the seminal vesicle. The seminal vesicles secrete a fluid which, with the fluid secreted by the prostate gland, forms the semen, or the material ejaculated in sexual intercourse. During intercourse the seminal vesicles and the prostate gland contract and force their contents out through the urethra. When the glands become full they sometimes empty themselves in what are known as seminal emissions or nocturnal emissions, that is, emission of seminal fluid during sleep. Nocturnal emissions are very common and sometimes quite regular among adolescents or other males who are not having regular sexual intercourse. They are a natural result of glandular activity and are in no way harmful. The penis, through which the urethra makes its way to the exterior, is the male copulatory organ, corresponding to the vagina in the female. It is composed of special tissue, in reality a spongy network of blood vessels that become tense when congested, causing the penis to enlarge, harden, and become erect in position. This condition occurs during sexual excitement and allows intromission of the penis to deposit semen within the vagina.

Conception

Approximately once each month, from puberty until the menopause, ovulation takes place in the female reproductive system. That is, an egg is released from the ovary and starts its course to the uterus. When the egg, or ovum, is released, it is swept into the fallopian tube by the fingerlike projections which lie closely about the ovary. If sperm are present, the egg usually meets with the sperm somewhere in its course through the tube and is fertilized there.

During sexual intercourse innumerable spermatozoa are deposited in the vagina near the entrance to the uterus. The sperm cells are extremely motile and begin moving rapidly in all directions, some of them entering the uterus, and traveling on into the tubes. If an egg is encountered, the sperm cell unites with the egg cell and conception has occurred. The fertilized egg continues through the fallopian or uterine tube to the uterus, where it implants itself, and development of the embryo proceeds. If sperm do not appear while the egg is progressing toward the uterus and fertilization does not take place, the egg soon dies and, together with other elements that were involved in its production, is later cast off during the menstruation process.

Menstruation

Throughout the ages, menstruation in women has been the subject of much speculation and superstitious belief on the part of both laymen and medical men. Only within the last 85 years has any reliable scientific information been available on the subject. Even now research continues to add answers to some of the baffling questions that have existed about this function. In general, however, it may be said that menstruation is the result of failure of conception to occur. During the time that the egg is becoming mature and ready to be released from the ovary, elaborate preparations are being made within the uterus to receive a fertilized egg. The exact manner of these preparations and the factors that initiate them are complicated and very interesting. For our purposes, it is sufficient to say that within the ovary are produced hormones which are carried through the blood stream to the uterus, where they cause certain changes to take place. A steadily increasing growth of the mucous membrane lining of the uterus (endometrium) occurs, and also a gradually increasing supply of blood in the endometrium. Another change takes place in the endometrium specifically designed to provide anchorage for the fertilized egg (zygote) if it arrives, to insure that it will not be cast off before it is firmly implanted. All these preparations are completed in each monthly cycle in time to receive the egg. If no sexual intercourse takes place, or if sperm have been deposited but have failed to make contact with and fertilize the egg, then the egg soon dies and fails to arrive in the uterus as expected. It has been said that menstruation is evidence of "disappointment on the part of the endometrium at the failure of pregnancy to occur." Since all the preparations for the egg are useless, the uterine lining, which has enlarged and become full of blood, is cast off and makes its way out of the body in what we call menstruation.

Some women experience a measure of discomfort just preceding or during menstruation, because the body tissues may tend to retain fluids. Sometimes there is also a tendency toward feelings of emotional unevenness or depression at this time. However with most women such factors, if they occur, are not prolonged or seriously uncomfortable. To get a better understanding of what are some of the physical and mental-emotional changes accompanying the menstrual cycle, 400 women in family sociology classes were asked to cooperate in keeping daily records of their changes in feelings for from one to three months.[1] When the study was completed, we had fairly complete records on 334 cycles as reported by 181 women whose cycles had ranged from 20 to 42 days. A summary of the study is given in Tables 27 and 28. The first quarter would begin with the first day of menstruation, the fourth quarter would be the one leading up to menstruation. It will be noticed from the tables that certain physical and mental-emotional symptoms were reported with much greater frequency during the first and fourth quarters of the cycle.

[1] Judson T. Landis, "Physical and Mental-Emotional Changes Accompanying the Menstrual Cycle," *Research Studies of the State College of Washington, Proceedings of the Pacific Sociological Society,* 25:2 (June, 1957), 155-162.

TABLE 27 DAILY PHYSICAL CHANGES DURING 334 MENSTRUAL CYCLES,
AS REPORTED BY 181 WOMEN,
SUMMARIZED BY QUARTERS OF THE CYCLE

Physical symptoms	First quarter N-334	Second quarter N-334	Third quarter N-334	Fourth quarter N-334
Decreased energy (easily fatigued)	63.5%	25.4%	27.8%	44.0%
Skin eruptions	52.7	26.9	29.0	57.8
Headache	40.1	20.4	18.9	32.6
Increased appetite	29.6	21.9	23.1	30.2
Decreased appetite	44.9	17.4	16.8	21.0
Chills	22.5	3.6	4.8	16.5
Cramps	56.6	3.3	3.9	22.5
Nausea	24.0	4.5	6.0	9.9
Poor coordination	19.2	9.6	5.4	14.7
Swelling or tenderness in breasts	30.2	3.6	10.2	44.0
Weight gain	24.3	6.9	12.0	21.3

TABLE 28 DAILY MENTAL-EMOTIONAL CHANGES
DURING 334 MENSTRUAL CYCLES,
AS REPORTED BY 181 WOMEN,
SUMMARIZED BY QUARTERS OF THE CYCLE

Mental-emotional state	First quarter N-334	Second quarter N-334	Third quarter N-334	Fourth quarter N-334
Depressed	47.9%	29.0%	31.7%	48.2%
Tendency to worry	34.4	25.4	24.9	35.9
Tendency to cry easily	35.9	16.8	22.2	36.8
Inability to concentrate	48.8	25.4	26.3	38.6
Inability to make decisions	20.4	12.6	11.7	19.2
Forgetfulness (absentmindedness)	23.1	11.7	16.2	16.8
Disorganized at work	32.9	15.6	17.1	21.0
Irritable (touchy, argumentative, quarrelsome)	41.3	21.0	26.9	42.8
Uncooperative toward others	18.3	9.6	14.1	18.0
Tendency to nag	13.8	8.4	8.7	20.1
Critical of others	24.6	14.4	19.2	28.1
Feeling of being unloved or unappreciated	17.7	9.9	12.9	26.3
Affectionate toward others	47.9	40.7	36.8	36.5
Increased sex desire	44.3	29.9	29.0	38.0
Decreased sex desire	24.9	10.5	11.7	18.3

The evidence seems to show that certain changes in feelings and in physical functioning do accompany stages in the menstrual cycle. But menstruation is not an illness and usually is not accompanied by pain. If pain does occur, a medical examination will reveal that abnormal conditions are responsible. Some mothers condition their daughters to consider themselves "unwell" during menstruation, and so help to build attitudes and habits that may contribute to painful or difficult menstrual periods. However, most girls look on menstruation as a normal, if not always pleasant, function related to their femininity. If menstrual periods are regularly accompanied by pain, medical help should be obtained, for such pain is evidence of abnormal functioning, whatever the cause.

The "safe period"

The rhythm method or "safe period," sometimes depended upon as a means of conception control, is based on the principle that conception can take place only at the time when the egg is in the fallopian tubes. If intercourse is limited to other periods of the month, then conception will not occur. This theory is sound, but, since many factors remain unknown at the present time, it is of limited effectiveness.

Research biologists are agreed that conception can take place only when the egg is present, but they do not know exactly when the egg will be expelled from the ovary. In general, it is during the middle of a regular 28-day menstrual cycle. However, not all cycles are regular, and ovulation is believed to take place about 14 days before the onset of the next menstruation. This of course means that ovulation is not in the middle of the cycle in a 21-day or a 40-day cycle, or in any other cycle which regularly or temporarily varies from the 28-day cycle. For some years, women have been taught to use a temperature chart to establish the time of ovulation. A sudden rise in body temperature of about three-fifths of a degree in mid-month was thought to indicate ovulation.

However, it is now known that the temperature rise indicates the hormonal changes that take place near the time of ovulation.

Research at Sloane Hospital for Women [2] found that the interval between ovulation and temperature rise may vary as much as four days. In some cases evidence seems to show that ovulation may occur at times other than about two weeks preceding the next menstruation. We know that more than one egg can mature at one time, since this occurs when fraternal twins are conceived. It is also possible then that more than one egg may be released at different times in the cycle. Moreover, it is now known that some women do not ovulate during every cycle.

Authorities are not agreed on the length of time the egg lives if it is not fertilized or on the length of time the sperm cells will survive in the uterine cavity. One researcher [3] believes that the spermatozoon retains its capacity to fertilize the egg cells no longer than 24 hours and that the egg is capable of fertilization no longer than 12 hours. All these uncertainties or unpredictable factors mean that the "safe period" as a method of conception control is unreliable.

Tests for pregnancy

Although it is usually impossible for a doctor to determine pregnancy with certainty during the first two months after conception, tests have been devised which are almost 100 per cent accurate if administered properly. The best known of these tests, the Friedman and the Aschheim-Zondek, work on the same principle. After conception takes place, a new hormone is secreted and excreted in the urine. If the urine is injected into a virgin female animal, it will cause the genital tract to mature and ovulation to take place within from one to four days. The Friedman test uses

[2] C. L. Buxton and E. T. Engle, "Time of Ovulation," *American Journal of Obstetrics and Gynecology*, 60:3 (September, 1950), 539-551.

[3] Edmond J. Farris, *Human Fertility and Problems of the Male*, p. 145. White Plains, New York: The Author's Press, Inc., 1950.

rabbits; the Aschheim-Zondek uses mice or rats; and a more recent test uses frogs. One advantage of the frog test is that ovulation takes place in from 6 to 18 hours. Consequently, this test will show the existence of pregnancy almost at once.

Another pregnancy test, which does not use animals, is the cervical color test. In pregnancy, the cervix deepens in color and by the 40th day a test matching cervical color with prepared color slides is usually strongly positive.[4]

Usually, only those women whose commitments make it necessary for them to know at once, go to the trouble and expense of having a test for pregnancy. Most women wait until other evidence indicates whether or not they are pregnant.

Presumptive signs of pregnancy

Signs that are not based on biological tests or the doctor's diagnosis after an examination are said to be presumptive. In the early months of pregnancy, the following are presumptive signs of pregnancy: (1) skipping of menstrual period, (2) nausea or "morning sickness," (3) increased frequency of urination, and (4) increasing tenderness of the breasts. None of these by itself is conclusive, since each may be due to some other cause. A combination of these signs, however, could be considered fairly conclusive evidence that pregnancy exists. However pregnancy may exist without some of these signs appearing at all. In some cases of pregnancy, menstruation may continue for one or two periods. Conversely, failure to menstruate cannot be taken as an absolute sign of pregnancy because failure to menstruate may be due to nervous tension or worry, or even to climatic changes, as well as to pregnancy. Also many women have no nausea during pregnancy. Although more than half of all pregnant women report nausea or morning sickness, some women have had nausea when they thought they were pregnant but actually were not; on dis-

[4] Edmond J. Farris, *Human Ovulation and Fertility*, pp. 133-136. Philadelphia: J. B. Lippincott Company, 1956.

covery that they were not pregnant, the nausea disappeared. Nevertheless, in our study of 212 couples who had gone through their first pregnancy, we found many cases in which the wife began to have nausea before she suspected that she was pregnant.[5] Those findings suggest that the nausea of early pregnancy may have a basis in metabolic changes or in changes in glandular balances which occur with conception. However, no one of the presumptive signs alone may be taken as conclusive evidence of pregnancy, for most of them can occur at other times and for other reasons.

Positive signs of pregnancy

By the third month, the doctor's examination will usually be accurate in determining whether pregnancy exists. By this time there will be an enlargement of and a softening of the cervix. The fetal heart beat can be heard during the fourth or fifth month, and the mother can "feel life," or the movement of the fetus. Shortly after this time, changes in the mother's figure will also become evident.

Boy or girl?

Since parenthood begins with conception, couples find themselves in the position of having a child some months before they know its sex. They usually are curious on this point, but so far there is no reliable way of knowing before birth what the sex of the child is. Superstition and "folk" explanations are common. Some of these say that if it is a boy it will be carried high, will kick the mother's right side, will cause the mother to prefer sour foods, will cause more nausea, or will be more active; and that a girl will cause the opposite effects. Guttmacher [6] points out that

[5] Shirley Poffenberger, Thomas Poffenberger, and Judson T. Landis, "Intent Toward Conception and the Pregnancy Experience," *American Sociological Review*, 17:5 (October, 1952), 616-620.

[6] Researchers continue to seek ways to tell the sex of an infant before birth, such as saliva tests. Such tests are still inconclusive.

HOW SEX IS DETERMINED

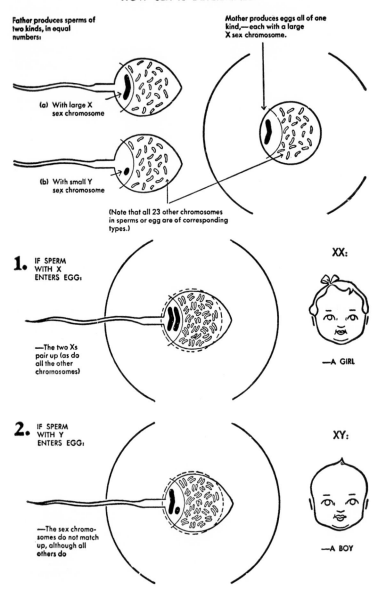

Fig. 91 By permission, Amram Scheinfeld, *Women and Men*,
p. 12. New York: Harcourt, Brace and Company, 1943.

516

all these beliefs are without foundation. Some doctors make predictions as to what the baby will be just as they bet on the horses. One doctor had a policy he felt worked to everyone's satisfaction. When a couple asked his opinion as to whether their child was to be a boy or a girl, he took pains to find out which was their preference. Then if they preferred a girl he would predict a boy. If it turned out to be a boy, his reputation as a prognosticator was established. If, however, it was a girl, the couple would be so happy at getting exactly what they wanted that their reaction would be: "The doctor happened to be wrong this time, but how glad we are that he missed," and their feeling of appreciation toward him for helping them get their wish would be favorable anyway. His comment was: "By my system you can't lose."

Sex determination

The sex of the baby is determined at the time the sperm unites with the egg, and nothing can be done to change the sex after that. All eggs are alike, but there are two types of sperm cells, those with an X chromosome and those without the X chromosome; sperm cells without the X chromosome are designated as Y. If the egg is fertilized by a sperm having an X chromosome, the baby is a girl; if fertilized by a sperm with a Y chromosome, a boy. Scheinfeld [7] has worked out a simple chart which explains the process by which sex is determined (see Fig. 91). Since it is all chance whether an X or Y sperm will fertilize an egg, it might be expected that an equal number of boys and girls would be born. However, the sex ratio at birth is 105.5 boys to 100 girls, and at conception it has been estimated to be between 120 and 150 boys to 100 girls. Several theories have been advanced to explain why more Y sperm cells than X reach their mark. Some of these theories are that the Y sperm cells are able to move faster

[7] Amram Scheinfeld, *Women and Men*, p. 12. New York: Harcourt, Brace and Company, 1943.

or that the acidity of the female genital tract is more fatal to X sperm.

Twins and triplets

Many gaps still exist in our knowledge of the causes of multiple births. In identical twins the egg seems to divide into two individuals at a very early stage of cell division. (Siamese twins develop if the egg does not completely divide.) Identical twins, then, are developed from a single egg and a single sperm and usually grow with one placenta. It is often difficult to know whether twins are identical or fraternal but a series of tests have been developed which can make the distinction. Twins that are not identical grow when two eggs are fertilized at the same time. The reason why this variation should occur is not known, but in

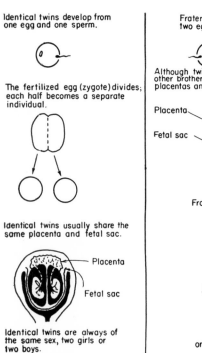

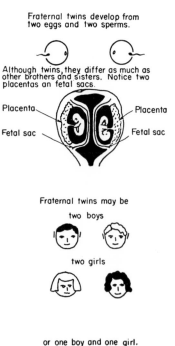

Fig. 92 THE WAY IN WHICH MULTIPLE BIRTHS DEVELOP.

some cases two or more eggs are released from the ovary at the time of ovulation and all may be fertilized, producing a multiple birth. Individuals produced by this type of multiple birth are no more alike than are other brothers and sisters who are produced

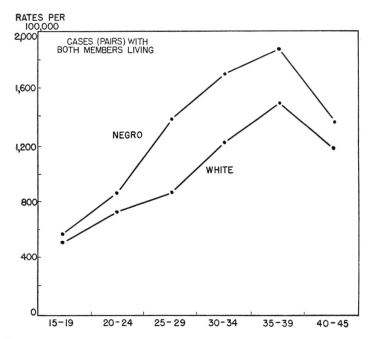

Fig. 93   RATES OF TWIN CASES PER 100,000 TOTAL CASES OF BIRTH, BY RACE, AGE OF MOTHER, AND NUMBER OF TWINS BORN ALIVE WITH BOTH MEMBERS LIVING, UNITED STATES, 1944. "Twinning" increases with the age of the mother up to the age of 40. The same principle holds for other higher multiple births. U.S. Bureau of Census, *Vital Statistics Special Reports*, 25:18 (July, 1947), 346.

by single births. Fraternal twins may be of different sexes, whereas identical twins are always of the same sex, since they are the result of an egg fertilized by a single sperm, either X or Y.

Other multiple births, such as triplets, quadruplets, and quintuplets, may be identical, fraternal, or a combination of the two.

The Dionne quintuplets are thought to be the result of one fertilized egg that divided and produced five individuals. Division into two would have produced identical twins.

Evidence indicates that twinning runs in families, but just why or how has not been established. The fact that one mother may have a number of multiple births seems to indicate that in some women the ovaries tend to bring to maturity and release more than one egg at each ovulation. Twins occur once in 92 births, triplets once in 9,000, and quadruplets once in 500,000.[8] Multiple births occur much more frequently among Negro mothers than among white mothers. The incidence of twins is 25 per cent higher, triplets 74 per cent higher, and quadruplets 600 per cent higher among Negro mothers.[9]

Pregnancy

Choosing a doctor.   As soon as pregnancy is suspected, the couple faces the necessity of finding a doctor. The task is relatively simple for those who have lived in the same community or city for many years. They will already have a family doctor who will either take the case or suggest an obstetrician. The problem is more complicated for the couple newly located and without a family doctor. Today in the United States a great many young couples begin married life away from the places where they have grown up. To such couples the choice of a doctor may present a puzzling problem. It is essential that they find a doctor whom they believe to be competent to handle any complications that might arise. Otherwise, worries and doubts may disturb their peace of mind unnecessarily during the pregnancy. In many communities the couple may inquire at a hospital and secure a list of the doctors in the area who take obstetrical cases. Most hospitals will not make any specific recommendations. The most satisfac-

---

[8] Metropolitan Life Insurance Company, *Statistical Bulletin,* 27:3 (March 1946), 9.

[9] *Ibid.,* p. 10.

tory procedure is to consult the latest edition of the *Directory of Medical Specialists*. This directory may be found in public libraries. The directory lists specialists in obstetrics and gynecology who have been certified by the American Board of Obstetrics and Gynecology.

If more than one qualified obstetrician is available, the prospective parents may then consult one or two and make a choice. A well-qualified obstetrician will be glad to talk with them in a frank manner before taking the case. He will take a little time to get acquainted with them. He will also tell them what his fees are, whether or not he has a preference as to hospitals, and he will answer other questions they may wish to ask before they make their final choice of a doctor. Some young prospective parents are too timid here. The better-qualified doctors recognize the importance of rapport between the obstetrician and his patients and will welcome this preliminary consultation. Once a doctor has been chosen, his decisions should be followed in all matters concerning the pregnancy and birth.

Early in the pregnancy the doctor will give the expectant mother a thorough physical examination to determine the condition of her general health. He will be interested in her health background, including the obstetrical history of her mother and sisters. He will check blood pressure and make tests for venereal disease. He will also take the pelvic measurements to be sure there is sufficient room for the baby to be born normally. Throughout the pregnancy he will keep a close check on all conditions and developments so that if any complication is likely to arise at the time of the birth he will be able to anticipate it and be prepared to cope with it. All these things are an important part of the services of the obstetrician.

Physical and psychological developments

Pregnancy is accompanied by a number of physical changes, some of which are readily apparent. The one of which both husband and wife are usually most conscious is the wife's gaining weight and her change in figure. With the physical changes, there are also emotional and psychological effects which sometimes cause difficulty in the adjustment of the couple. If the child was desired by both and the pregnancy resulted after it had been planned for, difficulties may be somewhat less likely to arise, for both enter the experience with a feeling of sharing and mutual responsibility. They feel that, although it is the wife's part to go through the physical processes of pregnancy and birth, the whole undertaking is as vitally important to the husband as to the wife. Such couples often find the months preceding the birth of their child to be among the happiest in their lives. Even in these cases it sometimes comes as a shock to them to find that the wife may have lost all sexual desire early in the pregnancy. This often occurs. Occasionally a woman becomes aware of an increase in sexual desire during pregnancy, but research shows that many women report that although they feel excellent physically and are conscious of great affection for their husbands they seem incapable of their usual sexual response.

If the couple did not desire a child and if conception occurred without their having planned for it, they sometimes experience more problems of adjustment, although some of these difficulties may arise regardless of whether the child was desired or not. Some wives consider pregnancy as an illness and demand all the privileges of a semi-invalid. Other wives may be resentful of the loss of their figure and react emotionally, blaming the husband for all the inconveniences of pregnancy. Some couples have their first difficulties in sex adjustment at this time.

In the previously quoted study of 212 pregnancies, information was secured on changes in sex desire of husbands and wives during the first pregnancy.[10] Half the wives and three out of four of

---

[10] Judson T. Landis, Thomas Poffenberger, and Shirley Poffenberger, "The Effects of First Pregnancy Upon the Sexual Adjustment of 212 Couples," *American Sociological Review*, 15:6 (December, 1950), 767-772.

the husbands said they saw no change in sex desire during the first trimester, but that the desire of both decreased rapidly through the next two trimesters. More than one-fourth of the wives noticed a marked decrease in sex desire with the onset of pregnancy, and less than one in five noticed an increase in sex desire with pregnancy. We do not know why this change in sex desire takes place, but since the pattern of the husband is similar to that of the wife it appears that there must be a strong psychological basis for it. However, in some cases the wife's sudden loss of interest in sex comes as a shock to a couple. Unable to appreciate that it is only a temporary condition, they may lose

Fig. 94 PERCENTAGES OF 212 HUSBANDS AND WIVES RATING SEXUAL DESIRE IN THREE PERIODS OF PREGNANCY AND SINCE BIRTH, AS COMPARED WITH DESIRE BEFORE PREGNANCY.

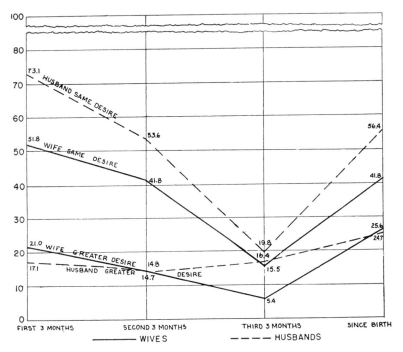

perspective and decide that the marriage is headed for the rocks. The husband may show his frustration by becoming critical of his wife or acting irritable. His wife is in no mood to take such behavior, since she feels she is the one who is carrying the family burdens at the moment. Thus, sometimes tensions and unhappiness result that could be avoided if both had a better understanding of pregnancy and could maintain a better perspective of the situation.

The wife is only occasionally an invalid and usually can live normally and happily during these months. Our study of pregnancy showed that over half of the wives noticed no change in their health, one-third said their health was better, and only one in ten said her health was poorer during pregnancy. It is true that nausea is a common discomfort, especially during the first three months. Over half the wives in our pregnancy study reported having had nausea in the first trimester, but only 15 per cent reported it during the last three months of pregnancy.[11] Most of those who had nausea considered it a discomfort rather than "ill-health."

In many of the adjustments during pregnancy, it is logical that the husband should be the one most willing to compromise and sacrifice his personal desires. Our research among the young couples indicated that the husbands did identify closely with their wives; the wives found their husbands more helpful, thoughtful, and affectionate than ever before. However, if the husbands noticed any change in the dispositions of their wives, it was that some wives were harder to live with than before pregnancy.[12] This is not surprising, for a wife may need more than the usual assurance of affection if she is to keep her feeling of poise and self-confidence during pregnancy.

A woman is not likely to feel very kindly toward her husband if he shows any embarrassment or unwillingness to be seen with her when her pregnancy is apparent. And any husbandly remarks about the clothes she must wear when pregnant will not be taken

[11, 12] *Ibid.*

lightly by the average wife. Fortunately, nature seems to offer compensation in that many women have an unusual feeling of well-being during pregnancy—their complexions are better; and in general their appearance, with the exception of their figures, improves during pregnancy. One study of pregnancy found that the majority of husbands rated their wives as attractive or more than usually attractive to them physically during pregnancy.[13]

Within about six weeks after the birth of the baby, sex desire returns to about the same level as before conception took place and normal sexual relations can usually be re-established. Of course, a baby in the house means extra work and loss of sleep, factors which may have an effect on the sex life of new parents.

Prenatal influences

Some prospective parents worry over the possibility that their child may be "marked" or abnormal in some way. Since hospital records show that only one baby in 200 is born with any kind of a blemish, the individual mother's chances of having a normal baby are about 199 to 1. Among the exceptions are included babies with only minor and unimportant blemishes, so that in reality the individual chances of having a normal baby are much greater than 199 to 1. Old wives' tales abound with examples of infants who are born with various types of marks or deformities that were presumably caused by some experience of the mother during the months of pregnancy. A child is born with a red birthmark, and the mother in trying to explain it remembers that during the prenatal period she was frightened by a fire, or a red car. She concludes that the scare caused the child to be marked. But the facts of fetal development from conception to birth discount any possibility of truth in such stories. No nervous connection exists between mother and child. The incidents that are

[13] Leland Stott, Research Report on Pregnancy Study at Merrill-Palmer School, Annual Meeting National Council on Family Relations, Rutgers University, September 1, 1952.

supposed to "mark" the child usually occur during the months when the pregnancy is well advanced, at which time the baby is completely formed. So anything the mother might see or experience during that time could not affect the child even if there were a nervous connection.

In the past, mothers were urged to cultivate in themselves traits they desired in their child, in the belief that they could impress such traits on the unborn child. Such self-discipline by the mother was doubtless all to the good, although it could not affect the unborn child. Its value lay in the fact that the self-cultivation might have desirable effects on the mother herself, who was to be the most important factor in the child's environment during his most impressionable years after birth. The expectant mother who spent her time going to concerts, reading the lives of great musicians, and letting her mind dwell on music, concluded later that her behavior during pregnancy had a great effect in causing her child to become a master musician. In reality, the behavior of the mother during pregnancy had no effect on her unborn child. However, the mother who tries to influence her child before birth will continue to influence the child after birth, and so her interests and activities may be important in shaping the interests of the child.

Fetal development

After fertilization, the egg immediately begins the process of division and growth, and continues through the tube where it met the sperm. It is believed that about three days are required for the fertilized egg to reach the uterus. Once there, it appears to rest for several more days. During this time, however, a process is taking place by which a part of the ovum is preparing to continue its development into a new individual, and another layer of cells is preparing for its special function of securing nourishment for the fetus during the months of its growth in the uterus.

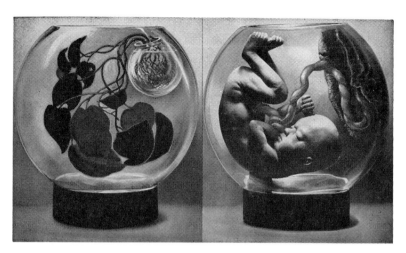

Fig. 95 THE BABY GROWS LIKE A PLANT. By permission, Dickinson-Belskie, *Birth Atlas*. New York: Maternity Center Association, 1943.

This second layer of cells forms the placenta, which becomes a flat, broad structure attached to the side of the uterus. It has numerous villi which penetrate the uterine lining and through osmotic action secure nutritive substances from the mother's blood. Waste products of the developing fetus are also given off by the same process to be carried away by the mother's blood. All nutritive substances and waste products pass through a membrane by absorption. The placenta is connected to the umbilicus of the fetus by means of a cord containing the blood vessels that carry the nourishment and waste products back and forth. After the placenta has formed and established itself, membranes develop which arise from the margin of the placenta and surround the fetus. This membranous sac fills with a watery fluid in which the fetus lives until almost time for birth. This fluid is called the amniotic fluid and serves to protect the fetus from outside shocks, as well as to keep the temperature constant. This sac of fluid breaks sometime during the birth process. Whether it breaks early or late has nothing to do with the ease or difficulty of the birth.

The length of time required from conception to birth is about

527

Fig. 96 ACTUAL SIZE OF THE FETUS AT ONE, TWO, AND THREE MONTHS. By permission, Nicholson J. Eastman, *Expectant Motherhood*, p. 30. Boston: Little, Brown and Company, 1940.

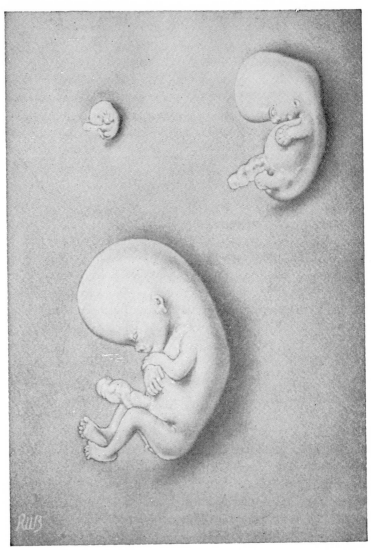

266 to 270 days, or roughly nine calendar months.[14] Doctors usually figure that the birth is due 280 days from the beginning of the last menstruation. However, since conception in a 28-day cycle takes place approximately 12 days after the last menstruation, 268 days is a more accurate figure. A recent study in which women had conceived by artificial insemination or where coitus had taken place only once during the month found that age may have something to do with length of gestation. In the age group 20-23, gestation had averaged 272 days; in the age group 36 to 39 it had averaged 263 days.[15] During this time, the embryo develops in size and complexity. By the end of the fourth week it is about ¼ inch long and is composed of a body and small buds that will later be the arms, legs, eyes, ears, and nose. By the end of the sixteenth week the fetus is approximately five inches long and quite well developed; the sex organs, which until this time have appeared much the same for both sexes, have now differentiated, so the sex of the fetus is evident. During the first two months the new individual is called an embryo, after that and until birth, a fetus. From this time on the fetus grows in length and in weight, most of the weight increase coming during the later weeks of the prenatal period. The weight is approximately doubled in the last four weeks before birth.

The Rh blood factors

During the early part of pregnancy, when the doctor tests for venereal disease he may also make a test for the Rh factor in the blood of the mother. This factor was first discovered in the blood of Rhesus monkeys. Like many other discoveries, its importance in childbearing has been exaggerated in the minds of many peo-

[14] H. L. Stewart, "Duration of Pregnancy and Postmaturity," *Journal of the American Medical Association,* 148 (March, 1952), 1079-1093.

[15] Edmond J. Farris, *Human Ovulation and Fertility,* p. 119. Philadelphia: J. B. Lippincott Company, 1956.

ple. At first it was even proposed that tests for this factor should be required before marriage and that people with incompatible blood should not marry. Now the Rh blood factors are better understood and can be coped with in childbearing.

About 85 per cent of white persons have the Rh factor in their blood and are called Rh positive; 15 per cent do not have such a factor and are called Rh negative. The Rh negative mother who conceives by a Rh positive father in some cases has a Rh positive child. In such a case if any minute amount of the baby's blood elements get into the mother's circulation—an occurrence that is extremely rare no matter what the blood types are—the mother's blood stream builds up antibodies against the incompatible blood elements. The presence of these antibodies in the mother's blood will not affect, usually, first or second pregnancies; it may cause jaundice and anemia in later babies. It is estimated that in cases of couples with the father Rh positive and the mother Rh negative only one in 300 pregnancies is actually affected by the wrong combination. Where periodic tests during pregnancy show that the mother's blood is building up the antibodies to the point of danger, doctors now prepare for the emergency and at birth the baby is given transfusions which gradually replace the blood with which the child was born. Thus most of the small percentage of babies that would be affected by the incompatibility of their parents' blood can be saved.

Prospective parents do much needless worrying if they know they have the "wrong combination" of blood. Typical is the mother of four healthy children, all born before tests for the Rh factor were being made, who learned during her fifth pregnancy that she was Rh negative and her husband Rh positive. She worried all through her pregnancy and, although this child also was healthy and unaffected, she was afraid to attempt another pregnancy. She would probably have been afraid to have any children after the first one had she known about the Rh factor at that time.

Birth

After approximately 40 weeks of growth, the fetus is ready to be born. Authorities differ as to just what forces initiate the birth process. Some theorize that it is due to hormone action similar to that which initiates the shedding of the uterine lining in the process of menstruation when pregnancy has not occurred. Whatever the force that starts it, the birth process begins in due time and proceeds through three definite stages, which result in release of the child from the mother's body.

In the first stage, the cervix undergoes changes and dilates until it is large enough to permit the baby to pass through. In the second stage, the baby is expelled from the uterus and passes through the cervix and the vagina to be born. The third stage is the expelling from the uterus of the placenta, known as the "afterbirth." As soon as the birth process is over, the tissues of the mother begin to return to their former state. The uterus goes through a series of contractions and gradually returns to approximately its original size and shape. This process usually takes about six weeks.

There are many conflicting opinions among both medical men and other interested authorities concerning the pain accompanying the birth process, or labor. Many mothers say that the process of giving birth to their children was little different from menstruation in the pain involved; that they experienced a series of cramping sensations that could hardly be called pain. Other mothers beg for anesthetics almost from the onset of labor and consider the pain to be severe. Many doctors are quite free in giving anesthetics to mothers in labor, and most doctors give an anesthetic at least during the last moments when the baby is being born.

There has been a cycle in the use of anesthetics. From the viewpoint that they should be used little or not at all, there was a swing to the other extreme. All kinds and types of anesthetics were used and much was said about achieving "painless births"

Fig. 97 (*top*) BEFORE LABOR: THICK PELVIC FLOOR, CERVIX CLOSED, UTERUS RELAXED. Figures 97, 98, 99, 100, and 101 are reproduced by permission from Dickinson-Belskie, *Birth Atlas*. New York: Maternity Center Association, 1943.

Fig. 98 (*bottom*) LABOR: UTERUS CONTRACTING, CERVIX DILATING, BAG OF WATER BELOW HEAD.

Fig. 99 *(top)* FULL DILATION: HEAD DEEP IN BIRTH CANAL, PULL OF UTERINE CONTRACTIONS DRAWS CERVIX UP.

Fig. 100 *(bottom)* HEAD TURNS UPWARD, PELVIC FLOOR SLIPS BACK OVER FACE.

through new types of anesthesia. The medical profession is now swinging back to a more conservative stand. Some doctors have taken the position that the pain that goes with the birth process is due to the fact that in our culture birth is generally accepted to be a process involving severe pain, so that most mothers go into labor in a state of great tenseness because of their fear of pain and of the unknown.

Progress is being made now toward a better understanding on the part of both doctors and laymen of the facts about the birth process. Formerly the idea was accepted that it was the *doctor* who "delivered" the baby, the implication being that the mother was simply present and probably quite thoroughly anesthetized while the doctor engineered the birth process. Now more emphasis is given to the fact that if nature takes its course the mother, not the doctor, gives birth to the baby.

More mothers now realize that during the first stage of labor it is best to relax and rest, for this stage will proceed more smoothly and quickly if the mother is not tense. In this first stage the cervix gradually opens to allow the baby to begin to pass through into the birth canal. The muscles of the uterus automatically contract as the cervix opening enlarges, and the mother experiences the sensations similar to the cramping sensations that sometimes accompany menstruation. A relaxed attitude of mind and body is of greatest importance at this stage.

After the first stage of labor is over, the mother is taken into the delivery room for the second stage, or the actual birth of the baby. It is in this stage that the mother "labors" to help give birth to her baby. This stage is much shorter than the first. One obstetrician says of this stage, "It is certainly work, just as playing a game of football or running a foot race is work. How much of it is 'pain' is a matter of viewpoint or definition, and that differs with different women." Certainly the facial expressions of many athletes in action could be interpreted as expressions indicating pain, but few of them would call their sensations pain. So it is with mothers during childbirth. Many of them insist that they be given no anesthetic because they want to be fully conscious, for they look on giving birth to a child as an achievement that they accomplish at least in part by their own efforts. This viewpoint among mothers is increasing because of the work of certain doc tors who are known as advocates of "natural childbirth." These doctors believe that if mothers are thoroughly informed about what actually takes place in the birth process, if they are familiar with how the birth of the baby is to be handled—including some knowledge of hospital conditions and routines—and if they have confidence that the doctor will be standing by ready for any emergency, they will go into the birth process free of tension and able to give birth naturally to the child with little need or desire for anesthetics.

Support is given to these views by research studies carried out at certain medical schools. A study was made of 1,000 consecutive deliveries in the Yale University Service of the Grace-

Fig. 101 BIRTH OF THE SHOULDERS, TURNING TO FIT PASSAGE.

New Haven Community Hospital. All the mothers took part in the Training for Childbirth Program, which gave both physical and psychological preparation. Doctors Thoms and Wyatt say of the program, "The educational aspects of our program consist of four talks given to prospective parents, and four exercise classes given by a nurse. . . . Following the fourth class, which is given in the third trimester of pregnancy, the women visit the obstetrical division of the hospital, meet members of the personnel, see the labor and delivery rooms, and learn how the delivery tables and anesthesia apparatus operate. The patient in labor is in a room by herself; during this period she may have her husband with her if she wishes. The patient is kept informed of her progress and during active labor is not left alone. Attention is focused upon her needs and what she is trying to accomplish. Any therapy or instruction is in the hands of a nurse or a physician. Activity and busyness on the part of those attending her are kept to a minimum." [16]

Of the 1,000 consecutive births reported in the Yale study, the average length of total labor, whether the birth was of a first baby or not, was 10.3 hours; only 8 babies out of 1,000 died.

Helen Heardman studied the duration of labor among 1,000 women who were having their first baby; 500 of the mothers had gone through the "natural childbirth" training program and a control group of 500 had had no special training. The average length of labor was approximately six hours shorter for the 500 who had gone through the training program, and there was a much larger percentage of normal deliveries in this group.[17]

Many doctors now consider it routine to conduct classes or to have an assistant conduct classes for expectant mothers. Training similar to that described in the Yale program is usually given.

[16] Herbert Thoms and Robert H. Wyatt, "One Thousand Consecutive Deliveries Under a Training for Childbirth Program," *American Journal of Obstetrics and Gynecology*, 61:1 (January, 1951), 205-209.

[17] Herbert Thoms, *Training for Childbirth*, p. 76. New York: McGraw-Hill Book Company, Inc., 1950.

One company has prepared a series of films showing normal labor and childbirth, and these films are used at the conclusion of the training programs.[18]

The education of young people should emphasize the normality of the birth process and of the launching of a new individual into life. In the past too much emphasis was given to possible pain and risk. Parents have sometimes tried to inspire gratitude in their children by repeated references to the sacrifices and suffering that were necessary to bring the children into the world. The picture

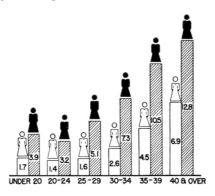

Fig. 102 MATERNAL MORTALITY BY AGE AND RACE. Age 20-24 is the safest age for women to bear children. At younger or older ages, the maternity death rate increases for both white and Negro mothers. Adapted from Metropolitan Life Insurance Company, *Statistical Bulletin,* 26:12 (December, 1945), 8.

given by such references is not accurate, for the truth is that to have children and to give them a good start in life, physically and emotionally, is one of the unparalleled experiences that come to human beings.

Nor is giving birth to a child today dangerous for the mother, as was true at one time. In 1956, in the United States, only one mother died for every 2,700 live births. The discovery and devel-

[18] Medical Arts Productions, Inc., 414 Mason St., San Francisco, California. "Prenatal Care," "Labor and Childbirth," "A Normal Birth," and "Postnatal Care" are four films in the series.

opment of new drugs to prevent infection have done most to reduce the dangers that once existed in childbirth. More progress is still needed to make good medical care available to non-white mothers and mothers from the lower socio-economic classes. Childbirth risks are four times greater among this group. Almost all white mothers are attended by a physician and have their babies in hospitals. The most favorable age for giving birth to children is between 20 and 24 years, although if there is adequate medical care the risk is not great at any age.

Rooming-in

It is becoming recognized that certain things can be done from the very moment of birth to give children a good start emotionally. The earliest experiences an individual has with his mother are believed to be the basis for his later human relationships and to influence his total personality. Many hospitals are now following a plan designed to give children a better start in life emotionally than they were given in the past. This is called the rooming-in plan. In the Yale University program described above, "rooming-in" is an important part of the plan in the hospital. According to the rooming-in plan, the babies are not kept in a central nursery but remain in the rooms with their mothers. Mothers are encouraged to do as much as they want to in caring for their newborn babies. Mothers get confidence in caring for their babies while in the hospital under direction of a nurse, and they learn from one another, since several may be in one unit of rooms. Breast-feeding is encouraged. More mothers seem to be able to nurse their babies when the babies are with them and when the mother and baby are able to work out their own schedule than when the baby is fed only at stated intervals according to hospital schedules.[19]

[19] Thaddeus L. Montgomery, Robert E. Steward, and Pauline Shenk, "Observations on the Rooming-in Program in Ward and Private Service," *American Journal of Obstetrics and Gynecology*, 57:1 (January, 1949), 176-186.

New mothers may be more enthusiastic about rooming-in than mothers with several children. The latter may look forward to a vacation when they go to the hospital. Some hospitals are constructing rooms that allow the mother to have her baby with her and still turn it over to the care of nurses when she wants to be free to rest. But even mothers of several children are likely to prefer to have their babies with them because they want to know that their babies are comfortable at all times. Under the system in which babies are all kept in a central nursery, mothers often can hear babies crying and each one may worry over whether it is her baby that needs attention.

Hospitals and doctors using the rooming-in plan believe that a close relationship between mother and baby is important during the first days and weeks of the baby's life and that better mental and emotional health will result for both mothers and babies.

Review questions

1. Explain the basis of menstruation.
2. What are some of the physical states more commonly experienced during the first and fourth quarters of the menstrual cycle?
3. What are some of the mental-emotional states more commonly experienced during the first and fourth quarters of the menstrual cycle?
4. What are some of the unknowns that make the "safe period" or rhythm method unreliable for conception control?
5. What are some of the tests now being used for pregnancy?
6. What is the principle of the pregnancy tests?
7. Is it possible to determine the sex of an unborn child?
8. How is sex determined? Why are more boys than girls conceived?
9. Explain how twinning takes place.
10. Is twinning more common among Negro or white mothers?
11. Where can one find help in choosing an obstetrician?
12. What are some of the common problems facing a couple during pregnancy?
13. Is it possible for a pregnant woman to influence the future behavior of her child by the activities she engages in during pregnancy? Explain.

14. What is the origin of the many old wives' tales about "marking" babies?

15. Draw a diagram on the blackboard to show how the fetus secures nourishment from the mother.

16. Explain the Rh blood factors.

17. What are the three stages in the birth process? At which stage is the mother encouraged to help in giving birth to her child?

18. Explain the theory of "natural childbirth" as you understand it.

19. How are expectant mothers prepared for "natural" childbirth?

Project

Ask an obstetrician who believes in "natural" childbirth to come to class and give a talk on pregnancy and childbirth.

Films

Biography of the Unborn. Shows actual union of human sperm and ovum and early development of embryo. Encyclopaedia Britannica Films, 15 minutes, sound.

Human Reproduction. Factual film on human reproductive systems and on process of normal birth. McGraw-Hill Book Company, Inc. 23 minutes, sound.

Suggested readings

Becker, Howard, and Reuben Hill, eds., *Family, Marriage, and Parent·hood.* Boston: D. C. Heath and Company, 1955. Ch. XIV, "Heredity and the Family," and Ch. XV, "Caring for Mother and Child Before and After."

Eastman, Nicholson J., *Expectant Motherhood.* Boston: Little, Brown and Company, Revised 1957. A scientific treatment of the prenatal period by a professor of obstetrics at The Johns Hopkins University and Obstetrician-in-Chief to The Johns Hopkins Hospital.

Farris, Edmond J., *Human Fertility and Problems of the Male.* White Plains: The Author's Press, Inc., 1950. Laboratory research largely on human male, but also on female, to determine real cause of infertility. Should be of interest to all couples having difficulty conceiving.

————, *Human Ovulation and Fertility.* Philadelphia: J. B. Lippincott Company, 1956. Companion book to the above giving latest research on ovulation and fertility.

Genné, William H., *Husbands and Pregnancy.* New York: Association Press, 1956.

Goodrich, Frederick W., *Natural Childbirth*. Englewood Cliffs, N. J.: Prentice-Hall, Inc., 1950. A manual containing information on natural childbirth, diet, exercise, relaxation, and the labor experience. For expectant parents.

Heardman, Helen, *Natural Childbirth*. Baltimore: The Williams & Wilkins Company, 1949. A manual describing methods used to prepare mothers for natural childbirth. Includes illustrated instructions for exercises designed to aid in the relaxation necessary for uncomplicated childbirth.

Landis, Judson T., and Mary G. Landis, eds., *Readings in Marriage and the Family*. Englewood Cliffs, N. J.: Prentice-Hall, Inc., 1952. Part IX, Reading 4, "The Rh Blood Factors," Curt Stern; Reading 5, "Effects of First Pregnancy on Sex Adjustment," Judson T. Landis, Thomas and Shirley Poffenberger; Reading 8, "Birth Control: The Fortune Survey," Elmo Roper.

Read, Grantley Dick, *Childbirth Without Fear*. New York: Harper & Brothers, 1944. The thesis of this book is that by doing away with fear through knowledge and understanding of childbirth, birth will be the natural, comparatively painless function nature intended it to be.

Thoms, Herbert, and Lawrence Roth, *Understanding Natural Childbirth*. New York: McGraw-Hill Book Company, Inc., 1950. Describes Yale University training program.

Family Planning

From the viewpoint of society, a major function of marriage is reproduction. All groups have found it necessary to regulate the sex behavior of men and women so that offspring will be guaranteed care and protection during the long period of immaturity. There are variations from society to society, but whether the recognized type of marriage be monogamy, polygyny, or polyandry, the system attempts to guarantee some measure of family stability for the children. A secondary object of regulation of husband-wife behavior is protection of the personal and material rights of the husband and wife.

Although the chief function of the family is to perpetuate the race by producing and nurturing offspring, some married couples, by choice, have no children. Throughout history, couples who married expected to have children; if no children came, the marriage could be dissolved. Such marriages can still be dissolved in some countries, and in two states in the Union [1] inability to have children is a legal reason for divorce.

.. 23

Desirable family size

For a number of years we have queried college students concerning the number of children they consider desirable in the ideal family, and the number given has gradually increased. Figure 106 compares our most recent study on the number of children desired with a previous study in 1947, and with one by Bell in 1936. Bell found that over half of the young people thought one or two children constituted the ideal family, whereas of the students queried in 1947 approxi-

[1] Pennsylvania and Tennessee.

543

mately one-fourth named one or two, and only 18 per cent of the students queried in 1957 named this number.[2] The average size of the family considered ideal by the young people in 1936 was 2.3; in 1947, 3.0; in 1957, 3.4. It is possible that the contrast in economic conditions between the depression 30's and the prosperity of the 1950's caused young people to think differently about the desirable number of children. War and threat of war may also have brought about a shifting of values toward greater emphasis on family living and the presence of children as essential to happiness.

Although young people in 1957 stated they wanted large families, each couple will not necessarily have three or four children

[2] Howard M. Bell, *Youth Tell Their Story*, pp. 36-38. Washington, D. C.: American Council on Education, 1938.

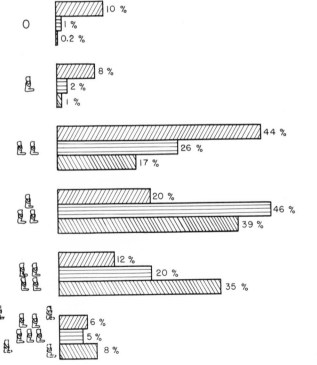

Fig. 103 SIZE OF THE FAMILY CONSIDERED IDEAL BY YOUNG PEOPLE, IN 1936, 1947, 1957. Are family values changing, or is the difference in the number of children desired explained by various economic factors?

when they face the realities of parenthood. In a study of 212 couples who had had their first child, we asked whether they planned to have the same number, more, or fewer children than they had originally hoped to have. About one in five wanted fewer. Our study in 1957 and studies by the Purdue Opinion Panel show that girls say they want larger families than boys want, and both boys and girls show a preference for boy babies. A family of two boys and one girl seems to be considered the ideal family by the young people polled.[3]

The birth rate

The birth rate in the United States decreased steadily for many years, but started increasing after the worst depression years of the 30's. It has continued to be high since that time. Whether this is a permanent trend or a temporary increase resulting from prosperity, hot and cold wars, and the increased marriage rate, cannot be stated positively. Some years ago, advertisements and other pictures featuring family life showed the mother and father and two children, a boy and a girl. Today, however, the typical family is pictured as having three or more children.

Birth rates vary in relation to certain socio-economic factors. In urban areas the birth rate is far lower proportionately than in rural areas. Birth rates are proportionately higher among lower-income groups than among high-income groups in both city and country. College-educated people have fewer than their proportionate share of children. However, educated people who live in rural areas have more children than people of equal education living in cities. There is some evidence to indicate that people with more education have been having a larger proportion of the babies in recent years.

Broad religious classifications differ in number of children born. Studies show that Catholics are most prolific, Protestants

[3] *The Purdue Opinion Panel, Report 43*, Lafayette, Ind.: Purdue University, 15:1 (February, 1956), 4-5a.

next, and Jews least. Mixed marriages of Catholics and Protestants have fewer children than Protestant or Catholic marriages. But within all three religious groups, as in the population in general, those with higher incomes and more education, and those in urban areas, have proportionately fewer children than do the others of their faith.

Contraception

One factor which must be taken into consideration in explaining the difference in the birth rate of different socio-economic groups is the belief in, and the successful use of contraception. Contraceptive information has been disseminated quite rapidly throughout the United States during the last 30 years. This information has been more readily accepted and more effectively used

Fig. 104   Source: U.S. Census Bureau Study, based on 1950 census. Courtesy of *U.S. News and World Report*.

THE HIGHER THE EDUCATION, THE FEWER THE CHILDREN

NEW OFFICIAL REPORT DISCLOSES THAT MARRIED WOMEN IN U.S.—

—with less than 7th-grade education have	**2,905 children** per 1,000 women
—with 7th and 8th-grade education have	**2,341 children** per 1,000 women
—with 1 to 3 years of high school have	**1,865 children** per 1,000 women
—with high-school diplomas have	**1,511 children** per 1,000 women
—with 1 to 3 years of college have	**1,533 children** per 1,000 women
—with 4 or more years of college have	**1,412 children** per 1,000 women

Note: Figures for white women 15 to 44 years of age, married once and living with husband.

by the families of higher income and education. Studies by Pearl [4] show that approximately 80 per cent of women in the higher-income groups, aged 20 to 24, having their first baby in the 1930's practiced some form of contraception, whereas of the lowest-income groups only 25 per cent practiced contraception. The same study shows that the effectiveness of contraception increases with the increase in economic status among both white and Negro women. Educated people are not only more likely to know about contraception, but their birth rate is lower because they tend to marry at a later age, thus having fewer years for childbearing.

The difference in the birth rate of Catholics and Protestants is explained partially by the difference in the practice of birth control. Although the Catholic clergy had opposed birth control, no official pronouncement was made by the Pope on the subject until 1930. In that year, Pope Pius XI made an official pronouncement in which he stated that birth control was "unnatural and intrinsically evil and therefore not to be justified for any reason however grave." The Catholic church does recognize the right to limit the size of the family under certain circumstances by limiting intercourse to the so-called "safe period." However, in 1951 Pope Pius XII warned Catholics against the abuse of this practice.

Catholic couples who follow the teachings of their church on birth control are expected to have children and to have them early in marriage. The young Catholic couple who find that they are sterile or relatively infertile may feel a measure of defensiveness because they know that their Catholic friends will believe that they are practicing contraception. Members of most other faiths do not experience quite the same pressure.

Although Protestants have not taken a united stand on the

[4] Raymond S. Pearl, *The Natural History of Population,* pp. 234-244. New York: Oxford University Press, 1939. (Data summarizing interviews with 30,000 women during the years 1931 and 1932, after their confinement in urban hospitals.)

question of birth control, the Federal Council of Churches of Christ in America, through its Commission on Marriage and the Home, has gone on record as favoring birth control. The Federal Council represents 25 of the largest Protestant denominations. The Council's report expresses recognition of a two-fold function of sex as divinely instituted. We quote from their statement:

> A majority of the committee holds that the careful and restrained use of contraceptives by married people is valid and moral. They take this position because they believe that it is important to provide for the proper spacing of children, the control of the size of the family, and the protection of mothers and children; and because intercourse between the mates, when an expression of their spiritual union and affection, is right in itself. They are of the opinion that abstinence within marriage, except for the few, cannot be relied upon to meet these problems, and under ordinary circumstances is not desirable in itself.[5]

In taking this position, the Council recognizes the dangers involved in a more widespread acceptance of contraception. However, it goes on to state:

> Society faces a new problem of control with each fresh advance of knowledge. If men generally cannot properly use the knowledge they acquire, there is no safety and no guarantee of the future. These members of the committee believe that the undesirable use of contraceptives will not be indulged in by most people, and that if the influence of religion and education is properly developed the progress of knowledge will not outrun the capacity of mankind for self-control. But if the sex impulse and the use of contraceptives are to be kept under moral control, the church and society, including parents, must give greater attention to the education and character building of youth and to the continued education of adult opinion.[6]

Orthodox Jews have not made any official pronouncement on the subject of birth control in modern times. However, the Jewish Orthodox point of view is opposed to birth control. The Talmud

[5] *Moral Aspects of Birth Control*, p. 5. New York: Federal Council of the Churches of Christ in America, Committee on Marriage and the Home, 1938.
[6] *Ibid.*, p. 6.

states that where the health of the woman is involved contraception may be practiced within certain specified limitations.[7]

Reformed Jews have taken a favorable attitude toward birth control through the Central Conference of American Rabbis. In 1929, the Central Conference wrote into its social justice program its recognition of "intelligent birth regulation as one of the methods of coping with social problems." Such social problems are those that arise when parents do not have the health, economic resources, or intelligence to guarantee their children a worthy heritage.[8]

The Rabbinical Assembly of America, the Conservative Jewish group, passed a resolution on birth control in 1934:

> As rabbis we are deeply concerned with the preservation and extension of the human values inherent in the institution of the monogamous family. Careful study and observation have convinced us that birth control is a valuable method for overcoming some of the obstacles that prevent the proper functioning of the family under present conditions.
>
> Jewish tradition explicitly recognizes the desirability of the use of contraceptives when health of the mother or the children is involved. It is obvious that there is an intimate connection between the economic status of the family and the physical and psychic health of the members. We therefore regard it as legitimate and completely within consonance with the spirit of Jewish tradition to permit the use of contraceptives on economic grounds, as well as where the earning capacity of the family makes the postponement of child-bearing wise and necessary.
>
> Hence we urge the passage of legislation by the Congress of the United States and the State Legislatures to permit the dissemination of contraceptive information by responsible medical agencies. We maintain that proper education in contraception and birth control will not destroy but rather enhance the spiritual values inherent in the family and will make for the advancement of human happiness and welfare.[9]

[7] Personal letter from Uri Miller, President, Rabbinical Council of America, December 11, 1947.

[8] Mary A. Cannon, *Outline for a Course in Planned Parenthood*. New York: Planned Parenthood Federation of America, p. 20.

[9] Personal letter from Ira Eisenstein, Chairman, Social Justice Committee, The Rabbinical Assembly of America, December 26, 1947.

Although the Catholic church and certain Protestant denominations oppose the use of contraceptives, not all members of these religious groups abide by the teachings of the churches. This situation is evident when we observe the differential birth rate between Catholics with higher incomes and more education and those with lower incomes and less education. Studies of the religious affiliation of clients of birth control clinics reveal that all faiths are well represented.

Legality of contraception

With the change in public opinion on the question of birth control, there has followed a change in the laws pertaining to the giving of contraceptive information. There has also been a gradual lessening of efforts to enforce existing laws. The Comstock Act, passed in 1873 to prohibit the sending of information on contraception through the mails, was virtually nullified by a decision of the United States Circuit Court of Appeals in 1936. Some states have laws to control the giving and printing of contraceptive information. However, the laws in most states are not enforced. Nineteen states make no mention in their statutes of the prevention of conception; 14 states have statutes that restrict the distribution and dissemination of information regarding the prevention of conception, but expressly exempt medical practice; 13 states have statutes aimed at indiscriminate advertising and distribution of information regarding the prevention of conception, but exempt medical practice by implication or construction; in Massachusetts and Connecticut, state courts have interpreted state laws as prohibiting physicians from advising patients on contraception for any reason whatsoever.[10] In Connecticut, the law forbids any person to use a contraceptive.

A change in thinking concerning use of contraceptives is reflected in the establishment of birth-control clinics. The United

[10] *The Legal Status of Contraception.* New York: Planned Parenthood Federation of America, Inc., p. 6.

States Public Health Service has adopted the policy of helping to set up family planning clinics as a part of the public health facilities of the states. A number of states have taken advantage of this assistance and have established such clinics.

Present indications are that dissemination of contraceptive information will be more open in the future. Especially will it be made available to the poorer classes, and to those who in the past could not get reliable information. Since these groups are the ones that have had a high birth rate, greater availability of contraceptive information may tend to depress the birth rate in the future.

Contraception and health

Considerable discussion has developed over the effects of contraception on the health of those using contraceptive devices. People opposed to the use of contraceptives have maintained that contraceptives are not only physically injurious but also tend to cause sterility. Those in favor of contraceptives have argued that no harmful results follow their use. Clinical evidence shows that some unapproved mechanical and chemical methods may lead to physical injury, but that clinically approved methods do not result in physical injury. Clinicians believe that people who conclude that they have been made sterile through the use of contraception were probably sterile before they started using the control measures. Clinics have found that normal, healthy women of the childbearing age will usually conceive soon after they abandon the use of clinically approved contraceptives.

The psychological effects of the use of contraceptives will depend on the individual couple. If a couple is using contraceptives even though one spouse feels that it is wrong to limit conception, emotional conflict may arise that will make it difficult for the couple to achieve a good sex adjustment in their marriage. On the other hand, if neither spouse has scruples against birth control, contraception may make sex adjustment easier in cases where the wife's response might be affected by fear of pregnancy. If this fear is removed and if no feeling of moral condemnation exists, then a good relationship should be easier to achieve.

Effectiveness of contraceptives

Although people have been interested in contraception for centuries, serious research is relatively recent. Papyrus rolls of as early as 1850 B.C. contain formulas to induce abortion, and by the fourth century B.C. measures had been found to prevent conception. It was not until 1937 that the American Medical Association accepted contraception as an integral part of medical practice and education. Since that time, some systematic research has been undertaken to find contraceptives that are harmless, effective, and acceptable. Nevertheless, some young couples approaching marriage with no scruples against birth control still find it difficult to get the best information on contraceptives. Private companies are manufacturing hundreds of different products and all claim that their products are the best. Some of these devices are not only ineffective but harmful. Doctors are subjected to high-pressure salesmanship through advertising and have no accurate way to judge products. A nationwide poll of the medical profession by Dr. Alan F. Guttmacher of the Johns Hopkins Medical School showed that three out of four practicing physicians had received no training in medical school about contraceptives. But the practices of medical schools are changing, and now about two-thirds of them give some training on the theory and clinical aspects of fertility control.

There is little objective research today on the effectiveness of different contraceptives. Much of the so-called research is done by the manufacturers of the products. Few carefully controlled experiments have been set up. It is certain that the effectiveness depends on many factors, such as proved fertility on the part of the people using the contraceptive, willingness to follow instructions carefully, and a desire on the part of both to control fertility.

FAMOUS LAST WORDS . . . . .

"Let's plan on two, dear, a boy
for me and a girl for you."

Fig. 105 By permission, Irwin Caplan and *The Saturday
Evening Post.*

If one couple in ten is sterile, that ten per cent would find any
contraceptive effective; many more couples are relatively infertile,
and these would also find little difficulty in controlling conception.
To be productive, research would have to be done with a group
of couples who are highly fertile. A study of 212 college couples
at Michigan State University [11] who had gone through their first
pregnancy, and a similar study by Christensen at Purdue University among 346 couples,[12] showed that only slightly over one-third

[11] Judson T. Landis, Thomas Poffenberger, and Shirley Poffenberger, "The
Effects of First Pregnancy Upon the Sexual Adjustment of 212 Couples,"
American Sociological Review, 15:6 (December, 1950), 767.
[12] Harold T. Christensen and Robert E. Philbrick, "Family Size as a
Factor in the Marital Adjustment of College Couples," *American Sociological
Review,* 17:3 (June, 1952), 309.

of the pregnancies were definitely planned. In contrast, one producer of contraceptives claims that its product is 99.4 per cent effective, a claim that is unquestionably an exaggeration. Human error in failing to use a product as directed would result in a certain percentage of failures even if the contraceptive were theoretically perfect. Failure would not usually be so great as among the college couples in the two studies cited above, for they were using assorted contraceptives and were, in general, fertile couples. At least they all had had children.

For couples who have good reasons to postpone their first pregnancy and who wish to plan their families, the best source of information is the Planned Parenthood Federation of America, which has offices in most of the large cities. These clinics can be helpful to married couples, whether the problem is the postponement of pregnancy or the inability of sterile or relatively infertile couples to have children.

Abortion as a form of birth control

Abortion is a common form of controlling births in the United States. Abortion is not contraception, since contraception prevents the uniting of the sperm with the egg; abortion destroys the fertilized egg sometime before birth. Abortions are of three types: spontaneous, therapeutic, and criminal. Spontaneous abortions, or miscarriages, are produced by various causes and are more or less accidental or unpreventable. It is now believed that most spontaneous abortions are nature's way of disposing of imperfect embryos that are not developing properly, whether from a defective egg or sperm or from improper implantation in the wall of the uterus. The belief that miscarriage is due to movements or activities of the mother is now largely discounted.

Therapeutic or legal abortions are cases in which the pregnancy is interrupted by a qualified doctor in order to protect the health or life of the mother.

Criminal or illegal abortions include all others in which the mother, a doctor, a midwife, or any other person interrupts pregnancy by any means.

Many abortions are of the third type, but it is impossible to know how frequently they occur, since they are illegal and those who perform such abortions keep no records. It has been estimated that a great many illegal abortions are performed on women who are not pregnant. The menstrual cycle is often upset in unmarried girls who are having coitus. When such girls go to an abortionist, naturally he will not give a pregnancy test since his actions are illegal and solely for criminal financial gain. Even if he suspects that the girl is not pregnant, he can go through the motions of performing an abortion and collect money from the victim. Doctor Rock, of the Harvard Medical School, reports that 40 per cent of the women who came to one clinic thinking they were pregnant found that they were mistaken. He states that if the proportion of nonpregnant women visiting abortionists is as high as at that clinic, a high proportion of illegal abortions are performed each year on women who are not pregnant.[13]

Illegal abortions involve extreme danger for the women undergoing them. Since reputable doctors will not perform them, they are usually performed by unqualified doctors, quacks, or devious characters who depend on such illegal business for a living. The operations are performed under conditions regulated by the necessity for secrecy rather than by surgical standards, with the result that the mortality rate is high. One-third of all maternity deaths are the result of abortions. Where death does not result, the effect of the illegal abortion may be permanent impairment of health, or sterility.

Qualified doctors are permitted to perform therapeutic abortions in certain justifiable cases, such as when the life of the mother depends on terminating the pregnancy or when demonstrated abnormality in the pregnancy indicates that it could not

[13] John Rock and David Loth, *Voluntary Parenthood*, p. 156. New York: Random House, 1949.

result successfully in any event. State laws usually stipulate that therapeutic abortions cannot be performed except when advised by a consultation of licensed medical practitioners. This provision not only works toward control of illegal abortions but also serves to protect the reputation of the individual doctor who finds it necessary to perform therapeutic abortions at times to save the lives of mothers. In these cases the danger to the mother's life is decreased, because the operation is performed without secrecy, and under conditions that meet the surgical standards of the medical profession.

The argument is sometimes presented that the high abortion death rate indicates the need for more widespread distribution of contraceptive information. Proponents of this viewpoint believe that since some women will go to any extreme to prevent the birth of unwanted babies, it would be better to provide contraceptive information more widely so that women would not risk their lives through illegal abortions. Russia tried to solve the abortion problem by legalizing abortion operations. For 16 years, between 1920 and 1936, Russian women could have abortions performed by registered physicians at little or no cost. The Russian abortion rate increased rapidly until it was almost equal to the birth rate. In 1936, the Russian government went back to its former position, making abortion illegal. The reason given for the change in attitude was that scientific observation had demonstrated that it was desirable to prohibit abortions since sterility, invalidism, and psychological shock often resulted. It is possible that the desire for soldiers and workers preceding World War II also had something to do with the change in policy. Sweden, a non-militaristic country, adopted a law in 1938 and amended it in 1942 and in 1946 to permit legal abortion, on the recommendation of the Royal Medical Board in Stockholm, upon certain medical and genetic conditions, or in cases of rape, or under certain social and economic conditions.

The abortion problem in the United States needs to be faced

realistically. Whatever the legal status of abortion, more general education is needed on the dangers involved.

Some eugenic considerations

The question of how many children a couple should have has been discussed pro and con. If parents were to have enough children to replace themselves, each couple producing children would have to bear an average of more than two children, since some will not grow to maturity; some of those that mature will not marry; some who marry will not have children.

The eugenists for some years decried the fact that people living in the worst environments are producing a disproportionate share of the future population. Some eugenists believe that this condition will slowly lead to biological and cultural degeneracy. They advocate efforts to cut down the birth rate among the less fit and to increase it among the more fit. This is a sound position, but who are the fit? In our society there is some tendency to consider the ones who have accumulated economic wealth as the fit. And yet, ability to accumulate economic goods in a competitive society is not necessarily an indication of fitness for parenthood.

Visher's [14] study of *Who's Who in America,* a listing of individuals who have achieved fame, showed that the children of clergymen had the best chance to achieve success. Ministers as a group have modest incomes, yet their children, as judged by listings in *Who's Who,* have a very high ratio of achievement when compared with other groups. Children of other professional groups, such as teachers, lawyers, and doctors, rate second to children of clergymen in achievement. Some years ago, studies by Terman showed that the professional group produced 1,003 per cent of its proportionate quota of gifted children, the public service group produced 137 per cent, the commercial group 128

---

[14] S. S. Visher, "A Study of the Type of the Place of Birth and of the Occupation of Fathers of Subjects of Sketches in *Who's Who in America,*" *American Journal of Sociology,* Vol. 30 (1925), 551-557.

per cent, and the industrial group produced 35 per cent of its proportionate quota. Although the professional class seems to be the most qualified, it is not producing enough children to reproduce its own numbers.

Postponing parenthood

Most people who marry hope to have children eventually. But a great many young couples plan to wait a while before having the first child. In a study of a national sample of high-school students in 1956, the Purdue Opinion Panel found that approximately one-fifth would want their first child in the first year of marriage, 38 per cent the second year, and 12 per cent the third year.[15] The thinking of these students would seem to represent the trend at the present time, that is, people are not only marrying at a younger age but they are also starting their families earlier in marriage. However, many people say that they do not wish to have a child during the first year because "We need a year to become adjusted to each other and to continue our good times together." They do not want to be tied down to the responsibilities of parenthood too early in marriage.

Since fertility decreases with age, the danger exists that some couples will not be able to have any children if they postpone the first pregnancy too long. This is especially true of couples who have low fertility or who are older than average when they marry.

Some of the reasons for postponing parenthood are financial. Young people sometimes feel that in fairness to themselves and to their children they should be out of debt, have a home, and be established economically before they have children. Standards of what constitutes the required economic condition differ. Many couples who postpone having children for economic reasons learn that their standards change; they raise their level of living to keep pace with increased income, so that after a few

---

[15] *The Purdue Opinion Panel, Report 43,* Lafayette, Ind.: Purdue University, 15:1 (February, 1956), 10a.

years of marriage they do not feel any more able to afford children than at the beginning. Society's experience has proved that,
although financial stability is not to be minimized as a factor in
successful family life, it is one of the more minor considerations
in determining whether a couple is ready for parenthood. Some
couples who have achieved the happiest and most successful
family life with their children would never have had children at
all if they had waited to have the first baby until they could afford
the luxury of a family.

Far more important than financial stability is the emotional
maturity of the parents. Available evidence suggests that happier
marriages result and that children get off to a better start in life if
couples have time to make the early marital adjustments before
the coming of the first child. Since the time required for reaching
a good marital adjustment varies, some couples are ready to
have children within a year after marriage, whereas others will
be occupied with growing up emotionally themselves for a long
time after marriage.

Do children prevent divorce?

Because the divorce rate is much higher among childless
couples than among those with children, some authorities have
suggested that the sooner children arrive in the home, the better.
It is true that 60 per cent of the divorcing couples have no children. But it does not follow that if these couples had had children
they would not have divorced. Nearly half of all divorces are
secured within the first six years of marriage. Many of the frictions
which result in divorce start within the first months of marriage,
although the couple may not resort to divorce until months or
years later. Some divorcing couples do not have children because
they conclude early that the marriage will fail.

Some people are emotionally and temperamentally unsuited to
be parents for the same reasons that they cannot adjust happily in
the married state. An emotionally unstable spouse can wreck a

marriage whether children are present or not. If there are children, the complications are greater. The presence of children will not transform maladjusted individuals into happy husbands and wives.

Why have children?

Basically, the purpose of human reproduction is to perpetuate the species. But few people feel a personal responsibility for the perpetuation of the species. A great many couples have children simply because nature takes its course. They marry with the expectation that it will be so; they give little thought to whether or not they actively wish to have children, and they welcome the children that come. Some others desire children because of a wish to have a stake in the future. They may feel a conscious desire to keep a grasp on youth and life through the lives of their children, or they may feel an undefined urge toward self-perpetuation. People may desire children also because they believe that children are necessary to a complete and happy home life. Studies of college students show that almost all of them hope to have children eventually. The majority in the study in 11 colleges in 1952-1955 said also that they would hesitate to marry a person who did not want children.

Whatever the reason back of the desire for children, it is true that having children does give married people not only a stake in the future but an interest in the present. Matters that we may shrug away as of no concern to us suddenly take on importance after we become parents.

Children and happiness of parents

Do children contribute to the happiness of marriage? Several attempts have been made to determine the relationship between happiness in marriage and the size of the family. Terman, Hamilton, and Bernard found no significant differences between the happiness scores of childless and non-childless husbands and wives. In our study of 409 couples, couples without children tended toward the extremes in their adjustments, being either very happy or very unhappy, while those with children approached an average in happiness.

Several difficulties are involved in trying to determine the effects of children on the happiness of a marriage. Of importance is the duration of the marriages studied. Studies of people who are in the early months or the first year of marriage may show a high percentage of happy marriages, most of which will be childless, but in these marriages of short duration the childlessness is not significant. In marriages of short duration, the partners

Fig. 106 "I'm up! I'm up! Call 'em off!" By permission, Harry Mace and *The Saturday Evening Post.*

are likely to rate the marriage as very happy simply because they are still in the honeymoon stage. Even if they suspect that their marriage is less happy than they had anticipated, they are not so likely to admit it as are couples who have been married longer. With couples who have been married for longer periods of time, the fact of desiring or not desiring children may be of greater importance than the actual presence or absence of children. If the coming of undesired children forces a couple to give up the type of life they had planned, or if unwanted children

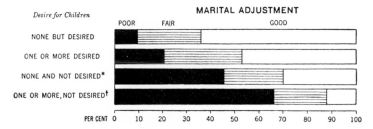

Fig. 107 DESIRE FOR CHILDREN AND MARITAL ADJUSTMENT. People who do not desire children are poor marital risks. Children may serve as a bond to hold husband and wife together, or the coming of unwanted children may serve as an added handicap to marital adjustment. From Ernest W. Burgess and Leonard S. Cottrell, *Predicting Success or Failure in Marriage,* p. 260. Englewood Cliffs, N. J.: Prentice-Hall, Inc., 1939.

come to a couple who are already unhappy in marriage, the coming of the children may increase the adjustment problems. Burgess and Cottrell found that couples who had no children but desired them, and couples who had one or more children because they desired them, were the happiest in marriage.[16] It seems that for a couple to be in agreement in desiring children is

[16] Ernest W. Burgess and Leonard S. Cottrell, *Predicting Success or Failure in Marriage,* p. 260. Englewood Cliffs, N. J.: Prentice-Hall, Inc., 1939.

an indication of good marital adjustment. Consequently, whether or not they are successful in having children, they are among the happier couples. Burgess found that those who had no children because they did not want them, and those who had children in spite of their contrary intentions, were among the less happy.[17] Reed, in a careful study of 1,444 Indianapolis couples, found "an increase in marital adjustment with increasing success in controlling fertility according to the desires of the couples."[18]

Review questions

1. What are some of the factors that have caused young people to change their estimate of the size of the ideal family?
2. How is the birth rate affected by residence? Income? Educational level? Occupation?
3. What is revealed by studies of the birth rates among different religious groups?
4. What are the official attitudes of different religious faiths on the use of contraceptives?
5. What is the legal status of the giving of contraceptive information?
6. What position has the United States Public Health Service taken on the giving of contraceptive information?
7. What are the physical and psychological effects of using contraceptives?
8. How does abortion differ from contraception?
9. Explain the difference between spontaneous, therapeutic, and criminal abortions.
10. Why did Russia return to a position of making abortions illegal?
11. Almost two out of three couples who divorce have no children. Consequently, the suggestion is sometimes made that it is best to have children early in marriage. Criticize.
12. What are some of the reasons why people desire to have children?
13. Discuss the effect of children on happiness in marriage.
14. What did Burgess and Cottrell find to be the important factor in determining whether children contributed to the happiness of marriage?

[17] *Ibid.,* p. 260.
[18] Robert B. Reed, "Social and Psychological Factors Affecting Fertility, Part VII," p. 423. New York: Milbank Memorial Fund, 1948.

Projects and activities

1. Make a tally of what the students in your class consider the ideal number of children in a family. How does it compare with the figures given in the text?

2. Make a diagram of your family tree for as many generations as you can. List the number of children born to each couple for each generation. Do you find a gradual decrease in the number of children in each generation?

Suggested readings

Baber, Ray E., *Marriage and the Family*. New York: McGraw-Hill Book Company, Inc., 1953. Ch. XV, "Determinants of Family Size."

Becker, Howard, and Reuben Hill, eds., *Family, Mariage, and Parenthood*. Boston: D. C. Heath and Company, 1955. Ch. XXV, "Larger or Smaller Families for America?"

Cooper, Lillian, "Predisposition Toward Parenthood: A Comparison of Male and Female Students," *Sociology and Social Research*, 42:1 (September-October, 1957), 30-36.

Farber, Bernard, and Leonard S. Blackman, "Marital Role Tensions and Number and Sex of Children," *American Sociological Review*, 21:5 (October, 1956), 596-601.

Kanin, Eugene J., "Value Conflicts in Catholic Device-Contraceptive Usage," *Social Forces*, 35:3 (March, 1957), 238-243.

Childless Marriages and Adoption

In 1952 almost one-fifth (19.4 per cent) of American women past the childbearing age had borne no children.[1] It is almost impossible to know what proportion of childlessness is due to biological causes and what proportion is due to contraception. Some authorities have concluded that from one-half to two-thirds of childless marriages are involuntarily sterile.[2] Many more couples are relatively infertile or become so after the birth of one or two children. The problem of sterility is faced by almost 150,000 newly married couples each year. Many young people who marry are concerned only with making sure that they do not have children until they are ready to have them. Some people are shocked and disappointed to find, when they are at last ready, that because of low fertility or infertility they cannot have children at all.

Throughout history folk-beliefs have assumed that the cause of a sterile marriage is always to be found in the wife. Even within this generation in many cases when no children are born to a married couple the wife seeks medical advice, but the couple refuse to entertain doubts about the ability of the husband to father offspring. However, more accurate information about the reproductive processes, and the results of modern medical research offer a different picture. It is now recognized that in the majority of cases of

.. 24

[1] U.S. Bureau of the Census, "Fertility of the Population" (April, 1952), 11.
[2] P. K. Whelpton, "Reproduction Rates Adjusted for Age Parity, Fecundity, and Marriage," *Journal of the American Statistical Association*, 41 (1946), 501-516. Warren S. Thompson, *Population Problems*, pp. 212-215. New York: McGraw-Hill Book Company, Inc., 1953.

sterile or relatively infertile marriages, both the husband and the wife show some evidence of infertility; the cause is not necessarily wholly in one or the other partner. When causes can be definitely discovered, it has been found that at least a third of the causative factors are in the husband.

There are a number of specific causes of sterility. The female genital tract is normally acid, but it may be too acid for the sperm to survive, especially if the sperm are not overly vigorous. Extra secretions from the cervix may prevent the sperm from entering. Some failure in glandular functioning may hinder implantation of the egg after it has been fertilized, so that the fertilized egg does not remain to grow in the uterus. Since the sex cells are very susceptible to the effects of X-ray and radium, either partner may become temporarily sterile after exposure to radiation. The sex cells of a particular couple may be incompatible and destroy each other, a condition called genetic incompatibility. The general health, mental or physical, of one or both may be such that it is impossible or unlikely that conception will occur. Age is also a factor, younger women being much more likely to conceive than older women. Some cases of sterility are due to the failure of the couple to have intercourse during the time of the month during which the egg is present in the tube and available for fertilization. Recent research indicates that normally fertile women will produce a normal egg cell in slightly over 8 out of 10 menstrual cycles, whereas women of subfertility ovulate normally in less than half of the menstrual cycles. Some wives in this second group who were tested regularly in every cycle for more than a year ovulated normally only three or four times in that period of time.[3] In many men, spermatozoa are not produced in sufficient quantity or of vigorous enough quality, and the result is lowered fertility. Fallopian tubes

[3] Edmond J. Farris, *Human Fertility and Problems of the Male*, p. 191. White Plains, N. Y.: The Author's Press, Inc., 1950.

may be closed by infection, injury, or disease, so that the sperm cannot meet the egg to permit fertilization.

Since any one of these factors, or a combination of several of them may play a part, fertility may be seen to be relative. A couple may be infertile temporarily, or they may have a low fertility so that they are unlikely to have many children but still may have one or two.

Progress in overcoming sterility

Determining the time of ovulation. Progress is being made in studies of infertility; conception now occurs in from one-fourth to one-third of the couples who go to infertility specialists for help. The Planned Parenthood Federation has found, in a study of over 8,000 couples who came for aid, that 23 per cent achieved pregnancies. Probably the greatest aid in effecting pregnancy is by helping subfertile couples to determine the exact time of ovulation. One detailed study of 240 infertile couples revealed that 26 per cent of the wives became pregnant largely as a result of having determined the exact time of ovulation.[4] There are doubtless many couples who are fertile for only a few hours of the month, and the newer methods to determine time of ovulation are important in effecting conception with these couples. Dr. Farris of the Wistar Institute of Anatomy and Biology has published the results of ten years of study on human ovulation at the Institute.[5] This research has promise for making conception possible among many childless couples. The Institute developed the rat hyperemia test by which urine from the subject is injected into young female rats on each of the days when ovulation is most likely to take place; the ovaries of the rats show reactions indicating exactly when ovulation is occurring. After two months of testing, the exact day of ovulation can be determined for

[4] Richard Frank, "A Clinical Study of 240 Infertile Couples," *American Journal of Obstetrics and Gynecology*, 60:3 (September, 1950), 645-654.

[5] Edmond J. Farris, *Human Ovulation and Fertility*. Philadelphia: J. B. Lippincott Company, 1956.

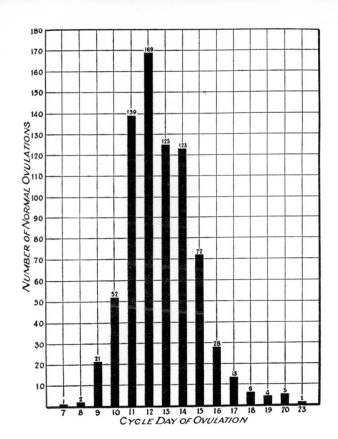

Fig. 108 THE DAY OF OVULATION, AS DETERMINED BY THE RAT TEST. The day of the menstrual cycle in which 761 ovulations occurred in 232 women prior to conception. Ovulation took place between days 7 and 23, with cycle day 12 being the most common. Edmond J. Farris, *Human Ovulation and Fertility*, p. 70. Philadelphia: J. B. Lippincott Company, 1956.

an individual and conception can be attempted in the third month. In order to test this prediction of ovulation, couples cooperating with the Institute attempted conception only once during the month, or artificial insemination was attempted but once. The rat hyperemia test was found to be accurate in determining ovulation.

For several years, a temperature reading has been recommended to determine the time of ovulation. This has been used by people who could not effect pregnancy as well as by those who desired to postpone conception by relying on the "safe period." The Farris research supports the findings of Buxton, Engle,[6] and

[6] C. L. Buxton and E. T. Engle, "Time of Ovulation," *American Journal of Obstetrics and Gynecology*, 60:3 (September, 1950), 539-551.

others, which show that a rise in temperature may or may not indicate ovulation. In one experimental group of women, Farris found in predicting ovulation by the rat test that almost half conceived before there was any change in their temperature reading, 15 per cent when the temperature was at its lowest point and the remainder during a rise in temperature. Farris concludes that although the temperature reading has helped some people to achieve pregnancy, it also contributes to infertility because it cannot be depended on to indicate ovulation.

For some time it has been thought that in a regular cycle of 28 days, ovulation would be most likely to take place on the 14th day. However, the researchers at the Wistar Institute have found that it is more likely to take place on the 12th day. Figure 109 has been worked out to show when 364 conceptions actually took place among couples who came to the Wistar Institute for help. Clearly there is great variation in when the fertile period occurs in women having the same length cycle, the most fertile period in women with a 20-day cycle being from the 6th to the 13th day after the onset of menstruation, and the most fertile period for women on a 40-day cycle being from the 15th to the 23rd day after the onset of menstruation. In general, the Wistar Institute research places the most likely day of ovulation as the middle day of the menstrual cycle minus two days, with fertility extending from approximately two days before that time until about five days afterward.

Thus there is only a period of about eight days or less in any given month when the average couple may hope to achieve pregnancy. The findings in this area of research should make it possible for many couples to have children who might otherwise pass the childbearing age without ever achieving pregnancy. However, it will be some time before informed help from fertility clinics will be available to the average couple. And the average physician is too busy with a general practice or with the pursuit of his own specialty to be able to be adequately informed and ready to offer as much help in this field of practice as might be desired. Meanwhile, in many cities the Planned Parenthood League offices can provide some information or suggest sources of information and help for couples who fail to have children.

Artificial insemination. Some couples who have been unable to have a child attempt conception through artificial insemination with the husband as donor. In cases where this attempt is not successful, couples may decide on artificial insemination and trust their doctor's judgment in the choice of donor. Staff

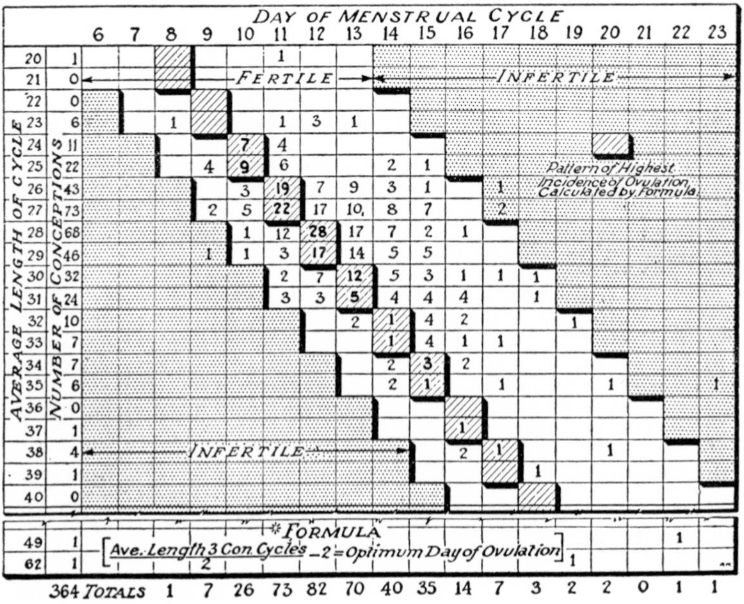

Fig. 109 THE FERTILE AND INFERTILE PERIODS. Day on which 364 conceptions took place, in relation to the length of the menstrual cycle. (Study based on 100 donor inseminations, 30 husband artificial inseminations, and 234 cases in which only one coitus occurred during cycle.) Rat hyperemia test used to determine time of ovulation. Edmond J. Farris, *Human Ovulation and Fertility*, p. 103. Philadelphia: J. B. Lippincott Company, 1956.

DAY OF MENSTRUAL CYCLE

Avg. Length	No. of Conceptions	6	7	8	9	10	11	12	13	14	15	16	17	18	19	20	21	22	23
20	1						1												
21	0			FERTILE							INFERTILE								
22	0																		
23	6					1		1	3	1									
24	11						7	4											
25	22					4	9	6		2	1								
26	43						3	9	7	9	3	1		1					
27	73					2	5	22	17	10	8	7		2					
28	68						1	12	28	17	7	2	1						
29	46					1	1	3	17	14	5	5							
30	32						2	7	12	5	3	1	1	1					
31	24						3	3	5	4	4	4		1					
32	10								2	1	4	2		1					
33	7									1	4	1	1						
34	7								2	3	2								
35	6								2	1		1		1					1
36	0																		
37	1										1								
38	4			INFERTILE								2	1			1			
39	1													1					
40	0																		
49	1																	1	
62	1																		

Pattern of Highest Incidence of Ovulation Calculated by Formula

FORMULA
$$\left[\frac{\text{Ave. Length 3 Con. Cycles}}{2}\right] - 2 = \text{Optimum Day of Ovulation}$$

364 TOTALS 1 7 26 73 82 70 40 35 14 7 3 2 2 0 1 1

members of the Wistar Institute report that many couples decide on donor insemination when every other procedure to accomplish pregnancy has failed. In a follow-up study of 38 couples who had had a child by artificial insemination, the researchers found that the couples had the following reasons for making their decision: (1) the wife's urgent desire to experience pregnancy, (2) dissatisfaction with adoption agencies, (3) benefits the couple believes the child will derive from maternal heredity even though paternal heredity will not be from his "father", (4) the couple's belief that they will have a closer relationship with the infant than would be possible in adoption, (5) the desire to conceal infertility.[7]

The legal status of artificial insemination by donor is not clear. A Chicago judge held that artificial insemination is adultery when the donor is a third party. However, the New York Supreme Court held that a test-tube child is legitimate. Since artificial insemination is becoming more common the legal aspects will doubtless be cleared up through new court decisions and new laws.

The Catholic church forbids use of any artificial method to aid in conception on the same basis that it forbids artificial methods for preventing conception. Pope Pius XII in 1957 declared artificial insemination to be immoral and illicit. For Catholics or for other couples who remain sterile in spite of all medical assistance, and who for various reasons do not want to attempt artificial insemination, only two alternatives remain. They can accept childlessness or they can seek to adopt a child.

Adoption of children

Not only childless couples, but many couples who fail to have more than one or two children before the childbearing age is

---

[7] Edmond J. Farris and M. Garrison, "Emotional Impact of Successful Donor Insemination," *Obstetrics and Gynecology,* 3:19-20 (1954). Or Farris, *Human Ovulation and Fertility,* p. 146.

past, wish to adopt a child or children. The number of couples who wish to adopt is far greater than the number of children available for adoption.

Several factors operate together to make it increasingly difficult for couples to find children for adoption. Most of these factors represent progress in the development of programs providing for the needs of dependent children. In early American history, all needy children, those who were orphaned or those of illegitimate birth, were herded into institutions, at first "almshouses" and later orphanages. Here they received the minimum essentials of physical care until they were old enough to be released to make their own way in the world. In those days adoption of a child was looked upon as an act of philanthropy and it was assumed that few adopted children would be expected to have the capacity to bring credit to their adoptive parents. In 1909, President Theodore Roosevelt called the first White House Conference to consider the problems of child welfare. Out of that first conference and the succeeding ones has grown an entirely new understanding of the needs of children, with new programs for providing for them.

Social agencies dealing with adoption now generally assume that the best place for a child is in his own home, if that is possible. Therefore, more provision is made for aid to mothers. Children are not available to adoptive parents until all possible attempts to help the children's own parents to keep them have failed. When it is not possible for natural parents to keep their children, foster homes are used, under the supervision of social agencies, for as long as there is any hope that the child might eventually be returned to his own parents. When no other arrangement is possible, a child becomes available for adoption.

The application of that principle to the offering of children for adoption has materially decreased the number of children who can be adopted during infancy, and most couples prefer to adopt infants rather than children who have already had the experience of being for several years in foster homes or with parents under unstable circumstances.

Another factor reducing the number of children available for adoption to the average couple is that many states now have stricter legislative control of the processes of adoption than formerly. Attempts are made to make sure that all adoptions take place under the supervision of legally constituted agencies, and to prevent the making of informal adoptive arrangements by unwed mothers and their doctors and lawyers.

At the same time that the newer attitudes on the part of public agencies have reduced the number of children for adoption, many of the old superstitions and prejudices about inferiority of adopted children have been quite generally discarded. To adopt children has become accepted and approved among people of all social levels but especially among the middle and upper-middle classes. More and more couples seek, without much hesitation, to adopt children. Many of the couples are disappointed when they find it difficult or impossible to find a child available to them through the legally constituted agencies.

Some couples who cannot adopt through the usual channels arrange private adoptions through their family doctor or through a lawyer. If great care is not taken to become acquainted with and follow legal regulations in the state in which the adoptive parents live and in which the adoption occurs, future developments may bring sorrow to the adoptive parents and the child. All of those involved need to be protected by careful legal procedures in order to insure that the adoption cannot be later challenged and the child removed from his adoptive parents. Occasionally court cases arise in which a natural mother seeks to regain custody of a child whom she gave for adoption at birth several years previously. Some judges tend to attach major importance to the claims or the wishes of the natural mother and in some cases adoptive parents have been ordered to relinquish a child after they have had the child since its birth. Such a situation can be tragic for the child as well as for the adoptive parents, and could be avoided if people were careful to follow legal adoptive procedures and thus make secure the status of the child.

Points to be faced before adopting

Before a couple adopts a child there are some important questions they need to face. These same questions must be considered also by any agency or organization before a child is entrusted to the care of adoptive parents. The questions go much deeper than merely, "Do we want a child?" or "Are we disappointed that we have not had a child of our own?"

1. *Why do we wish to adopt a child?*

Are we hoping that a child will be a possible source of ego satisfaction to ourselves? Are we emotionally mature enough so that we will faithfully help a child to grow in his own way toward development of his own abilities, however broad or limited they may be? Or will we seek to make him a reflection of ourselves—projecting onto him our ambitions and interests?

Sometimes investigators for welfare agencies and couples themselves assume that if a couple are educated, are of the professional class, and have adequate financial means, they are qualified to adopt children. But frequently very unhappy situations arise for both children and parents because couples of this type may be determined to fit the adopted child into a certain mold according to their standards. One of the most essential qualifications of adoptive parents should be their ability to allow the adopted child to be himself and to develop according to his own capacities, free of pressure designed to fit him into some predetermined mold. Many children brought up by their own parents become warped and unhappy adults because of the pressure put on them by parents who are determined to fulfill their ambitions through the lives of their children. The danger is even greater with adopted children, because the parents may have as one of their primary motives for adoption the desire to see their own specific successes perpetuated in the child.

2. *Are we thinking of the needs and rights of the child we might adopt or are we looking to him to provide companionship or fulfill other needs for a child we already have?*

Couples who are thinking primarily of the needs of an "only" child who is already in the home are likely to overlook many of the needs of the adopted one. Each child must be understood and loved for himself, whether or not he meets needs of another child and even if his presence in the family may create problems for the other child. Quite often, bringing another child into the home does create new problems, or at least the situation brings into the open problems that were potentially there all the time. People who have the capacity to be wise parents will be able to help both children to work through problems that arise, but this can be done only if they adopt a child for himself, and study his personality and his needs, without unrealistic expectations about what his presence will do for the home or for another child. The following case illustrates the kind of situation that may develop:

> Mr. and Mrs. A. were professional people in their late thirties in comfortable financial circumstances. They were, in other words, "typical" of those who adopt. They desired a companion for their five-year-old daughter, so they adopted a four-year-old boy. From the beginning, the children did not get along well together. Since the parents felt that their daughter needed to learn to play with others, they went ahead with the final adoption.
>
> Whenever the children quarreled, the parents were inclined to see the side of the little girl; having had her from birth, they understood her and made allowances for all her faults. They were careful to apply justice in their dealings with the two children, but the love they felt for the girl was lacking in their attitude toward the boy; consequently, he was often punished for his naughtiness, whereas the little girl could get by without her misdeeds being noticed. When issues between the children had to be decided, it

was much easier for the parents to see the viewpoint of the little girl than of the boy, so rulings were seldom in his favor.

The little boy was extremely desirous of affection and often showed an aggressive attitude toward his foster sister when the parents were around. He was always punished for this, for he was bigger and stronger than she was, and the parents feared he would hurt her. They pointed out that the little girl never resorted to such behavior. As time passed, the boy became accustomed to being always the loser and always in the wrong. He withdrew to himself and avoided playing with his adopted sister or with other children as much as possible. When he did play with other children he was sly in his dealings, taking what he wanted by stealth rather than ever facing an open issue. As he grew older, his adopted parents bewailed the fact that he was untruthful, underhanded, lacking in self-confidence, and lacking in affection for others. At school he was over-aggressive with those younger than he, but was constantly the victim of those his own age, being frequently chased by the other boys.

It was impossible for the parents to see that their own treatment was responsible for the development of the undesirable traits. They had adopted him thinking only of the needs of their daughter, and giving little thought to the needs of the boy; they had not loved him for himself but had maintained an attitude of comparing him with the other child. Their conception of justice was to judge both children by the same rules, all of which had been made to fit the needs of the girl.

The boy became a very unhappy child and a serious disappointment to the parents. The girl developed traits of smug self-righteousness. Her assumption that the scales of justice would always be weighted in her favor created later problems for her also.

3. *Are we capable of carrying through undertakings once begun, or are we likely to make alibis for our mistakes and refuse to accept the responsibility if the child's emotional growth is not satisfactory?*

Sometimes adoptive parents, with problems like those in the case above, resist accepting responsibility for the directions in which the child develops. There is a temptation to blame undesirable traits on something in the child's hereditary background rather than to work with patient perseverance and love to help the child develop in the best possible way. The couple who would adopt need to settle in their own minds, before they take a child, the fact that they are undertaking exactly the same degree of responsibility for an adopted child that they would have if they gave birth to the child.

4. *Are we capable of making a success of our marriage with or without a child, or are we expecting an adopted child to salvage our marriage for us?*

Marriage counselors not infrequently hear from couples having trouble in marriage: "We are trying to find a child to adopt. We feel that if only we had a child it would bring us closer together."

A child should never be adopted by a couple who have not been able to build a satisfactory relationship between themselves. If they cannot cope with their two-way relationship, to add a third person would probably complicate their situation and intensify their pressures. Successful parenthood requires more cooperation and self-sacrifice than marriage itself requires. Babies need protection against being placed with adopted parents whose search for a foster child is an attempt to escape from their own problems and frustrations in life, or their inability to cope with the requirements of marriage. Sometimes the very desperation with which a couple seeks to adopt a child is evidence of a neurotic adjustment to life.

5. *Are we too old to adopt?*

That may be a hard question for people to face. Sometimes people put off having children until late in the childbearing years and then decide that they wish to have children by adoption; or they wait for years, hoping to have a child of their own, and at last when they are approaching middle age, seek to adopt. Some simple mathematics will help find the answer to this question. How old will the parents be when the child is an adolescent? When he or she is fifteen or sixteen and behaves like any normal adolescent—noisy, exuberant or depressed, sometimes irresponsible, often unreasonable, delighting in crowds, confusion, and activity—will his parents be too old "to take it"? Over-age parents are likely to resist and feel impelled to thwart the quite normal behavior of extreme youth; in such cases the resulting pressures may result in delinquent behavior on the part of the young person and in sorrow and grief for the parents.

Another aspect of the parental age question is the fact that if the parents are middle-aged when they adopt, their life expectancy is less than that of the average parent; their child will be orphaned at a younger age than if he were adopted by young parents. Thus, it may not be fair for people who are beyond the early thirties to adopt. Some adoption agencies seek to protect children by refusing to allow placement with over-age parents, but many couples resent the age limitation and, if they can, go ahead to adopt children through sources that impose no age limitations.

The child's background and status

Once a couple have reached the point where they are ready and qualified to undertake adoptive parenthood, they should be able to approach parenthood with as much confidence as they would approach the birth of a child to them as natural parents. If they adopt children through authorized channels, which exercise at least a minimum of care in investigating the physical and mental background and condition of the child before placing it, they are taking no more risk of getting an inferior child than they would take if they gave birth to their own child. Few of us check carefully into the hereditary background of our mates before we marry; in almost every combination of parents there is the possibility that undesirable traits may appear in the offspring. With adopted children, parents at least have the protection of a thorough physical and mental examination for the child before it is adopted. They also have in almost all states a required trial period during which the adoption is not final. If valid objections are discovered during the trial period, the child need not be adopted.

Natural parents have no such protection. They must take what nature gives them.

Once a child is legally adopted, he is a member of the adopting family just as if he had been born to them. He is entitled to all the rights and subject to all the obligations that would have come with his natural birth into the family. People who would make any reservations in the matter of name or inheritance should not adopt children.

Special tasks of adoptive parents

Certainly many adoptive parents do as well with adopted children as they would have done with any children born to them. Nevertheless, adoptive parents need, in some ways, to be supermen and superwomen, for parenthood is always a challenging job and there *are* more potential problems in being a successful parent of adopted children.

Honesty with the child about adoption. Some parents have tried to avoid telling a child that he is adopted. Such a policy has resulted in shock and sorrow for many children when they later learned they were adopted. A child's loss of confidence in the truthfulness of the parents he has trusted can be extremely damaging to his emotional development. Most adoptive parents recognize that a child should know that he is adopted, while he is still very young, so that he lives with and accepts the fact that he was not born physically to his parents, before that fact has much specific meaning for him.

But one of the most challenging, even difficult, tasks the parents face is to handle the facts of his origin with a child in a way that will help him make the best possible emotional development, not only when he is a little child listening to bedtime stories, but later when he is in the teens and is deeply aware of all the implications of his birth and adoption.

Many adopted children are told lovely stories about being "chosen" children, with great emphasis and detail given to how carefully their parents searched for them and chose them. But it is very doubtful whether the story of a child's being chosen and adopted should be used as a bedtime story any more often than parents would use the story of his physical birth as a bedtime story if the child had been born to them. There are some good reasons for this statement.

Telling about adoption can be overdone. First, some parents in their zeal to impress the child with the fact that he was wanted and chosen, overdo their emphasis on his adoption, and in the end the child may be just as troubled as if they had tried to hide his adoption from him. In either case, they succeed in impressing on the child that he is *different* from other children, and it is almost always painful or upsetting to a child to feel that he is different from others.

> A little boy of three whose parents had conscientiously told and retold the story of his being a chosen child, seemed to delight in hearing the story. At bedtime he would cuddle into his bed and say, "Now, tell me about when you got me." But his mother became aware that he was very intense about the story and sometimes would be slow to go to sleep afterwards, then would sleep restlessly and cry out in his sleep. This mother said, "All the books told us to be sure to let him know he was a chosen child. But no one warned us not to make too big a thing of it. We had to learn the hard way how complicated the thoughts and feelings of a little child are, and to try not to overdo what we thought was being truthful with him about his origin."

So parents of a small child need to be realistic about this. They should see that he knows he is adopted, but they should be careful not to give any more emphasis or attention to the subject while he is little than they would normally give to all the facts of his natural birth—a subject it is safe to say most parents do not pursue and dwell on unduly with a child. Any specific questions the child asks should be honestly and accurately answered just as parents try to answer questions he asks about all other subjects. Far more important than how they got him is that they love him now and as he is.

To overdo the "chosen" aspect of adoption is not really being accurate or honest, no matter what the intentions. For the truth is that most parents would have chosen to give birth to a child of their own if that had been possible. What has that truth to do with the adjustment of the child? Perhaps not very much while the child is little, but far more as he grows up.

The adolescent's feelings about adoption

As a child grows older and becomes aware subjectively that most children are born to their parents, he will think of many things; he will not restrict his thoughts to what has been said in bedtime stories. He will wonder why his natural parents let someone else have him, if parents love their children; he will wonder what his first parents were like, and whether he is like them. The thought is bound to occur to him that his adopted parents might have preferred to have a child of their own in his place; and he is likely to have some envious feelings toward other children who live with their "own" parents and have to face no questions or puzzles about their background.

During adolescence, when the child feels a great need to be like others in all possible ways, some of the questions in his mind will suggest answers to him that may not fit with the picture his parents have tried to give him of adoption. If he begins to think that on even one point they have tried to give him a picture not exactly true to the facts, serious doubts may begin to trouble him, not only about his parents but about himself. One girl in her teens who was almost frantically seeking information about her natural relatives said, "I can't ask my mother anything. She's always seemed to think that everything about my adoption was so won-

derful that I can't let her know about all the things that bother
me. Sometimes I think she just doesn't know the facts of life, or
she'd *know* that people are luckier to be born to their own parents
and get to grow up where they're born. Either she doesn't know
that, or she's lied to me all my life!"

Importance of honesty and free communication

Two things are absolutely necessary in families in which children, whether adopted or natural, make good emotional growth
without turmoil and parent-child conflict. These things are honesty between the parents and child, and keeping lines of communication open so that troublesome feelings and experiences
can be talked about. Lack of honesty at any point will block the
possibility of free communication. Almost no problem or question need be too upsetting if the child and parents can talk it
over with complete trust and confidence. Thus the parent who
tries to build in an adopted child's mind the belief that everything connected with being adopted is sweetness and joy, is
setting up a block that may later cause loss of confidence on the
part of the child. The truth is that there is sadness for at least
some one person back of every adoption. Regardless of the circumstances of the birth or the release of a child for adoption,
someone has experienced disillusionment and sorrow of some
sort. But is that so bad? None of us ever gets to choose exactly
every circumstance in life; we must accept the less-than-ideal
along with the delightfully perfect in the circumstances of our
lives. Children reared by the parents who gave birth to them
may easily look about and see other families into which they
might have been more fortunately born, just as adopted children
may sometimes wish their situation were different. But a good
adjustment to life means accepting circumstances that are not
controllable, and making the most of the advantages that do exist
in every life.

Handling questions constructively

If a relationship built on confidence and trust has been firmly established during the child's early years, the adolescent or teenage child will be able to bring out into the open his doubts and seek the reassurance that a wise parent can give. We quote here two examples of answers given to children by adoptive parents. An eleven-year-old boy said, "My parents must have been no good." His adopted mother answered, "I know almost nothing about the people you were born to, I haven't seen the records. But I do know this: No matter what unfortunate thing happened that meant they didn't keep you, there were surely some very fine things about them. I know that, because I know you so well, and a boy like you certainly has some wonderful people among his ancestors. I think you'll be like the best of your ancestors and like the best that we are, too." This mother faced openly the feelings of self-doubt that accompanied the boy's doubtful feelings about his natural parents.

A nine-year-old girl said, "Why did my mother give me up, if mothers love their children?" The answer was, "I don't know all the circumstances. But I do know there was some reason why she couldn't keep you, and she did the best she could under the circumstances so that you could have a better and happier life as our child. I'm sorry that she is missing getting to know you and live with you, but I never could be too sorry about it because I'm so happy and thankful that you are our child. Sometimes even sad things in life turn into happy things and that's the way it is with us and you. So let's try not to worry too much about how it came about, and just enjoy being together."

Both of these parents answered difficult questions with directness and sincerity and their answers would probably help the child to feel better about himself and his background, and also contribute to his sense of being valued and loved for himself in his family.

Naturally, parents might prefer, if they could, to eliminate all doubtful thoughts and questions from the mind of a child and give him only a happy conception of his origin. But unfortunately, neither adopted nor natural parents can control the thoughts of children. Children will have doubts and questions; if the parent accepts the child's feelings and meets questions with honesty and love, the parent-child relationship will be such that it contributes to the child's security and adequacy. The adopted child, like any other child whose parents can manage to keep lines of communication open throughout childhood and the teens, is able to cope with difficulties that life offers.

Review questions

1. How common a problem is infertility in marriage?
2. What seems to be an accurate assessment of the partners' responsibility in a sterile marriage?
3. Give some of the most common causes of infertility.
4. What proportion of supposedly sterile marriages may be successfully treated?
5. What is the purpose of the rat hyperemia test?
6. Does a rise in temperature necessarily indicate ovulation? Explain.
7. When could ovulation be expected in a 20-day cycle? a 28-day cycle? a 40-day cycle?
8. What is the legal status of a child conceived by donor artificial insemination? What is the position of the Catholic church on this?
9. Why is it becoming increasingly difficult for those who wish to adopt children to find children to adopt?
10. What are five important questions that prospective adoptive parents should answer before they seriously consider adopting a child?
11. Is it "safe" to adopt a baby? Explain.
12. What will be the most important factor in determining how the adopted child develops? What mistake did Mr. and Mrs. A. make when they adopted their second child?
13. Does the adopted child have the legal rights of other children?
14. What are some of the special tasks adoptive parents have that natural parents do not have? How might some of these tasks be handled?

15. What questions are adoptive children likely to raise sooner or later? How might these questions be answered by the parent?

16. What two things are necessary in families if children are to make a good emotional growth? Why?

Suggested readings

Brooks, Lee M., and Evelyn C. Brooks, *Adventuring in Adoption.* Chapel Hill: University of North Carolina Press, 1939.

Cady, Ernest, and Frances Cady, *How to Adopt a Child.* New York: William Morrow and Company, 1956.

Farris, Edmond J., *Human Fertility and Problems of the Male.* White Plains, N. Y.: The Author's Press, Inc., 1950.

——, *Human Ovulation and Fertility.* Philadelphia: J. B. Lippincott Company, 1956.

Landis, Judson T., and Mary G. Landis, eds., *Readings in Marriage and the Family.* Englewood Cliffs, N. J.: Prentice-Hall, Inc., 1952. Part IX, Reading 6, "Artificial Insemination," Joseph H. Greenberg; Reading 7, "Effect of Adoption on Fertility," Frederick M. Hanson and John Rock.

Latz, Leo J., *The Rhythm of Fertility and Sterility in Women.* Chicago: Latz Foundation, 1947.

Lockridge, Frances, *Adopting a Child.* New York: Greenberg Publisher, 1947.

Prentice, Carol S., *An Adopted Child Looks at Adoption.* New York: Appleton-Century-Crofts Company, Inc., 1940.

Vincent, Clark E., "The Adoption Market and the Unwed Mother's Baby," *Marriage and Family Living,* 18:2 (May, 1956), 124-127.

When Children Come

Sometimes husbands and wives who have lived together for two or three years and have worked out satisfactory relationships in all areas are baffled to find, after the first baby arrives, that new and unexpected differences arise, requiring readjustments in their relationships. The arrival of the first baby is one of the first major occasions calling for readjustments.

This period would be easier if young parents were able to be objective about the social-psychological-interactional changes that take place in husband-wife relationships when the first baby arrives. A level of adjustment has previously been reached in the relationships of the couple. That is, they have in the first two or three years of associating together arrived at working arrangements in their personal relationships that are fairly satisfactory and quite clearly understood by both. The arrival of the third person in the home upsets the status quo and again the couple must achieve a satisfactory working arrangement. The new interaction pattern involves different roles for each. The husband has been used to his wife's playing the part of a devoted wife who centered her attention chiefly on him. Or she may have been the career wife who helped support the home. Now he must adjust to her as the mother who gives much of her time to the baby, or as the ex-career wife who now may show inexperience and helplessness as the mother of his child. Similar readjustments will be necessary for the wife. Gradually a new interaction pattern will be established, which, however, will never become static. Changes will occur as the child matures, and as other children are born.

... 25

Rearing children—a marital problem

Studies of marriage adjustment among long-married couples and among people in the early years of marriage agree in finding that training the children ranks high with both groups as a problem in marital adjustment. Our study of 409 marriages of parents of college students revealed that the care and disciplining of the children had ranked next to sex among those problems on which couples had failed to reach satisfactory adjustments. In the study of marriages of younger couples, disagreements over child training ranked next to trouble with in-laws and economic difficulties as focal points of friction. The explanation is understandable. When two young people enter marriage, each comes with a vast array of "old wives' tales," superstition, hearsay, and very little scientific information. After the arrival of the first baby, the differences in their attitudes, produced by different family backgrounds, will become evident.

Our study of young parents who were students in college, attempted to discover just what points were causes of friction in the care of the children. Since most of the children involved were under three years of age, the picture is one of early parenthood.

The most common cause of tension was the feeling on the part of one parent that the other "pampers and spoils" the baby. This complaint was made more often by the young father. Fathers said that it seems that the wife always gives in to the child, and does not use enough disciplinary measures. The wives often complained that the husbands were strict or harsh with children. Wives were critical because they felt that husbands demand too much obedience from a small child, frighten the child by scolding, or show irritation with the child over trivial things.

When parents differ over child training both are inclined to react emotionally to their differences. Neither can appreciate the way the other believes. One may believe in "reasoning" with the child, and the other may believe in requiring instant obedience.

One may believe in a rigid schedule, and the other may not. The wife may feel the husband is not applying any principles of psychology to situations; and the husband may complain that the wife shows affection for the child whom she has just spanked. On all these points there is a conflict in the "folk" methods that

Fig. 110 "I changed my mind—I want a red bike instead of a blue one." By permission, Roy L. Fox and *The Saturday Evening Post.*

Fig. 111 "I gave him away." Reproduced, courtesy of *Ladies' Home Journal*, Curtis Publishing Company. By permission, Sivic.

the young people have taken into their marriage. Couples who read together some of the more sensible books on child training are sometimes able to compromise and agree on methods recommended by an outside expert. However, some will not change their ideas. One parent may feel he has lost face if he finds his theories are not supported in the literature, and he may decide to stick to his "folk" methods regardless of the consequences. That is evidence of immaturity.

A common complaint among the younger couples as well as among the parent generation in the research studies was that one spouse would countermand orders given by the other. That habit is always irritating and usually causes trouble in marriage. If the wife tells Johnny to stop throwing the ball against the house and the husband tells Johnny to go ahead, it won't hurt anything, several undesirable effects have been achieved. The wife feels defeated not only because the ball continues to hit the house, but because her authority has been undermined by the husband. Johnny has learned that it is possible to pit one parent against the other in order to do as he pleases. And the husband, besides incurring his wife's displeasure and weakening her authority, has also weakened his own future authority with his son.

If discipline is to be effective, the parents must present a united front to the children. It is almost impossible for one parent to do anything with the children if the other is issuing different orders. Not only does such variance cause failure with the children, but it creates increasing marital tension between the husband and wife. Parents will differ, but successful parents will discuss these differences and reach compromises when the children are not present.

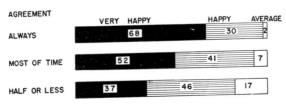

Fig. 112 AGREEMENT ON CHILD TRAINING AND MARRIAGE HAPPI-NESS (544 COUPLES). Young parents who see eye to eye on the training and disciplining of their children will find greater harmony in their marriage relations.

A common complaint among wives is that husbands do not take enough responsibility in training and caring for the children. Many husbands go into marriage with the attitude that training the children is the responsibility of the wife and that the husband's duty is to support the family. Too often the father becomes absorbed in his work and is almost unconscious of the fact that he has other family responsibilities. If children are to be well reared, the father and the mother must work together.

Sometimes a young mother becomes so absorbed in the new baby that the father feels he has lost out in his wife's affections. He may complain that she spends too much time with the child and that she is too anxious about minor details of the child's life. He may criticize the wife and all her methods in training and disciplining the child because he feels that he has to take second place in her affections. Such behavior on the part of a husband is evidence of immaturity, but is nevertheless common. If the young father could analyze his feelings and identify them for what they are, he would be taking a long step toward solving the problem. Objectivity concerning one's own actions is not easy, but it can be achieved.

What is a happy home?

We have been considering the coming of children in relation to the happiness of parents. But what of the children? One hundred and fifty university students made free lists of the specific home circumstances that brought greatest happiness to them when they were between the ages of 5 and 12. The 15 factors listed most frequently were then arranged in a list for a second group of 200 students to check. The order in which the second group of students ranked these home circumstances is as follows:

1. Happiness of parents
2. Parental expression of love for me
3. Sense of the family's interest in me
4. Sense of parents' trust
5. Mother a good cook
6. Companionship with parents
7. Family unity and fellowship
8. Meals always on time and house always clean
9. Family able to provide adequate financial means
10. Pride in accomplishments of family
11. Pleasure in doing things together as a family
12. Parents' approval of friends
13. Religion in the home
14. Family cooperation
15. Feeling that I had a responsible part in our family

It is interesting that happiness of the parents rated highest. For the parents to be happily married seems to be of fundamental importance to the happiness of the children. Other studies have shown that the happiness of the parents not only contributes to the happiness of the children in the home but also conditions them for successful family living in their own homes later.

Second to happiness of parents, the students named items that emphasize the importance to the children of overt expressions of parental love for them. In many homes the parents take it for granted that their parental care and their efforts to provide for all the needs of the children will be recognized by the children as evidence of parental love. It may not be so. Children must be reassured that they are loved through open expression of affection. Parental care is something that they accept as part of their background, and many young children will make no connection between that and parents' love for them. The desire for emotional security is strong in children and they need reassurance and evidence that they are loved.

It is interesting to note that young people gave adequate finances ninth place in the list. It seems to be true that a sense of being loved and trusted, and a feeling that one is a companion with his parents is more important to the development of the child than being showered with numerous or expensive possessions. Some parents mistakenly think that they have taken care of their children's needs simply because they have given them the material things that money can buy. But nothing can be substituted for parental happiness, love, and companionship in the life of the young child.

The same students were asked to list specific factors that caused greatest unhappiness in their lives as children. The order in which the students ranked the home circumstances that brought them greatest unhappiness between the ages of 5 and 12 is as follows:

1. Death and illness in the family
2. Parents' quarreling
3. Conflict with parents' views

    4. Quarreling of brothers and sisters
    5. Inability of parents to see my point of view
    6. Loneliness
    7. Misunderstanding in the family
    8. Parents' unhappiness
    9. Quarreling with parents
  10. Feeling of being misunderstood
  11. Being compared with other children
  12. Parents nagged me
  13. Lack of companionship with parents
  14. Afraid parents would separate
  15. Father hard to get along with
  16. Lack of association with those my own age
  17. Lack of adequate finances

Illness and death ranked first as a major cause of unhappiness for children. It is understandable that serious illness or death usually represents a family crisis which threatens or destroys the security of the children. The students ranked a quarreling pattern in the home second to illness and death as a source of unhappiness. Quarrels between parents caused greatest unhappiness but quarrels between siblings also rated high. Not very much can be done to keep children from worrying about illness and death, but families can do something about quarreling. Parents who quarrel easily, without considering their quarrels to be serious, would be shocked to learn the extent of emotional tension created for children by parental quarreling.

Another source of unhappiness for children has to do with conflicts between parents' and children's point of view. A measure of conflict on this score will be inevitable in parent-child relationships. Sometimes parents do know best even though they may find it impossible to make clear to the child the reasons for their attitudes. Again, parents may make arbitrary rulings with a total lack of understanding of the young person's point of view. Some parents attempt to solve the problem of conflict by relaxing all efforts at control or guidance and escaping into an attitude of "If you won't bother me, I won't bother you." This is hardly a constructive solution. It is an attempt to evade responsibility. Successful parents accept their responsibility for guiding their children. They try to avoid making arbitrary rulings and they work for understanding and agreement with their children about what is desirable or undesirable behavior.

Situations causing anxieties in children

Even children from happy homes have certain fears and worries that are rather universal. If the home is happy, these troubles are not permanently serious. If the home is not happy, and if the child lacks the inner confidence that comes with family solidarity, the childhood problems assume greater importance.

A common worry in childhood has to do with physical appearance. A third of all the college students included this item in their free list. Why are children so acutely conscious of physical characteristics that they suffer over their real or imagined defects? In many cases the reason goes back to thoughtless remarks and comments made within the family circle while the child is small. A parent or relative may remark that Junior has inherited those ears from the other side of the family. Junior may be a handsome, attractive child, but that has nothing to do with his reaction to comments on his ears. He begins to feel that his ears are big and conspicuous. When Sister begins to grow tall in early adolescence before her boy cousins have started their adolescent growth, the parents and relatives remark over and over, "How tall she is! I believe she is going to be taller than the others." And Sister begins to slouch over and try to make herself inconspicuous. Or while she is still a toddler, mother and aunts remark, "It is too bad her hair is straight." After she hears that a few times, she feels that her hair is a serious handicap to her looks. Since any deviation in the shape of a child's jaw and the regularity of his teeth occasions comment in the family, innumerable children and young adults go about with the feeling that they have horribly prominent teeth.

A child's actual appearance seems to have little to do with whether or not he worries over how he looks. Some children do have features or defects that might be expected to be handicaps, yet, if the matter has been handled right in the family, the child may be entirely unconscious of the characteristic so that it handicaps him not at all. Individual features are a handicap only if the child feels conscious of them and considers them as handicaps.

One of the finest gifts a father and mother can give to a child is a feeling within himself that he is a credit to the family; that they like him and are proud of him. Whether he happens to be tall or short, fat or slim, curly-haired or straight-haired, with big ears or small, should be supremely unimportant as far as family love is concerned.

Other childhood troubles have to do with situations in which the child feels that he has "lost face" before others. If he is punished before others, if his parents discuss him and his traits in the presence of others, or if he is forced to dress or act in ways that are noticeably different from those about him, he will feel that he has lost face. Table 29 gives a more complete listing of home circumstances causing anxiety in children.

People approaching marriage and parenthood should give some thought to these things that affect the happiness and sense of well-being of children in the home. The happiness of the children is important not only to the happiness of the parents but because of the influence it will have on the future marriages of the children.

Parents need above all to try to take the long view of their children's growing up. Their continuous task is to look beyond immediate problems that may seem baffling and to decide which childish actions or attitudes have significance in determining what kind of a man or woman this child will eventually be. They need to see in today's fascinating and frustrating two-year-old the prophecy of tomorrow's twenty-year-old. While they are busy coping with specific details of child rearing,[1] they can also have clearly in mind the contribution they can make to the personality development of their children.

TABLE 29   STUDENT RANKING OF SPECIFIC CIRCUMSTANCES
THAT CAUSED ANXIETY DURING CHILDHOOD *

Physical features	Losing face before others
1. Afraid I would always be homely	1. Had to wear long stockings or un- derwear
2. Crooked teeth	2. Scoldings before other children
3. Awkwardness	3. Had to perform for others
4. Too fat or too slim	4. Parents made me apologize for things
5. Wearing glasses	5. Parents bragged about me
6. Complexion	6. Didn't dress as other children did or had to wear hand-me-down clothes
7. Unattractive hair	7. Teasing
8. Not growing any taller	8. Being left out of things
	9. Couldn't do things others did
	10. Mother always let everyone know I was the baby

Conditioned fears	Desire for security
1. Darkness	1. That our house would burn
2. Lightning and thunder	2. That my father would die
3. Animals, snakes, bugs, etc.	3. That my mother would die
4. Being left alone	4. That my brothers or sisters would die
5. Fires	5. That I would die
6. Deep water	6. That I was adopted
7. Being locked in closet	7. That my parents would separate
8. Old empty houses	8. Being kidnaped
9. Fear of not getting to heaven	9. That the world would come to an end
10. Fear of going to hell	
11. Fear of being punished by God	
12. Ghosts	

* Three hundred and fifty college students listed the specific factors that caused great anxiety in their lives when they were between the ages of 5 and 12. These common fears and worries have been classified under four headings in the above table. In each grouping, the items are listed in descending order, from those mentioned most frequently to least frequently. Some of these fears are quite universally conditioned in small children, others reflect a child's feelings of insecurity in the home, and still others are natural reactions to "losing face" before one's friends.

[1] *The Pocketbook of Baby and Child Care,* by Benjamin Spock, offers an excellent guide for parents in dealing with many details of child training.

Trends in child-care practices

For some years authorities on infant care have laid much stress on such matters as breast-feeding, toilet-training, and methods of weaning, as important factors in the development of the basic personality pattern of the child. Many young mothers feel that if they cannot breast-feed their babies they may be handicapping the child's development of feelings of security.

In the 1930's the "good" mother put her child on a three- or four-hour feeding schedule and allowed nothing to interfere with it. She let the baby "cry it out" if he attempted to upset the schedule. She weaned him from the breast or bottle to a cup as early as possible, and she felt that his toilet-training must begin while he was but a few months old and be completed by a set time. Now, mothers are advised to do the opposite, to let nature take its course in the development of the child lest they create tensions, fears, and frustrations in him that will handicap his personality throughout life.

An investigation of some 644 articles written between 1890 and 1949 on the subject of child care showed that most of the articles written in 1890 suggested that the mother "loosely schedule"; most of those written in 1920 advocated that she "tightly schedule" and let the child "cry it out"; and most in 1949 urged that she permit the child to "self-regulate." [2] In this period of about 60 years there was a swing of the pendulum from one extreme to the other on many matters of infant care.

Today the emphasis is on the relationship between details of the infant's physical care and his psychological and emotional growth. Sewell attempted to test the importance of that relationship through a study of the personalities of a group of children and an examination of the methods that were used in their care as infants. He found few significant relationships between infant-

[2] Clark E. Vincent, "Trends in Infant Care Ideas," *Child Development,* 22 (September, 1951), 199-209.

care practices and later personality. He reports, "Such practices as breast feeding, gradual weaning, demand schedule, and easy and late induction to bowel and bladder training . . . were almost barren in terms of relation to personality adjustment as measured in this study." [3]

However, Sewell's findings should not be interpreted to mean that it does not matter what methods are used in the early months of a child's life. The findings suggest, rather, that certain other factors may be of more fundamental importance in personality development. In the years when infant-care practices were characterized by rigidity, just as in the years when the opposite methods were considered best, a great many children still managed to develop well-adjusted and basically secure personalities. That fact alone suggests that successful parenthood goes far beyond following specific "right" or "wrong" methods of infant care.

Basic principles in child-care practices

Basic in determining the personality of the child is the *quality of the total relationship* between parent and child. This is something which defies examination in a study, even in such an excellent one as that conducted by Sewell. To illustrate: A mother may nurse her baby because of a strong sense of duty, although she may reject the child emotionally and actually may have little understanding of its total needs. Another mother may not be able to nurse her baby, but she may show greater warmth and affection for the child than the resentful, nursing mother. When it was popular to put the baby on a schedule and let him "cry it out," there were still a great many babies whose total emotional relationships with their mothers led to their feeling loved and secure. These babies could therefore adjust to the rigid schedules without emotional damage.

Certainly today's emphasis upon a close relationship between

---

[3] William H. Sewell, "Infant Training and the Personality of the Child," *The American Journal of Sociology*, 58:2 (September, 1952), 150-159.

mother and baby from the earliest days of a child's life is right. Other sound practices are less rigid feeding schedules, and more flexibility in toilet-training and in some matters of discipline. However, no amount of doing certain things right in infant care will ever take the place of the more intangible and more important things—really wanting the child, understanding him as an individual, and making him feel valued.

Children may have all their physical needs satisfied from the time they are born until they reach adulthood and yet turn out to be unhappy, maladjusted people, simply because their emotional needs were never met in the parent-child interactional pattern. Moreover, a few mistakes in method will not ruin a child if the total parent-child relationship is sound and healthy. We do not accept the theory that a child's personality is absolutely set at a very young age and that early mistakes in method made by parents are inevitably disastrous to personality. Children are amazingly tough, both physically and emotionally; parents who, through lack of experience, knowledge, or understanding, make mistakes with their children when the children are young can overcome their mistakes as they themselves mature and gain insight into their children's development. Evidence of this fact is to be seen in the cases of adults who may have been handicapped by their early life experiences, but who, with motivation and increased insight, later are able to overcome their handicaps and become flexible, more fully functioning personalities.

Review questions

1. What readjustments in husband-wife relationships are often required when the first child is born?

2. What seems to be the basic factor underlying conflict between husbands and wives over the training and discipline of their children?

3. What are some of the more common differences concerning child training?

4. Why is it essential for parents to present a united front in child training?

5. What home circumstances seem to be important to the happiness of children?

6. Cite some home situations that make for the unhappiness of children.

7. What are some of the most common fears and worries of children?

8. How can a child be made to feel that his physical features are not a handicap?

9. What have been some of the trends in child care during the past 70 years? What is the trend today?

10. What is the relationship between child-care practices and personality?

11. What elements are basic in the personality development of the child?

Projects and activities

1. Write a case history of parental conflict over the training and disciplining of children. Bring out the effect of the conflict on the relationship of the parents as well as the reaction of the children to the conflict.

2. Write an analysis of your own home, bringing out the circumstances that made for happiness or unhappiness and the things you worried about as a child.

3. *Role-playing.* Jack and Elizabeth have been married ten years. They have three children ages two months, three, and seven years. Scene: Jack has just spanked John, the 7-year-old, when Elizabeth comes into the room and says to Jack, "You shouldn't spank John. He didn't mean to break the window!"

Films

Life with Baby. Shows how children grow, mentally and physically, as charted by Dr. Gesell. March of Time. 18 minutes, sound.

Palmour Street. Child-care practices in lower-class Negro family. Health Publication Institute. 27 minutes, sound.

Preface to a Life. Shows effects of different methods of child training on the child. Castle. 29 minutes, sound. Secured from most film rental services. If only one film is to be used here, we suggest this one.

Suggested readings

Baber, Ray E., *Marriage and the Family.* New York: McGraw-Hill Book Company, Inc., 1953. Chs. VIII and IX, "Parent-Child Interaction."

Burgess, Ernest W., and Paul Wallin, *Engagement and Marriage*. Chicago: J. B. Lippincott Company, 1953. Ch. XXI, "Children and Marital Success."

Duvall, Evelyn Millis, *Family Development*. Chicago: J. B. Lippincott Company, 1957. Part II, "Expanding Families."

Kirkpatrick, Clifford, *The Family: As Process and Institution*. New York: The Ronald Press, 1955. Ch. IV, "Family Types and Dilemmas."

Landis, Judson T., and Mary G. Landis, eds., *Readings in Marriage and the Family*. Englewood Cliffs, N. J.: Prentice-Hall, Inc., 1952. Part X, Reading 1, "How Family Forces Affect the Individual," O. Spurgeon English; Reading 2, "The Practical Application of Basic Mental Hygiene Principles by the Cornelian Corner," Leo H. Bartemeier; Reading 3, "Child-Rearing and Social Status," Martha Ericson Dale; Reading 4, "Maternal Over-Protection and Rejection," David M. Levy; Reading 5, "Adolescent-Parent Adjustment," Ivan Nye; Reading 6, "Some Neglected Areas in Family Life Study," Bossard, Boll, and Sanger.

Levy, John, and Ruth Munroe, *The Happy Family*. New York: Alfred A. Knopf, Inc., 1938. Ch. VII, "Children: The Consummation of Marriage," and Ch. VIII, "All Children Have Difficulties."

Nimkoff, Meyer, *Marriage and the Family*. Boston: Houghton Mifflin Company, 1947. Ch. XVI, "Parents and Children."

Spock, Benjamin, *The Pocketbook of Baby and Child Care*. New York: Pocket Books, Inc., 1957.

Waller, Willard, *The Family* (Revised by Reuben Hill). New York: The Dryden Press, 1951. Part V, "Parenthood: Imposing Relationships."

Bringing Up Children

How can parents help the child develop characteristics that will enable him eventually to be a marriageable person? And what traits characterize the personality that is able to function adequately at each stage of life? Many of the traits that need to be developed in a child are interrelated and tend to be found together as a personality pattern.

To explore this subject we must review, from the chapters on marriageability, some of the characteristics of people who have made a success of their marriages. The research shows that happily married people tend to have certain traits: [1]

They are optimistic, having the "habit of happiness" rather than being given to moodiness, depression, or wide swings in emotional levels.

They show self-reliance and initiative.

They are responsible and able to apply themselves dependably to work-tasks that life requires of them.

They are inclined to be unselfish and considerate.

They have a sense of proportion about their own rights and the rights of others.

They can live comfortably with the sex mores and social conventions in our culture.

They are reasonably self-confident and secure as indicated by lack of jealousy and by the ability to assess fairly accurately their own strengths and weaknesses.

They have learned constructive ways to work through problems.

In addition to personal characteristics, some of the life circumstances found by Terman and his associates to be predictive of successful marriage are also pertinent to our further dis-

[1] Lewis M. Terman, *Psychological Factors in Marital Happiness,* pp. 142-166. New York: McGraw-Hill Book Company, 1938. Ernest W. Burgess and Leonard S. Cottrell, *Predicting Success or Failure in Marriage.* Englewood Cliffs, N. J.: Prentice-Hall, Inc., 1939.

cussion. These circumstances are: superior happiness of parents; childhood happiness; lack of conflict with mother and with father; home discipline that was firm but reasonable and not harshly restrictive; parental frankness about matters of sex.

Parental perspective

The best parents are those who can take the long view of their children's development. Young parents need to think through their specific responsibility as parents. In simplest terms, their responsibility is to help the child develop attitudes and char-acteristics that will enable him to live successfully, without his parents, in the world in which he finds himself. One aspect of their helping is not to hinder the child's development by letting too many of their own emotional pressures or handicaps dictate their policies with their children. In almost all areas of child-rearing, thoughtful parents can recognize tendencies toward certain courses of action arising out of their own past experiences. By the time we become parents emotional pressures have been built into us regarding many subjects, and it is easy to act blindly rather than to make rational choices of policy in dealing with a child. Some of these "inherited" or built-in-by-experience attitudes influence parental action in sound and constructive ways; others have a negative effect on the child's development.

A task of parents is to try to interpret childish behavior in the light of whether an act is a logical, though perhaps annoying, expression of childish nature, or whether it indicates development of an undesirable tendency that has bearing on the adult personality into which the child will grow. A parent without perspective may punish a child for getting his clothes dirty at play, for breaking a dish when he is trying to help, or for making too much noise in crowded living quarters, but overlook the fact that the child lies easily and frequently not just because of his pleasure in fantasy, but because lying enables him to avoid facing unpleasant facts or situations. The same parents may punish a child for trivial acts that are annoying to themselves, but take no notice of the fact that the child is destructive of property belonging to others or is cruel and unkind in his relationships with other children. Such parents are unaware of the relative importance of events, or of the traits that need to be cultivated if a child

"I don't expect you to make her beautiful. Just concentrate on making her look like a girl!"

COLLIER'S   FRANK OWEN

Fig. 113   By permission, Frank Owen and *Collier's*.

is to be happy and well adjusted in childhood, and if he is to achieve the maturity he will need for making a success of his own relationships throughout life.

The habit of happiness

It seems clear that the first and probably the most important advantage that can be given to children is a background of happily married parents.[2] The couple who can apply self-discipline and objectivity to their own marital relationships in order to work out happy adjustments will find no insurmountable difficulties in bringing up their children. Happiness in the home and optimistic attitudes toward the circumstances of life strongly influence children. The habit of happiness is learned, not inherited.

Self-reliance and initiative

Self-reliance can begin to develop early, when the child first shows an interest in doing things for himself. He should be encouraged, but not pushed, in his attempts to dress himself and to feed himself. It is here that parents often fail, for it is much easier to take over and do for the child than to wait for him to muddle through at his own pace.

Many parents, with their first child, do not realize at how early an age a child's urge toward independence may appear. The mother of a nine-month-old baby was struggling through dinner-time with the baby in his highchair. Each time she offered him food in a spoon, he swung at her hand and frequently succeeded in knocking either the spoon or the food to the floor. She said, "I don't know why he's so naughty lately. I have a terrible time feeding him." A friend said, "Why don't you just let him go it alone? He may be swinging at the spoon because he'd like to get hold of it and feed himself instead of having you

[2] *Ibia.*

Fig. 114 CHILDREN DEVELOP SELF-RELI-ANCE AND INITIATIVE BY BEING ENCOURAGED TO DO THINGS FOR THEMSELVES. Courtesy of Rondal Partridge.

thrust the food at him." The mother protested that the baby was far too young to feed himself, but she decided to give him a chance. She began setting his food before him with a spoon beside it and going about her other work. Of course he tried the handle of the spoon, and his fingers, and various other methods of getting his food to his mouth, but in a very short time he was feeding himself with no worse spillage than had been occurring when his mother had been trying to feed him. And his great satisfaction in being able to do for himself independently was easily apparent in the enthusiasm with which he welcomed mealtimes. How better can a young child be spending his time and energy than in learning, even by hit and miss, to do for himself? If parents can curb their impatience and allow the child to go ahead and learn for himself with a minimum of help or interference, they will be allowing him to make progress toward achieving self-reliance.

As the child grows a little older, he often wants to take part in his parents' activities, to "help" with whatever work he sees them doing. If Dad is pounding with a hammer, the small child wants to pound too. His efforts are not always helpful, especially if Dad's pounding is a hurried attempt to fix something in the apartment that Mother has been requesting for many weeks past. A too frequent result of the child's efforts to help is, "Come get this child out of my hair if you want me to fix anything."

Small children who follow their mothers around wanting to "help" sometimes meet the same kind of rebuff. One young mother was washing the kitchen floor when in came her three-year-old son with a small pan of water and a clean towel from the bathroom. He put down his pan of water with a big splash on the part of the kitchen floor that she had just nicely finished cleaning, and began scrubbing the floor with great swishing of the towel and splashing of water. Thinking only of the work to be done over, his mother descended upon him angrily, snatching the pan and towel away from him with a "No, no, naughty boy to get

Fig. 115 "Okay—three eggs well beaten. Now what?" Reproduced, courtesy of *Ladies' Home Journal*, Curtis Publishing Company. By permission, Walt Wetterberg.

the clean floor all wet again," which sent him crying from the kitchen.

There are undoubtedly too many incidents such as this in the background of older children whose mothers complain bitterly, "He never shows any initiative or willingness to take his share of responsibility." The wise parents will, from the earliest years, respect and encourage evidences of initiative in the child, even if his attempts to help are not always helpful. It remains a matter of perspective. Which is of more permanent importance, getting the housework or repair work done exactly according to schedule, or helping a little boy feel that he is needed by his parents and useful to them, that his ideas and help can make a contribution to running the home? It is not reasonable to squelch evidences of a child's initiative for years because "he is too little," and then suddenly to assume that "now he is old enough" and expect him to show initiative. Growth is not that simple.

The same principle applies to making decisions. No one certain day or particular age marks the point at which a child becomes old enough to think for himself. It would be easier for parents if that were the case. Parents must decide frequently in individual situations, "Is this a situation that calls for guidance and direction? Is it a decision that is so entirely beyond the child's experience that it should be decided for him? Is it one of the many cases that in itself is not so important, the important thing being that the child should make the decision for himself?"

Helping the child to think for himself

Some children seem to shrink from making their own decisions and depend on parents too much. These children need to be encouraged toward self-reliance. Here again, objectivity on the part of the parent is important. Sometimes parents, especially mothers, become so wrapped up in the lives of their children that they are too much occupied with making all the child's decisions for him. The wise mother will realize that it is better for the child to make his own decisions insofar as it is possible because the time is not far ahead when he will have to make his own choices. He will need confidence in his own judgment if he is to take his place with others in the outside world. If a child shrinks from making his own decisions, parents can help him by talking over his possible choices with him and then encouraging him to feel that he is ready to decide for himself. They can help especially by showing respect for his judgment and by withholding criticism when he makes choices that are not exactly the same ones the parents would make if they were doing his thinking for him.

Responsibility

In considering the ways in which children develop a sense of responsibility and become able to cope with tasks, the subject of handling money arises, for money and its use is quite inevitably tied up with developmental experiences of children in our culture. Parents need to evaluate their own attitudes about money and the responsibilities and obligations involved in its use. A child's conception of his responsibility in the family and in the outside world will be influenced by his experiences regarding money. Giving a child an allowance, and guiding him in spending that allowance are effective teaching devices, whether or not the parents intend it that way.

In one family, the four children, ranging in age from eight to fifteen, received allowances sufficient to take care of all their needs. They were expected to work out a yearly budget, including their clothing, recreation, books, and all expenses except food and shelter. The father spent many hours with them assisting them with their budgets.

In another family the two children, ten- and twelve-years-old, received allowances of one dollar a week. The allowance was paid to them every Saturday morning and the procedure was always the same. They collected their allowances and rode their bicycles to town in time to be waiting when the dime stores opened. A half-hour later their money was gone. Sometimes they brought home a small toy or gadget, and sometimes they found nothing that could hold their interest even long enough to get all the way home with it. The rest of the week, if they saw something they wanted or needed, they "begged mother" for it and—except for the rare occasions when she argued with them, and usually came off second best—she either bought it for them or gave them the money for it. This mother once said, "We have closets full of the junk the children have bought. I have sometimes wanted to give some of it away when the Christmas toy drives have come along, but the children won't let me. They never use any of it, but after all it does belong to them; they bought it."

These cases represent two extremes. Some would question whether young children should be expected to take as much responsibility as the children in the first case. Many adults shrink from struggling with a budget, and it would be an unusual child who would enjoy coping with the problem as part of his regular responsibility. In the second case, the logical outcome of the policy would be that the children would develop no responsibility in handling money nor any awareness of the needs of other people. Many cases could be cited to show how such early experiences affect the child's sense of responsibility and also help to form the code of ethics that will dominate his dealings with other people.

A young man who was engaged to be married, with the wedding date set for December, was saving ten dollars each week in a special fund to pay for the honeymoon. In November he was invited to go on a hunting trip with some friends, and on impulse he spent the whole honeymoon fund for a new deer rifle and an expensive hunting jacket. He could not understand why his fiancée was upset over his action, even though it did mean that the wedding would have to be postponed or their long-standing plans for a wedding trip changed. In their discussion of his action his fiancée remarked that she was beginning to see why her parents felt that he was irresponsible and undependable. This seemed to him unfair, for his pattern had always been to indulge his immediate wants if possible, regardless of plans for the future, and without thought for the effect his actions might have on another person.

Many other experiences not related to money matters can help children learn to be responsible and dependable, if their parents are alert to the importance of these traits, and *if the parents are dependable themselves*. Parents handicap their children's development if they make promises and then change their minds without an urgent and unavoidable reason, or if they are capricious instead of consistently reliable in all their dealings with their children. Parents can help children to learn by their example, and by teaching, that it is important to keep promises and to finish tasks undertaken rather than quitting if the going gets rough or boring. A man who had achieved success and fame in life once said, "When I was a little boy I used to help my grand-father in his shoe-repair shop, and he often said to me, 'John, you are a *dependable* boy!' I grew up thinking that it was very important and necessary to be dependable—and I still think so."

Consideration for others

The happiest married couples are those in which both partners are able to look at the other person's viewpoint and are not self-centered in relationships with others. The habit of consideration for others usually was developed in these happily married people long before they married. It begins in early childhood and is very important to the happiness of the individual and those about him throughout life. The very young child can understand that sometimes it is necessary to play quietly because Daddy is tired and needs to rest; and that he should not run and play across the line in the neighbor's yard because his feet might trample flowers that she has worked hard to raise. It is important for a child to begin early to be conscious of the rights and interests of others. A child does not need to be suppressed or too much inhibited in order to learn to be considerate. He can see that consideration is a two-way thing in his family, if it is. Just as he tries to let his father sleep, or not to interrupt when his parents are talking, so his parents are careful to respect his rights, too. They do not interrupt him. They also respect his property; they would not lend or give away his things without consulting him. They respect *him;* they would not laugh at his serious thoughts, or embarrass him in front of other people. If parents do not treat a child with respect and consideration, they cannot expect to succeed in teaching him to show respect and consideration for themselves or for others. Always in child-rearing there must be a balanced share of example and teaching; neither one alone will suffice. The parent may need to point out to the child, "Billy, I would not act to you as you are acting now, and you are not to act that way to me. We owe each other respect." The parent who is firm but reasonable about such matters is not likely to be complaining when the child reaches adolescence, "He's rude and disrespectful and *talks back* to me."

Many mothers in their desire to be good mothers, regularly tolerate inconsiderate behavior on the part of their growing children. They are not doing the child a kindness to allow him to develop selfish, demanding attitudes toward life, for such attitudes will make trouble for him in his contacts with other people. He will be far happier if he learns to think of the wishes and feelings of others.

Fig. 116 "We've always encouraged Junior to take part in the conversation!" By permission, Jeff Keate and *Collier's*.

The child's sex attitudes

A difficult part of child-rearing for many parents is what policy to follow with regard to the child's developing sex nature. How can they help him to grow up with wholesome attitudes about sex and a healthy understanding of the place of sex in life? The problem for most parents arises from three sources.

Sex is an emotional subject. First, the subject of sex is an emotionally weighted subject for almost all adults. It is not, for adults, as casual a subject as the blue sky or the high mountains. The adult's personal experiences, his urges and impulses, are factors realistically present. Moreover, in our culture, in spite of what might superficially appear to be emancipated attitudes about sex, the subject of basic sex relationships is loaded with taboos, restrictions, fears, exaggerations, and folklore. So, for the average parent, the question of how to overcome personal and cultural handicaps and handle the sex phase of life with the young child is not easy.

Parents lack information. The second basis for the problem is that most parents simply do not have enough accurate information about sex to be able to answer with confidence many of the questions small children ask. They become confused or embarrassed. Many of us grow up thinking we know all about the facts of life and then we are shaken, if not overwhelmed, to realize when confronted with a child's questions that we do not have the words or the specific knowledge to give answers that will stand up under the impact of the child's later knowledge and experience.

Social patterns have an influence. The third part of the problem arises because parents who may have prepared themselves to answer the child's questions truthfully are confronted with the realization that *the facts of life are not all sex facts.* The mechanics of sex functioning are not half so important for the child as the social values involved and the cultural patterns with which he must live, sex nature and all. The task of giving sex facts and at the same time preparing the child to live in a complicated and not always reasonable social world, is a major challenge.

Parental policy toward questions

Many parents are surprised at the very early age at which a child may ask questions about sex. By the time a child is two or three years old—or as soon as he can talk—he is asking questions about everything, the questions becoming more involved as he grows a little older. "How do birds fly?" "Why can't I fly?" "How do fathers and mothers make babies?" "What makes apples red?" "How was I born?" "What makes thunder?" "If I swallow this seed will a baby grow in me?" A little child is a true scientist in that he is curious about every unexplained thing in his world. Sex has no more emotional connotations for him than any of the other interesting things in the world, but it is hard for parents to be as objective as the child is. They may feel convinced that Johnny is a budding genius because of some of his questions, but be confused or shocked when he asks other questions—specifically about sex facts—at so young an age.

The parents' reactions to a child's first questions affect the direction that the child's attitudes about sex begin to take. For the parent to be evasive or shocked immediately makes the child feel that here is a loaded subject, a subject in some way different from all the other interesting things to learn about. If the parent tries to get by with a tale about a stork or a cabbage, or about the doctor bringing babies, or about babies being sent down from heaven, a step is taken toward losing the child's confidence. The child will, sooner or later, find out that the parent told him a false tale in answer to a serious question, and from that time on the child will seek information from what he hopes will be more reliable sources than his parents.

There is no better way than to answer a child's questions about sex as accurately as one can, *when the questions are asked,* even if a child starts asking as soon as he can talk. To think that the responsibility for teaching sound sex attitudes can be met in one big facts-of-life session when the child is "old enough to understand" is a delusion. The young child is able to understand, at least in a measure, the answers to whatever questions he is capable of asking about sex, at any age.

Fig. 117 "Dr. Jones brings good ones—do your folks take offen him?" By permission, Mrs. Crawford Young and *The Saturday Evening Post.*

The realistic viewpoint is to recognize that the question is not whether children should or should not know about sex. The choice that parents have is between the child's getting garbled information from random sources or receiving sex information from the parents who are interested in his healthy emotional development.

Answering specific questions

The most common question asked by the pre-school child has to do with the origin of babies. "Where did I come from?" Or "Where was I before I was born?" When the child first asks this question, a satisfactory answer is usually simply that the baby grew in his mother's body. There is nothing shocking to the child about the answer. He may not be much impressed, and his next question may be on some subject far removed, such as why the sky is blue, or why water is wet. He may come back three weeks later and again ask where babies come from.

When children first start asking questions, biologically complete answers are not needed, any more than a complete explanation is needed of the functioning of the internal combustion engine the first time the child asks what makes the car go. Some children ask more specific questions that call for more detailed answers. "How does the baby get out?" The child may be told that there is a special place in the mother where the baby grows until it is ready to come out into the world through the passageway that is provided for it. This explanation or a similar one will satisfy many young children. But some will ask more, especially as they get a little older. Whenever he asks specific questions that show he is ready for specific information, the child should be given a more complete answer and the correct terms should be used for various parts of the reproductive system.

The most difficult question for parents to answer is the one about what part the father plays in getting a baby started. Not all young children ask this question. One study made of the questions asked by 2,000 children in 1,000 homes showed that only 5 per cent of the questions from small children had to do with the father's part in reproduction.[3] When an exceptional child asks this question, it is wise to answer it accurately. He

[3] Katherine W. Hattendorf, "A Study of the Questions of Young Children Concerning Sex," *Journal of Social Psychology,* 3 (February, 1932), 37-65.

may be reminded that mothers and fathers are different physically and that the father is constructed with a special organ with which to unite his cells with the mother's to start the new baby. This is not hard for a child to understand and is in no way shocking to him if the facts are given in a straightforward manner at the time when the question has arisen in his mind. The average child will have observed already that his father is constructed differently from his mother.

It is natural for parents to feel hesitant, even alarmed, at the idea of an eight- or nine-year-old daughter's knowing exactly how babies are conceived. The fear is likely to be: What if she experiments with other children now or in two or three years when such experimentation could mean trouble? But children do wonder how conception comes about, and the mother whose small child asks her the question can only appreciate her child's confidence in her and go ahead to do her best to give an honest explanation. (We say the mother, here, because she is the parent more often at hand to be asked.) As the parent tells the facts, the explanation may be given that the act through which fathers and mothers start the life of a baby is an act for men and women who can provide a home and take care of the babies that they have. The child who is aware enough to ask the question certainly has enough understanding to think about what it means to

Fig. 118 "Can't you just tell them the facts of life without all these visual aids?" By permission, Lafe Locke and *Family Circle.*

bring a baby into the world and take care of it, to give it a home and the loving care that make life comfortable and happy. In terms of her own happy family life, the child will interpret what is learned, and there is little reason to worry about dangerous experimentation. The fearful parent can be glad at this point that, because of the child's confidence, the parent was permitted to present the facts in a wholesome way, rather than the child's having sought the information from some source that might have given an unwholesome view of the matter.

Vocabulary to use

One reason many parents have difficulty keeping lines of communication about sex matters open as children approach the adolescent period is that the parents have no language they can use in discussing sex with their children. They have used a baby language for bodily functions and parts of the body. As the child grew older he learned to say "hand" and not "patty," "foot" and not "tootsie"; but he may not have been given the right names for his sex organs or for processes of bodily elimination. In fact, many parents themselves do not use accurate language; all they know is the street language or words they learned as children. Since they would feel ridiculous using this language with their children, there is actually an area in which parents and children cannot converse without great awkwardness. They do not have the vocabulary. If terms such as bowel movement, urinate, penis, vulva, nipple, are used from the very first with children, they will accept the terms just as readily as they accept feet, hands, stomach, arms, and legs, and the family will have a language that is understood by all and available when needed.

Kinds of information given by parents. In our study of the 3,000 university students, each student was asked to specify the type of sex and reproduction information he had received from parents. Table 30 shows the percentage of students stating the different types of information their parents had given them. Less than one-third of the parents gave their children any sex and reproduction education beyond telling girls about menstruation and telling both boys and girls where babies come from. We recognize that it is difficult for many parents to go beyond this elementary stage. But, since one great worry of the parents is that the young people will not be able to control their sex emotions during the dating years, it would seem that the pleasure of sex experience and the consequent difficulty of controlling the sexual impulses should be discussed with sons and daughters. By

TABLE 30   PERCENTAGES OF 3,000 STUDENTS FROM 11 COLLEGES STATING SPECIFIC SEX AND REPRODUCTION INFORMATION GIVEN BY PARENTS

Information given	Men (N-1,056)	Women (N-1,944)
Where babies come from	57.0%	74.0%
Menstruation	25.0	90.0
Venereal disease	30.0	33.0
Difficulty of controlling sexual emotions	21.0	38.0
Coitus (sexual intercourse)	26.0	37.0
Masturbation	22.0	17.0
Sex perversions	14.0	19.0
Pleasure of sexual relations	13.0	23.0
Nocturnal emissions	22.0	15.0
Contraceptives	13.0	21.0
Orgasm	10.0	10.0
No information given	30.0	6.0

such discussions, parents can help their children to appreciate that sex is a valuable, constructive force that enhances relationships, but which—like any other powerful force in life—needs to be understood in its relevance to all other facets of personality and experience. Because of their own emotional reactions, many parents cannot or do not discuss this phase of sex. They worry about their children's ability to cope with the strong sex urges that are new to them in adolescence, and some parents may offer negative warnings and admonitions. The entire matter might be handled more effectively if an honest and direct approach is taken, openly recognizing the urgency of sex drives and the positive aspects of sex in life.

Facing the subject of sexual deviation

Another subject that few of the parents of the university students in our research had ever discussed with their children is sexual deviation. It is understandable that many parents would avoid the subject, hoping the child need never know anything about it. But that is not a realistic point of view. A study among 1,800 university students revealed that one-third of both the men and the women had as children or in their teens had one or more encounters with sex deviation.[4] The most common encounters for girls were with exhibitionists or older persons who made improper sexual advances, and for boys, homosexuals.

Most parents know that such things happen; they would like to make sure that their children are prepared to avoid or resist such undesirable experiences, but they do not want to cause a child to be fearful and distrusting in his attitudes toward others, nor to be overimpressed with the negative and threatening aspects of sex behavior in the world. The goal of parents should be first to try to help the child develop normal and healthy attitudes concerning sex; that will constitute a most important form of protection. But just as children need to know that there are dishonest or unkind people in the world, and that part of growing up is learning to cope with whatever kinds of people one encounters, so they ought to know that there are people with unhealthy and warped attitudes about sex, and they should

---

[4] Judson T. Landis, "The Nondelinquent Child and the Sexual Deviate," *Research Studies of the State College of Washington, Proceedings of the Pacific Sociological Society,* 23:2 (June, 1955), 92-101. Also, Judson T. Landis, "Experiences of 500 Children with Adult Sexual Deviation," *The Psychiatric Quarterly Supplement,* Part 1 (1956).

know how to cope with these people also if they should encounter them. All frightening or "scare" talk should be avoided, for that can contribute as much or more to unwholesome attitudes in the child as an encounter with some types of deviates might do. In fact, the evidence seems to show that much of the trauma following a child's experience with the more common types of deviates is caused by the handling of the matter after it has happened. The shock and horror of parents and adults may be more frightening in many cases than the experience itself was.[5]

One of the best protections a child can have is for lines of communication to be kept open all along the way. The child who will not hesitate to say to the parent, "Say, I heard a queer thing today, some of the kids were saying . . ." and then go on to tell what it was that seemed "queer" to him, is not in much danger of having his ideas about sex too distorted by the mistaken ideas or the warped attitudes of others. Similarly, the child who has discussed all subjects freely with his parents will not only be more alert to avoid undesirable sex experiences with deviated persons, but can allow the parent to help protect him or her from such experiences. A ten-year-old girl went home from school and reported, "On the way home today there was a man sitting in a car when I passed. He opened the door and asked me very politely to come over there because he said he wanted to ask me a question. I didn't like his face; he smiled like he was trying to be *so nice,* but the way he looked at me kind of scared me. Did I do right just to not answer him and walk on home as fast as I could?" Even if in this case the man was harmless and the child over-cautious, the mother had an excellent opportunity to discuss the subject of deviation and help her child to think about ways to avoid such people without having to feel that she was being rude or mistrustful toward strangers.

[5] *Ibid.*

Recognizing the social aspects of sex

Always, a complicating factor in parental policy in sex education of children is the matter of social values and cultural patterns. When a parent talks about sex with the child, the parent is usually aware that because of social attitudes the child may have sad experiences of different kinds as he grows older; he may break rules and bring down upon himself social disapproval that will hurt him seriously, or he may go through emotional experiences that handicap him. That is why the social aspects of sex should be as openly faced within the family as are the social aspects of all other areas of living. Parents teach values relative to all other phases of life almost from the beginning of a child's life. They use all kinds of situations and incidents in daily living to emphasize with children that some things are done and some things are not done; that one has certain obligations, and that the world expects certain kinds of behavior. But, with regard to cultural patterns and values surrounding sex, many children live in a vacuum as far as parental teaching goes. If sex is a hush-hush subject, parents have no occasion to interpret social values, patterns, or attitudes. Rather, attitudes and values are communicated negatively or by default, the child formulating his ideas on the basis of the implications of taboos and restrictions.

In the study of the 3,000 college students in 1952-1955, the factor of chastity was related to childhood sources of sex information. A larger percentage of those who had maintained socially acceptable standards of behavior had gained their sex information from parents or from school classes, and they were more likely to have had most of the information in Table 30 given to them by their parents. Those who reported having had premarital sexual experience were more likely to have had no information from parents and to have learned about sex facts from brothers or sisters or from other children. The research supports the belief that parents who give their children rather complete sex information also influence their children toward developing attitudes and standards with which they can live comfortably in our society.

In the average family, some problems may arise because sex activities and attitudes are subject to so many outside influences.

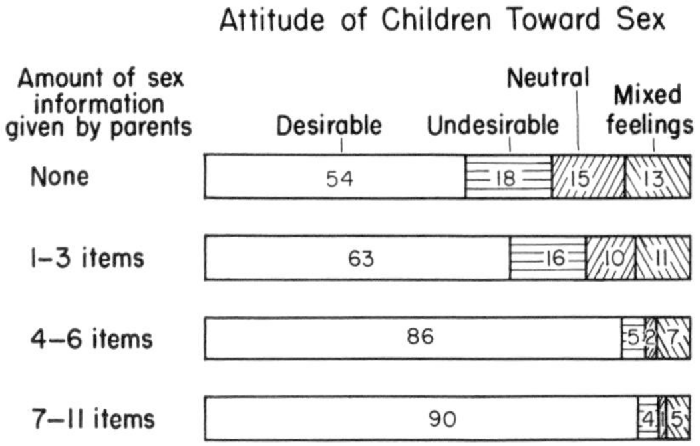

Attitude of Children Toward Sex

Fig. 119 RELATIONSHIP BETWEEN CHILDREN'S ATTITUDES TOWARD SEX AND THE AMOUNT OF SEX INFORMATION GIVEN BY PARENTS. Attitudes were rated according to responses of 3,000 students to a check list of items, such as: "Sex is dirty and vulgar." "Sex is for mutual husband and wife enjoyment." See Table 30 for a summary of what sex information was given by parents.

Children may become involved with other children in activities that are not socially acceptable, such as undressing at play, exercising the functions of elimination in public, public masturbation, or attempts at sex experimentation with other children. It is important for the parent to maintain his objectivity and to handle the situations in such a way that he does not do more harm than good. He should remember *why* he is trying to prevent some actions: that often it is because of social unacceptability and not because in itself there is anything bad or shocking in the child's act.

Sometimes children who have been freely told the facts of

birth and reproduction create neighborhood friction by telling the neighbors' children things their own parents consider them too young to know. Actually, the talking about sex that children almost inevitably do, whether or not their parents approve, will not do any harm, especially if the children have been armed with accurate information by their parents. But parents who are worried about what other parents are going to think may usually prevent difficulty by handling the matter honestly with their children.

In one family where the facts of life had been frankly faced from the children's infancy, the mother told her children, "We think all these things are an interesting part of life and worth talking about sometimes. But not all families have the same ideas about what can be talked about and what can't. Some people would be shocked if we talked to them about how babies are started and how they are born, so let's try not to offend people who may feel that way." That her children understood and accepted this difference in views was shown by the fact that her six-year-old son said one day, after coming home from a neighbor's, "Johnny's mother is one of the people who think a lot of ordinary things are hush-subjects. She made us go outside to play when she gave their baby her bath."

Masturbation as a problem

Most parents are confronted with decisions when they observe masturbation in a child. Almost all children masturbate at some time during the process of maturing. The practice may begin when the child is six-months-old, six-years-old, or not until later. At one time parents quite universally punished their children for masturbating, believing that the habit would cause feeblemindedness, insanity, softening of the brain, stunted growth, and other horrible effects.

Even today some people hold such opinions. But students of child development recognize that there are no harmful physical and mental effects of masturbation per se; rather, some form of bodily exploration is a normal part of infancy and childhood. Emotional damage may result if the child is severely censured and made to feel guilty and fearful about the habit.

Although masturbation, occurring as an accompaniment of certain phases of development, is not in itself harmful, it is true that any such activity may create problems since the child lives in a social world. Parents are conscious of how others who deal with the child may react when they observe the habit. The child may be severely censured or ostracized by others, with resulting emotional damage to him. In general, it is best to take a constructive approach. Parents need to make sure that the child is provided with interests and activities that fill his time adequately. They must see that he has the security that comes with knowing that he is appreciated and loved. Excessive masturbation may be an indication that the child has not enough satisfying interaction with other people, or that his general activities are restricted, to the point of boredom.

Sex attitudes and the whole personality

It is important that children grow up with an appreciation of the fact that healthy sexual development is social and emotional as well as physical, and that sex with all its implications is one of the positive forces in personality. Successful parents approach this phase of bringing up their children with the same common sense and affection that is evident in all their other dealings with their children. Clearly many variables other than how much information about sex functioning has been given affect the development of sexual attitudes and behavior.

A large and intensive study in San Francisco of teen-age people who were promiscuous in their sexual behavior revealed that their promiscuity was an indication of other serious problems in their lives, and that the promiscuity was an attempt to find a solution to inner conflicts.[6] Many of the girls had been rejected by their parents, and felt unloved and unwanted; their promiscuity was a striving for a satisfaction of other personality needs that had not been met in their relationships at home.

Family companionship

Many of the goals parents hope to achieve with their children will be easier to attain if the family associates together as people who like each other and enjoy doing things together. This requires a specific effort in today's world. Pressure is upon all members of the family to participate in activities that are specialized for age and sex. Consequently, members of the family do not participate in many of the same groups outside the home. Although many of the organized activities for children and adults are excellent in purpose, they leave little time for family life unless people are intelligent in determining where to draw the line in their participation.

There is no substitute for family companionship as a source of happiness and security for the child. To small children it is not important what the activity is, or how much time is occupied with it, just as long as it is one in which all participate and one that can be depended upon to have its regular place in the daily or weekly routine. Children gain great pleasure from looking forward to pleasant family activities that they know will take place without fail. The knowledge that the parents will not let them down by allowing unimportant outside interests to displace the family activities is important to a child's sense of security.

Some parents who establish the precedent of spending Sunday evenings together when the children are little find to their surprise that even when their children are adolescent and have many interests outside the home they prefer to save Sunday evenings to spend with the family. Often the children bring their friends

[6] Benno Safier, *et al., A Psychiatric Approach to the Treatment of Promiscuity,* pp. 77-78. New York: American Social Hygiene Association, 1949.

so that the circle is enlarged; such an arrangement adds to the pleasure of family activities as the children grow older. Invariably children from families who have little or no family life as such are anxious to be welcomed into the activities of other families who do things together. It is not always easy or convenient for parents to be consistent about spending time with their children, but parents who make it a practice find that it pays.

A sense of humor

No discussion of child-rearing would be complete without some attention to the importance of a sense of humor in parents and in children. The best possible tension reliever is laughter. The ability to see the humor that is inevitably present even in one's own difficulties, helps one to face problems and be more effective in discovering solutions. Parents are giving their children an ad-

Fig. 120 DOUBTS ABOUT CHANCES FOR SUCCESSFUL MARRIAGE AND PARENTAL MARITAL HAPPINESS AS REPORTED BY 3,000 STUDENTS. The children from happy homes reported much greater confidence in their ability to have successful marriages.

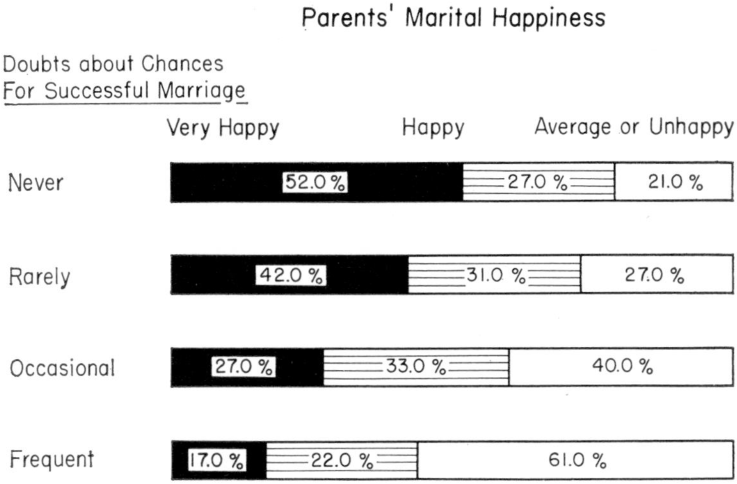

Parents' Marital Happiness

Doubts about Chances
For Successful Marriage

	Very Happy	Happy	Average or Unhappy
Never	52.0 %	27.0 %	21.0 %
Rarely	42.0 %	31.0 %	27.0 %
Occasional	27.0 %	33.0 %	40.0 %
Frequent	17.0 %	22.0 %	61.0 %

vantage in life if they themselves can keep in mind that some things are better laughed about than wept over or shouted about. Parents can help their children see the humor in many situations in daily life that are potentially tension producing.

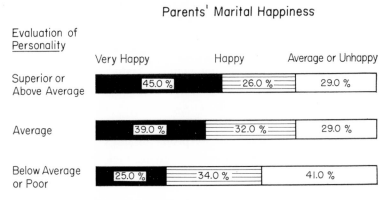

Fig. 121 EVALUATION OF THEIR OWN PERSONALITIES IN EARLY ADOLESCENCE AND PARENTAL MARITAL HAPPINESS, AS REPORTED BY 3,000 STUDENTS.

Like the habit of happiness, a sense of humor is a learned characteristic; it is not inherited or presented as a ready-made gift. Even people who are naturally serious minded and humorless can overcome their handicap if they recognize the value of humor and shared laughter in family life. What laughter means in a child's life was expressed by a little boy whose parents had been undergoing a period of unusual strain. He said unexpectedly at dinner one day, "What's the matter with us all? Are we sick? We haven't had a good laugh for a week!"

What is successful parenthood?

People who would evaluate their effectiveness as parents must look at the whole child, not just at some of his faults or virtues. Is he generally a happy child? Is he developing resources within himself so that he is not too dependent on outside circumstances for contentment? Does he have a feeling that others like him and value him? Is he dependable? Is he self-reliant, with confidence in himself and his ability to cope with life as it comes? A part of his self-confidence is a recognition of his personal responsibility for his own acts. Can he accept the consequences of his own acts without offering alibis, or blaming other people or circumstances? If his parents are people who do their best but are not afraid to say, "I was wrong," he will appreciate the fact that although his parents are not infallible they are able to work things out in spite of mistakes. This realization will help him to have the same attitude toward himself.

In order to help a child develop desirable traits, parents need to be sure of their own attitudes toward the child. They must love him for himself, the individual that he is now, not as a reflection of their own personalities. Objectivity does not come naturally to parents. It must be cultivated. When it is achieved, one's role as a parent is more easily understood. There must be warmth of love so that from the cradle all the way along the child has the security that comes with a consciousness that he is loved and valued. But this parental love must not be so overwhelming and smothering that it stands as a wall between the child and the realities of the world about him.

The ultimate responsibility of every parent is to contribute to the child's physical, mental, and emotional growth so that in due time he becomes an independent, autonomous person, able to create and maintain satisfactory relationships with others in his world.

Review questions

1. List some personality characteristics that parents might keep in mind in training their children, which would make the children more marriageable.

2. What home circumstances might the parents keep in mind as they think of the future marriageability of their children?

3. Why is it hard for parents to see the behavior of their children in its proper perspective?

4. Why do parents often defend the faults of their children to neighbors and relatives?

5. How can one help his child develop initiative and self-reliance? Illustrate.

6. Criticize the allowance systems used by the two families described in the text. Did either of these approach the allowance system you had in your family?

7. Why is it important for parents to give their children accurate sex information?

8. Criticize the viewpoint of parents who say, "I don't believe children should know about sex; they aren't old enough to know."

9. When is a child old enough to receive his first sex information?

10. What are the most common first questions asked by children about sex?

11. Why do many parents fail to use a scientific vocabulary when talking to their children about sex, reproduction, and bodily elimination?

12. How does a parent establish rapport with his children in discussing sex and reproduction?

13. How commonly do children encounter adult sexual deviation? Why is it difficult to prepare the child for such experiences?

14. Will knowledge about sex lead to sex experimentation?

15. Why is it so difficult for parents to have the proper perspective on common sex problems of normal children?

16. How can development of a sense of humor be encouraged?

17. Why is doing things together as a family important to the development of the child?

18. What questions might a parent ask himself in deciding whether he is pursuing the right course in training his child?

Projects and activities

1. Give a case from your acquaintance in which the parents always defended the faults of their children.

2. Give a case from your acquaintance in which the parents were careful to train their children on unimportant behavior but permitted the children to engage in other quite serious behavior without comment.

3. Either from your own family or from a family you know, cite how doing things together as a family contributed to the security and happiness of the children.

4. Write your own case history of learning about sex: how it was handled in the home; what you learned from playmates or reading; and your reaction to what you learned.

5. *Role-playing.* Steve and Lucy have been married ten years and have four children, ages 2, 4, 6, and 8.

a) John, aged 8, has not shown good judgment in the way he spends his allowance. He received his 50¢-a-week allowance this morning and at noon is back from town with all the money gone. His mother and father decide to make an issue of it.

b) Mary, aged 4, told Mrs. Smith to go home this morning when Mrs. Smith was talking to Mary's mother.

c) Henry, the 6-year-old boy, insists on helping his father build things in the shop. The father is annoyed with Henry's taking his tools all the time, getting in the way, and delaying the work.

d) Mary, aged 4, tells the family that a neighbor's child has told her that storks bring babies. She then asks her mother where babies come from. Other questions follow from all the children after the first one is answered. (For the types of questions asked by children of different ages, see Frances Bruce Strain, *New Patterns in Sex Teachings,* pp. xiii-xvi. Ways to answer are given in this book.)

Films

Angry Boy. One of the few films that show the effects of the husband-wife adjustment on the child. Also shows adequate child-guidance facilities in treating child. Association Films. 33 minutes, sound.

Human Beginnings. Designed to give first-grade children normal attitudes toward reproduction. Probably of more value to use with people approaching parenthood. 20 minutes, sound.

Human Growth. Designed to explain the process of reproductive maturity to children in grades 4 to 6. 20 minutes, sound.

(Association Films, *Human Beginnings* and *Human Growth* are excellent for use with college young people to show them how to handle the sex and reproductive education of children. The films were the outgrowth of the reproductive education program in Oregon.)

Meeting Emotional Needs in Childhood. Film emphasizes the needs of children for security, complete love, a sense of belonging and independence. New York University, 32 minutes, sound.

Over-Dependency. This is the case history of Jimmy, an attractive young man whose life is crippled by the behavior patterns carried over from a too-dependent childhood. National Film Board of Canada. McGraw-Hill Book Company, Inc., 30 minutes, sound.

Suggested readings

Aldrich, C. Anderson, and Mary M. Aldrich, *Babies Are Human Beings.* New York: The Macmillan Company, 1938.

Bossard, James H. S., and Eleanor S. Boll, *Ritual in Family Living.* Philadelphia: University of Pennsylvania Press, 1950.

Cavan, Ruth Shonle, *The American Family.* New York: Thomas Y. Crowell Company, 1953. Ch. XVIII, "Parents and Children."

Duvall, Evelyn Millis, *Family Development.* Chicago, J. B. Lippincott Company, 1957. Part II, "Expanding Families."

Eckert, Ralph G., *Sex Attitudes in the Home.* New York: Association Press, 1956.

English, O. Spurgeon and Constance J. Foster, *Fathers are Parents, Too.* New York: G. P. Putnam's Sons, 1951.

Gesell, Arnold, and Frances L. Ilg, *Infant and Child in the Culture of Today.* New York: Harper & Brothers, 1943.

Kirkendall, Lester A., *Sex Education in Human Relations.* New York: Inor Publishing Company, Inc., 1950.

Landis, Judson T., and Mary G. Landis, eds., *Readings in Marriage and the Family.* Englewood Cliffs, N. J.: Prentice-Hall, Inc., 1952. Part XI, Reading 4, "The Stepmother," and Reading 5, "The Stepchild," William C. Smith. Part XII, Reading 5, "Children of Divorce," Kingsley Davis. Part XIV, Reading 2, "Sound Attitudes Toward Sex," Lester A. Kirkendall.

Ribble, Margaret A., *The Rights of Infants.* New York: Columbia University Press, 1943.

Spock, Benjamin, *The Common Sense Book of Baby and Child Care.* New York: Duell, Sloan and Pearce, Inc., 1957. A manual on all phases of the physical and emotional development of the infant and young child. A good book for mothers to own.

———, *The Pocketbook of Baby and Child Care.* New York: Pocketbooks, Inc., 1957. (Pocketbook printing of *The Common Sense Book of Baby and Child Care.*)

Strain, Frances Bruce, *New Patterns in Sex Teachings.* New York: Appleton-Century-Crofts, Inc., Revised 1951.

———, *The Normal Sex Interests of Children.* New York: Appleton-Century-Crofts, Inc., 1948.

Strecker, Edward A., *Their Mother's Sons.* Philadelphia: J. B. Lippincott Company, 1946.

U.S. Department of Labor, *Your Child from One to Six.* Children's Bureau Publication 30. Superintendent of Documents, Washington, D.C. (Latest revision.)

Wolf, Anna W. M., *The Parents' Manual.* New York: Simon & Schuster, Inc., Revised 1951.

Building a Successful Marriage

A backward look at the many topics discussed in this book brings the realization that to build a successful marriage is an accomplishment unlimited in its implications. It goes far beyond the horizons of the two who marry, and reaches into the lives of future generations.

Where does successful marriage begin? Not with the wedding. Rather it begins somewhere in an unending circle made up of many parts—childhood experiences and feelings, parents who knew cooperation, learning experiences in youth and adulthood, attitudes in every area of living. It includes romance and responsibility, sacrifice, drudgery, and the acceptance of disappointments, as well as fundamentally rewarding fulfillments—sexual, social, psychic, emotional, and even material.

Always an essential condition for successful marriage is growth in the two who marry, a continually expanding perception of the needs and feelings of others, and an increasing ability and willingness to give acceptance, respect, and cooperation. Those who build successful marriages reject any conception of life or relationships as static; they perceive that people change and that relationships are never absolutely set and unimprovable. They become able to live creatively with the mate, their children, and all others in the circle. They will not settle for less than the best that marriage can be. They therefore study to learn; they observe and try to understand; they learn to bend and adjust in order to develop relationships that give meaning to life. In other words, building a successful marriage is living creatively at every stage in life.

639

Selected Readings on Marriage and Family Relations

The list of annotated books is grouped to make it easier for the reader to find the ones to fit his particular needs.

PREPARATION FOR PARENTHOOD

Getting ready to be parents

Cady, Ernst, and Frances Cady, *How to Adopt a Child.* New York: William Morrow and Company, 1956.

Gives practical advice on matters relative to the adoption process.

Eastman, Nicholson J., *Expectant Motherhood.* Boston: Little, Brown and Company, Revised 1957.

A scientific treatment of the prenatal period by a professor of obstetrics at the Johns Hopkins University and Obstetrician-in-Chief to the Johns Hopkins Hospital.

Farris, Edmond J., *Human Fertility and Problems of the Male.* White Plains: The Author's Press, Inc., 1950.

Reports on laboratory research largely on human male, but also on female, to determine real causes of infertility.

———, *Human Ovulation and Fertility.* Philadelphia: J. B. Lippincott Company, 1956. 159 pp.

Summary of the research of the Wistar Institute on ovulation and fertility.

Genné, William H., *Husbands and Pregnancy, The Handbook for Expectant Fathers.* New York: Association Press, 1956. 127 pp.

Describes the classes for expectant fathers conducted by the Clara Elizabeth Fund for Maternal Health in Flint, Michigan.

Goodrich, Frederick W., *Natural Childbirth*. Englewood Cliffs, N.J.: Prentice-Hall, Inc., 1950. 176 pp.

A manual containing information on natural childbirth, diet, exercise, relaxation, and the labor experience. For expectant parents.

Heardman, Helen, *Natural Childbirth*. Baltimore: The Williams & Wilkins Company, 1949. 128 pp.

A manual describing methods used to prepare mothers for natural childbirth. Includes illustrated instructions for exercises designed to aid in the relaxation necessary for uncomplicated childbirth.

Lockridge, Frances, *Adopting a Child*. New York: Greenberg, Publisher, 1947. 216 pp.

Answers given on where and how to obtain a child for adoption. Appendix gives adoptive agencies in each state.

Portnoy, Louis, and Jules Saltman, *Fertility in Marriage*. New York: Farrar, Straus and Company, 1950. 250 pp.

A guide for childless couples. Discusses methods being tried to help overcome sterility.

Read, Grantley Dick, *Childbirth Without Fear*. New York: Harper & Brothers, 1953.

The thesis of this book is that by doing away with fear through knowledge and understanding of childbirth, birth will be the natural, comparatively painless function nature intended it to be.

Thoms, Herbert, and Lawrence Roth, *Understanding Natural Childbirth*. New York: McGraw-Hill Book Company, Inc., 1950. 112 pp.

Describes natural childbirth program at Yale University.

Child care and training

Aldrich, C. Anderson, and Mary M. Aldrich, *Babies Are Human Beings*. New York: The Macmillan Company, 1954.

Good on the development behavior of babies. Outlines practical suggestions for managing the infant. Not as light reading as some of the books on the subject, but valuable for parents who will read it.

Bacmeister, Rhoda W., *Your Child and Other People*. Boston: Little, Brown and Company, 1950. 299 pp.

A guidebook to the social life of children from one to eight.

Bro, Margueritte Harmon, *When Children Ask*. New York: Harper & Brothers, 1956.

Deals with ways of answering children's questions on many subjects. Puzzled parents will find help here.

Gesell, Arnold, and Frances L. Ilg, *Infant and Child in the Culture of Today*. New York: Harper & Brothers, 1943. 399 pp.

A reliable treatment of techniques for child guidance.

Gruenberg, Sidonie Matsner, *We the Parents*. New York: Harper & Brothers, 1948.

Considers parent relationships with growing children. Includes such subjects as discipline in the home; the child's handling of money; meeting the challenge of movies and the radio; explaining the facts of birth, death, marriage, and divorce; any many other topics.

Spock, Benjamin, *The Common Sense Book of Baby and Child Care*. New York: Duell, Sloan and Pearce, Inc., 1956.

A manual on all phases of the physical and emotional development of the infant and young child. A good book for mothers to own.

————, *The Pocketbook of Baby and Child Care*. New York: Pocket Books, Inc., 1956.

(Pocketbook printing of *The Common Sense Book of Baby and Child Care*.)

Strecker, Edward A., *Their Mothers' Sons*. Philadelphia: J. B. Lippincott Company, 1946. 220 pp.

A psychiatrist analyzes the factors in parent-child relationships that contribute to the development of emotional maturity in children. Based on his observation of great numbers of young men at induction centers in wartime.

————, and Vincent T. Lathbury, *Their Mothers' Daughters*. Philadelphia: J. B. Lippincott Company, 1956. 255 pp.

Companion volume to the above book.

Tenney, H. Kent, *Let's Talk About Your Baby*. Minneapolis: The University of Minnesota Press, Revised 1947. 115 pp.

A guide for young mothers. Written in a refreshing style.

U.S. Department of Labor, *Your Child from One to Six.* Children's Bureau Publication 30 (revised). Superintendent of Documents, Washington, D.C. (Latest edition)

Examines both the physical and emotional development of the child. Much improved over the earlier editions in that it gives greater emphasis to the relationships involved in living together in a family.

Wolf, Anna W. M., *The Parents' Manual.* New York: Simon & Schuster, Inc., Revised 1951. 331 pp.

Handles the emotional development of the child and his relationships with others.

SEX EDUCATION OF CHILDREN

References for teachers and parents

Beck, Lester R., *Human Growth.* New York: Harcourt, Brace & Company, 1949. 124 pp.

Book to be used with the film "Human Growth."

Bibby, Cyril, *Sex Education. A Guide for Parents, Teachers, and Youth Leaders.* New York: Emerson Books, Inc., 1946. 311 pp.

American edition of an English book that discusses many phases of sex education, especially as it might be developed in the schools. Questions of children and youth with suggested answers.

Eckert, Ralph G., *Sex Attitudes in the Home.* New York: Association Press, 1956. 242 pp.

Excellent discussion of sex education in the home, from the first questions children ask until marriage.

Gilbert, Margaret Shea, *Biography of the Unborn.* Baltimore: The Williams & Wilkins Company, Revised 1943. 132 pp.

This is the story of the development of a human individual from the moment of conception through birth.

Hymes, James L., *How To Tell Your Child About Sex.* New York: Public Affairs Committee, 1949. Pamphlet No. 149.

Kirkendall, Lester A., *Sex Education as Human Relations.* New York: Inor Publishing Company, Inc., 1950. 351 pp.

Excellent background information on the basic principles of sex education. Description of programs, methods, and materials.

Strain, Frances Bruce, *New Patterns in Sex Teachings.* New York: Appleton-Century-Crofts, Inc., Revised 1951. 262 pp.

Classifies most of questions children ask about sex and suggests answers. This is still among the best of the books in this field. Recommended for the family library.

————, *Sex Guidance in Family Life Education.* New York: The Macmillan Company, 1942. 340 pp.

For parent, teachers, and community leaders interested in organizing a program of sex education in the public schools. Outlines a program of sex education from the first grade through the high school. Includes much of the good information given in *New Patterns in Sex Teachings.*

————, *The Normal Sex Interests of Children.* New York: Appleton-Century-Crofts, Inc., 1948. 210 pp.

Considers the developing sex nature of children from birth to adolescence.

Readings for grade-school children

de Schweinitz, Karl, *Growing Up.* New York: The Macmillan Company, 1953.

Explains clearly how we come alive, are born, and grow up. Similar to *The Wonder of Life,* but written in more simple terms.

Gruenberg, Sidonie M., *The Wonderful Story of How You Were Born.* Garden City, N.Y.: Hanover House, 1952. 38 pp.

Written to be read to children. Illustrated.

Levine, Milton I., and Jean H. Seligmann, *The Wonder of Life, How We Are Born and How We Grow Up.* New York: Simon and Schuster, Inc., 1940. 114 pp.

Contains an unusually good approach to and treatment of the sex facts that children should know. Will be read with interest and understanding by young children if it is available in the home.

Strain, Frances Bruce, *Being Born, a Book of Facts for Boys and Girls.* New York: Appleton-Century-Crofts, Inc., 1954.

Suited to somewhat older children than the books by de Schweinitz, and Levine and Seligmann.

Readings for junior-high-school children

Beery, Mary, *Manners Made Easy*. New York: McGraw-Hill Book Company, Inc., 1954.

Discusses behavior for all types of social occasions. Supplementary text for junior- and senior-high-school classes.

Bibby, Cyril, *How Life Is Handed On*. New York: Emerson Books, Inc., 1947. 159 pp.

A description of reproduction, courtship, and family life in animals with some attention given to human reproduction. Interestingly written and illustrated.

Crawford, John E., and Luther Woodward, *Better Ways of Growing Up*. Philadelphia: The Muhlenberg Press, 1948. 270 pp.

Excellent in treatment of personal, social, and life adjustment problems of teen-agers.

Dickerson, Roy E., *Into Manhood*. New York: Association Press, 1954.

A discussion of maturing sexually and its meaning. Deals with desirable habits of eating, sleeping, exercising, and so forth, for growing boys.

Fedder, Ruth, *A Girl Grows Up*. New York: McGraw-Hill Book Company, Inc., Revised 1957.

Designed to help the adolescent girl understand the problems that face her day by day as she grows into maturity. Stresses the problems of physical and emotional maturity rather than the sexual phase.

Keliher, Alice V., *Life and Growth*. New York: Appleton-Century-Crofts, Inc., 1938. 245 pp.

Explains social usages for high-school students and then treats physical and sexual development.

Kirkendall, Lester A., and Ruth F. Osborne, *Dating Days*. Chicago: Science Research Associates, 1949.

Discusses common problems of boy-girl relationships during early teens.

Landis, Judson T., and Mary G. Landis, *Teen-Agers Guide for Living*. Engelwood Cliffs, N.J.: Prentice-Hall, Inc., 1957. 218 pp.

Discusses adjustments of teen-agers to friends, family, school, sex, dating, and future marriage.

McKown, Harry C., *A Boy Grows Up*. New York: McGraw-Hill Book Company, Inc., Revised 1949. 333 pp.

Considers relationships of junior-high-school boys with the family and outside groups and gives lists of social usages to follow on all occasions.

Novikoff, Alex, *From Head to Foot*. New York: International Publishers Co., Inc., 1946. 96 pp.

Interestingly written book showing clearly how the body functions. Unusually well illustrated.

Strain, Frances Bruce, *Teen Days*. New York: Appleton-Century-Crofts, Inc., 1946. 183 pp.

Bridges the gap between the two books, *Being Born* and *Love at the Threshold*.

PREPARATION FOR MARRIAGE AND FAMILY LIVING

Textbooks for high-school classes

Duvall, Evelyn Millis, *Family Living*. New York: The Macmillan Company, 1955. 410 pp.

Landis, Judson T., and Mary G. Landis, *Personal Adjustment, Marriage and Family Living*. Englewood Cliffs, N.J.: Prentice-Hall, Inc., 1955. (11th or 12th grade) 364 pp.

———, *Building Your Life*. Englewood Cliffs, N.J.: Prentice-Hall, Inc., 1954, Revised, 1959. (9th and 10th grade).

Landis, Paul H., *Your Marriage and Family Living*. New York: McGraw-Hill Book Company, Inc., 1954. 388 pp.

Moore, Bernice M., and Dorothy M. Leahy, *You and Your Family*. Boston: D. C. Heath and Company, 1953. 440 pp.

Textbooks for college classes

Blood, Robert O., *Anticipating Your Marriage*. Glencoe, Ill.: The Free Press, 1955. 482 pp.

Bowman, Henry A., *Marriage for Moderns*. New York: McGraw-Hill Book Company, 1953. 562 pp.

Butterfield, Oliver M., *Planning for Marriage*. Princeton, N.J.: D. Van Nostrand Company, Inc., 1956. 343 pp.

Christensen, Harold T., *Marriage Analysis*. New York: The Ronald Press Company, 1958. 645 pp.

Duvall, Evelyn Millis, *Family Development*. Chicago: J. B. Lippincott Company, 1957. 533 pp.

Duvall, Evelyn Millis, and Reuben Hill, *When You Marry.* Boston: D. C. Heath and Company, 1953. 466 pp.

Himes, Norman E., and Donald L. Taylor, *Your Marriage.* New York: Rinehart & Company, Inc., 1955. 384 pp.

Hirning, J. L., and Alma L. Hirning, *Marriage Adjustment.* New York: American Book Company, 1956. 456 pp.

Koos, Earl Lomon, *Marriage.* New York: Henry Holt and Company, Inc., 1957. 441 pp.

Landis, Judson T., and Mary G. Landis, *Building a Successful Marriage.* Englewood Cliffs, N.J.: Prentice-Hall, Inc., 1958.

———, *Youth and Marriage, A Student Manual.* Englewood Cliffs, N.J.: Prentice-Hall, Inc., 1957. 286 pp.

Landis, Paul H., *Making the Most of Marriage.* New York: Appleton-Century-Crofts, Inc., 1955. 542 pp.

Peterson, James A., *Education for Marriage.* New York: Charles Scribner's Sons, 1956. 429 pp.

General books for young people

Dickerson, Roy E., *So Youth May Know.* New York: Association Press, 1948. 259 pp.

Deals with sexual maturity in boys and the problems associated with it.

Duvall, Evelyn Millis, *Facts of Life and Love.* New York: Association Press, 1956. 426 pp.

Rather complete discussion of the problems of teen-agers, interestingly written.

Kirkendall, Lester, *Understanding Sex.* Chicago: Science Research Associates, 1947. 48 pp.

This is an outstanding pamphlet which presents sex facts for the 14- to 16-year-old in understandable language.

Scheinfeld, Amram, *The Human Heredity Handbook.* Philadelphia: J. B. Lippincott Company, 1956. 276 pp.

Shultz, Gladys Denny, *Letters to Jane.* Philadelphia: J. B. Lippincott Company, 1948. 224 pp.

A mother writes a series of letters to her daughter and her college friends answering their many questions about love and sex.

Strain, Frances Bruce, *Love at the Threshold.* New York: Appleton-Century-Crofts, Inc., 1942. 349 pp.

Presents material on dating, romance, and marriage. Addressed to young men and women as they approach the age for marriage.

PREPARATION FOR MARRIAGE ADJUSTMENT

For engaged and married couples

Bentley, Marguerite, *Wedding Etiquette*. Philadelphia: John C. Winston Company, 1947. 383 pp.

Offers complete information on weddings. Includes the wedding requirements of the different religious faiths.

Butterfield, Oliver M., *Sex Life in Marriage*. New York: Emerson Books, Inc., 1952. 192 pp.

A manual for people about to be married or those who are married, but who want a good book on sex expression in marriage. This is one of the best books written on sex in marriage.

———, *Sexual Harmony in Marriage*. New York: Emerson Books, Inc., 1953. 96 pp.

Booklet giving much of the information in the above book by the same author.

Castallo, Mario A., and Cecelia L. Schultz, *Woman's Inside Story*. New York: The Macmillan Company, 1948. 203 pp.

Similar to the book listed in this section by Novak.

Exner, M. J., *The Sexual Side of Marriage*. New York: W. W. Norton & Company, Inc., 1932. 127 pp.

Treats both the physical and psychological phases of sex in marriage in a frank and scientific manner.

Fishbein, Morris, and Ruby Jo Reeves Kennedy, *Modern Marriage and Family Living*. New York: Oxford University Press, 1957. 545 pp.

Groves, Ernest R., Gladys Hoagland Groves, and Catherine Groves, *Sex Fulfillment in Marriage*. New York: Emerson Books, Inc., Revised 1943. 308 pp.

Reviews frankly and clearly the scientific knowledge about marital relations.

Hamblen, E. C., *Facts About the Change of Life*. Springfield: Charles S. Thomas, 1949. 86 pp.

This book dispels superstitions and false ideas based upon folklore concerning the menopause.

Novak, Emil, *The Woman Asks the Doctor*. Baltimore: The Williams & Wilkins Company, 1944. 130 pp.

An authoritative discussion of special problems of women presented in a clear, understandable style.

Popenoe, Paul, *Marriage Is What You Make It*. New York: The Macmillan Company, 1950. 221 pp.

Largely a collection of articles that have appeared in popular magazines.

Stone, Hannah, and Abraham Stone, *A Marriage Manual*. New York: Simon & Schuster, Inc., Revised 1952.

A practical guide to sex in marriage. Probably the best on this subject.

PREPARATION FOR LEADERSHIP IN FAMILY LIFE EDUCATION

Textbooks for college courses in the sociology of the family

Baber, Ray E., *Marriage and the Family*. New York: McGraw-Hill Book Company, Inc., 1953. 719 pp.

Becker, Howard, and Reuben Hill, editors, *Family, Marriage, and Parenthood*. Boston: D. C. Heath and Company, 1955. 849 pp.

Burgess, Ernest W., and Harvey J. Locke, *The Family*. New York: American Book Company, 1953. 743 pp.

Cavan, Ruth Shonle, *The American Family*. New York: Thomas Y. Crowell Company, 1953. 658 pp.

Folsom, Joseph K., *The Family and Democratic Society*. New York: John Wiley & Sons, 1943. 755 pp.

Groves, Ernest R., and Gladys Hoagland Groves, *The Contemporary American Family*. Philadelphia: J. B. Lippincott Company, 1947. 838 pp.

Kane, John J., *Marriage and the Family: A Catholic Approach*. New York: The Dryden Press, 1952. 341 pp.

Kirkpatrick, Clifford, *The Family*. New York: The Ronald Press Company, 1955. 651 pp.

Landis, Judson T., and Mary G. Landis, *Readings in Marriage and the Family*. Englewood Cliffs, N.J.: Prentice-Hall, Inc., 1952. 460 pp.

Mihanovich, Clement Simon, Gerald J. Schnepp, and John L. Thomas, *Marriage and the Family*. Milwaukee: The Bruce Publishing Company, 1952. 502 pp.

Nimkoff, Meyer F., *Marriage and the Family*. Boston: Houghton Mifflin Company, 1947. 767 pp.

Thomas, John L., *The American Catholic Family*. Englewood Cliffs, N.J.: Prentice-Hall, Inc., 1956. 471 pp.

Truxal, Andrew G., and Francis E. Merrill, *The Family in American Culture*. Englewood Cliffs, N.J.: Prentice-Hall, Inc., 1953. 587 pp.

Waller, Willard, *The Family* (Revised by Reuben Hill). New York: The Dryden Press, Inc., 1951. 637 pp.

Winch, Robert F., *The Modern Family*. New York: Henry Holt and Company, 1952. 522 pp.

———, and Robert McGinnis, *Selected Studies in Marriage and the Family*. New York: Henry Holt and Company, 1953. 578 pp.

Books for adult education leaders, ministers, teachers, and counselors

Cuber, John F., *Marriage Counseling Practice*. New York: Appleton-Century-Crofts, Inc., 1948. 175 pp.

Davis, Allison W., and Robert J. Havighurst, *Father of the Man*. Boston: Houghton Mifflin Company, 1948. 245 pp.

Dyer, Dorothy T., *The Family Today, A Guide for Leaders*. Minneapolis: The University of Minnesota Press, 1950.

English, O. Spurgeon, and Gerald H. J. Pearson, *Emotional Problems of Living*. New York: W. W. Norton & Company, Inc., 1945. 438 pp.

Foote, Nelson N., and Leonard S. Cottrell, Jr., *Identity and Interpersonal Competence*. Chicago: The University of Chicago Press, 1955. 305 pp.

Landis, Paul H., *Adolescence and Youth*. New York: McGraw-Hill Book Company, Inc. Revised, 1952. 482 pp.

Levy, John, and Ruth Munroe, *The Happy Family*. New York: Alfred A. Knopf, Inc., 1938. 320 pp.

Matteson, William J., and E. C. Harwood, *Life Insurance from the Buyer's Point of View*. Great Barrington, Mass.: American Institute for Economic Research. Revised each year.

Mudd, Emily H., *The Practice of Marriage Counseling*. New York: The Association Press, 1951. 336 pp.

Skidmore, Rex A., Hulda Van Steeter Garrett, and C. Jay Skidmore, *Marriage Consulting*. New York: Harper & Brothers, 1956. 417 pp.

Vincent, Clark E., ed., *Readings in Marriage Counseling*. New York: Thomas Y. Crowell Company, 1957.

RESEARCH REPORTS ON FAMILY LIFE

Bernard, Jessie, *Remarriage.* New York: The Dryden Press, 1956. 372 pp.

Bossard, James H. S., and Eleanor S. Boll, *Ritual in Family Living.* Philadelphia: The University of Pennsylvania Press, 1950. 228 pp.

————, *One Marriage, Two Faiths.* Philadelphia: University of Pennsylvania Press, 1957. 180 pp.

————, *The Large Family System.* Philadelphia: University of Pennsylvania Press, 1956. 325 pp.

Burgess, Ernest W., and Leonard S. Cottrell, *Predicting Success or Failure in Marriage.* Englewood Cliffs, N.J.: Prentice-Hall, Inc., 1939. 472 pp. (Out of print.)

Burgess, Ernest W., and Paul Wallin, *Engagement and Marriage.* Chicago: J. B. Lippincott Company, 1953.

Duvall, Evelyn Millis, *In-Laws: Pro and Con.* New York: Association Press, 1954. 400 pp.

Glick, Paul C., *American Families.* New York: John Wiley & Sons, Inc., 1956. 240 pp.

Goode, William J., *After Divorce.* Glencoe, Ill.: The Free Press, 1956. 381 pp.

Hill, Reuben, *Families Under Stress.* New York: Harper & Brothers, 1949. 443 pp.

Hollis, Florence, *Women in Marital Conflict.* New York: Family Service Association of America, 1949. 236 pp.

Koos, E. L., *Families in Trouble.* New York: King's Crown Press, 1946.

Locke, Harvey J., *Predicting Adjustment in Marriage.* New York: Henry Holt and Company, 1951. 407 pp.

Terman, Lewis M., *Psychological Factors in Marital Happiness.* New York: McGraw-Hill Book Company, Inc., 1938. 474 pp. (Out of print.)

Waller, Willard, *The Old Love and The New.* New York: Horace Liveright, 1930. 344 pp. (Out of print.)

Index

A

Abortion:
  criminal, 554-555
  harmful effects of, 223, 555-556
  non-pregnant women and, 555
  Russian policy on, 556
  spontaneous, 554-556
  Swedish policy on, 556
  therapeutic, 554-556
Accommodation and marriage adjustment, 350-352
Adams, Clifford, 383
Adaptability, 124-126
Adjustment in marriage (*see* Marriage adjustment)
Adolescence:
  age of puberty, 26
  mental achievements in, 30-31
  puberty and age of dating, 60-61
  rate of growth in, 26; *figure,* 27
Adoption:
  adolescents and, 583
  considerations for adoptive parents, 576-580
  evils of, in past, 574
  honesty in adoptive relationships, 584
  premarital pregnancies and, 223-224
  risks in, 580-581
  standards for, 574-575
  telling child of, 581-583
  unwed mother and, 224
Affection (*see also* Love):
  a function of marriage, 11-12
  child's need for, 594-595
  grievances in marriage and, 121-123
Affinity, marriage prohibitions and, 327-328
Age, maternity death rate by, 537-538; *figure,* 537
Age at marriage:
  annulments and, 336-337
  divorce and, 152-154; *figure,* 156
  emotional maturity and, 152-154
  in-law adjustments and, *figure,* 413
  marital happiness and, 154-157; *table,* 153
  median, 55-56; *figure,* 56
  time to adjust in marriage and, 154
Age for marriage:
  legal, 324-326

Age for marriage (*cont.*):
  minimum, 322-326; *table,* 322-324
  without parental consent, *figure,* 325
Allen, Frederick Lewis, 37
Allowances, children's, 614-617
American Bar Association, 335
American Board of Obstetrics and Gynecology, 521
American College of Life Underwriters, 498
American Institute of Economic Research, 491
American Medical Association, 552
Annulled marriages:
  legitimacy of children of, 338-339
  number per year, 337
  void and voidable marriages, 336-337
Annulment:
  contrasted to divorce, 336
  most common grounds for, 337
Ante-nuptial agreement, 238-240
Artificial insemination:
  Catholic position on, 573
  couples' reasons for, 573
  legal status of, 573
  research on, 572-573
Aschheim-Zondek test for pregnancy, 513, 514

B

Baber, Ray E., 16, 51, 77, 97, 139, 245, 253, 254, 265, 268, 318, 319, 367, 375, 400, 426, 564, 603
Baby, average cost of having a, 186
Barron, Milton L., 253
Becker, Howard, 16, 77, 139, 176, 209, 257, 315, 344, 400, 438, 456, 476, 540, 564
Bell, Howard M., 244, 544
Bernard, Jessie, 209, 560
Bigamous marriages:
  annulment and, 336-338
  legitimacy of children of, 338-339
  void marriages as, 336-337
Bigelow, Howard F., 446
Birth certificates:
  illegitimacy shown on, 338-342
  short form of, *figure,* 339
Birth control (*see also* Contraception):
  ante-nuptial agreement on, 238-239